Future of Business and Finance

The Future of Business and Finance book series features professional works aimed at defining, describing and charting the future trends in these fields. The focus is mainly on strategic directions, technological advances, challenges and solutions which may affect the way we do business tomorrow, including the future of sustainability and governance practices. Mainly written by practitioners, consultants and academic thinkers, the books are intended to spark and inform further discussions and developments.

More information about this series at http://www.springer.com/series/16360

Satinder K. Dhiman • Joan F. Marques
Editors

Leadership After COVID-19

Working Together Toward a Sustainable Future

Springer

Editors
Satinder K. Dhiman
School of Business
Woodbury University
Burbank, CA, USA

Joan F. Marques
School of Business
Woodbury University
Burbank, CA, USA

ISSN 2662-2467 ISSN 2662-2475 (electronic)
Future of Business and Finance
ISBN 978-3-030-84869-9 ISBN 978-3-030-84867-5 (eBook)
https://doi.org/10.1007/978-3-030-84867-5

This Springer imprint is published by the registered company Springer Nature Switzerland AG
The registered company address is: Gewerbestrasse 11, 6330 Cham, Switzerland

This volume is humbly dedicated to
our sisters and brothers,
our true heroes,
serving in the
health care field and other vital industries
who are working together toward a
sustainable future
by keeping hope and trust alive during these
trying times.

Preface

These are uncertain times indeed; perhaps the toughest that humanity has ever experienced before in recent memory. A tiny virus has shaken the whole world like nothing else and has brought the whole humanity to its knees. It is a humbling revelation that we are not in charge of the show. Even more than a threat to our physical bodies, it represents a challenge to our consciousness, an attack on human psyche. We all need to work together with each other, albeit with stoic calm, to combat this pandemic and stay strong-willed. Only then we can hope for a shared, sustainable future for humanity.

Indeed, the COVID-19 pandemic has brought countless challenges and changes to the world. In addition to a serious health crisis (more than 5.6 million deaths so far, as of January 31, 2022) and myriad economic issues, the social distancing policies due to the pandemic have substantially changed how we work. Thousands of people suffered profound work-related changes, shifting the work dynamic to home office. All those changes, in addition to the greater risk of infection itself, have brought fear, uncertainties, and a great stress at work.

Perhaps it is too early to arrive at post-pandemic *leadership theory and practice*. At the time of this writing (February 28, 2021), the new normal is barely emerging alongside the global vaccine rollout: the framework within which leaders will operate is not yet knowable, nor is the full measure of requirements of leadership practice determinable. Perhaps the disruption of the COVID-19 pandemic is one case of a wider pattern of systemic disruptions and challenges that leaders will increasingly face over the next decade.

Nevertheless, during this moment of crisis, we *must* build on the lessons we have learned so far and help leaders to embrace universal, holistic leadership principles—self-evident, self-validating laws that govern how leaders should lead change: *be authentic, have integrity, serve selflessly, and create communities of care, together.* The current context has increased the need for new leadership perspectives in the organizations that demand a more fluid, less encumbered, and more participative kind of leadership.

When leaders understand the context and embody these guiding principles as they start to practice within the emerging new normal, they will be *ready* to lead authentically—which in present volatile and precarious world is indeed something toward which we should aim.

It is not that the former leadership styles and change methodologies have become entirely redundant. It is just that we will need to reharness and reconfigure them to address in a sustainable manner the challenges posed by the emergent new normal. We call it leadership after post-COVID-19.

This book is our humble offering in this direction.

Burbank, CA, USA

Satinder K. Dhiman
Joan F. Marques

Introduction

These are uncertain times indeed; perhaps the toughest that humanity has ever experienced before in recent memory. A tiny virus has shaken the whole world like nothing else and has brought the whole humanity to its knees. It is a humbling revelation that we are not in charge of the show. Even more than a threat to our physical bodies, it represents a challenge to our consciousness, an attack on human psyche. We all need to work together with each other, albeit with stoic calm, to combat this pandemic and stay strong-willed. Only then we can hope for a shared, sustainable future for humanity.

Indeed, the COVID-19 pandemic has brought countless challenges and changes to the world. In addition to a serious health crisis (more than 2.3 million deaths so far, at the time of this writing—February 7, 2021) and myriad economic issues, the social distancing policies due to the pandemic have substantially changed how we work. Thousands of people suffered profound work-related changes, shifting the work dynamic to home office. All those changes, in addition to the greater risk of infection itself, have brought fear, uncertainties, and a great stress at work.

Perhaps it is too early to arrive at post-pandemic *leadership theory and practice*. At the time of this writing (February 28, 2021), the new normal is barely emerging alongside the global vaccine rollout: the framework within which leaders will operate is not yet knowable, nor is the full measure of requirements of leadership practice determinable. Perhaps the disruption of the COVID-19 pandemic is one case of a wider pattern of systemic disruptions and challenges that leaders will increasingly face over the next decade.

Nevertheless, during this moment of crisis, we *must* build on the lessons we have learned so far and help leaders to embrace universal, holistic leadership principles—self-evident, self-validating laws that govern how leaders should lead change: *be authentic, have integrity, serve selflessly, and create communities of care, together.* The current context has increased the need for new leadership perspectives in the organizations that demand a more fluid, less encumbered, and more participative kind of leadership.

When leaders understand the context and embody these guiding principles as they start to practice within the emerging new normal, they will be *ready* to lead authentically—which in present volatile and precarious world is indeed something toward which we should aim.

It is not that the former leadership styles and change methodologies have become entirely redundant. It is just that we will need to reharness and reconfigure them to address in a sustainable manner the challenges posed by the emergent new normal. We call it leadership after post-COVID-19.

This book is our humble offering in this direction.

Truly global in scope and strength, this volume highlights the concerted efforts of more than 40 scholar-practitioners to understand and share their findings regarding the broader themes of post-COVID-19 leadership and change for a sustainable future.

The following pages provide a synoptic overview of the various chapters in this volume.

Part I, comprising five chapters, focuses on *Organization Studies*.

- In Chap. 1, Dhiman opines that the COVID-19 pandemic has permanently changed lives around the world and no dimension of life and leadership seems to have been spared from its wrath. Masks, social distancing, and zooming have become the new norms, turning much of the world into "a collection of reluctant shut-ins." And yet, this pandemic has also stirred us into thinking about novel approaches to lead organizations and societies toward a shared, sustainable future. Perhaps it is too early to arrive at post-pandemic leadership theory and practice. Nevertheless, the current context has heightened the need for renewed leadership perspectives in the organizations that demand a more fluid, less encumbered, and more participative kind of leadership. This chapter offers one such engaging prospect in the form of holistic leadership. This chapter concludes with the ancient Greco-Roman philosophy called Stoicism as a choice perspective in life and leadership and also as a survival toolkit in the time of pandemic.
- In Chap. 2, Förster and Duchek aim to provide insights into the functioning and promotion of leaders' resilience. Based on previous resilience research in the fields of psychology and management, as well as their own empirical work, they develop a leaders' resilience model that points to central resilience factors in the leadership context. Their model focuses on behavioral resilience factors that leaders need to survive crises productively as well as healthily. These factors refer to the phases before, during, and after the critical event and depend on the leaders' traits and abilities as well as the leaders' private and work-related environment. The authors use the COVID-19 crisis to illustrate the individual parts of the model and draw lessons learned for future leadership practice.
- In Chap. 3, Dent notes that during the COVID-19 pandemic, Peter B. Vaill passed away at age 83. Although most of his scholarly output was in the twentieth century, Vaill remains a leading voice for the post-COVID-19 generation for insisting that managing, organizing, and leading are performing arts not just skills, behaviors, or competencies. He questioned the dominant unsustainable paradigms of the field and often found them inaccurate or insufficient. He observed over 60 years that the field has made little progress in producing actionable research and effectively teaching it. This chapter presents his vision, philosophy, and perspective for more sustainable organizations, which are arrayed in five

sections: (1) "Permanent Whitewater"—VUCA, (2) Manager-Leaders not Management Competencies, (3) Practice, (4) Management is Purposing, Learning, Encouraging, and (5) Management Education.

- In Chap. 4, Roberts explores how the attributes of Christian servant leadership reinforce sustainable leadership practices from a conceptual, empirical, and Christian social justice theological perspective. Sustainable practices are embedded and integrated within organizational macro, intermediate, and micro levels that entail producing goods and services that promote the greater good and in a fashion that facilitates the well-being and growth of all the key stakeholders. The key focus of the chapter is the micro leadership and human resource policies and practices that stimulate employee long-term sustainability on the job to reduce burnout and the associated negative physical, emotional, spiritual, and organizational performance outcomes. The chapter concludes with recommendations for future research and development.
- In Chap. 5, Chaskalson, Nichols, and Hardman take the system disruption of the COVID-19 pandemic to be one case of a wider pattern of systemic disruptions that leaders will increasingly face. Their fieldwork observation of their clients' responses to the crisis has showed them that some ways of leading work better than others in adaptive times. The authors have identified that less egotistic forms of leadership—which we call here Quiet Ego Leadership—help in forming agile and collaborative responses to systems shifts. This chapter describes the AIM model of Quiet Ego Leadership—Allowing, Inquiry and Meta-awareness—and shows how this type of leadership can be developed and applied in practice.
- In Chap. 6, Delves suggests that we can't yet teach post-pandemic *leadership practice*. The new normal is only just emerging alongside the global vaccine rollout: the framework within which leaders will operate is not yet knowable, how they need to practice is unknowable. But in this moment of hiatus, this global inflection point, we must help leaders to embrace *leadership principles*: self-evident, self-validating laws that govern how leaders should lead: be authentic, have integrity, behave with emotional intelligence. When leaders understand and embrace these principles before they start to practice within the emerging new normal, they will be ready to lead transformationally—which in a world where every industry, every activity, every endeavor in which we are engaged must change if it is to survive is surely something toward which we should aim. In a volatile world, this is how to aim for a future in which leaders take us beyond striving toward thriving.
- In Chap. 7, Lopes and Hayashi aver that the world after COVID-19 is strongly transformed by the digital revolution and industry 4.0 and it demands a new leadership style. Younger, connected, restless, and convicted people do not want to work for someone: they want to work with someone. Coevolutive leadership proposes to be a positive answer at this new social, cultural, and economic moment, based on three key elements: Vision, Conviction, and Motivation. This leadership model seeks progression over time from people who are freed from the ungrateful task of receiving orders to build together, with active shared responsibilities and who seek, in a changing and still unclear future, to cooperate

in the mind, in the hands, and in the heart. These are probably the legacies of the pandemic, a better world for everyone with the obligation of being each day a better person. A struggle for life and a life for struggling to help others.

- In Chap. 8, Song and Ford observe that the COVID-19 pandemic has made it imperative to practice social distancing, making technology-mediated leadership more needed than ever before. E-leadership sheds light on coordinating and re-shaping the workforce through the integration of leadership and advanced information technology. However, extant e-leadership literature is still based on the assumption that it is a technology-assisted natural intelligence (i.e., human intelligence) system. Artificial intelligence (AI)-simulated leaders can be a viable alternative to human leaders because of their abilities to learn and apply learning to works. The pandemic, coupled with AI technology, drives us to revisit and rethink e-leadership from an AI perspective. By integrating AI into e-leadership, we propose "e-leadership 2.0," which explores the possibility of substituting natural intelligence with AI in a leadership context.
- In Chap. 9, Luning and Ledford explore a series of questions triggered by the Global pandemic: what does it take for organizations to persist through such an unparalleled global situation? What role do leaders play in enabling organizations to persist during a crisis? How can leaders foster an environment where the organization is able to be resilient through such a crisis? This chapter proposes that organizations with gritty cultures are better equipped to persist through crisis and demonstrate organizational resilience in the face of obstacles. This chapter highlights the elements of a culture of organizational grit and how those elements contribute to resilience. Further, the chapter emphasizes the role that leaders play in establishing a culture of organizational grit, enabling their organization to be resilient when overcoming catastrophic events.
- In Chap. 10, Makka opines that the COVID-19 pandemic has revealed many areas of strength, weakness, opportunity, and potential threat in businesses, organizations, and societies around the world. The COVID-19 crisis has laid bare the need for leaders who have integrity and moral leadership. Extant theories on leadership pay scant attention to the moral dimension of leadership. This chapter contends that to re-set and re-build businesses, industries, organizations, and societies after COVID-19 in a sustainable manner, moral leadership is imperative. Moral leaders are those who demonstrate compassion and respect for others, they are humane and humble, they value and speak the truth, and they actively listen. In today's world, such leaders are more important than ever before. In this chapter, moral leadership is defined, the traits of moral leaders are examined, the case for moral leadership is made, and the consequences of a lack of moral leadership in a post-COVID-19 world are considered.
- In Chap. 11, Marques reviews the need for ongoing expansion of and reflection on one's internal locus of control as a personal skill toward perseverance and creative reinvention in challenging times. Using the COVID-19 global pandemic, as well as previous global challenges as instigators, the chapter will discuss some critical tools for self-preservation, sustainable growth, and overall excellence in personal and professional settings. The chapter first discusses the need for posi-

tive leadership as a necessary mode of operation in a post-COVID-19 world, with an emphasis on awakened leadership. In extension to setting this stage, the chapter discusses the positive practice of COURAGE, which alludes to an understanding of having a Choice, nurturing an Open mind, keeping aware of the Usefulness of every experience, engaging in regular Reality checks, positivizing one's Attitude, honing the inner Genius (creative skills), and continuing to Educate oneself.

- In Chap. 12, Caro observes that as the world prepares for recovery after the COVID-19 pandemic, it will be clear that the world community is evolving into a cogent and unified planetary society. Humankind will continue to confront existential threats, including those demographic, environmental, pandemic, and technological in nature, as well as war conflicts. These threats will require cogent transformational leadership to meet extraordinary planetary system challenges effectively and proactively. In evoking the possible contours of the future landscape, this chapter underscores the need for cogent and ethical leadership values that will drive and transform the emerging integrated planetary society toward the end of the twenty-first century. Transformational leaders will transcend national paradigms and form the foundations and shape of future planetary solutions and systems. Such systems will not be a panacea but will allow for more humane and integrated collaboration and coordinated approaches to humankind development and foster greater environmental integrity, harmony, justice, and peace.
- In Chap. 13, Xu and Niu aver that as we re-imagine normalcy together, there is an increased need for modification of leadership style and tasks at work. Faster business cycles caused by COVID-19 accelerate the shift away from classic authoritarian leadership to more bottom-up models. With disruptions from the global pandemic, employees facing new challenges also seek out more self-initiated adjustments to their jobs. The authors suggest that transformational leaders could develop and cultivate employee job crafting to increase work engagement and utilize it as a communication tool to create shared visions. Transformational leaders can guide employees to initiate changes and connect individual tasks or jobs to the organization's overarching purpose. The authors propose that shaping a climate of psychological safety is crucial for the organization to craft and update their journey together during this volatile time.
- In Chap. 14, Gingerich notes that during the time of COVID-19, there has been speculation on whether a global shutdown has impacted the release of Greenhouse Gas (GHG) emissions into the atmosphere and whether there is hope for a reversal of CO_2 emissions if certain practices are permanently altered—e.g., less air travel, the provision of alternate forms of clean-fuel energy, and limiting livestock farming. Noticeably, as a result of COVID-19, foot traffic is on the increase, flights have been limited in passenger bookings and destination choice, and skies have been noticeably clearer—from Shanghai to Los Angeles. And global CO_2 emissions are on track to drop by 5.5% by the end of 2020—such a drop would be the largest yearly change on record, surpassing the financial crisis of 2008 and World War II. But even with the global economy gridlocked, science indicates

that the world is still on track to release 95% of the carbon dioxide emitted in a typical year, continuing to heat up the planet and intensify climate change even with so many still at home. In this chapter, the author explores questions such as: What can be done to lead the world from this seemingly inevitable calamity and implement the measures necessary to effect meaningful change? What already has been in the works since the signing of the Paris Agreement in 2015 that might be expanded now?

- In Chap. 15, Mayer and Wilke provide insights into the views of experts with regard to changes in the global automotive industry during VUCA times. They present findings from a qualitative, international study in the automotive industry, based on 30 qualitative interviews conducted with experts in the field. Findings show that crucial areas of leading employees and organizations in VUCA times refer to driving organizational change and applying specific leadership values, developing organizations toward social enterprises, based on faith, passion, meaning, and purpose in the context of ethical, action-driven leadership. The chapter provides a conclusion and recommendations for future research into both organizational and leadership practice.
- In Chap. 16, Gupta and Reina develop a conceptual framework of mindful leadership in crisis to explain how leader mindfulness influences follower outcomes. They draw from and advance mindfulness theory and the high-quality connections literature to propose that mindful leaders better manage crisis situations by expressing empathetic behaviors, actively listening, and empowering their followers. These leader behaviors significantly color followers' emotional experiences and contribute to improved follower work outcomes including job satisfaction, satisfaction with their leader, relationship quality, and job performance. Throughout the chapter, they refer to the COVID-19 pandemic as an example crisis situation in which mindful leaders can be especially helpful in shaping followers' experiences.
- In Chap. 17, Schockman and Ravani aver that the pandemic has exposed the dearth of Crisis Global Leader (CGL) competencies. The massive amounts of food loss and waste in both case countries have created food deserts, an epidemic of hunger/food insecurity, and a huge carbon footprint. The AFSC has both upstream and downstream factors that have added to poverty and food scarcity by increasing prices, further creating widespread food insecurity for the masses. Government intervention (lack of) has added a burden to provide a solution to this severe and immediate food shortage problem. Although food systems are deteriorating worldwide, innovation such as blockchain technology, inculcating competency skill sets for our future global leaders, a systematic approach to improving local organic farming, and the involvement of nonprofit organizations at all state levels are needed to regulate this massive break in the food supply system in both developing and developed nations.
- In Chap. 18, Sum explores the significance of information literacy within leadership practice in schools, and its implications for school leadership during a crisis such as COVID-19. Education, and more specifically schooling, has faced many calls for change and accountability. While not the first crisis for school leaders,

COVID-19 challenged many day-to-day aspects of school life. The speed, impact, and levels of uncertainty addressed by school leaders, during such times of crisis, highlighted the significance of information literacy as critical to leadership practice. This chapter draws on data from two different case studies of school leaders, one pre-COVID and one during COVID-19, both providing illustrations of leadership during crisis. The illustrative examples provide insight into how school leaders currently enact information literate practice as a means of developing sustainable leadership.

- In Chap. 19, Bayat and Cissna opine that since executive coaches often serve as trusted advisors, it is thus imperative for them to not only understand the nature and impact of VUCA conditions on a leader's wellness and mental clarity, but also build their skillset to ensure leadership effectiveness through such uncharted times. This book chapter summarizes findings from a qualitative research study that examined the best practices for executive coaches who support global leaders. The results combine insights and advice from 39 highly successful, in-demand executive coaches, representing nine different countries, from a wide array of disciplines and professional backgrounds who provide strategies for leadership success in a VUCA world. Findings suggest nine key best practices, centered on presence and open-mindedness, as the basis to support leadership success as we collectively address the challenges during the COVID-19 pandemic and beyond.
- In Chap. 20, Leonelli and Primavera present a study that aims to identify nurses' abilities and behaviors affecting their adaptability to change in crisis periods. Adaptability to change is widely recognized as the main reason for difficulty in implementing change initiatives. Nevertheless, little is known about the factors triggering such a behavior in the workplace. An original research model is developed and empirically tested using primary data collected from Italian nurses between April and May 2020. In total, the final sample includes the responses of 281 nurses. Linear regression models are employed to test the hypotheses. Through the lens of change management, results show that nurses' positive behavior and their coping and leadership/authority abilities positively affect their adaptability to change. By analyzing the different dimensions of individual evaluation toward change, and also considering the environmental crisis given by COVID-19, their study expands the knowledge in the fields of change management and nursing management, thus adding something to previous works.
- In Chap. 21, Pestonjee and Pastakia observe that the COVID-19 pandemic has brought about an unprecedented emphasis on the slogan "Work from Home!" We must however ask ourselves, "Are our homes truly designed to act as workplaces?" Most "lockdowns" did not provide enough advance warnings for the workforce and HR professionals to even contemplate about reimagining their home as their office. Apart from an in-depth exploration of novel post-pandemic workplace adaptations for the OB/HR profession in several sectors, this chapter shall also explore, in conjunction, other impacts relevant to these novel workplace adaptations, which "shelter-in-place" or "lockdown" restrictions have had such as the sudden brakes on excessively materialistic lifestyles of the urban

populace, disruptions in population density, likely changes in labor migration patterns, etc. and all other changes that are likely to stay. Lastly, the various trends in general mental health of the populace as ramifications of the lockdowns (both positive and negative) have been discussed.

- In Chap. 22, Emirza notes that the COVID-19 outbreak has dramatic effects on organizations and organizational members across the globe. Many organizational members have gone through a drastic change and become remote workers almost overnight. Because this abrupt shift to remote working was mandatory rather than optional, the extant knowledge on remote working might not be easily generalized in such an unprecedented context. By drawing on Job Demands Resources theory, this chapter aims to explore how leaders have attempted to motivate employees enforced to remote working. For this purpose, semi-structured interviews with 12 employees working from home were conducted. Accordingly, two job demands (long working hours and work overload) were identified as demotivating factors. On the other hand, five job resources (communication of supervisor, technical support, social support, rewards and recognition, and flexibility and job control) were identified as motivating factors.
- In Chap. 23, Owens notes that after experiencing the global pandemic of COVID-19, there remains no doubt that our world is volatile, complex, and uncertain. In this environment, there is no perfect leader—no ideal set of personality traits or leadership strategies that is perfect for every situation. To be successful, leaders must identify their strengths and weaknesses, and then adapt to the situation at hand. Upon the advice of Ancona et al. (2007) who praise the "incomplete leader," we must recognize that not only is it acceptable to be "incomplete," but we can grow stronger together through distributive leadership. The chapter introduces new integrated framework of leader-personality to help the reader identify their own leader-personality profile, and then identify others who can compensate where they are weak. The seven-part framework is grounded in personality psychology and leadership theory, and underpinned by a biblical definition of personality.
- In Chap. 24, Sharififard proposes to assess how the local food environment and the uncertainty of food security in areas affected by a lack of food sources affect the ability to have food and nutrition security. Based on the author's dissertation research conducted during the doctoral program, this chapter further identifies how the regional food supply chain is affected by social determinants in the food system by using a qualitative and philosophical approach to food security and urban geography. The author also analyzes food accessibility among the local and systemic level through (a) the emerging rise of food pantries, (b) changes to food waste and food policy, and (c) food system activities related to food services more likely to affect the likelihood of food insecurity issues. The author also explains the benefits of a structurally, economically, and geographically diverse food system that includes food products needed for sustainable food banks and food services.
- In Chap. 25, Dean states that the author was at center stage when planning for Y2K in a global organization and maintained the plan for over 20 years. As

COVID-19 unfolded in early 2020, those skills were in high demand as organizations without a plan scrambled to figure out what to do. This chapter will walk through the basics of developing a Business Continuity Plan that will help reduce fear and uncertainty in schools, organizations, communities, churches, and households. This chapter will also discuss the whole person (body, heart, mind, and soul) aspect of such a strategy. From a theoretical perspective, it will discuss leadership theory, change management, crisis management, and social responsibility.

- In Chap. 26, Aboramadan and Kundi observe that sophisticated planetary difficulties, extraordinary turbulence, and unforeseen chaos of COVID-19 have exposed the world of today. Although this current state amplifies the difficulties that organizational leaders face, it also offers fertile ground of opportunities for leadership that promote new approaches of thinking, leading, and learning. Therefore, progressive thoughts on leadership practice and theory, and relevant leadership strategies to manage the current crises and emergencies, are therefore an urgent must for organizations. The significance of emergency management in leading an organization and the vital role that emergency-oriented leaders play within organizations require the creation of a leadership framework relevant to emergency. Given this discussion, the authors propose in this chapter a model of emergency-oriented leadership developed based on a literature review pertaining to emergency and leadership. Furthermore, this chapter provides a roadmap to leaders and policymakers insights on the leadership qualities needed to deal with emergencies such as crisis, epidemics, etc.
- In Chap. 27, Lang and Sutton present an innovative leadership model that builds upon a framework for repackaging a proven Swiss Army Knife of tools to approach digitized workplaces affected by COVID-19 and the VUCA (volatility, uncertainty, complexity, and ambiguity) ecosystem our world has been thrust toward. Today our organizations are challenged to improve creativity, originality, initiative, innovation, critical thinking, and complex problem-solving. Leaders in the post-COVID-19, VUCA world require a different mindset than those of the Third Industrial Revolution, which is achievable, according to the authors, by applying the proposed framework of techniques in the Internal Leadership model. The tools of the External Leadership model, on the other hand, could support leaders in building rapport and gaining authenticity and credibility within the Fourth Industrial Revolution, making them able to inspire and empower their communities. The authors bring it together within the proposed Internal-External Leadership Model.
- In Chap. 28, Kaushal analyzes the wisdom-related ideologies through narratives and their relevance in the context of today's volatile, uncertain, complex, and ambiguous environment after COVID-19 of the organizations for the development of strategies and represents an indigenous concept of sustainable leadership. The world's bizarre, peculiar, and the constant changing environment has presented new challenges for leaders, which act as new possibilities to validate their expertise and explore distinct strategies. It requires the implementation of a viable leadership approach, including vigorous, effective, and rational policies in

the organizational setting. Ancient scholars have acknowledged the soulful, intense, harmonious, and spiritual pedagogy embodied in the Upanishads of Indian civilization as an extensive notion of knowledge that has provided strength and human values to the people in managing the dynamic and varying circumstances. Spiritual perception develops an energetic and positive sentiment by reducing psychological strain during a crisis and provides new insight and unique vision with a prospective solution.

- In Chap. 29, Sarkar states that leadership determines the outcome in a crisis. To be sustainable it must be based on perennial principles. The chapter defines spiritual economics based on the eternal concepts of Vedanta and differentiating it from religious economics, establishes its efficacy in the light of the shortcomings of the conventional economics. The notion of sustainable development is delineated as per the definitions of WCED and in the light of this philosophy. An attempt is made to establish that this spiritual economics can make the development really sustainable. In this backdrop, this chapter investigates whether there has been any suitable time-tested leadership theory which can support this endeavor. Given this interconnected background of spiritual economics and sustainability, this chapter examines whether and to what extent this evolving concept can be applied in the present COVID-19-induced pandemic whose all-encompassing impact has made the world increasingly volatile, uncertain, complex, and ambiguous (VUCA). It presents many representative illustrations and opines that the socially responsible *Rājarshi* leadership concept can be an Indian response to the world crisis, which can bring some peace and order in the chaotic post-COVID-19 world.
- In Chap. 30, Brown and Schockman observe that the COVID-19 pandemic and resulting social, economic, and political crisis has unleashed an avalanche of uncertainty and unique challenges on the global stage. Within a constructivist theoretical lens, this chapter explores the failures of pandemic global leadership. These failures include that global leadership has been xenophobic, siloed, and fraught with mixed messages that make followership problematic. Nevertheless, triumphs of global leadership have also emerged against the backdrop of the coronavirus, such as accelerated digital transformation and the recognition of a cadre of influential young women leaders internationally. Lessons can be gleaned from the coronavirus experience for application in the post-pandemic era. Global leaders will need to be more agile, connected, and empathetic. A preliminary empirical research study concludes that core leadership factors of focusing on collective over individual interests, communicating optimism and a sense of purpose, and having concern for the moral and ethical impact of decisions will be more important post-pandemic than in the pre-pandemic era. Overall, the roadmap for post-pandemic leadership as designed by the citizen voice is grounded in notions of transformational leadership.
- In Chap. 31, Kumar and Modi observe that COVID-19 has compelled the leaders to think and lead differently in the present volatile, uncertain, complex, and ambiguous (VUCA) environment with new challenges like loss of comfort zones, disorganization, unpredictable speed and magnitude of change, sudden

and severe fluctuations due to lockdowns, etc. They need to leverage compassion and creativity for taking decisions that will impact on large number of people. Positive leadership deeply rooted in spirituality, ethical and moral values like interconnectedness, universal responsibility, courage, meaning in life, patience and tolerance, learning and sharing, selfless service, and self-awareness that have contributed to happiness and well-being of people can promise shared and sustainable future. This chapter attempts to explore the role of positive leadership in the present VUCA environment.

- In Chap. 32, Craddock observes that some organizations and leaders struggle with balancing decisions regarding financial, societal, and environmental contributions, the three traditional components of sustainability. While some leaders pursue "the infinite game," many focus primarily on the near term by necessity. This chapter explores the relationships among an organization's leadership, its pursuit of excellence, the balance of traditional sustainability components, and ultimately its longevity. Then, it reexamines those relationships through the lens of the COVID-19 pandemic, a global existential threat that has affected both organizations and individuals in unequal ways. Insights from both failed and surviving organizations may provide lessons for future organizational resiliency.

Satinder K. Dhiman
Joan F. Marques

Contents

About the Editors

Satinder K. Dhiman Recognized as a lead thinker for his pioneer contributions to the field of transformational leadership, workplace spirituality, workplace well-being, sustainability, and fulfillment in personal and professional arena, Professor Dhiman is a sought-after keynote speaker at regional, national, and international conferences. In 2013, he was invited to be the opening speaker at the prestigious TEDx Conference @ College of the Canyons in Santa Clarita, California. Since then, he has led several major national and international conferences as co-organizer and/or as track chair. With an instructional and research focus on leadership and organizational behavior—and with specific concentration on sustainability, workplace spirituality, and well-being—Professor Dhiman holds a PhD in Social Sciences from Tilburg University, the Netherlands, an EdD in Organizational Leadership from Pepperdine University, Los Angeles, an MBA from West Coast University, Los Angeles, and a Master's degree in Commerce from Panjab University, Chandigarh, India, having earned the Gold Medal. *He has also completed advanced Executive Leadership Programs at Harvard, Stanford, and Wharton.* Recipient of several national and international academic and professional honors and awards in teaching, scholarship, and service, Professor Dhiman won the Woodbury University Ambassador of the Year Award in 2015 and 2017 and MBA Professor of the Year Award in 2015; Scholarly and Creative Writing Award, 2019; Most Valuable MBA Professor Award, 2018; Most Inspirational and Most Charismatic MBA Teacher Award 2012, 2013/2014/2018; the Steve Allen Excellence in Education Award in 2006; and the prestigious ACBSP International Teacher of the Year Award in 2004. Most recently, he chaired a symposium at the Academy of Management that received 2019 Best Symposium Proposal and Showcase Symposium Award. Professor Dhiman is committed to an interdisciplinary research agenda and has published scholarship in many fields including organization behavior, holistic leadership, workplace spirituality, workplace well-being and fulfillment, sustainability, servant leadership, mindfulness, social entrepreneurship, education, organization development, and Eastern and Western philosophy. Professor Dhiman has done over 65 Conference Presentations and more than 55 Invited Keynotes, Plenary Sessions, Conference Track Chair Sessions, Distinguished Key Guest Lectures, and Creative Workshops—*nationally and internationally*—and has published over 60 peer-reviewed journal articles and book chapters. Author, translator, editor, co-author, and co-editor of over 35 management, leadership, spirituality, sustainability, and accounting-related books and research monographs, his recent books include: *New Horizons in Management, Leadership and Sustainability* (Springer, 2021; with Samaratunge); *New Horizons in Positive Leadership and Change* (Springer, 2020); *Social Entrepreneurship and Corporate Social Responsibility* (Springer, 2020; with Marques); *Bhagavad Gītā and Leadership: A Catalyst for Organizational Transformation* (Palgrave Macmillan, 2019); *Managing by the Bhagavad Gītā: Timeless Lessons for Today's Managers* (Springer, 2018; with Amar); *Holistic Leadership* (Palgrave, 2017); *Gandhi and Leadership* (Palgrave, 2015); *Seven Habits of Highly Fulfilled People* (2012); and *Engaged Leadership* (Springer, 2018; with Marques); *Spirituality and Sustainability* (Springer, 2016); and *Leadership Today* (Springer, 2016). He has also translated several Indian spiritual classics into English, including the *Sahaja Gītā*. He is the *Editor-in-Chief* of seven multi-author *M*ajor *R*eference *W*orks: *Springer Handbook of Engaged Sustainability* (2018—Springer International, Switzerland) and *Palgrave Handbook of Workplace Spirituality and Fulfillment* (2018—Palgrave Macmillan, USA); *Routledge Companion to Mindfulness at Work* (2020); *Palgrave Handbook of Workplace Well-Being* (2021—Palgrave Macmillan); *Routledge Companion to Leadership and Change* (2022—Routledge, UK); *The Palgrave Handbook of Servant Leadership* (2022—Palgrave Macmillan, USA; with Roberts); *The Springer Handbook of Global Leadership and Followership* (2022—Springer International, Switzerland; with Marques, Schmieder-Ramirez, and Malakyan). Additionally, he serves as the *Editor-in-Chief* of *Palgrave Studies in Workplace Spirituality and Fulfillment; Routledge Frontiers in Sustainable Business*; the *General Editor* of a series entitled *Routledge Frontiers in Sustainable Business Practice* (the Series); and co-editor of *Springer Series in Management, Change, Strategy and Positive Leadership*.Some of his select forthcoming titles include *Leading without Power: A Model of Highly Fulfilled Leaders* (2022—Palgrave Macmillan); *Conscious Consumption: Healthy, Humane and Sustainable Living* (2022—Routledge, UK); *Wise Leadership for Turbulent Times* (2021—Routledge, UK); and *Creative Leadershift: Discover. Innovate. Enact.* (2022—Routledge, with Chandra Handa). He has published research with his colleagues in the *Journal of Values-Based Leadership, Organization Development Journal, Journal of Management Development, Journal of Social Change, Journal of Applied Business and Economics*, and *Performance Improvement*. Currently, Professor Dhiman serves as the Associate Dean, Chair, and Director of the MBA Program; and as the Professor of Management at Woodbury University, Burbank, California. He has served as the Chair for a special MBA Program for the Mercedes-Benz executives, China. He was invited as Distinguished Visiting Professor at the Tecnológico de Monterrey, Guadalajara campus, Mexico, and has served as E-Commerce curriculum lead advisor, Universidad Francisco Gavidia, El Salvador, and coordinator for LA Fieldtrip for MBA students for the Berlin

University for Professional Studies (DUW). He was also invited by Monash University, Australia, to lead a track in Spirituality in Management in the 16th International Conference in Business Management, held during Dec. 12–15, 2019. He has served as the President (2016–2018) and now serves as a distinguished *Patron*, International Chamber for Service Industry (ICSI). Professor Dhiman has served as Accreditation Consultant, Evaluator, and Site Visit Team Leader for the Accreditation Council for Business Schools and Programs (ACBSP) for more than 25 universities in America, Canada, Europe, and Asia. He is the Founder-Director of Forever Fulfilled, a Los Angeles-based Well-being Consultancy that focuses on workplace wellness, workplace spirituality, and self-leadership.

Joan F. Marques has reinvented herself from a successful media and social entrepreneur in Suriname, South America, to an innovative "edupreneur" (educational entrepreneur) in California, USA. Her entrepreneurial career spans over four decades and includes the creation and successful management of companies in Public Relations and Advertising, Import and Export, Real Estate, Media Productions, and a Nonprofit, focused on women's advancement. In the United States, she has been a co-founder of the *Business Renaissance Institute* and the *Academy of Spirituality and Professional Excellence* (ASPEX). Based on her impressive career and ongoing influence, Dr. Marques was awarded the highest state decoration of her home country, Suriname: *Commander (Commandeur) in the Honorary Order of the Yellow Star*, in 2015. That same year, she was also awarded the *Dr. Nelle Becker-Slaton Pathfinder Award* from the Association of Pan-African Doctoral Scholars in Los Angeles, for her exemplary and groundbreaking professional performance. In 2019, she was awarded the *Kankantrie Life Time Achievement Award* for her accomplishments in Education from the Suriname American Network Inc. in Miami, FL. In 2016, she was granted the *Faculty Scholarly-Creative Award* as well as the *Faculty Ambassador Award*, both awarded by Woodbury University's Faculty Association. Dr. Marques is a frequent speaker and presenter at academic and professional venues. In 2016, she gave a TEDx Talk at College of the Canyons in California, titled "*An Ancient Path Towards a Better Future*," in which she analyzed the Noble Eightfold Path, one of the foundational Buddhist practices, within the realm of contemporary business performance. In recent years she has conducted presentations and workshops on multiple forums, such as at the Management, Spirituality and Religion research colloquia at the Academy of Management Annual Meetings in 2018 and 2019 on *Phenomenology as a Qualitative Research Method*; a keynote address titled "*Ethical Leadership: How Morals Influence Your Communication*" at the Center for Communication and Public Relations, in Paramaribo, Suriname; and an interactive workshop with thought leaders and development coaches at the Knowledge and Expertise Center Suriname, titled "*On Leadership, Ethics and Social Responsibility*." In 2019 and 2020 she also represented her home country Suriname on the annual CALIFEST literary festival in Los Angeles, where she conducted workshops on successful publishing. In 2016, she presented at the Kravis Leadership Institute at Claremont McKenna College, on female leadership during the annual *Women and Leadership Alliance* (WLA) conference, resulting in the collective work, "Women's Leadership Journeys: Stories, Research and Novel Perspectives" (Routledge, 2019) in which she contributed the chapter, "*Courage: Mapping the Leadership Journey.*" Dr. Marques further conducts regular presentations at the Academy of Management, and at business venues in Los Angeles as well as for professional audiences in Miami and Suriname. Joan's research interests pertain to Awakened Leadership, Buddhist Psychology in Management, and Workplace Spirituality. Her works have been widely published and cited in both academic and popular venues. She has written more than 150 scholarly articles, which were published in prestigious scholarly journals such as *The Journal of Business Ethics, Business and Society, International Journal of Organizational Analysis, Leadership & Organization Development Journal, The International Journal of Management Education, Journal of Communication Management, Journal of Management Development, Organization Development Journal,* and *Human Resource Development Quarterly*. Dr. Marques has (co)authored and (co)edited more than 32 books, among which, *New Horizons in Positive Leadership and Change* (Springer, 2020); *Social Entrepreneurship and Corporate Social Responsibility* (Springer, 2020; with Dhiman); *The Routledge Companion to Happiness at Work* (2020); *The Routledge Companion to Inclusive Leadership* (2020); *Lead with Heart in Mind* (Springer, 2019); *The Routledge Companion to Management and Workplace Spirituality*; *Engaged Leadership: Transforming through Future-Oriented Design* (with Satinder Dhiman—Springer, 2018); *Ethical Leadership, Progress with a Moral Compass* (Routledge, 2017); *Leadership, Finding Balance Between Acceptance and Ambition* (Routledge, 2016); *Leadership Today: Practices for Personal and Professional Performance* (with Satinder Dhiman—Springer, 2016); *Business and Buddhism* (Routledge, 2015); and *Leadership and Mindful Behavior: Action, Wakefulness, and Business* (Palgrave MacMillan, 2014).Joan currently serves as Dean at Woodbury University's School of Business, in Burbank, California, where she works on infusing and nurturing the concept of "*Business with a Conscience*" into internal and external stakeholders. She is also a Full Professor of Management and teaches business courses related to Leadership, Ethics, Creativity, Social Entrepreneurship, and Organizational Behavior in graduate and undergraduate programs. Joan holds a PhD in Social Sciences (focus: *Buddhist Psychology in Management*) from Tilburg University's Oldendorff Graduate School and an EdD in Organizational Leadership (focus: *Workplace Spirituality*) from Pepperdine University's Graduate School of Education and Psychology. She also holds an MBA from Woodbury University and a BSc in Business Economics from MOC, Suriname. Additionally, she has completed postdoctoral work at Tulane University's Freeman School of Business. Dr. Marques is a member of the executive committee of the *Management, Spirituality and Religion* interest group of the Academy of Management, where she serves as the officer for Membership and Community Building.

About the Contributors

Mohammed Aboramadan received his PhD in economics and management (major: management) from the University of Pavia, Italy. Currently, Dr. Aboramadan works as a postdoctoral research fellow at the Department of Economics, Management and Statistics with areas focused on human resource management (HRM), leadership, employee and organizational performance. Dr. Aboramadan has published in the area of servant leadership in service-based sectors. Furthermore, Dr. Aboramadan has published in the *International Journal of Contemporary Hospitality Management*, *Journal of Management Development*, *Voluntas*, *Academy of Management Proceedings*, *International Journal of Organizational Analysis*, *International Journal of Educational Management*, *Journal of Higher Education Policy and Management*, *International Journal of Public Administration*, and *Journal for Global Business Advancement*.

Noushin Bayat is the founder of Engaging Wisdom, Inc, a consultancy organization that provides change management, leadership development, and executive coaching services within agile organizational environments that require stakeholder management and engagement across all business functions. Dr. Bayat strives to create healthy work cultures and operational strategies that empower individuals and teams to thrive. Dr. Bayat's clients include: Children's Hospital Los Angeles, University of Southern California (USC), Gap USA, Nestle Globe, Nestle USA, Kaiser Permanente, Tesco's Fresh & Easy Markets, and Deloitte & Touche, among others. Dr. Bayat has a doctorate in organizational leadership from Pepperdine University where her research focused on how complex global systems impact not only leaders but also operational and decision-making systems and how coaching best practices need to adapt to support leaders to thrive within this web of complexity. Findings point to "presence" as a key factor in thriving through VUCA conditions.

Natasha Brown is a PhD student in the Global Leadership and Change program at Pepperdine University in the Graduate School of Arts and Sciences. She holds an MA in International Relations from Yale University and a BA in Political Science from Occidental College. Natasha also studied at the University of Helsinki in Finland with a Fulbright fellowship. Professionally, she works in organizational development and business strategy and brings a deep passion for and expertise in large-scale enterprise transformation. Natasha has a background in international business, management consulting, and nonprofit. Her research interests include Post-Pandemic Global Leadership, Mentorship and Transformational Learning, Self-Awareness in Executive Development, Post-M&A Organizational Culture, and Crisis Leadership. Natasha lives in Portland, Oregon.

Denis H. J. Caro is a Professor Emeritus with the Telfer School of Management at the University of Ottawa in Ottawa, Canada. His alma mater is McGill University, and he holds degrees in mathematics, management information systems, and a Doctorate in Hospital and Health Care Administration from the School of Public Health of the University of Minnesota. He has extensive professional and teaching experience across Canada and the United States in emergency management, health care management, and e-health systems. Author of extensive scholarly publications, he is also the recipient of numerous awards in research, teaching, and leadership. He has a passionate love for teaching and students, whom he regards as the "Hope of the twenty-first Century." Dr. Caro leads a very simple life and admits to being a man of prayer and faith.

Michael Chaskalson is a pioneer in the application of mindfulness to leadership and workplace contexts. He is a Professor of Practice adjunct at Hult Ashridge Executive Education; an Associate at the Møller Institute at Churchill College in the University of Cambridge; founding director at Mindfulness Works Ltd.; and a Partner at GameShift. He is the author of several books, papers, and book chapters on mindfulness, in general and in organizations, as well as mindful leadership. He co-led the training on a world-first waitlist controlled trial of the effects of an 8-week Mindful Leader program with senior business leaders at Ashridge. He is the author of *The Mindful Workplace* (Wiley-Blackwell, 2011), *Mindfulness in Eight Weeks* (Harper Thorsons, 2014), and co-author of *Mindfulness for Coaches* (Routledge, 2018) and *Mind Time* (Harper Thorsons, 2018).

Kerri Cissna is a Postdoctoral Fellow with the Program for Leadership and Character at Wake Forest University where she teaches entrepreneurship. She earned a PhD in global leadership and change from Pepperdine University where she also teaches Leading the Philanthropic Enterprise. Dr. Cissna is also a lecturer at Cal State Long Beach. She formerly served as Executive Director of Leadership Long Beach and as Assistant Vice-Chancellor, Director of Housing and Residence Life, and the Leadership Development Coordinator at Pepperdine University.

William T. Craddock is a global trainer, author, and consultant. He previously led staff and operations groups for a Fortune 300 company, and now works with organizations to improve their organizational effectiveness and sustainability. Assignments have included strategic planning, organizational excellence, and various workshops. His certifications include Lean Six Sigma Black Belt (LSSBB) and Project Management Professional (PMP). Bill has made presentations at various

Global Congresses and authored a PMI Thought Leadership White Paper on Change Management. He has served as a Master Examiner for the Baldrige Performance Excellence Program as a team leader and site visit team leader. He has been a member of two US Delegations for ISO international Committees—TC/176 (Quality Assurance & Quality Management) and TC/279 (Innovation Management) and has served in leadership roles for the respective US ISO committees. Bill has undergraduate/graduate Engineering degrees, a Doctorate in Higher Education, and is a Registered Professional Engineer (PE).

Debra J. Dean is an adjunct professor at Regent University. She has 25+ years of experience in corporate with responsibilities including, but not limited to, business continuity plans, business transformation, quality control, and operations excellence. She is a published researcher and sought-after speaker with topics related to faith at work, followership, organizational metaphors, respectful pluralism, and social responsibility. She holds a PhD in Organizational Leadership from Regent University. Dean holds many titles including the 2020 Woman of Influence, Most Influential Business Consultancy CEO, Operational Excellence Leader of the Year, and Top Female Leader of the Year.

Roger Delves is currently a Fellow of the RSA and educated at Oxford with a first career with international ad agency DMB&B, where he was a board director of the London office. Roger taught at Cranfield University School of Management before joining Ashridge in 2008. He is the Associate Dean of Faculty and a Professor of Practice, specializing in leadership. His academic interests are around authenticity and emotional intelligence, transformational leadership, and team engagement. Co-author of *Fifty Management Dilemmas* and co-editor of *Inspiring Leadership*, he is a regular contributor of articles to professional journals and recently co-wrote a paper delivered at Euram 2020. He has taught all over the world, delivering material for tailored, open and degree qualification programs. At Ashridge he has at various times been Director of the Ashridge MBA, Director of Ashridge General Management portfolio of degree programs, and Dean of Degree programs. He sat on the Academic Board of Hult from June 2015 to June 2019.

Eric B. Dent serves as Professor and Uncommon Friends Endowed Chair in Ethics at Florida Gulf Coast University. He is committed to an interdisciplinary research agenda and has publications in journals of leadership, consulting, philosophy, workplace spirituality, science, history, communications, psychology, education, and others. Dr. Dent has been honored for his teaching, scholarship, and service including two best paper awards at the Academy of Management Conference and North Carolina's highest designation of appreciation for distinguished volunteer service bestowed by the governor. Dr. Dent has served in many capacities in academia, ranging from Faculty Senate Chair to Business School Dean. He is a consultant to Fortune 500, government, and nonprofit organizations as well as an invited speaker to national audiences. Prior to earning his PhD, Dr. Dent served as a corporate vice president in the financial services industry. He began his career as a computer scientist with IBM.

Satinder K. Dhiman Woodbury University, Burbank, CA, USA

Stephanie Duchek is currently working as a Guest Professor at the Brandenburg University of Technology (BTU) Cottbus-Senftenberg (Germany). She is head of the Chair of Organization and Corporate Governance at the Faculty of Business, Law, and Social Sciences. Her main research fields are the development and dynamization of organizational capabilities, innovation management, strategic human resource management, and qualitative research methods. Currently, her research focuses on resilience at different levels within organizations (e.g., organizational, team, and individual resilience). In her empirical research projects, she studies resilience processes, resilience resources as well as measures of resilience promotion. Stephanie Duchek received her PhD in Business Administration at the Free University of Berlin and worked as a Junior Professor at the Technical University of Dresden. She also works as a resilience coach, consultant, and trainer.

Sevgi Emirza is a research assistant in management and organization studies at the Faculty of Business, Dokuz Eylül University, where she conducts and contributes to research studies particularly in the field of organizational behavior. She completed her MSc in the field of Business Administration in 2015 and studied the effect of regulatory focus on trust between strangers. She received her PhD degree in Business Administration from Dokuz Eylül University in 2020. Her doctoral research focused on the leader and follower cognitive similarity and its effect on dyadic relationship quality. She has previously published in *International Journal of Stress Management*, *Leadership and Organization Development Journal*, and *Current Psychology*. Her current research interests include leader-member exchange (LMX), political skill and behavior at workplace, and leader characteristics and behaviors.

Michael Ford is an Associate Professor in the Department of Management at the University of Alabama. He earned his PhD from the George Mason University. Dr. Ford's research interests include Occupational Health, Stress, and Safety, Emotions and Motivation, Employee-Organization Relationship, and Work-Life Balance.

Charlotte Förster is currently working at the Johannes Kepler University in Linz (Austria), where she investigates Resilience of Health Care Organizations in the COVID-19 crisis. Starting in spring 2021, she will be a junior professor of European management at the Technical University of Chemnitz (Germany), where she will focus her research on European pandemic management. Her research addresses leadership, leaders' resilience, and organizational resilience. She received her PhD from the Technical University of Dresden and also works as a consultant for the University of Applied Sciences for Social Work, Education and Care in Dresden. Previously, she studied at the University of Paderborn (Germany) and the University of Seville (Spain).

Elizabeth F. R. Gingerich teaches graduate and undergraduate courses in business law and is editor-in-chief of Valpo's *Journal of Values-Based Leadership*. She completed her JD from Indiana University, Indianapolis. She brings nearly three decades of law experience into the classroom, most recently as a law partner with the Terrell & Thrall LLP. She has lectured at national and international conferences on intellectual property, and her work has been published in *The Indiana Law Review*, *Res Gestae*, and *Employee Relations Law Journal*. She is a member of both the Indiana and Virginia State Bar Associations and maintains a limited practice in corporate law.

Alisha Gupta is a doctoral student at Virginia Commonwealth University where she is pursuing a PhD in Business with a concentration in Management. Her research interests are mindfulness, well-being, and emotions in the workplace.

Philippa Hardman specializes in working with organizations to help them have better quality discussions about strategy and change. While she frequently consults to Boards and senior management teams, Philippa's work also focuses on enabling wider participation across the organization to ensure that any changes are not only achieved but sustainable. She has extensive experience of working strategically with a wide range of private and public sector organizations in many countries. Philippa's career started as a translator with Volkswagen before joining PwC to train as a Chartered Accountant. She then moved into strategy consulting and held various positions at PwC and PA Consulting before moving to Ashridge Business School. There Philippa jointly led Ashridge Consulting's Strategy Engagement Practice and subsequently was its Director of Resourcing and Performance. She is co-Founding Partner of GameShift, a collaborative hub which helps individuals, teams, and organizations deliver better results through a creative process of reframing issues to allow new thinking to flourish.

Paulo Hayashi Jr. is an assistant professor at the State University of Campinas. His main areas of interests include organizational behavior, organizational theory and strategy. He holds a PhD in Business Administration from Federal University of Rio Grande do Sul (UFRGS). He is the co-founder and coordinator of Lab of People and Marketing (LPM) of School of Applied Science (University of Campinas—Unicamp).

Nidhi Kaushal is a PhD holder in Management Studies from Indian Institute of Technology, Roorkee. She holds a Master's degree in Business Administration and a Bachelor's degree in Computer Science from Kurukshetra University, India, as well. She has been interested and indulged in the research works related to Entrepreneurship, Leadership, Literature, Management, and Indigenous Studies. During her PhD, she has identified the indigenous studies of literature and folklore related to Leadership and Management and presented her work in various international conferences and research publications across the globe. She has also worked at many managerial and academic positions. Being a researcher, she is also an event organizer and has organized conferences and other related events in the Institute. She is exploring Leadership with the study of creative writings and ancient Indian texts, and this is her contribution to her academic research. This area will not only enrich management studies but also become immensely useful for entrepreneurs.

Varinder Kumar is Associate Professor of Commerce in the Post Graduate Department of Commerce, Government College, Kapurthala (North India), where he also serves as the Head of the Department of Commerce. He holds an MCOM from Panjab University, Chandigarh (having earned the Gold Medal), and is currently working on his PhD in the area of workplace spirituality. He has authored more than 30 books on Business Communication, Soft Skills, Human Values, and Professional Ethics, which are prescribed in syllabuses of different Indian universities. His areas of interest include spirituality at workplace, transformational leadership, and creativity.

Yasir Mansoor Kundi is a PhD researcher at IAE—Aix-Marseille université, France. His research interests relate primarily to leadership, work-related behaviors, and career success. Mr. Yasir has published in *Academy of Management Proceedings*, *International Journal of Organizational Analysis*, *Journal of Career Assessment*, and *VOLUNTAS: International Journal of Voluntary and Nonprofit Organizations*.

Sonja Lang inspires business leaders and executives across industries, continents, and cultures. Her coaching and training are based on Western and Eastern sciences combined with proven business practices. Sonja motivates leaders to transform internally and externally, as a certified coach and certified NLP master and trainer. She developed and promoted her "*Internal-External Leadership*" *Model* for the digital VUCA world, combining internal clarity with high-end communication: for unbiased processing, authentic behavior, and influencing with integrity. After achieving a master's degree in business economics, Sonja enjoyed a successful 20-year career in investment banking in London. Sonja's monk-like Eastern sciences training at the Isha Institute of Inner Sciences in meditation, breathing, and courses on yoga psychology helps her clients to adopt and successfully apply unique tools and techniques, and develop new competencies. Her speaking techniques and exemplary presentation skills position her as an exceptional keynote speaker and conceptual modeler.

Andrew Ledford is a Permanent Military Professor and an Assistant Professor of Leadership and Ethics at the United States Naval Academy. He teaches the core class of leadership and the Code of the Warrior elective. His past research has been on social movement in Iran as well as the nexus of religion and politics in the Middle East. He currently leads a research group on mindfulness, grit, hardiness, and resilience. Dr. Ledford has a master's degree in International Relations with a focus on Irregular Warfare from the Naval War College, where he was the honor graduate. He spent over 20 years as a Naval Special Warfare officer, which included several tours to both Iraq and Afghanistan in addition to other regions before receiving a master's degree in sociology and his PhD from Princeton University where he studied political sociology and social network analysis.

Simona Leonelli is Research Fellow at the University of Padova (Italy). Previously, she was Postdoctoral Research Fellow at the University G. d'Annunzio Chieti-Pescara (Italy) where she received her PhD in Accounting, Management, and Finance in 2017. She was visiting at Skema Business School (Nice—France). Her main research interest lies in the area of Entrepreneurship and Business Organization. She focuses on the existing relationship between entrepreneurs' personality traits (e.g., narcissism) and innovative performance, survival and growth of start-ups and SMEs. She published in the *Journal of Small Business and Entrepreneurship*, *Journal of Entrepreneurship and Small Business*, *Sinergie*, and *Prospettive in Organizzazione*. She has also published two books: one with Edward Elgard Publishing entitled *Entrepreneurial Personality and Small Business Management* and one with Emerald Publishing entitled *Sustainable Entrepreneurship*. She is adjunct professor of Business Organization, Behavior in Organization and Organization Design and Governance of Human Capital at the University of Padova.

Derson Lopes Jr. is an assistant professor, author, consultant, and speaker in the areas of leadership, productivity, project management, spirituality, and volunteering. He acts as Vice President of R&D/e-Learning at Aspectum; Trainer at VitalSmarts; Dean of Graduation, Research and e-learning at FAAMA; Leader Partner at GOTT; and co-founder at Instituto Aksioss. He holds a PhD in Business Administration from Unicamp, PMP certification, specialization in Finance, and degrees in Administration, Accounting, and Theology. He worked in different areas as manager and leading big teams and volunteered in several countries, including Bangladesh, Mozambique, Egypt, Uruguay, and USA.

Anoosha Makka is a Senior Lecturer in Business Management at the University of Johannesburg, South Africa. She has earned one bachelor and two master's degrees (an MBA in International Business from Leeds University Business School, UK, and an MRes in Educational Research at the University of London, UK). Anoosha has earned her PhD in Business Management from the University of Johannesburg, South Africa. She is a recipient of the Nelson Mandela Scholarship and Chevening Scholarship. Her areas of interest include spirituality and management, spirituality and leadership, CSR and multinational corporations, and mindfulness. She currently teaches Strategy and International Management at postgraduate level at the University of Johannesburg. Prior to joining academia, Anoosha spent 10 years in the corporate sector in banking and 6 years in the public sector in South Africa.

Joan F. Marques Management, Woodbury University, Burbank, CA, USA

Claude-Hélène Mayer is a Full Professor of Industrial and Organizational Psychology at the Department of Industrial Psychology and People Management, University of Johannesburg, Johannesburg, South Africa. She holds Master's degrees from Germany and England and Doctorates from Germany and South Africa (Management, Psychology, and Political Sciences). Her research areas are workplaces of the Fourth Industrial Revolution, mental health and well-being, women in leadership, conflict management and mediation, creativity, and psychobiography.

Sanjay Modi is Professor and Executive Dean, Social Sciences, Lovely Professional University, Phagwara (India). He received his PhD from Punjabi University, Patiala (Pb), India. He has been Associate Editor of *Indian Management Studies Journal*, Punjabi University, Patiala, and has been author of three research books and 12 research papers published in different Indian journals. His areas of interest are Human Resource Management, Employee Engagement, Trade Unionism, Life Skills, and Spirituality and Work Behavior.

Chris Nichols has consulted to governments, NGOs, and corporate organizations in over 50 countries over the past 30 years. He works mostly with executive teams and individual leaders using collaborative approaches to strategy formation, innovation, and change. He has a particular interest in the use of extended epistemology in organizational work—bringing a wide array of creative approaches to enrich organizational dialogue and extend leaders' view of the systems they work in and across. He is influenced by Buddhist and Quaker approaches to human development, alongside contemporary organizational psychology, and by the psychosynthesis work of Roberto Assagioli. He has written widely on organizational strategy and leadership issues, and also writes fiction and poetry.

Yuanlu Niu is an Assistant Professor of Human Resource and Workforce Development at the University of Arkansas. She holds a PhD in Education with a concentration in the Workforce Education and Development and an MBA from Southern Illinois University Carbondale. Her research focuses on discrimination in the workplace, career development, human resource development, and workforce diversity. Her papers have been published in *Asia Pacific Business Review*, *International Journal of Chinese Culture and Management*, *Journal of Education*, *International Journal of Chinese Culture and Management*, etc.

Courtney E. Owens is a Chartered Organizational Psychologist and serves as the Deputy Director of the Engineering Leadership Development Program and Lecturer in Leadership and Organization at Alliance Manager Business School, University of Manchester, United Kingdom. She holds a PhD in Organizational Psychology from the University of Manchester, UK, and an MBA from the University of Washington, WA, USA. She teaches and presents on work-personality, leader-personality, leadership, and self-awareness. Her research interests focus on personality traits in the context of the workplace, biblical psychology, and leader development.

Taronish A. Pastakia is currently serving as Assistant Professor in the Department of Psychology at St. Xavier's College (Autonomous), Ahmedabad, Gujarat, India, having obtained his MSc in Cognitive Science from the Indian Institute of Technology (IIT) Gandhinagar and BA in Psychology from St. Xavier's College, Ahmedabad. He has qualified the UGC-NET examination in the subjects of Psychology (with JRF), Criminology, Sociology, and Anthropology.

Dinyar M. Pestonjee served the Indian Institute of Management (IIM), Ahmedabad, as Professor of Organizational Behavior (1979–2001). In 2000 he was conferred the title of Honorary Professor of the Albert Schweitzer International University, Geneva. He was Chairman of Organizational Behavior Area for three terms and L&T Chair Professor of Organizational Behavior (1992–1999). He is a Psychologist by training having obtained his MA and PhD in Industrial Psychology from the Aligarh Muslim University. He has been conferred Doctor of Letters (Honoris Causa) by the Banaras Hindu University in 2003 after serving there as Professor of Psychology (1964–79). A year later, he was awarded the Albert Schweitzer Medal for Science and Peace in April 2004 at the 50th Anniversary of the Nobel Peace Prize. He has over five decades of teaching experience. Since 2009, he is the GSPL Chair Professor at School of Petroleum Management, Pandit Deendayal Petroleum University, Gandhinagar.

Emanuele Primavera is a Registered Nurse of AUSL Romagna (Italy). He has a master's degree in management for health professions. He published several papers in national and international journals. His research interests are nurses' fundamental care, workload, and stress perception. In collaboration with Simona Leonelli, he has created a model to organize geriatric units following the positive aging culture. During the pandemic period, he works in a COVID-19 medical ward.

Anita Ravani is the founder of APR Investment and Management, a leading management and consulting firm based out of Los Angeles, California, that specializes in finance and accounting to drive consumer decision making. She is a member of senior management at Stifel Financial Corporation and has more than 20 years of finance and accounting experience working with Fortune 500 companies to solve their most important financial challenges. Anita is a two-time inductee of the prestigious Beta Gamma Sigma Honor Society and holds an MBA from Pepperdine Gradzadio School of Business. Anita is currently in her final year of Global Leadership and Change PhD program at the Graduate School of Education and Psychology at Pepperdine University.

Celeste Raver Luning is the Class of 1967 Leadership Research Fellow in the Department of Leadership, Ethics, and Law at the United States Naval Academy. Broadly, her research focuses on understanding the dynamic nature of organizations. Dr. Raver Luning's current research centers on resilience and grit at the individual, team, and organizational levels of analysis. She also teaches one of the core leadership courses at the United States Naval Academy. Prior to her academic career, she was part of a team that built and ran a successful multi-location service business in Southern California, in which she served as the Chief Operating Officer. Dr. Raver Luning obtained her PhD in Organizational Leadership from the University of Maryland Eastern Shore, holds a Master of Business Administration with an emphasis in Entrepreneurship from Pepperdine University, and a Bachelor of Arts in Philosophy from the University of Maryland, Baltimore County.

Christopher S. Reina is an Assistant Professor in the Department of Management and Entrepreneurship at Virginia Commonwealth University (VCU), and the Founder and President of Leading Without Ego, LLC. He consults and leads trainings on mindfulness and mindful leadership. His research focuses on the intersection of leadership, mindfulness, and emotions in the workplace and how they bring about employee and organizational well-being. Christopher received his PhD in Business Administration from the W. P. Carey School of Business at Arizona State University and he has extensive industry experience in leadership training and development as well as sales and marketing in the health care and food industries. His research has been featured in such outlets as *Harvard Business Review*, *Leadership Quarterly*, *Organizational Behavior and Human Decision Processes*, *Journal of Applied Psychology*, and *Organization Science*, and he is an author of several book chapters on the topics of mindfulness, emotions, and neuroscience.

Gary E. Roberts is a Professor and Director of the Master of Public Administration (MPA) Program in the Robertson School of Government at Regent University with teaching interests in human resource management and nonprofit administration. Professor Roberts' research interests include servant leadership within the human resource management system and the influence of spiritual intelligence on personal and organizational well-being. With five books and 50 plus articles and book chapters, he has published extensively primarily in the area of human resource management with direct relevance to the public and nonprofit sectors. His latest books include *Working with Christian Servant Leadership Spiritual Intelligence* and *Servant Leader Human Resource Management: A Moral and Spiritual Perspective*. He is an active member of St. Nicholas Greek Orthodox Church and Vineyard Community Church. He has been married to his beautiful wife Connie for 37 years and has three wonderful daughters.

Bidyut K. Sarkar has 23 years of formal teaching and administrative experience in reputed management institutions of India. He has been the Vice-Principal and Member-Secretary of Tagore Centre for Human Values. As a Corporate Educator he has conducted 75 workshops across India and abroad with top- and middle-level executives of public and private sector companies on Values, Ethics, Leadership, and Stress Management. As a Visiting Professor he has also delivered 48 courses and workshops at various academic institutions across India. His publications include 48 papers/articles, three monographs, four book chapters, and one book. His academic and professional qualifications include MBA, MCA, MS (Psychotherapy), PGDCA, PGDI (Indology), BS (Physics), PG Diploma in International

Understanding and Human Unity, Major World Religions, Functional Sanskrit, UGC-NET, AIMA-TEM, AIMA-AMT, etc. He takes interest in social work and conducts spiritual discourses on Bhagavad Gita, Sri Sri Chandi, and Upanishads.

H. Eric Schockman is a Professor of Political Science and International Relations and Director of the Center for Leadership, Equity and Diversity at Woodbury University. He also teaches in the PhD program in Global Leadership and Change at Pepperdine University. A public policy expert, Dr. Schockman previously served as Associate Dean and Associate Adjunct Professor at the Sol Price School of Public Policy at the University of Southern California. He is President and founder of the Global Hunger Foundation, dedicated to helping women in the developing world break the chains of poverty by funding projects designed to provide sustainable development and organic farming. He has also written several books and edited many articles on leadership and politics in California, the nation, and international affairs, and presented on panels on these same topics. Dr. Schockman holds a PhD in Political Science and International Relations from the University of California.

Sonya Sharififard currently serves as the inaugural Managing Editor of *The Scholarship without Borders Journal* in the Center for Global Partnerships and Learning at Pepperdine University, as well as Adjunct Faculty in the Excellence and Innovation Program in the Graduate School of Education and Psychology. In her roles, Dr. Sharififard advises doctoral dissertation candidates and facilitates higher learning seminars and distinguished speaker series colloquia about education-related topics focusing on advancing leadership, organizational change, teaching and learning philosophy, and scholarly communications. She has coauthored a chapter in *New Horizons in Positive Leadership and Change* (Springer 2020) and in the *Handbook of Workplace Spirituality and Fulfillment* (Palgrave 2018), and has presented her research findings at major international conferences. Her research focuses on advancing student success, workplace well-being, and law and policy. In 2020, Dr. Sharififard earned her PhD in Global Leadership and Change from Pepperdine University.

Xiaochuan Song is an Assistant Professor in the Business Department at Misericordia University. He earned his PhD from the University of Alabama. Dr. Song's research interests include Organizational Justice, Workplace Mistreatment, Employee Well-being, and Crowdsourcing.

Nicola Sum is a lecturer in Educational Leadership within the Faculty of Education at Monash University. Her work in the faculty draws on over 20 years of school experience, having worked in the Victorian, UK and International school systems. Following her work as a school principal, Nicola completed her doctoral studies on the interconnected nature of glocalization (global-local) and educational leadership practice. She teaches in postgraduate programs of principal preparation, educational leadership, educational research and globalization, alongside undergraduate studies in teaching and learning and teacher leadership. Her research interests include school leadership, principal preparation, international education, education systems, and global education policy.

Michael J. D. Sutton is an innovative researcher, knowledge scientist, and learning engineer. Over the past 50 years he has distinguished himself as an interdisciplinary generalist working across several business and educational fields: Game-Based Learning, Online and Distance Education, Executive Coaching and Mentoring, Entrepreneurship/Edupreneurship, and Leadership and Executive Development. He has extensive experience in educating learners and leading strategic business and educational initiatives. He was an entrepreneur for over 40 years and a Practice Director for over 15 years in the emerging field of Knowledge Management. He holds a PhD in Knowledge Management from McGill University. When he joined the academy, he motivated his learners in Business Schools to adopt an "entrepreneurial spirit" that is necessary to succeed in our complex world of volatility, uncertainty, complexity, and ambiguity (VUCA). He has coached and mentored founders of start-ups, SMEs, as well as executives and managers. As a life-long learner, Michael works to instill his vision of *Edupreneurship* in those he coaches and mentors.

Katharina Wilke holds a Master's degree and a PhD from the European University Viadrina in Germany in the fields of Intercultural Communication Studies and Talent Management. Her research areas are talent management, change management, leadership, and the future of work. She works as Organizational and People Excellence Manager in Singapore.

Xu Xu is an Associate Professor of Economics and Data Analytics in the School of Business at Henderson State University. She received her PhD in economics from Southern Illinois University Carbondale. Her research focuses on the impact of perception on various social, economic outcomes such as migration, education, and tourism. Her papers have appeared in *Growth and Change*, the *Journal of Continuing Higher Education*, *Kyklos*, *Economic Modelling*, *Economic Inquiry*, *Tourism Management Perspectives*, etc.

Holistic Leadership for Post-COVID-19 Organizations: Perspectives and Prospects

1

Satinder K. Dhiman

Introduction

Between stimulus and response there is a space.
In that space is our power to choose our response.
In our response lies our growth and our freedom.

— Author Unknown (attributed to Victor Frankl)

In their article in *Harvard Business Review* (April 13, 2020) titled "What Good Leadership Looks Like During This Pandemic," Michaela J. Kerrissey and Amy C. Edmondson opine that "the speed and scope of the coronavirus crisis poses extraordinary challenges for leaders in today's vital institutions."[1] Based on their review of how two different leaders handled the situation [Adam Silver, the commissioner of the National Basketball Association (NBA) and New Zealand's Prime Minister Jacinda Ardern], these authors distil five lessons for leaders to handle novel crisis: (1) *Act* with urgency; (2) *Communicate* with transparency; (3) *Respond* productively to missteps; (4) *Engage* in constant updating; and (5) *Tap* into suffering to build meaning.

These are important lessons for leaders to take heed during these turbulent times.

The COVID-19 pandemic has permanently changed lives around the world and no dimension of life and leadership seems to have been spared from its wrath. Quarantines and lockdowns have become ubiquitous. Masks, social distancing, and zooming have become the new norms, turning much of the world into 'a collection

[1] Kerrissey, M. J., & Edmondson, A. C. (2020). What good leadership looks like during this pandemic. *Harvard Business Review*.

S. K. Dhiman (✉)
Management, Woodbury University, Burbank, CA, USA
e-mail: satinder.dhiman@woodbury.edu

S. K. Dhiman, J. F. Marques (eds.), *Leadership After COVID-19*, Future of Business and Finance, https://doi.org/10.1007/978-3-030-84867-5_1

of reluctant shut-ins.' And yet, this pandemic has also stirred us into thinking about novel approaches to lead organizations and societies toward a shared, sustainable future. Jamie Dimon, JP Morgan CEO, has rightly called the pandemic 'a wake-up call … for business and government to think, act and invest for the common good.' It is our decisions, individually and collectively, that will determine the future course of humanity as well as the fate of our organizations. Humanity seems to have arrived at a point where, moving forward, every organization, every activity, every enterprise in which we are engaged *must* change if it is to survive in this volatile world.

COVID-19 pandemic has brought countless challenges and changes to the world. In addition to a serious health crisis (more than 2.4 million deaths so far) and myriad economic issues, the social distancing policies due to the pandemic have substantially changed how we work. Thousands of people suffered profound work-related changes, changing the work dynamic to home office. All those changes, in addition to the risk of infection itself, have brought fear, uncertainties, and heightened stress levels at work. It has changed the future of work in the organizations.

COVID-19 and Future of Work

Besides serious health hazard, in terms of its social impact, the pandemic has turned our dwellings into home-shift offices and social distancing has disrupted work, school, and gatherings with family and friends. Although the new 'normal' for future of work is still emerging, COVID-19 pandemic has 'normalized' remote work, necessitated the hybrid way of working, and fostered a mix of 'synchronous and asynchronous' communication. The pandemic has also brought challenges in its wake, such as hidden social inequalities embedded in working from home, escalation of job-related stress and the potential to magnify the gender gap.

A study published during the month of July, 2020, investigated psychological repercussions and psychiatric symptoms of the Chinese workforce associated with the COVID-19 pandemic (Tan et al., 2020). The study indicated that the psychological effects of returning to work during the COVID-19 pandemic are largely unknown. Surprisingly, the study found that returning to work had not caused a high level of psychiatric symptoms in the workforce: Of 673 respondents, 10.8% attended to post-traumatic stress disorder (PTSD) diagnosis criteria after returning to work. Only 12.0% revealed moderate to severe concerns about their physical health. The researchers observed that the low prevalence of psychiatric symptoms could be due to confidence instilled by psychoneuroimmunity prevention measures before the resumption of work. In general, researchers found relative low levels of anxiety, depression, stress and insomnia while no significant differences found with regard to psychiatric symptomology among workers/technicians and executives/managers. The researchers believe that these findings would provide guidance for other countries during the COVID-19 pandemic.

The restructuring of workplace due to the pandemic have led to several major changes within the organization and work environment. The International Labour Organization (ILO) (2020) monitored some studies about the COVID-19 pandemic impact on the working world. ILO reported that four out of five people (81%), from

3.3 billion global workforce, are affected by the total or partial shutting of workplaces, with an estimated reduction of about 6.7% of their work assignments, which equals 195 million full time workers. Likewise, Global Workplace Analytics—GWA (2020) estimates that 25–30% of work force is working from home several days a week by the end of 2021 because of COVID-19 pandemic.

Additionally, a recently published flagship report (February 23, 2021) by International Labor Organization (ILO) explores world employment and social outlook in terms of how the contemporary platform economy is transforming the way work is organized, analyzing the impact of digital labor platforms on organizations, workers, and society as a whole. Drawing on surveys and interviews with some 12,000 workers and representatives of 85 businesses around the world, in multiple sectors, this report offers a comprehensive picture of the experience of workers and businesses on online web-based and location-based platforms.

Guy Ryder, ILO Director-General, states in the preface to this comprehensive report,

> It is widely considered that the COVID-19 pandemic has accelerated changes that were already under way, both in society and at work. These include the expanded use of digital platforms….The result has been innovative ways of working, and flexibility for both workers and businesses….Many businesses have relied on digital labour platforms to keep operating, reach new markets and reduce costs.

However, this new operating model has brought challenges in its wake. Enumerating some of these challenges, Ryder (2021), states that

> This new business model allows platforms to organize work without having to invest in capital assets or to hire employees. Instead, they mediate between the workers who perform the tasks and clients, and manage the entire work process with algorithms. Workers on digital labour platforms often struggle to find sufficient well-paid work to earn a decent income, creating a danger of working poverty. Many do not have access to social protection, which is particularly concerning during a pandemic.

Since digital labor platforms operate across multiple borders and jurisdictions, it has resulted in regulatory uncertainty for workers, businesses and governments alike. Ryder (2021) concludes his prefatory remarks stating that

> Digital labour platforms have the potential to benefit both workers and businesses – and through them, society more generally. But they will only fulfil this positive potential, and help us achieve the Sustainable Development Goals, if the work opportunities they provide are decent. A clearer understanding of the operation of digital labour platforms, and a more effective and consistent approach to them, are therefore essential.

Sustainable Leadership After covid-19

Perhaps it is too early to arrive at post-pandemic *leadership theory and practice*. At the time of this writing (March 1, 2021), the new normal is barely emerging alongside the global vaccine rollout: the framework within which leaders will operate is not yet knowable, nor is the full measure of requirements of management and leadership practice determinable. Perhaps the disruption of the COVID pandemic is one case of a wider pattern of systemic disruptions that leaders will increasingly face over the next decade.

Nevertheless, during this moment of crisis, we *must* build on the lessons we have learned so far, help leaders to embrace universal, holistic leadership principles—self-evident, self-validating laws that govern how leaders should lead: be authentic, have integrity, serve selflessly and create communities of care, together. The current context has increased the need for new leadership perspectives in the organizations that demands a more fluid, less encumbered and more participative kind of leadership. In this chapter, we propose one such innovative leadership style called Holistic Leadership.

Holistic leadership is voyage of *inner discovery* that begins with *knowing* oneself and culminates in *living* one's deepest values at the personal, team, and organizational level. Effective leaders and managers *holistically* engage the body, mind, heart, soul, and spirit of those whom they lead. It starts with self-awareness and self-mastery, progresses with living authentically one's core values and culminates in leaving a legacy by fulfilling life's purpose through selfless service for the greater good. This mindset is critical in managing and leading organizations successfully during these turbulent times. Guided by self-knowledge, holistic leaders and managers immerse their total, authentic self in all that they do, and surpass themselves by serving for the good of others, thereby enhancing the human condition.

When leaders understand the context and embody these guiding principles as they start to practice within the emerging new normal, they will be *ready* to lead authentically—which in present volatile and precarious world, is indeed something toward which we should aim.

It is not that the former leadership styles and change methodologies have become redundant. It is just that we will need to reharness and reconfigure them to address the challenges posed by the new normal.

Holistic Leadership: A *New* Paradigm for Future Leaders

> *In a small crisis power moves to the center, but in a big one, it moves to the periphery.* ~ cited in Bohmer et al., *HBR*, November 2020

In a recent article in the *Harvard Business Review*, authors Bohmer et al., present insights and strategies from two hospitals which have handled the COVID pandemic most effectively. These authors suggest, "Instead of returning to the old leadership and management style, we should continue to encourage the kind of innovation leadership that characterized the acute response."

These authors further observe that the successful COVID-19 response of these hospitals can be attribute to 'flatter hierarchies, easier access to senior leaders, a sharper focus on what really matters, quicker decision-making, rapid experimentation and tolerance of experimental failure, and less-experienced staff spontaneously stepping up to lead.' Some pointers for leadership under uncertainty as practiced at both Boston Hope and NHS Nightingale London as discussed by these authors are: (1) Publicly acknowledge the uncertainty; (2) Delegate authority; (3) Don't delay making the difficult (and unpopular) decisions; (4) Look after your people; and (5) Be there!

The Need for a More Integrative Perspective

In wake of increasing uncertainty and ambiguity triggered by global pandemic and social unrest of today, the managers and leaders of organizations need to adopt a more integrative, holistic approach in leading and managing virtual organizations and build trust and understanding. The traditional forms of leadership and management characterized by command and control model of management and hierarchical organizational structures are proving inadequate to deal with emerging reality that is increasingly volatile, complex, multidimensional, and virtual. We need new thinking, new structures, and new metaphors of resonance to dance with the emergent reality. We need *holistic systems* and *inclusive organizations*; and we need agile managers and leaders who are able to integrate the spiritual and the material perspectives in a *dialectical* manner.

The scholarship on leadership and management is vast and continues to grow. Several new approaches have been developed recently that cover the whole spectrum of management process—from transformational leadership to servant leadership, including the emergent approaches influenced by positive psychology such as authentic leadership and self-leadership. While holistic leadership builds upon these myriad strands of growing leadership literature, it focuses more on the personal development of a leader in a holistic manner. Very few leadership approaches really explore the self, spirit, and service dimensions of leadership process in an integral manner, much less their relationship to professional excellence and optimal performance within contemporary organizations (Dhiman, 2017).

Three Dimensions of Holistic Leadership and Management: Self, Spirit, Service

This holistic leadership journey is denoted by three S's: Self, Spirit, and Service, each signifying three overarching dimensions of holistic leadership—Self-Leadership, Authentic Leadership, and Legacy Leadership. Each leadership competency presents two sides—simultaneously representing leader's and follower's perspective. Therefore, when self-motivation is discussed, it pertains to leader's own motivation as well as to the motivation of those who are led. The integral nature of the function of leadership vindicates Lao Tzu's matchless wisdom: *To lead, one must follow*. Figure 1.1 represents the cycle of holistic leadership and its various dimensions:

Three *Integral* Circles of Holistic Leadership

Figure 1.1 presents three integral circles of holistic leadership signified by their three defining dimensions—Self (nurturing), Spirit (aligning), and Service (contributing) and three corresponding leadership types—Self-leadership, Authentic Leadership, and Legacy Leadership. Each leadership type has three dimensions.

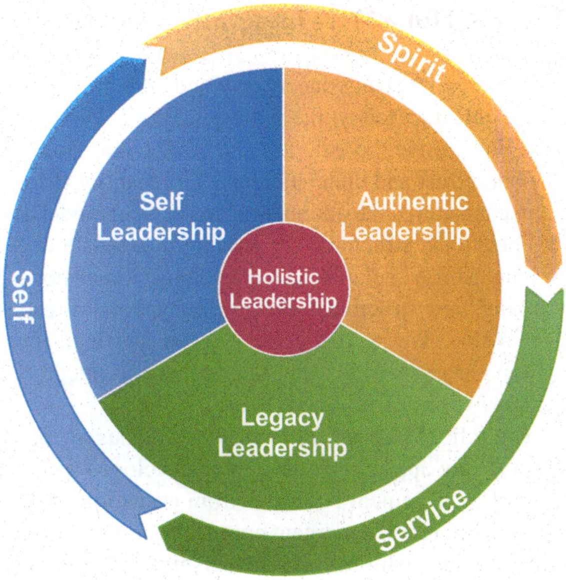

Fig. 1.1 Cycle of holistic leadership, Satinder Dhiman (2017). (Source: Conceptual cycle of leadership, Manoj Chandra Handa (2015); personal communication, September 18, 2015)

Self-leadership represents the preparation phase on the path of holistic leadership and comprises self-motivation, self-mastery and self-creativity. Authentic leadership comprises self-awareness informed by internalized moral perspective expressed as unity and purity in thought, speech and action. It comprises harnessing the spirit through emotional intelligence and appreciative inquiry guided by strong moral compass. Service leadership presents the quest for meaning and fulfillment through selfless service culminating in a leader's enduring legacy (Dhiman, 2017).

The journey of holistic leadership starts with the development of the leader as a person. Warren Bennis, who has authored and coauthored some 30 books on leadership and has been hailed as the "The 'Dean' of Leadership Gurus," contends that to become a leader, a person first has to develop as an individual (See: Asghar, 2014; McGregor, 2014). Peter Senge (2006, pp. 129–162; Senge et al., 2008, p. 92) concurs and regards self-mastery to be the key aspect of growing as a leader. According to Bennis, the real task of becoming a leader boils down to becoming an authentic individual first: "At bottom, becoming a leader is synonymous with becoming yourself. It's precisely that simple, and it's also that difficult" (2009, p. xxxvii).

Gandhi (Cited in Easwaran, 1989, p. 20) once said, "Our greatness lies not so much in being able to *remake the world* as being able to *remake ourselves*" [*emphasis added*]. It is only through internalizing self-knowledge that leaders are able to truly "remake" themselves and fulfill their mission. Guided by Self-knowledge, holistic leaders express their total, authentic self in all that they do and surpass themselves by serving for the good of others.

Turing to Stoicism in the Time of Pandemic[2]

If your philosophy doesn't work in the most dire circumstances, then abandon it now, because it is a Starbucks philosophy. ~ Major Thomas Jarrett[3]

At the time of this writing (February 20, 2021), more than 2.4 million people around the world have succumbed to the COVID-19 infection so far, and many more have been hospitalized. Overall, the hazard of serious illness, the impending fear of loss of job security, and the challenging adjustments to our normal work routine have created extraordinarily high levels of stress.

To deal with anxiety and stress caused by the pandemic, we turn to Stoicism, a philosophy that has its roots in ancient Greece and Rome. Stoicism is a school of ancient Greco-Roman philosophy whose influence has persisted to the present day. It lays great emphasis on resilience and mental freedom gained from living a life of moral virtue in accordance with nature, thereby gaining a state of "imperturbable tranquility." It offers a deep philosophical framework and an ethical scaffold, especially relevant during hard times such as these. From Seneca, Epictetus to Marcus Aurelius during these early times to Victor Frankl and James Stockdale in our times, Stoicism has endured as a "tough-love" philosophy to live a fulfilling, meaningful life, even amidst adversity. The early Stoics learned all about managing crises, first-hand: they lived through exiles, wars, pandemics and loss of loved ones. Using universally applicable, rational principles to understand life, the Stoics devised various mind-hacks that can be used to cope with stress, misfortune, and grief. As Tim Ferriss said in a 2017 TED Talk that Stoicism is "the most reliable safety net for emotional free fall."

The COVID-19 pandemic has affected all of us and raised many questions about the ways we work, live our lives, and lead our organizations. During such turbulent times, the older wisdom traditions such as Stoicism can be helpful. Now that the impending danger of the COVID-19 pandemic is slowly giving way to a protracted state of caution and restraint, we can benefit from taking a Stoic perspective in dealing with its slings and arrows.

As a robust philosophy and way of life, through the ages, Stoicism has inspired a wide range of writers, thinkers, and practitioners such as Shakespeare, Montaigne, Goethe, Kant, Pascal, Descartes, Ralph Waldo Emerson, Walt Whitman, Thomas Jefferson, Pierre Hadot, JK Rowling, and Admiral James Stockdale. Stoicism is especially an excellent philosophy for those in positions of power and leadership and for those in high-stress jobs. Additionally, Stoicism has inspired many modern approaches to personal development (such as "Self-Help" movement), influenced logotherapy and psychotherapy (in particular, cognitive behavioral therapy and its

---

[2] This section partially draws upon author's recent work: Dhiman S. (2021). More than Happiness: A Stoic Guide to Human Flourishing. In: Dhiman S. (ed.) *The Palgrave Handbook of Workplace Well-Being*. Palgrave Macmillan, Cham. https://doi.org/10.1007/978-3-030-02470-3_51-1.

[3] Cited in Jules Evans, *Philosophy for Life and Other Dangerous Situations* (London: Rider, 2013), 70.

precursor, rational emotive behavior therapy). It is also popular with the US military and the National Health Services (NHS) in the UK.

Stoicism seems ideally suited for leadership development and the pursuit of well-being since it has its core as character, self-mastery, and purposeful action—the hallmarks of resilient leadership and flourishing. The life example of Admiral James Stockdale serves as a beacon of resilient leadership. Stockdale endured 7 1/2 years of extreme torture as naval POW in Hanoi Hilton, Vietnam, sustained by the teachings of Stoicism as his unassailable "inner citadel" and main survival kit.

Of all the Western philosophies, Stoicism seems perhaps the most immediately relevant and useful for our turbulent times. Today it is popular within several groups such as the military, Silicon Valley, and people interested in secular alternatives to religion. The practice of stoic philosophy will benefit medical doctors, psychotherapists, nurses, military service men and women, entrepreneurs, politicians, attorneys, social workers, and law and order personnel, to name a few.

The Stoics equated *eudaimonia* (flourishing) with virtue and recognized that happiness can be achieved through living a life of "value" (and not "valuables"); that is, by cultivating the four cardinal virtues of wisdom, courage, righteousness, and self-control. Accordingly, Stoicism can provide us with best coping strategies to deal with the stress and maintain mental peace in a state of exception like pandemic. It operates from two fundamental set of axioms, by way of reminders to us: (1) It could be worse. (2) You are not the first one to experience this. Armed with these two prompts, we can deal with all arrows and slings of outrageous fortune and circumstance with Stoic calm.

Additionally, Stoicism counters our general habit of complaining with the attitude of gratitude by reminding us that things could always be worse. As one writer put it: "Instead of complaining that you can't go to a concert, bar, or sporting event, be thankful that you do not have to go to the hospital" (Sullivan, 2021).[4] The Stoics also considered our duty to humanity takes precedence duty to oneself. What is good for the beehive is good for the bee. This simple understanding can help us to diligently follow social distancing and using mask, etc. for the preservation of the greater good of the society.

Stoicism emphasizes that you can't control events, but you can control your responses to them. We present below four Stoic techniques/exercises to deal with the stress caused by events such as the pandemic:

Dichotomy of Control: The Trump Card of Stoicism

One of the most robust psychological scaffolds that Stoics use is called 'dichotomy of control:' some things are in our control (our thoughts and actions) and some aren't (our health, property, reputation). The Stoic refrain: Focus on what is within

[4] Sullivan, B. (2021). Manage the stress of COVID-19 with stoicism: psychological tools from the ancient Stoics can help you endure the pandemic. *Psychology Today*. https://www.psychologytoday.com/us/blog/pleased-meet-me/202101/manage-the-stress-COVID-19-stoicism.

your sphere of choice, and take the rest as it comes, with equanimity. The Stoic approach to eudaimonia hinges on understanding this distinction clearly. Whoever wants to be free, says Epictetus, should wish for nothing or avoid nothing that is up to other people (*Enchiridion*, 14).

By focusing on what is in our control and taking the rest as it comes with stoic calm can go a long way in alleviating stress. What happens to us is never directly under my control, never completely up to us; however, our own thoughts and actions are. The pandemic is *not* really under my control—virus' mutation into various strands is not under my control—but the way I behave in response to it is in my control (wearing a mask, hand-sanitizing, practicing social distancing).

One of the basic psychological principles of Stoicism states that "It's not events that upset us but rather our judgment about them." More specifically, our judgment that something is really bad, or even catastrophic, causes our distress. Once understood in the right manner, it can brace us to deal with any adversity, including the post COVID-19 environment, with Stoic calm.

View from the Above: Taking a Cosmic Perspective of Human Situation

This exercise consists of the act of reflecting on things from a larger perspective or taking a cosmic view of our human condition. In the grand scheme of things, everything is so small, so miniscule. Even our planet is a mere fraction of a dot! Seneca advises Lucilius in letter XCIX to "place before your mind's eye the vast spread of time's abyss, and embrace the universe; and then compare what we call human life with infinity."[5]

A variation of this exercise is to remember that we are not the first to experience adversity. Humanity endured several health pandemics such as cholera, the Spanish flu, and HIV/AIDS, to name just a few. Somehow, we do not seem to remember that in the past people have gone through such conditions as we ourselves have been since March 2020. Approached thus, we realize that things don't matter as much as or in the manner that we initially thought that they do. This practice enjoins us to look at external things dispassionately, not referring everything back to our own individual hopes and fears. Approaching life situations this way, we can preserve our tranquility, our most precious possession.

Marcus Aurelius refers to this practice at several places in his *Meditations* (e.g., IV.33, V.23, V.24). In this exercise, we strive to take a dispassionate view of our worldly concerns and weigh them in the cosmic scale: as the minute, passing, repetitive, and, in a word, "indifferent" affairs that they are, relative to the Stoic perspective for which virtue is the only true good.[6] Marcus Aurelius assures us that this

[5] Cited in Pierre Hadot, *Philosophy as a Way of Life* (Malden, MA: Blackwell Publishing, 1995), 182.

[6] See Pierre Hadot's Stoicism by Matthew Sharpe. Retrieved February 20, 2021: https://modernstoicism.com/pierre-hadots-stoicism-by-matthew-sharpe/.

view from the above will relieve us from the daily burdens of our human existence and foster a sense of wonder: Dwell on the beauty of life. Watch the stars, and see yourself running with them (*Meditations* VII.47).

This exercise is all about transcending one's individual perspective for a more total perspective that sages from all ages have bidden us. In his work *Human, All Too Human*, Friedrich Nietzsche, remembering Plato's words in the *Republic* (604c), says, "All in all, nothing in human affairs is worth taking very seriously, nevertheless."[7]

Memento Mori: The Finitude of Human Existence

This exercise is about reminding ourselves about the impermanence of things, relations, and events, including our own mortality. It said that in the ancient Rome, according to a practice hankering back to the more virtuous days of the Republic, Roman emperors had people whispering "*sic transit gloria mundi*" (worldly glories are fleeting) and "memento mori" (remember you are mortal) into their ears and their generals' ears during the parades and the chariot rides celebrating their triumphs.

Epictetus is succinct, "Continually remind yourself that you are a mortal being, and someday will die. This will inspire you not to waste precious time in fruitless activities, like stewing over grievances and striving after possessions."[8] This exercise is not about obsessively brooding over death all the time. Rather, it is about living urgently and authentically making the most with what we have in the time we have. It is about reminding ourselves how transient life yet precious life is and living it fully, without getting too attached to things, people, and positions. The moment we realize how fragile life is, we stop making "to-do" lists and start working on "to-be" list.

Apple ex-CEO Steve Jobs' Stanford commencement speech, given 6 years before his death, was a moving meditation on mortality. He reminded the graduating class that

> death is the destination we all share. No one has ever escaped it. And that is as it should be, because death is very likely the single best invention of life. It is life's change agent.[9]

Far from being morbid, frequently meditating on the finitude of our human existence could help us appreciate the time we have and make the most of life by becoming aware of its inherent fragility, precariousness, and preciousness.

---

[7] Nietzsche, F. (1996). *Human, all too human: A book for free spirits* (M. Faber & S. Lehmann, Trans., p. 260). University of Nebraska Press.

[8] Torode, S. (2019). *The manual: A philosopher's guide to life, a new rendering* (p. 25). CreateSpace Independent Publishing Platform.

[9] See Steve Jobs' 2005 Stanford Commencement Address (with intro by President John Hennessy). Retrieved February 16, 2021: https://www.youtube.com/watch?v1/4Hd_ptbiPoXM.

Premeditatio Malorum: Negative Visualization

Negative visualization is a mental exercise—an experiment in imagination: we contemplate bad things so that we will be better prepared for them when they actually occur. The basic idea is to be prepared rather than sorry. Stoics use negative visualization to train themselves to stay calm and stay free from emotional anguish in the face of adversity. Also referred to as *premeditatio malorum* (literally, pre-meditating on future evils), this exercise is about imagining worst that could happen. Why it is essential to practice negative visualization? Because whatever fate has given us, fate can take away without a moment's notice. The idea is not to make ourselves depressed, but contemplating on these things takes away their impact when they do happen.

As Seneca explains in his essay To Marcia on Consolation, ix.5, "He robs present ills of their power who has perceived their coming before-hand."[10] The very act of thinking about these things beforehand lessens their blow when such things happen. Seneca further explains that we should so brace ourselves beforehand through this practice that nothing ever takes us by surprise in letter XCI to his friend Lucilium:

> What is quite unlooked for is more crushing in its effect, and unexpectedness adds to the weight of a disaster. The fact that it was unforeseen has never failed to intensify a person's grief. This is a reason for ensuring that nothing ever takes us by surprise. We should project our thoughts ahead of us at every turn and have in mind every possible eventuality instead of only the usual course of events.[11]

That is why it is said that nothing happens to the wise person against his expectation. Such a person undertakes everything "with a reserve clause" … in his most steadfast decisions, he allows for uncertain events.[12] The wise person prefaces every undertaking with a reserve clause—'God willing' or 'circumstances permitting.'

To summarize the Stoic perspective about dealing with adversity and living a life of fulfillment, the Stoic literature provides us with some good formulations of some "truths" to live by. We present one such formulation as follows:

1. Some things are within our control and some things are not.
2. We are not disturbed by events but by our opinions about them.
3. Life is what you make of it. It's up to you.
4. The universe is changing. Nothing lasts forever.
5. Do not act as if you had 10,000 years still to live … rather while you still can, while there is still time, make yourself good.

---

[10] Seneca, To Marcia on Consolation. In John W. Basore, trans., *Essays* Vol. II. Retrieved February 20, 2021: http://stoics.com/seneca_essays_book_2.html.

[11] Campbell, R. (2014). Seneca, *Letters from a stoic: Epistulae morales ad lucilium* (p. 205). Penguin Classics. Selected and Trans. with an Introd.

[12] Seneca cited in Pierre Hadot, *The Inner Citadel: The Meditations of Marcus Aurelius*, 194.

Living a Life of Flourishing and Fulfillment is in our Own Hands: Pointers for Leaders

As is evident from the foregoing, the Stoic approach is aimed at living a life that is impervious to external exigencies. As the great American historian Will Durant has observed in his exposition of the philosophy of Epictetus: "The essence of the matter is that a man should so mold his life that his happiness shall depend as little as possible upon external things."[13] External things are not within our control and pursuing them will make us vulnerable. "Who, then, is the invincible human being?" Epictetus once asked and answered the question himself: "One who can be disconcerted by nothing that lies outside the sphere of choice" (*Discourses* 1.18.21, tr. Robin Hard). Any misfortune "that lies outside the sphere of choice" should be considered an opportunity to strengthen our resolve, not an excuse to weaken it. This is one of the truly great mind-hacks ever devised, this willingness to convert adversity to opportunity.[14]

Stoicism prepares us to deal with whatever happens by using the virtues that we have cultivated over many years. Stoics believe that our real good resides in our own character and virtuous actions. Happiness, they maintained, only depends on virtue, i.e., the mindset that makes you "do the right thing." And no one can truly take away this moral freedom from us. Victor Frankl (2006) rights in the manner of a Stoic: "Everything can be taken from a man but one thing: the last of the human freedoms—to choose one's attitude in any given set of circumstances, to choose one's own way."[15] This freedom to stay calm, to be good and to do good trumps all else in fostering happiness. As free moral agents, we remain the masters of our fate and captains of our soul, to paraphrase William Ernest Henley.[16] Reminiscent of Victor Frankl, the following quote from Wolfe's novel underscores the ultimate freedom that we have, the freedom to assent to what is true and to deny what is untrue:

> One of the few freedoms that we have as human beings that cannot be taken away from us is the freedom *to assent to what is true* and *to deny what is false*. Nothing you can give me is worth surrendering that freedom for.[17]

---

[13] Durant, W. (1972). *The story of civilization: 3 Caesar and Christ* (p. 491). Simon and Schuster.

[14] https://aeon.co/essays/why-stoicism-is-one-of-the-best-mind-hacks-ever-devised.

[15] Victor E. Frankl, *Man's Search for Meaning* (New York: Beacon Press, 2006), 66. This book, which has sold over 12 million copies worldwide, is a required reading for anyone looking for some proven pointers on the art of living meaningfully, under all conditions, including extreme unfavorable ones.

[16] See the last lines of *Invictus* by William Ernest Henley (Retrieved February 20, 2021: https://www.poetryfoundation.org/poems/51642/invictus):

It matters not how strait the gate,
How charged with punishments the scroll,
I am the master of my fate,
I am the captain of my soul.

[17] Wolfe, T. (1998). *A man in full: A novel* (1st ed., pp. 671–672). Farrar, Straus and Giroux. [Emphasis added].

Concluding Thoughts and Remarks

Given the current pandemic crisis, we believe that there is a greater need for holistic leadership approach and the role models that embody it to illustrate such leadership. We also think that the philosophy of Stoicism can offer a resilient framework to wade through these tough times, both personally and professionally speaking.

Holistic leadership harnesses the synergistic energy fashioned by the coming together of the self, spirit, and service that creates a whole that is greater than the sum of its parts. It presents a unique perspective on self-leadership which is defined as leading from one's highest authentic self. Holistic leadership is approached as an expression (and as an extension) of who we are. Exemplary leaders recognize that the most important challenges confronting organizations and society at large are so profound and pervasive that they can only be resolved at the fundamental level of the human spirit—*at the level of one's authentic self.*

> *While we recognize the importance of the role of leaders in fostering hope and nurturing trust during such volatile times, holistic leadership also places such responsibility on the shoulders of every member of the organization. It garners the unique view that managing and leading organization is a shared venture, a collaborative affair, individually and collectively. Only then can we hope to bring about happy individuals and harmonious communities and improve the overall human condition and state of our planet.*

To lead others, one must first lead one's self. To lead one's self, one must first know oneself. To know oneself, one must first "be" oneself. To be oneself is the first and last step on a leader's journey. Strictly speaking, it is not a journey in the strict sense of the word; rather, it is a home-coming. This is called self-discovery—a journey of recognition, from *here* to *here*.

> *The spiritual quest is journey without distance*
> *You travel from where you are right now*
> *To where you have always been*
> *From Ignorance to recognition* ~ Anthony de Mello

The following story[18] connects the cosmopolitan message of Stoicism with living a life of virtuous contribution, a life over which we have full control. In choosing such life of serving the greater good, in good times as well as in times of crisis, lies our collective glory.

> "When the Titanic hit the iceberg on April 15, 1912, there were three more ships in its periphery. The nearest one was "The Sampson," merely 11 kilometers away from Titanic. Though its crew saw the distress signals from the Titanic, "The Sampsons" did not rush to help, because they were involved in the illegal hunting of seals and were afraid of being caught and they sailed away in the opposite direction.
>
> *The Sampson represents egocentric people. People who are so self-absorbed that they are unable to see past their own gains and comforts. These are the people who choose to ignore the pain and suffering of the others and work only toward bettering their own lives.*

[18] Retrieved February 20, 202: https://www.youtube.com/watch?v=dhbFS19IIfiU.

22 kilometers away from the Titanic was the "SS Californian," which was surrounded by ice on all sides and chose to wait till the next day morning as its crew felt that maneuvering the ship through the ice fields at night would have been challenging.

The "SS Californian" is a metaphor for those individuals who say "I can't do anything." "These are people who believe that their hands are tied because the time and situation isn't right", the Court remarked.

If we wait like the "Californian" for the "right time" we will keep waiting all our lives. We can find hundreds and thousands of reasons and excuses to run way from our responsibilities to help our neighbors. But whoever can find it in their hearts to rise above all these frivolous excuses will always be remembered fondly in history.

Farthest away from the sinking Titanic was "The Carpathia." Almost 94 kms away, Captain Arthur Rostron heard the distress cries over the radio but was unsure what direction the cries were coming from.

Not allowing hopelessness to take over, he (Captain Arthur Rostron) prayed to God to guide him. He knew he was taking a chance when he ordered his ship to turn around and sail full steam in the opposite direction through the dangerous ice fields. That fateful night "Carpathia" was the first ship to respond to the distress of the Titanic. This nine-year-old ship took three and & half hours to reach the Titanic. She managed to sail at 31 kilometers per hour which was way beyond her quoted top speed. Determined to fight against all odds, that night the "Carpathia" managed to save 705 passengers from the freezing to their deaths.

Captain Arthur Ronson was honored in England and the United States not only for his valor and Gallantry but also for his unshaken determination to help those in danger."

The tragic saga of the Titanic teaches us that our fate is uncertain, governed by the powerful forces of nature. We face a similar tragedy today in the form of a global pandemic caused by a contagious virus we barely have any power over. *What we do have power over is ourselves.*

We all need to do the needful to help the community in every manner possible.

We all should become the "Carpathia."

5 Take Away Lessons from the Chapter

1. Though it may be too early to arrive at post-pandemic *leadership theory and practice*; nevertheless, this chapter builds on the lessons we have learned so far to help leaders to embrace holistic leadership principles that guide how leaders should lead toward a sustainable future. Holistic leadership is an integrative model of leadership that represents a more fluid, less encumbered and more participative kind of leadership suitable for these turbulent times.
2. As a survival toolkit to deal with the stress triggered by COVID-19 pandemic, this chapter also briefly discusses the ancient Graeco-Roman philosophy called Stoicism. Stoicism lays great emphasis on resilience and mental freedom gained from living a life of moral virtue in accordance with nature, thereby gaining a state of "imperturbable tranquility." It offers a deep philosophical framework and an ethical scaffold, especially relevant during hard times such as these. Stoicism seems ideally suited for leadership development and the pursuit of well-being since it has its core as character, self-mastery, and purposeful action—the hallmarks of resilient leadership and flourishing.
3. Stoicism uses several "mind-hacks" such as 'dichotomy of control:' some things are in our control (our thoughts and actions) and some aren't (our health, property, reputation). It urges us to focus on what is within our sphere of choice, and take the rest as it comes, with equanimity. Another Stoic technique is to remember that we are not the first to experience adversity. Humanity endured several

health pandemics such as cholera, the Spanish flu, and HIV/AIDS, to name just a few. Somehow, we do not seem to remember that in the past people have gone through such conditions as we ourselves have been since March 2020. Taking such cosmic view, we realize that things don't matter as much as or in the manner that we initially thought.

4. Holistic leadership harnesses the synergistic energy fashioned by the coming together of the self, spirit, and service that creates a whole that is greater than the sum of its parts. It presents a unique perspective on self-leadership which is defined as leading from one's highest authentic self. Holistic leadership is approached as an expression (and as an extension) of who we are. Exemplary leaders recognize that the most important challenges confronting organizations and society at large are so profound and pervasive that they can only be resolved at the fundamental level of the human spirit—*at the level of one's authentic self.*
5. While we recognize the importance of the role of leaders in fostering hope and nurturing trust during such volatile times, holistic leadership also places such responsibility on the shoulders of every member of the organization. It garners the unique view that managing and leading organization is a shared venture, a collaborative affair, individually and collectively. Only then can we hope to address sustainably not only the challenges posed by these uncertain crises, but also bring about happy individuals and harmonious communities and improve the overall human condition and state of our planet.

5 Reflection Questions

1. In what manner has the COVID-19 pandemic reconfigured how we work and lead organizations. Discuss briefly the challenges posed by this new normal?
2. How can we address these challenges in a sustainable at the individual, team, and organizational level?
3. Briefly explain how holistic leadership is pertinent during these turbulent times?
4. Briefly discuss how Stoicism may help us manage the stress caused by pandemic.
5. Four Stoic exercises to manage stress are presented in this chapter. Which Stoic exercise would you recommend to manage the uncertainty and loss of control one feels during these times? And why? Explain briefly.

References

Asghar, R. (2014). *The 'dean' of leadership gurus passes at 89*. Forbes. http://www.forbes.com/sites/robasghar/2014/08/01/the-dean-of-leadership-gurus-passesat-89/

Bennis, W. (2009). *On becoming a leader*. Basic Books.

Bohmer, R. M. J., Erickson, J. R. I., Meyer, G. S., Blanchfield, B. B., Mountford, J., Vanderwagen, W. C., & Boland, G. W. L. (2020). 10 Leadership lessons from Covid field hospitals. *Harvard Business Review*. https://hbr.org/2020/11/10-leadership-lessons-from-covid-field-hospitals

Dhiman, S. (2017). *Holistic leadership: A new paradigm for today's leaders*. Palgrave Macmillan.

Easwaran, E. (1989). *The compassionate universe: The power of the individual to heal the environment*. Nilgiri Press.

Frankl, V. E. (2006). *A man's search for meaning*. Beacon Press.

Global Workplace Analytics (GWA). (2020). *A future of work research*. Author.
ILO. (2020). *Monitor: COVID-19 and the world of work* (6th ed.). Author. https://www.ilo.org/global/topics/coronavirus/impacts-and-responses/WCMS_755910/lang%2D%2Den/index.htm
ILO. (2021). *World employment and social outlook: The role of digital labour platforms in transforming the world of work*. Author. https://www.ilo.org/wcmsp5/groups/public/%2D%2D-dgreports/%2D%2D-dcomm/%2D%2D-publ/documents/publication/wcms_771749.pdf
Kerrissey, M. J., & Edmondson, A. C. (2020). What good leadership looks like during this pandemic. *Harvard Business Review*.
McGregor, J. (2014). Remembering leadership sage Warren Bennis. *The Washington Post*. http://www.washingtonpost.com/blogs/on-leadership/wp/2014/08/04/remembering-leadership-sage-warren-bennis/
Senge, P. M. (2006). *The fifth discipline: The art & practice of the learning organization* (pp. 129–162). Doubleday. Revised and updated edition. See chapter 8: Personal Mastery.
Senge, P. M., Scharmer, C. O., & Jaworski, J. (2008). *Presence: Human purpose and the field of the future*. Crown Books.
Sullivan, B. (2021). Manage the stress of COVID-19 with stoicism: psychological tools from the ancient Stoics can help you endure the pandemic. Psychology Today. https://www.psychologytoday.com/us/blog/pleased-meetme/202101/manage-the-stress-COVID-19-stoicism.
Tan, W., Hao, F., McIntyre, R. S., Jiang, L., Jiang, X., Zhang, L., Zhao, X., Zou, Y., Hu, Y., Luo, X., Zhang, Z., Lai, A., Ho, R., Tran, B., Ho, C., & Tam, W. (2020). Is returning to work during the COVID-19 pandemic stressful? A study on immediate mental health status and psychoneuroimmunity prevention measures of Chinese workforce. *Brain, Behavior, and Immunity, 87*, 84. https://doi.org/10.1016/j.bbi.2020.04.055. S0889-1591(20)30603-6.

2 Leaders' Resilience: What Leaders Can Learn from the COVID-19 Crisis

Charlotte Förster and Stephanie Duchek

Introduction

At the beginning of 2020, the world was hit by a global pandemic that was triggered by the spread of a new coronavirus, SARS-CoV-2. Despite a short phase of flattening the COVID-19 infection curve, this crisis is still not over, whereby economic prospects continue to be gloomy. This suggests that the crisis will be worse and longer than the financial crisis in 2008 initiated by the Lehman bankruptcy, probably the worst crisis since the Great Depression of the 1930s.

Living and operating in a global world, the risk for a global economic crisis has never been greater, thus pressuring leaders to get their companies ready for any economic situation. Drawn from these circumstances, extraordinary leaders are increasingly characterized by how they deal with adversity, if they are able to find meaning in negative events, and if they can learn from the trying circumstances (Bennis & Thomas, 2002). Since leaders, through a trickle-down-effect, have a major impact on their employees' health, well-being, and productivity (e.g., Avey et al., 2011; Gooty et al., 2009; Walumbwa et al., 2010), their psychological health status emerges as a real competitive factor during the COVID-19 crisis. The ability to effectively deal with critical situations and, ideally, grow in the face of adversity, is not, as often mistakenly assumed, magical; it is resilience (e.g., Masten, 2001). It can be said that leaders' resilience is exactly the stuff true leadership is made of

C. Förster (✉)
Juniorprofessorship for European Management, University of Technology Chemnitz, Chemnitz, Germany
e-mail: charlotte.foerster@wiwi.tu-chemnitz.de

S. Duchek
Fraunhofer Institute for Industrial Engineering IAO, Berlin, Germany
e-mail: stephanie.duchek@iao.fraunhofer.de

S. K. Dhiman, J. F. Marques (eds.), *Leadership After COVID-19*, Future of Business and Finance, https://doi.org/10.1007/978-3-030-84867-5_2

(Bennis & Thomas, 2002). Nonetheless, and even if there are a lot of recommendations for how leaders should lead their businesses through the coronavirus crisis (e.g., Reeves et al., 2020) or what good leadership should look like during this pandemic (e.g., Kerrissey & Edmondson, 2020), little is known about how leaders themselves can stay resilient in this exceptional situation.

Our chapter aims to help in closing this research gap. Building on previous resilience research in the fields of psychology and management as well as our own empirical work, i.e., several interview studies concerning leaders' resilience (e.g., Foerster & Duchek, 2017) and an online survey with 403 leaders belonging to different leadership levels and working in multiple industrial sectors, we are able to provide insights into how leaders can overcome major crises healthily and productively. We develop a leaders' resilience model that points to central behavioral resilience factors in the leadership context. These factors refer to the phases before, during, and after the critical event and depend on the leaders' traits and abilities as well as their private and work-related environments. Although the COVID-19 crisis is not over yet, it is time to draw first conclusions and summarize what we can learn from this extreme crisis. Thus, we use the COVID-19 crisis to illustrate the individual parts of the model and draw lessons learned for future leadership practice. Thereby, we not only show what is important while dealing with grand challenges such as the COVID-19 crisis (Howard-Grenville, 2020) but also contribute to what McKiernan and Tsui (2019) labeled as responsible management research (Tourish, 2020), especially since this will probably not be the last global pandemic. With our theoretical model on leaders' resilience, we provide a helpful starting point for future research as well as for leaders' resilience promotion in practice.

Defining Resilience

Referring to its original research discipline, developmental psychology, definitions of individual resilience are numerous and diverse. Notably, two concepts in those definitions are fundamental: *adversity* and *positive adaptation* (e.g., Luthar & Cicchetti, 2000; Wright et al., 2013). Incorporating both of these concepts, resilience can be defined as "positive adaptation in the face of risk or adversity" (Wright et al., 2013: 17). In addition, resilience needs to be conceptualized as a process that varies *contextually* (i.e., depending on the various spheres of life), *situationally* (i.e., from situation to situation), and *temporally* (i.e., across the lifespan) (Foerster & Duchek, 2018; Fletcher & Sarkar, 2013; Gu & Day, 2007; Luthar et al., 2000; Vanderbilt-Adriance & Shaw, 2008; Windle, 2011).

Resilience in the Leadership Context

Although academic interest in resilience—not only in developmental psychology but also in the organizational context (Linnenluecke, 2017; Luthar et al., 2000; Robertson et al., 2015; Williams et al., 2017)—has increased in recent years, resilience research in the leadership context is still at a preliminary stage (for review, see Foerster & Duchek, 2018). Considering the current state of research on leaders' resilience, Foerster and Duchek (2018) point to the imbalanced research on factors influencing leaders' resilience, in which researchers mainly focus on the identification of resilience-promoting individual factors instead of resilience-promoting and resilience-impeding situational and behavioral factors. Regarding a proper definition, leaders' resilience can, with reference to the main psychological literature, be depicted as the leaders' ability to not only effectively deal with critical situations, challenges, and crisis but also to grow through it (e.g., Fletcher & Sarkar, 2013; Foerster & Duchek, 2017, 2018; Wright et al., 2013).

Although there is no specific model of leaders' resilience available so far, certain theoretical approaches in the work context can help in developing a model of leaders' resilience. In particular, three frameworks are worth being mentioned:

1. King and Rothstein's (2010) model, used by McLarnon and Rothstein (2013), depicts workplace resilience as a collection of protective factors and dynamic processes. Their model distinguishes personal characteristics, forms of social support, and self-regulatory processes that, when combined, help individuals overcome adverse situations and maintain well-being and performance. In particular, self-regulatory processes, as part of the resilience process, can be differentiated into affective mechanisms related to controlling and regulating emotions, behavioral mechanisms related to understanding and controlling behaviors, and cognitive self-regulation mechanisms related to understanding and controlling thoughts and thinking patterns.
2. Cooper et al.'s (2013) framework for understanding employees' resilience to workplace pressure describes resilience as a dynamic process involving interactions between personality and situations. Whereas the model describes personality primarily in terms of the five-factor model of personality, it describes situations as either sources of workplace pressure and support or other situational factors (e.g., home life). The model contains 12 personal characteristics important for resilience in the workplace and assigns them to four categories: confidence (e.g., positive emotions and optimism), purposefulness (e.g., self-control and conscientiousness), adaptability (e.g., intelligence, problem-solving, and improvisational skills), and forms of social support (e.g., self-awareness and sociability).
3. Kossek and Perrigino's (2016) integrated occupational resilience framework shows that resilience is not only influenced by individual but also occupational factors, in which resilience can be both generalized across occupations as well as job-specific with regard to "occupation triggers or pressure points" (p. 732). Based on their review, the authors depict resilience as a multi-level framework, where occupational resilience is described as the "synthesis of an individual's traits, capacities or coping strategies, and processes" that are used to positively adapt to adversity and risks arising from one's organizational and occupational context (p. 764). Thus, occupational resilience is depicted as a dynamic framework where "stressors are mediated by resilience and moderated by occupational and organizational contexts" (p. 765).

Taken together, these models imply that resilience in the workplace rests upon the interaction of various factors that can be both individual and context-specific. In particular, the three presented frameworks illustrate that resilience outcomes result from the interaction of individual factors, situational factors, and resilience processes and thus provide a deeper explanation of the relationship between resilience factors (risk and protective factors) and resilience processes.

Until now, most studies on resilience in the workplace have focused on individual or person-related resources (e.g., Rees et al., 2015; van Doorn & Hülsheger, 2015), whereby the social environment in which the individual interacts, in particular regarding his or her occupational context, has often been neglected (Kossek & Perrigino, 2016). In this sense, scholars have merely underscored the importance of social support for individual resilience (e.g., Kearns & McArdle, 2012; Wang et al., 2014; Zunz, 1998), but did not examine how the situational factors differ depending on the occupational context (Kossek & Perrigino, 2016). Based on the review of management studies and examination of 11 occupations, Kossek and Perrigino (2016) showed that due to stress triggers that can be general or job-specific, resilience can be as well. This means, based on the "occupational task and contextual demands," we need to distinguish what resilience means and, thus, consider that resilience can be both "individually and occupationally determined" (Kossek & Perrigino, 2016: 729). Although leaders are not an occupational group per se (Kossek & Perrigino, 2016), there are various stress triggers that can be summarized as "leadership stress triggers," for instance, the "loneliness of command" (Quick et al., 2000: 39f.), thus, probably influencing leaders across industries.

Despite the importance of leaders' resilience not only to the leaders themselves, but also to their employees and organizations, and although we know that resilience is context-dependent and findings cannot simply be transferred from one context (e.g., employees) to another (e.g., leaders), hardly any authors have attempted to create a resilience model specific for the leadership context. Furthermore, knowledge is limited about resilience processes, especially in the leadership context. What processes, capabilities, and behaviors help leaders cope effectively with crises? To answer this question, we develop a new model of leaders' resilience. In compliance with the described frameworks, we understand the resilience of leaders as a process dependent not only on individual characteristics (i.e., traits and abilities) but also on environmental features (i.e., factors related to private environments and workplace environments), which together contribute to resilience outcomes (e.g., psychological health and well-being). In detail, we take Cooper et al.'s (2013) workplace resilience framework as well as Kossek and Perrigino's (2016) integrated occupational resilience framework as a foundation and add deeper insights from organizational resilience research into resilience processes. Further, we explain these processes in detail and illustrate their functioning using the COVID-19 situation.

The Leaders' Resilience Model

In order to visualize how leaders deal effectively with a critical situation, we developed a process-oriented model of leaders' resilience (Fig. 2.1). Building on findings from organizational resilience research (Duchek, 2019; Williams et al., 2017), we

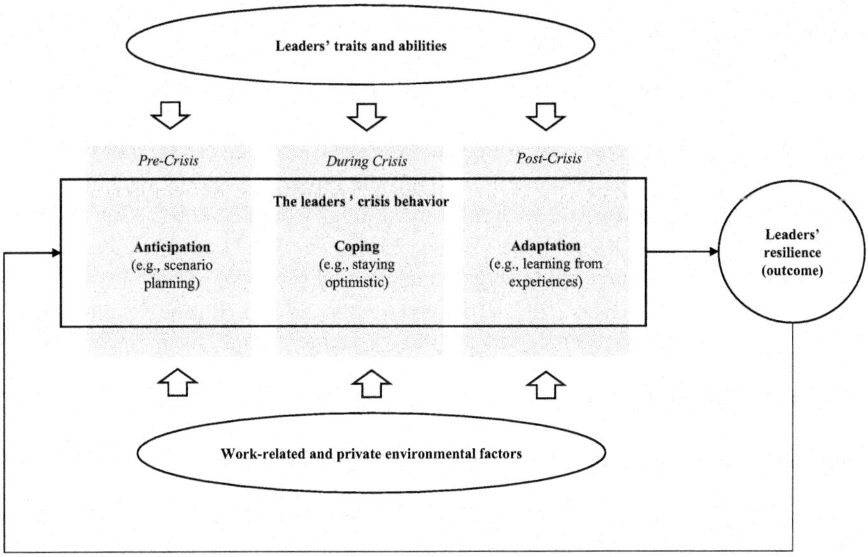

Fig. 2.1 The leaders' resilience model

define three successive stages of the resilience process, i.e., pre-crisis, during crisis, and post-crisis. Since the demands and challenges within these three stages are completely different, the leader must demonstrate specific behaviors to master these stages successfully. In stage one, the leader must anticipate critical developments and prepare for potential crises; in stage two, the leader must cope with an acute crisis situation, and in stage three, the leader must reflect on and learn from the crisis.

Only if the leader is able to anticipate crises, cope with them effectively, and learn from them can he or she reach high levels of resilience. It is not enough to anticipate crises and prepare carefully. The leader must also be able to use developed resources in times of crisis and use crisis experiences to become better afterward. Since leaders' resilience is a dynamic process, the leaders' crisis behavior benefits greatly from prior crisis experience. The broader the knowledge, the better the leader is able to see and understand critical developments as well as act on them. Nevertheless, caution is advised here because crises are hardly always the same. Therefore, the learned behavior must always be critically questioned and adapted to the current crisis; otherwise, it leads to rigidity and arrogance that will not help in any critical situation.

Although the COVID-19 crisis is still not over yet, and leaders must especially demonstrate effective coping behavior, the stages before and after the crisis are equally important to leaders' resilience. This means leaders should also be aware of their anticipation and adaptation capabilities and invest in their enhancement.

In the next sections, we highlight important behaviors needed by leaders to anticipate, cope with, and learn from major crises. We use the COVID-19 crisis to illustrate the different resilience phases, related challenges, and important resilience resources before drawing lessons learned for future leadership practice.

Anticipation

In the first stage ("pre-crisis"), leaders need to anticipate potential crises and make themselves ready. Referring to the COVID-19 crisis, for almost all countries outside Asia, the current crisis was hardly unexpected because China was hit weeks before the virus reached Europe or the U.S. Further, the threat of a global pandemic was definitely far from unexpected, with several warnings from Bill Gates (Gates, 2015) and the World Health Organization (WHO, 2019). The WHO even released a specific guide "to inform and harmonize national and international pandemic preparedness and response" (WHO, 2017: 2; Rouleau et al., 2020). Initially published in 2009, the guide was revised based on the "lessons learned from the influenza A(H1N1) 2009" (WHO, 2017: 8).

To realize threats early, thorough scanning activities, and risk analyses are needed (Faustenhammer & Goessler, 2011). Based on that, leaders can engage in scenario planning and resource building ("slack resources") to get ready. Lessons from past crises have shown that preparation can be essential. In this sense, Coutu (2002) illustrated how the investment bank Morgan Stanley recognized, after the first attack on the World Trade Center in 1993, the danger of operating in a building that had become such a symbol for U.S. commercial power. By introducing a preparation program, including a fire drill that was taken seriously and multiple backup sites, only seven of the 2700 employees working in the south tower died in the terrorist attack in 2001. Even though it is an important fact that the south tower was hit by the second plane only, preparation saved many lives. Referring to the COVID-19 crisis, preparation could have also been crucial to the extent of the crisis. In light of the several pandemic warnings as well as with regard to the requirements of a global and diverse workforce, solutions could have been developed and introduced years ago (e.g., home office regulations, tools for virtual communication, compatibility of work and family life).

Beyond that, leaders need to make themselves mentally ready. This means that leaders, completely aware of the crucial role they have in their team's and their company's resilience, need to engage in resilience-building measures. For this purpose, leaders have to be aware of their strengths and weaknesses. For instance, based on prior crisis experience or simulated crisis situations, leaders should honestly consider what works and what brings them to their limits. The support of an experienced resilience coach might be useful for this task. Subsequently, leaders can expand their resilience, for instance, by using experience-based learning methods (e.g., Kolb, 2014). Learning here is understood as a process in which knowledge is generated through concrete experiences and their transformation. In order to enable this kind of experience, various active learning methods, such as cooperative learning, role play, or simulations, can be used (Snyder, 2003). For instance, a computer-based company simulation could be developed (Gopinath & Sawyer, 1999) in which the leader is confronted with a specific crisis situation and thus can develop crisis behavior strategies.

Coping

In the second stage ("during crisis"), adversity becomes real, which means the leader has to cope with it. Leaders need to remain self-confident and optimistic to manage the situation successfully, especially when it gets tricky (Bossmann et al., 2016; Christman & McClellan, 2008; Sarkar & Fletcher, 2014; Lazaridou & Beka, 2015).

In particular, having a certain level of self-confidence with regard to their own decisions and actions is important; otherwise, leaders will be caught in self-doubts, which will certainly diminish their resilience. Unfortunately, there is always another side of the coin, particularly when it comes to self-confidence. In this sense, being self-confident is undoubtedly crucial for leaders navigating through crisis, but when being overconfident becomes hubris, this harms not only the leaders' resilience but also that of the organization (e.g., Wray, 2016). Referring to the historically greatest corporate scandals, for instance, that of the U.S. company Enron or the decline of Lehman Brothers, several leaders in the past suffered from such hubris (e.g., Wray, 2016). This can easily lead to situations in which a crisis is not assessed correctly and no preparations are made, for example, when corporate leaders did not expect the coronavirus could hit us the same way, or even worse, than China.

Equally, being optimistic is demonstrably important for the leader to stay resilient during the crisis; otherwise, one could give up right away. Nonetheless, being optimistic without a certain sense of reality can be dangerous because it keeps one from taking precautionary measures (Coutu, 2002). In this context, Giustiniano et al. (2020) argued that dealing with highly uncertain and ambiguous situations, such as the current COVID-19 crisis, can lead to contradictory demands. For instance, leaders have to remain optimistic but cannot lose their sense of reality even though staying realistic can certainly be depressing. Depending on what the crisis demands, switching between optimism and realism can be difficult. For the COVID-19 crisis, this could mean leaders need to be optimistic that the pandemic will end soon but also prepare for the fact that it could continue and, thus, always be ready to change the plan.

Further, research shows that not losing one's head even if the house is on fire is of the highest priority to remain resilient during the crisis. Along this line, resilient leaders realize an *effective task fulfillment* by dedicating themselves to a rational, analytical and structured way of working and always considering the possible consequences their actions might have (Foerster & Duchek, 2017; Bossmann et al., 2016). By doing so, leaders are less likely to panic and more likely to keep track and control. As the COVID-19 crisis has shown, decisions made during the crisis were often vital and far-reaching, including some of them even caused strong protest. Therefore, acting in the midst of the crisis and still not losing one's head requires the leader to act in a rational, analytical, and structured way and make decisions thoroughly. Unfortunately, every critical situation also requires that decisions must be made quickly at times. To do that, leaders need to rely on their (crisis) experiences and be guided by their intuition. Considering all the decisions that had to be made during the COVID-19 crisis, being able to decide quickly, thus preventing major damages, is one of the most important qualities of leaders (Kerrissey & Edmondson, 2020). Nonetheless, being intuitive can also be misleading because sticking too closely to what was learned from prior crises might not be appropriate for managing the current crisis (Reeves et al., 2020). Consequently, to remain resilient during an actual crisis, leaders should trust their gut feelings but always critically question their own knowledge. Further, behaving in a rational, analytical, and structured way can help leaders keep their emotions under control and decide thoroughly.

In addition, leaders should also bear in mind that crises are usually highly sensitive phases that demand a lot from them and their surroundings. Therefore, *professional and private networks* are even more important for leaders in times of crisis. Based on the conservation of resources theory (Hobfoll, 2002), the positive and moderating effect of social support on work stress has been well documented (Westman & Chen, 2017). Along this line, empirical findings showed that having a reference person within the firm, trust, a positive work climate, support, and appreciation are factors that positively influence leaders' resilience (Foerster & Duchek, 2017). Nonetheless, leaders also experience a certain loneliness, particularly, the higher the leader is in the hierarchy. Thus, several studies pointed to the importance of leaders' networks, where they could exchange with kindred spirits (e.g., Bossmann et al., 2016; Bullough & Renko, 2013; Sarkar & Fletcher, 2014; Foerster & Duchek, 2017; Quick et al., 2000). Due to competitive factors, such an exchange is more difficult when the leaders are operating in the upper echelon and the company gets in trouble. In these situations, leaders can also turn to their private networks consisting of family and long-lasting friends where they can talk openly about problems and get honest feedback (e.g., Christman & McClellan, 2008; Sarkar & Fletcher, 2014; Quick et al., 2000). Thus, private networks become even more important as the situation becomes tougher and when the leader has more responsibility. Bearing the importance of those professional and private networks in mind, leaders in the actual crisis, such as the COVID-19 crisis, should pay special attention to maintaining a good working atmosphere and taking care of their professional and private networks because they are the people who support the leaders in tough times like this. Although the development of such networks usually takes place long before the crisis happens, and thus is normally part of the anticipatory behavior, long-term contacts and work atmosphere can be easily destroyed during a crisis, especially since people in critical situations are in general more susceptible to leaders' failure and tough in their judgments. Therefore, acting empathically and reflectively and communicating openly are beneficial not only to the leaders' resilience but also to the resilience of their teams, their companies, and their families.

Apart from that, *health* is also an important topic of leaders' resilience (e.g., Bossmann et al., 2016; Buell, 2014; Koen et al., 2013; Quick et al., 2000). Especially in times of crisis, leaders might neglect a healthy diet or sports, but doing that is like driving without enough air in the tires—it will exact revenge at some point. Therefore, just drive to the next rest stop and put air in the tires, which means leaders should pay extra attention to not neglect their sports, healthy diet, and relaxation. Although people's normal places for sports, relaxation, or eating were closed in the COVID-19 crisis, there are plenty of possibilities for all this to be done from home.

In this sense, instead of running to the cafeteria as usual, one could go for a run during lunch break, and instead of the common business dinners, cook dinner with the family in the evening. In this context, coping also refers to making the best of the current situation, and even during a crisis, leaders need a break sometimes to recharge their batteries.

Adaptation

During the last stage ("post-crisis"), leaders recover from the crisis and learn from it for the future. Since leaders are often intertwined with their companies, the learning phase takes place with the leaders and their companies. As already addressed in the anticipation phase, leaders should learn from each crisis by reflecting on what went right and what went wrong, and more importantly, what could have been done better (e.g., Sarkar & Fletcher, 2014). Although this requires leaders to be open to criticism and suggestions (e.g., Bullough & Renko, 2013) and take responsibility for their actions (e.g., Lazaridou & Beka, 2015), reflection should occur without a guilty conscience since this hinders learning. Leaders are, as everyone, only human beings trying their best. If leaders act according to this standard, they should not stick to what happened in the past—hindsight is always 20/20—but learn for the future.

Based on reflection and learning, a change in the leader's behavior can occur, in which crises, as recently depicted by Seidl and Whittington (2020), represent specific opportunities to change one's practice. This reflection and learning can, in turn, be particularly beneficial in terms of a possible future crisis. In this sense, every crisis is an opportunity. A potential opportunity arising from the COVID-19 crisis might be the insight that leading from a distance is sometimes possible, and not all business trips are actually required. This could be groundbreaking for the future of leadership. Even though this will certainly create new challenges, it may solve various challenges leaders struggle with today. Leading from home, at least sometimes, enables leaders to spend more time with their families, which could lead to a general improvement in the compatibility of work and family life. Having a solid family foundation also benefits leaders' resilience, thus helping them cope with future adversities. Nonetheless, since leading from a distance and working from home will certainly pose new challenges to leaders, especially to their resilience, these challenges might better be addressed before the next pandemic hits the world.

Conclusion

Based on the explanations above, it becomes clear that the leaders' resilience process is as dynamic as the crisis itself. Thus, leaders need to apply different behavioral strategies in different phases of the crisis. In the following, we summarize what we have learned from the COVID-19 crisis in terms of our leaders' resilience model (see Fig. 2.1) and how leaders can navigate healthily and productively through crises. Nonetheless, one should be aware that these are generalized behavioral strategies for leaders that must always be examined critically against the background of the actual crisis and the individual leader who wants to apply these strategies.

First, before a crisis even occurs ("pre-crisis"), leaders need to anticipate potential crises and make themselves ready. For this purpose, leaders can apply scanning activities, risk analysis, scenario planning, and resource building, whereby leaders also have to make themselves ready by engaging in resilience-building measures. *Second*, when the crisis becomes real ("during crisis"), leaders have to cope with acute adversities. Leaders can do this by remaining self-confident and optimistic, engaging in an effective task fulfillment, using their professional and private networks, and taking care of their health. Due to the quickly changing demands of the crisis, it is no surprise that necessary behaviors in this phase are sometimes contradictory (Giustiniano et al., 2020). *Third*, when the crisis is over ("post-crisis"), leaders need to recover and learn from the crisis. For this purpose, leaders need to be open to criticism and suggestions, and, more importantly, must be able to convert the gained knowledge into a changed leader's behavior. *Fourth*, the leaders' conscious and unconscious behavioral reactions to crises are certainly influenced by their personalities. However, it does not matter if these underlying individual features are developed through personal or leadership training or available through predisposition. Empirical findings clearly show that the lack of certain innate characteristics (e.g., self-confidence) can be compensated by the development of related skills (e.g., the ability to trust oneself) (Foerster & Duchek, 2017). *Fifth*, the crisis behavior of leaders also depends on their surroundings. In this sense, it is up to leaders to create surroundings in which they feel safe and supported. Even if the work and private environment do not provide an optimum of protective factors, leaders can do the best for themselves (e.g., time outs, sports), especially since research has shown that resilience is influenced by various factors, both work-related and non-work-related (e.g., Kossek & Perrigino, 2016; Cooper et al., 2013). Nonetheless, and in particular, since research has emphasized that individual resilience is not only embedded in the occupational but also the organizational context (Kossek & Perrigino, 2016), organizations should create a resilience-promoting atmosphere, especially in times of crisis. For instance, this can be done by providing flexible work schedules or offering resilience training. Based on our explanations above, this training should consider the three resilience phases since these are the foundation for a holistic leaders' resilience promotion. Only if leaders learn to anticipate potential risks, cope with crises, and adapt afterward are they able to survive crises not only efficiently but also healthily. In order to train these kinds of behavior, various approaches are available, especially experienced-based (Kolb, 2014) and active learning methods (Snyder, 2003). Which training approach is most appropriate depends on the occupational, organizational, and individual context.

Since dealing with unexpected events can be considered a fundamental challenge in daily organizational life (e.g., Linnenluecke, 2017), and future pandemics are more than likely due to our global interdependence (e.g., Li, 2020), learning from the COVID-19 crisis is highly important. Therefore, we pose five reflection questions that might help us learn from the crisis and simultaneously prepare for the next. First, since most leaders were required to stay at home and rely on online technologies to lead their teams, leaders need to address the question of *how to lead from a distance?*. In this context, a related question could be *What technologies can support me in leading from a distance?*. In addition, leaders need to reflect on the COVID-19 crisis by asking, *What major risks and challenges did I face when leading from a distance, and how can they be met in the future?*. Furthermore, since many leaders were required to stay at home during the COVID-19 crisis and, thus, could not use their homes as a retreat any longer, leaders should consider *how to live and work at home?*. To stay not only efficient but also healthy, leaders need to find ways to separate or combine professional and personal issues as well as discover how to relax when working at home. Finally, since leaders' resilience is a concept that is influenced by both occupational as well as individual factors (Kossek & Perrigino, 2016), leaders need to think about what is important for their personal resilience. Some might need a structured work environment; others might need a chaotic one. Some may need to separate their personal and professional lives; others might appreciate a more flexible but interrelated life. Some need endurance sports, and others need relaxation techniques. What is right for one is far from right for the other. Nonetheless, leaders must ask themselves early, *What helps me build resilience for myself?*.

References

Avey, J. B., Avolio, B. J., & Luthans, F. (2011). Experimentally analyzing the impact of leader positivity on follower positivity and performance. *The Leadership Quarterly, 22*(2), 282–294.

Bennis, W. G., & Thomas, R. J. (2002). Crucibles of leadership. *Harvard Business Review, 80*, 39.

Bossmann, U., Ditzen, B., & Schweitzer, J. (2016). Organizational stress and dilemma management in mid-level industrial executives: An exploratory study. *Mental Health and Prevention, 4*(1), 9–18.

Buell, J. M. (2014). The resilient leader: Mind, body and soul. *Healthcare Executive, 29*(6), 10–18.

Bullough, A., & Renko, M. (2013). Entrepreneurial resilience during challenging times. *Business Horizons, 56*(3), 343–350.

Christman, D., & McClellan, R. (2008). "Living on barbed wire": Resilient women administrators in educational leadership programs. *Educational Administration Quarterly, 44*(1), 3–29.

Cooper, C., Flint-Taylor, J., & Pearn, M. (2013). *Building resilience for success: A resource for managers and organizations*. Palgrave Macmillan.

Coutu, D. L. (2002). How resilience works. *Harvard Business Review, 80*(5), 46–56.

Duchek, S. (2019). Organizational resilience: A capability-based conceptualization. *Business Research, 13*, 215–246.

Faustenhammer, A., & Goessler, M. (2011). Preparing for the next crisis: What can organizations do to prepare managers for an uncertain future? *Business Strategy Series, 12*(2), 51–55.

Fletcher, D., & Sarkar, M. (2013). Psychological resilience. A review and critique of definitions, concepts, and theory. *European Psychologist, 18*(1), 12–23.

Foerster, C., & Duchek, S. (2017). What makes leaders resilient? An exploratory interview study. *German Journal of Human Resource Management, 31*(4), 281–306.

Foerster, C., & Duchek, S. (2018). Leaders' resilience-A systematic literature review and future research agenda. *Academy of Management Annual Meeting Proceedings, 2018*, 13879.

Gates, B. (2015). *The next outbreak? We're not ready*. TED Talk. https://www.ted.com/talks/bill_gates_the_next_outbreak_we_re_not_ready/transcript

Giustiniano, L., Cunha, M. P., Simpson, A. V., Rego, A., & Clegg, S. (2020). Resilient leadership as paradox work: Notes from COVID-19. *Management and Organization Review, 16*, 971–975.

Gooty, J., Gavin, M., Johnson, P. D., Frazier, L., & Snow, D. B. (2009). In the eyes of the beholder: Transformational leadership, positive psychological capital, and performance. *Journal of Leadership and Organizational Studies, 15*(4), 353–367.

Gopinath, C., & Sawyer, J. E. (1999). Exploring the learning from an enterprise simulation. *Journal of Management Development, 18*(5), 477–489.

Gu, Q., & Day, C. (2007). Teachers' resilience: A necessary condition for effectiveness. *Teaching and Teacher Education, 23*(8), 1302–1316.

Hobfoll, S. E. (2002). Social and psychological resources and adaptation. *Review of General Psychology, 6*(4), 307–324.

Howard-Grenville, J. (2020). Grand challenges, Covid-19 and the future of organizational scholarship. *Journal of Management Studies, 58*, 254–258.

Kearns, S., & McArdle, K. (2012). 'Doing it right?' – Accessing the narratives of identity of newly qualified social workers through the lens of resilience: 'I am, I have, I can'. *Child & Family Social Work, 17*(4), 385–394.

Kerrissey, M. J., & Edmondson, A. C. (2020). What good leadership looks like during this pandemic. *Harvard Business Review*. https://hbr.org/2020/04/what-good-leadership-looks-like-during-this-pandemic

King, G. A., & Rothstein, M. G. (2010). Resilience and leadership: The self-management of failure. In M. G. Rothstein & R. J. Burke (Eds.), *Self-management and leadership development* (pp. 361–394). Edward Elgar.

Koen, M. P., du Plessis, E., & Watson, F. G. (2013). Exploring leadership hubs as an intervention in strengthening the resilience of health caregivers. *Journal of Psychology in Africa, 23*(3), 495–499.

Kolb, D. A. (2014). *Experiential learning: Experience as the source of learning and development*. Pearson Education.

Kossek, E. E., & Perrigino, M. B. (2016). Resilience: A review using a grounded integrated occupational approach. *The Academy of Management Annals, 10*(1), 729–797.

Lazaridou, A., & Beka, A. (2015). Personality and resilience characteristics of Greek primary school principals. *Educational Management Administration and Leadership, 43*(5), 772–791.

Li, P. P. (2020). Organizational resilience for a new normal: Balancing the paradox of global interdependence. *Management and Organization Review, 16*(3), 503–509.

Linnenluecke, M. K. (2017). Resilience in business and management research: A review of influential publications and a research agenda. *International Journal of Management Reviews, 19*(1), 4–30.

Luthar, S. S., & Cicchetti, D. (2000). The construct of resilience: Implications for interventions and social policies. *Development and Psychopathology, 12*(4), 857–885.

Luthar, S. S., Cicchetti, D., & Becker, B. (2000). The construct of resilience: A critical evaluation and guidelines for future work. *Child Development, 71*(3), 543–562.

Masten, A. S. (2001). Ordinary magic: Resilience processes in development. *American Psychologist, 56*(3), 227–238.

McKiernan, P., & Tsui, A. (2019). Responsible management research: A senior scholar legacy in doctoral education. *The Academy of Management Learning and Education, 18*, 310–313.

McLarnon, J., & Rothstein, M. (2013). Development and initial validation of the workplace resilience inventory. *Journal of Personnel Psychology, 12*(2), 63–73.

Quick, J. C., Gavin, J. H., Cooper, C. L., & Quick, J. D. (2000). Executive health: Building strength, managing risks. *Academy of Management Executive, 14*(2), 34–44.

Rees, C., Breen, L., Cusack, L., & Hegney, D. (2015). Understanding individual resilience in the workplace: The international collaboration of workforce resilience model. *Frontiers in Psychology, 6*, 73.

Reeves, M., Lang, N., & Carlsson-Szlezak, P. (2020). Lead your business through the coronavirus crisis. *Harvard Business Review, 27*.

Robertson, I. T., Cooper, C. L., Sarkar, M., & Curran, T. (2015). Resilience training in the workplace from 2003 to 2014: A systematic review. *Journal of Occupational and Organizational Psychology, 88*(3), 533–562.
Rouleau, L., Hallgren, M., & de Rond, M. (2020). Covid 19 and our understanding of risk, emergencies, and crises. *Journal of Management Studies, 58*, 245–248.
Sarkar, M., & Fletcher, D. (2014). Ordinary magic, extraordinary performance: Psychological resilience and thriving in high achievers. *Sport Exercise and Performance Psychology, 3*(1), 46–60.
Seidl, D., & Whittington, R. (2020). How crisis reveals the structures of practices. *Journal of Management Studies, 58*, 240–244.
Snyder, K. D. (2003). Ropes, poles, and space: Active learning in business education. *Active Learning in Higher Education, 4*(2), 159–167.
Tourish, D. (2020). The triumph of nonsense in management studies. *The Academy of Management Learning and Education, 19*(1), 99–109.
Van Doorn, R., & Hülsheger, U. (2015). What makes employees resilient to job demands? The role of core self-evaluations in the relationship between job demands and strain reactions. *European Journal of Work and Organizational Psychology, 24*(1), 76–87.
Vanderbilt-Adriance, E., & Shaw, D. S. (2008). Conceptualizing and re-evaluating resilience across levels of risk, time, and domains of competence. *Clinical Child and Family Psychology Review, 11*(1–2), 30–58.
Walumbwa, F. O., Peterson, S. J., Avolio, B. J., & Hartnell, C. A. (2010). An investigation of the relationships among leader and follower psychological capital, service climate, and job performance. *Personnel Psychology, 63*(4), 937–963.
Wang, J., Cooke, F., & Huang, W. (2014). How resilient is the (future) workforce in China? A study of the banking sector and implications for human resource development. *Asia Pacific Journal of Human Resources, 52*(2), 132–154.
Westman, M., & Chen, S. (2017). Crossover of burnout and engagement from managers to followers. In C. L. Cooper & J. C. Quick (Eds.), *The handbook of stress and health: A guide to research and practice* (pp. 236–248). Wiley-Blackwell.
WHO. (2017). *Pandemic influenza risk management: A WHO guide to inform and harmonize national and international pandemic preparedness and response*. Author.
WHO. (2019). *Ten threats to global health in 2019*. Author. https://www.who.int/news-room/feature-stories/ten-threats-to-global-health-in-2019
Williams, T. A., Gruber, D. A., Sutcliffe, K. M., Shepherd, D. A., & Zhao, E. Y. (2017). Organizational response to adversity: Fusing crisis management and resilience research streams. *Academy of Management Annals, 11*(2), 733–769.
Windle, G. (2011). What is resilience? A review and concept analysis. *Reviews in Clinical Gerontology, 21*(2), 152–169.
Wray, T. (2016). The role of leader hubris in the decline of RBS and Lehman Brothers. In P. Garrard & P. Robinson (Eds.), *The intoxication of power* (pp. 229–251). Palgrave Macmillan.
Wright, M. O., Masten, A. S., & Narayan, A. J. (2013). Resilience processes in development: Four waves of research on positive adaptation in the context of adversity. In S. Goldstein & R. B. Brooks (Eds.), *Handbook of resilience in children* (pp. 15–37). Springer.
Zunz, S. J. (1998). Resiliency and burnout: Protective factors for human service managers. *Administration in Social Work, 22*(3), 39–54.

Charlotte Förster is junior professor of European Management at the University of Technology Chemnitz (Germany), where she focuses her research on pandemic management. She also works for the Johannes Kepler University in Linz (Austria), where she investigates Resilience of Health Care Organizations in the COVID-19 crisis. Her research addresses leadership, leaders' resilience, extreme contents, and organizational resilience. She received her PhD from the Technical University of Dresden and also worked as a consultant for the University of Applied Sciences for Social Work, Education and Care in Dresden. Previously, she studied at the University of Paderborn (Germany) and the University of Sevilla (Spain). For more information, visit http://www.charlotte-foerster.com.

Stephanie Duchek is currently working as a researcher at the Fraunhofer Institute for Industrial Engineering IAO in Berlin (Germany). Her main research fields are the development and dynamization of organizational capabilities, innovation management, strategic human resource management, and qualitative research methods. Currently, her research focuses on resilience at different levels within organizations (e.g., organizational, team, and individual resilience). In her empirical research projects, she studies resilience processes, resilience resources as well as measures of resilience promotion. Stephanie Duchek received her PhD in Business Administration at the Free University of Berlin and worked as a junior professor at the Technical University of Dresden. She also works as a resilience coach, consultant, and trainer.

A Paean to the "Poet Laureate of Management" Peter B. Vaill

3

Eric B. Dent

> *When Peter spoke, everyone listened.* – Matt Minahan (2020, p. 5), *Organizational Development Review* Editor.

Let me settle one point right away. This chapter is an essay. It may even be a manifesto (Vaill, 1996a, p. xv). Peter B. Vaill (1936–2020) considered himself primarily an essayist, much to the chagrin of several of his colleagues who were aghast that his work never included a structural equation model, multivariate analysis, or even a *p*-test. Vaill, the "poet laureate of management" (Kramer, 2016, p. 642), was the leading voice of his generation for insisting that managing, organizing, and leading are performing arts not only skills, behaviors, or competencies. *Training & Development Journal* listed him as one of the top ten organization development specialists in the United States (Vaill, 1996a, p. xxii).

There will likely never be another Peter Vaill. I don't just mean that in an honoring, obsequious way but in the sense that the business school academy, AACSB accreditation, and the norms of Academy of Management scholarship largely mitigate against a next-generation Peter Vaill. Still, from my perspective, Vaill's life and work merit this chapter as one last siren call to impact the field of organizational behavior (OB) and management according to Vaill's vision.

Brief Career Summary

For those who may be unfamiliar with Vaill's career I will provide some overly brief experiences and accomplishments. As an undergraduate student in the 1950s, Vaill studied under Kenneth Clark (1914–2000; author of seminal works in psychology and a key figure in the establishment of the Center for Creative Leadership (CCL)).

E. B. Dent (✉)
Uncommon Friends Endowed Chair Professor of Ethics, Florida Gulf Coast University, Fort Myers, FL, USA

S. K. Dhiman, J. F. Marques (eds.), *Leadership After COVID-19*, Future of Business and Finance, https://doi.org/10.1007/978-3-030-84867-5_3

Next, he went to the Harvard Business School (HBS) where he worked with faculty including Fritz Roethlisberger (1898–1974) for an MBA and doctorate. The work of Carl Rogers had the greatest impact on Vaill during his doctoral program (Vaill, 1996b).

Vaill's first faculty appointment was at UCLA in the department headed by Bob Tannenbaum (1915–2003), of NTL (then, National Training Laboratories) and T-group fame. His early education and experience with such luminaries in the field created fertile ground for his own pioneering work in first describing the field of organizational excellence and high-performing systems (HPS) in his early 30s. At age 36, he started serving 5 years as Dean, School of Business and Public Management, at The George Washington University (GWU: where he also worked with OB stars Gordon Lippitt (1920–1985) and Jerry Harvey (1935–2015)). Shortly thereafter he was one of the "four horsepeople" (Minahan, 2020, p. 4) who "saved" NTL. Also, in the 1970s he began playing with the idea of "managing as a performing art," which became the title of a later book. In 1978, Vaill stepped down as dean and remained professor of Human Systems at GWU until 1997.

In the 1980s, he introduced the idea of "permanent whitewater" (PWW) that caused a shift in OB focus to a greater appreciation of the dynamic context in which managers and employees were working. Vaill edited *Organizational Dynamics* from 1986 to 1989 publishing some of the most celebrated works in the annals of that journal. Vaill also reprinted his favorite (1996b) poem, "Corson's Inlet" by A. R. Aamons (1962) that he described as "an inexhaustible mine of thoughts and feelings about systems and systems change" (Vaill, 1986, p. 3).

He was a member of the Board of Directors of the Organizational Behavior Teaching Society (OBTS) 1988–1991. In 1989, he published his first book *Managing as a Performing Art: New Ideas for a World of Chaotic Change*, which was also released in German, Russian, Chinese, and Spanish.

In 1992, Vaill began a 5-year term as a Member of the Board of Governors at CCL, whose international headquarters are in Greensboro, NC, USA. He served a second term beginning in 1999.

Tragically, in 2001, Vaill had what was thought to have been routine back surgery and acquired meningitis in the hospital and became paralyzed from the waist down for the remainder of his life. Further health incidents greatly slowed his professional work, though, they never dimmed his intellect or upbeat spirit.

Most of his scholarly outputs in the 2000s were book chapters in handbooks, such as "Organizational Epistemology – Wisdom, Culture, and Organizations" in *Handbook of Organizational and Managerial Wisdom* (2007a) and "Process Wisdom? The heart of Organization Development" in *Handbook of Organization Development* (2007b). Vaill remained an active scholar until his last days, adapting to the world of podcasts. He collaborated with Dave Fearon, his doctoral student from the 1960s/1970s in producing weekly episodes (Fearon & Vaill, 2021) on the subject of "practice." The overarching question addressed in many episodes is "What is the nature of Practice? Why does it matter?" He also left a complete, unpublished book entitled *On Practice as a Way of Being* (2019).

In short, Vaill's career has many characteristics not found in top scholars of the next generation. First, he was trained at the HBS that was known for long-term studies in the bowels of the workplace. Roethlisberger's work on the Hawthorne Project, for example, was a major effort from 1927 to 1932. Vaill's dissertation was an in-depth study of five industrial settings. Compare that with the opposite extreme, the keynote speaker at a recent academic conference who stated, "But there is a choice to be made: sit in my office and make up problems or go out and find real ones," and that certainly untenured faculty should "stay in their offices and make up problems to solve … addressing real-life problems should be taken care of by tenured professors" (Koskela, 2017, p. 4).

Consider the organizations that he affiliated with and led—OBTS, the Organization Development Network (ODN), NTL, CCL. These are organizations that all place a premium on practice. CCL and the others all produce high-quality scholarship, but it is not of the same genre, for example, as *Academy of Management Journal*. Vaill also got his hands dirty as a practitioner. He served as a business school dean and director of a doctoral program he transformed. He worked as part of a team of four to rescue the dying NTL. He served on several boards of directors. For many faculty today, these "service" roles would be shunned or taken on minimally. For Vaill, having his hand in practice was important for him as a scholar.

In the remainder of this chapter I will attempt to share Vaill's vision for the management field, explaining the key influences on his own thinking and explicating the challenges he saw in the practice of management and the field of OB. Vaill was ahead of his time in advocating sustainable approaches that are suitable for a post-COVID world. In short, Vaill concluded that in many ways our field is "barking up the wrong tree." I use that idiom from the vernacular because Vaill was extremely gifted at using terms that were both poignant and simple, terms such as "running an organization" (Vaill, 1992). Because of space limitations, I will write little about Vaill's seminal contribution to the field of HPS, his metaphor of PWW, "process wisdom," and his writings on spirituality, although like his colleague Jerry Harvey (Dent, 2017), Vaill (1987) was writing about workplace spirituality long before the Academy of Management launched the Management, Spirituality, and Religion (MSR) Special Interest Group (SIG) in 2000.

Although Vaill advocated for many viewpoints that are counter-cultural among mainstream professional managers, executive education leaders, classroom teachers, and MBA students, some continue to exemplify his vision, so encouraging examples will be provided. In the same way that Servant Leadership became much more widely accepted after Robert Greenleaf's death, I am hopeful that Vaill's ideas will be embraced more thoroughly posthumously.

Vaill's Philosophy and Perspective

> *American behavioral science has been - we have been - saying the wrong thing. For decades we have tried to say the wrong thing better and better… As long as we continue to say the wrong thing - no matter how well we say it, no matter how "reliably" and "validly," no matter how elegantly and mesmerically - it still will be the wrong thing. It will not feel right to the most honest ones among us, and it will not achieve any influence among practitioners.* (Vaill, 1998, p. 11).

Commentators for decades have lamented the same state of affairs: practicing managers don't read business research, business research is stove-piped and not relevant enough, practicing managers don't even apply the time-tested solid research findings about basics such as meeting management or providing feedback. Tourish (2020) characterized the management discipline as "in crisis. We neglect really important issues in favor of bite-sized chunks of research that are more likely to find quick publication in leading journals" (p. 99). His further concern is that management as a discipline has become primarily about boosting academic careers. In the current environment it makes sense for faculty scholars to become "imposters," not conducting research that addresses truly significant issues and seeks to make a difference (Harley, 2019; McKiernan & Tsui, 2019).

In a similar critique, Koskela (2017) reported that *Harvard Business Review* articles in 1984 and 2005 came to strikingly similar conclusions about the state and deficiencies of management research. Koskela noted, "the consequential irrelevance of research done and published is funnily enough discussed in almost the same format, 'to be fair …, but …', with emphasis on what comes after 'but': a strong statement on the irrelevance of 'most' or 'much' of research" (p. 5). Regarding basic, solid research findings, I will simply testify that the meetings of the Management Department that I attend today are no more productive or fun than those I attended at the beginning of my career at another university. Also, my young undergraduates working part-time jobs routinely make the same complaints about their supervisors (bossy, not thoughtful, don't want to listen, etc.) that my friends and I would have about our part-time supervisors more than 40 years ago. Vaill (1998) observed that throughout history, legions of leaders have been successful without knowing the research findings of OB and that current practicing leaders seem to find our research only marginally useful and not particularly interesting (p. 12).

Peter Vaill may not have had the proper vision that would have, and still might, change this state of affairs (although he's convinced it could help kids continue with piano lessons (Vaill, 1989, p. 48)). Still, it is provocative vision and the remainder of the chapter will elucidate his guidance. First, his philosophy and perspective will be outlined in five sections: (1) "Permanent Whitewater" (VUCA); (2) Manager-Leaders not Management Competencies; (3) Practice; (4) Management is Purposing, Learning, En-courag-ing; and (5) Management Education that all feature Vaill's unique vision for the practice and study of management beyond his lifetime.

Permanent Whitewater—VUCA

> *I think the messiness, contingency, sprawl, and indeed danger of the real managerial world ought to be the* centerpiece *of our thinking, not an afterthought* (Vaill, 1992, p. 133).

Peter Vaill is, perhaps, most famous for coining the term *permanent whitewater* (PWW) to describe the constantly changing organizational context that seemed to pick up pace in the 1980s. He and I created a "Change Assessment Inventory" and among thousands of respondents over many years, only three reported working in a less turbulent context than 5 years earlier. Questions ranged from asking whether people had more, or less, deadline pressure, unexpected interruptions, technological complexity, aggressive objectives, adequacy of information for decisions, and so forth. Vaill saw as "the grand paradox of management" the idea that managers are asked to bring greater control to their objectives, which, by definition, are less and less controllable.

Vaill christened *whitewater events* as the most extreme aspects of this turbulence characterized as surprising, novel, messy or ill-structured, costly or obtrusive, recurring (although not in exactly the same way) or unpreventable (Vaill had a good enough sense of humor to chuckle at the irony of his death occurring during the most extreme whitewater event of his lifetime, the COVID-19 pandemic). Vaill was preceded by Emery and Trist (1965) whose metaphor was "the ground itself is moving" to describe the phenomena of a destabilized context that prevents predictable plans of action from being viable. Vaill loved the metaphor of Siu (1980) who wrote about "Chinese baseball," a sport in which, when the ball is in the air, any player can move any base anywhere.

In the 2020s, PWW is more often referred to as the VUCA (volatile, uncertain, complex, and ambiguous) Model. This appellation was first coined by the U.S. military and Col. Eric G. Kail (2010) published a series of articles in the *Harvard Business Review* each featuring one aspect of VUCA. Kail together with experts in the public and private sectors have noted that the context often dominates the particular subject at hand. Post-COVID, organizational decisions must incorporate the VUCA environmental characteristics, which lead to counterintuitive recommendations such as building slack into a system rather than optimizing it. Leaders are commended for thinking divergently, thinking cross-culturally, and developing keen situational awareness.

Manager-Leaders Not Management Competencies

> *The problem as I see it exists at the level of basic philosophies of inquiry. I am trying to take big bites out of the CM [competency movement], not just nibble at its edges. ... The CM makes a basic assumption which it does not question, and which it probably is not even aware of as an assumption (or presupposition). It is this:* Competencies exist. *The fundamental question then is, what is the basis for assuming that competencies exist?* (Vaill, 1989, p. 45).

Despite Vaill's admonition, the textbook my university uses for the "Principles of Management" course (Kinicki & Williams, 2020) differentiates between "leaders" and "managers," as if an individual in an organization could be one or the other. The same mindset is found in corporate training programs. Vaill, however, preferred the term "leader-manager" when discussing those with managerial responsibility in organizations.

For Vaill, even our use of language creates an ontological issue. For example, the Harvard Business School in the 1920s adopted as its primary focus for the school's mission first "the administrator" and later "the general manager," as if this one person could be extracted from an organizational context. Vaill pointed out the logical inconsistency in the work of someone he considered a giant in the field, Chester Barnard. Barnard's most famous book is entitled *The Functions of the Executive*, yet within that book, first published in 1938, Barnard wrote, "The executive functions, which have been distinguished for purposes of exposition and which are the basis for much functional specialization in organizations, have no separate concrete existence. They are parts of aspects of a process of organization as a whole" (Barnard, 1968, p. 235). Because we don't have techniques for studying wholes, we study parts, but Vaill concluded that our study of the parts was often fallacious.

The problem compounded over the years. In 1960 Douglas McGregor published *The Human Side of Enterprise*, a title that suggests there is a non-human side of enterprise. By 1973 the split into what are often called "management competencies" (Vaill, 1992, p. 131) was complete with the Mintzberg's publication of *The Nature of Managerial Work*. The "management competencies" body of work contains many assumptions Vaill questioned such as that learning a competency largely means the student knows how and when to use it, downplaying the contextual considerations of PWW (Vaill, 1983).

This reductionism was present with the founding of MSR in the Academy of Management. Note that spirituality is listed separately from religion in the title of the SIG. Research that led to the most cited book in MSR asked survey participants about the main differences between religion and spirituality (and not similarities) and asked them to rate religion and spirituality separately on a seven-point scale. Voila! The epistemology used has defined religion and spirituality separately and the field is framed, no matter contrary facts such as the religion of Islam, with the second-highest number of practitioners on earth, makes absolutely no distinction between spirituality and religion (Dent, 2019). Neither do many people outside the northeastern and western United States, where the surveys were conducted. The field is now blinded to the possibility that the fusion of spirituality and religion may be the most interesting and insightful aspect of study.[1]

CCL, a highly-regarded, international leadership development organization, touts 52 leadership competencies that are important for managerial success. This list has been vetted and refined over a period of decades. Yet, glancing at the list, it is easy to take issue with the framing of much of what managers "do" or "are." For example, research has shown that successful leaders are emotionally intelligent. The CCL list includes factors such as "compassion and sensitivity," "interpersonal savvy," and "resilience," which, even collectively, don't adequately capture the emotional intelligence requirements of top managerial success. The only factor that approximates working virtually in a multinational environment is "global team management." Finally, "spirituality" is not on CCL's list. The closest competencies might be "balance" or "vision." Spirituality may be too loaded a word, but for Vaill (1992) those "running an organization" successfully clearly transcended its

[1] For most of his career, Jerry Harvey, of "Abilene Paradox" fame was Vaill's closest colleague. In a memorial tribute to Harvey, Vaill reported the following conversation—"I asked him, 'Jerry, would you agree that golf and spirituality are two quite important things about you?' he would reply, 'Dr. Vaill, yes, and by the way they are not two things'" (Vaill, 2017, 107–108).

activities, policies, and practices and conveyed a deeper meaning to its employees and customers. Vaill might agree that such a list of factors provides most of the bricks needed for the foundation of a structure of managerial success, but he would contend that most of the mortar is missing.

Vaill was so insistent on not prematurely being reductionist that when he launched the field of organizational excellence or high-performing systems in 1972 with 47 descriptive characteristics, he wrote that he was not interested in doing conventional research to continue to validate the characteristics. This work is more accessible in a 1976 book chapter where he explained "I feel this way because behind the hypotheses is some kind of dimly perceived gestalt that will evaporate entirely if I become analytical too soon" (p. 103). This would be an entirely foreign notion to nearly all management researchers today. Vaill lamented that he was handicapped in trying to conceptualize wholes by language, which forces a sequential, discrete rendering and that his own writings were forced to be reductionist. Still, he would argue that our field is missing the target by focusing on management competencies rather than the overall managerial experience. Running an organization is exceedingly intricate, and certainly not a mastery of a variety of managerial competencies.

A philosophical successor to Vaill is Michael Beer (2009), who has described his approach in books such as *High Commitment High Performance* (HCHP). Rather than focusing on management competencies, he counseled companies including Johnson & Johnson, Hewlett Packard, and Goldman Sachs that leaders must think in terms of a multistakeholder perspective, for example. They must lead-manage with their hearts and provide "employees at all levels with a sense of higher purpose, meaning, challenging work, and the capacity to make a difference" (p. 51). HCHP makes no distinction between management and leadership, focusing holistically on resilience, sustainable action, and viewing their behaviors and the organization as a total system. Beer advocates both/and, not or/either thinking.

Practice

> *Theory and practice do not "integrate;" they dance with each other, sometimes lustily, but just as often ploddingly or with one lording over the other or warily and with stony indifference. But it also must be said that in a school of administration, management, leadership, or practice, if theory and practice do not dance with each other somehow, the learner will graduate not knowing much about practice not having gained any increment in concrete skill nor remembering any of the theories that were intended to be relevant in the future* (Vaill, 2007c, p. 327).

In his last months, Vaill joined Dave Fearon in hosting 22 podcasts about "practice" and was intending to publish his next book, *On Practice as a Way of Being* (2019). The podcast website is entitled "Choosing a Practiced Way of Life." For Vaill, theory and practice were inextricably linked. The phrase "that's fine in theory, but what about in practice" is commonly expressed, yet researchers focus nearly all of their energies on developing and understanding theory, not practice (p. 13). This notion is foreign to most modern scholars who even distinguish between practitioner journals and scholarly journals.

At Vaill's (2010) last conference presentation he spoke about learning, co-inquiry and practice, but referred to the topic of practice as his "biggie." He introduced the provocative metaphor of dark matter. Dark matter comprises 85% of the matter of the universe but it cannot be detected with existing instrumentation. Dark matter prevents galaxies from flying apart and has a strong influence on the structure and ongoing unfolding of the universe. Dark energy plus dark matter constitutes 95% of the universe's total mass-energy content ("Dark matter," 2020). Vaill provocatively asserted that "practice is the dark matter and energy of social science. Practice is everywhere" (Vaill, 2010). Moreover, practice, like dark matter, does not get *nearly* the attention it deserves.

Just as dark matter can't be seen by scientific instruments, Vaill believed that practice remains largely undetected by the current tools commonly in use by management researchers who operate primarily in a positivist, objectivist paradigm. He offered six characteristics about practice that allow it to remain mostly hidden from such research techniques. For example, practice *happens in real time outside a controlled setting* where many variables are changing simultaneously. Vaill also imagined more research of the duration of the Hawthorne studies. He recommended that every researcher have one project that essentially followed an organization or a leader for that researcher's entire career. This would allow for a richness of data that simply isn't available in OB research today.

Near the end of his life, Vaill's advice to us about the field was to "*turn to practice to reinvigorate scholarship*" [italics in the original] (Jamieson & Milbrandt, 2017, p. 1399). A worthy successor to Vaill's work on practice are Joseph Raelin (2016) and colleagues who contributed chapters to *Leadership-as-practice*. Their goal is to change the conventional view of leadership. They eschew perspectives of leadership that focus on traits, behaviors, or competencies. They also do not recognize or demark pre-established roles, or focus on leader-member relations. Instead, they place their lens primarily on practice, the "interaction with the environment through both individual and collective sensorimotor processing" and engage in process-oriented studies that "consider cultural, historical, and political conditions embedded with the leadership relationship." They view themselves as a "movement" with a change agenda for the field of management, so, perhaps, this view will further blossom.

Management Is Purposing, Learning, En-courag-ing

> *An organization would not have "management" ... it would have* "encouragement." *You'd no longer have schools of management; you'd have schools of encouragement. A promotion would not be to move into management; it would be to move into* encouragement *– and the difference is almost break-taking* (Vaill, 2006, p. 3).

Our field does not have a theory of leadership or management that is independent of performance. Coaches who win games are considered great. Coaches who lose games are not. It's that simple. The management field does not have a model or theory that can delineate when leader-managers have performed outstandingly while their organizations have not, even though it is not difficult to list reasons largely outside the leader-manager's purview, such as macro-economic factors.

Vaill was critical of the framing of most popular management and leadership theories. Vaill wrote that he had seen outstanding leaders that ranged from "tyrants [with] almost maniacal commitment that would get them locked up in other contexts to laid-back managers who seem outwardly to do very little (1982, p. 38)." Drucker (2004) agreed noting that in 65 years he had seen exceptional CEOs who were "all over the map in terms of their personalities, attitudes, values, strengths, and weaknesses. They ranged from extroverted to nearly reclusive, from easygoing to controlling, from generous to parsimonious" (p. 59).

From the beginning of his career until the end Vaill (2010), Vaill was still inspired and informed by Chester Barnard's statement that "sensing of the organization as a whole and the total situation relevant to it. It transcends the capacity of merely intellectual methods, and the techniques of discriminating the factors of the situation. The terms pertinent to it are 'feeling,' 'judgment,' 'sense,' 'proportion,' 'balance,' 'appropriateness.' It is a matter of art rather than science, and is aesthetic rather than logical. For this reason, it is recognized rather than described and is known by its effects rather than by analysis" (Barnard, 1968, p. 235). Similarly, Vaill bemoaned that just because some activities in an organization lent themselves to quantitative analysis, as Deming clearly demonstrated, management researchers assumed "running an organization" was seen that way.

Vaill's thinking evolved over the years, but began with the argument that management is a performing art. As noted above, he began using that metaphor in the early 1970s and etched it into OB with a book of that title (Vaill, 1989). Then, he started characterizing what is commonly thought of "managing" as "purposing," which he defined as "that continuous stream of actions by an organization's formal leadership that has the effect of inducing clarity, consensus, and commitment regarding the organization's basic purposes" (1982, p. 29). He would later contend that "all management is people management" (1989, p. 126) because all managing and leading happens with and through people and the meaning that these people attach to the leader-manager's action.

Vaill's (2006) final thoughts on the subject are quite provocative. He wondered whether management is, surprisingly, encouragement. He built the case based on Ackoff's notion that what top leaders really needed was "guts" (Detrick, 2002) and Deming's admonition to "drive out fear." Consequently, what leader-managers need is courage. He thought of courage as "the capacity and process of maintaining one's identity and values in the face of psychic challenge" (Vaill, 1988, p. 9). Vaill then referenced a leadership theory he *did* appreciate, Kouzes and Posner's Leadership Challenge, in particular, their later appreciation that of their five practices of exemplary leadership, the most important might be "Encourage the Heart" (Kouzes & Posner, 1999). He sometimes spelled it as en-courage-ment to emphasize *courage*, because encouragement in the vernacular has a softer, cheerleading connotation, which is only a small aspect of instilling courage. Leadership, he mused, might be "leading people out of superficial tranquility and *into* anxiety and then into a feeling of a need for courage and then along the courage-formed path itself" (Vaill, 1988, p. 10). As noted in the quotation opening this section, he saw this reframing as breath-taking. He also believed this framing was consistent with the research on emotional intelligence and servant leadership (Vaill, 2006).

Management Education

> *How can you make a class sweat over a complex concept or formula or software application while at the same time communicating, "Be aware, however, that we are in a hothouse here. This problem and this algorithm don't look anything like this when they surface in an organization. You won't have the right data; you won't have enough time; key people will think you're crazy and may take steps to prevent this approach; your own energy for this approach may be very mixed; the technique's reputation in the organization may have preceded your use of it and you will have to deal with those stereotypes; the situation may be moving so quickly that by the time you get the problem set up according to the algorithm the need has passed; there will be others with different, equally sophisticated approaches competing with you ...," and so on.* (Vaill, 1992, p. 133).

Vaill defined the field of management/organizational behavior as consisting of the responses to two questions "'how is it that men and women get things done in organizational contexts?' and, 'How can we help them do what they're trying to do better?'" (Vaill, 1979, p. 3). The second question essentially encompasses management education, so Vaill thought and wrote extensively about the question of how OB faculty teach, including writing the book *Learning as a Way of Being* (1996a). The field of OB has had a long-running dialogue about what percentages of teaching are devoted to content and to process. Vaill recommended placing significantly more weight on the latter. In fact, he considered too much emphasis on content as "losing focus" (1992, p. 133). He saw the Ford and Carnegie Foundation reports of the late 1950s as basically mandates to teach subject matter. They assumed that passing on more content would lead to better education. In his words, this assumption is fallacious and the promised better education "didn't happen" (p. 133). Another fallacy Vaill saw in management education is embodied in the opening quotation for this section and can be clarified in distinguishing between *inside* and *outside* knowledge. Inside knowledge is very context-dependent. Outside knowledge is mostly context-independent and is what faculty and trainers teach when they cover feedback skills, leadership approaches, teaming, etc. Yet another fallacy is that we teach outside knowledge with the assumption that the learner can automatically transform it into inside knowledge. This mostly doesn't happen either, though.

Vaill described his own teaching not as instructing, but as "engaging in, a *conversation about human beings as they are in organizations*" (1996b, p. 262). The conversation covers problems/issues, theorizing and modeling processes, and resulting working theory. Part of the dialogue in OB is how much of the class is about personal growth. Vaill would applaud personal growth, but he didn't conceive any part of what he was doing as functioning like a therapist. He also eschewed the approach of a classroom comprised of fun and games or entertainment. He strongly recommended that faculty engage in experiential activities but believed that faculty needed to create the activities for novel behavior to learn from, not run canned experiential activities such as a version of Desert Survival, that is designed to produce a predetermined behavior in the participants. He believed that just below the surface of such approaches was a touch of authoritarianism by the teacher and manipulation of the students.

Vaill also abjured the teaching frame commonly placed on management that excludes moral agency. Vaill claimed that "everything we think we should be teaching - is about values and standards and morals" (1992, p. 137). To teach leadership, human behavior, and values, Vaill included non-management sources. He taught courses specifically on these topics through the lenses of movies, poetry, and novels. In all his courses, students were likely to encounter "Bach… Goethe… Augustine… Heidegger… Lao Tzu…de Tocqueville… Kierkegaard…or Shakespeare" (1979, p. 4). He asked of the field, "Do we really believe that Henry Mintzberg (I'm sorry, Henry) is more important than Tacitus? Are we so bold as to say that a good post-1970 text will do the job?" (p. 4).

Vaill identified three hallmarks to his own teaching style, (a) his personal fascination with the subject matter, (b) his "desire to achieve a genuinely collegial relationship with participants" (1996b, p. 280), and (c) his hope that participants would want to develop their own versions of love for the subject matter and desire for collegiality in all their other learning contexts. To these ends, for example, Vaill worked hard at reducing the power and status imbalance between himself and the students, who he referred to as participants. He wrote extensively on a "co-inquiry model of teaching" in which "a professor and students achiev[e] a genuine collaboration in seeking to understand the subject matter of the course or program" (Vaill, 1999, p. 3). Still, without using the language of evidence-based management (EBM), Vaill (1996b) felt obligated to teach what was grounded in the best peer-reviewed research and theory available.

Management education is a $160 billion business in the United States and $356 billion globally. For the most part, this "training clearly had not worked." The "context in which [participants] work makes it difficult for them to put what they're taught into practice" (Beer, 2016, p. 52). The training is typically directed at an "aggregation of individuals" when what is needed is training focused on the "systems of interacting elements" (i.e. the context). I'm working with a multinational Aerospace and Defense corporation, that provides an excellent example of a Vaill- and Beer-recommended approach to senior leadership development. Their Leadership Program (LP) is a 2-year experience for a global cohort of 14–16 potential C-Suite leaders. Program features that highlight Vaill's recommendations include: an emphasis on the overall context of the leader-in-organization; executive coaching, one-on-one conversations with the executive team, and peer consulting that all underscore the specific circumstances of each leader; a focus not on increasing management competencies, but developing the whole executive through relationship building that is forged among participants and with the executive team, emotional intelligence, and on-the-job "stretch" assignments.

The MLP also includes an "Experience to Lead" session at the beaches of the WWII Normandy Battle site. This session is framed by Kolb's experiential learning model of meaning-making and links emotion to cognition for more impactful learning. Finally, current MET leaders are extremely encouraging, as the program gives them storytelling opportunities about their own leadership journeys, particularly emphasizing the challenges they faced and the setbacks they had to overcome.

Vaill's Legacy

Now that Vaill is gone, what torches would he want us to carry forward in a post-COVID world? In one of his last recorded interviews, Vaill's answer was threefold: "transform the image of people-in-the-organization to people-as-the-organization … resurrect the idea of a *spirit* and *purpose* into organizational thinking … define leadership as a landscape of practice" (Jamieson & Milbrandt, 2017, pp. 1409–1410). Fortunately, Vaill was a frequent speaker to professional audiences, usually taught a heavy course load, wrote prolifically, and directed numerous dissertations, so there are many people picking up this torch and continuing to question for our field, some of the guiding assumptions that may be fallacious or incomplete.

Allow me to create an analogy using William Ely Hill's famous perceptual image, "My Wife and My Mother-in-Law," to explain how Vaill's vision for the field of management is so different from where the field is today. Contained within the single image are pictures both of an older and younger woman, but our perception typically forces us to see only one or the other initially. Once someone points out to us that there are two women, we can move our perception back and forth between them. If someone is shown this image and given the task of finding greater beauty, she or he should try to "see" the wife, not the mother-in-law. Likewise, in the practice and education of management, reductionism and holism are present, the person and the context are present, and rational management and feeling-judgment-sense management are present. Vaill's career is a plea that if our task is to create greater productivity and workplace satisfaction, we must not keep the mother-in-law (reductionist, context-free, rational, etc.) as our primary focus. The more we can also see the wife (holistic, context-laden, judgment, etc.), the better off society will be.

As noted above, there are corners of the management field where Vaill's vision persists and thrives. To expand those corners, management education and practice need to focus on the whitewater or messiness of context. Rather than focusing on management competencies (competency-based learning and competency-based education are ascendant), training and education should emphasize running an organization with Barnard's insistence on feeling, judgment, sense, proportion, balance, and appropriateness. Consider how poetry (Vaill, 1981), music, and novels might hasten the process. In practice and teaching we must blur the distinction between human and business sides of enterprise. My hope is that this essay will provoke some reconsideration of Vaill's vision. Others made his points before him, and others will after him. However, he crafted the vision with such an elegance of writing and an insight into the current *zeitgeist*.

I will conclude with a quotation that Vaill wrote about someone with vision, in an introduction to an issue of *Organizational Dynamics* he edited, and simply say that for me, Vaill was someone with tremendous vision. Each encounter I had with him stretched my mind and enflamed my passion for my work. "When we meet someone who does indeed have a vision, our sense of its essence is its noncontrived, nonoccasional, noninstrumental quality. We feel that we are in the presence of something very deep about the person, something unmistakably genuine, something that lies close to the person's core values and beliefs" (Vaill, 1987).

Chapter Takeaways/Lessons

1. Managing/leading seems to be an activity that is partly a performing art and partly learned competence. As you grow as a manager/leader, consider honing your skills in a competency, such as giving feedback, but also in systematically noticing your feeling, judgment, sense, proportion, balance, and appropriateness.
2. To grow as a manager/leader attend training and read business books. Also, though, read poetry and novels and listen to symphony. Try your hand at doing some writing about your situation. Notice leadership all around you—at a restaurant, in a store, in your community, and in the other contexts of your life.
3. Barnard, Vaill, and others have long advocated for the importance of actual experience, rather than vicarious experience in a mediated way. There is a difference between walking through The Louvre and viewing the paintings online. In addition to giving money to charity, do you also offer charity, perhaps delivering a service to the poor that brings you into close contact with them?
4. Is more of your management/leadership activity planning, organizing, staffing, directing, and controlling or dealing with ambiguity, messiness, and novelty? Consider how you spend your day. For "messy" challenges, are you ultimately able to bring them under control or can you only "steer" them in the manner whitewater rafters deal with the rapids? Do you thrive in the rapids or dread them? Gaining more appreciation for the rapids might enhance your overall managing/leading.
5. If you are a trainer or teacher, what do you try to accomplish through your training/teaching process? Does it matter whether you have a relationship with those you are instructing? Does it matter whether you have actually practiced the concepts you are teaching? How can you better include the context of those in your classroom? Ponder these questions.

Reflection Questions

1. Consider a manager at Starbucks, a manager at a shoe factory, and a manager at Google. How much of their management work is similar and how much is different? How do we know?
2. The question that seemed to dominate Vaill's mind is, "What is practice?" Consider the various practices in your life. How do you interact with your pet? How do you plan and eat your meals? How do you keep your mind, body, and spirit healthy and thriving? You may discover insights into your managing/leading.
3. Why isn't the work of the Academy of Management read by practitioners? Why do they accept as gospel (and buy) business books that are almost exclusively anecdotal information?
4. Why is management considered a role that someone can assume with little or no formal preparation? Why don't most organizations bother to require managers know, and practice, even the most basic management research findings?
5. If you are a management researcher, are you functioning as an "imposter" producing research that is publishable but has almost no practical relevance and applicability?

References

Aamons, A. R. (1962). *Corson's inlet*. https://www.poetryfoundation.org/poems/43073/corsons-inlet

Barnard, C. A. (1968). *The functions of the executive*. Harvard University Press. (Thirtieth Anniversary Edition).

Beer, M. (2009). *High commitment high performance*. Jossey-Bass.

Beer, M. (2016). Why leadership training fails – And what to do about it. *Harvard Business Review, 94*(10), 50–57.

Dent, E. B. (2017). Jerry Harvey: The quintessential life of sense and nonsense. *Journal of Management, Spirituality & Religion, 14*(2), 109–116.

Dent, E. B. (2019). MSR 2.0: Spirituality plus religion. In J. Marques (Ed.), *The Routledge companion to management and workplace spirituality* (pp. 74–87). Routledge.

Detrick, G. (2002). Russell L. Ackoff. *Academy of Management Learning & Education, 1*(1), 56–63.

Drucker, P. F. (2004). What makes an effective executive. *Harvard Business Review, 82*(6), 58–63.

Emery, F. E., & Trist, E. (1965). The causal texture of organizational environments. *Human Relations, 18*, 21–32.

Fearon, D. S., & Vaill, P. B. (2021). *Practice?* Enaction Research. https://enactionresearch.com/podcast-page/ [Audio podcast]

Harley, B. (2019). Confronting the crisis of confidence in management studies: Why senior scholars need to stop setting a bad example. *Academy of Management Learning & Education, 18*(2), 286–297.

Jamieson, D. W., & Milbrandt, J. M. (2017). Peter B. Vaill: A life in the art of managing and leading change. In D. B. Szabla, W. A. Pasmore, M. A. Barnes, & A. N. Gipson (Eds.), *The Palgrave handbook of organizational change thinkers* (pp. 1389–1414). Palgrave Macmillan.

Kail, E. G. (2010). Leading in a VUCA environment: V is for volatility. *Harvard Business Review*. https://hbr.org/2010/11/leading-in-a-vuca-environment-1

Kinicki, A., & Williams, B. K. (2020). *Management: A practical introduction* (9th ed.). McGraw-Hill.

Koskela, L. (2017). Why is management research irrelevant? *Construction Management and Economics, 35*(1–2), 4–23.

Kouzes, J. M., & Posner, B. Z. (1999). *Encouraging the heart: A leader's guide to rewarding and recognizing others*. Jossey-Bass.

Kramer, R. (2016). Dialogic organization development: The theory and practice of transformational change. *Academy of Management Learning & Education, 15*(3), 639–643.

McGregor, D. (1960). *The human side of enterprise*. McGraw-Hill.

McKiernan, P., & Tsui, A. (2019). Responsible management research: A senior scholar legacy in doctoral education. *Academy of Management Learning & Education, 18*(2), 310–313.

Minahan, M. (2020). Remembering Peter Vaill. *Organization Development Review, 52*(1), 4–6.

Mintzberg, H. (1973). *The nature of managerial work*. HarperCollins.

Raelin, J. A. (2016). *Leadership-as-practice*. Jossey-Bass.

Siu, R. G. H. (1980). Management and the art of Chinese baseball. In H. J. Leavitt & L. Pondy (Eds.), *Readings in managerial psychology*. University of Chicago Press.

Tourish, D. (2020). The triumph of nonsense in management studies. *Academy of Management Learning & Education, 19*(1), 99–109.

Vaill, P. B. (1976). Toward a behavioral description of a high-performing system. In M. W. McCall Jr. & M. M. Lombardo (Eds.), *Leadership: Where else can we go?* Duke University Press.

Vaill, P. B. (1981). Thoughts on using poetry in the teaching of OB. *Exchange: The Organizational Behavior Teaching Journal, 6*(3), 50–51.

Vaill, P. B. (1982). The purposing of high-performance systems. *Organizational Dynamics, 11*(2), 23–39.

Vaill, P. B. (1983). The theory of managing in the managerial competency movement. *Exchange: The Organizational Behavior Teaching Journal, 8*(2), 50–54.

Vaill, P. B. (1986). *To our readers, Organizational Dynamics, 15*(1), 2–3.

Vaill, P. B. (1987). To our readers. *Organizational Dynamics, 16*(2), 2–3.
Vaill, P. B. (1988). A note on the idea of courage. *Organizational Behavior Teaching Review, 12*(3), 9–11.
Vaill, P. B. (1989). *Managing as a performing art: New ideas for a world of chaotic change*. Jossey-Bass.
Vaill, P. B. (1992). Notes on "running an organization". *Journal of Management Inquiry, 1*(2), 130–138.
Vaill, P. B. (1996a). *Learning as a way of being: Strategies for survival in a world of permanent white water*. Jossey-Bass.
Vaill, P. B. (1996b). Meditations on a poet's overalls. In P. Frost & R. Andre (Eds.), *Researchers hooked on teaching* (pp. 258–282). Sage Publications.
Vaill, P. B. (1998). *Spirited leading and learning: Process wisdom for the new age*. Jossey-Bass.
Vaill, P. B. (1999). *Notes on a co-inquiry model of teaching*. University of St. Thomas. [Unpublished manuscript].
Vaill, P. B. (2006). *Notes on "encouragement"*. Antioch University. [Unpublished manuscript].
Vaill, P. B. (2007a). Organizational epistemology – Wisdom, culture, and organizations. In E. H. Kessler & J. R. Bailey (Eds.), *Handbook of organizational and managerial wisdom* (pp. 327–356). Sage.
Vaill, P. B. (2007b). Chapter 13 Process wisdom? The heart of organization development. In T. G. Cummings (Ed.), *Handbook of organization development* (pp. 219–236). Sage.
Vaill, P. B. (2007c). F. J. Roethlisberger and the elusive phenomena of organizational behavior. *Journal of Management Education, 31*(3), 321–338.
Vaill, P. B. (2010). *Three organization behavior legacy statements* [Video]. https://vimeo.com/13203879. [Prepared for the Organizational Behavior Teaching Conference, 2010].
Vaill, P. B. (2017). Let us now praise Jerry B. Harvey - The down home scholar. *Journal of Management, Spirituality & Religion, 14*(2), 105–108.
Vaill, P. B. (2019). *On practice as a way of being*. Antioch University. [Unpublished manuscript].
Wikipedia. (2020). *Dark matter*. Author. https://en.wikipedia.org/wiki/Dark_matter

Eric B. Dent serves as professor and Uncommon Friends Endowed Chair in Ethics at Florida Gulf Coast University. He is committed to an interdisciplinary research agenda and has publications in journals of leadership, consulting, philosophy, workplace spirituality, science, history, communications, psychology, education, and others. Dr. Dent has been honored for his teaching, scholarship, and service including two best paper awards at the Academy of Management Conference and North Carolina's highest designation of appreciation for distinguished volunteer service bestowed by the governor. Dr. Dent has served in many capacities in academia, ranging from Faculty Senate Chair to Business School Dean. He is a consultant to Fortune 500, government, and nonprofit organizations as well as an invited speaker to national audiences. Prior to earning his PhD, Dr. Dent served as a corporate vice president in the financial services industry. He began his career as a computer scientist with IBM.

4 The Compatibility of Christian Servant Leadership and Sustainable Leadership in a Post-Covid-19 World

Gary E. Roberts

Introduction

One of the greatest challenges of leadership is to promote sustainable organizational success while preserving employee well-being. Sustainability is a multidimensional construct, but for the purposes of this chapter, sustainability is defined by the ability of the organization to achieve its mission while promoting the greater good and cultivating the wellbeing of all key stakeholders over an extended period. Sustainable leadership systematically cultivates effectiveness in a patient, long-term perspective using the agricultural analogy of an organic produce farmer that lovingly cultivates the land through such practices as natural fertilizers and pest control with crop rotation and regular cycles of allowing the land to lie fallow versus the short-term gain approach of "slash and burn" agriculture that depletes the soil. From a Christian theological perspective, servant leadership embraces this agricultural and animal husbandry perspective through the metaphors of leadership beginning with the identity of a faithful servant and a leader as the altruistic servant shepherd in I John 10:11. Jesus stated "I am the good shepherd. The good shepherd lays down his life for the sheep." The secular and Christian worldview literature on servant leadership further supports the elements of patient, long-term mission and 360-degree stakeholder cultivation in which leaders promote the greater good (Greenleaf, 1977; Spears, 1998; Roberts, 2015). Servant leadership anticipates threats to employee safety and wellbeing, and systematically invests in health and safety practices to minimize the threat (Roberts, 2015). Hence, servant leadership led organizations are prepared to address the threats posed by the current Covid-19 crisis as well as future outbreaks. The key focus of the chapter is the micro leadership and human resource

G. E. Roberts (✉)
Robertson School of Government, Regent University, Virginia Beach, VA, USA
e-mail: garyrob@regent.edu

S. K. Dhiman, J. F. Marques (eds.), *Leadership After COVID-19*, Future of Business and Finance, https://doi.org/10.1007/978-3-030-84867-5_4

policies and practices that promote employee long-term sustainability in a post Covid-19 world by protecting employee health thereby reducing burnout and the associated negative physical, emotional, spiritual, and organizational performance outcomes. These key elements of servant leader sustainability include ongoing implementation of policies and practices that enhance employee wellbeing including employee empowerment, fair employee treatment, and conducting a workplace health, safety, and stress audit to identify and solve problems.

General Research Support for Servant Leadership

Before we address the specific elements of servant leadership sustainability in a post Covid-19 world, it is important to clearly present the impressive and robust evidence of the efficacy of servant leadership across the globe. This section will summarize two aggregate sources of information, a summary of the meta, systematic, and literature reviews on the effectiveness of servant leadership, and the author's own ongoing research on the empirical servant leader literature.

Five meta-analyses have demonstrated the robust and significant beneficial effect of servant leadership across a wide range of employee attitudes, behaviors and performance outcomes. Aaron et al. (2020) found positive effects sizes for servant leadership on job performance, organizational citizenship behavior, creative behavior, affective commitment, job satisfaction, and leader-member exchange. The meta-analysis by Kiker et al. (2019) demonstrated the positive influence of servant leadership on job performance, organizational citizenship behavior, job satisfaction, organizational commitment, and follower trust. Marinova and Park's meta-analysis (2014) demonstrated the favorable influence of servant leadership on leader-member exchange, trust in leader, global leadership effectiveness, perceived organizational support, fairness perception, organizational commitment, collective identification, self-efficacy, job satisfaction, task performance, organizational citizenship behavior, group justice climate, group performance, group organizational citizen behaviors, and organizational effectiveness while being negatively related to turnover intention, deviance, and group deviance.

Lee et al. (2020) and Hoch et al. (2018) demonstrated that servant leadership explains a significant amount of the variance in leadership effectiveness over and above transformational leadership in a variety of outcomes and found roughly equivalent positive effect sizes for the United States and other Anglo countries when compared to China (Aaron et al., 2020). The positive effects of servant leadership are also reflected in four systematic and literature reviews (Setyaningrum et al., 2020; Bavik, 2020; Chon & Zoltan, 2019; Parris & Peachey, 2013).

The author has assessed published empirical servant leader research studies using the Business Source Complete data base as well as reviewing the table of Contents of key servant leader journals such as the *International Journal of Servant Leadership* and *Servant Leadership Theory and Practice*. The analysis (Table 4.1) identified 211 empirical articles published from 2004 to 2020. The complete list of reviewed studies is available from the author. Table 4.1 demonstrates the increasing

Table 4.1 Frequency count of servant leader empirical studies

United States and non-US studies by year	US alone studies	US alone %	Joint US and Inter. studies	Joint US and Inter. studies %	Non-US alone studies	Non-US alone studies %	Non-US joint studies	Non-US joint studies %	Total number of studies	% of Total
2004–2008	12	85.7	1	7.1	1	7.1	0	0.0	14	6.6
2009–2013	16	39.0	1	2.4	22	53.7	2	4.9	41	19.4
2014–2020	31	19.9	2	1.3	117	75.0	6	3.8	156	73.9
Total	59	28.0	4	1.9	140	66.4	8	3.8	211	100.0

Table 4.2 Frequency count of servant leader empirical studies by continent

Frequency	*n*	Percent
African	8	3.6%
Asia	79	35.1%
Australia/New Zealand	7	3.1%
Caribbean	4	1.8%
Europe	38	16.9%
Middle East	20	8.9%
North America	69	30.7%
Total	225	100%

Table 4.3 Servant leader empirical variable assessment analysis

US, positive effect hypothesis confirming	**US, not significant**	**US, significant effect, negative influence**	**Total US studies**	**US% positive effect hypothesis confirming**	
142	0	1	143	99.3%	
Global, positive effect hypothesis confirming	**Global, not significant**	**Global, significant effect, negative influence**	**Total global studies**	**% Global positive effect hypothesis confirming**	
277	13	5	295	93.9%	
Total positive effect, hypothesis confirming	**Total, not significant**	**Total, significant effect, negative influence**	**Total US and global studies**	**Total positive effect hypothesis confirming %**	*n*
419	13	6	438	95.7%	438

global scope of servant leadership. Servant leadership empirical research began in the early portion of this century. The first 5 years of research (2004–2008) was dominated by the United State with 93% of the empirical studies originating in the United States. This percentage has decreased dramatically to 41% from 2009 to 2013 and 26% from 2014 to 2020. Table 4.2 provides a summary by continent with the highest percentage of studies from Asia at 35.1% (primarily China) followed by North America (mostly U.S.) at 30.7%, and Europe at 16.9%. The regions that are underrepresented are Africa at 3.6% and Central and South America at 0%.

The breadth, depth, and scope of the positive influence of servant leadership are consistent, robust, and global. The analysis (See Table 4.3) identified 438 total instances when the effect of servant leadership was tested as a direct independent variable or as a mediator or moderator. Approximately 96% of the measured relationships were in the favorable direction. When divided into United States versus international studies, there was a slight discrepancy with 99.3% of United States studies deemed favorable versus 93.9% for international studies.

Tables 4.4, 4.5, 4.6, 4.7, 4.8, 4.9 and 4.10 summarize the specific results by area. In terms of employee attitudes (Table 4.4), servant leadership manifests a universally positive influence on organizational and community citizenship, organizational and customer service commitment, job satisfaction, various forms of

Table 4.4 Positive effects of servant leadership: employee attitudes

Positive servant leader effect: employee attitudes	US	Global	*n*
Organizational (community) citizenship	9	27	36
Organizational (customer service) commitment	11	17	28
Job satisfaction	16	10	26
Organizational trust (trust, affective, cognitive trust)	5	14	19
Employee engagement (disengagement)	5	10	15
Procedural/interactive/distributional justice/informational	3	5	8
Motivation (public service, motivational rewards, proactive, prosocial)	0	8	8
Self-efficacy/psychological capital	1	6	7
Need and life satisfaction	1	4	5
Commitment to change	1	3	4
Organizational identification	1	3	4
Organizational culture	1	2	3
Loyalty	1	1	2
Organizational cynicism	1	1	2
Job embeddedness	1	0	1
Follower/person organizational fit	1	0	1
Organizational change	1	0	1
Organizational support	1	0	1
Sum	60	111	171

organizational trust (trust, affective trust, cognitive trust), and employee engagement, among other important employee attitudinal variables. Table 4.5 addresses the influence of servant leadership with positive effects on turnover, in-role performance, employee creative, innovative and helping behavior, promoting a climate for creativity and management innovation, and encouraging employee voice and negative feedback behavior that promotes organizational learning.

Table 4.6 addresses the influence of servant leadership on key leader competency areas with favorable effects on perceptions of leader competence/effectiveness, leader/supervisor trust, beneficial leader/member exchange relationships, and the cultivation of employee empowerment, participation and collaboration. Table 4.7 reflects that servant leaders are perceived to possess desirable character traits such as agreeableness, empathy, extraversion, hope, integrity, and vitality.

Table 4.8 summarizes the impressive breadth and depth of servant leadership's influence on employee wellbeing. The research demonstrates lower levels of stress and burnout, improved health outcomes, better work and family balance, higher levels of employee well-being, and more ethical and moral work climates, more effective interpersonal relations, higher levels of group trust, healthy work relationships, a more positive work climate, employee thriving, higher levels of social capital, and greater career satisfaction. Table 4.9 summarizes the favorable influence of servant leadership on the human resources management system. These beneficial attributes including developing systems that enhance intrinsic motivation through job crafting, green human resource practices, more robust job resources, and the

Table 4.5 Positive effects of servant leadership: employee behavior outcome variables

Positive servant leader effect	US	Global	*n*
Turnover	10	7	17
In-role performance	4	12	16
Employee creative/innovative and helping behavior/climate for creativity, management innovation	6	10	16
Voice and negative feedback seeking (promotive and prohibitive)	0	6	6
Green work behaviors (crafting, creativity, resource seeking, role identity)	0	4	4
Organizational learning/knowledge sharing	0	4	4
Proactive behavior	0	3	3
Observer/self-reported deviance	0	2	2
Tardiness	0	2	2
Team cohesion	0	2	2
Extra-role performance	0	2	2
Adaptability to change	0	1	1
Adaptive performance	0	1	1
Customer service recovery failures	0	1	1
Developmental goal orientation	1	0	1
Employee deviancy	0	1	1
Employee productivity	0	1	1
Extra-effort	0	1	1
Job social support	0	1	1
Leadership avoidance	0	1	1
Pro-environmental behaviors	0	1	1
Service climate	0	1	1
Service-sales ambidexterity	0	1	1
Serving driven capabilities	0	1	1
Socialization	0	1	1
Tacit knowledge	1	0	1
Team functional conflict	0	1	1
Team identification	0	1	1
Sum	22	69	91

development of task and development I-deals, or personalized work arrangements. Servant leadership practices also enhance the workplace diversity climate, the effectiveness of diversity management and developing career skills.

Table 4.10 explores the few nonsignificant and negative effects of servant leadership. Even with the likely presence of publication bias associated with accepting positive results, the overall consistency and depth of support demonstrates servant leadership's efficacy. In terms of the negative effects, the six studies that have demonstrated a negative effect are all from international settings. The common theme is that servant leadership can in some circumstances motivate employees to devote excessive levels of time and energy in the workplace leading to burnout, lower levels of commitment, and higher levels of work and family conflict. However, these

Table 4.6 Positive effects of servant leadership: leadership quality variables

Positive servant leadership outcome variables	US	Global	*n*
Leader competence/effectiveness	6	1	7
Leader/supervisor trust	3	4	7
Leader/member exchange	1	4	5
Empowerment/participation	1	4	5
Collaboration	3	0	3
Commitment to supervisor	1	2	3
Goal and process clarity	2	1	3
Leadership identification	0	2	2
Women higher in servant leadership	1	1	2
Servant follower development	2	0	2
Leader development	1	0	1
Leader respect	0	1	1
Leader span of control	0	1	1
Leadership style alignment	0	1	1
Leadership style preference	0	1	1
Leadership/relationship quality	0	1	1
Satisfaction with supervisor	1	0	1
Succession planning	1	0	1
Supervisory support	1	0	1
Total	24	24	48

Table 4.7 Positive effects of servant leadership: leader character

Positive servant leader outcome variables: leader character	US	Global	*N*
Agreeableness	2	0	2
Empathy	1	1	2
Extraversion	1	0	1
Hope	1	0	1
Integrity	1	0	1
Vitality	0	1	1
Total	6	2	8

negative effects are isolated and rare given that servant leaders promote healthy levels of work effort and do not take advantage of the intrinsic motivation and mission commitment of employees. In terms of the nonsignificant findings, there is no pattern other than servant leadership may not always enhance organizational performance given the many variables that influence outcomes, and secondly that in some settings servant leadership may not be valued by employees given their preference for other leadership styles.

In summary, the analysis demonstrates the consistency of servant leadership in cultivating a more effective, healthy and moral work environment. The next section will summarize the elements of Christian social justice that promotes sustainability.

Table 4.8 Positive effects of servant leadership: employee holistic health and well-being

Positive servant leader effect: employee holistic health and well-being	US	Global	*n*
Stress/burnout/health	2	8	10
Work/family	1	6	7
Employee well-being	3	3	6
Ethical/moral work climate	2	2	4
Interpersonal/group trust/healthy work relationships	1	2	3
Positive work climate	2	1	3
Employee thriving	0	2	2
Social capital	0	2	2
Career satisfaction	0	2	2
Collective thriving	0	1	1
Emotional regulation (deep acting)	0	1	1
Gratitude	0	1	1
Job boredom	0	1	1
Psychological capital	0	1	1
Resource loss	0	1	1
Spirituality	0	1	1
Psychological withdrawal	0	1	1
Proactive personality	0	1	1
Surface acting	0	1	1

Table 4.9 Positive effects of servant leadership: human resources practices

Positive servant leader outcome variables: HR practices	US	Global	*n*
Job crafting	0	2	2
Diversity climate	0	1	1
Diversity management	0	1	1
Career skills	0	1	1
Green HR practices	0	1	1
Job resources	0	1	1
Task and development I-deals (personalized work arrangements)	0	1	1
Sum	0	8	8

Table 4.10 Nonsignificant and negative effects of servant leadership

Organizational outcomes (nonsignificant)	**US**	**Global**	***n***
Firm performance	0	2	2
Leadership style preference	0	2	2
Organizational citizenship	0	2	2
Anti-social behaviors	0	1	1
Lean practices	0	1	1
Organizational culture (in excellent service, innovation, modeling, professionalism)	0	1	1
Organizational justice	0	1	1
Prohibitive voice	0	1	1
Satisfaction	0	1	1
Team dysfunctional conflict	0	1	1
Total (nonsignificant)	0	13	13
Negative effects of servant leadership	**US**	**Global**	***n***
Burnout	0	1	1
Commitment	0	1	1
Empowerment	0	1	1
Lean tools, negative	0	1	1
Performance	1	0	1
Work/family conflict	0	1	1
Sum	1	5	6
Total nonsignificant	0	13	13
Totals negative	1	5	6
Totals nonsignificant or negative	1	18	19

Definition of Sustainable Leadership from a Christian Servant Leadership Perspective

Sustainable leadership from a Christian worldview begins with the history and nature of work as detailed in the first three chapters of the bible in Genesis. In the Garden of Eden, the original dwelling place of Adam and Eve, the first humans created in the image of the triune God were endowed with four key attributes, decision-making free will, the ability to reason, the capacity for creativity, and most importantly, to love and have rich and meaningful, transcendent fellowship with God and each other. The charge was to be fruitful and multiply (Genesis 1:28), as God's nature is to work and create, and the primary element of Adam's "job description" was to tend the garden (Genesis 2:15) and name the animals (Genesis 2:20) a process of discovery, the merging of faith and reason. With free will comes the ability to make ethical and moral choices and embrace short-term or long-term success, and to promote self-interest or the greater good. Adam and Eve chose to disobey God and embraced self-interest to achieve short-term gain by eating from the tree of the knowledge of good and evil given their desire to "secure the power now" and obtain independent, God-like status, an identity-based separation from the creator

(Genesis 2:4–3:24). God responded to this decision to focus on short-term self-interest by expelling them from the Garden of Eden (Genesis 3:24), ending the prior state of harmony between God and nature in which short- and long-term greater good was aligned. In our present state of fallen creation the proximal and distal interests fail to align and work becomes ambiguous, uncertain, and inherently stressful when divorced from moral and ethical motives, means and ends (Chewning, 2011). However, all is not lost. From a Christological and eschatological perspective, God sent His son to redeem fallen creation by dying on the Cross for humanity's sins, providing a new spiritual nature and the ability to overcome the hedonistic and materialistic worldviews that resist the key character virtues of altruism and delaying gratification.

From a Christian worldview perspective, all organizations irrespective of the sector (public, private, nonprofit), exist to help humanity collectively and individually achieve their God-given purpose, calling and creative identity (Greek Orthodox Archdiocese of North America, 2020; Canadian Conference of Catholic Bishops, 2005). What is vital to grasp from a Christian worldview on sustainably is that it posits equality of identity in terms of inherent worth and dignity of every human being, but God endows each person with differential abilities, interests and gifts producing disparate life outcomes, hence a rejection of equality of outcomes inherent in other social justice and political philosophy frameworks such as communism. Organizations provide employment and volunteer opportunities to help the relevant stakeholders realize their individual and collective potential as they exercise their respective talents, gifts, skills, and abilities and produce and provide goods and services that benefit society and promote the greater good.

Consistent with servant leadership's emphasis on stewardship and fiduciary responsibility, Christian worldview posits that all of creation is "God's property." Hence, all elements, all matter, all human, animal, labor and capital resources are gifts of God and His possession (Greek Orthodox Archdiocese of North America, 2020; Canadian Conference of Catholic Bishops, 2005). Private property is not owned but is a fiduciary stewardship resource that is to be managed prudently to promote the common good. Secondly, in Christian worldview on social justice, individual, group and organizational effectiveness is not simply a product of atomistic individual character and merit, but a product of a synergetic community web of interconnected relationships. The surplus or profit generated by private and nonprofit organizations is therefore a means to a greater end of glorifying God, meeting the basic life necessities of the key stakeholders, and very importantly, a resource to help the poor and reduce human suffering, Hence, the financial resources are not owned by the capitalist or by the investors, but reflects a collective good that is a resource used to invest in an ecosystem of linked stakeholders (Greek Orthodox Archdiocese of North America, 2020; Canadian Conference of Catholic Bishops, 2005).

More specifically, Catholic social justice as reflected in the Rerum Novarum (2020) reinforces that Christian social justice is founded upon the following seven principles, (1) the inherent dignity of every human person made in the image of God, (2) the promotion of the common good linked to the personal good of the organization, (3) the principle of subsidiarity which states that the locus of authority for decision-making should be decentralized to the lowest level possible, (4) the principle of participation in which all stakeholders possess voice or the ability to influence the decision-making process, (5) solidarity, or the obligation to help others, (6) the right to private property, and (7) the universal destination of goods which states that all sectors of society both nationally and globally should have access to the resources to provide a decent standard of living (Frémeaux & Michelson, 2017).

These macro social justice principles are linked to the common good of an individual organization through the following sustainability enhancing principles: (1) an enduring commitment to promoting a broadly defined mission success in which profit is a means, not an end, (2) a long-term time commitment in which time is viewed as more important than space, or the success of the present (be an investor over a gambler focusing on short-term returns), (3) promoting the totality principle that embraces a collective, team-based approach to success in which the whole is greater than sum of its parts, (4) the unity principle in which truth telling or voice is encouraged, in which conflict is confronted openly and not suppressed, and (5) the reality principle in which the concrete present condition of the key stakeholders is more important than abstract ideas (Frémeaux & Michelson, 2017).

One of the most challenging aspects of Christian social justice from a Christian worldview is the definition of the common good. At an abstract level the common good entails the sharing of the fruits of organizational success through investing in the commons, or the public square that benefits society as a whole, the commonality of the common good, or equality of access to common goods for all members of society, and the good of the common good or the balance of benefits that are produced between individuals, families, and the community (Frémeaux & Michelson, 2017).

Melé (2009) provided a more practical definition of the common good with four elements listed below:

1. Economic conditions that produce a reasonable level of well-being
2. Organizational conditions that respect human freedom, justice, and solidarity
3. Sociocultural values shared in a community (human rights and dignity, for example)
4. Environmental conditions that provide a safe environment for current and future generations.

In addition to the factors listed above, Orthodox and Catholic social justice emphasizes living wage compensation practices, supporting unions and collective bargaining to combat market failure and increasing social inequity, promoting global governmental organization regulation to address market failure and exploitation of labor, and an overall awareness and promotion of knowledge and civic education on the perils of globalism and income inequity (Greek Orthodox Archdiocese of North America, 2020; Canadian Conference of Catholic Bishops, 2005). The following section explores the specific Christian servant leader practices that promote sustainability in organizations.

Elements of Sustainable Leadership: Macro Variables

In order to fully integrate Christian worldview principles on sustainability into an organization's culture at both the micro- and macro-levels, six key factors are vital. They are character virtue, emotional intelligence, spiritual intelligence, systems and critical thinking, social justice, and corporate responsibility. The first is that without character virtue, it is impossible to cultivate and integrate the degree of altruism necessary to sacrifice for future generations and to promote an ascetical cultural ethos that rejects the temptations of immediate gratification (Roberts, 2015; Roberts, 2016). Hence, it is vital that a systematic organizational cultural value is to hire, promote, and reward leaders based upon character, ethical conduct and character virtue, as organizational researcher Jim Collins (2001), would state, to get the "right people on the bus" and move them to the right seats.

In order to practice authentic Christian servant leadership, a well-developed and healthy personality and moral reasoning system is foundational (Roberts, 2015; Roberts, 2016). This begins with the five-part foundation of emotional intelligence, self and other awareness in terms of understanding moods, motives and drives, self-regulation or the ability to manage emotional states and respond appropriately, an internal motivation system that emphasizes growth, learning, development and higher order thinking, cultivating and practicing empathy to understand the emotional state of others, and the development of social skills that enable leaders to solve problems, navigate conflict, and positively influence others (Goleman, 1998; Lu et al., 2019).

With the foundation of emotional intelligence, Christian servant leaders are led by the Holy Spirit to embrace spiritual intelligence, which is the highest form of ethical and moral decision-making in which the leader adroitly integrates the three forms of ethical of reasoning, deontology (rule-based), teleological (promoting the greater good), and the cultivation of character virtue (arete) ethics (Roberts, 2016). Spiritual intelligence enables the leader to thoughtfully reflect on the larger ethical and moral antecedent factors in cause and effect relationships and more clearly identify and the true motives, means and ends that are being pursued. Hence, the goal is to promote organizations that are self-conscious and aware of their true underlying virtuous and God-honoring motives in order to promote epistemological integrity or orthodoxy of knowledge, authentic internalization of belief, which in turn, promotes the adoption of moral means that are implemented with integrity (orthopraxis), under the authority of the penultimate virtue of wisdom. A great example from scripture appears on Matthew 12: 9–14 in which Jesus heals the man with the withered hand balancing all three forms of ethical reasoning reinforcing orthodoxy of belief and orthopraxis of action. The Pharisees (the Jewish religious leaders) in their ongoing conflict with the ministry of Jesus are seeking opportunities to publicly invalidate His self-proclaimed identity as the son of God thereby discrediting his credibility in the eyes of His followers. The account begins with Jesus entering the synagogue on the Sabbath and encountering a man with a withered or crippled hand. The Pharisees were ready to condemn Jesus if he healed on the Sabbath, given that the rigid Pharisees had legalistically defined healing on

Saturday a form of prohibited work. Jesus employed the three forms of ethical reasoning by posing a question. If your sheep, a valuable resource, fell into a pit on the Sabbath, would you not rescue the sheep (the law permitted such actions)? Jesus then stated, isn't a man worth more than a sheep, rebutting the overreliance on deontological reason with a teleological logic statement reinforcing that human life is even more valuable, hence a greater good. In healing the man with the withered hand, it enabled him to resume a trade and provide for his family demonstrating character virtue in helping and loving your neighbor. Jesus demonstrated that ethical reasoning entails a balanced assessment of ethical approaches with the higher order value of promoting love overriding adherence to rules. This has direct application to the workplace in which bureaucratic regulations frequently overcome mission integrity and the overall greater good.

Christian servant leaders must also think and reason in a complex, system-oriented fashion employing critical thinking skills to discern the relevant cause and effect relationships (Roberts, 2015; Roberts, 2016). This entails being aware of the cognitive and attributional biases that plague reasoning and decision-making and practicing a humility about his or her abilities (Tversky & Kahneman, 1974). Servant leaders recognize the inherent limits to decision-making in terms of information, time, knowledge and understanding and embrace the presence of making decisions with imperfect information and the inevitable presence of paradoxes. Christian servant leaders use the most powerful form of intuition, which is prayer and being directed by God's Holy Spirit to provide the necessary balance of rationalism and intuition/inspiration. Christian servant leaders embrace a long-term form of reasoning that recognizes the presence of intended and unintended consequences of decisions in the proximate, mid-range, and distal time periods relevant to the decision. For example, micromanagement may solve the immediate problem of a poorly performing employee (proximate), but it inhibits learning, growth and development (mid-range) and the succession planning process (distal). In addition, Christian servant leaders "test the spirits" and refuse to judge upon appearance and promote critical thinking in using the internal and external threats to validity in assessing casual claims and research (Shadish et al., 2002). For example, a police chief in analyzing the reason for a steep increase in burglaries needs to assess a complex set of endogenous and exogenous variables such as the state of the economy, the presence of gang activity, and random events that will not be repeated such as a high number of crimes committed by one skilled and motivated burglar.

As was discussed in the previous section on Christian worldview, the promotion of social justice is a vital and foundational Christian servant leader value. It includes a variety of dimensions and approaches including promoting environmental sustainability or "creation care" that derives from the Garden of Eden in which Adam and Eve tended a perfectly harmonious garden eco-system (Spence & Brown, 2018). Christian servant leaders understand the importance of providing products and services that promote a healthy eco-system in terms of all components of the service or production causal chain. This includes eliminating or reducing the negative externalities associated with air, water, sound and light pollution, among other environmental hazards for the supply chain that provides the essential resources to produce goods and services, for all direct (employees) and indirect stakeholders (community), and for direct and indirect consumers of the product. This entail providing services and producing goods that promote the greater good of individual consumers, their families and the larger community. In other words, a mindful reflection on how the goods and services influence or effect consumers from a physical, mental and spiritual health and wellbeing standpoint. For example, Christian servant leaders would reject leading a tobacco company that sells a product that manifests adverse effects on consumers, their families, hence a public health hazard. Another example is to eliminate all deceptive, manipulative marketing and advertising that employs fear, ego and pride to cultivate materialism, competitive consumption (keep up with your neighbors), and defining success and wellbeing by possession of status enhancing products and services. In essence, defining luxuries as necessities. Christian servant leaders cultivate a communitarian orientation in the organization's culture emphasizing the value of simplicity and the importance of relationship building internally, with customers, and the greater community.

In addition, the moral obligation of Christian servant leaders is to advocate, model, and practice corporate/organizational social responsibility (Frémeaux & Michelson, 2017; Wisler, 2018, Wang, 2013; Mackey & Sisodia, 2013; Tuan, 2018; Sengupta & Sengupta, 2018; Afsar et al., 2018; Tuan, 2020; Francisco et al., 2020; Luu, 2019). This includes such elements as living wages for all employees, generous compensation levels of suppliers, investing in the local community through volunteerism and philanthropy, an active program to create employment and training opportunities for the poor and the disenfranchised. In summary, these macro approaches set the foundation for the micro sustainability practices that promote employee wellbeing that are discussed in the next section.

Elements of Sustainable Leadership: Micro Variables

Microlevel employee sustainability entails a wholistic workplace culture from a Christian servant leader perspective that produces three forms of wellbeing, hedonic (life pleasure and enjoyment) (Czerw, 2019), eudemonic (meaning purpose and growth) (Czerw, 2019), and shalom or mind, body and spiritual wellbeing (Fisher, 2016). From a human resource management perspective, employee sustainability incorporates four elements, (1) a secure, safe, and stable work environment, (2) an intrinsically motivating job that produces growth, transcendence, meaning and purpose, (3) a reasonable and sustainable set of work performance expectations in terms of quantity, quality, and timeliness of work that promote life and work balance, adequate rest and paid time off, and (4) protection from explicit workplace hazards such as Covid-19 (Roberts, 2015). The literature on servant leadership demonstrates its favorable influence on employee wellbeing (van Dierendonck & Nuijten, 2011; Russell et al., 2018; Reinke, 2004; Maula-Bakhsh & Raziq, 2018; Jaramillo et al., 2009; Chan, 2018), employee and collective thriving (Walumbwa et al., 2018; Wang et al., 2019a) and on other wellbeing elements including lower levels of burnout (Upadyaya & Salmela-Aro, 2020; Zhang et al., 2019; Hakanen & van Dierendonck, 2011; Coetzer et al., 2017; Bande et al., 2015; Babakus et al., 2011).

A Secure, Safe and Stable Work Environment

Let us begin this paragraph by discussing how to promote a secure, safe, and stable work environment. This increases perception of employee stability and safety which reduces the physical, mental and spiritual causes of elevated stress levels and their negative effects. A safe work environment from a Christian servant leader worldview begins with a sustained and integrated commitment in policy and practice to employee wellbeing, growth and development producing a clear workplace covenant, or organizational contractual commitment (Roberts, 2015). Christian servant leaders formally integrate a pledge to employee wellbeing within the formal mission, vision and values statements. For example, a clear value statement would state "our organization commits to empowering and developing employees in a patient and supportive fashion to cultivate their personal and professional growth." A second example is "Our organization is committed to providing a healthy, balanced, and sustainable work environment that promotes employee mental and physical health." Secondly, this commitment to employee wellbeing is reinforced by leadership in a multi-method media communications campaign to reinforce the integrity of the espoused policy. For example, leaders need to emphasize their commitment to work life balance in meetings with employees, information on company/organizational websites, and a summary of concrete policy implementation in organizational reports.

The second major element of microlevel sustainability for a safe and stable work environment is the promotion of a covenantal workplace environment that provide employees with credible organizational commitment to a long-term employment relationship in which all forms of justice are authentically practiced and adverse personnel actions (terminations, layoffs, wage and benefit reductions, etc.) are last resort options (Roberts, 2015). The first aspect of the workplace covenant entails a systematic focus on dignified, respectful, and fair employee treatment that emphasizes the three major forms of organizational justice that servant leadership models, interactional (Kool & van Dierendonck, 2012), distributive (Schwepker, 2016), and procedural (Chung et al., 2010; Ehrhart, 2004; Hakanen & van Dierendonck, 2011; Shim et al., 2016; Walumbwa et al., 2010). The Christian servant leader human resource management system employs a variety of attitudinal, behavior and performance-based organizational justice metrics that are linked to all aspects of the human resource management system including 360-degree evaluations that serve as the basis for management and leadership performance appraisals (Roberts, 2015).

As per addressing fiscal stress, the Christian servant leader embraces a triage of methods to tackle fiscal stress and reduction situations, for example. As noted in Table 4.11, the first option is productivity enhancing and labor-saving options that entail employee empowerment. Using the Stephen Covey quadrants of time framework (Covey, 2004), servant leaders are proactive in anticipating the normal fiscal cycles and cultivate a learning culture in which employees are empowered through formal and informal quality improvement policies and practices that generate creative and innovative practices to increase efficiency, productivity and lower costs thereby enhancing fiscal margin (Roberts, 2015). In other words, engaging in the long-term planning that is not urgent from a present time perspective, but is vital for

Table 4.11 Christian servant leader "triage" response options for human resource fiscal stress situations

1. Covenant-based employment relationship: layoffs and adverse personnel actions are last resort options. First choice methods to increase efficiency and effectiveness include:
(a) Labor-saving tools through technology
(b) Gainsharing (bonus for reducing costs or increasing efficiency and effectiveness)
(c) Productivity improvement (quality management programs)
(d) Flexi-place, virtual workplace (tele-commuting)
(e) Flextime/flexible schedule/compressed work week
(f) Cross-training
(g) Volunteers
(h) Performance-based compensation (merit pay and bonus)
2. Strategies that increase efficiency but manifest some degree of loss of worker income or jobs
(a) Job sharing
(b) Work rule buyouts
(c) Personnel complement controls and hiring freezes
(d) Reductions in compensation through lower overtime levels or substituting compensatory time
(e) Wage and benefit reductions to base salary and benefits
(f) Use of part-time/temporary employees
3. Personnel reductions:
(a) Furloughs, layoffs, and buyouts
(b) Privatization/contracting out/regional service consolidations

long-term growth and development. One example is to institute a gain sharing system in which productivity increases are used to reduce the budget deficit and when financial circumstances improve can be shared with employees in the form of increases in wages or benefits. However, for these programs to be efficacious, there must be an authentic cultivation of forgiveness of good-faith failures and mistakes that promote long-term growth and learning and open access to data and a transparency of information (Roberts, 2015).

The second quadrant of practices are strategies that increase efficiency but manifest some degree of loss of worker income or employment such as job sharing, work rule changes and using part-time or temporary employees. The third quadrant is the last resort set of options of furloughs, buyouts and layoffs. One of the most frequently overlooked, but vital tangible demonstrations of servant leader empathy and servanthood is sharing the cost and burdens related to budget reductions or other adverse organizational decisions. When leadership reduces their own benefits or salary, or terminates members of their staff first, it reinforces an empathy and solidarity of spirit (Roberts, 2015). This is a Christ like action of demonstrating your willingness to sacrifice for the mission and "walk the talk" and lead by example. The obligations for sustainable Christian servant leadership clearly do not end there. With wage and benefit reductions and terminating or laying off employees, it is vital that the organization plan the transition in a timely manner to provide advanced notice to employees, offer severance pay, job placement assistance, counseling for terminations, and communicate personal and public statements of gratitude for their service in conjunction with genuine regret for severing the covenantal relationship to reduce employee shock and stress and provide dignity and respect to the departing workers (Roberts, 2015). In addition, the Christian servant leader systematically and proactively addresses the effects on the remaining employees to help them cope with the increased workloads and new responsibilities along with the emotional stress produced by "survivors' guilt" and lower levels of personal job security. The remaining employees require ongoing reassurance of leadership's support, care and concern through direct and indirect communication methods. In addition, if the remaining staff is experiencing higher workloads and new job duties, training support must be provided to help employees adapt. Secondly, Christian Servant leaders assess the effects of the terminations on their clients and customers to ensure that their needs are addressed, and quality of service is not eroded (Roberts, 2015).

Intrinsically Motivating Work

The next set of practices that enhances sustainability is intrinsically motiving work that engenders meaning, purpose and transcendence. The first element is ensuring that every employee and volunteer possesses a clear and compelling understanding of how their specific job and its constellation of duties promotes the mission (Roberts, 2015). This is a foundational element for providing each employee with an enduring sense of dignity. For example, the custodial staff of a hospital cannot view its works as low-level and unskilled, but as a professional team member equal to physicians and nurses in providing invaluable medical services. If rooms are not cleaned effectively, patients and the staff are placed at risk for disease. Dignity promotes wellbeing. This in turn, encourages and attracts employees that possess higher degrees of altruism as demonstrated by servant leadership's cultivation of public service motivation (Tuan, 2016; Shim & Park, 2019).

Secondly, it is vital to develop positions that embrace intrinsic motivation using the Job Characteristics framework of Hackman and Oldham (1976). Each job should be designed to provide job identity (an identifiable work product is provides the employee's "signature"), task significance, or duties that are vital to the success of the organization, task and skill variety that engenders growth and challenge, providing autonomy and empowerment of decision-making, and clear, specific, timely, behavioral and actionable feedback that comes from a credible source (Ilgen et al., 1979).

Performance feedback, or knowledge of results, consists of two forms, intrinsic feedback and external feedback (Roberts, 2015). Internal feedback is directly generated by the job itself and is perceived by the employee as the duty/task is performed. For example, direct feedback are cues that an elementary school teacher receives from student demeanor or body language while teaching or grading the results of scores on assignments. The second form, external feedback, is knowledge of results from the judgements and assessments of supervisors that provide a formative or summative assessment of performance data or metrics. One other element is needed to support the intrinsic motivational model, and that is developing clear, specific, accepted, and self or jointly developed performance goals (Locke & Latham, 1990; Lee, 2019; Rodríguez-Carvajal et al., 2019; Carter & Baghurst, 2014; Hu & Liden, 2011). Goal setting provides the essential motivational foundation by directing energy and focus toward the activities and tasks with the highest priorities providing an inner compass to avoid distraction and diffusion of effort. One common acronym that is used in the goal setting process is SMART, or specific, measurable, achievable, relevant, and timely. To support the intrinsic motivational model, Christian servant leaders embrace a long-term, empowerment-based, patient employee development process that entails the necessity of mistakes, setbacks, and failures as an essential component of the learning process. Servant leadership research reinforces its favorable effects on such elements as developing servant followers (Parris & Peachy, 2012; Reed, 2015), career skills development (Wang et al., 2019b), career satisfaction (Kaya & Karatepe, 2020; Ilkhanizadeh & Karatepe, 2018) and general life satisfaction (Prottas, 2013; Li et al., 2018; Ilkhanizadeh & Karatepe, 2018; Hakanen & van Dierendonck, 2011). When employees believe that their supervisors genuinely support and retain confidence in their abilities and potential in the presence of challenges and an absence of perfection, it drives fear from the workplace bestowing employees with the psychic capital to be creative, innovate and grow. Other key human resource practices that support Christian servant leader investment orientation is providing employees with generous and sustained training, education and development support through individual learning accounts (ILA) that provide a designated dollar value budget for training along with individual development plans (IDP) that systematically identify employee strengths, weakness, and performance gaps (Roberts, 2015).

Reasonable and Sustainable Set of Work Performance Expectations

The third element of micro sustainability is a reasonable and sustainable set of work performance expectations in terms of quantity, quality and timeliness of work that promote life and work balance, adequate rest and paid time off (Roberts, 2015). The literature on servant leadership demonstrates it encourages lower levels of work and family conflict (Prottas, 2013; Tang et al., 2016), enhances the quality of family life (Haar et al., 2017; Tang et al., 2016) and reduces employee stress (Pfrombeck & Verdorfer, 2018; Prottas, 2013). Sustainability begins with Christian servant leaders that model healthy and sustainable practices. Unless leadership models and sets the standards, employees and other stakeholders will defer to traditional norms that view work as the ultimate end leading to workaholic behavior. Christian servant leaders recognize that employees possess other important domains in their lives beginning with their relationship with God, their families, and the larger community. In order to achieve balance, Christian servant leaders need to exercise self-care in terms of limited work hours, and model the recommended sleep, exercise, physical activity, and dietary practices and encourage others in the workplace to follow their example.

In addition to personal modeling, Christian servant leaders formally integrate these practices into the human resource management system through developing clear work sustainability metrics that are used in the recruitment, selection, promotion, and the general performance management system. In other words, managers and employees are held responsible and rewarded for developing a work environment that provides sufficient rest and work/life balance through such factors as adequate staffing and a generous compensation and benefits systems, especially work/life benefits that promote flexibility and the virtual workplace (Roberts, 2015). With a realistic work pace and sufficient margin built into work demands, employees are more productive and effective, hence, "less is more." When employees are provided with a reasonable workload in terms of quantity and quality of work with adequate rest during the workday and paid time off, they possess both the reserves and the motivation to engage in periodic high intensity work effort situations, assuming that they are limited in frequency and duration and followed by times of rest (Roberts, 2015). Servant leaders proactively plan to reduce the number and intensity of such episodes to the absolute minimum. The Covid-19 pandemic has increased another potentially wellbeing enhancing change in the nature of work, the virtual workplace. In the virtual workplace, employees work remotely reducing commuting time and costs, enhancing choice in domicile, thereby providing increased autotomy and higher empowerment levels. There are significant challenges associated with the virtual workplace including the absence of adequate and secure computer broad band service, isolation and reduced interpersonal interaction, and excessive family conflict, especially with young children present. In addition, servant leaders must reject the tendency to develop a dual class of employees in which traditional modes of work (facetime) are valued more highly from a motivational and commitment standpoint. This will entail training and supporting managers in learning to how lead in a virtual setting and cultivating a community setting that generates supportive interpersonal relations (Green & Roberts, 2010).

In addition to addressing the overall nature of work, the sustainability efforts of Christian servant leaders develop formal wellbeing enhancing programs such as employee-assistance programs including an emphasis on mental health as a vital component of workplace wellbeing (Roberts, 2015). Amid the Covid-19 outbreak, the anxiety, depression and other mental health conditions have increased dramatically, and it is vital to end the stigma associated with mental illness and the associated treatment options. The goal is to cultivate an inspiring, challenging, and supportive work environment that promotes employee eustress, or beneficial stress to reduce negative stress.

The final element of sustainability in promoting reasonable and sustainable work expectations in terms of concrete organizational practices, is the advancement of the religious and spiritually friendly workplace in which voluntary and noncoercive religious and spiritual practices and activities are viewed as an essential element of human diversity and human flourishing (Roberts, 2015; Posner & Boone, 2006). Research clearly indicates the benefits of religious and spiritual practices for mental and spiritual wellbeing (Koenig, 2012; Koenig et al., 2012). However, boundaries need to be respected as religion and spirituality can become divisive and produce dysfunctional conflict. To preserve the appropriate boundaries, Hicks (2003) summarizes the foundational principles as follows:

1. A forced compartmentalization of religion and spiritualty in the workplace disenfranchises those with genuine religious and spiritual beliefs.
2. *All religious/spiritual expression must observe and honor the dignity of all persons with equal respect.*
3. All religious and spiritual expression is voluntary and noncoercive.
4. There can be no formal establishment of a "state" religion or spiritual practice.

The specific practices of the religious friendly workplace are summarized by Roberts (2015):

- Promote religious and spiritual events, retreats, seminars, service, and volunteer opportunities
- Develop an employee website or bulletin board to promote religious/spiritual activities (not available to the public)
- Draft a policy that permits the display of religious objects in the office and in employee dress
- The adoption of a workplace chaplain program either through the creation of a formal full- or part-time position, contracting with a chaplain consulting firm, or securing volunteers from churches
- Develop religious mental health counseling programs
- Develop religious-based wellness and employee-assistance program
- Permit employees to transmit religious information on company email or intranet system

These policies and practices are not exhaustive but demonstrate a range of institutionally supported means for enabling employees to express a vital element of their humanity.

Protection from Explicit Workplace Hazards

The final aspect of promoting a sustainable workplace from a Christian servant leader perspective is to engage in a proactive workplace policy of systematically gathering data on the overall health and wellbeing of the labor force. For example, in terms of protecting employees in the current Covid-19 environment, an analysis would indicate the need for:

1. Adequate protective equipment (PPE) for all employees.
2. Training on how to use PPE equipment properly and minimize risks to the employee and others that they interact with (peers, clients, etc.).
3. The provision of hazardous duty pay.

4. Providing virtual work options including the proper equipment and training.
5. Providing mental health counseling and employee-assistance programs.
6. Providing paid leave and other accommodations as needed.

Christian servant leader organizations possess an ironclad commitment to protecting employee health and safety and utilize a learning organization framework that is presented in Roberts (2015) based upon the workplace stress model of Jex (1998) including the following elements:

- An integrated workplace hazard monitoring and audit process that identifies the source and cause of excessive levels of workplace mental, physical and spiritual stress ranging from health and safety threats including accidents, illness, disease, chemical exposure, noise, and other factors.
- Empower employees to jointly identify, diagnose and develop solutions for the identified hazards.
- Empower employees to jointly identify, diagnose and develop means for maintaining and enhancing employee wellbeing.
- Employees would be regularly surveyed on the presence of risk factors, with teams of employees working with management to develop, implement and evaluate strategies to address the problems and maintain areas of strength. Surveys would be supplemented with data from focus groups, retention and exit surveys to provide a more robust data base.

Table 4.12 below summarizes some of the key job stress related factors that adversely affect employee sustainability and wellbeing based upon Jex (1998) and Roberts (2015). The audit process would review the various sources of archive and attitudinal data to ascertain the risk factors and engage in ongoing research to identify the root cause and effect relationships along with the appropriate solutions. The first set of factors relate to job characteristics. Christian servant leaders focus considerable investments of human capital, job design, and human resource strategic management focus on promoting harmony on role responsibilities, clarity of job expectations, providing reasonable performance demands in terms of the quantity, quality and timeliness of work, placing employees into areas of strength, providing ample training and job growth opportunities, both vertically through promotion and horizontally through job enlargement and enrichment (Harju et al., 2018; Bavik et al., 2017). With the elevated presence and importance of virtual work arrangements, Christian servant leaders ensure employees possess adequate equipment, are supported, and train leaders and managers on how to effectively develop a cohesive and supportive virtual work environment while being sensitive to the work/life challenges and conflicts posed by working at home (Green & Roberts, 2010).

The second dimension presented in Table 4.12 are the leadership attributes that promote a healthy and virtuous work environment (Prottas, 2013). It begins with providing employees with a confidence in the moral and ethical integrity of leadership enhancing trust and providing a credible and authentic workplace covenant that

Table 4.12 Job stress audit factors

Job characteristics and attributes
• Role Responsibility Conflicts (managerial and leadership pressures from supervising, meeting work deadlines, and achieving performance standards)
• Role Ambiguity: vague or unclear job duties and/or performance standards
• Role Conflict: competing job requirements that create tensions and stress such as concurrent high quality and quantity performance standards
• Role Overload: Excessive performance requirements and demands
• Role Incongruity: job duties not matched to skills and interests
• Role Incapacity: inability to perform at an acceptable level given lack of essential training, equipment, or resources (fiscal, information, etc.)
• Career Growth Limits: limited career development and progression opportunities
• Virtual Workplace:
– Role incapacity: lack of adequate broadband, computer support, supplies, etc.
– Lack of support by management
– Family conflicts: child and dependent care
Leadership attributes: the adverse effects of the absence of servant leader character elements such as integrity, trust, and honesty
• Lack of employer covenant related to job security, workplace forgiveness, and transparency
• Biased employee treatment from leaders, peers, and clients
– Absence of empowerment, autonomy, and the presence of micromanagement
– Lack of procedural, distributive, and interactional justice (unfair human resource management decision-making in training and development, performance appraisal, compensation, and employee staffing, etc.)
– Protected class bias and discrimination (race, gender, religion, etc.)
– Hostile work environment from sexual harassment, workplace bullying/violence
– Excessive levels of office politics
– Unethical, immoral work climate and actions related to fraud, waste, abuse, conflicts of interest, and insider trading, etc.
– Favoritism producing in-groups and out groups
Adverse physical and social working conditions
• Hazardous temperatures
• Safety hazards that produce accidents and illness
• Exposure to dangerous chemicals, noise levels and hazardous electrical, microwave and other forms of harmful radiation
• Regular interactions with angry or abusive clients or customers
Work/life balance issues
• Absence of adequate dependent care support (child, elder care, disabled or sick family members)
• Absence of adequate transportation
• Absence of adequate health care

provides emotional and concrete job security in which employees are empowered and possess the necessary levels of autonomy (Roberts, 2015; Jaramillo et al., 2015; Burton et al., 2017; Washington et al., 2006; Miao et al., 2014; Schaubroeck et al., 2011; Sendjaya & Pekerti, 2010). Christian servant leaders promote a healthy work environment that cultivates harmonious work interpersonal relationships minimizing and eliminating all forms of biased employee treatment including procedural, distributive and interactional injustice, protected class bias and discrimination (race, gender, age, religion, disability, etc.), sexual harassment, workplace bullying, office politics, favoritism and corruption from fraud, waste, and abuse (Carter & Baghurst, 2014; Khattak et al., 2019). Servant leaders reinforce harmony through such character elements as empathy (Washington et al., 2006; Elche et al., 2020), providing hope and offering encouragement (Taylor et al., 2007). In addition, servant leaders promote employee voice to enhance two-way communication, learning, and workplace fair treatment and justice (Arain et al., 2019; Sun et al., 2019; Ruiz-Palomino et al., 2019).

The third dimension is adverse physical and social working conditions including chronic interactions with angry or abusive clients and customers. Christian servant leaders are good shepherds of the flock and ensure that employees are supported and trained in techniques to calm anger and resolve conflict productively. Secondly, it is vital that workers are not exposed to hazardous working conditions without proper equipment, support, and rest (Roberts, 2015). The final dimension is work/life balance which reflects that employees do not work in isolation, they are embedded within supportive systems and networks of family, work, and community. Christian servant leaders attempt to identify and solve transportation, dependent and health care issues as well. The final section addresses the barriers to Christian servant leadership.

Barriers to Sustainable Christian Servant Leadership

There are two major barriers to ongoing sustainable Christian servant leadership. The first is the absence of organizational commitment and support, and the second is self-interested, sinful human nature. The absence of a deeply embedded organizational sustainability ethos leads to superficial adherence that creates what Argyris and Schön (1974) noted a conflict between espoused theory and the theory in use. When the evitable financial, political, or social conflict or threat situations arise, without a genuine internalized integration the stress produced will lead organizational leadership to revert to its default and traditional instrumental leadership approaches. With chronic or acute fiscal stress that adversely affects organizational stability, effectiveness and viability, the path of least resistance is to revert to reducing human resource costs through layoffs, wage and salary reductions, and increasing job workloads. Hence, the many years of cumulative growth can be erased either gradually or suddenly if the foundation of Golden Rule leadership practices are compromised. This occurred with Whole Foods when they were faced with increasing competition in the organic foods industry and leadership eliminated local suppliers and health benefits for employees to reduce production costs (Cheretis & Mujtaba, 2014; Aschoff, 2017).

The microlevel barriers include character flaws, personality weaknesses, and competing worldviews. As human beings from a Christian worldview, our human nature is influenced by the presence of our sinful nature producing self-interested motives, behaviors and actions (Roberts, 2016). The common character flaws including pride, fear of man through "people pleasing" and the presence of ego weaknesses such as interpersonal comparison, jealously, envy and revenge as we take pleasure when our competitors or those we dislike fail or suffer challenges (Schadenfreude), while we respond with anger, fear, envy, or jealousy when they prosper. When these tendencies are not recognized and checked, it generates a powerfully damaging form of hypocrisy that destroys the credibility of servant leaders (Roberts, 2015). It erodes the foundation of character integrity like termites slowly undermining the foundation of a home, contributing to an ultimate fruit of Darwinian survival of the fittest and empire building in which employees are means to an end and disposable resources. These character flaws erode the ability to engage in agape love actions that promote the long-term best interests of the key stakeholders inhibiting the presence of moral and ethical systems thinking. The only viable means to address these character flaws is to engage in a sustained commitment to self-reflection and analysis of our motives, means and ends that entails seeking and receiving feedback on how our attitudes, actions and behaviors are perceived by others, and assume responsibility for our sins and failures (Roberts, 2016). From both a religious and research-based perspective, self-perceptions are subject to many forms of bias related to rationalization of motives, protection of the ego, and self-esteem issues. Hence, servant leaders actively seek data and information to validate their self-perceptions welcoming information that exposes contradictions, failures and weaknesses. As scripture states, we must remove the "log from our eye" (Matthew 7:5) in order to see the issues of others more clearly (Roberts, 2016). This entails utilizing 360-degree appraisals, cultivating ongoing authentic relationships in which the leader sincerely asks employees what they need to start doing, stop doing, or continue doing to better lead and serve their growth, development and effectiveness. Employees must never be punished for truth telling to avoid self-censorship and superficial relationships. One other key personality and character barrier is perfectionism and the fear of failure that impedes creativity, innovation, and learning from mistakes (Roberts, 2016). Growth entails an inevitable time of trial, imperfection, and perseverance in the presence of obstacles.

The next barrier is the presence and influence of competing worldviews such as hedonism, materialism, and atomistic individualism that impede altruism and the ability to delay gratification in self and others. Atomistic individualism promotes the mythology of "self-made" men and women underemphasizing the communal team-based nature of organizational success. Another key barrier in this category is the presence of traditional economic models of free-market capitalism that overlook the presence of market failure and negative externalities.

Future Research Recommendations

The area of sustainable Christian servant leadership in a post Covid-19 world will require ongoing research and development in three areas. The first is how to develop and maintain an altruistic, Golden Rule organizational culture that is resistant to reverting to self-serving instrumental employment practices. What are the policies, practices and character elements that promote organizational resiliency in the face of changing adverse circumstances? A second area is more research on the factors that promote and attenuate moral character and ethical reasoning development that are foundational for sustainable Christian servant leadership. The final area are the subordinate and stakeholder attributes that enhance or detract from sustainable Christian servant leadership. Clearly the reaction and support of employees and other key stakeholders is vital element as servant leaders require servant followers for long-term success.

Conclusion

Sustainable Christian servant leadership in a post Covid-19 world is a vital component to promote the long-term wellbeing of employees and other stakeholders. Sustainable leadership practices honor the Christian biblical commands for leaders to be "good shepherds" of the flock in which they seek the wellbeing and benefit of each employee. This is reflected in Matthew 18:12, when Jesus states "What do you think? If a shepherd has a hundred sheep, and one of them has gone astray, does he not leave the ninety-nine on the mountains and go in search of the one that went astray?" The ethos of sustainable Christian servant leadership is to promote the best interests of the micro- and macro-levels, individual employee wellbeing and achieving the mission, balancing servanthood and stewardship. This is an ongoing aspirational process that requires patience, perseverance, and resilience, but the fruits are sweet and beneficial to employees, the relevant stakeholders and society as a whole.

References

Aaron, M. S., Bell, C. M., & Min, Y. A. (2020). Does "the servant as leader" translate into Chinese? A cross-cultural meta-analysis of servant leadership. *European Journal of Work and Organizational Psychology, 29*(3), 315–329. http://eres.regent.edu:2048/login?url=https://www.proquest.com/scholarly-journals/does-servant-as-leader-translate-into-chinese/docview/2410668442/se-2?accountid=13479

Afsar, B., Cheema, S., & Javed, F. (2018). Activating employee's pro-environmental behaviors: The role of CSR, organizational identification, and environmentally specific servant leadership. *Corporate Social Responsibility and Environmental Management, 25*(5), 904–911. https://doi.org/10.1002/csr.150

Arain, G. A., Hameed, I., & Crawshaw, J. R. (2019). Servant leadership and follower voice: The roles of follower felt responsibility for constructive change and avoidance-approach motivation. *European Journal of Work and Organizational Psychology, 28*(4), 555–565. https://doi.org/10.1080/1359432X.2019.1609946

Argyris, C., & Schön, D. (1974). *Theory in practice: Increasing professional effectiveness.* Jossey-Bass.

Aschoff, N. (2017, May 29). Whole foods represents the failures of 'conscious capitalism'. *The Guardian.* https://www.theguardian.com/commentisfree/2017/may/29/whole-foods-failures-conscious-capitalism#:~:text=Same%2Dstore%20sales%20have%20declined,away%20during%20the%20same%20period

Babakus, E., Yavas, U., & Ashill, N. J. (2011). Service worker burnout and turnover intentions: Roles of person-job fit, servant leadership, and customer orientation. *Services Marketing Quarterly, 32*(1), 17. http://0-search.proquest.com.library.regent.edu/docview/821292896?accountid=13479

Bande, B., Fernández-Ferrín, P., Varela, J. A., & Jaramillo, F. (2015). Emotions and salesperson propensity to leave: The effects of emotional intelligence and resilience. *Industrial Marketing Management, 44*, 142–153. https://doi.org/10.1016/j.indmarman.2014.10.011

Bavik, A. (2020). A systematic review of the servant leadership literature in management and hospitality. *International Journal of Contemporary Hospitality Management, 32*(1), 347–382. https://doi.org/10.1108/IJCHM-10-2018-0788

Bavik, A., Yuen Lam, B., & Pok Man, T. (2017). Servant leadership, employee job crafting, and citizenship behaviors: A cross-level investigation. *Cornell Hospitality Quarterly, 58*(4), 364–373. https://doi.org/10.1177/1938965517719282

Burton, L. J., Welty Peachey, J., & Wells, J. E. (2017). The role of servant leadership in developing an ethical climate in sport organizations. *Journal of Sport Management, 31*(3), 229–240. https://doi.org/10.1123/jsm.2016-0047

Canadian Conference of Catholic Bishops. (2005). *Compendium of the social doctrine of the church*. Author.

Carter, D., & Baghurst, T. (2014). The influence of servant leadership on restaurant employee engagement. *Journal of Business Ethics, 124*(3), 453–464.

Chan, K. W. C. (2018). Servant leadership supports wellness development in adolescents. *Servant Leadership: Theory and Practice, 5*(2), 41–52.

Cheretis, D., & Mujtaba, B. G. (2014). Maximizing long-term value and conscious capitalism at whole foods. *SAM Advanced Management Journal, 79*(3), 4–16.

Chewning, R. C. (2011). Capitalism: From its genesis to its eschatology its compatibilities with Christianity; its insidious challenges to godliness. *Journal of Biblical Integration in Business, 13*(1), 30. https://cbfa-jbib.org/index.php/jbib/article/view/191/191

Chon, K. K.-S., & Zoltan, J. (2019). Role of servant leadership in contemporary hospitality. *International Journal of Contemporary Hospitality Management, 31*(8), 3371–3394. https://doi.org/10.1108/IJCHM-11-2018-0935

Chung, J. Y., Jung, C. S., Kyle, G. T., & Petrick, J. F. (2010). Servant leadership and procedural justice in the U.S. national park service: The antecedents of job satisfaction. *Journal of Park and Recreation Administration, 28*(3), 1–15.

Coetzer, M. F., Bussin, M. H. R., & Geldenhuys, M. (2017). Servant leadership and work-related well-being in a construction company. *SAJIP: South African Journal of Industrial Psychology, 43*, 1–10. https://doi.org/10.4102/sajip.v43i0.1478

Collins, J. (2001). *Good to great*. Harper Collins.

Covey, S. R. (2004). *The 7 habits of highly effective people: Restoring the character ethic*. Free Press.

Czerw, A. (2019). Diagnosing well-being in work context – Eudemonic well-being in the workplace questionnaire. *Current Psychology, 38*, 331–346. https://doi.org/10.1007/s12144-017-9614-8

van Dierendonck, D., & Nuijten, I. (2011). The servant leadership survey: Development and validation of a multidimensional measure. *Journal of Business and Psychology, 26*(3), 249–267.

Ehrhart, M. G. (2004). Leadership and procedural justice climate as antecedents of unit-level organizational citizenship behavior. *Personnel Psychology, 57*, 61–94.

Elche, D., Ruiz-Palomino, P., & Linuesa-Langreo, J. (2020). Servant leadership and organizational citizenship behavior: The mediating effect of empathy and service climate. *International Journal of Contemporary Hospitality Management, 32*(6), 2035–2053. https://doi.org/10.1108/IJCHM-05-2019-0501

Fisher, J. (2016). Selecting the best version of SHALOM to assess spiritual well-being. *Religions, 7*(5), 45. https://doi.org/10.3390/rel7050045

Francisco, F. M. B., Emilio, D. E., Ricardo, C. G., & Rafael, L. A. (2020). Promoting firm innovativeness through servant leadership and corporate social responsibility to employees. *Leadership and Organization Development Journal, 41*(4), 615–633. https://doi.org/10.1108/LODJ-03-2019-0127

Frémeaux, S., & Michelson, G. (2017). The common good of the firm and humanistic management: Conscious capitalism and economy of communion. *Journal of Business Ethics, 145*(4), 701–709. https://doi.org/10.1007/s10551-016-3118-6

Goleman, D. (1998). *Working with emotional intelligence*. Bantam.

Greek Orthodox Archdiocese of North America. (2020). *For the life of the world: Toward a social ethos of the Orthodox Church*. Author. https://www.goarch.org/social-ethos

Green, D., & Roberts, G. (2010). Personnel implications of public sector virtual organizations. *Public Personnel Management, 39*(1), 47–57.

Greenleaf, R. K. (1977). *Servant leadership: A journey into the nature of legitimate power and greatness*. Paulist Press.

Haar, J., Brougham, D., Roche, M., & Barney, A. (2017). Servant leadership and work engagement: The mediating role of work-life balance. *New Zealand Journal of Human Resources Management, 17*(2), 56–72.

Hackman, J. R., & Oldham, G. R. (1976). Motivation through the design of work: Test of a theory. *Organizational Behavior and Human Performance, 16*(2), 250–279.

Hakanen, J., & van Dierendonck, D. (2011). Servant-leadership and life satisfaction: The mediating role of justice, job control, and burnout. *The International Journal of Servant-Leadership, 7*(1), 253–261.

Harju, L. K., Schaufeli, W. B., & Hakanen, J. J. (2018). A multilevel study on servant leadership, job boredom and job crafting. *Journal of Managerial Psychology, 33*(1), 2–14. https://doi.org/10.1108/JMP-08-2016-0237

Hicks, D. A. (2003). *Religion and the workplace: Pluralism, spirituality, leadership*. Cambridge University Press.

Hoch, J. E., Bommer, W. H., Dulebohn, J. H., & Wu, D. (2018). Do ethical, authentic, and servant leadership explain variance above and beyond transformational leadership? A meta-analysis. *Journal of Management, 44*(2), 501–529. https://doi.org/10.1177/0149206316665461

Hu, J., & Liden, R. C. (2011). Antecedents of team potency and team effectiveness: An examination of goal and process clarity and servant leadership. *Journal of Applied Psychology, 96*(4), 851. Retrieved from http://0-search.proquest.com.library.regent.edu/docview/878997586?accountid=13479.

Ilgen, D. R., Fisher, C. D., & Taylor, M. S. (1979). Consequences of individual feedback on behavior in organizations. *Journal of Applied Psychology, 64*(4), 349–371.

Ilkhanizadeh, S., & Karatepe, O. M. (2018). Does trust in organization mediate the influence of servant leadership on satisfaction outcomes among flight attendants? *International Journal of Contemporary Hospitality Management, 30*(12), 3555–3573. https://doi.org/10.1108/IJCHM-09-2017-0586

Jaramillo, F., Grisaffe, D. B., Chonko, L. B., & Roberts, J. A. (2009). Examining the impact of servant leadership on salesperson's turnover intention. *The Journal of Personal Selling & Sales Management, 29*(4), 351–365. http://0-search.proquest.com.library.regent.edu/docview/506525219?accountid=13479

Jaramillo, F., Bande, B., & Varela, J. (2015). Servant leadership and ethics: A dyadic examination of supervisor behaviors and salesperson perceptions. *Journal of Personal Selling & Sales Management, 35*(2), 108–124.

Jex, S. M. (1998). *Stress and job performance: Theory, research and implications for managerial practices*. Sage.

Kaya, B., & Karatepe, O. M. (2020). Does servant leadership better explain work engagement, career satisfaction and adaptive performance than authentic leadership? *International Journal of Contemporary Hospitality Management, 32*(6), 2075–2095. https://doi.org/10.1108/IJCHM-05-2019-0438

Khattak, S. I., Jiang, Q., Li, H., & Zhang, X. (2019). Corporate social responsibility (CSR) and leadership: Validation of a multi-factor framework in the United Kingdom (UK). *Journal of Business Economics and Management, 20*(4), 754–776. https://doi.org/10.3846/jbem.2019.9852

Kiker, D. S., Callahan, J. S., & Kiker, M. B. (2019). Exploring the boundaries of servant leadership: A meta-analysis of the main and moderating effects of servant leadership on behavioral and affective outcomes. *Journal of Managerial Issues, 31*(2), 172. http://eres.regent.edu:2048/login?url=https://www.proquest.com/scholarly-journals/exploring-boundaries-servant-leadership-meta/docview/2319666235/se-2?accountid=13479

Koenig, H. G. (2012). Religion, spirituality, and health: The research and clinical implications. *ISRN Psychiatry*, 1–33.

Koenig, H. G., King, D. E., & Carson, V. B. (2012). *Handbook of religion and health* (2nd ed.). Oxford University Press.

Kool, M., & van Dierendonck, D. (2012). Servant leadership and commitment to change, the mediating role of justice and optimism. *Journal of Organizational Change Management, 25*(3), 422–433. https://doi.org/10.1108/09534811211228139

Lee, Y. H. (2019). Emotional intelligence, servant leadership, and development goal orientation in athletic directors. *Sport Management Review, 22*(3), 395–406. https://doi.org/10.1016/j.smr.2018.05.003

Lee, A., Lyubovnikova, J., Tian, A. W., & Knight, C. (2020). Servant leadership: A meta-analytic examination of incremental contribution, moderation, and mediation. *Journal of Occupational and Organizational Psychology, 93*(1), 1–44. https://doi.org/10.1111/joop.12265

Leo, III. (2020). *Rerum Novarum. Encyclical of Pope Leo XIII on capital and labor*. Vatican.va. http://www.vatican.va/content/leo-xiii/en/encyclicals/documents/hf_l-xiii_enc_15051891_rerum-novarum.html

Li, Y., Li, D., Tu, Y., & Liu, J. (2018). How and when servant leadership enhances life satisfaction. *Personnel Review, 47*(5), 1082–1098. https://doi.org/10.1108/PR-07-2017-0223

Locke, E. A., & Latham, G. P. (1990). *A theory of goal setting and task performance*. Prentice Hall.

Lu, J., Zhang, Z., & Jia, M. (2019). Does servant leadership affect employees' emotional labor? A social information-processing perspective. *Journal of Business Ethics, 159*(2), 507–518. https://doi.org/10.1007/s10551-018-3816-3

Luu, T. T. (2019). Building employees' organizational citizenship behavior for the environment. *International Journal of Contemporary Hospitality Management, 31*(1), 406–426. https://doi.org/10.1108/IJCHM-07-2017-0425

Mackey, J., & Sisodia, R. (2013). *Conscious capitalism: Liberating the heroic spirit of business*. Harvard Business Review Press.

Marinova, S. V., & Park, H. (2014). Does it matter if leadership is about us? A meta-analysis of other-oriented leadership. *Academy of Management Annual Meeting Proceedings, 2014*(1), 1082–1087. https://doi.org/10.5465/AMBPP.2014.267

Maula-Bakhsh, R., & Raziq, A. (2018). Relationship between servant leadership and subjective well-being: Evidence from manufacturing and services based SMEs in Pakistan. *Journal of Management Sciences, 5*(1), 62–85. https://doi.org/10.20547/jms.2014.1805104

Melé, D. (2009). Integrating personalism into virtue-based business ethics: The personalist and the common good principles. *Journal of Business Ethics, 88*(1), 227–244.

Miao, Q., Newman, A., Schwarz, G., & Xu, L. (2014). Servant leadership, trust, and the organizational commitment of public sector employees in China. *Public Administration, 92*(3), 727–743.

Parris, D. L., & Peachey, J. W. (2013). A systematic literature review of servant leadership theory in organizational contexts. *Journal of Business Ethics, 113*(3), 377–393. https://doi.org/10.1007/s10551-012-1322-6

Parris, D. L., & Peachy, J. W. (2012). Building a legacy of volunteers through servant leadership: A cause-related sporting event. *Nonprofit Management & Leadership, 23*(2), 259–276.

Pfrombeck, J., & Verdorfer, A. P. (2018). How psychological capital and sense of coherence enhance servant leadership and buffer leader stress: Preliminary insights from an empirical study. *Servant Leadership: Theory and Practice, 5*(1), 25–48.

Posner, B., & Boone, M. (2006). Spirituality and leadership among college freshmen. *The International Journal of Servant-Leadership, 2*(1), 165–180.

Prottas, D. J. (2013). Relationships among employee perception of their manager's behavioral integrity, moral distress, and employee attitudes and well-being. *Journal of Business Ethics, 113*(1), 51–60. https://doi.org/10.1007/s10551-012-1280-z

Reed, L. (2015). Servant leadership, followership, and organizational citizenship behaviors in 9-1-1 emergency communications centers: Implications of a national study. *Servant Leadership: Theory and Practice, 2*(1), 71–94.

Reinke, S. J. (2004). Service before self: Towards a theory of servant-leadership. *Global Virtue Ethics Review, 5*(3), 30–57. http://0-search.proquest.com.library.regent.edu/docview/235111370?accountid=13479

Roberts, G. (2015). *Christian scripture and human resource management: Building a path to Servant leadership through faith*. Palgrave Macmillan.

Roberts, G. (2016). *Working with Christian servant leader spiritual intelligence: The foundation of God honoring vocational success*. Palgrave Macmillan.

Rodríguez-Carvajal, R., Herrero, M., van Dierendonck, D., de Rivas, S., & Moreno-Jiménez, B. (2019). Servant leadership and goal attainment through meaningful life and vitality: A diary study. *Journal of Happiness Studies, 20*(2), 499–521.

Ruiz-Palomino, P., Hernández-Perlines, F., Jiménez-Estévez, P., & Gutiérrez-Broncano, S. (2019). CEO servant leadership and firm innovativeness in hotels: A multiple mediation model of encouragement of participation and employees' voice. *International Journal of Contemporary Hospitality Management, 31*(4), 1647–1665. https://doi.org/10.1108/IJCHM-01-2018-0023

Russell, E. J., Broomé, R., & Russell, J. (2018). Servant leadership and the wellbeing of police officers: A case study. *Servant Leadership: Theory and Practice, 5*(2), 73–92.

Schaubroeck, J., Lam, S. S. K., & Peng, A. C. (2011). Cognition-based and affect-based trust as mediators of leader behavior influences on team performance. *Journal of Applied Psychology, 96*(4), 863. http://0-search.proquest.com.library.regent.edu/docview/879030243?accountid=13479

Schwepker, C. H., Jr. (2016). Servant leadership, distributive justice and commitment to customer value in the salesforce. *Journal of Business & Industrial Marketing, 31*(1), 70–82. https://doi.org/10.1108/JBIM-07-2014-0143

Sendjaya, S., & Pekerti, A. (2010). Servant leadership as antecedent of trust in organizations. *Leadership and Organization Development Journal, 31*(7), 643–663. https://doi.org/10.1108/01437731011079673

Sengupta, J., & Sengupta, S. S. (2018). Service-oriented leadership style for CSR: A perceptions-based view. *IUP Journal of Business Strategy, 15*(2), 7–30.

Setyaningrum, P. R., Setiawan, M., & Irawanto, D. W. (2020). Servant leadership characteristics, organisational commitment, followers' trust, employees' performance outcomes. *A literature review European Research Studies Journal, 23*(4), 902–911.

Shadish, W. R., Cook, T. D., & Campbell, D. T. (2002). *Experimental and quasi-experimental designs for generalized causal inference*. Houghton, Mifflin and Company.

Shim, D. C., & Park, H. H. (2019). Public service motivation in a work group: Role of ethical climate and servant leadership. *Public Personnel Management, 48*(2), 203–225. https://doi.org/10.1177/0091026018806013

Shim, D. C., Park, H. H., & Eom, T. H. (2016). Public servant leadership: Myth or powerful reality? *International Review of Public Administration, 21*(1), 3–20. https://doi.org/10.1080/12294659.2016.1147753

Spears, L. (1998). *Insights on leadership: Service, stewardship, spirit, and servant leadership*. John Wiley & Sons.

Spence, B. M., & Brown, L. W. (2018). Theology and corporate environmental responsibility: A biblical literalism approach to creation care. *Journal of Biblical Integration in Business, 21*(1), 45–54.

Sun, J., Liden, R. C., & Ouyang, L. (2019). Are servant leaders appreciated? An investigation of how relational attributions influence employee feelings of gratitude and prosocial behaviors. *Journal of Organizational Behavior, 40*(5), 528–540. https://doi.org/10.1002/job.2354

Tang, G., Kwan, H., Zhang, D., & Zhu, Z. (2016). Work-family effects of servant leadership: The roles of emotional exhaustion and personal learning. *Journal of Business Ethics, 137*(2), 285–297. https://doi.org/10.1007/s10551-015-2559-7

Taylor, T., Martin, B. N., Hutchinson, S., & Jinks, M. (2007). Examination of leadership practices of principals identified as servant leaders. *International Journal of Leadership in Education, 10*(4), 401–419.

Tuan, L. T. (2016). How servant leadership nurtures knowledge sharing. *International Journal of Public Sector Management, 29*(1), 91–108. https://doi.org/10.1108/IJPSM-06-2015-0112

Tuan, L. T. (2018). Activating tourists' citizenship behavior for the environment: The roles of CSR and frontline employees' citizenship behavior for the environment. *Journal of Sustainable Tourism, 26*(7), 1178–1203. https://doi.org/10.1080/09669582.2017.1330337

Tuan, L. T. (2020). Environmentally-specific servant leadership and green creativity among tourism employees: Dual mediation paths. *Journal of Sustainable Tourism, 28*(1), 86–109. https://doi.org/10.1080/09669582.2019.1675674

Tversky, A., & Kahneman, D. (1974). Judgment under uncertainty: Heuristics, and biases. *Science, 185*, 1124–1131.

Upadyaya, K., & Salmela-Aro, K. (2020). Social demands and resources predict job burnout and engagement profiles among Finnish employees. *Anxiety, Stress, and Coping, 33*(4), 403–415. https://doi.org/10.1080/10615806.2020.1746285

Walumbwa, F. O., Hartnell, C. A., & Oke, A. (2010). Servant leadership, procedural justice climate, service climate, employee attitudes, and organizational citizenship behavior: A cross-level investigation. *Journal of Applied Psychology, 95*(3), 517. http://0-search.proquest.com.library.regent.edu/docview/347854572?accountid=13479

Walumbwa, F. O., Muchiri, M. K., Misati, E., Wu, C., & Meiliani, M. (2018). Inspired to perform: A multilevel investigation of antecedents and consequences of thriving at work. *Journal of Organizational Behavior, 39*(3), 249–261. https://doi.org/10.1002/job.2216

Wang, C. (2013). Response to commentary: On the scientific status of the conscious capitalism theory. *California Management Review, 55*(3), 97–106.

Wang, Z., Meng, L., & Cai, S. (2019a). Servant leadership and innovative behavior: A moderated mediation. *Journal of Managerial Psychology, 34*(8), 505–518. https://doi.org/10.1108/JMP-11-2018-0499

Wang, Z., Yu, K., Xi, R., & Zhang, X. (2019b). Servant leadership and career success: The effects of career skills and proactive personality. *Career Development International, 24*(7), 717–730. https://doi.org/10.1108/CDI-03-2019-0088

Washington, R., Sutton, C., & Feild, H. (2006). Individual differences in servant leadership: The roles of values and personality. *Leadership and Organization Development Journal, 27*(8), 700–716. https://doi.org/10.1108/01437730610709309

Wisler, J. C. (2018). U.S. CEOs of SBUs in luxury goods organizations: A mixed methods comparison of ethical decision-making profiles. *Journal of Business Ethics, 149*(2), 443–518. https://doi.org/10.1007/s10551-016-3069-y

Zhang, K., Jia, X., & Chen, J. (2019). Talent management under a big data induced revolution: The double-edged sword effects of challenge stressors on creativity. *Management Decision, 57*(8), 2010–2031. https://doi.org/10.1108/MD-06-2018-0711

Gary E. Roberts is a professor and director of the Master of Public Administration (MPA) Program in the Robertson School of Government at Regent University with teaching interests in human resource management and nonprofit administration. Professor Roberts' research interests include servant leadership within the human resource management system and the influence of spiritual intelligence on personal and organizational well-being. With five books and 50 plus articles and book chapters, he has published extensively primarily in the area of human resource management with direct relevance to the public and nonprofit sectors. His latest books include Working the Christian Servant Leader Spiritual Intelligence and Servant Leader Human Resource Management: A Moral and Spiritual Perspective. He is an active member of St. Nicholas Greek Orthodox Church and Vineyard Community Church. He has been married to his beautiful wife Connie for 37 years and has three wonderful daughters.

5 Quiet Ego Leadership After Covid-19: Releasing Compassion, Confidence and Creativity

Michael Chaskalson, Chris Nichols, and Philippa Hardman

The world seems to reward loud-ego leadership, but that form of leading is not necessarily what the world needs.

Highly self-confident, risk-seeking, and callous leaders say O'Reilly and Chatman (2020) have profiles matching what the American Psychiatric Association (American Psychiatric Association, 2013) classifies as narcissistic personality disorder. Yet in the pre-Covid world it was people with just those characteristics to whom we often gave the highest power and the biggest jobs along with the right to mould the world the rest of us live and work in. We sometimes spoke of them as transformational players—the makers and shapers of our world. In several notorious cases, including some cited by O'Reilly and Chatman (2020), dysfunctional organisational leaders such as this created organisational cultures that led to the destruction of value amounting to many billions of dollars.

More often perhaps, and certainly less visibly, the consequences of such attitudes are less dramatic but no less serious. Employees in organisations run by narcissistic

M. Chaskalson (✉)
Ashridge Executive Education at Hult International Business School, Berkhamsted, UK

Mindfulness Works Ltd, Cambridge, UK

GameShift, Berkhamsted, UK
e-mail: michael@mindfulnessworks.com

C. Nichols
Ashridge Executive Education at Hult International Business School, Berkhamsted, UK

GameShift, Berkhamsted, UK
e-mail: chris@gameshift.co.uk

P. Hardman
Ashridge Consulting, Berkhamsted, UK

GameShift, Berkhamsted, UK
e-mail: philippa@gameshift.co.uk

S. K. Dhiman, J. F. Marques (eds.), *Leadership After COVID-19*, Future of Business and Finance, https://doi.org/10.1007/978-3-030-84867-5_5

leaders often suffer in a bullying culture (Hoel & Salin, 2002) and organisations as whole can come to manifest a loss of curiosity and consequent creative possibility as contrary views are silenced. There is a disappearance of nuance and difference as people try to follow, and second-guess, the leader. Thinking and acting within the guardrails of the dominant style becomes the unconsciously enforced norm (Lipman-Blumen, 2006). Noisy egos, at all levels in organisations, can bring chaos or stifled compliance in their wake.

As educators and consultants working in the process of leadership development, we have come increasingly to recognise some of the problems inherent in one of the most commonplace conceptions of leadership itself: the notion that leadership comes with a peculiar status—that the leader is always somehow special. This attribution to leaders of special status tends to create a pattern of self-selection, one which privileges a louder and more overtly confident form of personal style.

In response to this we have been working to develop an alternative. In our work with many different organisations through the recent crisis, we have noticed that loud and large ego leading has often not been the most successful. Many of the better outcomes we have seen have come from a different way of operating. One of the shared characteristics of the excellent leaders we have witnessed over this period has been that they have quieter egos.

This is not to say that they are ego-less. Barring a very few exceptional saints and sages, all of us have an ego—that inner voice which nature has endowed us with and which, for thousands of years, has played a key part in our rise to dominance as a species. That voice, abstracted from present-moment experience, helps us plan for the future, reflect on the past and stay safe. It enables us to navigate our surroundings, understand ourselves in relation to others and create effective social groups.

Before moving on, we need to make it clear that we are not using the term 'ego' here as Freud did to refer to the arbiter between the id and superego (Freud, 1961). Nor do we mean the excessively positive view of oneself, or the centre of will and self-control that Freud also sometimes referred to.

Rather, our use of the term relies simply on the original Latin meaning of 'ego,' which is synonymous with 'I.'

In our usage, an egoic state is one in which people are excessively focused on themselves and their personal concerns. It's a state in which 'I' and 'me' figure prominently in one's thoughts and reactions (Leary et al., 2016).

Of course, people are necessarily interested in their own well-being and in outcomes that are favourable to themselves. It seems obvious that natural selection would have filtered for organisms that focused on themselves and their own interests.

The problem we draw attention to is a subset of the more general issue that people often focus on and think about themselves and on self-relevant outcomes even when such thoughts are not needed or are counterproductive. Such egoicism often creates emotional and behavioural difficulties (Leary et al., 2016) and, we suggest, those difficulties are amplified and broadcast when they take place in leadership contexts.

James (1890, p. 333) observed, "My thinking is first and last and always for the sake of my doing," yet, he noticed, people waste a great deal of their thinking on self-relevant topics that actually inhibit effective action.

Almost all of us run an inner narrative, linked—as Farb and his colleagues (2007) have noted—to our brains' Default Mode Network (DMN). That narrative is part of the way in which we create our sense of identity over time.

"Will I be OK?"
"Will they like me?"
"What did I do that she looks at me like that?"
"Have I got all the slides prepared for that presentation next week? Is it going to go well? Have I done everything I need to do? Have I?"
"One day they're going to find out I'm not good enough..."
"This is a good experience. I'm having a good experience right now. I'm fine. This is great, this is great..."

On and on and on.

When most of us spend a few minutes alone with ourselves in silence and turn our attention inwards to listen, we discover the noise of irrelevant self-focussed thinking. That is the DMN turning over and over and over. It's where we default to.

It is that persistent self-focussed narrative that we have in mind when we speak of the ego.

Because egos are generally disposed to seek out and prioritise self-interest, it is vital that leaders find ways to quieten excessive self-focussed thoughts in order to attend at times to the needs and opinions of others.

Failure to do this leads to the kind of self-serving attitudes to leadership we see reflected, for example, in the soaring levels of senior executive remuneration and increasingly problematic income disparity.

To lead well, leaders must learn to quieten their egos.

The quiet ego is not a fragile, squashed or unwillingly silenced ego. It is deeply resilient, attuned to its own and others' inner dynamics. It has no inherent need to assert itself over others. Loud egos, on the other hand, draw sustenance primarily from the world of external appearances to which they constantly turn for reassurance (Bauer, 2008).

Wise leaders have quieter egos. In consequence, they are not taken in by their social image. They see that the self is simply a construction—a story that enables a sense of unity and purpose but throws the shadows of illusions that may sometimes be destructive (Wayment & Bauer, 2008). Noisier egos, by contrast, expend considerable energy in identifying and defending their constructed selves as if they were somehow real—asserting themselves into the world.

As Bauer (2008) shows, there is a virtuous relationship between ego quietening and personal growth. Quiet Ego Leaders are therefore also those who are able to build on their own strengths and to recognise, and engage in development around, areas where they are weaker.

Quiet Ego Leaders seek to grow and develop—and growth and development can produce wiser leaders. Quiet Ego Leadership, we suggest, is a trainable skill.

Later sections of this chapter will set out in detail what we mean by Quiet Ego Leadership and show both how it can be developed and why this is essential in addressing some of the organisational challenges ahead. Before that, we will set out our approach and some of the fieldwork observations on which this chapter is based.

Our Intention in Writing This Chapter

We have written this chapter for practicing leaders working in organisational life, for the consultants who work with them and the academics who research and write in this field. Our intention, since this volume is a companion handbook on leadership and change, is to produce a chapter that is, above all, a contribution to practice and to thoroughly grounded practical knowledge in the field. We therefore have chosen to write this as a piece of action research (Reason & Bradbury, 2001; Marshall et al., 2011), based on our day-to-day work as consultants to, and as leaders ourselves in, a range of organisations.

We are ambitious for the potential for this practical knowledge as an important contribution to organisational thinking. Although we have prepared this chapter based on direct experience of, and reflection about, organisations in a time of response to the pandemic, we do not believe (nor do the organisations or leaders we have worked with believe) that the learning is specific or limited to the COVID-19 crisis.

Our intention is to draw out practical lessons, perspectives and practices in leadership and change that are applicable to the wider forms of systemic shock of which the pandemic is only one example (Hardman & Nichols, 2020). We believe that this is vital and necessary because organisations today face several impending systemic shifts that have the potential to be as significant and disruptive as the COVID-19 pandemic. These systemic shifts include, but are not limited to, disruptions in the fields of climate and earth systems, geopolitics and trade patterns, economic and financial shocks, food security, microbial resistance arising from the widespread systemic medical and food system use of core antibiotic agents, the application of digital and connected technologies including AI and machine learning (the Internet of Things), and demographic shifts.

Each of these systems shifts, individually, has the potential to offer seismic and existential threats to the forms of organisation and to organisational practice. Taken together, since there is every likelihood of these shifts playing out in parallel and in combination, they offer an unprecedented challenge and opportunity to all aspects of life in organisations and in society (Marshall et al., 2011).

We are convinced that the pandemic crisis is merely one, potentially short term and containable, subset of a wider pattern of shifts and challenges. Learning lessons from the immediate challenges of COVID-19, seems to us to be essential preparation for a wider and more testing frontier of organisational transformation that lies on a near horizon.

Our Basis for Writing This Chapter

It seems appropriate to say some words of orientation about the foundations on which we have created this chapter, including the nature of the research and evidence that underpin our observations.

We position ourselves in the field as both scholar-practitioners and scholar-activists (Marshall et al., 2011) working with the organisational application of mindfulness practice in leadership and change, using an action research/action inquiry approach.

The challenges of large-scale systems shifts are in the heartland of our practice. We work with boards, executive teams, and whole organisations, to help develop strategic and leadership responses in times of uncertainty, turbulence, and incomplete information. Our client organisations are usually large and complex organisations, working across multiple geographies and cultures, and often with diverse business activities to coordinate. A common characteristic of our work is that we accompany leaders and organisations in situations where the future has become sufficiently unclear that rapid and deep learning is required, and where the only certainty is that existing knowledge and practice has become insufficient.

During 2020 we worked with several organisations where addressing the organisational and leadership response to the COVID crisis was a significant facet of the work we were engaged in with them. These organisations spanned several sectors and locations but included the following:

- UK hospitals in the National Health Service
- The Danish health sector, hospitals, non-hospital clinical care, medical sciences
- NGOs in the medical research and public health arena
- Government agencies and central government departments in the UK
- Regional and local government bodies
- Global businesses in material science, technology, engineering, automotive and pharmaceutical
- Retail and hospitality businesses
- Professional and financial services

Our observations in this article are drawn from our research in practice with these clients rather than from any form of empirical study. It is deeply engaged reflective research, focused on practical challenges and on experiments in live situations as these clients responded to the challenges and opportunities of their situation. We believe that what has arisen from this is an extremely robust set of cross-sectoral observations and reflections that offer some practical perspectives underpinned by both rigorous practice and robust theory.

The Theoretical Basis of Our Work

We are not neutral—we come to our work with a set of beliefs, assumptions and biases about "what the world is" and about how we can know it and act in it. We are explicit about these when we frame our work with clients. In brief an outline of our framing might be the following:

- The world is complex in that it consists of many interacting elements, forces and influences that do not have a linear, predictable and deterministic pattern (Hutchins, 2014).
- The world in which we work consists of participants beyond the human and when we work, we work with awareness of the wider earth and of the living systems of which we are part (Hutchins, 2014; Reason & Bradbury, 2001)

- The world of society and organisation is complex and is largely socially constructed (Gergen, 1999): that is, it is made up of the stories we co-construct and the meanings we make (Denzin & Lincoln, 2000). We are at the same time makers and consumers, weavers and woven
- We need therefore to take a systemic view (Whittington, 2020; Hawkins & Turner, 2020; Senge et al., 2005; Scharmer & Kaufer, 2013), seeing the world as an everchanging pattern in the form of a complex responsive process, where actions and reactions are connected but not necessarily in predictable or linear ways (Stacey, 2003; Boulton et al., 2015)
- There is much that cannot be known and much that cannot be seen at least in its entirety: so collaborative working (Salas & Tillmann, 2010) and diversity becomes essential in that this allows us to see more, know more and explore more that is seen by others but not by ourselves. We gain more insight together.
- Not all that we need to know can be accessed by conventional modes of research nor can it be contained in the conventional leadership or organisational vocabulary. So, we believe in the power of seeking insight from diverse and richer ways of knowing (Seeley & Thornhill, 2014). No way of knowing has a monopoly on the truth

Over the years we have adopted action research (and action inquiry) as a foundational approach for our way of understanding systems and intervening in them alongside our clients.

We define Action Research as a way of "being in the world" that is both empirically rigorous and at the same time promotes worthwhile social change. It is a tested and highly practical way for senior leaders to apply discipline to learning in real time in the heat of their actual work arena. It is also the mechanism that suits many forms of executive and organisational development work in the fields of practical learning, innovation and change. While there is no *one* definition of Action Research, most practitioners would accept the following.

Action Research, following Marshall et al. (2011) who draw on Reason & Bradbury (2001), is based on these five dimensions (and if one of the dimensions is absent, the work is NOT Action Research as we understand that):

- It **addresses practical challenges** often framed as "How do I …?" kinds of question: Such as "How do I increase genuine diversity and participation in my organisation?"
- It **focuses on worthwhile purposes** and is thus unashamedly value laden. We act and research on things we care about to improve society, organisation and the world.
- It **favours participation and democracy** and is based on the belief that people are social, learn better together and create change best if that change is co-created.
- It **features many and diverse ways of knowing** and believes that the questions we face can better be addressed by using a range of data sources, techniques and perspectives that sometimes lie outside the traditionally legitimate range of research.
- It is **emergent in form**. Later stages of research respond to what has gone earlier. It is hugely improvisational AND rigorous.

Torbert and his associates, developed the closely related concept of Action Inquiry which can be seen as an attempt to raise awareness in real time of the effectiveness, validity and legitimacy of our own behaviour and, through that, of framing and guiding purposeful change (Torbert & Cook-Greuter, 2004).

Action Inquiry argues that to be effective in all of our communities and organisations we need to pay rigorous attention to the congruence between our intentions and strategies, and the behaviours and outcomes we get. Being alert to this in the moment and acting creatively with others in way that are continually curious and seek to achieve worthwhile outcomes is at the heart of Action Inquiry.

Specifically, the transformational learning from action inquiry allows individuals, teams and organisations to become more capable of listening deeply; increasingly alert to current opportunities and challenges; and, from this, to become more capable of achieving effective and sustainable outcomes (Torbert & Cook-Greuter, 2004).

In working like this we are responding to one of the most powerful critiques ever made of traditional management education. Sumantra Ghoshal, the late and eminent academic and professor of business wrote "Bad Management Theory Is Destroying Good Management Practice" (2005). In this seminal piece Ghoshal provided a critique of the traditions of mainstream business education, arguing that by reducing management theory to a form of pseudo-physics, through trying to make everything empirical and mathematical, management schools have assumed away most of the more difficult and important issues in leadership and organisation including ethics and judgement. He called for this "pretence of knowing" to be replaced by a more modest, but more useful practical way of being rigorous about leadership knowledge that was more like 'temporary walking sticks', contingent practical knowledge to help real managers handle genuine complexity.

Our work is about using action research and action inquiry to develop a community of leaders with the skills to advance this kind of practice, day in and day out, and in doing so change the world in which we live (Salas & Tillmann, 2010; Marshall et al., 2011; Seeley & Thornhill, 2014).

The following section takes the work we have been doing with action research and action inquiry in a large range of organisations during the time of the pandemic and draws out some of the leadership and organisational challenges that have emerged and which we have been working to address.

What We Have Found in Our Client Organisations

During the initial days and weeks of the COVID crisis, most client organisations mobilised quickly to respond to the sudden, often existential, threat.

Health Sector Stories

Our health service (UK and Denmark) clients swiftly mobilised onto an emergency footing, rapidly prioritising COVID provision in new ways of working. It was stressful and turbulent work.

We recorded some of the descriptions of this initial response period. People talked about:

"I am wearing so many different hats"
"The spotlight is really on us"
"Every day is a shitstorm"
"There are so many plates spinning—all of them different"
"I am struggling but my head is mostly above water"
"I feel like I am a healer on the warpath"
"We are short of doctors at every level—I spend all of my day trying to find more people"
"The laundry never stops coming, no matter what else is happening in the world"

Despite the difficulties people found great joy from working together in new ways to serve a shared purpose. They reported sentiments such as:

"We have achieved more change in a month than we've been able to get in 5 years"
"We have worked together—politics and organisational blockages simply dissolved"
"I realised that being a doctor is like being in a marriage for life—I'm here for love, however hard it gets"
"We're doing a lot of beautiful things every day"
"I believe in this"
"I've realised that the pharmacy department can learn to dance to many different tunes"

Once the immediate crisis was over, the same people noticed that many of the behaviours they'd enjoyed quickly began to move back into old patterns—as you would expect in complex systems. Much inertia was temporarily overcome by the crisis but, once the temporary impetus passed, there was considerable pull towards old relationships and structures, old priorities and previous patterns of working.

They reported things like:

"The old patterns have re-emerged. My boss is more remote than the Pope"
"I find that I am a lone wolf—I am used to standing out in a large field of men, but I do feel that no one has my back"
"It is a daily struggle to make ends meet"
"Our systems pull in the opposite direction to many of our aspirations"
"We've gone from priority number one to being the ugly duckling again"
"I've realised that if I want to keep any of the gains we made I have to be very loud to get attention"
"I want to keep the collaboration going—but it seems to take so much energy because it involves fighting against the way things are organised"

Our work with these health sector clients had parallels with those working in corporate environments.

Large Non-health Clients

Many of our commercial clients had an initial period of "panic/paralysis" where everything stopped apart from the effort to work out, in crisis mode, how to manage their businesses under new arrangements—usually on the assumption that there would be a "return to normal" after a few weeks. Within a month or two, most realised that there would be at least a prolonged dislocation and began preparing to work in new ways.

Over time, it became clear that organisations would need to adapt rapidly to new ways of working, often based on a rapid shift to virtual/digital and remote ways of working.

After several months we inquired into the experience of these new ways of working. There were many highly positive responses. Clients reported:

- Significant improvements in efficiency: an increased focus in meetings—online meetings are quicker with less social time and fewer distractions
- An increase in personal "effectiveness"—with the ability to do more, to "be in more than one place at a time"—coupled to "novelty leading to high levels of energy in the team"
- There's a real focus on sustainability—"there is far less carbon, fewer commuting miles"

Some also reported gains in work life balance, with more flexibility and autonomy, allowing more integration of family time and work time. But this was not evenly distributed. Some aspects of privilege appeared—younger employees tended to lack suitable workspaces and suffer more from the burdens of loneliness of remote work.

There were also reports of important changes in culture—which were similar to those reported in the health sector. These included:

"There's a lot more empowerment—trust levels are definitely up"
"There's much more autonomy"
"Teamwork is stronger—much more support among colleagues"

But people also spoke very strongly about the challenges they've faced in adopting new ways of working. Among the most commonly described challenges were these:

- Dealing with inequalities: flexible working doesn't suit everyone and not all team members have equally adaptable home situations. Staff may face difficult challenges in doing their work safely and healthily, and these may be difficult for bosses to see.
- Although virtual working feels accessible and "flat", new forms of exclusion and power dynamics have sometimes emerged and have exacerbated existing inclusion/exclusion issues in organisations. It is less easy to spot the politics of informal power as it flows in virtual space. People can be at formal meetings online and yet be excluded very easily from informal side conversations (in chat spaces,

on WhatsApp or Slack, on separate calls). Sometimes this is harder to see online than it is in the office.

- Maintaining the social fabric of teams is harder, with the loss of "watercooler conversations". The informal connective tissue of teams can suffer, it can be harder to include and "onboard" new members, and sometimes some team members health and well-being can suffer.

In addition to these challenges, the move to flexible work locations and meeting forms has presented some real challenges for more senior leaders. In some global clients, for example, very senior (group/divisional) leaders vested a lot of their identity in (almost constant) international travel, visiting offices and sites, and in hosting regional meetings. We have seen some clear examples of top management being an obstacle to new ways of working largely through anxiety about the loss of power and status in the familiar organisational rituals associated with their roles in the old ways of working.

Some teams also expressed a challenge in terms of finding ways to explore new thinking together. For many, teams had become increasingly slick and effective in terms of dealing with operational priorities and in addressing problem situation in crisis mode. In some ways, the slickness at "solving problems effectively" online also became an obstacle to exploring alternatives well. Finding a slick way of resolving a complicated challenge is NOT the same discipline as exploring a wider range of perspectives to allow new ideas to emerge. Sometimes the difficulty of the latter was expressed to us as a lack of time and space. The new rhythm of short virtual meetings simply didn't encourage the expression of open curiosity. But it was also expressed in terms of the inability to do even basic collaborative exploration well in the virtual space. Many leaders don't feel comfortable inviting large teams to explore the unknown in a virtual meeting—and many lack the technical knowledge of their organisational collaboration tools to do this well online.

Overcoming these challenges is important work as we all learn the lessons from the COVID crisis and prepare to address the challenges of the wider raft of systems shifts that lie ahead. The work needed includes many important edges for the future of leadership and change that should be on the agenda for anyone in Learning and Development and Organisational Development (Hardman & Nichols, 2020)—and needs to be on the risk register of all executive teams (Brissett et al., 2020; Whittington, 2020; Hawkins & Turner, 2020).

It is for this reason that we have brought together our work on mindfulness and strategic exploration. The bringing together of these strands into what we call Quiet Ego Leadership has direct application to all of the challenges we have found in making the most of new ways of working, as well as in addressing the creative response to significant systems change.

Quiet Ego Leadership

Drawing on our informal findings working with clients through the COVID-19 pandemic, as set out above, we have come to see over and again that in times of rapid change and uncertainty it is all too easy for leaders to default to safety-seeking, or to self-referential 'me first' styles of leadership. The ego, as we have described it above, is in part a safety-seeking mechanism. Self-referential thought, after all, is often targeted on what best serves one's own perceived best interests. The ability to step apart from such self-referential thinking, allow that one has not got all the answers and openly explore new territories along with others is a vital skill in times of rapid change.

At times of crisis, moreover, when all are asked to give beyond previously contracted obligations, it is crucial that leaders are seen authentically to put others' interests ahead of their own. That applies outside of crisis as well. Leaders who are observably less self-referential will engage a more willing and therefore more engaged followership.

To lead well, leaders need to quieten their own egos.

Drawing on Wayment and Bauer (2008) we propose there are four factors which help the ego to quieten. These four factors should therefore be seen as crucial elements in any programme of leadership development. They are mindfulness; a sense of interdependence; compassion; and a framework of values that spring from these and which support continuous personal growth.

Considerable research over the past decade tells us that both mindfulness and compassion are trainable skills (Goleman & Davidson, 2017). A sense of the interdependent nature of phenomena can be conceptually taught. And training and/or coaching can help leaders to discover and become clearer about the values they hold which support the development of wisdom.

Let us turn to each of these factors in factors in turn.

Mindfulness

First described by the Buddha 2600 years ago (Wynne, 2007), what Buddhists long described using terms such as the Pāli word *sati* began to emerge in clinical (and therefore researchable) contexts in the mid-1970s following the pioneering work of Kabat-Zinn (1990) and colleagues. Since then, tens of thousands of research papers looking into the efficacy of mindfulness training in a wide variety of contexts have been published and the approach is consequently finding increasing acceptance in the workplace in general. A meta-analysis of Mindfulness-Based Programs (MBPs) carried out by Vonderlin et al. (2020) suggests that MBPs effectively reduce stress, burnout, mental distress and somatic complaints, while improving mindfulness, well-being, compassion and job satisfaction.

In leadership contexts, research into the outcomes of mindfulness training is relatively scant. But there seems to be no reason on the face of it why the workplace-related outcomes found by Vonderlin et al. (2020), and in the more generic or clinical studies carried out in the population at large, would differ for those who occupy leadership positions.

Out of the few leadership-specific studies available, we can turn to a wait-list controlled multi-method study carried out by Chaskalson and colleagues (2020) with 57 self-described senior business leaders. This study found that those leaders who attended an 8-week Mindful Leader program, and who meditated for at least 10-min per day, experienced increases in their overall resilience, their capacity to collaborate with others and their ability to manage effectively in conditions of complexity.

Based particularly on their analysis of qualitative data from that research, Chaskalson and Reitz (2018) ascribe the changes experienced by participants on the Mindful Leader course to increases in three meta-capacities which they describe using the acronym AIM—Allowing, Inquiry and Meta-awareness.

"Allowing" refers to the ability to accept present-moment reality as it actually is and to approach the situations one finds oneself in openly and compassionately. This is not the same as passivity. Rather, the attitude we describe here springs from a deep reality-orientation. Many of us spend much of our time *not* allowing what is the case to be the case. "If only it were not like this—everything would be OK." If only I had a different job, a bigger house, a different partner, a different boss… If only I hadn't made that decision 2-weeks ago—everything would be OK.

But, as participants on the Quiet Ego Leader Process learn, the truth is that things are as they are and when, with an allowing, open-hearted attitude, we can allow things to be as they are then choice opens up for us. "It's like this—now what shall I do?" The allowing attitude carries over to the next step in the process. Because the interesting question is what would be best? Best for me, best for others, best for the situation. By implication, what would be kindest?

As one participant on Chaskalson and Reitz's Mindful Leader course put it:

> So [I think], "'Ooh, this is all a bit uncertain, and I'm quite unsure';" that's actually an okay place to be, and from there you can explore. (Chaskalson et al., 2020, p. 136)

"Inquiry" stands for an attitude of curiosity and open-hearted engagement with whatever presents in each moment.

As another participant on the Mindful Leader course put it:

> I think that bit of stepping back and just saying, "'What's actually is the problem here? What is it that's getting at me?"' I find really helpful, actually. (Chaskalson et al., 2020, p. 136)

"Meta-awareness" is akin to the more commonly used psychological term meta-cognition, but the broader use of 'awareness' rather than 'cognition' in the phrase draws attention to the fact that its target is more than thought—although that is included. It also refers to feelings, to sensations and to impulses. It is the ability to choose, when needed, simply to observe what you are thinking, feeling, and sensing. This allowed the participants on the Mindful Leader program to see that their thoughts, feelings, sensations, and impulses are just that—a combination of thoughts, feelings, sensations and impulses. "Thoughts are not facts," as Teasdale (1999) puts it. Nor are the other components of the experiencing mind.

Taken together, these three meta-capacities open up a vital space in the automated flow of a leader's experience.

Quiet Ego Leadership training uses mindfulness methods to help participants turn their attention inwards and observe their own minds at work. They learn to look *at* their minds, rather than just *through* their minds. With the consequent growth of meta-awareness, they begin to see their own the narrative self-focus for what it is: simply a flow of thoughts, feelings, sensations and impulses.

As participants on the Mindful Leader program put it:

> ... it gave me a way to take back, to own some of that control if you like, over my own thinking. So, recognizing that I'm choosing my thoughts, and they're not me, they're just the noise of what's going on. (Chaskalson et al., 2020, p. 136)

And:

> [The program has] allowed me to just be able to see these things—thoughts, feelings, sensations—separately from me, view them, explore them .... (Chaskalson et al., 2020, p. 136)

Participants on mindfulness-based courses often come to the realisation that "I am not my thoughts" (Kabat-Zinn, 2015). Insights like that allow the ego to begin to quieten.

A Sense of Interdependence

A novel virus somehow emerges in Wuhan in Central China and within a few short months more than a million people die and the world's economies suffer a huge collective recession. We live, and always have done, in a completely interconnected world. This is not a novel phenomenon—the product of the twenty-first century's highly mobile, globalised culture. Interconnection is a fundamental property of all phenomena.

From the 'butterfly effect' described by Lorenz (1963) who suggested that factors such as the exact time of formation, and path taken by a tornado might be influenced by minor perturbations such as the distant butterfly flapping of a butterfly's wings several weeks earlier, to the notion that the elements in the human body were made in distant stars a very, very long time ago and have come to us often by way several supernovas (Schrijver & Schrijver, 2015), popular culture is gradually absorbing the notion that all existence is an unthinkably vast, constantly interconnected and complex system—a web of life.

The need for this understanding has, arguably, never been higher. In the unfolding climate emergency, we all of us need to realise ever more deeply the implications each of our choices has on the delicately interconnected processes on which we depend. Our choices of whether or not to fly, even whether to stream video in high rather than standard definition all have implications for the climate (Griffiths, 2020).

We all affect one another all the time.

Quiet Ego Leadership training allows leaders by degrees to discover, in their experience, that we are not each of us separate, isolated, ego-identities constantly striving in competition for one another for scarce resources. Rather, we inextricably inter-depend on each other and all things in a vast process of systemic relatedness and the choices we make ramify far beyond ourselves alone.

Compassion

Coming to see the interconnected, interdependent nature of living systems is a cognitive matter that has, we suggest, an affective counterpart as compassion.

As evidenced by numerous studies (Gilbert, 2009; Neff & Germer, 2013; Fredrickson & Siegel, 2017) compassion is a trainable skill and compassion meditation trainings are an effective means of increasing compassionate attitudes—both to oneself and to others. The other-regarding attitudes that both support and emerge from a quieter ego depend in part on underlying attitudes of care and concern to oneself and others and such attitudes, it seems, can be trained.

Participants in Quiet Ego Leadership training processes learn and are encouraged to practice compassion-based meditations as part of the training.

Values

Ware (2011) says that the top five regrets she encountered in her many years working as a palliative care nurse are—

1. I wish I'd had the courage to live a life true to myself, not the life others expected of me;
2. I wish I hadn't worked so hard;
3. I wish I'd had the courage to express my feelings;
4. I wish I had stayed in touch with my friends;
5. I wish I had let myself be happier.

It can be argued that the last four of these regrets are in fact a subset of the first: I wish I'd had the courage to live a life true to myself. Or, in other words, I wish I had stayed more often true to my deepest values.

Quiet Ego Leadership training processes use a variety of methods to help participants uncover and express what most deeply matters to them. Our assertion is that when mindfulness, a sense of interdependence and compassion come together with what our participants most deeply value then the actions that follow from that will be less self-regarding, more other regarding.

We have no interest in prescribing a set of values or ethics. Rather, we suggest that they emerge naturally from the inner attitudes that our course participants discover and make explicit to themselves as the process unfolds.

Why Quiet Ego Leadership Is Vital to Creating the Future

We said earlier in this chapter that we see the COVID crisis as one specific form of a wider set of systems challenges that are in train. The ability to work to address these crises is, in our view, the most pressing leadership challenge of our time. We also argue that the development of Quiet Ego Leadership has an important role to play in equipping us to address these challenges well. This section explores why—in the specific connection between quiet ego states and the ability to engage in the exploration of the unknown, and essential skills for addressing post COVID systems challenges creatively and well.

The Difference Between Navigation and Exploring

It is clear that in any aspect of life some things are more certain and predictable than others (Stacey, 1993/2003; Boulton et al., 2015). We draw on a simple analogy to help get this thinking clearer. We call it the 'Navigate-Explore' framework.

- *The Navigation zone* is when things are relatively stable and familiar, when you're dealing with technical issues (even demanding ones) and your existing experience and expertise is a good guide for action. We call it Navigation because you already have a good enough 'map' to guide the actions you need to take. Navigation tasks may be lengthy and complicated, but they will feel familiar: the tasks of 'business as usual'—project management, resource allocation and so on—all with the aim of delivering specified outcomes.
- *The Exploration zone* is when things are more unfamiliar, for example when you're in times of change, when you're innovating, when you want different behaviours to get new outcomes. These times will all tend to have some elements of being 'beyond the known map'. In this type of activity your existing experience and expertise may or may not be quite so useful and may at times be a false friend.

We illustrate the Navigation and Exploration spaces in this 'yin and yang' form because we like the complementary and flowing form of relationship that it suggests. We also like the two black dots in either section which we take to denote that that each section is to some extent affected by what lies in the other. Navigation is never *totally* without Exploration—and vice versa. This is not a polar relationship of opposites. Very often you'll face issues that lie more in one zone than the other, but most of our professional lives involve becoming adept and working with both, often at the same time.

Many of the challenges we will face, as organisational leaders, and in wider society, will lie in the exploring space—because they will be novel challenges which cannot be fully solved through the application of known expertise. The future requires new knowledge creation, which will arise from rigorous exploration.

What makes for good exploration? In our field work we noticed a number of positive behaviours that support effectiveness in this working well with the unknown.

Effective exploration rests on some behaviours that benefit from the application of Quiet Ego style of leadership. We cannot give a full account here, but some of the most important characteristics are set out below.

Taking an appreciative stance Organisational life, and society in general, seems to have a huge appetite for looking at what's wrong, who failed, where the problem is. A lot of effort gets poured into deficit thinking, plugging the gap, fixing the problem. It's not obvious that this always works—after all, the railways still fail, the hospitals still have waiting lists. Adopting the appreciative stance is in itself a radical act and sets the foundations for people to step into exploration with a positive energy (Watkins & Mohr, 2001). This matters because it is important to involve diverse participation—and an appreciative framing helps to bring this about.

Encouraging effective participation You can't explore from one perspective. So, the quality of participation is vital to good exploration. The capacity to shift perspective and to take other perspectives into account is greatly enhanced when leaders are able to put their egos aside for a time and open to the views, opinions and perspectives of others.

We have noticed that the quality of the quieter ego participation is influenced by some characteristics that we summarise under the headings of our 5P model (Hardman & Nichols, 2020).

Quiet Ego Leaders notice:

- *Participation*: ask who is involved and why—and who is excluded and why?
- *Preferences*: notice the psychological preferences in the room
- *Power*: notice the power dynamics in conversation: who and what is noticed and who and what is ignored?
- *Past Patterns*: What are the past relationships being played out in this strategic discussion? What impact is there on the conversation and the thinking?
- *Parental games*: Is this an adult conversation? Does anyone harbour saviour or victim positions? Who is the 'us' and who is the 'other' and what do we fantasise about them?

Cultivating richer ways of seeing and knowing The language of everyday organisational life is often too small to allow the system to be fully seen or understood. Good exploration requires new and richer ways of seeing, ways of getting different sorts of data (Reason & Bradbury, 2001; Seeley & Thornhill, 2014).

Richer and more diverse work gives us the opportunity to go beyond the common-space, brain-only workings of the organisational world. There is a depth and a freshness that comes from experiencing something deeply, in the senses and in the body, that feeds the potential for profound learning. Even more so if that experience is used to make visible the usually unstated assumptions and frames of the organisation, context or situation.

The more deeply we allow our richly sensed and embodied experience to inform our questioning of the given frame, and to feed our creative reframing of things, the bolder and more fruitful our work is likely to be.

Part of the work of exploration is to become aware of the richer data all around us. Stepping into the experience of being a living part of a messy creative planet is a vital part of this kind of work. Intellectualising before experiencing guarantees a separation from the living reality: we need to step into action with all our senses alert.

To allow the sensory experience to do its work, we must give it some time and space. Part of the work of artful knowing is to create experiences and exercises that temporarily derail the ever present 'brainy' mode of organisation and leadership. This is essential if we are to stop the rush from experience directly into expertise and problem-solving based on old frames and existing ways of seeing.

Noticing the Impact of Your Own Actions on the Exploration

When a leader is exploring, they are part of the bigger system, not just an objective observer. So the leader must learn to notice the effects of their actions on that system.

We have created (Hardman & Nichols, 2020) a model that maps this onto a continuum.

Actions that support things as they are:

- **Action with a "push" energy**
- **Telling and prescription**
- **Enforcement and compliance**
- **Logic and analysis above all**
- **Managing delivery of plans**

Actions that support the search for new possibility in action:

- **Action with a "pull" energy**
- **Invitation and allowing**
- **Curiosity, looking deeper**
- **Respect many kinds of data**
- **Emotional, embodied work is legitimate**
- **Working with energy flows**

Reinforcement action Activity coming from the left-hand side of this continuum comes from a place of fixed knowing. It is often based on expertise and knowledge, and from having some kind of authority and power that comes from a role within that system. Very often this approach makes use of the prevailing logical language of organisations.

Regenerative action When there are significant systems challenges to be addressed, reinforcement action isn't enough: the attributes and skills from the right-hand side of the continuum become more important. Here the interventions are based on explicitly not knowing. This is a position of courage and authority, of clearly stating that this is a situation of not knowing so therefore good exploration is needed. Here it becomes especially important to state assumptions and to be deeply curious about the assumptions that others bring. This is an act of inviting curiosity about the deeper reasons for an action or a statement. Attention to these assumptions makes more of this usually hidden foundation visible and invites others into an understanding, sharing and exploration of what is communicated.

Each one of these attributes of good exploration are best supported by the approaches of Quiet Ego Leadership. The allowing of what actually is, lets us to see the situation more fully. It enables us to appreciate the limits of our knowledge and opens the door to exploration.

The nurturing of compassion and values lets us invite others into exploring, and to support them in bringing their full range of energies and fears. This, and the gentle setting aside of our egos insistence on being "right", is an essential cornerstone of richer ways of knowing, and is a foundation of cognitive diversity in a team or organisation.

The practice of meta-awareness allows us to see ourselves, individually and collectively, thinking while we are in the act of doing it—an important element in not getting stuck in the familiar round, but instead allows stuck patterns to be avoided, exited, and new conversations to be opened up.

Towards a Continued Practice of Quiet Ego Leadership

We end our chapter by making a bold claim. Although our human society and its many connected systems are deeply troubled, and many of them are in crisis, we remain optimistic about the possibility of human society sustaining itself and learning to solve the problems we face. We believe that organisations, particularly business organisations, but not only businesses, have a particular role to play in this, and that leaders at every level in those organisations have a central role in making this potential become realised.

Our capacity for reflection and inquiry makes such ambition possible and reasonable. All of us can play our part in keeping life, society, our organisations and institutions alive and fit for the future. We can do this because we are drawn to participate, to join in and imagine something better. Sure, we are a species that often gets this wrong. We can veer down blind allies of closed minds and false certainty, and deny our capacity for curiosity, sharing and learning.

We do not believe that the potential can be realised from positions of expertise alone, nor can mere heroic achievement deliver this for us. The time for the deep explorer, based on the AIM model of Quiet Ego Leadership is dawning.

Takeaways

1. The Covid-19 heralds the first in what we believe will be a series of impending systemic shifts that have the potential to be at least as significant and disruptive as the Covid pandemic.
2. To lead well in these conditions of uncertainty and turbulence, leaders must learn to quieten their egos.
3. Quiet ego leadership is a trainable skill consisting in four primary elements: mindfulness, a sense of interdependence, compassion and the values that flow from these and accord with them.
4. Leaders with quieter egos are better able to move between the modes of 'navigate'—where what is called for is known—and 'explore', where what is called for is currently unknown. They are also better able to bring their people with them on that journey.
5. Loud-ego leadership leads to an organisational loss of curiosity and creative possibility as contrary views are silenced. There is a disappearance of nuance and difference as people try to follow, and second-guess, the leader. Thinking and acting within the guardrails of the dominant style becomes the unconsciously enforced norm. Quiet ego leaders draw out the best in their people and are better able to lead in contexts where they themselves do not and cannot have all the answers.

Reflections

1. When I, or someone close to me, worked under a loud-ego leader what was the impact on my own, or their, performance?
2. Can I notice the voice of my own ego? What effect does it have on me at work (and at home)?
3. How much do I live, and act, in awareness of my being embedded in a completely interdependent web of life?
4. Might I be a little more compassionate in my daily life. What would that look like?
5. What *really* matters to me? What would I want people to say about me at my funeral? How does that compare with the ambitions I have for my developing career?

References

American Psychiatric Association. (2013). *Diagnostic and statistical manual of mental disorders* (5th ed., pp. 669–670). Author.

Bauer, J. J. (2008). How the ego quiets as it grows: Ego development, growth stories, and eudaimonic personality development. In H. A. Wayment & J. J. Bauer (Eds.), *Decade of behavior. Transcending self-interest: Psychological explorations of the quiet ego* (pp. 199–210). American Psychological Association. https://doi.org/10.1037/11771-018

Bloget, H. (2010). *Mark Zuckerberg, Moving fast and breaking things*. Business Insider. https://www.businessinsider.com/mark-zuckerberg-2010-10?r=US&IR=T

Boulton, J. G., Allen, P. M., & Bowan, C. (2015). *Embracing complexity: Strategic perspectives for an age of turbulence*. Oxford University Press.

Brissett, L., Sher, M., & Smith, T. L. (Eds.). (2020). *Dynamics at boardroom level: A Tavistock primer for leaders, coaches and consultants*. Routledge.

Chaskalson, M., & Reitz, M. (2018). *Mind time*. Thorsons.

Chaskalson, M., Reitz, M., Waller, L., & Olivier, S. (2020). Mindful leadership. In *The Routledge companion to mindfulness at work* (pp. 124–141). Routledge.

Denzin, N. K., & Lincoln, Y. S. (Eds.). (2000). *Handbook of qualitative research* (2nd ed.). SAGE.

Farb, N. A., Segal, Z. V., Mayberg, H., Bean, J., McKeon, D., Fatima, Z., & Anderson, A. K. (2007). Attending to the present: Mindfulness meditation reveals distinct neural modes of self-reference. *Social Cognitive and Affective Neuroscience, 2*(4), 313–322.

Fredrickson, B. L., & Siegel, D. J. (2017). Broaden-and-build theory meets interpersonal neurobiology as a lens on compassion and positivity resonance. In *Compassion: Concepts, research, and applications* (pp. 203–220). Routledge.

Freud, S. (1961). The ego and the id. In *The standard edition of the complete psychological works of Sigmund Freud, Volume XIX (1923-1925): The ego and the Id and other works* (pp. 1–66). The Hogarth Press.

Gergen, K. J. (1999). *An invitation to social construction*. SAGE.

Ghoshal, S. (2005). Bad management theories are destroying good management practices. *The Academy of Management Learning and Education, 4*(1), 79–91.

Gilbert, P. (2009). *The compassionate mind*. Robinson.

Goleman, D., & Davidson, R. (2017). *The science of meditation: How to change your brain, mind and body*. Penguin.

Griffiths, S. (2020). *Why your internet habits are not as clean as you think*. BBC. https://www.bbc.com/future/article/20200305-why-your-internet-habits-are-not-as-clean-as-you-think

Hardman, P. M. L., & Nichols, C. P. (2020). *Disrupted! How to create the future when the old rules are broken*. Matador.

Hawkins, P., & Turner, E. (2020). *Systemic coaching: Delivering value beyond the individual*. Routledge.

Hoel, H., & Salin, D. (2002). Organisational antecedents of workplace bullying. In *Bullying and emotional abuse in the workplace* (pp. 221–236). CRC Press.

Hutchins, G. (2014). *The illusion of separation: Exploring the cause of our current crisis*. Floris.

James, W. (1890). *Principles of psychology*. Henry Holt.

Kabat-Zinn, J. (1990). *Full-catastrophe living*. Delta Publishing.

Kabat-Zinn, J. (2015). *Mindfulness-based stress reduction: An interview with Jon Kabat-Zinn*. Huff Post. https://www.huffpost.com/entry/mindfulnessbased-stress--r_b_6909426?guccounter=1&guce_referrer=aHR0cHM6Ly93d3cuZ29vZ2xlLmNvbS8&guce_referrer_sig=AQAAAEpJntlqcpZROL-iPNZXG8T25vw8teKO2tGsOSqYb8zrlNAHY7rAKRO2vrY9iyah9VMpyzZHtbhBDSMQedB3pdd_8mRrAsTJdhcCkTBBCI2kte-cBQjT9YK9qJxTXQvJghGbUCoPeYyLd3_r4GC6lShSl1yr3st6CndMFmaOgkXF

Laloux, F. (2014). *Reinventing organisations*. Nelson Parker.

Leary, M. R., Diebels, K. J., Jongman-Sereno, K. P., & Hawkins, A. (2016). Perspectives on hypo-egoic phenomena from social and personality psychology. In *The oxford handbook of hypo-egoic phenomena* (p. 47). Oxford University Press.

Lipman-Blumen, J. (2006). *The allure of toxic leaders: Why we follow destructive bosses and corrupt politicians—And how we can survive them*. Oxford University Press.
Lorenz, E. N. (1963). Deterministic nonperiodic flow. *Journal of the Atmospheric Sciences, 20*(2), 130–141.
Marshall, J., Coleman, G., & Reason, P. (2011). *Leadership for sustainability: An action research approach*. Greenleaf.
Neff, K. D., & Germer, C. K. (2013). A pilot study and randomized controlled trial of the mindful self-compassion program. *Journal of Clinical Psychology, 69*(1), 28–44.
O'Reilly, C. A., & Chatman, J. A. (2020). Transformational leader or narcissist? How grandiose narcissists can create and destroy organizations and institutions. *California Management Review, 62*(3), 5–27. https://doi.org/10.1177/0008125620914989
Reason, P. (1988). *Human inquiry in action: Developments in new paradigm research*. SAGE.
Salas, M. A., & Tillmann, H. J. (2010). *Participatory action research: Embracing the knowledge perspective within field research*. The Regional Center for Social Science and Sustainable Development.
Scharmer, O., & Kaufer, K. (2013). *Leading from the emerging future*. Berrett-Koehler.
Schrijver, K., & Schrijver, I. (2015). Living with the Stars: How the Human Body is Connected to the Life Cycles of the Earth, the Planets, and the Stars. Oxford University Press, USA.
Seeley, C., & Thornhill, E. (2014). *Artful organisation*. Ashridge.
Senge, P., Scharmer, C. O., Jaworski, J., & Flowers, B. S. (2005). *Presence: exploring profound change in people, organisations and society*. Nicholas Brealey.
Stacey, R. D. (1993/2003). *Strategic management and organisational dynamics: The challenge of complexity* (4th ed.). Pearson/FT Prentice Hall.
Teasdale, J. D. (1999). Metacognition, mindfulness and the modification of mood disorders. *Clinical Psychology & Psychotherapy: An International Journal of Theory & Practice, 6*(2), 146–155.
Torbert, W. R., & Cook-Greuter, S. R. (2004). *Action inquiry: The secret of timely and transforming leadership*. Berrett-Koehler.
Vonderlin, R., Biermann, M., Bohus, M., & Lyssenko, L. (2020). Mindfulness-based programs in the workplace: A meta-analysis of randomized controlled trials. *Mindfulness, 11*, 1579–1598.
Ware, B. (2011). *The top five regrets of the dying: A life transformed by the dearly departing*. Hay House.
Watkins, J. M., & Mohr, B. J. (2001). *Appreciative inquiry: Change at the speed of imagination*. Jossey-Bass.
Wayment, H. A., & Bauer, J. J. (Eds.). (2008). *Decade of behavior. Transcending self-interest: Psychological explorations of the quiet ego* (pp. 199–210). American Psychological Association.
Whittington, J. (2020). *Systemic coaching & constellations* (3rd ed.). Kogan Page.
Wynne, A. (2007). *The origin of Buddhist meditation*. Routledge.

Michael Chaskalson is a pioneer in the application of mindfulness to leadership and workplace contexts. He is a professor of practice adjunct at Hult Ashridge Executive Education; an associate at the Møller Institute at Churchill College in the University of Cambridge; founding director at Mindfulness Works Ltd.; and a partner at GameShift. He is the author of several books, papers and book chapters on mindfulness, in general and in organisations, as well as mindful leadership.

He co-led the training on a world-first wait-list controlled trial of the effects of an 8-week Mindful Leader programme with senior business leaders at Ashridge. He is the author of *The Mindful Workplace* (Wiley-Blackwell, 2011), *Mindfulness in Eight Weeks* (Harper Thorsons, 2014) and co-author of *Mindfulness for Coaches* (Routledge, 2018) and *Mind Time* (Harper Thorsons, 2018).

Chris Nichols has consulted to governments, NGOs and corporate organisations in over 50 countries over the past 30 years. He works mostly with executive teams and individual leaders using collaborative approaches to strategy formation, innovation and change. He has a particular interest in the use of extended epistemology in organisational work—bringing a wide array of creative approaches to enrich organisational dialogue and extend leaders' view of the systems they work in and across. He is influenced by Buddhist and Quaker approaches to human development, alongside contemporary organisational psychology, and by the psychosynthesis work of Roberto Assagioli. He has written widely on organisational strategy and leadership issues, and also writes fiction and poetry.

Philippa Hardman specialises in working with organisations to help them have better quality discussions about strategy and change. While she frequently consults to Boards and senior management teams, Philippa's work also focuses on enabling wider participation across the organisation to ensure that any changes are not only achieved but sustainable. She has extensive experience of working strategically with a wide range of private and public sector organisations in many countries. Philippa's career started as a translator with Volkswagen before joining PwC to train as a chartered accountant. She then moved into strategy consulting and held various positions at PwC and PA Consulting before moving to Ashridge Business School. There Philippa jointly led Ashridge Consulting's Strategy Engagement Practice and subsequently was its director of Resourcing and Performance. She is co-founding partner of GameShift, a collaborative hub which helps individuals, teams and organisations deliver better results through a creative process of reframing issues to allow new thinking to flourish.

6 Leadership for an Unknowable Tomorrow

Roger Delves

Leadership is one of the most researched areas in the field of management studies; however, despite all the research effort, scholars and practitioners are still trying to determine the key attributes that generate leadership success (Avolio, 2011; Bryman, 2011; Yukl, 1989). An important aspect of the growth in scholarship over the past three decades has been the attempt to understand how future leaders are best developed (Bass, 1997; Day et al., 2014; DeRue & Wellman, 2009).

No research could however have anticipated the seismic events of 2020, events which plunged entire nations into chaos, stretching public health services to the limit and beyond, while almost casually inflicting deadly wounds on swathes of industry and commerce—entire sectors such as leisure, travel and tourism, retail shopping, personal care—and simultaneously wreaking havoc on education systems, including the public examinations on which so much hung for hundreds of thousands of students around the world.

The pandemic struck tsunami-like but lingers more in the manner of the fallout from a nuclear event. It is as yet hard, as the end of 2020 beckons, to discern an emerging new normal for in truth despite the beginnings of a rollout of a vaccine, we are far from post-pandemic yet. Nevertheless, if ever we needed leadership, within and across industry and commerce, let alone politics, it is now. Yet how do we prepare leaders to lead in a tomorrow which is in many vital aspects unknowable? How can leaders ask their teams to follow them into such a tomorrow? We are used to following leaders who argue with logic and conviction. When both go

R. Delves (✉)
Practice, Ashridge Executive Education at Hult International Business School, Berkhamsted, UK

Faculty, Ashridge Executive Education at Hult International Business School, Berkhamsted, UK
e-mail: Roger.delves@ashridge.hult.edu

S. K. Dhiman, J. F. Marques (eds.), *Leadership After COVID-19*, Future of Business and Finance, https://doi.org/10.1007/978-3-030-84867-5_6

missing in action, what are we left with? The words of W.B. Yeats ring down through the years:

> The best lack all conviction, while the worst/Are full of passionate intensity (The Second Coming, 1921a)

Where Were We?

The start of the second decade of the twenty-first century seems a very long time ago. 2020 indeed feels like the longest year. Our pre-occupations at the start of the year were as different as the days seem distant. In the UK, the talk was all about getting Brexit done, with a freshly minted government gloating over a majority of more than 80 seats. In America it was re-election year. Trump versus a yet to be identified Democrat candidate. It was Australian brush-fire season, and as they raged, talk turned again to climate change. Flash floods in Jakarta did little to assuage fears that our biggest global concern was not nuclear war (despite North Korea's threats) but global warming. Greta Thunberg proves to be thought more trustworthy and credible than any current leadership figure on the world stage. There were continued protests in Hong Kong over the extradition bill and fears for autonomy. The Israeli prime minister was indicted for corruption, while China and America signed phase one of a new trade deal, despite distant alarm bells in Wuhan city, Hubei Province, places unknown to most, soon to become wearily familiar. Icelandic fishing company Samherji announced it would cease operations in Namibia. The company was embroiled in a bribery scandal there that resulted in the resignation of the Namibian Fisheries Minister and Justice Minister, as well as the arrest of two employees of South African banking corporation Investec.

In that single month are captured the major themes of leadership which dogged the first 20 years of the century. One is the ethical failure of leadership—the role of the leader in frauds, scams and swindles. The other is the failure of leaders to lead with convincing amounts of emotional intelligence or humanity to persuade their teams that they are worthy of being followed.

Let's look at ethical failures of leadership. The millennium started badly with the Enron scandal. It declared bankruptcy on December 2nd 2001, with its shares trading at less than a dollar each, down from a high of just under 100 dollars a share. At the heart of the scandal were deceptively named Special Purpose Vehicles (SPVs) and Special Purpose Entities (SPEs) dreamed up by the corrupt leadership of the organization to hide mountains of debt and toxic assets. These innocent acronyms were the forerunners of the Collateralised Debt Obligations or CDOs which were at the centre of the sub-prime mortgages business which led to the credit crunch. This banking collapse of 2008 led to the fall of Lehman Brothers, then America's fourth largest bank, Bear Sterns, Carlyle Capital Corporation, the UK's Northern Rock and many more. It very nearly brought down Merrill Lynch (only saved by a takeover by Bank of America), AIG (saved by an $85 bn emergency government loan), Freddie Mac, Fanny Mae, HBOS (taken over by Lloyds. Following special dispensation and the setting aside of UK competition law), The Royal Bank of Scotland (bailed out by the British Government) and the Alliance and Leicester. It is not going too far to say that the entire American and British banking systems were in danger of collapse.

Lehman's problem was that it had a huge commercial property loan book, securitized on sub-prime debt. It was the commercialization of that sub-prime debt that was at the centre of the financial crisis—and the selling of it as if it were triple-A rated stock. Somewhere in the midst of it all was some very unethical decision-making based on questionable motives—until, perhaps, one looks at the huge bonus payments made to brokers who successfully sold CDOs for their employers during the first 7 or 8 years of this century. Faced with the perverse imperative of a temptation in the form of a bonus running into millions of dollars, few brokers could or would resist the chance to sell these self-evidently worthless bundles of debt.

While the world's financial markets (and much of the commercial world) were still in deep distress in 2009, with austerity the new buzzword, a peculiarly British scandal broke which engulfed many politicians serving at Westminster as Members of Parliament. A national newspaper's investigative journalism revealed that for years there had been serial abuse of the system of allowances and expenses allowed to Members of Parliament (MPs). Such self-serving greed aroused wide-spread anger among the British public, particularly as the effects of the credit crunch were being felt by many at exactly the time that this scandal broke. The result was many resignations, sackings, de-selections and early retirements across all political parties. Four of the more egregious offenders faced criminal proceedings. Described as Parliament's Darkest Day by no less an authority than The Times newspaper (it was rival publication The Telegraph which broke the story and ran with the revelations for several weeks) what was perhaps most striking about this scandal was that every political colour and every level of politician from Cabinet Minister to first-term newbie were represented in the Rogue's Gallery of miscreants. United by greed and a sense of entitlement to more than they were due, the politicians did much to undermine faith in public leadership because this misbehaviour was so tawdry; cheating on expenses and being caught is somehow simultaneously both mundane and belittling.

Equally questionable but in some ways even more incomprehensible is the VW Clean Diesel scandal which engulfed the very highest echelons of leadership of this global car manufacturer in 2015. In short, in an effort to boost sales, VW fitted so-called Defeat Devices to VW and Audi diesel cars manufactured for the US market designed to allow them to pass emissions tests when in fact the engines were emitting nitrogen oxide pollutants up to 40 times the legal limit. These pollutants were without doubt contributing to air pollution, exacerbating respiratory diseases in sufferers and leading to premature death. Martin Winterkorn, CEO at the time of the scandal, resigned in the face of the evidence that he was a knowing contributor. His replacement, Mattias Muller, ex-CEO of VW subsidiary Porsche, has subsequently been mired in accusations that he too was at least aware of the activity. As of June 2020, the scandal has cost VW $33 bn in fines, penalties, financial settlements and buyback costs. Winterkorn and Oliver Schmidt, former GM for VW's engineering and environmental operation in the US, have both faced criminal charges, but it is glaringly obvious that such activity could not take place without the knowing involvement of huge numbers of management figures across both Germany and the United States.

Staying with the automotive trade, we might end this sad review of leaders and leadership in the first two decades of this millennium by singling out Carlos Ghosn. He was CEO of Nissan-Renault-Mitsubishi and by the mid-twenty teens he'd amassed personal compensation of around $120 m over a period of a couple of decades. After a whistleblower reported him, he was accused of misreporting his salary and compensation and was fined $15 m by the SEC in 2018. He then fled Japan for The Lebanon rather than stand trial. His whistleblower was also found to be overcompensating himself during an investigation by an external law firm instigated by his own whistleblowing.

The share price consequences to Nissan-Renault-Mitsubishi, to VW and their family of brands, the reputational damage to the British House of Parliament, the loss of savings and damage done to pension funds and the loss of jobs caused across developed countries by the sub-prime mortgages/CDO mis-selling and associated credit crunch, by the collapse of Enron simply cannot be over-stated. Ethical failures of leadership were a cancer affecting the global corporate body as the second decade of the twenty first century drew to its close.

So what about the failures in emotional intelligence? Goleman and Boyatzis developed with the Hay Group (now part of Korn Ferry) the Emotional and Social Competence Inventory (ESCI). Its 12 scales map onto the four Competencies of the EQ model developed by Goleman and Boyatzis and published in *Emotional Intelligence – why it can matter more than IQ* (1996). The four competencies (Self-Awareness; Self-Management; Social Awareness; Relationship Management) neatly summarize the four areas in which the unsuccessful leader tends to come to grief. Leadership failures are rarely due to lack of cognitive skill; instead, leaders fail because they aren't self-aware enough to see their own shortcomings, or they lack the ability or willingness to self-manage into a better space, or they can't communicate adequately or build quality relationships, or create places of psychological safety (Edmondson, 2018), or see or prevent conscious or unconscious bias, or inspire or motivate individuals or groups.

Where Are We Now?

How can we help leaders to address these shortcomings in EQ, especially when we understand, as we must, that in the post-Covid emerging landscape the premium placed on emotional intelligence will be greater than ever, as followers look to leaders for guidance through a fraught environment for which the acronym VUCA seems utterly inappropriate.

An EFMD SIG (European Federation for Management Development Special Interest Group) set up in 2018 explored the future of leadership development. In its 2019 report it said, *In a world within which the complexity of running organizations in the 21st-century challenges tried and tested models of leadership, and disruption of whole industries is either a reality or an ever-present cloud in the contemporary business landscape, helping leaders to cope, perform and shape their organizations has become an acute and necessary challenge.*

Business schools, traditionally a cornerstone of established teaching and understanding, may not be as appropriate as they once were seen to be. Johan Roos, the Chief Academic Officer of Hult International Business School, sponsors of the SIG, had this to say as he launched it on its way:

> *For the most part, today's business schools are busy teaching and researching 20th century management principles and, in effect, leading the parade towards yesterday.* (Delves & Paine, 2019)

This report pre-dates the pandemic and of course examinations of the state of leadership and leadership development are hardly new. Moreover, as Bass and Steidlmeier (1999) memorably noted, leadership is a many-headed hydra, that alternately shows the faces of Saddam Hussein and Pol Pot, as well as those of Nelson Mandela and Mother Theresa. There is ample evidence that unethical leadership did not come to a sudden halt with the onset of Covid-19.

Nevertheless, what Covid-19 has done is change the landscape not only of business but the landscapes in which we live and learn and play, in which we get sick and try to get better, in which we try to keep our jobs, try to raise and educate our families, try to stay connected to our friends and loved ones, try to go on holiday. We will never see yesterday again, and we can barely glimpse tomorrow. To return to Yeats,

> All changed, changed utterly/A terrible beauty is born (1921b)

Our terrible beauty may be far more all-encompassing than Yeats's but like him we must find a way to come to terms with it. Here is where leaders must step forward. Unlike the credit crunch, this pandemic truly is global in reach and captures Presidents as readily as paupers. Leadership will need to be shown across all aspects of society, divergent thinking leading to a re-imagining of how we work, learn and play. Shibboleths must be shattered and the immediate impulse—to retrench, to shelter behind borders that are utterly invisible to a virus, or behind beliefs that are utterly inappropriate (*drink bleach*, or *this is the worst nature has got*)—cast aside in favour of collaborative, borderline-agnostic thinking, action and leadership. Easy to demand. Harder to deliver. But is there perhaps an approach to leaders and to leadership which, even in the fog of today's uncertainty, would serve tomorrow well?

What Do We Need for Tomorrow?

Stephen Covey's Principle-centred Leadership (1999) described principles as *self-evident, self-validating natural laws*. Covey's point was that principles apply at all times and in all places. Whether or not we believe in them, they have proved effective through centuries of human history. They are self-evident in that when we hear them, we tend to say, "well yes, of course!" and they are self-validating in that when we apply them, they prove themselves to be good and true. Importantly, unlike values which are strongly held, internal and subjective lasting beliefs that certain modes of conduct or end-states of existence are more desirable than others and are activated by, yet transcend any particular objective or situation (Rokeach, 1949), principles such as Covey's are objective and external.

Covey's famous analogy was to compare values with a map—useful for as long as the map was accurate, but like values, maps change over time, often due to external forces. Principles, meanwhile, are like a compass: north is now where it was millennia ago and where it will be long after this century has been forgotten even by antiquarians.

Covey's four principles were what he called four internal sources of strength: Security (sense of worth); Guidance (the direction we receive); Wisdom (the understanding we develop) and Power (the capacity to act).

We can look at these principles and develop them into a model for post-pandemic leadership principles which will serve leaders and leadership well for tomorrow and beyond.

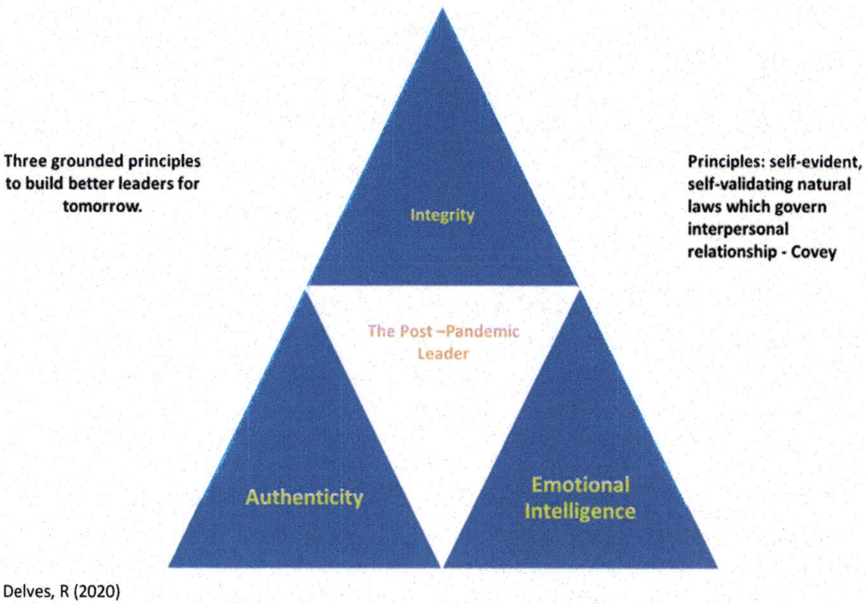

Delves (2020)

Act with Integrity

As Hannah et al. point out (2011) modern organizations have been characterized as morally complex environments that impose significant ethical demands on organizational actors. Leaders are required to make difficult choices. But the undeniable fact remains that were leaders only to act with integrity, so many of the frauds, scams and unacceptable behaviours of the past 20 years (and 20 millennia) would immediately become impossible for them to contemplate. One challenge with integrity is to agree a definition. *Adherence to moral and ethical principles; soundness of moral character; honesty* is the definition at dictionary.com and the issue is immediately obvious: what are "moral and ethical principles" and what is moral character? These are elastic and subjective concepts. Goleman, in his 1995 book *Emotional Intelligence* defines integrity as a three-part process:

1. Discerning right from wrong
2. Acting on what you discern
3. Saying openly that you are acting on your understanding of right from wrong

Evidently there are times when the first step is extraordinarily hard, and times when it is very straightforward. Equally, step two will sometimes be very easy to undertake and sometimes will require all our courage. Step three is the step that keeps us honest: we must be prepared to say that what we do we do because we believe it has integrity. We cannot try to hide our deeds or to describe them as something other than what they are, even if others will say that by their definition, that action lacks integrity.

We can discern and fail to act, and that makes us unfit to lead, particularly in the febrile atmosphere which is likely to prevail for the foreseeable future (insofar as any future is foreseeable from where we are today). Or we can fail to discern, which makes us unfit in a different way. If we can both discern and act appropriately but we lack the belief in our own integrity to lay claim to our discerning and our actions as having integrity, then we may lack the strength of character to lead.

When we act with integrity, we engage with two of Covey's four principles: **Wisdom**, in that we use the understanding we develop to discern right from wrong, and **Power**, in that we engage with the capacity to act, in this case acting on what we discern to be right.

Integrity is underpinned by our sense of personal values. Personal values are prescriptive beliefs about abstract ideal **modes of behaviour** (generosity, helpfulness, loyalty, fidelity) and **end-states of existence** (knowledge, comfort, skill, understanding) that are activated by, yet transcend any particular objective or situation (Rokeach, 1973).

Rokeach (1973) identifies two types of values: **Terminal Values** are the valued self-sufficient end-states of existence that a person strives to achieve. Examples are levels or degrees of knowledge, security, independence, skill, understanding which are sought. Meglino and Ravlin (1998) point out that a distinguishing feature of Terminal Values is that they are pursued for their own sake. **Instrumental Values** are valued modes of behaviour rather than states of existence. Consider courage, generosity, helpfulness, charity, consistency, loyalty or fidelity. Understandably there is often a link between Terminal and Instrumental. We pursue knowledge around sustainability (e.g. sustainable agriculture) because we want to help alleviate poverty and famine. The Terminal supports the Instrumental.

Positive values or ideals are therefore situation-independent, or what Schwartz (1994) describes as self-transcendent. These present themselves as other-directed values such as honesty, equality, social justice, consistency, reliability, loyalty. It is this self-transcendence that allows such positive values to support and underpin the sense of integrity which we have and the acts of integrity which we undertake. Schwartz (1994) also identifies self-enhancement values, which equate to self-directed values (consider personal success, power, gratification). These are positive values if well-managed and controlled.

Because values are strongly held subjective beliefs, values which others hold to be bad or wrong or challenging can of course be held by individuals and groups. When such beliefs underpin their sense of integrity, then others will challenge that integrity and the actions that stem from it.

Several scholars use the term Authentic Leader in association with values discussions to describe those leaders who rely on a set of values which are based on doing what is right and fair for all stakeholders (Bass & Steidlmeier, 1999; Luthans & Avolio, 2003; May et al., 2003).

Behave with Authenticity

May et al. (2003) take us back to the last quarter of the last century and remind us that even then losses due to ethical corporate meltdowns and inauthentic leadership cost the world economy hundreds of billions of dollars. Luthans and Avolio (2003) describe the contrasting authentic leaders as engaging in "self-transcending behaviours because they are intrinsically motivated to be consistent with high-end, other-regarding values that are shaped and developed through the leader's life experiences". George and Sims (2007) suggest that authentic leaders follow their own beliefs with courage and conviction, while serving others, being genuine and pursuing personal growth. Avolio et al. (2009) define authentic leadership as transparent and ethical, while encouraging openness and follower input to make decisions. Michie and Gooty (2005) define authenticity thus: "one acts in accordance with the true self, expressing oneself in ways that are consistent with inner thoughts and feelings". Luthans and Avolio (2003) see in the authentic leader a "seamless link between espoused values, behaviours and actions…building the moral capacity of leaders to make selfless judgements". This places values at the heart of an objective, codified code of conduct which will lead to predictable and consistent behaviours.

Authentic leadership can have no egotistic intent. The authentic leader's focused route to achieving the team or organization's objective must be an altruistic concern for others. This is not to say that leaders cannot be self-interested. A leader who has no personal ambition is unlikely to lead with the drive required by today's organizations. But an authentic leader's motive cannot be only self-interest. Self-examination is the surest way to know that your decisions are driven by a desire for mutual altruism or moral altruism. May et al. (2003) say that authentic leadership is ultimately about the leader knowing himself or herself and being transparent in linking inner desires, expectations, and values to the way they behave as leader every day, in each and every interaction and linking their own expectations and goals to those of the team. Knowing oneself and being true to oneself are the essential qualities of authentic leadership, and with those characteristics in place, the authentic leader is well-placed to provide the leadership that the post-pandemic emerging new normal requires.

May et al. (2003) capture the essence of authenticity in saying that authentic individuals are at the centre of authentic leadership and authentic leadership is at the base of all positive, socially constructive forms of leadership. Authentic leaders create authenticity in followers and create a culture of authenticity within organizations.

When we behave with authenticity, we engage with Covey's principle of **Security**, because we behave in a way that reflects our sense of worth, and with his principle of **Wisdom**, because our authenticity is grounded in the understanding that we develop.

It is important to believe that most leaders have the innate potential to become authentic leaders. Anecdotal evidence over many years suggests that authentic senior leaders can often recognize in others authentic leadership potential. Nevertheless, releasing and maximizing that potential requires a great deal of support through provision of, for example, coaching, through consistent modelling of best behaviour from senior leaders, and ideally though structured management development interventions to give emerging authentic leaders the opportunity to explore authenticity in a risk-free environment. These are of course not ideal times. The organizational challenge, when there is immense, often unexpected pressure on the bottom line form the effects of the pandemic (which in many industries is an extinction-level event) is to focus on the task of survival. However, critical to that task is the nature of the leadership that an organization experiences. The organization that survives, and in time may thrive, will be the one with the better leadership. Understanding what constitutes "better" therefore becomes itself a critical key to survival, and providing "better" with the space and the resources to grow and flourish becomes equally important.

Management development interventions are useful, if they are appropriately run, if they are an affordable activity and if there is the possibility to spare leaders from the business of leading. Alone they are not enough and often they will not be an option. What must exist is a committed, inter-connected approach utilizing modelled best behaviour from top management, ideally supported by internal workplace coaching and/or mentoring programmes (though to what degree past experience is relevant to an unknowable tomorrow is open to question), and workplace learning. Established and emerging leaders who seem able to offer authenticity should be nurtured and used to bring on other green shoots. Authenticity should be established as a benchmark for leadership behaviour within the organization.

Be Emotionally Intelligent

Peter Salovey and John Mayer first proposed their theory of EI in 1990, reframing it, first in 1997 then with David Caruso, in 2000. It was a model that discussed how we think about feeling: a model of *intelligence*. Goleman's 1995 EQ model of EQ shows the four competencies and the associated affective and cognitive skills and behaviours which later came to be honed to the 12 scales of the ESCI. He formulates EI as a theory of *performance*. The better your EQ, the better your performance.

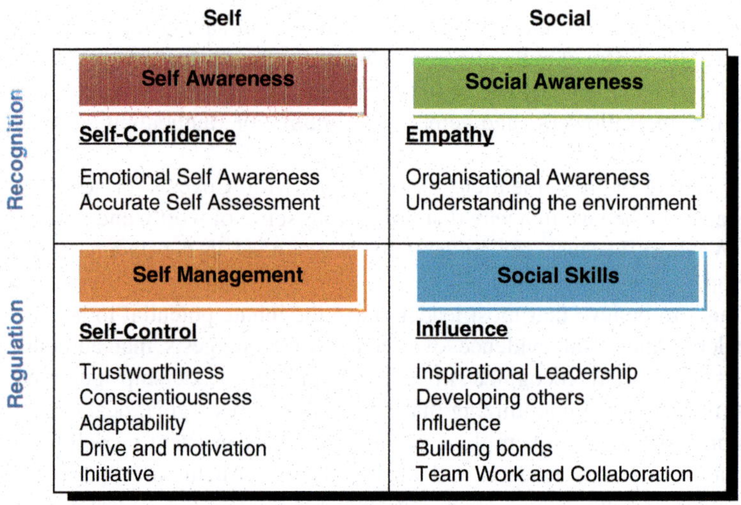

Goleman, D. (1995) *Emotional Intelligence: Why it matters more than IQ*

Goleman was always very clear that these skills can and could be developed—by anyone with the willingness to try. As students, Goleman and Boyatzis worked with the then-new concept of competencies with David McClelland at Harvard. Goleman's intention was to specify emotional intelligence competencies used by outstanding leaders which could be assessed objectively—hence his keen interest in an instrument such as the ESCI to support the research.

EQ is now long established as a differentiator in leadership success. Boyatzis's 1982 study of more than 2000 supervisors, middle managers and executives across 12 organizations showed that all but two of the 16 abilities setting the star performer apart from the average were emotional competencies (Boyatzis, 1982). An analysis of job competencies used by Spencer and Spencer (1993) across 286 companies worldwide showed that 18 of the 21 competencies in their generic mode for distinguishing superior from average performers were EI based.

Fleming (2018) tells us that emotionally intelligent leadership is not about sparkling levels of charisma, with no depth or sincerity, but is more about "living and exuding honest and values-led behaviors". These are the building blocks for effective leadership.

As EQ has gained a stronger and stronger mainstream foothold during the 20 years of this century, so have leaders' reasons for lacking emotional intelligence become less and less valid, convincing or sustainable. A deficiency in emotional intelligence is now seen as a significant career inhibitor, while the establishment of emotional intelligence as the differentiating factor in a leader's success continues to build momentum, even as the distinctions between being values-led, being inspirational, being adaptive, being a servant-leader become blurred. Increasingly, the term *being emotionally intelligent* seems to embrace all that is needed or required.

Emotionally intelligent leaders are engaging with each of Covey's Principles as they develop the two inward-looking elements of EQ, those of self-awareness and self-management: **Security** (a sense of worth developed through self-awareness); **Guidance** (the direction we receive, developed through the seeking of feedback, which also contributes to self-awareness); **Wisdom** (the understanding we develop which contributes to self-awareness) and **Power** (the capacity to act, which is evidenced through self-management).

Emotional competencies seem to operate most powerfully in synergistic groupings, with the evidence suggesting that mastery of a "critical mass" of competencies is necessary for superior performance (Boyatzis, Goleman & Rhee, 1999). Anecdotal evidence suggests that those who develop the skills and behaviours attached to the competence of Self-Awareness then find it easier to do the same within the competence of Self-Management. The competencies of Social Awareness and Relationship Management by their nature contain degrees of overlap, so once again developed skills and behaviours in one will lead to an increased ability to develop similar levels of skill and behaviours in the other.

Developing emotionally intelligent individuals can help to create emotionally intelligent teams and work spaces. Emotionally intelligent behaviour helps to foster a climate of trust and helps leaders to build places of psychological safety.

Where Do Principles Lead in Practice?

The challenge we are identifying here is that it is hard to help those who must lead through today and tomorrow in the way we normally have, because that normal way was to focus on leadership practice. As the landscape within which this practice took place has been swept away by the pandemic, we are left to ask if this practice has any role to play in the today and tomorrow we now inhabit.

We have established that our three principles are valid, not only because they are grounded in Covey's self-evident and self-validating natural laws, but also because they are supported by a body of academic literature. We might argue that our current inflection point makes neither the literature nor those natural laws valid any longer, but we need a starting point of some sort to develop a post-pandemic leadership practice. As Fleming (2018) points put, we all know that leadership is not what happens when the *status quo* is maintained, but when disruption happens. The starting point I am suggesting leads us to a leadership practice which exists already, but which needs to be re-stated so that we are clear both about what it means and what it demands of those who practice it.

Transformational Leadership

Transformational leadership is much more than the opposite of transactional leadership, but a useful starting point is to define that opposite. Bass and Steidlmeier (1999) called transactional leadership contingent reinforcement. Motivation is provided through promise, praise or reward (the carrot) while correction is provided by negative feedback, reprimands, disciplinary action or even dismissal (the stick). Whether in pursuit of the carrot or attempting to avoid the stick, those led transactionally can be infantalized by the style of leading, acting in a variety of ways which are wilfully childlike as they seek reward or seek to avoid punishment. This task-orientated leadership style is nevertheless time-efficient, has its place, and can seem particularly appropriate in environments where leaders feel they are only judged by results achieved. It is only when it is inappropriately used that it becomes inefficient or even damaging. Time-impoverished leaders can be drawn to it when it is not appropriate because it appears swift; however, when it is not suitable, and therefore when team members do not respond appropriately either to carrot or stick, it can too often be the embodiment of the old adage *more haste, less speed*. There is an overt risk that transactional leadership can be "grounded in a world view of self-interest" (Kanungo & Mendonca, 1996) or is "self-absorbing and manipulative" (Burns, 1978).

In contrast, transformational leadership is inclined to raise the level of human conduct. Kanungo (2001) describes transformational leadership as the development of a vision which informs and expresses the organization's mission, and lays the foundation for the organization's strategies, policies and procedures. It is therefore less tactical and more attitudinal—less about what we do than it is about how we do it. Where leaders are not at a level where they can influence corporate goals and ambitions, the transformational leader will create a sense of empowerment, and cause team members to feel a sense of being part of a shared vision around how to deliver their part of the bigger picture. Howell and Avolio (1992) make the point that only leaders who are concerned for the common good—who are fundamentally other-centric—can be transformational, excluding therefore those who are at heart self-interested. This sense of other-centricity is one of the hallmarks of authenticity, confirming the role of authenticity in transformational leadership.

Transformational leadership contrasts with transactional leadership in that it is time consuming and it puts the relational aspects of leadership at the centre of the leader's role. This makes it very challenging for the pandemic and post-pandemic leader, who is and will be overwhelmed with *things to do* and oftentimes even despite the best intentions of the organization will be more rewarded for task completion, or at least for overt attention to tasks, than for relationship management and overt attention to those whose responsibility it should be in reality to undertake and complete the tasks. The transformational leadership approach requires the leader to have a good deal of discretionary time, and the knowledge and understanding to spend that time with and on people, inspiring and motivating, cultivating places of psychological safety, building coaching cultures, allowing people to fail and learn, in short creating an environment where productivity could increase and performance could improve.

The Bass and Avolio (1995) view of transformational leadership was summarized into the four domains or competencies that underpinned their Multifactor Leadership Questionnaire (MLQ). These are:

1. Inspirational Motivation
   (a) Talks optimistically about the future
2. Intellectual Stimulation
   (a) Re-examines critical assumptions
   (b) Questions suitability of assumptions
3. Individualized Consideration
   (a) Helps others discover their strength
4. Idealized Influence
   (a) Considers moral and ethical consequences of decisions
   (b) Goes beyond self-interest for the good of the Group

The links to our three leadership principles—act with integrity, with authenticity and with emotional intelligence—are very clear, suggesting that the principled leader will be, or at least can be transformational.

The EFMD SIG report into innovations in leadership development completed in 2019 looked at live leadership development innovations taking place within some of the 12 member companies within the SIG. When the changes in leader behaviours and attitudes generated by the new approaches to leadership development were summarized by the members of the SIG, what emerged was this (Table 6.1):

Table 6.1 Shifts in leader behaviours and attitude that increased productivity and improved performance

From	To
Power and control	Facilitation and enablement
Being certain	Exploring uncertainty
Individual success	The power of the team
Perfecting process	Innovating process
Managing uncertainty	Living with uncertainty
Occasional experiment	Permanent testing and learning
Being omniscient	Admitting you don't know
Punishing failure	Learning from failure
Low trust environment	High trust environment
Working it out on your own	Peer empowerment and sharing
Learning from content	Learning from experience
Static roles	Dynamic roles

Source: EFMD SIG Report: *Innovations in Leadership Development* January 2020

Mindset change was critical in order to create leaders able to see beyond their team or function and work holistically. The focus is on the leaders' role in empowering and convincing others to commit to transition—a *transformational change* leadership role.

Conclusions

A challenge for any paper exploring leadership and change after Covid-19, and writing such a paper at a point in time when infection rates are still rising in many countries and the vaccines which appear to offer the best way out of the pandemic have only just begun to be delivered in one single country (the UK) is of course the fog of uncertainty which obscures the context within which the leader is expected to work.

In the pandemic and post-pandemic world, leaders may well lack a sense of their own authenticity, a feeling of being grounded in something secure and unchanging as they seek to offer convincing leadership to others through change at a time of volatility, uncertainty, complexity and ambiguity. The very mindset they need may be elusive because of the prevailing circumstances.

The teams they lead may themselves be operating in some hybrid version of their previous incarnation or may be transitioning into a new version of their old selves where there is much less time spent together. Generating those elements which Schaufeli and Bakker (2004), Schaufeli (2013) said led to a sense of engagement—autonomy and self-efficacy, a safe environment and a positive culture—may be significantly more difficult in the emerging environment for teams than it was in the pre-pandemic environment. They will need to be led in a carefully transformational way to embrace their new form while maintaining or building on their past performance levels.

So this is why it is important that now, while we wait for the new normal to take shape, what we do with our leaders is not focus on practice, but help them to explore their readiness to lead from these points of principle, to make the mindset change that will allow them to be transformational.

Five Chapter Takeaways

1. Remember that tomorrow is unknowable but it cannot be undoable
2. Accept that transformational change is at the centre of everything that leaders will be asked to do
3. Agree that the three post-pandemic leadership principles (behave with emotional intelligence, authenticity and integrity) provide a guide to how we can think about leadership even before the post-pandemic new normal emerges
4. Understand that transformational leadership takes time and prioritizes interpersonal relational skills
5. Realize that the shifts in leader behaviour and attitude that increase productivity and improve performance are mindset changes around empowering others to commit to transition.

Five Reflection Questions

1. What can our organization do at this inflection point to ensure that the tendency to behaviour that is fraudulent and/or lacks integrity is buried with the virus?
2. The availability of a vaccine creates a watershed: what are the inequities that we can, should and must address as we rebuild business and social landscapes?
3. Are we as an organization doing enough right now to prepare leaders to lead through transformational change and to prepare followers to follow?
4. Do we currently place enough value on leadership development within our organization?
5. Does our pandemic or post-pandemic culture create leaders who focus on task completion at the expense of investing time in building high performing teams?

References

Avolio, B. J. (2011). *Full range leadership development*. Sage.

Avolio, B. J., Walumbwa, F. O., & Weber, T. J. (2009). Leadership: Current theories, research and future directions. *Annual Review of Psychology, 60*(1), 421–449.

Bass, B. M. (1997). *Does the transactional-transformational leadership paradigm transcend organizational & national boundaries?* www.psycnet.apa.org

Bass, B. M., & Avolio, B. J. (1995). *The multifactor leadership questionnaire*. Mind Garden.

Bass, B. M., & Steidlmeier, P. (1999). Ethics, character and authentic transformational leadership behaviour. *The Leadership Quarterly, 10*, 1999.

Boyatzis, R. E., Goleman, D., & Rhee, K. (1999). *Clustering competence from emotional intelligence: Insights from the emotional competence inventory (ECI) handbook of emotional intelligence*. Jossey-Bass.

Bryman, A. (2011). Research methods in the study of leadership. In *The Sage handbook of leadership*. Sage.

Burns, J. M. (1978). *Leadership*. Harper and Row.

Covey, S. (1999). *Principle centred leadership*. Simon & Schuster.

Day, D. V., Fleenor, J. W., Atwater, L. E., Sturm, R. E., & McKee, R. A. (2014). Advances in leadership and leader development: A review of 25 years of research and theory. *The Leadership Quarterly, 25*(1), 63–82.

Delves, R., & Paine, N., (2019). *Innovation in leadership EFMD SIG report*.

DeRue, D. S., & Wellman, N. (2009). Developing leaders by experience: The role of developmental challenge, learning orientation and feedback availability. *Journal of Applied Psychology, 94*, 859. www.psycnet.apa.org

Edmondson, A. (2018). *The fearless organization: Creating psychological safety in the workplace for learning, innovation, and growth*. Wiley.

George, W., & Sims, P. (2007). *True north: Discover your authentic leadership* (1st ed.). Jossey-Bass, a Wiley Imprint.

Goleman, D. (1996). *Emotional intelligence: Why it can matter more than IQ*. Bloomsbury Books.

Goleman, D., Boyatzis, R., & McKee, A. (2001). Primal leadership: The hidden driver of great performance. *Harvard Business Review*.

Hannah, S. T., Avolio, B. J., & Walumba, F. O. (2011). Relationship between authentic leadership, moral courage and ethical, pro-social behaviours. *Business Ethics Quarterly, 21*(4), 555–578.

Howell, J. M., & Avolio, B. J. (1992). The ethics of charismatic leadership: Submission or liberation? *Academy of Management Executive, 6*(2), 43–54.

Kanungo, R. N. (2001). Ethical values of transactional and transformational leaders. *Canadian Journal of Administrative Sciences, 18*(4), 257–265.
Kanungo, R. N., & Mendonca, N. (1996). *Ethical dimensions in leadership*. Sage Publications.
Luthans, F., & Avolio, B. J. (2003). Authentic leadership: A positive development approach. In *Cameron, Dutton and Quinn's positive organizational scholarship: Foundations of a new discipline*. Berrett-Koehler.
May, D. R., Chan, A. Y. L., Hodges, T. D., & Avolio, B. J. (2003). Developing the moral component of authentic leadership. *Organizational Dynamics, 32*, 2003.
Meglino, B. M., & Ravlin, E. C. (1998). Individual values in organizations: Concepts, controversies & research. *Journal of Management, 24*(3), 351.
Michie, S., & Gooty, J. (2005). Values, emotions and authenticity: Will the real leader please stand up? *The Leadership Quarterly, 16*, 441–457.
Rokeach, M. (1973). *The nature of human values*. Free Press.
Schaufeli, W. B. (2013). What is engagement? In *Employee engagement in theory and practice*. Routledge.
Schaufeli, W. B., & Bakker, A. B. (2004). Job demands, job resources and their relationship with burnout and engagement: A multi-sample study. *Journal of Organizational Behavior, 25*, 293. https://doi.org/10.1002/job.248
Schwartz, S. H. (1994). Are there universal aspects in the structure and content of human values? *Journal of Social Issues, 50*, 19.
Spencer, L. M., & Spencer, S. M. (1993). *Competency at work: Models for superior performance*. John Wiley & Sons Inc.
Yeats, W. B. (1921a). *The second coming in Michael Robartes and the Dancer*.
Yeats, W. B. (1921b). *Easter 1916, in Michael Robartes and the Dancer*.
Yukl, G. (1989). Managerial leadership: a review of theory & research. *Journal of Management, 15*, 251. https://journals.sagepub.com/

Roger Delves is currently a Fellow of the RSA and educated at Oxford with a first career with international ad agency DMB&B, where he was a board director of the London office, Roger taught at Cranfield University School of Management before joining Ashridge in 2008. He is the Associate Dean of Faculty and a Professor of Practice, specializing in leadership. His academic interests are around authenticity and emotional intelligence, transformational leadership and team engagement. Co-author of *Fifty Management Dilemmas* and co-editor of *Inspiring Leadership*, he is a regular contributor of articles to professional journals and recently co-wrote a paper delivered at Euram 2020. He has taught all over the world, delivering material for tailored, open and degree qualification programs. At Ashridge he has at various times been Director of the Ashridge MBA, Director of Ashridge General Management portfolio of degree programmes and Dean of Degree programmes. He sat on the Academic Board of Hult from June 2015 to June 2019.

7 Coevolutive Leadership for an After COVID-19 World

Derson Lopes Jr. and Paulo Hayashi Jr.

Introduction: COVID-19 and the Need for a New Leadership Style

COVID-19 has brought countless problems and changes to the world. In addition to a serious health crisis, more than one million deaths in the world and economic issues, the isolation public policies due to the pandemic have substantially altered working conditions. Thousands of people suffered deep impacts work wise, as job loss, compulsory vacations, and journey and salary reduction, changing the work dynamic to home office, holiday anticipation, appointments' changes, goals adjustments, among others. All those changes, on top of family impacts and tensions provoked by the risk of infection itself, have brought uncertainties, fear and a great stress potential at work.

A recent study has investigated psychological repercussions and psychiatric symptoms of the Chinese workforce associated with the COVID-19 pandemic (Tan et al., 2020). Of 673 respondents, 10.8% attended to post-traumatic stress disorder (PTSD) diagnosis criteria after returning to work. Besides, 12.0% revealed moderate to severe concerns about their physical health. In general, low levels of anxiety (3.8%), depression (3.7), stress (1.5%), and insomnia (2.3%) were found, there were also no significant differences in respect with psychiatric symptomology among workers/technicians and executives/managers. The stress in professional

D. Lopes Jr. (✉)
Aspectum Business School, State University of Campinas – UNICAMP, Amazonia Adventist University – FAAMA, Campinas, SP, Brazil

Pinhais, PR, Brazil
e-mail: derson.lopes@aspectum.com.br

P. Hayashi Jr.
State University of Campinas – UNICAMP, Limeira, SP, Brazil
e-mail: paulo.hayashi@fca.unicamp.br

S. K. Dhiman, J. F. Marques (eds.), *Leadership After COVID-19*, Future of Business and Finance, https://doi.org/10.1007/978-3-030-84867-5_7

activities results in the individual perception of not being capable of attending work demands, with consequent psychic suffering, behavior changes, negative attitudes toward work, and cardiovascular risk augmented (Quick & Henderson, 2016).

The restructuring and management of professional activities due to the pandemic have led to significant changes within the organization and work management. The International Labour Organization (ILO) (2020) monitored some studies about the COVID-19 pandemic impact on the working universe. The organization reported that by now, 4 out of 5 people (81%), from 3.3 billion global workforce, are affected by the total or partial closing of workplaces, with an estimate reduction of about 6.7% of their work journey, that equals to 195 million of full time workers. Besides that, Global Workplace Analytics—GWA (2020) estimates indicate that 25–30% of work force is working from home several days a week by the end of 2021 because of COVID-19 influence.

This context increased the need for a new leadership style in the organizations. The change is already in place, aroused by the digital transformation and impacted by the ubiquitous presence of social media (Li, 2010), however, the COVID-19 pandemic has accelerated this process in 5 up to 10 years. With younger groups, influenced by the shared economy and currently adapting to physical, mental and socially to the social isolation impacts, leaders need to develop a new form of leadership, more participative, open and, above all, willing to share. A new leadership style does not abandon essential and consolidated concepts proposed by previous models, but it adapts its interpretation and language to the current situation of the organizations and the world (Putriastuti & Stasi, 2019).

This chapter will explore the coevolutive leadership, an updated proposal which aims to keep its relevance, as well as facing complex situations and emergencies such as the one experienced in the pandemic scenario.

Coevolutive Leadership: Initial Concepts

In spite of its theme's popularity and the leadership concept to be considered as a Holy Grail that solves (almost) every issue and transforms the way an organization operates drastically, taking it from a loss position to solvency and profit, gathering investors' trust, there is still room for development on this matter (Dries & Pepermans, 2012). That's due to the rapid and radical changes that many business scenarios have been facing, as well as a kind of a dense, provocative and threatening fog, which hangs over the future of society and consequently, of organizations. If in the 1980s the Organizational Ecology Theory, created and spread by Hannah and Freeman, was very popular, certainly 40 years later, the theme is recaptured with deeper changes' possibilities in both traditional and new sectors (Burt, 2009). For example, in the trainers and sports products segment, it is possible to customize a player's name on football boots by a derisory price. The name is printed, being part of the product. In a radical sense, Adidas starts to offer trainers' sole 100% customized to its clients' feet shape, through carbon 3D printing technology. However, not only mass customization will occur, a significant niche will also be occupied by companies that use 3D technology in a *gourmet* sense, such as Kathrien Herdewyn, from Continuum, Iris Van Herpen. So, with technology comes the emergence of new opportunities while so many others fade away, including new leadership challenges (Shapiro, 2019).

The coevolutive leadership is born precisely in this turbulent and troubled context, in new disruptive technologies, as well as in the pandemic scenario. Coevolution is a biology concept that consists in the process in which two or more species evolve simultaneously in response to selective pressures exercised by one another (Carmona et al., 2015). This process can explain why some species are co adapted, that is mutually adapted, as it happens with pollinizer insects and flowers (Friedman, 2009). Similarly, the coevolutive leadership considers leaders and employees in joint evolution and continuous collaboration. In other words, help yourself by helping others. The employees exercise influences on their leaders, the leaders influence their employees, the organization promotes influence upon all, though in these collaborations and partnerships, Coevolution happens. The coevolutive leader comprehends that his success depends on people, his integration with them, and in this symbioses lies everyone's growth: employees, leaders, and organizations. The important fact is the joint growth in the long term, as well as visualizing improvements as a whole, in an attempt to overcome barriers and difficulties. The coevolutive leadership foundation can be seen in the framework presented in Fig. 7.1.

As it can be seen, the foundation of the coevolutive leadership is the Leader Vision, developed from his purpose and connected to his Conviction, which, in its turn is formed by his personal magnetism and trust. Conviction enables the leader to co-create his Vision, which is the goal set to his team and organization, i.e., the future to be accomplished. It consists in a two-way street. Both Conviction influences Vision, as in the way around. In its turn, Motivation, coevolutive leadership's third dimension, is the channel that connects Vision and Conviction with people. People do not take over the Vision, but interact with it and transform it as well. To

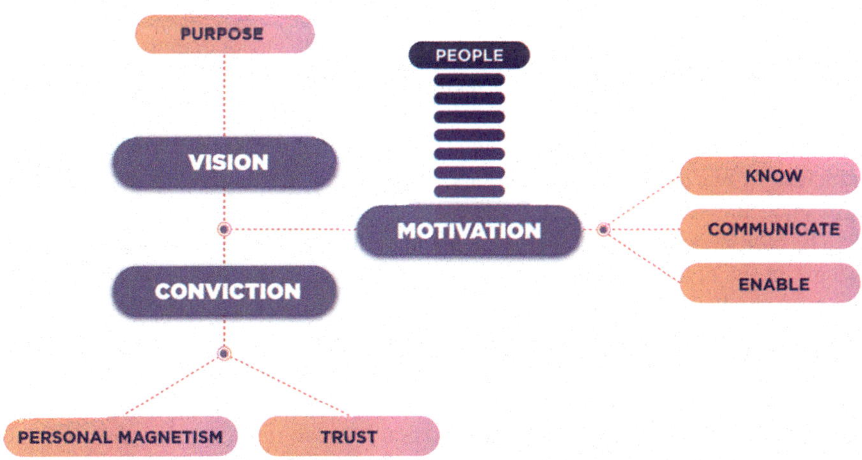

Fig. 7.1 Coevolutive Evolution Model. Fonte: Developed by the authors

create Motivation, the leader needs to get to know his group and respect their personal convictions, communicate properly with his team, allowing constant group interaction and enable his followers to reach the proposed goals. Each one of these elements will be approached further in details.

Vision

Business and administration books provide several definitions for the term *vision*. Some even believe it can be measured in the short term, others believe that it should always be feasible, but at the same time inspiring, among other variations. In a synthetic and practical way, we can understand vision as a scenario to be reached and pursued by the company (Dubrin, 2016). An inspiring vision has in its composition excellence factors, which also boost companies to a higher stage. It does not mean it cannot be reached, however, when it is sought for, it acquires a completely new meaning and with it, a new future scenario is automatically drawn. In a broader and unrestricted view, having a vision consists in not to settle with what you have and focus on progress and growth. The dream, the inspiration, the desire and the need are entry doors to compose a thought provoking and challenging vision (Mohler, 2012; Ulrich et al., 1999).

The vision aims to prospect the future and take a start, in a proactive and anticipatory manner, the forthcoming changes that, certainly, are not just a few and, in certain way, will change society and the individual's behavior toward the other human beings, machines, human machines, etc. (Dries & Pepermans, 2012). If we remember the lessons as one of the classical administration precursors, the French Henry Fayol, in the administration function, the vision is related to the planning activity (Williams, 2018). More than ever, and not the way around, looking at the future becomes a critical activity for the business survival. The future is co-built, not in a restrained way to be reached in a paranoiac way. The future will be built gradually as new technologies and competitors emerge. Considering those aspects, there will hardly be time of tranquility and to rest. On the other hand, it will also be necessary to organize the organization's members in a *loosely-coupled organizational* way (Weick, 1976). This type of organization is characterized for being more flexible and adapted to changes than a rigid structured organization, such as the military structure or many religious institutions. Loosely coupled organizations must seek efficiency and flexibility, synergy and the right speed.

The current problem with vision is that it is often restricted to the minds of a few people in the organization, if not the minds of just a single person. As previously seen, by analyzing the entrepreneur, in a business someone has a big vision for his product, service, or company and starts acting like this vision, however, the individual forgets to share it with his employees, that is why he cannot win their hearts for his plan. By not sharing properly, the vision will not be realized or persecuted in so little time. For Senge (2010), shared vision is much more than an idea. It is the force that drives people's heart, an impactful power. People can even get excited with simple ideas, but a great well shared vision will be seen as existing and tangible for the whole team.

Shared vision demonstrates to everyone what we desire to create in our work. We can say vision is really shared when people start to have a similar image in mind, when they think about the future of their organization and want to achieve that level together. We can say shared vision can free energy and courage in people, it works as a spark that ignites the inner flame of each individual (Senge, 2010).

How to Develop a Shared Vision

Sharing a vision is not an easy task, however, it is a highly rewarding activity. We will analyze some factors, which boost vision sharing below.

- **Have the right people on the boat**: Collins (2001) analyzed winning companies in different sectors and listed common characteristics among them, disregarding their segment. In other aspects, he highlighted that winning companies worry about having the right people first, so that they can worry about what they will actually do afterwards. That is a very important principle in the strategic change sphere. When the company is composed by a team which has committed and competent people, who are constantly seeking for professional enhancements and organizational growth, it will not be difficult to convince them about this change. However, how can we get the right ones? First, hire the right people. Most problems companies have with employees could have been foreseen through a competent recruiting and selection process. When seeking someone to work for your organization, set standards. Analyze the candidate's story, challenges he accepted and transformations provoked by him. Also, verify if his personal values align to the organization's. Second, to have the right people, it is necessary to lead in the right way. Qualified and committed people are highly targeted by the market, due to their rareness. Therefore, even if you hire the right people, if you do not lead them in the right way, they will leave. Offer autonomy and responsibility, personal and professional development and then, you will be able to demand results. Leading, and not controlling people, will attract the best talents. Finally, develop people. Continuous development programs keep people prepared, arouse new challenges and promote a responsibility bond between the employee and the organization.
- **Encourage personal vision:** companies cannot dream, people can. Therefore, an organization vision will always be born with people (Senge, 2010). Thus, it is fundamental for leaders to encourage people to create their own vision for the company, picture new scenarios and challenge current limits within the organization.
- **Transform personal vision in shared vision:** once individuals have visions for the company, it is time to conjugate these thoughts to synthetize them in the organizational vision. Although different indicators can be stablished, employees know the company and when there's integration between people and the organi-

zation, these scenarios will converge naturally to a common development point. It is important to listen to people in pursuit of improvement and innovation. Conjugating several thoughts will always be broader and more powerful than one person's thought. It is possible that one single person in a hierarchical position has a much clearer idea about where the company may find its blue ocean than the executive's vision.

- **Demonstrate the benefits of achieving vision:** to move forward toward a direction, people need to believe their new position will be better than the current one. To promote a strategic realignment and repositioning, you need to convince people that a new scenario to be reached will be better than the current level the company is at. The shared vision should show everyone the proposed strategic changes need to be done so the company continues to grow, being competitive and discovering new markets. Everyone needs to see they will be personally benefitted with the new strategy. Few people will be willing to engage in a change that will result in the end of their jobs or that accounts for personal losses. That does not mean strategic change cannot produce staff reduction, it is quite common in certain markets and segments, however, people who will be part of the change need to be the ones who will remain in the organization and changes need to be for the better.

Sharing vision is not just a technical exercise, but exercising leadership in a deeper level of taking people of their comfort zones and lead them toward growth (Ulrich et al., 1999). Without an aggregating vision, there will not be a meaningful strategic change. Not only an aggregating and shared vision, but a vision that causes discomfort with the present in which it generates beneficial changes and progress. As vision is built by everyone, conjugated in a common thought and inspired by its transformational power, the vision does not belong to people, if not people belong to the vision (Senge, 2010). It is exactly at this point in which the company goes beyond their founders or executives' identities and has its own life and energy to face the external market toward its goals. In coevolutive leadership, vision offers the direction to be followed. On the other hand, conviction and motivation offer the union and pace of execution. In addition, intrinsically in relation to vision and purpose, such as the relationship of the two sides of the same coin. With that, it is important to highlight the role of Viktor Frankl in the matter of life purpose.

Purpose

Viktor Frankl, Austrian psychiatrist born in 1905 in a Jewish family, created one of the main concepts related to having a meaningful life, which is worth living besides all setbacks. In the 1940s, Frankl was a young Viennese Jewish doctor, interested in psychoanalysis and psychology, who even attended circles of people interested in the works of Freud and Adler. Nevertheless, his life changed drastically in 1942 when he was taken to a Nazi concentration camp (Frankl, 2000). Although he had survived, he lost his wife, a brother and his parents in this period. From his life in three different camps, Frankl wrote a book named *Men's Searching for Meaning*

(Frankl, 2006). By observing people who lived in the concentration camp, he realized some could bear the suffering and survive longer than others. When comparing different behaviors and reactions (himself included), the psychiatrist noticed a fundamental factor lied in all people with greater suffering resistance: the purpose of life (Frankl, 2006).

People who cultivate this purpose, although they faced the same adversities the others did, were able to see their lives beyond that tough moment. For some, the purpose was to reencounter their family, for others, returning to their city, for Frankl, exercising his profession and contributing to people's mental health. The doctor imagined himself teaching and lecturing after the end of the war, studying, publishing research and being relevant to society, which indeed happened.

Within this context, Frankl references the sentences that opens the chapter in his book, attributed to Nietzche: "He, who has a why to live for can bear almost any how." Applying it to the organizational context, Deci (1996) considers purpose as a motivation factor. Sinek (2011) affirms that leaders do not engage people by presenting what they should do, or even how, but inspiring them with why, in other words, creating, inspiring, and uniting people on a purpose that justifies their efforts at work. Sinek (2011) names this process as Golden Circle (Fig. 7.2).

The golden circle allows us to go to the heart of "why?" and thereby strengthen the purpose. With the right and understood purpose, conviction is generated. Stablishing a life purpose is building meaning to your actions, bringing meaning to your victories and defeats, being sure that every step in your life is worth because you see the real reason that justifies your existence. Besides that, the purpose is the seed of Vision.

To visualize that, let's consider the World Health Organization (WHO) of March 11th 2020 statement, in which the Coronavirus pandemic (Covid-19) was officially declared. The Director-general Tedros Ghebreyesus puts his vision that besides rapid speed of transmission of new cases (more than 118,000 in 114 countries) the pandemic must be dealt with in a way that does not cause panic or fear. In the words of the Director-general himself: "We have therefore made the assessment that COVID-19 can be characterized as a pandemic. Pandemic is not a word to use

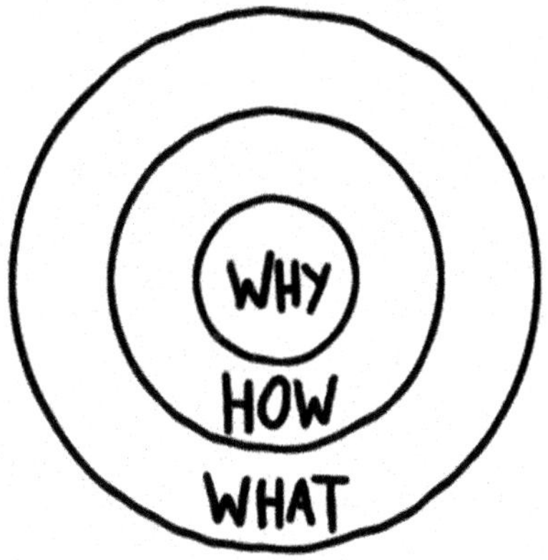

Fig. 7.2 Golden Circle. (Source: Sinek, 2011)

lightly or carelessly. It is a word that, if misused, can cause unreasonable fear, or unjustified acceptance that the fight is over, leading to unnecessary suffering and death" (Ghebreyesus, 2020). In this way, the WHO's purpose-vision is to create a joint effort to combat Covid-19, which can be done through people's conviction and motivation about its possibilities.

Conviction

Conviction can be acknowledged as a personal belief. It is developed within the leader, however, it also shapes the leader as a person (Mohler, 2012).

Nevertheless, conviction does not mean hardness, nor stubbornness. It is possible to unite through the reasons behind perception, that is, the story that makes it have sense and justifies the actions. As soon as something makes sense, the employee starts to adopt the idea as something natural and welcome. He changes his behavior to become useful. It is no use gathering people in a project that you do not believe in or you are not capable of showing direction. Certain coordination is necessary to execute the activities. That is why the WHO director reports clearly: "We have never before seen a pandemic sparked by a coronavirus. This is the first pandemic caused by a coronavirus. And we have never before seen a pandemic that can be controlled, at the same time" (Ghebreyesus, 2020).

Thereby, conviction brings structure and base to the vision, being shaped by two elements: personal magnetism and trust. Personal magnetism reflects your beliefs and values to others, attracting them to your ideas, while vision and trust keep them by your side, demonstrating your credibility (Berticelli, 2017; Gibson et al., 1998).

Personal Magnetism

Personal or animal magnetism, topic researched by German doctor Franz Mesmer in the eighteenth century (Herr, 2005), represents the component of leadership that connects with the vital force of our physical-biological body with the unconscious of other people, and it represents the energy that amplifies or cancels the reciprocity, sympathy and affinity that can exist between people. In other words, the leader's energy can be broaden or lost according to this personal and interpersonal care (or lack of it). Good nourishment, rest routines, noble purposes, uplifting readings, frequent mental and physical exercises are some of the activities which might raise the leader's personal magnetism and reinforce the conviction process. An energized person can expose arguments more clearly, as much as obtaining sympathy and commitment from others more easily. With high levels of personal magnetism, human beings have higher capacity of using physical, psychic and mental resources in favor of having a broader and accurate perception on the context, as well as having conditions of adopting right attitudes and actions to face the issue. It is not possible to talk the talk, if the leader walks the walk with his/her collaborators (Berticelli, 2017). That is the personnal magnetism. A force that drives and attracts people.

Trust

Lencioni (2002) states lack of trust as number one team dysfunction and as the cause for other five. Essentially, lack of trust comes from the indisposition of showing vulnerability. People who are not capable of speaking openly about their mistakes and weaknesses become impossible of creating a solid trust base. Reaching a high trust level based in vulnerability is difficult, for the reason that in the educational and career formation process, most well succeeded people learn to be competitive and protective of their own reputation. Undoing this pattern for the group's good is a great challenge, but essential.

Trust can be a gamechanging in leadership (Monzani et al., 2015). Covey (2006) defines trust as the combination of two key elements: Character and Competence. Character refers to the individual values, what he is, for instance. People with good character and who we know on a daily make us have trust in them. Values do not need to be said, but experienced. It is important to walk the talk! (Berticelli, 2017). Character has to do with what we are (Mohler, 2012). It is related to integrity, maturity and an abundant mindset.

Integrity has to do with coherence, being correct in all spheres of your life (Ulrich et al., 1999). A story is told about a couple who went to a fast food restaurant drive-thru to buy a sandwich. When leaving with the package, they opened and noticed there was a large amount of money inside. They returned to give it back. The employees were surprised and very happy because someone has wrongly given them the package with money that should have been taken to the bank instead of their sandwich.

After elucidating the fact, the employees sincerely thanked the man and asked him to register the moment on a photograph to be exposed at the store as a good character example. The man got embarrassed and did not permit his photograph to be taken, and soon he justified himself "this lady with me is not my wife." On this case, it was evident the man was honest with finances, but not with his wife, so he did not have integrity.

Maturity is developed when the person learns to deal with himself, stop being dependent on the environment and acts according to his own choices. That enables the person to be brave and kind, and can handle life difficulties in a compassionate manner (Covey, 2004).

The abundancy mentality eliminates the scarcity and competitiveness view, that is, holding the idea someone needs to win and another one needs to lose and there are not resources for everyone. People with abundancy mindset seek for solutions that attend both sides equally, that's why they possess character (Covey, 2004).

Those people who possess suspicious character and value flaws cannot count with complete and unworried commitment from his employees. If there is any true that the leader is the one who stands an example, so character is a key component in order to convince someone to do what is asked.

Competency has to do with the individual's abilities, what he can do. Competency is frequently defined by the combination of three elements: Knowledge, Ability and Attitude. More recently, an item was added to the Competency definition: Result (Hogan & Kaiser, 2005).

Knowledge means knowing, the formal knowledge acquired during life, at schools, universities, courses, professional experience: everything that refers to theory, data and information. Ability means knowing how to do, that is, all knowledge we practice and gradually is improved in the usage and challenge process. Theoretical knowledge itself does not take us far, it is necessary to put this knowledge into practice and use it effectively. Attitude is connected to wanting to do, the behaviors we have in face of our day-by-day situations and the tasks we develop daily. It is no use to have a lot of knowledge and have used this knowledge through abilities. In the last instance, we will bump into attitude, the intention and will that every individual has to accomplish what is proposed. Finally, Result completes the definition. In fact, we can only consider someone as a competent individual if he delivers the desired results for his position. Deliveries are crucial for the organization's survival, therefore, the employees need to focus on the converging goals toward this result (Ulrich et al., 1999).

Why is Credibility defined by Character and Competency? People will not believe you unless they understand they can trust your integrity reasons, as well as you can deliver what you propose. The combination of these two concepts makes someone reliable, both in his essence and in his responsibilities.

Vision and conviction aligned, motivation is the next step in ensuring the due executing.

Motivation

With conviction, your identity defines itself and the leader can connect with his employees (Mohler, 2012). With vision we have the direction to be followed and the ideal to be achieved. But these two factors, separated, are not able to move employees. Engagement and its maintenance are great leadership challenges. To engage employees through vision and based in conviction there is an enhancer: motivation. To create and keep motivation, the coevolutive leadership practices three fundamental actions: know, communicate, and enable. Specifically on the WHO director's speech, "This is not just a public health crisis, it is a crisis that will touch every sector—so every sector and every individual must be involved in the fight […] We're in this together, to do the right things with calm and protect the citizens of the world. It's doable" (Ghebreyesus, 2020).

Know

The first step to develop motivation properly is by deeply knowing people you are leading. It is necessary to remember people also have their convictions, based on their purpose, personal magnetism and credibility. It is also relevant to notice people have personal lives and, being concerned with your employees' lives is often connected to the opportunity of expressing to them how import they are. The leader needs to comprehend that, in order to promote his vision and engage people, he will have to respect their personal convictions, as well as personal issues. For this, it will be necessary to know your employees and seek alignment among their convictions and proposed vision.

Perhaps one of the most useless efforts posed to a leader is to unify people's purposes with the organization (Mohler, 2012). That is not only complex, as virtually impossible. Some time ago, Uber has shown to have understood that. In a campaign launched to gather partners in a large capital in Brazil, the company presented different people with various purposes which led them to work with Uber. "I want to pay my daughter's university, that's why I work with Uber," "I need to buy my own house, that's why I work with Uber," "I want to get married, that's why I work with Uber," "I want to make extra money at the weekend, that's why I work with Uber." The company made very clear that is possible to unify people in reaching a vision, respecting different purposes.

It is an illusion to put all people under the same purpose. People are different, have their own intentions, aspirations and challenges (Buckingham & Goodall, 2019). That is why leaders need to demonstrate employees can pursue their purposes and reach them, at the same time as they seek the organization's vision. This process is only possible when leaders know their employees.

In order to get to know your employees, it is necessary to live with them, listen to them, invest time on them and seek to understand their convictions, to find ways for their purpose to be achieved at work by seeking the organizational vision.

Communicate

Communication represents the way the leader will listen and tranquilize his employees in respect to his proposals (Mohler, 2012) Communication presents a strong relational element and, if it is horizontally built, will provide a kind of friends' talk. If the opposite happens, the communication purpose might lose itself, because fear makes many good ideas to get lost during long meeting silence periods (Patterson et al., 2011). Besides the topic complexity, the great key to success can be established as the creation of an environment with psychological safety, where trust, reciprocity and mainly, sensibility do not make listeners and participants to grow a mental blockage on the matter. Communication can be like a river, flowy and pleasant, where people shower, or, as a strong storm, where there are life risks and drowning warnings. On the same metaphor, maybe the communication vision as a light rain, continuous and recurrent is the proper way to approach this issue coherently. Communicating is sharing and sharing only when there is interest and profit is noticed. The leader has to attain to details that involve the communication act, in which attitudes, several times, count more than the content.

Enable

While carefully studying motivation and its theoretical development, Daniel Pink listed three elements that developed Motivation 3.0: Excellence, Purpose and Autonomy. Enabling is related to the third item. People need to feel some autonomy level so they can feel motivated to develop their jobs and work for the vision. However, unprepared and irresponsible autonomy can bring serious issues to people and the organization (Pink, 2011).

Enabling means offering people skills necessary to carry out their activities, offering authority and empowerment so that they can make decisions independently and quickly, and creating a cycle of accountability, so that people are held accountable for their activities.

Grenny et al. (2013) have developed an important study on the art of influencing people. According to the authors, people do things for two reasons: either because they want or do not feel capable of doing it. These two reasons can be promoted through three spheres: personal, social and structural. Thus, there are six influence sources, as follow:

- **Personal motivation:** It is related to people's deepest motives, their values, purposes, and aspirations. It can be awakened by communicating the reasons why the proposed action is aligned with the person's values and what the ultimate goal is to be achieved.
- **Personal ability:** It defines how much the person is qualified to carry out the activity that is proposed. People are more likely to perform tasks as they have skills required. This sphere is activated through training, teaching, and workshops.
- **Social motivation:** We are all part of social groups, whether professional or personal. The pressure from these groups will drive people to perform certain activities. Within the organizational context, people will only adopt changes in case their group also do. Therefore, it is important to locate opinion makers in the groups to engage them in the activities, in order to ease the group's acceptance.
- **Social ability:** People are more likely to perform tasks when their group provides support, that is, if they find people who help the task execution or who can teach and support them. It is necessary to guarantee people are able to teach each other to ensure the group strengthening toward the expected goal.
- **Structural motivation:** Many leaders expect certain behaviors and actions from their employees, but do not demonstrate through structure the importance of the desired activity. Structural motivation has to do with the system of rewards and punishments established by the leader. Rewards and punishments are not limited to financial returns and layoffs. Words of praise, promotions, employee prominence, etc. need to be tied to the desired behaviors, otherwise they will not stimulate people.
- **Structural ability:** As people around you, also the structure around people needs to facilitate action in order to propel it. Proper tools, efficient software, reminders on the walls, etc. make the structure to favor the proposed behavior by the leaders. When the physical structure turns into an obstacle, the power of influence is minimized.

It is possible to acknowledge 50% of the influence and motivation strategy is anchored in enabling people. Studies show that, if used properly, these sources can increase up to 10 times the influence of a leader.

Motivation, as part of the coevolutive leadership, is a major contributor in pursuit of achieving results.

Conclusion

The world after COVID-19 is strongly transformed by the digital revolution and industry 4.0 and it demands a new leadership style. Younger, connected, restless, and convicted people do not want to work for someone: they want to work with someone. Coevolutive leadership proposes to be a positive answer at this new social, cultural and economic moment. World Health Organization actions, mainly the ones through the Director-general, Tedros Ghebreyesus, and his speeches seem to be aligned to a coevolutive leadership approach. On the issue of transforming the pandemic in a syndemia and involve social and economic issues, in the case defended by the general editor of The Lancet magazine, Richard Horton (2020), it also seems to value the model of coevolutionary leadership even more, as it deals with this issue more broadly. Vision, Conviction and Motivation are components which represent the coevolutive leadership. A leadership based not on oppressing and hierarchy, but an approach that envisages a style with a vision for the future and another for the execution. Increasingly, leadership will be rethought not as an innate factor, but as a competence to be learned, developed and disseminated at its various levels. Coevolutionary leadership seeks progression over time from people who are freed from the ungrateful task of receiving orders to build together, with active shared responsibilities and who seek, in a changing and still unclear future, to cooperate in the mind, in the hands and in the heart.

The current scenario demands a more fluid, less hindered and more participative kind of leadership. This is coevolutionary leadership: it frees employees from the ungrateful task of taking orders and seeks their progress so that they can build a better future together. These are probably the legacies of the pandemic, a better world for everyone with the obligation of being each day a better person. A struggle for life and a life for struggling to help others.

Five Takeaways

1. The world changes bring new leadership challenges: The 4.0 industry was changing the organizational environment, and COVID-19 accelerated these changes. Leaders are now facing new challenges.
2. Coevolutive is imperative: There is no place for lonely heroes or selfish leaders. To engage people in a new paradigm, leaders must be worried about growing for all.
3. Vision brings inspiration and direction: Leaders need to be even more effective in show people the right direction and big picture for the future.
4. The leader's personality matters: When leaders have conviction based on personal magnetism and trust, they have the power to engage people.
5. Motivation is all about them: to create a motivational environment, leaders need to know, communicate, and enable people, then they will be willing to work together.

Five Reflection Questions

1. How were your company and team affected by COVID-19 changes? Are you prepared for that?
2. The COVID-19 changes will remain, or after its consequences, companies will come back to their traditional "modus operandi"?
3. How a Coevolutive mindset and posture can change the relationship between leaders and followers?
4. Reflecting on your leadership style, how close or far are you from coevolutive leadership? Why?
5. How probably will you adopt the coevolutive leadership model? How may this proposal change your results? Are you willing to change your status quo to achieve sustainable and long-term results?

References

Berticelli, A. (2017, April). The Magnetism of Leadership. *SDM Maganize*. https://www.sdmmag.com/articles/93741-the-magnetism-of-leadership

Buckingham, M., & Goodall, A. (2019). *Nine lies about work: A freethinking leader's guide to the real world*. Harvard Business Review Press.

Burt, R. S. (2009). *Structural holes: The social structure of competition*. Harvard United Press.

Carmona, D., Fizpatrick, C. R., & Johnson, M. T. J. (2015). Fifty years of co-evolution and beyond: Integrating co-evolution from molecules to species. *Molecular Ecology, 24*, 5315–5329.

Collins, J. (2001). *Good to great: Why some companies make the leap and others don't*. HarperColins.

Covey, S. R. (2004). *The 8th habit: From effectiveness to greatness*. FreePress.

Covey, S. M. R. (2006). *Speed of trust*. FreePress.

Deci, E. (1996). *Why we do what we do: Understanding self-motivation*. Penguin Books; Reprint edition.

Dries, N., & Peperman, R. (2012). How to identify leadership potential: Development and testing of a consensus model. *Human Resource Management, 51*(3), 361–385.

Dubrin, A. (2016). *Essentials of management*. Newbooks.

Frankl, V. (2000). *Recollections: An autobiography*. Basic Books.

Frankl, V. (2006). *Man's search for meaning* (1st ed.). Beacon Press.

Friedman, W. E. (2009). The meaning of Darwin's 'abominable mystery'. *American Journal of Botany, 96*(1), 5–21.

Ghebreyesus, T. A. (2020). *WHO Director-General's opening remarks at the media briefing on COVID-19—11 March 2020*. https://www.who.int/dg/speeches/detail/who-director-general-s-opening-remarks-at-the-media-briefing-on-covid-19%2D%2D-11-march-2020

Gibson, J. W., Hannon, J. C., & Blackwell, C. W. (1998). Carismatic leadership: the hidden controversy. *The Journal of Leadership Studies, 5*(4), 11–28.

Global Workplace Analyticsn (GWA). (2020). *A future of work research*. GWA.

Grenny, J., Patterson, K., Maxfield, D., Mcmillian, R., & Switzler, A. (2013). *Influencer*. McGrawHill.

Herr, H. W. (2005). Franklin, Lavoisier, and Mesmer: Origin of the controlled clinical trial. *Urologic Oncology, 23*(5), 346–335.

Hogan, R., & Kaiser, R. B. (2005). What we know about leadership. *Review of General Psychology, 9*(2), 169–180.

Horton, R. (2020). Offline: COVID-19 is not a pandemic. *The Lancet, 396*(10255), 874.

International Labour Organization - ILO. (2020). *Monitor: COVID-19 and the world of work. Second edition updated estimates and analysis*. ILO.
Lencioni, P. (2002). *The five dysfunctions of a team: A leadership fable* (1st ed.). Jossey-Bass.
Li, C. (2010). *Open leadership: How social technology can transform the way you lea* (1st ed.). Jossey-Bass.
Mohler, A. (2012). *The conviction to lead: 25 principles for leadership that matters*. Bethany House Publishers.
Monzani, L., Ripoll, P., & Peiró, J. M. (2015). Winning the hearts and minds of followers: The interactive effects of followers' emotional competencies and goal setting types on trust in leadership. *La Revista Latinoamericana de Psicología, 47*(1), 1–15.
Patterson, K., Grenny, J., McMillan, R., & Switzler, A. (2011). *Crucial conversations* (2nd ed.). McGraw-Hill Education.
Pink, D. (2011). *Drive: The surprising truth about what motivates us*. Riverhead Books.
Putriastuti, B. C. K., & Stasi, A. (2019). How to lead the millennials: A review of 5 major leadership theory groups. *Journal of Leadership in Organizations, 1*(2), 96–111.
Quick, J. C., & Henderson, D. F. (2016). Occupational stress: Preventing suffering, enhancing wellbeing. *International Journal of Environmental Research and Public Health, 13*(5), 459. https://doi.org/10.3390/ijerph13050459
Senge, P. M. (2010). *The fifth discipline* (Revised & Updated Edition). Currency Press.
Shapiro, G. (2019). *Ninja Future: Secrets to success in the new world of innovation* (1st ed). HarperCollins Publishers.
Sinek, S. (2011). *Start with why* (1st ed.). Portfolio Press.
Tan, W., Hao, F., McIntyre, R. S., Jiang, L., Jiang, X., Zhang, L., Zhao, X., Zou, Y., Hu, Y., Luo, X., Zhang, Z., Lai, A., Ho, R., Tran, B., Ho, C., & Tam, W. (2020). Is returning to work during the COVID-19 pandemic stressful? A study on immediate mental health status and psychoneuroimmunity prevention measures of Chinese workforce. *Brain, Behavior, and Immunity, 87*, 84–92. https://doi.org/10.1016/j.bbi.2020.04.055
Ulrich, D., Zenger, J., & Smallwood, N. (1999). *Results-based leadership*. Harvard Business Review Press.
Weick, K. (1976). Educational organizations as loosely coupled systems. *Administrative Science Quarterly, 21*, 1–9.
Williams, C. (2018). *MGMT (with MindTap Printed Access Card) (New, Engaging Titles from 4LTR Press)* (11th ed.). Cengage Learning.

Derson Lopes Jr is an assistant professor, author, consultant, and speaker in the areas of leadership, productivity, project management, spirituality, and volunteering. He acts as the vice president of R & D/e-Learning at Aspectum; trainer at VitalSmarts; dean of Graduation, Research and e-learning at FAAMA, leader partner at GOTT, and co-founder at Instituto Aksioss. He holds a PhD in Business Administration from Unicamp, PMP certification, specialization in finance, and degrees in administration, accounting, and theology. He worked in different areas as manager and leading big teams and volunteered in several countries, including Bangladesh, Mozambique, Egypt, Uruguay, and USA.

Paulo Hayashi Jr is an assistant professor at the State University of Campinas. His main areas of interests include organizational behavior, organizational theory and strategy. He holds a PhD in Business Administration from Federal University of Rio Grande do Sul (UFRGS). He is the co-founder and coordinator of Lab of People and Marketing (LPM) of School of Applied Science (University of Campinas—Unicamp).

8 E-leadership 2.0: Meet Your AI Leader

Xiaochuan Song and Michael Ford

Introduction

As an indispensable component within organizations, leaders are critical to organizations' prosperity. Extant literature has indicated important roles played by leaders. For instance, as indicated by Kotter (1990), leaders contribute to organizations' prosperity by engaging in both organization-oriented and people-oriented activities. Specifically, these activities include directing, evaluating, and coaching followers (Eisenberger et al., 2002; Shoss et al., 2013), but also supporting followers' work, fostering followers' abilities, and empowering followers to reach high job performance and achieve career goals (Cascio & Shurygailo, 2003; House, 1996). These examples indicate that leadership is a critical building block of a successful organization. In their study, Hogan and Kaiser (2005) defined leadership as the "responsibility to in charge of the organizations and their units" (p. 171). Based on this definition, people who assume this responsibility are considered to be leaders. Hogan and Kaiser (2005) also posited that leadership is a ubiquitous phenomenon in human society, with the capacity to solve problems and enhance followers' job performance.

Being broadly acknowledged as an important contributor to organizational success, leadership has attracted considerable attention from both business researchers and practitioners. In his book *Leadership in Organizations*, Yukl and Uppal (2018) posited that leadership builds up a process for guiding, structuring, and facilitating

X. Song, Ph.D. (✉)
Department of Management, Nova Southeastern University, Fort Lauderdale/Davie, FL, USA
e-mail: xsong@nova.edu

M. Ford, Ph.D.
Department of Management, University of Alabama, Tuscaloosa, AL, USA
e-mail: mtford@cba.ua.edu

S. K. Dhiman, J. F. Marques (eds.), *Leadership After COVID-19*, Future of Business and Finance, https://doi.org/10.1007/978-3-030-84867-5_8

followers' activities within a group or organization. Similarly, Dansereau et al. (2013) indicated that leadership is an interpersonal process, such that leaders employ this process to influences followers' behaviors and promote followers' performance (Cascio & Shurygailo, 2003). Taken together, these researchers intended to reveal there is a mechanism that leaders use to influence followers' attitudes and behaviors when it comes to leadership (Avolio et al., 2001).

Extant studies also suggested that leadership establishes connections between leaders and followers to enhance organizational effectiveness. For instance, as indicated by Avolio et al. (2001), leaders use communication channels (physical or electronic) to connect followers, such that communication channels establish links between leaders and followers and reflect leadership within the organization. Similarly, Walvoord et al. (2008) suggested that connecting to followers is one of the most critical skills that leaders need so that they can transmit information clearly and effectively to followers.

Therefore, it is evident that the quality of leadership, especially in terms of process and connection, can significantly contribute to organizations' prospective outcomes, such that good leadership leads to organizations' survival and prosperity (Cascio & Shurygailo, 2003; Day & Antonakis, 2012), whereas problematic leadership leads to uncertainty, inconsistencies, mistrust, perishing, and demise (Avolio & Kahai, 2003).

The Current Circumstance

In retrospect to the past three decades, communication media, such as fax, email, instant message, video conference, and remote work, has made it possible for the dispersed workforce to work together virtually. Communication via certain types of information technologies, also known as IT-mediated interaction, has enhanced and expanded human-to-human communication immensely (Thurlow et al., 2004). In his book *Distributed Work*, Cramton (2002) defined distributed work as tasks that "distributed to each working individual (either evenly or non-evenly) across different locations…that remote from each other" (pp.191–212). This definition implies that individuals in distributed work settings can work together on the same task or project without necessarily being geographically and/or temporally close to each other (Burn & Barnett, 1999). This flexibility (Boudreau et al., 1998) can remove the geographic and temporal constraint that exists in the traditional work environment and help organizations to achieve competitive advantages (Lurey & Raisinghani, 2001) and respond promptly to the external environment (Cascio, 2000).

The COVID-19 pandemic has made it imperative for organizations to practice social distancing (Farboodi et al., 2020; Fong et al., 2020; Jones et al., 2020), modify existing business models (Bauer et al., 2020; Mims, 2020; Isenberg & Di Fiore, 2020; Scheepers & Bogie, 2020), and redesign workflows (Nassauer, 2020; Quraishi et al., 2020; Simon, 2020)—these changes bring challenges to leaders in terms of adapting to hyper-dynamic working context and managing tasks, resources, and workflows wisely. The COVID-19 pandemic also brings about a movement from a co-located workforce to a dispersed one, and this movement has made technology-mediated leadership more imperative than ever before, making questions such as how to manage employees that work from home effectively and efficiently in the remote working environment become critical (Bartik et al., 2020; Choudhury et al., 2020; Howell et al., 2005).

In response to these challenges, organizations have been applying different types of information technologies (IT) to enhance communication medium among dispersed workforces, including online meeting (e.g., Zoom and Skype meeting), data transmission/sharing (e.g., Dropbox and Google Drive), and teamwork coordination (e.g., Asana and Trello). With the assistance of IT, leaders can organize and manage tasks and projects from remote locations and communicate with workers without being physically present (Avolio & Kahai, 2003), making it possible to coordinate the work beyond time and space boundaries (Jarvenpaa & Tanriverdi, 2003). In fact, since the advent of IT, many of leaders' jobs and functions have been fulfilled by IT, which over time, has been referred to as "Advanced Information Technology," or AIT, by leadership researchers (Avolio et al., 2001), and AIT establishes a link between leader and distributed workforce and makes it possible for dispersed workforce to collaborate beyond temporal and geographical boundaries. Therefore, the co-existence of AIT and leadership constitutes an organic integration of AIT and leadership, and this type of integration, as indicated by previous studies, builds up electronic leadership (i.e., e-leadership, Avolio et al., 2001).

E-leadership

As a typical application of AIT in leadership, e-leadership sheds light on coordinating and reshaping workforces by capitalizing technologies. The concept of e-leadership was initially coined by Elaine Kerr in 1986. In her research report, Kerr (1986) used the term "electronic leadership" to describe leadership techniques that applied to electronic interactions within a certain working group. Although distinct from the ways we understand e-leadership today, Kerr indicated essential components of e-leadership and shed light on the subsequent research in this area. More recently, Avolio et al. (2001) defined e-leadership as "a social influence process mediated by AIT to produce a change in attitudes, feelings, thinking, behavior, and performance with individuals, groups, and/or organizations" (p. 617). This definition posits that technology is an indispensable component when influencing working individuals. This definition also suggests that when implementing e-leadership, the social influence processes and outcomes need to co-evolve with AIT infrastructure so that worker's psychological states and behaviors can be adjusted to optimize their job performance within the organization. Therefore, when implementing e-leadership, instead of considering it merely an extension of traditional leadership, it is a fundamental change regarding how leaders and followers relate to each other (Avolio & Kahai, 2003) and how to integrate AIT with leadership.

Unsolved Problems: Natural Indigence vs. Artificial Indigence

E-leadership provides a solution for organizations to guide workforces through the integration of leadership and AIT. With the help of newly developed technologies, e-leadership has been broadly applied in multiple areas, such as public administration (Banerjee & Chau, 2004), healthcare (Holland et al., 2009), education (Van Ryssen & Godar, 2000), and mentoring (García, 2009). These applications of e-leadership, in essence, are computer-assisted human intelligence (Amabile, 2020), which is germane to that of traditional face-to-face leadership (DasGupta, 2011) with the assumption that both leaders and followers are human beings. In other words, similar to traditional leadership in a face-to-face context, e-leadership connects one natural intelligence (leader) to another natural intelligence (follower).

However, when moving beyond natural intelligence, a meaningful question to ask and examine is whether technologies are capable of simulating and substituting natural intelligence and play leaders' roles in the e-leadership context. In other words, will that be possible to move from existing "technology-assisted" leadership systems to "technology-centered" intelligence systems, as a new form of e-leadership? One possible and viable answer is artificial intelligence (a.k.a. AI). Unlike natural intelligence, a type of intelligence rendered by human beings, AI refers to the intelligence rendered by man-made systems that can learn from human beings and make human-like decisions.

Research and development in the AI domain can be dated back to the 1950s, the time when computer science researchers intended to develop computer-assisted systems that can engage in human-related behaviors, such as playing games, solving problems, and speaking (Russell & Norvig, 2003). Since then, AI development experienced some twists and turns due to funding issues (Crevier, 1993) and finally commercialized in the 1980s, in the form of expert systems, which solve problems "within specific, prefixed applications" (De la Sen et al., 2004, p. 173). By looking at roles played by AI, it appears that AI has the potential to substitute human workers' roles in multiple industries. In their book, *Artificial Intelligence: A Modern Approach*, Russell and Norving (2003) defined AI as "the study agents that receive percepts from the environment and performed actions…and the agent implements a function that maps percept sequences to actions" (p. 7). This definition implies that AI systems have human-like cognitive abilities, which allow them to learn from human and data inputs and finish works such as planning, decision making, recognizing patterns, making a decision, and answering inquires based on what it learned from the inputs.

More recently, AI applications have been extended to multiple areas, such as logistics (Kurzweil, 2005), healthcare (Hanson & Marshall, 2001), automotive (e.g., self-driving vehicles, West, 2016), disaster prevention and relief (Council, 2020a, b; McCormick, 2020), and personal assistant (e.g., Google Assistant, Apple's Siri, Microsoft's Cortana, and Amazon's Alexa). In some circumstances, AI can even outperform human beings in programming (Barr & Nicas, 2016), gaming

(Hernandez, 2020), and medical diagnosis (Killock, 2020). In the recent 5 years, AI application has been further extended to business-related areas, such as project development, task processing, and some types of work that would have otherwise been finished by humans when AI is absent (Clark, 2015).

AI also allows us to rethink e-leadership fundamentally. Taking General Electric Aviation as an example, the company has successfully implemented a working system, which uses AI algorism as a leader to manage tasks that have been handled by its human counterparts (Schechner, 2017). Similarly, Uber has recently started using apps and algorithms to distribute tasks to self-employed workers (Schechner, 2017). These examples shed light on the possibility of substituting natural intelligence (i.e., human leader) with AI (Kiulian, 2017; Moore, 2017). These examples also indicate that using AI to simulate leaders within an e-leadership system appears to be a viable alternative to human leaders because of AI's abilities to learn from humans and the external environment and apply learning to works.

The COVID-19 pandemic brings about challenges to business organizations in terms of operation, planning, and coordination (Amankwah-Amoah et al., 2020; Donthu & Gustafsson, 2020; Gursoy & Chi, 2020), however, AI technology can provide us an opportunity to revisit and rethink e-leadership that goes beyond natural intelligence and explore the feasibility of integrating AI into an e-leadership system. Specifically, with AI technology integrated into e-leadership, AI has the potential to change e-leadership fundamentally.

Some researchers have provided an optimistic outlook on AI applications in the business domain. In her recently published book, *The Future of Leadership: Rise of Automation, Robotics, and Artificial Intelligence*, Hyacinth (2017) provided a comprehensive review of AI applications. Specifically, the author discussed the possibility of replacing human leaders with AI and pointed out that AI can play important roles in future leadership. Similarly, recent reports indicated that compared with human leaders, AI-simulated leaders are less likely to be biased and make mistakes, and are more likely to provide accurate instruction, information, and guidance to followers (e.g., Hernandez, 2020; Killock, 2020).

By integrating AI into e-leadership, in this chapter, we propose the concept of "e-leadership 2.0," which explores the possibility of substituting natural intelligence with AI in the e-leadership context. As indicated earlier, the most evident characteristic that makes AI different from other technologies is that AI has human-like learning abilities (Amabile, 2020; Liebowitz, 2001). This type of learning capacity, during the early days, was considered to be machine learning, which yields optimized outcome when the AI system has access to a large volume of the dataset (Sutton & Barto, 1998); and more recently, this learning ability was interpreted as advanced learning activities, such as deep learning (Deng, 2014; LeCun et al., 2015). Taken together, it is meaningful and important to move one step further in the e-leadership domain by incorporating AI technology so that e-leadership will encompass both natural intelligence-based interaction and human-to-AI interaction. We also suggest that now is the time for both leadership researchers and practitioners to revisit e-leadership from the standpoint of AI.

Plan of the Chapter

As indicated above, this chapter intends to explore the possibility and efficacy of AI-simulated leaders from both leader's and follower's perspective as leader and follower are two essential components in the leadership domain (Dansereau et al., 2013). Specifically, built upon the Substitute for Leadership Theory, the overarching theory in this chapter, we explore and discuss the possibility of substituting human leaders with AI-simulated leaders in the following three aspects. Firstly, from the leader's and follower's perspective, we explore and discuss the extent to which AI-simulated leaders will have equivalent efficacy as human leaders. We specifically focus on the concept of social presence (Schloerb, 1995) and intend to find out differences between human leaders and AI-simulated leaders from the perspective of social presence. This is because social presence is an essential part of leader-follower interaction (Kahai et al., 2012). Secondly, from a contextual factors' perspective, we explore and discuss how followers' job-related characteristics, task structure, and time pressure can create boundary conditions when applying AI-simulated leaders to the e-leadership context. The following figure represents the conceptual model that we will explore in the e-leadership context (Fig. 8.1).

Literature Review and Theoretical Background

As indicated earlier, leaders play important roles in organizations (Kotter, 1990) and influence organizational performance (Cascio & Shurygailo, 2003). Presence is the key factor for leaders to fulfill their roles effectively. The Social Presence Theory, which was originally introduced by Short et al. (1976), provides a theoretical foundation for the leader's presence. In their book, *The Social Psychology of Telecommunications*, Short et al. (1976) defined social presence as "the degree of salience of the person in the interaction and the consequent salience of the interpersonal relationships" (p. 65). This definition implies that the level of social presence is subject to the ways information transmits from one person (sender) to another (receiver), such that the higher quality of the transmitted information, the higher fidelity of social presence can be rendered (Gunawardena, 1995; Mantovani & Riva, 1999).

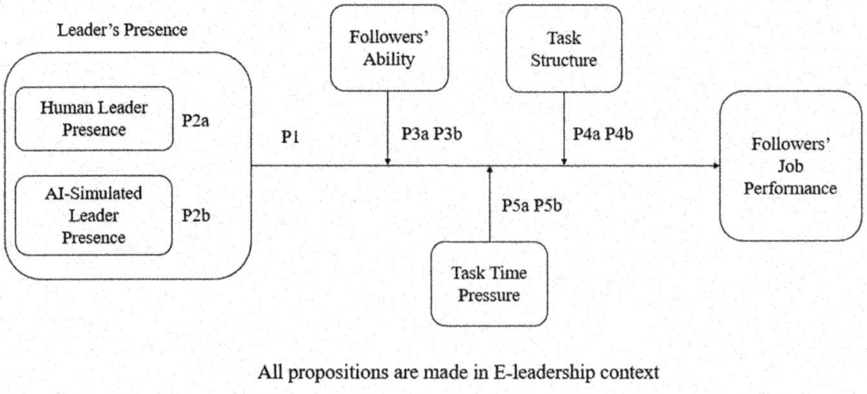

Fig. 8.1 Conceptual Model

Table 8.1 Types of presence and their corresponding covered aspects

Settings		Objective aspect	Subjective aspect
Face-to-face context	Physical presence (Schloerb, 1995)	X	
Technology-mediated context	Virtual presence (Steuer, 1992)		X
	Telepresence (Yan & Panteli, 2007)		X

When it comes to the traditional face-to-face work environment, a leader's social presence is inclined to physical presence, which is defined as "the existence of an object in some particular region of space and time … that is physically present in front of target people" (Schloerb, 1995, p. 68), implying that physical presence emphasizes the objective aspect of presence. Specifically, leaders render physical presence by physically attending meetings, sitting in the office, having a face-to-face talk with workers, etc.

On the other hand, in the technology-mediated working context, the absence of direct and face-to-face interaction between leader and follower makes a leader's social presence inclined to virtual presence, a sensation of "being there" for workers in the technology-mediated environment (Sheridan, 1992; Lombard & Ditton, 1997). Literature in this domain also describes virtual presence as telepresence, the feeling of "being there" under dispersed and mediated settings (Heeter, 1992; Sheridan, 1992; Steuer, 1992). Being different from physical presence, both virtual presence and telepresence represent are subjective presence, which emphasizes the "feeling of being attentive, connected, integrated and focused" (Kahn, 1992, p. 324) from the audiences' perspective. Taken together, to summarize different types of presence, it is clear that physical presence in the face-to-face context is relevant to the objective aspect of social presence, while virtual and telepresence presence in the technology-mediated context is relevant to the subjective aspect of social presence, as indicated in Table 8.1.

Leader's Presence and Followers' Performance

E-leadership is built on a technology-mediated environment and it can change workers' attitudes, feelings, and thinking (Avolio et al., 2001, 2014). To understand how e-leadership influences followers, we examine e-leadership from the standpoint of presence. Presence can be generally represented in three aspects. Sheridan (1992) proposed a three-dimension model that evaluates the level of presence. Specifically, Sherdian's model includes sensory information, which reflects the richness of a certain type of information transmitted from one to another; control of sensors, which refers to sender's ability to control how the information is transmitted; and control of the environment, which refers to sender's ability to manipulate the environment for information transmission. Based on these three aspects, a high level of presence occurs when all three elements are perceived to be high by a receiver (Sheridan, 1992). Sheridan's three-element model represents social presence in general, implying that it can be applied to both physical and virtual presence.

Steuer (1992) moved presence from general presence to telepresence, the type of presence in a technology-mediated environment. In the model he presented, Steuer (1992) posited that telepresence includes two elements: vividness, which refers to the "representational richness of a mediated environment as defined by its formal features, that is, how an environment presents information to the senses" (p. 11), such that the level of vividness depends on the breadth of information input (i.e., the extent to which the information includes comprehensive types of sensory) and the depth of information input (i.e., the level of quality of information). Another element is interactivity, which describes "the degree to which users can participate in modifying the form and content of a mediated environment in real-time" (p. 14). Such that the level of interactivity depends on the speed of information (i.e., the response time needed for receiving information), the range of information (i.e., the extent to which the communication channel can be modified), and the mapping of information (i.e., as controllability of the mediated environment). By taking vividness and interactivity together, it can be inferred that the higher level of vividness and interactivity a medium has, the higher level of leader's presence can followers perceive in the e-leadership context.

By integrating Sheridan (1992) three-dimension presence model and Steuer (1992) two-dimension telepresence model, several presence-related characteristics can be boiled down: (1) variety of the information sources, (2) richness of a certain information source, (3) level of synchronizability, and (4) level of manipulability. These key characteristics were described in Table 8.2.

Based on these characteristics summarized above, we posit that in the e-leadership context, leaders' presence influences followers' job performance. The Path-Goal Theory (House & Mitchell, 2007) can explain the important role played by presence when influencing followers' performance. The Path-Goal Theory suggests that leaders are more effective when they complement the environment in which followers work by providing cognitive clarification so that workers would be more productive in reaching job-related goals (House, 1996). In the traditional face-to-face working context, followers can receive guidance, clarification, and support from physical presence-based interaction with leaders, making it clearer for followers to understand job-related norms and expectations, which can facilitate and contribute to follower's higher job performance. Meanwhile, in a technology-mediated working context, e-leadership can provide followers with instruction, clarification, guidance, and other types of information that necessary for them to fulfill their duties and finish jobs, promoting followers' job performance—through different media.

Therefore, based on the Path-Goal Theory, increasing leaders' social presence in those four aspects can promote clarification, guidance, and support which will subsequently strengthen leaders' effect on followers' job performance. Also, leaders' social presence is positively related to followers' job performance in such a way that when leaders exert a high level of presence, followers are more likely to have a better understanding and less confusion about their jobs, thus assist followers to have higher job performance.

Proposition 8.1 *There is a positive relationship between a leader's presence and followers' job performance in an e-leadership context.*

Table 8.2 Key characteristics of each dimension of presence and telepresence model

Construct	Dimensions		Description	Key characteristics
Presence (general) (Sheridan, 1992)	Sensory of information		The level of the salience of certain information	#2: Richness of a certain information source
	Control of sensor		The extent to which the way of information transmission can be controlled by the sender	#4: Level of manipulability
	Control of physical environment		The extent to which the physical environment that information transmission depends on can be controlled by the sender	#4: Level of manipulability
Telepresence (Steuer, 1992)	Vividness	*Breadth*	The comprehensiveness of sensory (e.g., number of information channels, such as vision, smell, touch, taste, etc.)	#1: Variety of information sources
		Depth	The quality of certain information channels (e.g., the resolution of the image, legibility of text, the clarity of audio, etc.)	#2: Richness of a certain information source
	Interactivity	*Speed*	The response time that needed for one party to receive the information from another	#3: Level of synchronizability
		Range	The extent to which the communication channel can be modified (e.g., strengthen/weaken the current communication channel or change from one type of communication channel to another)	#4: Level of manipulability
		Mapping	The match between the controlling function in the mediated system and that in the real-world (e.g., use the office computer in the office vs. login to the office computer and use it remotely, drive the vehicle vs. control the vehicle remotely)	#4: Level of manipulability

Substitute for Human Leadership

The Substitute for Leadership Theory (Kerr & Jermier, 1978) provides a good theoretical framework to explain the extent to which AI-simulated leaders can substitute human leaders. The Substitutes for Leadership Theory posits that contextual and situational factors, such as follower characteristics (e.g., knowledge, skills, and abilities) and organizational factors (e.g., job/task structure, infrastructure, etc.), may attenuate the importance and necessity of having human leaders. Building upon the Substitutes for Leadership Theory, we consider AI technology to be a contextual/situational factor, which can establish and facilitate opportunities for AI-simulated leaders to work as human leaders' substitutes, in an e-leadership context. We built this proposition because AI-simulated leaders, in essence, are algorithms that operate within organizations' computerized systems (Schechner, 2017), implying that AI-simulated leaders are part of organizational infrastructure, in other words, a contextual factor that substitutes human leaders.

Proposition 8.2 *AI technology (a contextual factor) can substitute human leaders in e-leadership context, in the form of AI-simulated leadership, such that there is a positive relationship between AI-simulated presence and followers' job performance.*

Rendering Presence and Influencing Followers' Job Performance

In the subsequent sections, we explore the possibility and viability of substituting human leaders with AI-simulated leaders in terms of rendering presence, impacting followers' performance, and other contextual factors. In the technology-mediated working environment, leaders' presence can be rendered by either natural intelligence from human leaders or by artificial intelligence from AI-simulated leaders.

As indicated earlier, AI can learn from data inputs and human inputs and apply that to subsequent works as AI has human-like cognitive abilities (Amabile, 2020). In some circumstances, AI can even outperform its human counterparts in programming (Barr & Nicas, 2016), gaming (Hernandez, 2020), and medical diagnosis (Killock, 2020). Meanwhile, we should also note AI is less competent in some circumstances. For example, the AI system yields inferior outcome when learning from human input instead of learning from data input (Sutton & Barto, 1998), implying that AI may not work best when the data source is primarily based on human input (e.g., voice, facial recognition, touch, etc.). A recent wrongful arrest that reported by the New York Time indicates unreliable algorithm-based facial recognition can beget legal consequences when used inappropriately (Hill, 2020; Uberti, 2020). To compare the difference between human leaders and AI-simulated leaders in e-leadership context, we built Table 8.3 to compare human leaders and AI-simulated leaders based on four aspects that boiled down from the presence model (Sheridan, 1992) and the telepresence model (Steuer, 1992).

As shown in Table 8.3, to understand when AI-simulated leaders work better in an e-leadership context, we compared human leaders and AI-simulated leaders through the lenses of four characteristics of presence we summarized in Table 8.2. The following is an evaluation of four characteristics.

Table 8.3 The presence score of human leader and AI-simulated leader (in e-leadership context)

	Human leaders	AI-simulated leaders
#1: Variety of information sources	High (2)	Low (1)
#2: Richness of a certain information source	Low (1)	Low (1)
#3: Level of synchronizability	Low (1)	High (2)
#4: Level of manipulability	High (2)	Low (1)
Total score	**6**[a]	**5**[a]

[a]Values were assigned to reflect the level of presence in each aspect, for both human leaders and AI-Simulated leaders

1. Variety of information sources: in the e-leadership context, human leaders can communicate with followers in a variety of formats, such as video, audio, text message, email, etc. When it comes to AI-simulated leaders, however, it is unlikely to have as many information sources as human leaders because AI is a computer-based algorithm, which is unable to replicate all activities that human beings have in interpersonal interactions. In fact, the majority of AI-based systems available today are primarily built upon voice and text interaction, such as Amazon Alexa, Google Assistant, Apple Siri, and Microsoft Cortana, and any interactions beyond that level are still too nascent for prime time. Therefore, in Table 8.3, we assign "high" to human leaders and "low" to AI-simulated leaders in this characteristic.
2. Richness of a certain information source: the concept of information richness is from the Media Richness Theory, which was initially introduced by Daft and Lengel (1986), to describe the extent to which a communication medium can be sent over (from sender to receiver) without loss or distortion. Unlike face-to-face interaction, in the e-leadership context, both human leaders and AI-simulated leaders interact with followers via technology-mediated channels, which limit the quality and quantity of information exchanged between leaders and followers. For example, if workers have questions about certain tasks and need to ask their leaders for clarification, traditional face-to-face interactions accompanied with facial expressions, hand gestures, body language, etc. would be expected to reach better outcomes as face-to-face interactions can avoid information loss/distortion and miscommunication. However, when it comes to the e-leadership context, it is challenging for both human leaders and AI-simulated leaders to have direct interaction with workers, making information loss/distortion and miscommunication noticeable issues. Therefore, in Table 8.3, we assign "low" both human leaders and AI-simulated leaders in this characteristic.
3. Level of synchronizability: in the e-leadership context, AI-simulated leaders work better than human leaders in real-time communications. As computer-based algorisms that connected to the internet, AI-simulated leaders are always online and ready to work (except for system maintenance time)—they start working as soon as the message/data is received and send out completed works as soon as they are finished. Human leaders, on the other hand, have work schedules and cannot always be connected and ready to work. Therefore, in Table 8.3,

we assign "low" to human leaders and "high" to AI-simulated leaders in this characteristic.

4. Level of manipulability: in the e-leadership context, human leaders can simply switch communication channel, communication type, and even communication platform from one to another, whereas the AI-simulated leaders have limited abilities to switch because AI-simulated leaders, in essence, are algorithms that embedded within the e-leadership system. Therefore, in Table 8.3, we assign "high" to human leaders and "low" to AI-simulated leaders in this characteristic.

By evaluating these four characteristics, it indicates that in the e-leadership context, both AI-simulated leaders and human leaders can generate a certain level of presence. With that being said, we need to keep in mind that both AI-simulated leaders and human leaders have advantages and limitations when rendering presence in the e-leadership context. Also, by assigning scores to each characteristic (as indicated in Table 8.3), it indicates that AI-simulated leaders' efficacy of rendering presence is limited when comparing to human leaders, due to the limitation in information source variety and information manipulability. However, it is not the case that AI-simulated leaders are valueless. Instead, AI-simulated leaders can still play leaders' roles, take leaders' responsibilities, and finish the leader's jobs in the e-leadership context, in a comparable, similar manner. Therefore, we propose that in the e-leadership context, both AI-simulated leaders and human leaders can render a comparable level of presence, which is positively related to followers' job performance.

Proposition 8.3 *Both AI-simulated leaders and human leaders can render a comparable level of presence, which is positively related to followers' job performance in the e-leadership context, and the level of the positive relationship between leaders' presence and followers' job performance is subject to the type of leader, such that (a) the positive relationship becomes stronger when there is a human leader, and (b) the positive relationship becomes weaker when there is an AI-simulated leader.*

Followers' KSAs

In the previous section, we have compared the differences between human leaders and AI-simulated leaders in terms of their presence (in four characteristics) and the effect of presence on followers' job performance in the e-leadership context. In this section, built upon the Substitute for Leadership Theory, we move our focus from the leaders' perspective to followers' perspective and explore how followers' characteristics can influence the degree to which AI-simulated leaders can substitute human leaders.

As indicated earlier, Substitute for Leadership Theory suggested that the characteristics of workers and tasks can enhance, neutralize, or substitute the need for leaders, and these factors were proposed to serve as moderators that influence relationships between leadership and followers' outcomes (Dionne et al., 2002; Avolio et al., 2009). When seeing AI-simulated leaders through this theory, the extent to which AI-simulated leaders can substitute human leaders is subject to followers' differences in knowledge, skill, and ability (KSA), which can support their daily works (Stevens & Campion, 1994; Wooten, 1993). One of the important implications of workers' KSAs is that followers' KSAs influence their need for leaders' presence, such that followers are less likely to seek support and guidance from leaders when they can finish their jobs independently by utilizing their KSAs (Pearce & Manz, 2005). When followers have a higher level of KSAs, they can finish their jobs independently with less need for support, guidance, and clarification from their leaders, making it less necessary for followers to have job-related communication with leaders. Therefore, there will be a weaker relationship between leaders' presence and followers' job performance in the e-leadership context when followers have a higher level of KSAs, implying that there will not be a strong need for leaders' presence when followers' KSAs are high. Under this circumstance, AI-simulated leaders can be good substitutes for human leaders as rendering presence is not quite important when required leaders' presence is low.

On the other hand, when followers have a lower level of KSAs, they are less capable of finishing tasks independently and are more likely to ask for guidance, support, and clarification from leaders. Therefore, there will be a stronger relationship between leaders' presence and followers' job performance in the e-leadership context when followers have a lower level of KSAs, implying that there will be a strong need for leaders' presence when followers' KSAs are low. Under this circumstance, it is more challenging for AI-simulated leaders to serve as good substitutes for human leaders as AI-simulated leaders are less competent than their human counterparts in rendering presence when required leader presence is high. Therefore, in the e-leadership context, the extent to which AI-simulated leaders' presence can contribute to followers' job performance is subject to followers' KSAs.

Proposition 8.4 *In the e-leadership context, the capacity of rendering presence makes AI-simulated leaders (a) more likely to substitute human leaders when followers' followers' KSAs are high, whereas (b) less likely to substitute human leaders when followers' followers' KSAs are low.*

Job Tasks' Perspective

As indicated earlier, it makes human leaders unnecessary for followers when the level of substitutability is high (Schriesheim, 1997). Here, we move our focus on contextual factors that can potentially make human leaders unnecessary in the e-leadership context. Specifically, we mainly focus on task structure and time pressure.

Task structure. Task structure can influence the extent to which human leaders can be substituted by AI-simulated leaders. The Substitute for Leadership Theory suggests that job design can influence the need for leaders (Dionne et al., 2002; Avolio et al., 2009). As a specific area of job design, task structure can influence the impact of leaders' presence on followers' job performance in an e-leadership context. As indicated by Kerr and Jermier (1978), job design in terms of task structure refers to the nature of the task, which takes task routinization, predictability, and easiness into account. These aspects can indicate the possibility of substituting human leaders with AI-simulated leaders.

When tasks are routinized, they become relatively more predictable and easier for followers to complete so that leaders' support, guidance, and clarification get less indispensable. Therefore, there will be a weaker relationship between leaders' presence and followers' job performance in an e-leadership context when job tasks are routinized, implying that there will not be a strong need for leaders' presence when job tasks are routinized. Under this circumstance, AI-simulated leaders can be good substitutes for human leaders as rendering presence is not quite important when required leaders' presence is low.

On the other hand, when job tasks are not routinized, random issues may come up in the working process, making job tasks less predictable and more challenging, and followers will be more likely to ask for guidance, support, and clarification from leaders. Therefore, there will be a stronger relationship between leaders' presence and followers' job performance in an e-leadership context when job tasks are not routinized, implying that there will be a strong need for leaders' presence when job tasks are not routinized. Under this circumstance, it is more challenging for AI-simulated leaders to serve as good substitutes for human leaders as AI-simulated leaders are less capable than human leaders of rendering presence when required leaders' presence is high. Therefore, in the e-leadership context, the extent to which AI-simulated leaders' presence can positively affect followers' job performance is subject to task structure.

Proposition 8.5 *In the e-leadership context, AI-simulated leaders' capacity of rendering presence is (a) more likely to substitute human leaders when task structure is more routinized, whereas (b) less likely to substitute human leaders when task structure is less routinized.*

Time pressure of the task. In addition to the task structure we discussed above, another factor that can influence followers' job performance in the e-leadership context is the time pressure of the task, which is considered a contextual factor of a task that related to followers' perception of time strain (Munkvold & Zigurs, 2007), such that time pressure is more salient when a person experiences insufficient time to complete a task. A previous study has indicated that individuals within a workgroup are more likely to communicate with others when the time strain is high (Zigurs, 2003). Similarly, in a field study, Gersick (1989) found that when facing time pressure, group members tended to have more communication, compared to the situations that have little or no time pressure. Therefore, time pressure can be another factor that predicts the efficacy of substituting human leaders with AI-simulated leaders in an e-leadership context.

When the time pressure of a task is low, it becomes relatively easier for followers to finish job tasks so that they are less likely to contact leaders for support, guidance, and clarification. Therefore, there will be a weaker relationship between leaders' presence and followers' job performance in the e-leadership context when task time pressure is low, implying there is no strong need for leaders' presence when task time pressure is low. Under this circumstance, AI-simulated leaders can be good substitutes for human leaders as rendering presence is not quite imperative when required leaders' presence is low.

On the other hand, when task time pressure is high, it becomes more challenging for followers to finish job tasks without communicating with leaders. Therefore, there will be a stronger connection between leaders' presence and followers' job performance in the e-leadership context when time pressure is high, implying that there will be a strong need for leaders' presence when time pressure is low. Under this circumstance, it is more challenging for AI-simulated leaders to serve as good substitutes for human leaders as AI-simulated leaders are less capable than human leaders of rendering presence when required leaders' presence is high.

When it comes to the COVID-19 pandemic, time pressure is a major issue. For example, drug companies have time pressure to develop vaccines as quickly as possible, and essential businesses have time pressure to deliver needed products and supplies on time as well. However, because AI-simulated leaders are not as effective as human leaders when time pressure is strong, having AI-simulated leaders in the e-leadership context will not be a wise choice when time pressure is high.

Proposition 8.6 *In the e-leadership context, the capacity of rendering presence makes AI-simulated leaders (a) more likely to substitute human leaders when task time pressure is low, whereas (b) less likely to substitute human leaders when task time pressure is high.*

Discussion

This chapter provides multiple implications to leadership literature as well as leadership in challenging circumstances amid the COVID-19 pandemic. Firstly, applying AI technology to leadership is promising, and having the AI-simulated leaders to substitute human leaders would bring cost-effectiveness and enhanced reliability to organizations. However, as indicated in this chapter, different boundary conditions make AI technology becomes difficult to provide a "one size fits all" solution. This chapter explored factors that influence the effectiveness of AI-simulated leaders in the e-leadership context and provided insights about how to make the best use of AI-simulated leaders and how to utilize them wisely.

Secondly, this chapter extends existing theoretical frameworks of e-leadership. As discussed in this chapter, natural intelligence has dominated e-leadership in the past three decades. Building on the standpoint of the Substitutes for Leadership Theory, this chapter explored the possibility of simulating and substituting natural intelligence based on AI so that organizations can potentially move from the existing "technology-assisted" leadership systems to "technology-centered" intelligence systems.

Furthermore, by integrating AI technology into the e-leadership system and combine AI with natural intelligence, we propose the need for revisiting our existing understanding of e-leadership and introduce the concept of "e-leadership 2.0" that encompasses both AI and natural intelligence, to meet leadership challenges amid the pandemic.

In sum, it is not that the COVID-19 pandemic makes AI-simulated leaders less valuable, instead, AI-simulated leaders make it possible to free up human leaders from the tasks that can be done by AI-simulated leaders so that human leaders can spend their time on other jobs. If widely used in organizations, AI-simulated leaders can potentially drive down HR costs as well.

Five Chapter Takeaways/Lessons

1. The COVID-19 pandemic brings about challenges, such as the increased demand for leaders. AI-simulated leaders can provide a solution.
2. This chapter examined the factors that influence the effectiveness of AI-simulated leaders in an e-leadership context—there is no "one size fits all" solution because boundary conditions in different forms might exist, making AI technology difficult to be a "one size fit all" solution—AI-simulated leaders should be used wisely by taking these factors into account.
3. Workers with varying levels of KSAs join workforces. Business organizations should consider employees' KSA levels before adding AI-simulated leaders.
4. Businesses are transforming (e.g., retail, hospitality)—new business processes should take task structure into account and ensure new task structure is compatible with AI-simulated leaders added to working systems.
5. Many tasks are time-bounded amid the COVID-19 pandemic, meaning that certain tasks need to be finished in a timely manner. However, organization leaders should keep in mind that AI-simulated leaders may not applicable to tasks with tight timeframes.

Five Reflection Questions

1. This chapter discussed two types of leaders within organizations—human leaders and AI-simulated leaders. What is the essential difference between these two types of leaders?
2. Based on the discussion about virtual presence and telepresence, evaluate the following types of communication tools, and indicate the level of presence these tools can bring to workers:
   (a) Text message.
   (b) E-mail.
   (c) Telephone meeting.
   (d) Video meeting.
3. This chapter explores the possibility of substituting human leaders with AI-simulated leaders as well as factors that are likely to influence the efficacy of AI-simulated leaders. Briefly describe these factors. Based on these factors dis-

cussed in this chapter, describe three examples of works that can potentially use AI-simulated leaders.
4. In addition to these factors discussed in this chapter, build on the standpoint of (1) variety of information sources, (2) richness of a certain information source, (3) level of manipulability and (4) level of synchronizability, can you think about other possible influencing factors?
5. Despite their proven efficacy of AI in the healthcare industry (e.g., Dascalu & David, 2019; Hekler et al., 2019), emergency rescue (e.g., McCormick, 2020), financial services (e.g., Castellanos, 2020), etc., AI researchers have recently raised concerns about how to build tools for the future and take ethics into account when developing AI-based technologies, such that ethics need to be "baked into" the design of AI technologies instead of adding ethics aftermath, and it is important to take multi-disciplinary approach when building AI-based technologies so that all aspects that related to ethics will be considered and unintended ethical issues can be prevented (Council, 2020a, b). In the e-leadership context, what are the possible unintended ethical issues when implementing AI-simulated leaders? What do we need to "baked into" the design of AI-simulated leaders?

References

Amabile, T. M. (2020). Guidepost: Creativity, artificial intelligence, and a world of surprises guidepost letter for academy of management discoveries. *Academy of Management Discoveries, 6*(3), 351–354. https://doi.org/10.5465/amd.2019.0075

Amankwah-Amoah, J., Khan, Z., & Wood, G. (2020). COVID-19 and business failures: The paradoxes of experience, scale, and scope for theory and practice. *European Management Journal, 39*, 179–184. https://doi.org/10.1016/j.emj.2020.09.002

Avolio, B. J., Kahai, S., & Dodge, G. E. (2001). E-leadership. *The Leadership Quarterly, 11*(4), 615–668. https://doi.org/10.1016/s1048-9843(00)00062-x

Avolio, B. J., & Kahai, S. S. (2003). Adding the "E" to E-leadership. *Organizational Dynamics, 31*(4), 325–338. https://doi.org/10.1016/s0090-2616(02)00133-x

Avolio, B. J., Sosik, J. J., Kahai, S. S., & Baker, B. (2014). E-leadership: Re-examining transformations in leadership source and transmission. *The Leadership Quarterly, 25*(1), 105–131. https://doi.org/10.1016/j.leaqua.2013.11.003

Avolio, B. J., Walumbwa, F. O., & Weber, T. J. (2009). Leadership: Current theories, research, and future directions. *Annual Review of Psychology, 60*(1), 421–449. https://doi.org/10.1146/annurev.psych.60.110707.163621

Banerjee, P., & Chau, P. Y. (2004). An evaluative framework for analysing e-government convergence capability in developing countries. *Electronic Government, 1*(1), 29. https://doi.org/10.1504/eg.2004.004135

Barr, A., & Nicas, J. (2016, January 27). Google parent claims artificial-intelligence victory in go game win. *WSJ*. https://www.wsj.com/articles/alphabet-units-artificial-intelligence-program-wins-major-victory-1453917602

Bartik, A. W., Cullen, Z. B., Glaeser, E. L., Luca, M., & Stanton, C. T. (2020). *What jobs are being done at home during the COVID-19 crisis: Evidence from firm-level surveys* (w27422). National Bureau of Economic Research.

Bauer, L. B., Bloch, D., & Merkert, R. (2020). Ultra long-haul: An emerging business model accelerated by COVID-19. *Journal of Air Transport Management, 89*, 101901. https://doi.org/10.1016/j.jairtraman.2020.101901

Boudreau, M. C., Loch, K. D., Robey, D., & Straud, D. (1998). Going global: Using information technology to advance the competitiveness of the virtual transnational organization. *Academy of Management Perspectives, 12*(4), 120–128. https://doi.org/10.5465/ame.1998.1334008

Burn, J., & Barnett, M. (1999). Communicating for advantage in the virtual organization. *IEEE Transactions on Professional Communication, 42*(4), 215–222. https://doi.org/10.1109/47.807959

Cascio, W. F. (2000). Managing a virtual workplace. *Academy of Management Perspectives, 14*(3), 81–90. https://doi.org/10.5465/ame.2000.4468068

Cascio, W. F., & Shurygailo, S. (2003). E-leadership and virtual teams. *Organizational Dynamics, 31*(4), 362–376. https://doi.org/10.1016/s0090-2616(02)00130-4

Castellanos, S. (2020, August 26). Visa unveils more powerful AI tool that approves or denies card transactions. *WSJ*. https://www.wsj.com/articles/visa-unveils-more-powerful-ai-tool-that-approves-or-denies-card-transactions-11598436001

Choudhury, P., Foroughi, C., & Larson, B. Z. (2020). Work-from-anywhere: The productivity effects of geographic flexibility. *Academy of Management Proceedings, 2020*(1), 21199. https://doi.org/10.5465/ambpp.2020.225

Clark, J. (2015, December 8). Why 2015 was a breakthrough year in artificial intelligence. *Bloomberg*. https://www.bloomberg.com/news/articles/2015-12-08/why-2015-was-a-breakthrough-year-in-artificial-intelligence

Council, J. (2020a, October 26). Reid Hoffman and Fei-Fei Li on human-centered AI. *Tech News Briefing* [Audio podcast]. https://www.wsj.com/podcasts/tech-news-briefing/reid-hoffman-and-fei-fei-li-on-human-centered-ai-special-episode/5eb79c06-cfe7-435f-b0b2-7a17d1b20ed8

Council, J. (2020b, August 18). Microsoft, energy department to develop disaster-response AI tools. *WSJ*. https://www.wsj.com/articles/microsoft-energy-dept-to-develop-disaster-response-ai-tools-11597755601

Cramton, C. D. (2002). Attribution in distributed work groups. In P. Hinds & S. Kiesler (Eds.), *Distributed work* (pp. 191–212). MIT press.

Crevier, D. (1993). *AI: The tumultuous history of the search for artificial intelligence*. Basic Books.

Daft, R. L., & Lengel, R. H. (1986). Organizational information requirements, media richness and structural design. *Management Science, 32*(5), 554–571. https://doi.org/10.1287/mnsc.32.5.554

Dansereau, F., Seitz, S. R., Chiu, C., Shaughnessy, B., & Yammarino, F. J. (2013). What makes leadership, leadership? Using self-expansion theory to integrate traditional and contemporary approaches. *The Leadership Quarterly, 24*(6), 798–821. https://doi.org/10.1016/j.leaqua.2013.10.008

Dascalu, A., & David, E. (2019). Skin cancer detection by deep learning and sound analysis algorithms: A prospective clinical study of an elementary dermoscope. *eBioMedicine, 43*, 107–113. https://doi.org/10.1016/j.ebiom.2019.04.055

DasGupta, P. (2011). Literature review: E-leadership. *Emerging Leadership Journeys, 4*(1), 1–36.

Day, D. V., & Antonakis, J. (2012). Leadership: Past, present, and future. In D. V. Day & J. Antonakis (Eds.), *The nature of leadership* (pp. 3–25). SAGE.

De la Sen, M., Miñambres, J., Garrido, A., Almansa, A., & Soto, J. (2004). Basic theoretical results for expert systems. Application to the supervision of adaptation transients in planar robots. *Artificial Intelligence, 152*(2), 173–211. https://doi.org/10.1016/s0004-3702(03)00136-x

Deng, L. (2014). Deep learning: Methods and applications. *Foundations and Trends® in Signal Processing, 7*(3–4), 197–387. https://doi.org/10.1561/2000000039

Dionne, S. D., Yammarino, F. J., Atwater, L. E., & James, L. R. (2002). Neutralizing substitutes for leadership theory: Leadership effects and common-source bias. *Journal of Applied Psychology, 87*(3), 454–464. https://doi.org/10.1037/0021-9010.87.3.454

Donthu, N., & Gustafsson, A. (2020). Effects of COVID-19 on business and research. *Journal of Business Research, 117*, 284–289. https://doi.org/10.1016/j.jbusres.2020.06.008

Eisenberger, R., Stinglhamber, F., Vandenberghe, C., Sucharski, I. L., & Rhoades, L. (2002). Perceived supervisor support: Contributions to perceived organizational support and employee retention. *Journal of Applied Psychology, 87*(3), 565–573. https://doi.org/10.1037/0021-9010.87.3.565

Farboodi, M., Jarosch, G., & Shimer, R. (2020). *Internal and external effects of social distancing in a pandemic* (w27059). National Bureau of Economic Research.

Fong, M. W., Gao, H., Wong, J. Y., Xiao, J., Shiu, E. Y., Ryu, S., & Cowling, B. J. (2020). Nonpharmaceutical measures for pandemic influenza in nonhealthcare settings—Social distancing measures. *Emerging Infectious Diseases, 26*(5), 976–984. https://doi.org/10.3201/eid2605.190995

García, I. (2009, April). E-mentoring and e-leadership importance in the quality of distance and virtual education century XXI [paper presentation]. In *International Conference on Multimedia and Information and Communication Technologies in Education.*

Gersick, C. J. (1989). Marking time: Predictable transitions in task groups. *Academy of Management Journal, 32*(2), 274–309. https://doi.org/10.5465/256363

Gunawardena, C. N. (1995). Social presence theory and implications for interaction and collaborative learning in computer conferences. *International Journal of Educational Telecommunications, 1*(2), 147–166.

Gursoy, D., & Chi, C. G. (2020). Effects of COVID-19 pandemic on hospitality industry: Review of the current situations and a research agenda. *Journal of Hospitality Marketing & Management, 29*(5), 527–529. https://doi.org/10.1080/19368623.2020.1788231

Hanson, C. W., & Marshall, B. E. (2001). Artificial intelligence applications in the intensive care unit. *Critical Care Medicine, 29*(2), 427–435. https://doi.org/10.1097/00003246-200102000-00038

Heeter, C. (1992). Being there: The subjective experience of presence. *Presence: Teleoperators and Virtual Environments, 1*(2), 262–271. https://doi.org/10.1162/pres.1992.1.2.262

Hekler, A., Utikal, J. S., Enk, A. H., Hauschild, A., Weichenthal, M., Maron, R. C., et al. (2019). Superior skin cancer classification by the combination of human and artificial intelligence. *European Journal of Cancer, 120*, 114–121.

Hernandez, D. (2020, September 23). A robot beats humans at their own game—This time on the ice. *WSJ.* https://www.wsj.com/articles/a-robot-beats-humans-at-their-own-gamethis-time-on-the-ice-11600890345

Hill, K. (2020, June 24). Wrongfully accused by an algorithm. *The New York Times*. https://www.nytimes.com/2020/06/24/technology/facial-recognition-arrest.html?mod=djemTECH

Hogan, R., & Kaiser, R. B. (2005). What we know about leadership. *Review of General Psychology, 9*(2), 169–180. https://doi.org/10.1037/1089-2680.9.2.169

Holland, J. B., Malvey, D., & Fottler, M. D. (2009). Health care globalization: A need for virtual leadership. *The Health Care Manager, 28*(2), 117–123. https://doi.org/10.1097/hcm.0b013e3181a2cb63

House, R. J. (1996). Path-goal theory of leadership: Lessons, legacy, and a reformulated theory. *The Leadership Quarterly, 7*(3), 323–352. https://doi.org/10.1016/s1048-9843(96)90024-7

House, R. J., & Mitchell, T. R. (2007). Path-goal theory of leadership. *Leadership, 3*, 81–97. https://doi.org/10.2307/j.ctvpg85tk.25

Howell, J. M., Neufeld, D. J., & Avolio, B. J. (2005). Examining the relationship of leadership and physical distance with business unit performance. *The Leadership Quarterly, 16*(2), 273–285. https://doi.org/10.1016/j.leaqua.2005.01.004

Hyacinth, B. T. (2017). *The future of leadership: Rise of automation, robotics and artificial intelligence.* MBA Caribbean Organisation.

Isenberg, D., & Di Fiore, A. (2020). Entrepreneurs: How to change your business model in the pandemic. *LSE Business Review.*

Jarvenpaa, S. L., & Tanriverdi, H. (2003). Leading virtual knowledge networks. *Organizational Dynamics, 31*(4), 403–412. https://doi.org/10.1016/s0090-2616(02)00127-4

Jones, C. J., Philippon, T., & Venkateswaran, V. (2020). *Optimal mitigation policies in a pandemic: Social distancing and working from home* (w26984). National Bureau of Economic Research.

Kahai, S. S., Huang, R., & Jestice, R. J. (2012). Interaction effect of leadership and communication media on feedback positivity in virtual teams. *Group & Organization Management, 37*(6), 716–751. https://doi.org/10.1177/1059601112462061

Kahn, W. A. (1992). To be fully there: Psychological presence at work. *Human Relations, 45*(4), 321–349. https://doi.org/10.1177/001872679204500402

Kerr, E. B. (1986). Electronic leadership: A guide to moderating online conferences. *IEEE Transactions on Professional Communication, PC-29*(1), 12–18. https://doi.org/10.1109/tpc.1986.6449009

Kerr, S., & Jermier, J. M. (1978). Substitutes for leadership: Their meaning and measurement. *Organizational Behavior and Human Performance, 22*(3), 375–403. https://doi.org/10.1016/0030-5073(78)90023-5

Killock, D. (2020). AI outperforms radiologists in mammographic screening. *Nature Reviews Clinical Oncology, 17*(3), 134–134. https://doi.org/10.1038/s41571-020-0329-7

Kiulian, A. (2017, August 8). Why your next boss will be a robot? *Hacker Noon.* https://hackernoon.com/why-your-next-boss-will-be-a-robot-fbe6098de696

Kotter, J. P. (1990). *How leadership differs from management.* Free Press.

Kurzweil, R. (2005). *The singularity is near: When humans transcend biology.* Penguin.

LeCun, Y., Bengio, Y., & Hinton, G. (2015). Deep learning. *Nature, 521*(7553), 436–444. https://doi.org/10.1038/nature14539

Liebowitz, J. (2001). Knowledge management and its link to artificial intelligence. *Expert Systems with Applications, 20*(1), 1–6. https://doi.org/10.1016/s0957-4174(00)00044-0

Lombard, M., & Ditton, T. (1997). At the heart of it all: The concept of presence. *Journal of Computer-Mediated Communication, 3*(2).

Lurey, J. S., & Raisinghani, M. S. (2001). An empirical study of best practices in virtual teams. *Information & Management, 38*(8), 523–544. https://doi.org/10.1016/s0378-7206(01)00074-x

Mantovani, G., & Riva, G. (1999). "Real" presence: How different ontologies generate different criteria for presence, telepresence, and virtual presence. *Presence: Teleoperators and Virtual Environments, 8*(5), 540–550. https://doi.org/10.1162/105474699566459

McCormick, J. (2020, October 1). California firefighters tap AI for an edge in battling wildfires. *WSJ.* https://www.wsj.com/articles/california-firefighters-tap-ai-for-an-edge-in-battling-wildfires-11601544600

Mims, C. (2020, July 18). The next phase of the retail apocalypse: Stores reborn as e-commerce warehouses. *WSJ.* https://www.wsj.com/articles/the-next-phase-of-the-retail-apocalypse-stores-reborn-as-e-commerce-warehouses-11595044859

Moore, J. (2017, December 11). Your boss is probably going to be replaced by an algorithm too. *GQ.* https://www.gq.com/story/algorithm-bosses

Munkvold, B. E., & Zigurs, I. (2007). Process and technology challenges in swift-starting virtual teams. *Information & Management, 44*(3), 287–299. https://doi.org/10.1016/j.im.2007.01.002

Nassauer, S. (2020, May 20). Walmart's U.S. boss expects coronavirus to alter shopping permanently. WSJ. https://www.wsj.com/articles/walmarts-u-s-boss-expects-coronavirus-to-alter-shopping-permanently-11590005488

Pearce, C. L., & Manz, C. C. (2005). The new silver bullets of leadership. *Organizational Dynamics, 34*(2), 130–140. https://doi.org/10.1016/j.orgdyn.2005.03.003

Quraishi, M. I., Rizvi, A. A., & Heidel, R. E. (2020). Off-site radiology workflow changes due to the coronavirus disease 2019 (COVID-19) pandemic. *Journal of the American College of Radiology, 17*(7), 878–881. https://doi.org/10.1016/j.jacr.2020.05.008

Russell, S., & Norvig, P. (2003). *Artificial intelligence: A modern approach.* Prentice-Hall.

Schechner, S. (2017, December 10). Meet your new boss: An algorithm. *WSJ.* https://www.wsj.com/articles/meet-your-new-boss-an-algorithm-1512910800

Scheepers, C. B., & Bogie, J. (2020). Uber sub-Saharan Africa: Contextual leadership for sustainable business model innovation during COVID-19. *Emerald Emerging Markets Case Studies, 10*(3), 1–18. https://doi.org/10.1108/eemcs-05-2020-0165

Schloerb, D. W. (1995). A quantitative measure of telepresence. *Presence: Teleoperators and Virtual Environments, 4*(1), 64–80. https://doi.org/10.1162/pres.1995.4.1.64

Schriesheim, C. A. (1997). Substitutes-for-leadership theory: Development and basic concepts. *The Leadership Quarterly, 8*(2), 103–108. https://doi.org/10.1016/s1048-9843(97)90009-6
Sheridan, T. B. (1992). Musings on telepresence and virtual presence. *Presence: Teleoperators and Virtual Environments, 1*(1), 120–126. https://doi.org/10.1162/pres.1992.1.1.120
Short, J., Williams, E., & Christie, B. (1976). *The social psychology of telecommunications*. Wiley.
Shoss, M. K., Eisenberger, R., Restubog, S. L., & Zagenczyk, T. J. (2013). Blaming the organization for abusive supervision: The roles of perceived organizational support and supervisor's organizational embodiment. *Journal of Applied Psychology, 98*(1), 158–168. https://doi.org/10.1037/a0030687
Simon, R. (2020, August 1). COVID-19 shuttered more than 1 million small businesses. Here is how five survived. *MSN*. https://www.msn.com/en-us/money/smallbusiness/covid-19-shuttered-more-than-1-million-small-businesses-here-is-how-five-survived/ar-BB17r7co
Steuer, J. (1992). Defining virtual reality: Dimensions determining telepresence. *Journal of Communication, 42*(4), 73–93. https://doi.org/10.1111/j.1460-2466.1992.tb00812.x
Stevens, M. J., & Campion, M. A. (1994). The knowledge, skill, and ability requirements for teamwork: Implications for human resource management. *Journal of Management, 20*(2), 503–530. https://doi.org/10.1177/014920639402000210
Sutton, R. S., & Barto, A. G. (1998). *Reinforcement learning: An introduction. A Bradford Book*. MIT Press.
Thurlow, C., Lengel, L., & Tomic, A. (2004). *Computer-mediated communication*. Sage.
Uberti, D. (2020, June 1). Algorithms used in policing face policy review. *WSJ*. https://www.wsj.com/articles/algorithms-used-in-policing-face-policy-review-11591003801
Van Ryssen, S., & Godar, S. H. (2000). Going international without going international. *Journal of International Management, 6*(1), 49–60. https://doi.org/10.1016/s1075-4253(00)00019-3
Walvoord, A. A., Redden, E. R., Elliott, L. R., & Coovert, M. D. (2008). Empowering followers in virtual teams: Guiding principles from theory and practice. *Computers in Human Behavior, 24*(5), 1884–1906. https://doi.org/10.1016/j.chb.2008.02.006
West, D. M. (2016). *Moving forward: Self-driving vehicles in China, Europe, Japan, Korea, and the United States*. Center for Technology Innovation at Brookings.
Wooten, W. (1993). Using knowledge, skill and ability (KSA) data to identify career pathing opportunities: An application of job analysis to internal manpower planning. *Public Personnel Management, 22*(4), 551–563. https://doi.org/10.1177/009102609302200405
Yan, L., & Panteli, N. (2007). The politics of presence and absence in distributed organisations. In *ECIS 2007 Proceedings*.
Yukl, G. A., & Uppal, N. (2018). *Leadership in organizations*. Pearson Education.
Zigurs, I. (2003). Leadership in virtual teams: Oxymoron or opportunity. *Organizational Dynamics, 31*(4), 339–351. https://doi.org/10.1016/s0090-2616(02)00132-8

Xiaochuan Song is an Assistant Professor of Management in the Department of Management at Nova Southeastern University. He earned his Ph.D. from the University of Alabama. Dr. Song's research interests include Organizational Justice, Workplace Mistreatment, Employee Well-being, and Crowdsourcing.

Michael Ford is an Associate Professor of Management in the Department of Management at the University of Alabama. He earned his Ph.D. from the George Mason University. Dr. Ford's research interests include Occupational Health, Stress, and Safety, Emotions and Motivation, Employee–Organization Relationship, and Work–Life Balance.

The Role of Leaders in Enabling Organizational Resilience by Generating a Culture of Grit

9

Celeste Raver Luning and Andrew Ledford

The Role of Leaders in Enabling Organizational Resilience by Generating a Culture of Grit

Organizations have long faced the dilemma of how to endure hardship and emerge from organizational disruptions intact. For leaders of those organizations, facing crisis and challenge is part of their role. However, some organizational disruptions and crises are considerably more complex, requiring new and creative approaches to overcome the hurdles. In late 2019 and early 2020, as COVID-19 began to spread across the globe, organizations and their leaders were faced with increasingly *unprecedented* challenges. Hospital leaders were faced with questions of how to maintain the health and safety of their workforce, while finding ways to take care of the sick with shortages of supplies, equipment, and beds. Educational leaders faced the question of how to effectively educate their student body, while adapting to an external environment with increasing limitations. Restaurant owners and owners of service organizations confronted the question of how to remain in operation when their ability to provide services faced substantial restrictions. Retail organizations had to shift their focus to online sales and ensure product availability on new platforms. Religious organizations and their leadership had to adapt and find new methods to provide support to those in their congregation. Essentially no leader or organization across the globe was immune from the challenges imposed by the COVID-19 pandemic.

There have been global challenges with widespread impact, such as the flu pandemic of 1918, World War I, World War II, and even the HIN1 flu epidemic in 2009. However, in modern day society, this pandemic carries a much greater global impact

C. Raver Luning (✉) · A. Ledford
Department of Leadership, Ethics, and Law, United States Naval Academy, Annapolis, MD, USA
e-mail: luning@usna.edu; ledford@usna.edu

S. K. Dhiman, J. F. Marques (eds.), *Leadership After COVID-19*, Future of Business and Finance, https://doi.org/10.1007/978-3-030-84867-5_9

due to how interconnected global society has become both socially and economically (Brammer et al., 2020; Hsu et al., 2020). The COVID-19 pandemic illuminates how important it is to answer fundamental questions about how leaders enable organizations to persist through challenge. What does it take for organizations to persist through such an unparalleled global situation? What role do leaders play in enabling organizations to persist during such a crisis? How can leaders foster an environment where the people in the organization and the organization itself are able to be resilient through the disruption?

To begin to answer these questions, it is important to understand what researchers consider to be an organization's ability to persist or rebound through crisis. Many researchers (e.g., Barasa et al., 2018; Linnenluecke, 2017; Sutcliffe & Vogus, 2003; Vogus & Sutcliffe, 2007) consider organizational resilience to represent an organization's ability to persist through a crisis. Organizational resilience is a broad concept with numerous definitions and conceptualizations (Annarelli & Nonino, 2016; Duchek, 2020). It is often considered a process that emerges in organizations when they respond to disruptions (Carden et al., 2018). The ideas of organizational resilience emerged in the 1980s with research into how organizations adapt to environmental shocks (e.g., Meyer, 1982). However, the conceptualizations of organizational resilience are in their infancy and there is limited consensus as to what organizational factors and capacities enable an organization to be resilient (Duchek, 2020; Fisher et al., 2019; Linnenluecke, 2017). Yet, there is agreement (e.g., Barasa et al., 2018; Carden et al., 2018; Duchek, 2020; Ortiz-de-Mandojana & Bansal, 2016) that organizational resilience is necessary for an organization to persist through and rebound from disruptions.

The question is what can and should leaders do to generate an organizational environment that is primed for resilience. This chapter will highlight that creating a culture of organizational grit may serve as a foundation for how organizations are able to be resilient in the face of crisis. Organizational grit can be understood as an organization's ability to remain focused on its central purpose or mission and persevere through organizational failures and setbacks (Raver Luning, 2019). Organizational grit is a nascent concept in the organizational literature; however, it has been identified as a cultural aspect of an organization (Duckworth, 2016; Lee & Duckworth, 2018; Raver Luning et al., 2021). While the idea of organizational grit is still emerging, the concept of grit, passion and perseverance toward a long-term goal (Duckworth et al., 2007), is far from a new concept.

This chapter will outline what is currently understood about organizational resilience and a culture of organizational grit. It will then provide details of how a culture of organizational grit may enable an organization to be resilient through disruptions, such as the COVID-19 pandemic. After establishing this foundation, the chapter will address the role that leaders play in enabling an organization to persist through crisis; highlighting how leaders can forge a culture of organizational grit which may support an organization in being resilient through a time of crisis. Holistically, the chapter will address how leaders can foster a cultural environment primed for resilience; ultimately, enabling their organizations to persist through the COVID-19 pandemic and future obstacles of smaller and larger magnitude.

Organizational Resilience

The principles of resilience are ubiquitous within many research disciplines (King et al., 2016). No matter what the discipline, resilience captures the idea of adapting to changes in the environment, and overcoming and recovering from upheaval (Olsson et al., 2015). However, in most disciplines, the definitions and conceptualizations of resilience are broad. Organizational resilience perspectives can be grouped into three categories: resilience involves (1) resistance and recovery, (2) adaptation, or (3) anticipation (Duchek, 2020). Most often organizational resilience is considered an outcome, describing an organization that has rebounded from disruption (e.g., Boin & van Eeten, 2013; Gittell et al., 2006; Kendra & Wachtendorf, 2003). Yet, it is often unclear what is beneath the surface of organizations that enable them to be resilient when they face crises. Some researchers focus on the resources that enable an organization to be resilient (e.g., Kendra & Wachtendorf, 2003; Gittell et al., 2006), while others emphasize policies that enable organizational resilience (e.g., Lengnick-Hall et al., 2011; Riolli & Savicki, 2003). Duchek (2020) considered resilience to be a meta-capability consisting of anticipation, coping, and adaptation stages.

Despite these varied conceptualizations into organizational resilience, what is often missing from the discussion is an indication of the cultural dynamics of the organization that enable it to be resilient. Organizational culture is "central in all aspects of organizational life" (Alvesson, 2013, p. 1). It is generally understood as the values, beliefs, and patterns of behavior that lay at the underbelly of an organization (Schein, 2017). Weick (1987), in writing about high reliability organizations, highlighted the role of culture. He stated, "culture coordinates action at a distance by several symbolic means" (Weick, 1987, p. 125). Thus, if an organization's culture plays a vital role in its actions, then it is important to consider how an organization's culture may *coordinate action* as the organization is developing capacities for resilience or demonstrating resilience through a crisis.

Some researchers (e.g., Barasa et al., 2018; Boin & van Eeten, 2013; Carden et al., 2018; Williams et al., 2017) mention organizational culture as an important aspect in enabling an organization to be resilient, but few develop this further. Riolli and Savicki (2003) indicated that organizational culture may serve as a foundation for how an organization builds resiliency. Boin and van Eeten (2013) emphasized that culture can either enhance or detract from an organization's ability to be resilient. Williams et al. (2017) emphasized that certain features of a system may contribute to its resilience, such as culture. In their review of the literature, Barasa et al. (2018) provided that organizational culture is one of many factors that impact the resilience of an organization. Carden et al.'s (2018) study of McDonald's emphasized how strong organizational cultures may help to build capacities for organizational resilience. Fisher et al. (2019) pointed out that organizational factors, such as culture, may support resilience, but the focus was primarily resilience of individuals in the workplace. Duchek (2020) emphasized the need to better understand the role of culture in generating organizational resilience.

What is missing is an indication of the components of an organizational culture that enable an organization to be resilient. Organizational culture is complex and interwoven into how the organization and those within the organization operate (Alvesson, 2013). Thus, it is not enough to merely indicate that organizational culture may serve to enable organizational resilience. It is important to consider the manifestation of that organizational culture. While still an emerging area of research, one could argue that a culture of organizational grit may be what enables an organization to be resilient.

Culture of Organizational Grit

In the twenty-first century, the concept grit became popular following Duckworth et al.'s (2007) reintroduction of the term as a noncognitive personality trait, however, the idea of grit has long been established throughout global society (Ris, 2015). The idea of grit as a characteristic of an individual that displays tenacity and determination emerged in the early literary works of Hawthorne and Alger (Raver Luning & Ledford, 2020; Ris, 2015). In 1882, *Grit* was established as a rural newspaper in the United States (U.S.), which has remained in publication as a magazine in the twenty-first century (Teller, 2020). The newspaper came to symbolize small town traditions, with a focus on the courage, determination, and strength of rural communities (Van Auken, 2020). As many newspapers and magazines have ceased to exist over the last three decades, *Grit* survived, remaining true to its small town and rural roots, attributing its survival to the sheer grit of the organization (Teller, 2020). In many ways, the values and drive of this newspaper, turned magazine, represent the idea of grit as a cultural dynamic both of the organization and the communities which the magazine represents.

Duckworth (2016) wrote about the cultural idea of grit in Finnish society known as *sisu*. *Sisu* represents an energy and steadiness, which is tied to human endurance (Lahti, 2019). It is often considered an action mindset supported by extraordinary perseverance. The idea of *sisu* as a cultural aspect of Finnish society has long been discussed around the world. *Time* magazine, in 1940, ran a story on how *sisu* enabled Finland, the underdog, to remain steadfast during a battle with Russia in World War II (Duckworth, 2016). In the same timeframe, *The New York Times* ran a story describing *sisu* as a cultural ideal in Finnish society representing the society's extraordinary persistence and perseverance (Strode, 1940). Essentially, the concept of *sisu* has overlapping principles with the idea of grit and highlights how courage, strength, and fortitude can be embedded at the societal level. While the idea of grit is not new from either an individual or collective standpoint, it is important to review what is known about the concept of grit from an empirical and a theoretical perspective to understand how it might enable an organization to be resilient.

Grit at the Individual Level

From an empirical and theoretical perspective, grit is primarily considered an individual characteristic, representing one's *consistency of interest* toward a long-term goal and their *perseverance of effort* toward that same goal (Duckworth et al., 2007; Duckworth & Quinn, 2009). In numerous studies, higher levels of individual grit are linked to increased success (e.g., Duckworth et al., 2007, 2009, 2011; Mooradian et al., 2016; Pate et al., 2017), retention (e.g., Eskreis-Winkler et al., 2014; Kelly et al., 2014; Salles et al., 2017), and greater personal well-being (e.g., Datu et al., 2016; Jin & Kim, 2017; Vainio & Daukantaite, 2016). From a theoretical perspective, grit was recently linked to goal-setting theory (Jordan et al., 2019a). Gritty individuals use a hierarchical goal framework to achieve their superordinate long-term goal, which is achieved through accomplishment and readjustment of various subordinate goals as one works toward the superordinate, long-term end-goal (Duckworth & Gross, 2014).

Despite its popularity, the empirical and theoretical development of the individual grit construct does have critics (e.g., Credé, 2018; Credé et al., 2017; Ion et al., 2017; Rimfeld et al., 2016; Schmidt et al., 2020). The critiques of the individual grit construct center around the potential lack of discriminant validity from other personality traits, such as conscientiousness, as well as problematic construct validity. However, even critics of the individual grit construct (e.g., Credé et al., 2017) have indicated that grit warrants examination within organizational contexts and others (e.g., Jordan et al., 2019a, b) have made progress in reconceptualizing grit through new theoretical lenses, such as goal-setting and human resource theories. Thus, while the critiques of the individual grit construct are notable, the idea of grit as a cultural dynamic of an organization is distinct from the concerns of grit at the individual level of analysis.

Grit at the Organizational Level

The principles and tenets of organizational grit are still developing. However, there are conceptualizations of grit as a cultural dynamic of an organization (e.g., Duckworth, 2016; Lee & Duckworth, 2018) and initial exploratory research into the idea of a culture of organizational grit (e.g., Raver Luning et al., 2021) which provide indications of what constitutes a gritty culture, how to develop such a culture, and how a culture of organizational grit may enable an organization to be resilient. Duckworth (2016) explores the idea of a culture of grit through evaluating potentially gritty organizations and their leaders. Her focus is primarily on how culture, specifically a culture of grit, may influence one's individual grit. She stated,

> The bottom line on culture and grit is: *If you want to be grittier, find a gritty culture and join it. If you're a leader, and you want the people in your organization to be grittier, create a gritty culture.* (Duckworth, 2016, p. 245).

Duckworth's (2016) consideration of a culture of grit is limited in that the primary focus is on how culture may influence one's individual identity, or grittiness, rather than on the internal mechanics of the culture. However, there are a few insights that provide an initial framework to understand the dynamics of a gritty culture. One of Duckworth's interviewees, Anson Dorrance, University of North Carolina's head women's soccer coach, indicated that the core values everyone in the group lives by and believes are central to developing a gritty culture. Another interviewee, Jamie Dimon, the CEO of JPMorgan Chase, indicated that communication was central to creating such a culture. Seattle Seahawks head coach, Pete Carroll, created a culture of grit by stressing the importance of working together to strive for the best, respecting one another and the team, and always challenging oneself and the group to improve.

Lee and Duckworth (2018) reflected on grit at the individual, team, and organizational levels of analysis, linking grit at each level within an organization. From their perspective, for a team or organization to display grit, there must be a focus on a shared central purpose of the team or organization. That purpose is achieved through an interconnected goal framework, much like the goal framework used by gritty individuals. Moreover, for the group to know and work toward that purpose, there must be individual passion toward that purpose and clarity regarding the purpose itself. Further, commitment to that purpose from the leaders of the team and organization was considered to be central to generating grit in the team or organization. Relative to the organization, Lee and Duckworth indicated that the culture of the organization is what enables both the individuals and the teams within the organization to display grit.

In an interview study with U.S. military officers, Raver Luning et al. (2021) collected officers' perceptions of a culture of organizational grit. The study extended the theoretical tenets of individual grit to the organization level, and then used an organizational culture perspective to build a foundation for the concept of a culture of organizational grit. Officers were asked questions about how their units and commands overcame obstacles and how those same units and commands were able to remain focused on their mission both during normal circumstances and in the face of setbacks. In contrast to Duckworth's (2016) focus on how a culture of grit may enhance individual grittiness, Raver Luning et al.'s focus was on the cultural mechanisms that may represent grit at the organizational level.

Raver Luning et al. (2021) concluded that a culture of organization grit consisted of several organizational dynamics. Central to this culture was a focus on accomplishing the mission or central purpose of the unit, which tied to the mission of the organization. This focus on the mission seemed to form the foundation of a culture of organizational grit, which ties to Lee and Duckworth's (2018) idea that a central purpose would be a key component of a gritty organization. Similar to Duckworth's (2016) discussion of a culture of grit, strong organizational core values emerged as a component of a culture of organization grit and those strong core values were part of what enabled the team or organization to rebound from setbacks while remaining focused on their mission or central purpose (Raver Luning et al., 2021). The study also indicated that a collective growth mindset, a culture that supports a willingness to learn from mistakes and persist through the next challenge with openness (Murphy & Dweck, 2010), was a component of a culture of organizational grit. Strong team unity was said to be important for the group to overcome setbacks and deliberate practice around building skills centered on the central mission of the group seemed to build team unity (Raver Luning et al., 2021). Professional pride also emerged as a perceived dynamic in a culture of organizational grit, which may capture the tenet of passion that is foundational to the concept of grit at the individual level (Duckworth et al., 2007). Finally, in the study, collective determination was part of what enabled the group to be resilient in the face of obstacles (Raver Luning et al., 2021). While this early empirical work has limitations, its inquiry into leaders' perceptions of a culture of organizational grit does provide details of what may comprise such a culture.

The early conceptualizations (e.g., Duckworth, 2016; Lee & Duckworth, 2018) and empirical work into a culture of organizational grit (e.g., Raver Luning et al., 2021) provide support for the idea that an organization with such a cultural dynamic may be able to persist through catastrophic organizational disruptions; displaying resilience in the face of challenges such as the COVID-19 pandemic. Most central to a gritty culture appears to be a focus on a central purpose or mission of the organization or group. The organization's ability to remain focused on this central purpose seems to be supported by strong core values that are foundational to how the organization operates, as well as a pride or passion toward the purpose of the organization. Organizations with a culture of organizational grit are likely to be cohesive with all working closely as a team and unit. Finally, it seems as if there may be elements of learning from mistakes or hardships, growth mindset, at the team and organizational level, and a pattern of behavior of determined effort to work through both daily and more disruptive challenges. Ultimately, these factors seem to converge as the values, beliefs, and patterns of behavior that are representative of a culture of organizational grit.

How Organizational Grit Can Enable Organizational Resilience

Organizational grit seems to capture the cultural dynamics that many researchers (e.g., Barasa et al., 2018; Boin & van Eeten, 2013; Carden et al., 2018; Duchek, 2020; Williams et al., 2017) suggest are necessary for an organization to be resilient. This leads to the question of how might a gritty culture enable an organization to be resilient in the face of adversity. If culture is a catalyst for action (Weick, 1987), then it could be said that a culture of organizational grit may have environmental elements that encourage action when the organization is faced with crisis. Figure 9.1 represents how it is proposed a culture of organizational grit can facilitate this resilient action in the face of organizational disruption. A gritty culture may help an organization and its leaders resist and recover from crisis, as well as adapt to persist through the crisis. Central to this culture seems to be the purpose or mission focus of the organization; purpose and mission are used interchangeably, considered the central objective of organization and its reason for existence.

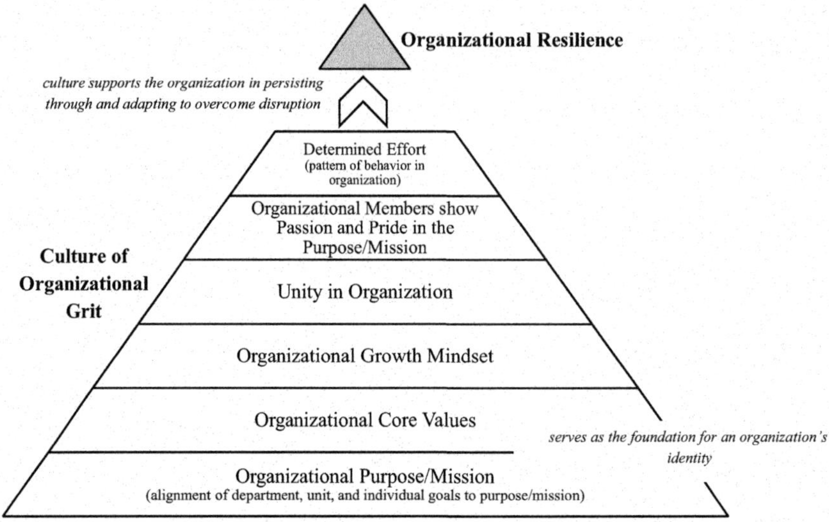

Fig. 9.1 Culture of organizational grit supporting organizational resilience

A central tenet of individual grit is the superordinate goal framework that one uses to achieve their long-term goal (Duckworth & Gross, 2014). It seems that in an organization this same superordinate goal framework may be applied with the purpose or mission of the organization serving as that superordinate goal that drives organizational performance. This focus on the purpose of the organization is embedded into the culture of the organization; it drives actions of those in the organization. Further, the focus on the purpose is what is a catalyst for action when there is disruption and facilitates the organization's ability to persist through, adapt to, and rebound from crisis.

In many ways, the focus on the central purpose or mission may serve to form the identity of the unit, team, or organization, which then embeds into the culture of the organization. Whetten (2006) defined the identity of an organization as "the central and enduring attributes of an organization that distinguish it from other organizations" (p. 220). The link between organizational culture and identity is explained by Hatch and Schultz (2002), where identity of an organization serves to embed values into an organizational culture and overtime culture becomes a representation of that organization's identity. Alvesson (2013) explained "organizational culture provides a framework for identity-formation projects. At the same time, identity provides important reference points to how to relate various cultural meanings" (p. 39). Essentially, the identity and culture of the organization are connected, in which feedback loops connect each element as the organization grows, changes, and ultimately deals with challenges. Relative to how a gritty culture enables an organization to be resilient in the face of crisis, it seems that a strong organizational identity centered upon the organizational purpose or mission is at the heart of that culture. As Schein (2017) indicated, organizational cultures with a strong identity have latent features that can empower, or diminish, an organization's ability to respond to their environment and challenges imposed by the environment in which they operate.

Other work (e.g., Denison, 1997; Denison & Mishra, 1995) supported the notion that purpose driven or mission focused organizational cultures enable organizational performance. Denison (1997) indicated that the mission contributes to organizational performance in two primary ways. First, it provides meaning and purpose to the role and goals of the organization, under which individual roles and goals should be defined and aligned. Second, an organizational mission that is embedded into the organization serves to provide clarity and direction. This clarity and direction not only help the organization collectively, but it also helps the individuals within the organization to operate both during times of calm and times of crisis. Schein (2017) highlighted the importance of goal alignment to the overall mission or purpose of the organization for culture to generate positive organizational outcomes. This sentiment was also emphasized by Denison in that individual goal alignment must be present in strong mission focused organizational cultures.

Aligning this principle with the Lee and Duckworth (2018) conceptualization of organizational grit and Raver Luning et al.'s (2021) exploration of a culture of organizational grit, it can be said that at the core of an organization with a culture of grit there must be alignment of individual, unit, department, and organizational goals to the purpose or mission of the organization. A representation of this alignment is provided in Fig. 9.2. It can then be argued that this mission focus and the alignment of the goals at all levels of the organization, can help serve as the force for action when the organization is faced with crisis. Essentially, it serves as the culture enabler for the organization to be resilient in the time of crisis. It seems to support the pattern of behavior of determined effort from those within the organization during the times of crisis that can help the organization to persist through an organizational disruption.

Thus, when an organization with a culture of organizational grit is faced with crisis, this embedded identity of the organization around its central purpose and the alignment at all levels of the organization to that central purpose is at the core of the organization's persistence or resilience. This is much like what acts as the core

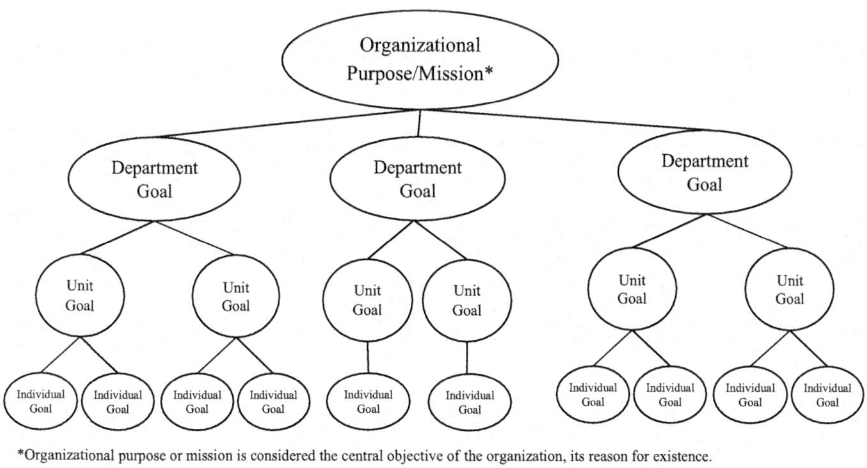

Fig. 9.2 Superordinate goal structure in a culture of organizational grit

driving force for a gritty individual; a gritty individual when faced with an obstacle is so driven by their particular long-term goal that they rebound by adjusting and reconfiguring lower order goals and then continuing to work toward their ultimate goal (Duckworth et al., 2007; Duckworth & Gross, 2014). Essentially, the purpose of the organization is so important and embedded into the functionality and culture of the organization, an obstacle, even as big as COVID-19, will not diminish the individuals in the organization, the leaders, or the organization, as a collective, in consistently working to accomplish the purpose that is central to its identity.

Further, it could be argued that the purpose-centered nature of the organization is what enables it to adapt in the face of challenge, which is part of how and why the organization is resilient. Carden et al. (2018) argued that McDonald's was able to be resilient as the fast-food industry changed by having an organizational culture that supported adaptation to a changing external environment. Carden et al. highlighted how core values, embedded into the culture, were tapped into when the organization needed to adapt to a changing external environment. This idea can be linked to Duckworth's (2016) indication that core values are central to a culture of grit. Further, it can be linked to Raver Luning et al.'s (2021) finding that core values embedded into the culture can support a unit rebounding from setbacks. Ultimately, a culture of organization grit appears to be one with strong core values; these core values may be central to the organization's ability to adapt to a challenging external environment. They seem to serve to guide the leaders and others in the organization around what is central to the value system of the organization, which allows change and adaptation to occur without losing sight of what are the foundational values of the organization.

Duchek (2020) indicated that a component of organizational resilience involved adaptation where reflection and learning occur, followed by change. This may link to the idea of a growth mindset that appears to be a dynamic of a culture of organizational grit (Raver Luning et al., 2021). Lee and Duckworth (2018) also indicated that gritty organizations would promote and cultivate growth mindset in the organization. Growth mindset captures the idea that "abilities can be cultivated" (Dweck, 2016, p. 50); those abilities can be of the individual or of a group. There is indication that growth mindset emerges as a cultural aspect of an organization (e.g., Delaney, 2014; Murphy & Dweck, 2010). Essentially, a growth mindset helps both individuals and the organization, holistically, to view setbacks as opportunities for learning, growth, and development. Thus, an organization with this cultural dynamic of viewing setbacks as a way to grow and learn may be more likely to adapt in a time of crisis, collectively learning and reflecting, then changing as needed to persist through the challenging experience.

Ultimately, it appears as if the mission-centered nature embedded into the culture of a gritty organization can be linked to the organization's ability to persist through crises both big and small; it supports the organization in displaying resilience in the face of challenge. Further, it seems as if the core values of the organization and a collective growth mindset serve as enablers to support the adaptation that is needed when an organization is faced with crisis. Essentially, it appears as if the dynamics of a culture of organization grit can serve as the catalyst for action when an organization faces a crisis and help to facilitate the organization in being resilient through such a disruption. Yet, the question remains as to how a leader enables and fosters these cultural dynamics.

Leaders' Role in Enabling and Fostering a Gritty Culture

Leaders' role within organizational culture is abstract; it is hard to extrapolate and explain (Alvesson, 2013). Despite this difficulty, Alvesson (2013) indicated that "leadership is a culture-influencing activity" (p. 111). In order for leaders to influence culture, they must be aware of the current organization culture in which they operate. Schein (2017) provides a framework for how leaders embed and transmit culture. In his framework, there are six primary and secondary embedding mechanisms. The primary mechanisms include: (1) what leaders pay attention to, measure, and control on a regular basis, (2) how leaders react to critical incidents and organizational crises, (3) how leaders allocate resources, (4) deliberate role modeling, teaching, and coaching, (5) how leaders allocate rewards and status, and (6) how leaders recruit, select, promote, and excommunicate (Schein, 2017, p. 183). The secondary mechanisms reinforce the cultural dynamics and serve to establish, or stabilize them, as part of the culture of the organization. The secondary mechanisms include: (1) organizational design and structure, (2) organizational systems and procedures, (3) rites and rituals of the organization, (4) design of physical space, facades, and buildings, (5) stories about important events and people, and (6) formal statements of organizational philosophy, creeds, and charters (Schein, 2017, p. 183).

Primary Methods to Influence Culture

With Schein's (2017) framework in mind, leaders may be able to create a gritty organizational culture, which over time could help to enable the organization to be resilient in the face of crisis. First, if the leader establishes, clarifies, and then continuously focuses on the central purpose or mission of the organization, it can begin to create an organization that is mission-centric and driven by a clear purpose. This can be done by paying regular attention to the mission and putting it at the forefront of both daily and long-term planning and operations. Further, the leader can introduce this mission-centered nature by ensuring alignment of goals around the purpose of the organization; develop an organizational goal hierarchy, much like the one presented in Fig. 9.2. The leader can use this framework to ensure that resources are adequately allocated at each level of the hierarchy. This allocation of resources can help to ensure continued alignment of the goals to the mission of that particular supporting unit of the organization and show the importance of that unit's role in supporting the mission.

The leaders should also focus on the people within the organization. Ensure that individuals' values align with the organizational values and core purpose. This is like Collin's (2001) principle of getting the right people on the bus, ensuring proper organizational fit, and then focusing on fitting individuals into the right roles within the organization. Once the right people are in the right positions in the organization, leaders should reward those that create and support an environment that is focused on the core purpose of the organization. Thus, reward the individuals who maintain and create goals both individually and for the groups that they lead that clearly fit in the superordinate goal structure of the organization. Relative to culture, this act, of making certain those in the organization are aligned with its central purpose and rewarding behavior that aligns with it, serves to further entrench the mission as central to the cultural value system of the organization.

Finally, the leader must realize that they serve as a representative of culture (Alvesson, 2013; Schein, 2017). Thus, when they respond to a critical event by emphasizing the core purpose of the organization, discussing how the organization can still achieve that core purpose, and then ultimately facilitating adaptation of the organization to continue to serve its core purpose, this shows all in the organization how to respond to crisis. In turn, the individuals in the organization follow suit, shifting individual and unit goals to adapt while still achieving the core purpose of the unit and ultimately organization. Thus, collectively the organization adapts in the face of crisis or displays resilience. This shifting is not easy, but the leader can help all to shift by being a role model, emphasizing having a growth mindset both individually and collectively, and supporting and encouraging those in the organization as they struggle to work around new requirements and changes.

To put this in the context of how organizational leaders dealing with COVID-19 can immediately embed and foster this culture, consider a school or university faced with restrictions relative to teaching students in its normal settings. First, the organizational leaders must make certain that they are clear about what the core purpose of the organization is. If not, leaders should communicate that core purpose to organizational members and emphasize the need to adapt in the time of disruption, while still fulfilling the organization's core purpose. Perhaps that core purpose is to educate students in a loving, learning environment, while maintaining a safe teaching environment for its educators. Next, leaders should consider how this core purpose is translated to all who are part of the organization, both the students and educators. The leaders should evaluate the alignment of goals of groups and departments within the organization and further the individuals (teachers) to the purpose of the organization. If there is misalignment, efforts should be taken to ensure alignment of the subordinate goals to the superordinate purpose of the organization. If individuals do not seem to align with the core purpose of the organization, perhaps they are not the right people on the bus (Collins, 2001).

Finally, the leaders should consider how the organization can still achieve its core purpose in light of external restrictions. How does the organization adapt, but not lose sight of what is the driving force behind the organization? In this case, perhaps leaders decide that keeping students in the classroom is the best way to optimally educate students in a loving, learning environment. However, doing this may require limiting class size, increasing distance between all students, imposing restrictions on movement throughout the facilities, and providing protective gear and COVID testing to all teachers on a regular basis to create a safe teaching environment for the educators. Once these adaptations are identified, the leaders should take steps to act and adapt in response to the crisis. First, proper alignment of all group and department goals should be considered relative to how the organization will adapt. Then, the leaders should begin the process of teaching and coaching those that will need to carry out these new methods of achieving the core purpose of the organization. The leaders should be present and role model this new approach with a realistic, yet positive attitude.

Secondary Methods to Influence Culture

The secondary methods to influence culture are what solidify culture as a part of the organization (Schein, 2017). They are what help the culture to be transferred to members of the organization. Considering the organizational design and structure, as well as the systems and procedures, one area in which leaders may introduce a culture of organizational grit is by limiting silos in their organization. This idea of limiting silos stems from Pete Carroll's emphasis on striving as a team in a gritty culture (Duckworth, 2016) and the importance of team unity that emerged as a perceived dynamic of a culture of organizational grit (Raver Luning et al., 2021). A siloed organization may have difficulty in clearly aligning around a hierarchical goal framework and working as a unified force against a challenge. Further, it may be hard to clearly identify how each department or unit goal aligns with the central purpose of the organization. By structuring the organization and creating policies that limit the creation of a siloed operating environment, it is easier for the leader to foster a culture that is mission centric or purpose driven. One simple way to do this is through the structure of the physical layout within the organization; creating an environment where there is overlap between various operating units so that cross discussion occurs and shared language around the central purpose emerges in the organization.

In the midst of the COVID-19 pandemic, leaders should assess their organizations for silos. If there are silos, leaders should first examine if the goals of each siloed unit align with the purpose of the organization, if not, take steps to shift the goals of the misaligned units or departments to align with the purpose. If there is alignment, but just siloed operating environments, create opportunities for integration between those separate units. For example, leaders can create shared goals between the units or departments that align with the purpose of the organization as it adapts to the challenging external environment. This should serve to help the siloed units have a shared purpose and operate in a more cohesive manner; thus, generating unity in the organization.

Other secondary embedding mechanisms of culture that may generate a gritty organization are through symbolic (rites, rituals, and stories) and indirect methods (formal statements and language). For example, to embed and foster the aspect of determination that emerged as a cultural dynamic in a gritty organization (Raver Luning et al., 2021), leaders should tell and retell stories about the organization persisting through a crisis. These stories become organizational folklore (Schein, 2017) which provide a representation of what the organization is capable of in a time of crisis; they also serve to set an expectation of how to act in a time of organizational disruption. For leaders dealing with the COVID-19 pandemic, one way to initiate this is to use stories of when the organization faced potentially devastating challenges in the past. Tell and retell those stories to show that the organization has displayed resilience in the past and will display resilience in this moment of crisis. Moreover, as the organization persists through and after the organization is resilient in the face of the COVID-19 pandemic, leaders should consider the stories that they will strategically tell and retell to further embed and foster that determination into the cultural dynamics of the organization. With these stories, consideration should be placed on how the purpose of the organization served to help the organization be resilient in the face of potentially devastating obstacles.

Another secondary embedding mechanism that should be considered is the use of language and formal statements to represent the organizational philosophy and purpose of the organization. This may be language that is tied to the core values of the organization. If the core values of an organization are a part of a culture of organizational grit (Duckworth, 2016; Raver Luning et al., 2021) and core values embedded into the culture can help an organization to be resilient (Carden et al., 2018), language that continually references the core values may serve to enable organizations to be resilient. In many ways this is done in the U.S. military, the core values of each military branch are emphasized continuously as individual soldiers, sailors, and airmen progress through the accession pipelines of their respective branches. The core values are emphasized by military leaders in their teams, units, and commands. As those teams, units, and commands adapt to a rapidly changing external environment, the core values are part of the driving force of why and how the groups are able to shift and continue to fulfill their mission. Further, language that focuses on highlighting the core purpose or mission of the organization should be used to embed and foster a culture of organizational grit. For example, if the core purpose is to create a high-quality product, then language should be continually used that emphasizes this goal.

To embed and foster this cultural dynamic during the COVID-19 pandemic, leaders should use language centered around the core values and mission if that was not already a norm within the organization. Leaders may find that organizational members quickly adopt such language and soon it becomes the norm to speak in terms of the core values and purpose of the organization. The core values and purpose of the organization should be made clear. Clarity around the mission or purpose of the organization is necessary for it to provide direction and enable organizational performance (Denison, 1997). If for some reason, the core values or purpose are not already transparent, then efforts should be made to make them transparent to those in the organization. For example, leaders can open organizational meetings by discussing the core purpose and values of the organization; then, discuss why highlighting them is so important in this time of crisis. Essentially, emphasize how the purpose can serve to provide direction for the organization. The language of the leaders should reflect that the ultimate purpose or mission of the organization does not change because there is a crisis; however, the organization may need to adapt to continue to achieve it.

Ultimately, while leaders are representatives of the culture of an organization (Alvesson, 2013), they also serve to embed cultural dynamics into an organization (Schein, 2017). While changing and shifting culture takes time and effort, leaders can immediately begin to embed and foster a gritty culture by being strategic in what they emphasize and focus upon. Specifically, leaders can highlight the core purpose or mission of the organization, putting it at the forefront of operations. They can emphasize and ensure alignment between all organizational goals to that core purpose or mission. Leaders can focus on reducing a siloed operating environment by creating shared goals between siloed units that align with the purpose of the organization. Finally, leaders can use stories of determined perseverance in the face of prior organizational obstacles and integrate language that represents the core values and purpose that are the driving forces of the organization.

Conclusion

The COVID-19 pandemic led and continues to lead to *unprecedented* challenges for organizations and their leaders (Brammer et al., 2020). While there is hope on the horizon with promising vaccines, the obstacles imposed by and repercussions of the pandemic will continue to be disruptive for years, if not decades, to come as society begins to understand the true impact of this pandemic to our global social network and economic infrastructure. As such, organizational leaders will continually face the question of how to be resilient in the face of this pandemic and its consequences. Beyond COVID-19 and its impacts, organizational leaders will always face organizational disruptions, some of grandeur, like this pandemic, others of small or more insular consequence. Nonetheless, organizational leaders must help their organizations to be resilient in the face of any organizational disruption.

A culture of organizational grit may serve to facilitate resilient action in an organization in the face of the COVID-19 pandemic and other organizational disruptions. Central to a culture of organization grit is the purpose or mission of the organization. The mission-centric nature of the organization seems to be a key enabler of the organization's ability to be resilient. An important aspect of this appears to be a clear alignment of goals of the individuals, units, and departments to the purpose or mission of the organization (Lee & Duckworth, 2018; Raver Luning et al., 2021). This alignment serves to create unity and helps to provide clarity and direction. Leaders can embed and foster the elements of a gritty culture to help their organization to be resilient as it continues to face the challenges from the COVID-19 pandemic and in preparation for future challenges. A key starting point is to create an organizational goal hierarchy, which will help to clearly identify the organization's core purpose and assess alignment of goals at all levels of the organization.

Leaders can and should act as role models displaying a determined spirit in the face of this disruption, constantly focusing organizational members on the ultimate purpose or mission of the organization, and highlighting how the organization can and will adapt while still fulfilling its purpose. In turn, organizational members that have pride in the mission of the organization will follow suit and display that determined spirit, realigning individual, team, and department goals to continue to achieve the core purpose of the organization while they adapt to the disruption in the external environment. Ultimately, while the COVID-19 pandemic presented and continues to present *unprecedented* challenges, leaders can support their organization in persisting through this disruption by enabling and fostering a culture of organizational grit which can aid those in the organization and the organization itself to be resilient in the face of challenge.

Chapter Lessons

There are many key lessons that can be taken from this chapter. However, they can be summarized as follows:

1. Organizational resilience is described as an organization's ability to rebound, adapt to, and recover from organizational disruptions (Annarelli & Nonino, 2016; Duchek, 2020).
2. An organization's culture may serve as a catalyst for action (Weick, 1987) and help an organization to be resilient in the face of adversity (Barasa et al., 2018; Boin & van Eeten, 2013; Carden et al., 2018; Duchek, 2020; Williams et al., 2017).
3. A culture of organizational grit may facilitate action and enable an organization to be resilient in the face of crisis.
4. Central to a gritty culture is the purpose or mission of an organization in which there is goal congruence or alignment throughout all levels of the organization (Lee & Duckworth, 2018; Raver Luning et al., 2021).
5. Organizational leaders can create a culture of organizational grit by focusing on primary and secondary mechanisms for influencing culture.

Reflection Questions

One fundamental way to enable an organization to be more resilient by generating a culture of organizational grit is to reflect upon the organization and the way it is being led. Below is a list of reflection questions that can help create a gritty organization; an organization that is primed for resilience.

1. What is the central purpose or mission of the organization?
   (a) Think beyond what is written in the mission statement and focus on what is at the core of what the organization is trying to achieve.
2. How central is that purpose to how the organization operates? Is that central purpose clear to the members of the organization?
3. How well do individual, unit, and/or department goals align with the organization's central purpose? Is the alignment of those goals clear to members of the organization?
4. What are the core values of the organization? Do those core values permeate the way the organization operates? How have those core values helped the organization to adapt in the face of crisis?
5. *Analyze the workforce.*

   (a) What drives individuals within this organization?
   (b) Do organizational members show passion toward the central purpose?
   (c) Are the individuals in the organization determined in the face of challenge?
6. *Consider past and present displays of resilience.*
   (a) How has the organization responded to challenges historically?
   (b) Are stories shared of the organization dealing with disruptions? How did the organization adapt during that time of crisis? What served as the driving force for the organization's adaptation?
   (c) What are current displays of organizational resilience? What stories should be strategically told and retold throughout the organization to represent those displays of resilience?

References

Alvesson, M. (2013). *Understanding organizational culture* (2nd ed.). SAGE.

Annarelli, A., & Nonino, F. (2016). Strategic and operational management of organizational resilience: Current state of research and future directions. *Omega, 62*(1), 1–18. https://doi.org/10.1016/j.omega.2015.08.004

Barasa, E., Mbau, R., & Gilson, L. (2018). What is resilience and how can it be nurtured? A systematic review of empirical literature on organizational resilience. *International Journal of Health Policy and Management, 7*(6), 491–503. https://doi.org/10.15171/ijhpm.2018.06

Boin, A., & van Eeten, M. J. G. (2013). The resilient organization: A critical appraisal. *Public Management Review, 15*(3), 429–445. https://doi.org/10.1080/14719037.2013.769856

Brammer, S., Branicki, L., & Linnenluecke, M. K. (2020). COVID-19, societalization, and the future of business in society. *Academy of Management Perspectives, 34*(4), 493–507. https://doi.org/10.5465/amp.2019.0053

Carden, L. L., Maldonado, T., & Boyd, R. O. (2018). Organizational resilience: A look at McDonald's in the fast-food industry. *Organizational Dynamics, 47*(1), 25–31. https://doi.org/10.1016/j.orgdyn.2017.07.002

Collins, J. (2001). *Good to great*. HarperCollins.

Credé, M. (2018). What shall we do about grit? A critical review of what we know and what we don't know. *Educational Researcher, 47*(9), 606–611. https://doi.org/10.3102/0013189X18801322

Credé, M., Tynan, M. C., & Harms, P. D. (2017). Much ado about grit: A meta-analytic synthesis of the grit literature. *Journal of Personality of Social Psychology, 113*(3), 492–511. https://doi.org/10.1037/pspp0000102

Datu, J. A. D., Valdez, J. P. M., & King, R. B. (2016). Perseverance counts but consistency does not! Validating the short grit scale in a collectivist setting. *Current Psychology, 35*(1), 121–130. https://doi.org/10.1007/s12144-015-9374-2

Delaney, S. (2014). *Why fostering a growth mindset in organizations matters*. http://knowledge.senndelaney.com/docs/thought_papers/pdf/stanford_agilitystudy_hart.pdf

Denison, D. R. (1997). *Corporate culture and organizational effectiveness*. John Wiley & Sons.

Denison, D. R., & Mishra, A. K. (1995). Toward a theory of organizational culture and effectiveness. *Organization Science, 6*(2), 204–223. https://doi.org/10.1287/orsc.6.2.204

Duchek, S. (2020). Organizational resilience: A capability-based conceptualization. *Business Research, 13*, 215–246. https://doi.org/10.1007/s40685-019-0085-7

Duckworth, A. L. (2016). *Grit: The power of passion and perseverance*. Scribner.

Duckworth, A. L., & Gross, J. J. (2014). Self-control and grit: Related but separate determinants of success. *Current Directions in Psychological Science, 23*(5), 319–325. https://doi.org/10.1177/0963721414541462

Duckworth, A. L., Kirby, T. A., Tsukayama, E., Berstein, H., & Ericsson, K. A. (2011). Deliberate practice spell success: Why grittier competitors triumph at the National

Spelling Bee. *Social Psychology and Personality Science, 2*(2), 174–181. https://doi.org/10.1177/1948550610385872

Duckworth, A. L., Peterson, C., Matthews, M. D., & Kelly, D. R. (2007). Grit: Perseverance and passion for long-term goals. *Journal of Personality and Social Psychology, 92*(6), 1087–1101. https://doi.org/10.1037/0022-3514.92.6.1087

Duckworth, A. L., & Quinn, P. D. (2009). Development and validation of the short grit scale (Grit-S). *Journal of Personality Assessment, 91*(2), 166–174. https://doi.org/10.1080/00223890802634290

Duckworth, A. L., Quinn, P. D., & Seligman, M. E. P. (2009). Positive predictors of teacher effectiveness. *The Journal of Positive Psychology, 4*(6), 540–547. https://doi.org/10.1080/17439760903157232

Dweck, C. S. (2016). *Mindset: The new psychology of success*. Ballantine Books.

Eskreis-Winkler, L., Shulman, E. P., Beal, S. A., & Duckworth, A. L. (2014). The grit effect: Predicting retention in the military, the workplace, school, and marriage. *Frontiers in Psychology, 5*(36), 1–12. https://doi.org/10.3389/fpsyg.2014.00036

Fisher, D. M., Ragsdale, J. M., & Fisher, E. C. S. (2019). The importance of definitional and temporal issues in the study of resilience. *Applied Psychology, 68*(4), 583–620. https://doi.org/10.1111/apps.12162

Gittell, J. H., Cameron, K., Lim, S., & Rivas, V. (2006). Relationships, layoffs, and organizational resilience: Airline industry responses to September 11. *Journal of Applied Behavioral Science, 42*(3), 300–329. https://doi.org/10.1177/0021886306286466

Hatch, M. J., & Schultz, M. (2002). The dynamics of organizational identity. *Human Relations, 55*(8), 989–1018. https://doi.org/10.1177/0018726702055008181

Hsu, L. Y., Chia, P. Y., & Vasoo, S. (2020). A midpoint perspective on the COVID-19 pandemic. *Singapore Medicine Journal, 61*(7), 381–383. https://doi.org/10.11622/smedj.2020036

Ion, A., Mindu, A., & Gorbănescu, A. (2017). Grit in the workplace: Hype or ripe? *Personality and Individual Difference, 111*(1), 163–168. https://doi.org/10.1016/j.paid.2017.02.012

Jin, B., & Kim, J. (2017). Grit, basic needs satisfaction, and subjective well-being. *Journal of Individual Differences, 38*(1), 29–35. https://doi.org/10.1027/1614-0001/a000219

Jordan, S. L., Ferris, G. R., Hochwarter, W. A., & Wright, T. A. (2019a). Toward a work motivation conceptualization of grit in organizations. *Group & Organization Management, 44*(2), 320–360. https://doi.org/10.1177/1059601119834093

Jordan, S. L., Wihler, A., Hochwarter, W. A., & Ferris, G. R. (2019b). The roles of grit in human resource theory and research. In M. R. Buckley, J. R. B. Halbesleben, & A. R. Wheeler (Eds.), *Research in personnel and human resources management, Vol. 37* (pp. 53–88). Emerald Group.

Kelly, D. R., Matthews, M. D., & Bartone, P. T. (2014). Grit and hardiness as predictors of performance among West Point cadets. *Military Psychology, 26*(4), 327–342. https://doi.org/10.1037/mil0000050

Kendra, J. M., & Wachtendorf, T. (2003). Elements of resilience after the world trade center disaster: Reconstituting New York city's emergency operations centre. *Disasters, 27*(1), 37–53. https://doi.org/10.1111/1467-7717.00218

King, D. D., Newman, A., & Luthans, F. (2016). Not if, but when we need resilience in the workplace. *Journal of Organizational Behavior, 37*(5), 782–786. https://doi.org/10.1002/job.2063

Lahti, E. E. (2019). Embodied fortitude: An introduction to the Finnish construct of sisu. *International Journal of Wellbeing, 9*(1), 61–82. https://doi.org/10.5502/ijw.v9i1.672

Lee, T. H., & Duckworth, A. L. (2018). Organizational grit. *Harvard Business Review, 96*(5), 98–105.

Lengnick-Hall, C. A., Beck, T. E., & Lengnick-Hall, M. L. (2011). Developing a capacity for organizational resilience through strategic human resource management. *Human Resource Management Review, 21*(3), 243–255. https://doi.org/10.1016/j.hrmr.2010.07.001

Linnenluecke, M. K. (2017). Resilience in business and management research: A review of influential publications and a research agenda. *International Journal of Management Reviews, 19*(1), 4–30. https://doi.org/10.1111/ijmr.12076

Meyer, A. D. (1982). Adapting to environmental jolts. *Administration Science Quarterly, 27*(2), 515–537. https://doi.org/10.2307/2392528

Mooradian, T., Matzler, K., Uzelac, B., & Bauer, F. (2016). Perspiration and inspiration: Grit and innovativeness as antecedents of entrepreneurial success. *Journal of Economic Psychology, 56*, 232–242. https://doi.org/10.1016/j.joep.2016.08.001

Murphy, M. C., & Dweck, C. S. (2010). A culture of genius: How an organization's lay theory shapes people's cognition, affect, and behavior. *Personality and Social Psychology Bulletin, 36*(3), 283 296. https://doi.org/10.1177/0146167209347380

Olsson, L., Jerneck, A., Thoren, H., Persson, J., & O'Byrne, D. (2015). Why resilience is unappealing to social science: Theoretical and empirical investigations of the scientific use of resilience. *Science Advances, 1*(4), 1–11. https://doi.org/10.1126/sciadv.1400217

Ortiz-de-Mandojana, & Bansal, P. (2016). The long-term benefits of organizational resilience through sustainable business practices. *Strategic Management Journal, 37*(8), 1615–1631. https://doi.org/10.1002/smj.2410

Pate, A. N., Payakachat, N., Harrell, T. K., Pate, K. A., Caldwell, D. J., & Franks, A. M. (2017). Measurement of grit and correlation to student pharmacist academic performance. *American Journal of Pharmacy Education, 81*(6), 105. https://doi.org/10.5688/ajpe816105

Raver Luning, C., Attoh, P., Gong, T., & Fox, J. (2021). A culture of organizational grit from the perspective of U.S. military officers: A qualitative inquiry. *Armed Forces & Society*. Advance online publication. https://doi.org/10.1177/0095327X20985197.

Raver Luning, C., & Ledford, A. (2020). The necessity of grit and hardiness in leading with character. *Journal of Character and Leader Development, 7*(1), 100–111.

Raver Luning, C. K. (2019). *Exploring organizational grit in mid-sized enterprises in the mid-Atlantic region: A multiple case study* (Publication No. 22588533) [Doctoral dissertation, University of Maryland Eastern Shore]. ProQuest Dissertation and Theses.

Rimfeld, K., Kovas, Y., Dale, P. S., & Plomin, R. (2016). True grit and genetics: Predicting academic achievement from personality. *Journal of Personality and Social Psychology, 111*(5), 780–789. https://doi.org/10.1037/pspp0000089

Riolli, L., & Savicki, V. (2003). Information system organizational resilience. *Omega, 31*(3), 227–233. https://doi.org/10.1016/S0305-0483(03)00023-9

Ris, E. W. (2015). Grit: A short history of a useful concept. *Journal of Educational Controversy, 10*(1), Article 3.

Salles, A., Lin, D., Liebert, C., Esquivel, M., Lau, J. N., Greco, R. S., & Mueller, C. (2017). Grit as a predictor of risk of attrition in surgical residency. *The American Journal of Surgery, 213*(2), 288–291. https://doi.org/10.1016/j.amjsurg.2016.10.012

Schein, E. H. (2017). *Organizational culture and leadership* (5th ed.). Wiley.

Schmidt, F. T. C., Lechner, C. M., & Danner, D. (2020). New wine in an old bottle? A facet-level perspective on the added value of grit over BFI-2 conscientiousness. *PLoS One, 15*(2), 1–25. https://doi.org/10.1371/journal.pone.0228969

Strode, H. (1940, January 14). Sisu: A word that explains Finland. *The New York times*, SM, 4.

Sutcliffe, K. M., & Vogus, T. J. (2003). Organizing for resilience. In K. S. Cameron, J. E. Dutton, & R. E. Quinn (Eds.), *Positive organizational scholarship: Foundations of a new discipline* (pp. 94–110). Berrett-Koehler.

Teller, J. (2020). *As American as mom, apple pie & grit*. Rural America Know-How. https://www.grit.com/grit-history

Vainio, M. M., & Daukantaite, D. (2016). Grit and different aspects of well-being: Direct and indirect relationships via sense of coherence and authenticity. *Journal of Happiness Studies, 17*, 2119–2147. https://doi.org/10.1007/s10902-015-9688-7

Van Auken, R. (2020). Sunday grit: A newspaper legacy. *Hands on Heritage*. https://handsonheritage.com/sunday-grit-a-newspaper-legacy/

Vogus, T. J., & Sutcliffe, K. M. (2007). Organizational resilience: Towards a theory and research agenda. In *IEEE International Conference on Systems, Man and Cybernetics, Canada* (pp. 3418–3422). https://doi.org/10.1109/ICSMC.2007.4414160.

Weick, K. E. (1987). Organizational culture as a source of high reliability. *California Management Review, 29*(2), 112–127. https://doi.org/10.2307/41165243

Whetten, D. A. (2006). Albert and Whetten revisited: Strengthening the concept of organizational identity. *Journal of Management Inquiry, 15*(3), 219–234. https://doi.org/10.1177/1056492606291200

Williams, T. A., Gruber, D. A., Sutcliffe, K. M., Shepherd, D. A., & Zhao, E. Y. (2017). Organizational response to adversity: Fusing crisis management and resilience research streams. *Academy of Management Annals, 11*(2), 733–769. https://doi.org/10.5465/annals.2015.0134

Celeste Raver Luning, PhD, is the Class of 1967 Leadership Research Fellow in the Department of Leadership, Ethics, and Law at the United States Naval Academy. Broadly, her research focuses on understanding the dynamic nature of organizations. Dr. Raver Luning's current research centers on resilience and grit at the individual, team, and organizational levels of analysis. She also teaches one of the core leadership courses at the United States Naval Academy. Prior to her academic career, she was part of a team that built and ran a successful multi-location service business in Southern California, in which she served as the Chief Operating Officer. Dr. Raver Luning obtained her PhD in Organizational Leadership from the University of Maryland Eastern Shore, holds a Master of Business Administration with an emphasis in Entrepreneurship from Pepperdine University, and a Bachelor of Arts in Philosophy from the University of Maryland Baltimore County.

Andrew Ledford, Ph.D., is a permanent military professor and an assistant professor of Leadership and Ethics at the United States Naval Academy. He teaches the core class of leadership and the Code of the Warrior elective. His past research has been on social movement in Iran as well as the nexus of religion and politics in the Middle East. He currently leads a research group on mindfulness, grit, hardiness, and resilience. Dr. Ledford has a master's degree in International Relations with a focus on Irregular Warfare from the Naval War College, where he was the honor graduate. He spent over 20 years as a Naval Special Warfare officer, which included several tours to both Iraq and Afghanistan in addition to other regions before receiving a master's degree in sociology and his PhD from Princeton University where he studied political sociology and social network analysis.

Moral Leadership in a Post-COVID-19 World

10

Anoosha Makka

Introduction

> *We are reminded that, in the fleeting time we have on this Earth, what matters is not wealth, or status, or power, or fame, but rather how well we have loved and what small part we have played in making the lives of other people better.*—Barack Obama

> *If you fight [external trends], you're probably fighting the future. Embrace them and you have a tailwind.*—Jeff Bezos, Founder and CEO of Amazon

In his popular 2015 TED Talk titled, "*The next outbreak? We're not ready,*" Bill Gates, the cofounder of Microsoft, forewarned that the next major threat to humanity would be a global epidemic of catastrophic proportions. He strongly cautioned that such an epidemic would have devastating consequences, particularly for the developing world (Gates, 2015). In his talk, Gates expressed concern and dismay about the general lack of preparation around the world for dealing with the outbreak of a global epidemic and predicted that when such an outbreak would occur (which he argued was inevitable), it would take the world by complete surprise (Gates, 2015). Unfortunately, this seemingly unlikely prediction of a global catastrophic pandemic became a nightmarish reality only 5 years later. As pointed out by Brammer et al. (2020), on 31 December 2019 the World Health Organization alerted the world about a pneumonia-like epidemic or "novel coronavirus" (p. 494), which was subsequently named COVID-19.

Most leaders, countries, governments, firms and organizations were woefully unprepared for the COVID-19 pandemic (Brammer et al., 2020). Their responses have largely been sluggish and reactive, the subject of widespread criticism from

A. Makka (✉)
Department of Business Management, School of Management, University of Johannesburg, Johannesburg, South Africa
e-mail: amakka@uj.ac.za

S. K. Dhiman, J. F. Marques (eds.), *Leadership After COVID-19*, Future of Business and Finance, https://doi.org/10.1007/978-3-030-84867-5_10

many quarters. The COVID-19 pandemic has had a huge impact throughout the world (Brammer et al., 2020). For example, Schwab and Malleret (2020), in their widely read book, *COVID-19: The Great Reset,* describe the impacts of the pandemic as being unprecedented and having "no parallel in modern history" (p. 12). They continue that the COVID-19 pandemic "is our defining moment" as humanity "and many things will change forever" (Schwab & Malleret, 2020, p. 12).

Throughout the world, countries, governments, communities, businesses, organizations and individuals have been thrown into a state of disarray, chaos and confusion, with life being totally disrupted and unpredictable. Change has occurred at every level of society, including an individual's way of life at home, at school, at work and within their community. In his best-selling book, *Ten lessons for a post-pandemic world*, prominent author, journalist and political commentator, Fareed Zakaria, discusses the consequences and the aftermath of the COVID-19 pandemic for the world. He supports the view that "[p]ost-pandemic, life will be different for countries, companies, and especially individuals. Even if economics and politics return to normal, human beings will not" (Zakaria, 2020, pp. 3–4).

Most notably, the COVID-19 pandemic has exposed weaknesses in the world, such as economic and social disparities in countries, the lack of unity and cooperation among leaders at a global and national level, inadequate global governance systems and the existence of ineffective, mediocre and amoral political and business leadership in many parts of the world (Schwab & Malleret, 2020). This view is supported by Brammer et al. (2020), who maintain that "COVID-19 has provoked heightened appreciation of the uneven impacts of the crisis on individuals and communities" (p. 502).

The role of leadership during and after the pandemic is at the forefront of determining the course of action countries, firms and organizations should be taking, both during and after the epidemic. The management consulting firm, McKinsey & Company, published an article titled *The CEO moment: Leadership for a new era.* The article states that "in a moment of crisis, everyone looks to their leader" (Dewar et al., 2020, p. 5). The *New York Times* best-selling author and acclaimed business professor, Scott Galloway, in his book, *Post Corona: From crisis to opportunity*, emphasizes that "in any crisis, there is opportunity; the greater and more disruptive the crisis, the greater the opportunities" (Galloway, 2020, p. xvi).

This chapter contends that the post-pandemic world will be extremely challenging but at the same time, there will be many opportunities to create positive changes in the world. The post-pandemic period will be characterized by volatility, uncertainty, complexity, ambiguity, risks and hidden opportunities. Numerous changes will occur—at the political, economic, social, technological, legal, and environmental levels. Leaders and followers should take note of the many lessons learned from the COVID-19 pandemic. This chapter argues that to successfully navigate the challenges and opportunities of the post-COVID-19 world, countries and organizations will need leaders who are agile, courageous, flexible, and who have a strong moral compass.

This chapter is structured as follows: the next section defines the meaning of moral leadership. Thereafter, the following topics are discussed: the character traits of a moral leader; moral leadership in the aftermath of the COVID-19 pandemic; macro and micro level changes after the pandemic; leadership behavior and skills after the pandemic; likely scenarios to occur after COVID-19; concluding thoughts, summary and reflection questions.

Meaning and Definition of Moral Leadership

In his highly acclaimed book, *Leadership*, the American historian, political scientist and leadership expert, James McGregor Burns, states that "leadership is one of the most observed and least understood phenomena on earth" (Burns, 1978, p. 2). Although extant research on leadership is extensive and varied, academic literature on "the nature of moral leadership" (Pijanowski, 2007, p. 2) remains limited and is not widely understood. Drouillard and Kleiner (1996) claim that the vast array of definitions of leadership discussed in business textbooks fall short in fully describing leadership "because of their lack of a moral stance" (p. 30). In other words, most definitions appear to lack a moral component. Banks et al. (2020) identify different leadership styles, such as authentic, ethical and servant, stating that these forms of leadership are all linked to moral leadership.

There are many examples in the literature of great leaders, who are regarded as being both effective and moral. For instance, figures such as Martin Luther King Jr., Mahatma Gandhi, Winston Churchill and Mother Theresa have all been admired for their contribution as leaders as well as for their moral stance. Fehr et al. (2015) observe that "all of them have demonstrated an ability to leverage morality as a means of garnering commitment to a cause" (p. 182). Spector (2019) notes that a key issue pertaining to how morality is defined is the ability to discern the difference "between good and bad" (p. 124).

Burns (1978) was a staunch proponent of moral leadership, defining it as "a process of morality to the degree that leaders engage with followers on the basis of shared motives and values and goals" (p. 54). This definition implies that when moral leadership is practiced, it leads to mutual benefits for both leaders and followers. Burns (1978) adds that moral leaders "raise the level of human conduct and ethical aspiration of both leader and led" (p. 20). Importantly, he clarifies what moral leadership is *not* about, stating that "moral leadership is not mere preaching, or the uttering of pieties, or the insistence on social conformity" (Burns, 1978, p. 4).

Cheng et al. (2004) describe moral leadership as "a leader's behavior that demonstrates superior personal virtues, self-discipline and unselfishness" (p. 91). Bernard Bass, a well-known expert in leadership, states that moral leadership is effective in promoting sustainability in an organization because:

> [m]oral leadership helps followers to see the real conflict between competing values, the inconsistencies between espoused values and behavior and the need for realignments in values, changes in behavior, or transformations of institutions … [However], the [moral] leader may be a breaker and changer of what society has regarded heretofore as right and wrong (pp. 182–184).

Ethical leadership is often associated with the moral behavior of leaders. Brown et al. (2005, as cited in Shakeel et al., 2019) describe ethical behavior as "the demonstration of normatively appropriate conduct through personal actions and interpersonal relationships, and the promotion of such conduct to followers through two-way communication, reinforcement, and decision-making" (p. 120). They highlight two aspects related to the duties of an ethical leader, namely, "the moral person and the moral manager" (Brown et al., 2005, as cited in Shakeel et al., 2019, p. 614). A manager as a 'moral individual' displays qualities "such as honesty and integrity" (Trevino et al., 2000, p. 128), which are considered very important. By contrast, a moral manager is the custodian of ethical behavior in an organization, crafting a persuasive ethics message that persuades employees to focus their "attention … thoughts … and behaviors" (p. 128) on being ethical (Trevino et al., 2000). Fehr et al. (2015) explain that ethical leadership involves "the demonstration and promotion of behavior that is positively moralized" (p. 184).

In a more comprehensive definition of ethical leadership provided by Shakeel et al. (2020), ethical leadership is characterized as:

> the implicit and explicit pursuit of desired ethical behavior for self and followers through efforts governed by rules and principles that advocate learning motivation, healthy optimism and clarity of purpose to uphold the values of empowerment, service to others, concern for human rights, change for betterment and fulfilling duties towards society, future generations, environment and its sustainability (p. 10).

However, the notion that leaders are good and moral individuals has been challenged by Harvard University academic and leadership expert, Barbara Kellerman. As argued by Kellerman (2004), it is an unrealistic assumption that all leaders are good and that they have positive intentions. Further, Kellerman (2004) asserts that "leadership is not a moral concept" (p. 45). Instead, she argues that "flawed leaders are everywhere" (p. 41). Adolf Hitler, Joseph Stalin, Benito Mussolini and Idi Amin are a good case in point of some of the world's worst political leaders who lacked a moral compass. In their book titled *Flexible leadership: Creating value by balancing multiple challenges and choices,* Yukl and Lepsinger (2004) advise that organizations should not rely entirely on one particular leader "because no single leader has the necessary knowledge and expertise to solve difficult problems for an organization" (p. 5). Therefore, as suggested by Yukl and Lepsinger (2004), for a leader to be effective, they should be flexible and adaptive, able to work together with others, collaborating with team members to address challenges.

Leaders are human beings, and human beings are not perfect. However, this does not excuse or minimize amoral behavior displayed by some leaders during the COVID pandemic. Take, for example, certain leaders who publicly and consistently denied the existence of the pandemic, purposely spread misinformation about COVID-19, downplayed the seriousness of the virus and deliberately and woefully ignored and disregarded the warnings, advice and findings of scientists. The consequences of this amoral behavior caused the unnecessary and painful loss of many lives due to the COVID-19 pandemic.

Questions that are being currently debated and discussed across the world include: What will happen after the pandemic if amoral and ineffective leadership persists? What will be the impact on the global economy as a whole, on individual economies (especially in developing countries), on people's lives and livelihoods, on businesses and other organizations, after COVID-19? Can the world and organizations afford to tolerate amoral leaders who are solely concerned with satisfying their self-interest, at the expense of everyone else after COVID-19? Or is the idea of moral leadership in a post-pandemic world a pipe dream? These questions will receive increasing attention over the next few months as leaders decide what courses of action are required at the global, national, regional, country and organizational levels after the coronavirus pandemic.

Character Traits of a Moral Leader

Moral leaders are also authentic leaders. As indicated by the *Encyclopedia of Leadership,* co-edited by leadership guru Burns, the traits associated with authentic leaders are "being trustworthy, and genuine, free from hypocrisy" (Goethals et al., 2004, p. 64). An authentic leader speaks and behaves in a consistent manner. An example of a firm's executive leaders demonstrating inauthentic behavior was at Enron, where leaders said one thing and did another, ultimately leading to the firm's demise (Goethals et al., 2004). When leader-follower interactions are based on mutual trust, respect, honesty and common purpose, this transcends the transactional nature of the leader-follower relationship (Goethals et al., 2004).

In his *New York Times* best-selling book, *The Righteous Mind: Why Good People Are Divided by Politics and Religion,* Professor Jonathan Haidt (2012) explains why individuals who have different ideological beliefs often do not see eye to eye. Further, he claims that there are series of six pillars to morality: "(1) care and harm, (2) fairness and cheating, (3) loyalty and betrayal, (4) sanctity and degradation, (5) authority and subversion and (6) liberty and oppression" (Haidt, 2012, p. 185).

Research was carried out by Maldonado and Lacey (2001) on 12 leaders, eliciting their views of what moral leadership entails and the characteristics of moral leaders. The study found that participants regarded moral leadership as "leading by example, taking a stand, speaking out, calling forth the best in others, and/or following one's own and/or prescribed definitions of right and wrong" (p. 79). Key findings of the study in relation to the character traits of moral leaders included "humility, listening, and personal truthfulness as well as actions related to justice" (p. 79).

In his research, Kiel (2015) found that a leader's character matters to their followers. In the study, CEOs were rated highly by their followers for principles related to their character and the way in which they treated followers. Four principles were mentioned most frequently—"integrity, responsibility, forgiveness, and compassion" (p. 20). Kiel (2015) concludes that moral leaders achieve superior financial performance, in contrast to leaders who were poorly rated in terms of character and achieved inferior financial performance. In her article in the *Harvard Business Review,* Doris Goodwin (2018) depicts moral leaders as being highly intelligent, "confident and humble, patient and persistent" (p. 128), having qualities such as "self-awareness, self-discipline and generosity of spirit" (p. 128).

Stogdill (as cited in Northouse, 2016) singles out ten character traits, which he argues are associated with good leadership. For example, these traits include:

> drive for responsibility, vigor and persistence, risk-taking and originality, drive to exercise initiative, self-confidence and sense of personal identity, willingness to accept consequences of decision and action, readiness to absorb interpersonal stress, willingness to tolerate frustration and delay, ability to influence other people's behavior and capacity to structure social interaction systems to the purpose at hand (p. 21).

In their survey of the impact of moral leadership on leaders and followers in a Chinese firm, Bao and Li (2019) conclude that there is a positive correlation between moral leaders and their influence on workers' behavior. They also describe the character traits of a moral leader, which include "honesty, integrity, unselfishness, justness, and caring" (p. 3). In their study, Shakeel et al. (2019) report that ethical leaders—who are also moral leaders—are focused on lifelong learning, have an optimistic outlook and a strong and clear purpose. They are committed to serving others, to promoting human rights, to sustainability and environmental issues, and they want to make a positive difference toward society as a whole (p. 615).

Moral Leadership in the Aftermath of the COVID-19 Pandemic

In a post-COVID-19 world, leaders will be confronted with many global, national and local issues—at the political, social, economic, technological, legal and environmental issues which may never be the same again. Leaders will need to address these issues and, in certain instances, bring about reform. The world after the pandemic will require a "reset" (Schwab & Malleret, 2020, p. 13), both at the macro and the micro levels. Let us now consider these changes at different levels.

Global Institutions and Multilateralism

Kentikelenis and Voeten (2020) indicate that due to the substantial changes that have taken place in the global economy over the past 50 years, the relevance of the current international economic order has been a source of constant debate and criticism, with calls urging reform of global multilateral institutions. At the macro level, there is a need to deepen and strengthen multilateralism and to ensure the immediate reform of global multilateral institutions such as the World Health Organization (WHO), the World Trade Organization (WTO), the International Monetary Fund (IMF), the World Bank and the United Nations (UN). The UN Committee for Development Policy, in its report titled *Development Policy and Multilateralism after COVID-19*, has cautioned that due to the pandemic, much of the progress made toward the Sustainable Development Goals (SDGs) may be eroded (UN,

2020, p. 10) and that the Paris agreement on climate change may not be implemented (UN, 2020, p. 11).

After the pandemic, there will be a great need for "global interdependence" so that no country or people are "left behind" by COVID-19 (UN, 2020, p. iii). This also means that the relevance of populist, right wing ideology—which emphasizes nationalism, isolationism, countries "going it alone," the rejection of globalization and globalism and the minimization of global cooperation and multilateralism in favor of unilateralism—is being challenged after the pandemic.

After the global COVID-19 pandemic, it is imperative to introduce "new rules" (UN, 2020, p. 2) in the global international order to ensure that there is "shared prosperity and environmental sustainability" (UN, 2020, p. 3) for all people throughout the world. For instance, urgent reform needs to take place within the WHO. The issue of whether the WHO provided the necessary moral leadership during the COVID-19 pandemic will be intensely debated for a long time after the pandemic. In other words, did the WHO assume moral leadership over global healthcare during the COVID health crisis? Was information regarding the pandemic communicated evenly and truthfully across the world, and in a rapid and transparent manner to all countries? What should the mandate of the WHO and its leadership be during an outbreak of another global epidemic (Hanrieder, 2020)? Considering the likelihood of further global epidemics occurring in the near future, should the WHO prioritize "infectious diseases"? (Hanrieder, 2020, p. 535) and develop strategic goals and objectives in global health care? (Hanrieder, 2020, p. 537). All of these questions need to be carefully considered by leaders after the pandemic, and a mandate and strategy need to be developed for the future role and relevance of the WHO in the new international order.

The vulnerability of global supply chains also came under scrutiny during the COVID-19 pandemic. Daugbjerg (2017) points out that ever since the failure of the Doha Round of trade talks in 2008, there have been strong calls to reform the WTO. The current mandate, relevance and clout of the WTO were challenged when Donald Trump imposed trade tariffs against China and pursued a policy of unilateral and bilateral trade over multilateralism. The global role and position of developing countries such as China and other emerging markets versus developed countries is being questioned. Issues such as free and fair trade among countries have once again become a topic of heated debate. Additionally, the dominance and voting rights of the IMF and the World Bank, which is largely skewed in favor of Western countries, is being questioned. It is clear that after the pandemic, developing countries and emerging market economies are demanding a more just, fair and equitable set of international rules, where every country has the same opportunities to promote economic development, sustainability and prosperity.

Macro Level Changes

Table 10.1 presents the macro level changes, anticipated after the pandemic that will require moral leadership.

Table 10.1 Possible areas for change and moral leadership

Theme	Potential areas that may require change
Political	Populism and isolationism; nationalism vs. globalism; strengthening global governance; immigration; xenophobia; systemic racism; strengthening democracy and democratic institutions; improving the quality of governments; managing the relationship and rivalry between China and the United States and failed and vulnerable nation states.
Economic	Promoting greater equity; income equality and distribution of economic resources; transforming capitalism to be more inclusive, fair and just; reforming business to be more conscious and sustainable; creating sustainable jobs and livelihoods; promoting fair wages and instituting minimum wages.
Social	Reducing poverty, global hunger, homelessness and inequality; improving access and affordability to decent education, universal and affordable healthcare; minimizing social unrest; addressing overpopulation in certain areas of the world; being more proactive in dealing with infectious diseases.
Technological	Accelerating digital transformation; adapting to an increasingly digital world; using technology to do business; using technology to promote economic prosperity and sustainability.
Legal	Government intervention; international and national laws; protection of property rights and intellectual capital; tariffs, quotas and protectionism.
Environmental	Air pollution; climate change; natural disasters; lockdown and carbon emissions; zoonotic diseases; excessive weather conditions; food and water crises.

Source: Adapted from Schwab and Malleret (2020) and Zakaria (2020)

Micro Level Changes

At firm and industry level in countries, the period after the pandemic will involve adaptation, change, flexibility and agility (Schwab & Malleret). Key issues and trends at firm level are (1) acceleration of digitization, (2) resilient supply chains, (3) governments and business, and (4) stakeholder capitalism and environmental, social and governance issues (Schwab & Malleret, 2020, pp. 123–129). At the industry level, notable trends after the pandemic include (1) social interaction and de-densification—the impact on the travel and tourism, hospitality, entertainment, retail, aerospace and even the automotive industries, (2) behavioral changes—effects on retail, real estate and education, (3) resilience of industries such as big technology, health, banking and insurance, automotive, electricity (Schwab & Malleret, 2020, pp. 133–142).

Leadership Behavior After the Pandemic

Moral leaders would need to behave in specific ways in the post-pandemic world. Table 10.2 outlines the leader memes and behaviors that will be of value in the post-pandemic era. Zaccaro (2014) explains leadership memes as "leadership prescriptions offered by successful leaders" (p. 18).

As can be seen in Table 10.2, leaders are regarded as warriors, problem-solvers, politicians, and also teachers (Zaccaro, 2014).

Table 10.2 Leadership memes and behaviors

Leadership meme	Leadership frame	Sample historical and cultural replication	Leader attributes
Leader-warrior	– Leadership as overcoming enemies Motivating and leading followers into battle	– Sun Tzu, *The Art of War* – Biblical story of David and Goliath – Early Greek and Roman war heroes (e.g., Alexander the Great; Julius Caesar) – von Clausewitz's *On War* – Modern war heroes (Washington, Napoleon, Churchill)	– Courage – Risk-taking – Honor – Integrity – Strategic cunning
Leader-problem-solver	– Leadership as generating wise solutions	– Lao Tzu, *Tao Te Ching* – Biblical story of King Solomon – Plato's *Republic* – Benjamin Franklin	– Complex problem-solving skills – Wisdom – Divergent thinking skills
Leader-politician	– Leadership as accruing the loyalty and leader role endorsement of followers	– Cicero – Machiavelli, *The Prince* – Leaders who were great communicators (e.g., Martin Luther King, Abraham Lincoln, Winston Churchill) – Leaders who enacted far-reaching political bargains (e.g., Thomas Jefferson, Abraham Lincoln, Franklin Roosevelt, Lyndon Johnson)	– Communication skills – Interpersonal skills – Social acumen – Political savvy – Negotiation skills
Leader-teacher	– Leadership as teaching, coaching, and empowering followers	– Lao Tzu, *Tao Te Ching* – Jesus	– Empathy – Integrity – Authenticity – Humility – Service orientation – Coaching and pedagogical skills

Source: Adapted from Zaccaro (2014)

Leadership Skills Required After the Pandemic

To successfully transition from the pandemic into the post-pandemic era, moral leadership is essential. The reason for this, as explained by Linzey (2015), is that moral leaders "tend to give others a sense of security" (p. 3). Moral leaders with the following skills will be invaluable to countries, firms, organizations, and communities.

Conceptual Skills

Northouse (2016) explains that it is important for leaders to possess conceptual skills, which are used to develop an organization's vision and strategic plan. As explained by Northouse (2016), conceptual skills refer to "the ability to work with ideas and concepts" (p. 45). A leader who possesses conceptual skills can easily document the organization's goals and is at ease when articulating ideas regarding the organization (Northouse, 2016).

Directing Skills

Effective leaders are able to direct their followers successfully in order to accomplish goals and objectives (Linzey, 2015). As stated by Bass and Riggio (2006), transformational leaders have a compelling vision and can motivate and inspire followers to implement their vision.

Human Skills

Human skills are also described as "people skills" (Northouse, 2016, p. 45). Northouse (2016) describes leaders with such skills as "being sensitive to the needs and motivations of others and taking into account other's needs in one's decision making" (p. 45).

Influencer Skills

Linzey (2015) foresees that leaders who are convincing and able to influence their followers in a positive way will have an important role to play after the pandemic. According to Bass and Riggio (2006), the world will need transformational leaders who inspire their followers, are charismatic and "have high standards of ethical and moral conduct" (p. 6); such individuals are risk-takers and have considerable influence over their followers. Bass and Riggio (2006) add that transformational leaders "are admired, respected and trusted" (p. 6) by their adherents who want to imitate them.

Technical Skills

Technical skills are essential to manufacture the products and produce the services that organizations offer (Northouse, 2016). Northouse (2016) explains that for leaders who have technical skills, this means having "competencies in a specialized area, analytical ability, and the ability to use appropriate tools and techniques" (p. 44). For instance, in a software firm, having technical skills would include understanding the firm's software and having programming skills (Northouse, 2016).

Likely Scenarios After COVID-19

As suggested by Brammer et al. (2020), there are three possible scenarios that could take place in the world after COVID-19.

Scenario 1: Life Goes Back to Normal. In this scenario, it is envisaged that life will return to how it was before the pandemic. In this perspective, the pandemic is regarded as an event that happens in every millennium. According to this scenario, there is little overall change that takes place. Structural and systemic inequalities, challenges and disparities in the world still exist, and is there is little attention paid to it by leaders. The role of political leadership during the pandemic is condemned widely, particularly in the context of the abysmal response of most leaders to the pandemic (Brammer et al., 2020, p. 500).

Scenario 2: Life As We Know It Will No Longer Be Normal or the Same. In the second scenario, there will be no going back to life as it was before the pandemic. In this scenario, change will occur and change will be inevitable. Interventions and innovations happen at many levels of society in response to the post-pandemic situation. Leaders are required to be proactive about what will happen during the next epidemic, what their response would be and the strategies they would implement in such a situation. The roles, responsibilities and accountability of leaders, firms and governments are scrutinized in this scenario in terms of predicting and preparing for the next crisis and the next epidemic (Brammer et al., 2020, p. 501).

Scenario 3: Let's Create a Reset and Develop a Better Normal. In the third scenario, issues such as collaboration, cooperation, unity and "interconnectedness of countries" (Brammer et al., 2020, p. 501) are emphasized and encouraged. Isolationism and divisiveness in the world are seen as counter-productive, hindering the creation of a sustainable and thriving world for everyone. To create a better world, moral leaders are required; change is also required. There is widespread recognition that inequalities, inconsistencies and discrepancies that exist at the global, national and country level must be addressed by leaders (Brammer et al., 2020, p. 501).

Conclusion

In this chapter, the role of moral leadership was considered in the context of the post-pandemic era. The chapter emphasized the need for moral leadership to successfully navigate the changes, complexity, challenges and opportunities confronting the world, after the pandemic. Additionally, areas requiring change at the macro and micro levels were put forward. Possible scenarios for moral leaders after the pandemic were forecasted; leadership traits, behaviors and skills were also deliberated in the chapter. In terms of future research in the area of moral leadership in the post-pandemic era, studies can be conducted on how moral leaders can prepare for the next global outbreak, what global strategies and actions need to be taken and a plan should be developed in terms of how the world should respond to another catastrophic external shock.

Moral Leadership Lessons

1. We are all connected and the world is globally interdependent. We are all in this together. Countries and people cannot isolate themselves from the rest of the world and operate in a vacuum. Therefore, moral leaders cannot ignore the suffering that takes place around the world.

2. Globalization and multilateralism are alive. Cooperation instead of conflict is the more desirable path to follow if humanity is to create positive and sustainable change in the world.
3. Moral leadership is required in the post-pandemic era in order to navigate the challenges and opportunities confronting the world today.
4. Business, political and other organizational leaders need to work together and collaborate instead of only competing with one another to achieve shared prosperity and sustainability for humanity.
5. Moral leaders need to implement the necessary changes to bring about a fairer, more equitable and just world by addressing systemic inequalities, inequities, inconsistencies and gaps at a global, country and organization level.

Reflection Questions
1. What role can moral leaders play after the COVID-19 crisis?
2. How can moral leaders institute the necessary changes after the pandemic in their countries and organizations?
3. How can moral leaders ensure a fairer, more equitable and sustainable world?
4. What actions should moral leaders take to promote global cooperation, interdependence and collaboration without compromising on national sovereignty?
5. How can business, political and organizational leaders prepare and respond to the next global epidemic?

References

Banks, G. C., Fischer, T., Gooty, J., & Stock, G. (2020). Ethical leadership: Mapping the terrain for concept cleanup and a future research agenda. *The Leadership Quarterly, 32*, 101471. https://doi.org/10.1016/j.leaqua.2020.101471

Bao, Y., & Li, C. (2019). From moral leadership to positive work behaviors: The mediating roles of value congruence and leader-member exchange. *Frontiers of Business Research in China, 13*(1), 1–18. https://doi.org/10.1186/s11782-019-0052-3

Bass, B. M., & Riggio, R. E. (2006). *Transformational leadership*. Lawrence Erlbaum.

Brammer, S., Branicki, L., & Linnenluecke, M. (2020). COVID-19, Societalization and the future of business in society. *Academy of Management Perspectives, 34*(4), 493–507. https://doi.org/10.5465/amp.2019.0053

Brown, M., Treviño, L. K., & Harrison, D. A. (2005). Ethical leadership: A social learning perspective for construct development and testing. *Organizational Behavior and Human Decision Processes, 97*(2), 117–134. https://doi.org/10.1016/j.obhdp.2005.03.002

Burns, J. M. (1978). *Leadership*. Harper and Row.

Cheng, B.-S., Chou, L.-F., Wu, T.-Y., Huang, M.-P., & Farh, J.-L. (2004). Paternalistic leadership and subordinate responses: Establishing a leadership model in Chinese organizations. *Asian Journal of Social Psychology, 7*(1), 89–117. https://doi.org/10.1111/j.1467-839X.2004.00137.x

Daugbjerg, C. (2017). Responding to non-linear internationalisation of public policy: The world trade organization and reform of the CAP 1992–2013. *Journal of Common Market Studies, 55*(3), 486–501. https://doi.org/10.1111/jcms.12476

Dewar, C., Keller, S., Sneader, K., & Strovink, K. (2020). The CEO moment: Leadership for a new era. *McKinsey Quarterly*. https://www.mckinsey.com/~/media/McKinsey/Featured%20Insights/Leadership/The%20CEO%20moment%20Leadership%20for%20a%20new%20era/The-CEO-moment-Leadership-for-a-new-era-v3.pdf?shouldIndex=false

Drouillard, S. E., & Kleiner, B. H. (1996). Good leadership. *Management Development Review, 9*(5), 30–33. https://doi.org/10.1108/09622519610131554

Fehr, R., Yam, K. C. S., & Dang, C. (2015). Moralized leadership: The construction and consequences of ethical leader perceptions. *The Academy of Management Review, 40*(2), 182–209. https://doi.org/10.5465/amr.2013.0358

Galloway, S. (2020). *Post Corona: From crisis to opportunity*. Portfolio Penguin.

Gates, B. (2015, March). *Bill Gates: The next outbreak? We're not ready* [Video file]. https://www.ted.com/talks/bill_gates_the_next_outbreak_we_re_not_ready?language=en

Goethals, G. R., Sorenson, G. J., & Burns, J. M. (2004). *Encyclopedia of leadership: Volume 1*. SAGE.

Goodwin, D. K. (2018). Lincoln and the art of transformative leadership. *Harvard Business Review, 96*(5), 126–134.

Haidt, J. (2012). *The righteous mind: Why good people are divided by politics and religion*. Pantheon/Random House.

Hanrieder, T. (2020). Priorities, partners, politics: The WHO's mandate beyond the crisis. *Global Governance, 26*(4), 534–543. https://doi.org/10.1163/19426720-02604008

Kellerman, B. (2004). Thinking about … leadership. Warts and all. *Harvard Business Review, 82*(1), 40–45.

Kentikelenis, A., & Voeten, E. (2020). Legitimacy challenges to the liberal world order: Evidence from United Nations speeches, 1970-2018. *The Review of International Organizations, 15*(4), 1–34. https://doi.org/10.1007/s11558-020-09404-y

Kiel, F. (2015). Measuring the return on character. *Harvard Business Review, 93*(4), 20–21.

Linzey, J. F. (2015). *Moral leadership: The 9 leadership traits*. Resource Publications.

Maldonado, N., & Lacey, C. H. (2001). Defining moral leadership: Perspectives of 12 leaders. *Florida Journal of Educational Research, 41*(4), 79–101.

Northouse, P. G. (2016). *Leadership theory and practice*. SAGE.

Pijanowski, J. C. (2007). Defining moral leadership in graduate schools of education. *Journal of Leadership Education, 6*(1), 1–13. https://doi.org/10.12806/V6/I1/TF1

Schwab, K., & Malleret, T. (2020). *COVID-19: The great reset*. ISBN Agentur Schweiz.

Shakeel, F., Kruyen, P. M., & Van Thiel, S. (2019). Ethical leadership as process: A conceptual proposition. *Public Integrity, 21*(6), 613–624. https://doi.org/10.1080/10999922.2019.1606544

Shakeel, F., Kruyen, P. M., & Van Thiel, S. (2020). Development of a broader conceptualization and measurement scale of ethical leadership. *The Journal of Values-Based Leadership, 13*(1), 1–20. https://doi.org/10.22543/0733.131.1299

Spector, B. (2019). Moral leadership? Be careful what you wish for. *Leadership, 15*(1), 123–131. https://doi.org/10.1177/1742715017736659

Trevino, L. K., Hartman, L. P., & Brown, M. (2000). Moral person and moral manager: How executives develop a reputation for ethical leadership. *California Management Review, 42*(4), 128–142. https://doi.org/10.2307/41166057

United Nations. (2020). *Development policy and multilateralism after COVID-19*. https://www.un.org/development/desa/dpad/publication/development-policy-and-multilateralism-after-covid-19/

Yukl, G., & Lepsinger, R. (2004). *Flexible leadership: Creating value by balancing multiple challenges and choices*. Wiley.

Zaccaro, S. J. (2014). Leadership memes: From ancient history and literature to twenty-first century theory and research. In D. V. Day (Ed.), *The Oxford handbook of leadership and organizations* (pp. 13–39). Oxford University Press.

Zakaria, F. (2020). *Ten lessons for a post-pandemic world*. W.W. Norton & Company.

Anoosha Makka is a senior lecturer in Business Management at the University of Johannesburg, South Africa. She has earned one bachelor and two masters' degrees (an MBA in International Business from Leeds University Business School, UK and the other an MRes in Educational Research at the University of London, UK). Anoosha has earned her PhD in Business Management from the University of Johannesburg, South Africa. She is a recipient of the Nelson Mandela Scholarship and Chevening Scholarship. Her areas of interest include: spirituality and management, spirituality and leadership, CSR and multinational corporations and mindfulness. She currently teaches Strategy and International Management at postgraduate level at the University of Johannesburg. Prior to joining academia, Anoosha spent 10 years in the corporate sector in banking and 6 years in the public sector in South Africa.

COURAGE as a Roadmap Toward Sustainable Practices in a Post-COVID World

11

Joan F. Marques

A Dire Need in Unparalleled Times

The year 2020 will not only linger in our collective memory as an easy number, a leap year, or a turmoil fraught election year, but even more because of the metanoia it instigated within large groups of the global society. The blend of an unprecedented pandemic and a series of human injustices that led to social unrest triggered a massive shift in our thinking, behaving, and our perceptions of reality. The stay-at-home orders that were globally mandated, along with the requirements of masking, social distancing, and regular testing did not only redefine daily life, but became a bedrock for widespread instances of stress, depression, rebelliousness, domestic violence, and other negative outflows. As the COVID-19 pandemic left a destructive trail within families but also entire communities, demanding more than 100 million victims with at least 2.5 million deaths at the time of writing this chapter, it became near impossible to distinguish anything positive from this manifestation. Indeed, the longitudinal struggle with an adjusted and not largely favored status quo has resulted in widespread moral injury. Williamson et al. (2020) explain moral injury as a physiological distress due to one's guilt for actions or no actions regarding the person's moral beliefs. Kuofie and Muhammad (2021) add that moral injury is associated with negative thoughts of oneself or others that can lead to mental illness and post-traumatic stress disorder (PTSD). They underscore that during the COVID-19 pandemic essential workers including healthcare professionals, fire services, police officers, and prison staff experienced moral injuries. Non-healthcare professionals such as educators, media workers, other service workers, as well as separated families, also experienced moral injuries.

J. F. Marques (✉)
School of Business, Woodbury University, Burbank, CA, USA
e-mail: joan.marques@woodbury.edu

S. K. Dhiman, J. F. Marques (eds.), *Leadership After COVID-19*, Future of Business and Finance, https://doi.org/10.1007/978-3-030-84867-5_11

Yet, it is exactly in times of major challenges that we need to find the strength to look behind the dark clouds and discover the silver lining that will carry us into a future of amplified insights and new opportunities. Understanding and accessing the strength of positive leadership becomes essential in these times. Positive leadership involves experiencing, modeling, and purposefully enhancing positive emotions (Avolio & Gardner, 2005). Avolio and Gardner (2005) further explain that positive leaders are interested in their employees' development as well as the bottom line. They harbor high self-awareness, optimism, and personal integrity. Multiple authors have underscored this finding in their research, such as Cameron (2012), who agreed that positive leadership induces positive emotion among members of an organization, promotes positive attitudes, and ultimately leads to the highest performance, and Youssef-Morgan and Luthans (2013), who affirmed that positive leadership encourages an organizational spirit among its members, fosters resilience, and enables them to develop their competencies by focusing on their strengths.

There are various positive leadership styles that address the essentials presented above. One that is of particular significance toward a rejuvenated collective spirit in a post-COVID world is Awakened Leadership. Awakened leaders lead from the heart and soul. They can be found in corporate, community, and household environments, and have in common that they refuse to put on different hats when it comes to their personality. They practice a holistic and authentic approach in every environment and at every time (Marques, 2009). Being awakened starts with the realization that we have the capacity to change our life. It also entails that we learn to adapt to different situations. Being awakened does not evolve through position, status, or financial affluence. It is not acquired through high education or through generational inheritance. Wakefulness is a skill that is developed by thinking, feeling, observing, experiencing, learning and unlearning, in other words, by living mindfully. It is an ongoing process—not an end result, achieved by the shifts that transpire within our minds and hearts over time (Marques, 2010).

Wakefulness particularly requires the ability of letting go, that is, unlearning and releasing things and thoughts that misguide us. This is critical in a post-COVID world, where many society members feel bogged down by long-term isolation and curtailment of socialization. Releasing any pattern or behavior requires courage, for it means that we may have to turn away from certain goods, habits, people and places, to which we have grown accustomed. Wakefulness is not an overnight accomplishment. It requires emotional intelligence, which gets sharpened by the losses we suffer and the failures we encounter. In fact, wakefulness is a paradox: we win it by losing. Every time we lose something precious, one of two things can happen: either we become more disillusioned and bitter, or we become more understanding and sensitive. Usually people first get bitter and disillusioned about their loss, and then start accepting and understanding. It is the second phase that results in a degree of wakefulness, which only elevates with the disappointment of each loss. There are people who never transcend the stage of bitterness over their losses. But the ones that reflect and allow themselves to feel and learn ultimately emerge into wakefulness (Marques, 2010).

While positive leadership styles such as Awakened Leadership are always critical, their purpose and meaning in times of societal and situational reinvention are particularly eminent. At this stage of our journey as living creatures on planet Earth, it is crucial for us to understand that we should transcend the boundaries of our reasoning and realize that all living beings deserve our respect and support toward a balanced and sustainable future. The era where flora and fauna were considered less important to our existence is forever behind us. Enhanced awareness has led us to understand the importance of boundless respect for all that lives, as it all contributes to the ecological balance that will safeguard our collective future. Behaviors and mindsets based on cruelty, vengeance, envy, injustice, faultfinding discrimination, greed, self-centeredness, and jealousy, should be placed in the museum of insufficient and destructive patterns, as a reminder to never access and utilize them again.

As we rise from the mental and emotional rubble of the COVID-19 pandemic, we have some important choices to make. The premise of these choices can be captured in one comprehensive perspective: victim-thinking or reinvention. Victim-thinking is an easy trap to fall into, as it warrants finger-pointing, or, as established in management circles, the manifestation of an external locus of control. People who harbor an external locus of control refuse to take ownership of their circumstances and will always find someone else to blame for their mishaps. On the other hand, reinvention is the fundamental aspect of stepping up and practicing an internal locus of control, whereby we take responsibility of our past, present and future, and develop a roadmap toward a future that is more promising than today's reality. In his book *Good to Great*, Jim Collins (2006) refers to this phenomenon as looking outside the window (external locus of control) versus looking in the mirror (internal locus of control). In a similar vein, Alex Patakos (2008), in his book, *Prisoners of our Thoughts,* encourages us to step away from self-imposed barriers in our thinking, and expanding our horizons in order to discover and access increased possibilities, while Daniel Quinn (1992), in "*Ishmael*" powerfully awakens our conscience toward respecting all living beings.

Because leadership starts with our own mindset and self-perception, our move toward a more rewarding and sustainable future will have to be based on courage, not merely in the true sense of the word, but also as an acronym that provides us a roadmap toward recurring reinvention. COVID-19 has been an unprecedented challenge, but our lifetime is not over yet, and no one knows what the future has in store. The most constructive approach to this recent pandemic is to take it as a clear lesson that the future is unpredictable, but that, for as long as we are alive, we can muster the resilience to overcome challenges. Let us now consider the elements of COURAGE as a guide toward practicing post COVID-19 Awakened Leadership.

Choice

The two most important facts every leader should remember in this regard are that, (1) there is *always* a choice, and (2) success often depends on what we do *after* we made our choice. Regarding the first fact: while the alternatives may not always be attractive, they still exist, so to say that we don't have a choice merely means that we don't consider all alternatives. More importantly, however, is the fact that we always make choices with insufficient information. The conclusion we can draw from this simple fact is that it's not the choice itself that leads to success or failure, but the actions we undertake afterwards. This means that even a poor choice can become useful in the long run, based on our follow-up actions.

In a post COVID-19 world, the first choice we are facing is how to retrospectively evaluate the time we had to mandatorily stay at home, the redesign of our work, or even the loss of our job. These are aspects that we cannot possibly take lightly, and while we cannot change reality, we can decide how we will interpret it. We all had to make decisions, and we did so with the best of intentions, even though some may not have ended in our favor. Fortunately, there is hope for as long as there is life, and anything can be redirected toward more promising outcomes. A key element in this practice is resilience, which can be defined as an individual's ability to "bounce back" despite adverse circumstances (Rutter, 2012). Rutter's resilience research reveals first and foremost that different people muster different levels of resilience in similar circumstances. This entails that not everyone will willfully and naturally be able to recover in the same way from the COVID-19 episode. Individuals who have been exposed to multiple adversities and stress incidents before have conjured a "steeling" effect, and will most likely have greater resilience than those who have not dealt with significant prior setbacks. Resilient individuals harbor "a complicated mixture of psychological habituation, changes in mental set, alterations in perceived and actual self-efficacy, hormonal changes (especially in the hypothalamic–pituitary–adrenal axis) and neural alterations" (Rutter, 2012, p. 341). Resiliency also becomes enhanced by the ability to reflect on prior successes, which may serve as positive affirmations toward pending improvement. Yet, whether we consider resiliency a personality trait or a process, it is an important skill for leaders. Awakened leaders understand the difference between "being strong" in the face adversity and being resilient. "Being strong is about enduring a tough situation, while resilience uses this strength as well as experience and intuition to cope effectively with adversity" (*What the COVID-19 Pandemic Tells Us…*, 2020, p. 23).

Merging the concepts of resiliency and choice, we may conclude that, especially in instances where we have lost our dignity and fear that we may have been scarred for a lifetime, we still have the choice to find resiliency and recover from our loss. Most of us experience suffering in multiple forms and at multiple stages in our lives, but we can invoke the inner capacity to fight for the preservation of our dignity in difficult times. Through self-responsibility we can grow and obtain a better understanding of freedom and choice (Hernandez, 2009). This holds true for most of the challenges in life, and the post COVID-19 world does not have to be an exception to that.

Open-Mindedness

Leading without an open mind has always been an inhibiting process, but in the fast-paced, volatile world of today it would be a downright disaster. Those who want to remain closed-minded will find themselves fallen by the wayside, chasing a dream or opportunity that never materializes. When we practice open-mindedness, we dare to accept options that we previously failed to consider, because we may have perceived them to be above or below our level, outside our comfort zone, or against our traditional perceptions.

Practicing open-mindedness means that we regularly have to inspect our principles in order to find out whether they are built on convictions that matter to us here and now or were adopted along the way without deeper considerations. Based on our upbringing, culture, generation, gender, religion, and a series of other potential influencing factors, we have developed a set of deeply embedded biases that determine how we perceive the world, and that can seriously limit our perceived options.

Implicit biases, also referred to as unconscious bias, implicit social cognition, or cognitive heuristics, are the unconscious cognitive shortcuts that we take to more rapidly process the world around us (Reeves, 2018). While a number of these cognitive shortcuts are beneficial to us and serve us toward living efficient and productive lives, these quick mental tactics of sizing up people based on assumptions and stereotypes that we developed over the course of our life are not particularly inclusive, and sometimes rather destructive. The destruction is not only done to others, which can be the case when we decide not to hire them based on our preconceived notions, but they can also be damaging to ourselves, when we exclude great opportunities due to our ideas that we would not fit within certain ethnic, age-based, geographical, or other types of groups. Cho (2020) shares the important awareness that most of us hold biases, some of which are counterintuitive to our very self, such as a person of color finding that she prefers white persons over individuals like herself. The *Harvard Implicit Association Test* site offers various tests to discover biases. It is only when we are aware of these biases that we will become able to address them. The most important thing to keep in mind there is that having biases is not unique. Yet, we should be aware when our biases result in destructive and limiting behaviors. Cho recommends Loving Kindness Meditation as a practice to enhance compassion and reduce such limiting biases. Loving Kindness Meditation (LKM) could be done in 15 daily minutes, and entails taking a relaxed, yet straight posture, breathing in and out, and envisioning loved ones from whom we receive loving kindness and to whom we send loving kindness in return (*Loving Kindness Meditation*, 2021).

Merging the concepts of biases and open-mindedness we may conclude that, while our biases serve important purposes in our lives, as they help us in making faster decisions, they can also be divisive, void of inclusivity, and limiting. Right in the heart of the COVID-19 pandemic we were jolted by repeated instances of social injustice in society, imposed by individuals whom we were supposed to trust. In the post COVID-19 world, we can take the stance of awakened leaders, and send compassionate feelings to all beings. In practicing the brief daily exercise of LKM, we will expand our acceptance of others, eliminate our mental barriers, and pave the way toward accepting more opportunities than we ever considered before.

Usefulness

A good way to explain the concept of usefulness is by referring to Steve Jobs' Stanford commencement speech, in which he shared how he discovered later in life what the purpose of earlier experiences was. He called it, "Connecting the dots." Jobs referred to a calligraphy class he took in college without any reason or intention, only to realize much later that taking this course enabled him to come up with the idea of multiple fonts on computers, an option we all happily use today (*Steve Job's* 2005 *Stanford Address*). Leaders should realize that even setbacks will once turn out to be useful. Once this awareness has sunk in, they will feel less devastated when things seem to go awry.

Reflecting on the deep impression COVID-19 made on humanity, Algafari (2020) shares some powerful thoughts on how she finds meaning in the pandemic. She reflects on numerous behaviors we had adopted as "normal," but might want to rethink based on the awareness the pandemic brought upon us. She pointed out our tendency to overconsume, shun silence, crave power, abuse our freedom, strive to dominate, and distance ourselves from one another, and invited for us to reconsider those patterns, and start gravitating again toward more emotional closeness, greater equality, and increased happiness. She also expressed hope that the restrictions of the pandemic would lead us to reconsider the simple pleasures we ignored in recent years, and that we would increasingly adopt critical thinking as a replacement of mindlessly absorbing intoxicating hypes. She pointed out the meaning of the pandemic in providing us a chance to reset our values and learn to turn inward to find our strengths rather than hoping to find it externally.

Kirshenbaum (2004), in her book *Everything Happens for a Reason: Finding the True Meaning of the Events in Our Lives*, explains that she found that, in retrospect, even the worst disasters harbor gifts, opportunities, and life lessons. Based on 25 years of clinical research, Kirshenbaum shares insights that may be of great value to us, one being that we should not try to find immediate explanations for things to happen. Sometimes the understanding and appreciation trickle in after months or even years. Yet, she states, once we realize that everything connects, and that nothing is an isolated matter, our understanding converts into wisdom, and our happiness increases. Most importantly, she alerts us that knowing that there is a reason for something to happen (even if we cannot understand it yet), helps take away the negative sense of blame to others or to ourselves.

Reality-Check

We all have our view of reality, influenced by our culture, religion, upbringing, education, character, and other determining factors. What we perceive may not be the same as what others see, even when we look at the same situation. Leaders should always keep this in mind, as it can help them better understand, or at least try to, where others come from. The difference in views of reality explains why some people can smile about something while others feel offended or disinterested about the same thing. Understanding that we all have our own mental model, which we call "reality," can make us more open and understanding to viewpoints from others, and can therefore guide us to a broader spectrum of alternatives.

Mental models are our internal pictures of how the world works. Because our mental models are our own deeply ingrained ideas about the world around us, they often form a major hurdle in accepting new ways of thinking and acting. If we are unaware of our mental models—and many people are—they can severely debilitate how we perceive the world.

Peter Senge (1992), a prominent thinker and author on mental models, explains, "Mental models can be simple generalizations, such as 'people are untrustworthy', or they can be complex theories. But what is most important to grasp is that mental models shape how we act. If we believe people are untrustworthy, we act differently from the way we would if we believed they were trustworthy" (p. 4).

In striving to do the right thing as leaders of ourselves and others, it is important to understand how mental models work and what they do: they are represented in the stories we believe and the assumptions we hold. Because we take them for granted, and assume they are the only way reality can be considered, our mental models shape—and can often distort—our interpretation of external impulses. Mental models don't just differ among people from different backgrounds or cultures: sometimes people from the same family or circle of friends can have very differing mental models. This is because our characters, personal experiences, and mindsets also play a major role in the shaping of our mental models.

Once we become aware of them, we should also notice that our mental models are highly imperfect. They are limited, unbalanced, and are often irrational and miserly. Yet, they evolved as a natural process: through our interactions with other people and a variety of situations. Human beings need their mental models because they provide simplified explanations to complex situations. We develop behavioral patterns on basis of our mental models. But while our mental models enable us to filter the abundance of information that comes to us, and helps us determine our stance with more ease and make quicker decisions, they may be inaccurate and withhold us from new paths and possibilities that could be advantageous.

In most Western nations, such as the US, people are taught that an individualistic mindset is the natural way for human beings to perform. A focus on self-progress and selfish gain, even if at the expense of others, is therefore highly preferred. This self-focus has even grown into a societal addiction, oftentimes creating a series of ignorant behaviors in personal and professional environments. Selfish gain is generally rewarded, because accumulating wealth or profits is a sign of having understood the dominant mental model. This shows that mental models, or perceptions, are not always internally created, but very often prompted by signals from our environment. Practicing critical thinking, we can engage in regular examinations of our mental models and change those that have become obsolete or destructive.

Attitude

Attitude can be defined as a relatively stable, general, and enduring evaluation of a group, person, object, issue, or concept on a dimension ranging from negative to positive (Potas et al., 2021). A positive attitude is one of the strongest assets of a leader. Even in the direst of times, our attitude is the only thing we have in our control. Our attitude cannot be determined by others, nor can it be taken away from us. We have the power to decide what it shall be. Our attitude is influenced by our mental models and our choices. How do we choose to look at the things that we encounter? Do we have a glass-half-full or glass-half-empty attitude? Do we find a solution for every challenge or a challenge for every solution? Do we see the clouds before the sun, or the sun behind the clouds? There are numerous ways to present this question, but it boils down to one thing: we cannot change the setbacks that life will present us, but we can decide what we will do once they have manifested themselves, because then we can decide whether we want to dwell on them and wallow in our misery, or pick ourselves up, dust off our clothes, and move on with a new lesson under our belt and a stronger backbone.

Our attitude oftentimes determines how others perceive us, and can influence the opinions they will hold about us, based on the behavior we display. This issue manifests itself in every layer and environment of society. Ochalla, Gall, and Casperson (2002) explain, for instance, that many business professionals are unaware of the attitude they convey. While they may be doing all the physical things correctly—such as giving firm handshakes, correctly saying the client's name and dressing appropriately—their attitude sabotages their business success. Ochalla, Gall, and Casperson then mention issues such as lack of respect, being preoccupied, interrupting others, displaying nervous or annoying mannerisms, and using unfavorable speech patterns. The abovementioned is just a detail of the attitudinal theme. The broader scope is even more compelling. It deals with everything that happens to us. It deals with life in general and what we make of it. Most of the problems we experience on a daily basis can be shifted into opportunities or useful lessons if we just care to adjust our attitude. Not everything that seems good is really good, and similarly, not everything that seems bad is actually bad. Sometimes we find out in hindsight, that a great opportunity was disguised as a challenge.

In his bestselling book *Man's Search for Meaning*, Victor Frankl (2006) made a number of immortal statements. But maybe the most unforgettable one was that everything can be taken from a person but one thing: the last of human freedoms—to choose one's attitude in any given set of circumstances, to choose one's own way.

The awareness that Frankl attempts to instill in his readers is similar to Algafari's (2020) and Kirshenbaum's (2004) opinions, earlier mentioned in this chapter: there is meaning to be found in anything. In a post-COVID-19 world, we may be even more aware of the power we have to determine our attitude toward what happened: we can decide to see the experience as a bad lemon, which we cannot recover from, or we can make a memorable lemonade from it, which we will cherish the rest of our life.

On a more cautionary note, it may be important for leaders to realize that there is a critical factor at the foundation of post-COVID-19 attitudes: Technology Addiction (TA). While researchers have described TA as the epidemic of the twenty-first century, the mandatory seclusion in the COVID-era amplified this concern. TA is now described as a behavioral problem that negatively affects human life due to its excessive use, enhancing the chance of problematic outcomes in one's life due to loss of control (Kuss & Griffiths, 2015). Young adults with TA addiction may acquire a range of physical and mental health problems, such as visual impairment, spinal disorders, finger numbness, arm pain, bulimia, obesity, insomnia, anger problems, aggression, antisocial behavior, suicide attempts, anxiety disorder, and depression, among many others (Potas et al., 2021). Potas et al. therefore recommend the development of support mechanisms to help combat a pending TA pandemic.

Genius

Whether we decide to accept this or not, there resides a genius in each of us. How to tap into this inner-genius is a very personal task and journey. Emerson (2019) refers to this effort as achieving self-reliance. What is referred to here as the "genius" is our intimate source of inspiration, verve, and creativity, which we rarely express for others to see and appreciate. The reason for that may be because life has beaten our inner-genius down so many times that we may think it has perished. Formal education, societal rules, pressure from work and relationships, they have all curbed our natural inner-genius. Yet, we can revive it if we choose to do so. It starts with the realization that our inner-genius *exists*, followed by the will to accept and explore it. Every day presents us thousands of miracles, which we no longer acknowledge as such. We can reconnect with our creative side by giving ourself a break from our computer and mobile device now and then, doing something out of the ordinary, going somewhere different, or talking to someone we've never talked to before. These small practices can help resurface and replenish our internal well of creative thinking.

Garnett (2015) admits that seeing and admitting our greatness remains a struggle for many of us. She warns that our inner-genius should not be equated to an extraordinarily high IQ, but rather to the unique way our brain addresses and works through challenges. She identifies several roadblocks to finding our inner-genius, which many of us have and offers solutions to them. We include the following two here:

1. Our subjective self-view prohibits us from acknowledging our inner-genius. In work settings we can resolve this by asking our colleagues about areas they have perceived as strengths in our performance, with an emphasis on our unique approaches to our work. When asking various people, we may start seeing a pattern, which will help us accept that there is something that makes us stand out.
2. Our human tendency to be cautious can be a hurdle in daring to demonstrate our full potential. We can overcome this by observing the negative messages our brain exudes, and ask whether they serve or hurt us. A critical analysis may assist us in reversing negative mental chatter into more positive internal messaging (Garnett, 2015).

Indeed, while we can all identify areas of passion within ourselves, we also know too well how easy it is to be overcome by anxiety. This is when we doubt whether we are good enough to do what we desire; when we doubt whether we will persevere, and may even fall prey to judgmental mindsets such as shame, guilt, and physical discomfort. Learning to connect with our authentic selves is a key element to pursuing our individual creative paths. It is thereby important to enhance positive emotions such as trust, openness to change, and the commitment essential for creativity, as well as practicing a calm physique in order to offset tension and develop self-compassion (Golden, 2007).

In a post-COVID-19 world we will need all the genius we can muster. The fact that we are aware that there is an immense source of wisdom inside, can serve as a strong encouragement to observe, think, and consider multiple directions toward a future, of which none of us knows the direction of substance yet. An even more encouraging thought in this context is, that we are not alone in the challenges we face, and if we decide to synergistically connect, our inner-geniuses may reach new, remarkable heights toward impressive future directions.

Education

Education should not necessarily be perceived as a formal path toward personal and professional development. It can be formal or informal, but it is critical that we maintain it. Education is the vehicle for leaders to stay ahead of the crowd. The more we learn, the sharper our critical and creative thinking skills get, the broader our scope becomes, and the more possibilities we see and create for ourselves. We live in unprecedented times, and have recently witnessed the manifestation of a complete societal change. If the COVID-19 era brought one thing to the forefront it is that continuing our education is no longer a luxury, but quite the contrary: failing to continuously educate ourselves will rob us from ceasing opportunities that others learn about.

The COVID-19 pandemic caused major disruptions in the supply and delivery of education (Bansak & Starr, 2021). Reviewing the case of public health education, Isley et al. (2021) note that the pandemic has mandated wide ranges of student populations to repeatedly adapt to new roadmaps for navigating their education. "First was the sudden switch to virtual coursework, followed by the more subtle adaptations that started to take place in the various corners of public health. "Flexibility" and "new normal" became the catchwords of 2020. Students have served as proof of the incredible human capacity to reorient in new conditions to survive" (Isley et al., 2021, p. 63).

Indeed, the pandemic brought along a massive shift to online education, conveying to our collective awareness that this trend is here to stay, and that it can bring some great advantages in regard to our range of choices, and the many directions in which we can be educated from the comfort of our homes or offices. At the same time, we became more abundantly aware than before of the discrepancy in access to technology, which is related to financial stability and job security. In times of great uncertainty, the need becomes crystal clear that we need to adopt policies to remedy the profoundly inequitable distribution of the basic necessities of life: employment, food, health care, housing, and education (El-Mohandes, 2020). El-Mohandes underscores that access to education is a key influence on health that has both short- and long-term consequences. This statement is corroborated by the Center for Disease Control and Prevention (2012), which published a press release that confirmed the interdependency between higher levels of education and health. The report stated that heads of households with higher levels of education had lower rates of obesity in their household, smoked less, had higher life expectancy rates, and had fewer uninsured children. The relationship makes sense: higher education usually leads to better jobs, resulting in higher earnings, thus enabling resources for

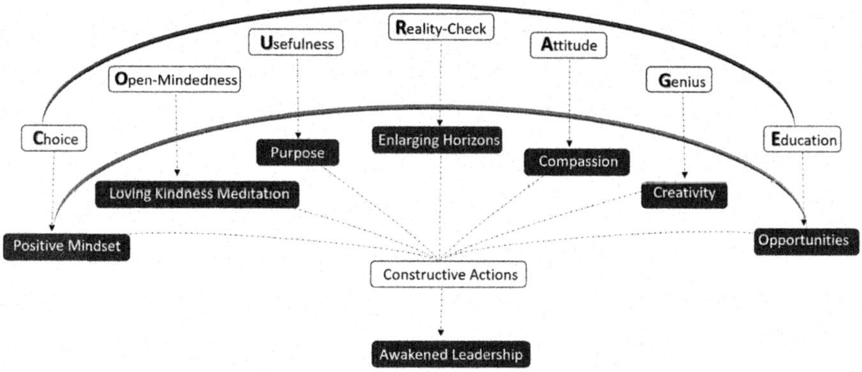

Fig. 11.1 COURAGE as a roadmap toward sustainable practices

good health. Unfortunately, the gaping discrepancies in access to necessary means leave large groups of Hispanic and Black Americans at a disadvantage. As an example, El-Mohandes presents the case of the March 2020 COVID-19 related public school closures in NYC, demanding a switch to online education. A large percentage of Hispanic households expressed difficulty supporting their children's education at home using distance learning methods, compared with far fewer English speakers. This is a reality that will undoubtedly have a negative effect on the futures of those children if not properly addressed (El-Mohandes, 2020).

Figure 11.1 below depicts the roadmap COURAGE provides toward sustainable practices.

Feature Case in Point: Dr. Kizzmekia Corbett

The COVID-19 pandemic brought into the limelight, an African American woman, who successfully served as the lead immunologist in the vaccine research center of the National Institutes of Health: Dr. Kizzmekia Corbett. With help of the massive knowledge acquired over the previous 6 years, applied to a vaccine platform in collaboration with Moderna, Dr. Corbett's team initiated the clinical trials in 2020.

Dr. Corbett became interested in science at an early age, and came to love the work she's doing and the immense contribution she is making. Born and raised in North Carolina, Kizzmekia had a large family of step- and foster siblings. After her K-12 education, she attended the University of Maryland, where she received a B.S. in biological sciences and sociology. She subsequently enrolled in University of North Carolina at Chapel Hill, where she received a PhD in microbiology and immunology.

As her awareness about the professional direction she wanted to choose took a solid shape, she began to work in research laboratories and as a summer intern in the science lab at Stony Brook University, where she studied Yersinia pseudotuberculosis pathogenesis. She also worked as a lab tech at the University of Maryland School of Nursing, and as a biological sciences trainer at the National Institutes of Health (NIH), where she worked on the pathogenesis of respiratory syncytial virus as well as on a project focused on innovative vaccine platform advancement. Toward her PhD, Corbett studied human antibody responses to dengue virus in Sri Lankan children under the supervision of Aravinda de Silva at University of North Carolina at Chapel Hill, and served as a visiting scholar at Genetech Research Institute in Colombo, Sri Lanka.

While her meticulous approach to science, and her growing knowledge are incredible assets, Kizzmekia is mostly praised for her ability to connect with people, a skill that more scientists should try to develop. According to the National Center for Education Statistics, only 18% of all students graduate with a STEM degree, among 2% are black (CBS, 2021). A brilliant scientist, Kizzmekia Corbett is accomplishing today what many of her equally talented black predecessors could not accomplish: acquiring the attention, respect, and support from supervisors and the community to make the significant contribution she can make to our collective well-being (CBS, 2021).

Corbett has been labeled an expert on the front lines of the global race for a SARS-CoV-2 vaccine, and someone who will go down in history as one of the key players in developing the science that could end the pandemic (Romero et al., 2020).

Dr. Corbett can count on the support of Dr. Anthony Fauci, director of the National Institute of Allergy and Infectious Diseases at the U.S. National Institutes of Health, who wrote in a February 2021 article in TIME, that Kizzmekia Corbett, the scientific lead of the Vaccine Research Center's coronavirus team at the U.S. National Institutes of Health, is widely recognized in the immunology community as a rising star. Dr. Fauci continued,

> For the past six years, she has focused on coronavirus biology and vaccine development. During the pandemic, those years of research led to the discovery that a stabilized version of a spike protein found on the surface of all coronaviruses can be a key target for vaccines, treatments and diagnostics. She and her colleagues have been central to the development of the Moderna mRNA vaccine and the Eli Lilly therapeutic monoclonal antibody that were first to enter clinical trials in the U.S. and now have authorization for emergency use. As a result, her work will have a substantial impact on ending the worst respiratory-disease pandemic in more than 100 years. (Fauci, 2021).

Dr. Kizzmekia Corbett has grown into one of the National Institutes of Health's leading scientists behind the government's search for a vaccine (Romero et al., 2020).

Case-Specific Reflection Questions

1. Evaluate the case of Dr. Kizzmekia Corbett, and share how she has implemented the elements of COURAGE in her life and career so far?
2. What personal inspirations can you gain from Dr. Corbett's story?
3. After reading this case, what do you consider to be Dr. Corbett's greatest asset toward her current success?

Positive Leadership/Change Lessons

COURAGE toward Sustainable Practices in a Post-COVID-19 world.

Several of the behaviors and mindsets in the above-used acronym, COURAGE, are interrelated. At the surface level it is easy to surmise that education can help us reignite our inner-genius, which can make us more receptive to the differences in mental models (reality-check), while practicing open-mindedness reveals more choices, and helps us see the usefulness of experiences more clearly. Moreover, an open mind is a great foundation for a constructive attitude, which can encourage us to explore more choices, and revive our inner-genius.

Within the more pronounced focus of a post-COVID-19 performance climate based on awakened leadership toward sustainable practices, this chapter offered the following suggestions

Choice

While the choices at our disposal are not always desirable, their effect is usually determined by our actions after we made them. Resilience, perseverance and grit will lead the way in making constructive choices, and more importantly, implement constructive outcomes. Our most important post-COVID choice is to recover and move on with a positive mind. Fortunately, the COVID challenge is not the first rodeo for many of us, and the good news is that resilience is a behavioral pattern that we can convert into a habit.

Open-Mindedness

Now that we are all aware of the implicit biases we hold, we can gracefully accept their existence and the purpose they serve in rapid decision processes, but we can also engage in constructive practices to overcome the natural sense of separate thinking that we harbor. Loving Kindness Meditation is a simple practice to enhance compassion and reduce limiting biases. It can enhance our awareness of social injustice, expand our ability to engage in critical thinking about our own contribution to these painful practices, and help us to become more accepting to others that we previously considered a non-option for collaboration.

Usefulness

Everything is useful in our lives, and if we choose to perceive the COVID-19 pandemic as such, we can discover numerous learning moments and opportunities for improvement that revealed themselves during the challenging era, varying from adjusting overconsumption and craving power to gravitate to more emotional closeness and appreciating the real and often immaterial paths toward greater happiness.

Reality-Check

The COVID-19 era confronted us with many previously ignored points of awareness. One is the concept of mental models, which feed into our biases, and create snapshots of how we see the world. Yet, our mental models are merely our viewpoint. A sustainable reality will be established when we understand and accept that others also have their own mental models, based on the many influencing factors that shaped them. Understanding this may expand our horizons and lead to the understanding that reality is a very personal phenomenon, for which no one can be blamed.

Attitude

In a post-COVID-19 world, we should be aware of the power we have to determine our attitude toward what happened: we can either choose to continue suffering from the effects, or take the pandemic-instigated lessons to heart and move on with greater insights. It is also important to understand that a pandemic of the COVID-19 magnitude may prompt mental and emotional issues within various layers of the working community, which will also require an understanding and compassionate approach.

Genius

There is a genius in all of us, but reality has made us self-conscious and doubtful about our qualities and creative skills. In a post-COVID-19 world we will need all the genius we can muster. The fact that we are aware that there is an immense source of wisdom inside, can serve as a strong encouragement to observe, think, and consider multiple directions toward a future, of which none of us knows the direction of substance yet.

Education

The COVID-19 pandemic brought along a massive shift to online education, conveying to our collective awareness that this trend is here to stay, and that it can bring some great advantages in regard to our range of choices, and the many directions in which we can be educated from the comfort of our homes or offices. At the same time, we became more abundantly aware than before of the discrepancy in access to technology, which is related to financial stability and job security. The proven interdependency between higher levels of education and health may serve as a strong inspiration to many to obtain higher education in order to enhance their professional applicability in a new, insecure, but exciting world.

Chapter-End Reflection Questions

1. This chapter focused on seven qualities and practices that can make a difference in your life (the elements of COURAGE). Please reflect on each of these seven aspects for yourself, and share in two or three sentences for each, how you feel they fit into your current circumstances?
2. Which of the seven elements comes easiest to you as an implementation of positive leadership in your life?
3. Which of the seven elements do you consider most challenging to implement as a positive leadership practice in your life?
4. After reading this chapter, what do you consider the greatest and most important lesson learned from the COVID-19 pandemic?
5. What do you consider the greatest challenge for yourself to overcome in a post-COVID-19 world?

References

Algafari, M. (2020). Everything has meaning. *International Body Psychotherapy Journal, 19*(1), 8–9.

Avolio, B. J., & Gardner, W. L. (2005). Authentic leadership development: Getting to the root of positive forms of leadership. *The Leadership Quarterly, 16*, 315–338.

Bansak, C., & Starr, M. (2021). Covid-19 shocks to education supply: How 200,000 U.S. households dealt with the sudden shift to distance learning. *Review of Economics of the Household, 19*(1), 63–90.

Cameron, K. (2012). *Positive leadership: Strategies for extraordinary performance*. Berrett-Koehler Publishers.

CBS News. (2021, January 9). *Meet the black female scientist at the forefront of COVID-19 vaccine development*. https://www.cbsnews.com/news/covid-19-vaccine-development-kizzmekia-corbett/

Center for Disease Control and Prevention. (2012, May 16). Higher education and income levels keys to better health, according to annual report on nation's health. *CDC Newsroom*. https://www.cdc.gov/media/releases/2012/p0516_higher_education.html

Cho, J. (2020). Tackling implicit bias. *ABA Journal, 106*, 11–12.

Collins, J. (2006). *Good to great: Why some companies make the leap. ..and others don't*. Random House Business Books.

Duncan, D. L. (2020). What the COVID-19 pandemic tells us about the need to develop resilience in the nursing workforce. *Nursing Management, 27*(3), 22–27.

El-Mohandes, A. (2020). COVID-19: A barometer for social justice in New York City. *American Journal of Public Health, 110*(11), 1656–1658.

Emerson, R. W. (2019). *Self-reliance*. Independently Published.

Fauci, A. (2021, February 16). Kizzmekia Corbett. *TIME*. https://time.com/collection-post/5937718/kizzmekia-corbett/

Frankl, V. E. (2006). *Man's search for meaning*. Beacon Press.

Garnett, L. (2015). 3 ways to unleash your inner genius (yes, you have one). *Inc.com*. https://www.inc.com/laura-garnett/3-ways-to-unleash-your-inner-genius-yes-you-have-one.html

Golden, B. (2007). *Unlock your creative genius*. Prometheus Books.

Hernandez, J. (2009). Servant-leadership as a cornerstone for restoration of human dignity. *The International Journal of Servant-Leadership, 5*(1), 303–320.

Isley, J. W., Gonzales, R., Drey, J., Ritter, E. Q., Lawrence, W. R., Rowe, B., & Sosa, P. (2021). Adaptability, change, hope: Student perspectives during the COVID-19 pandemic. *American Journal of Public Health, 111*(1), 63–65.

Kirshenbaum, M. (2004). *Everything happens for a reason: Finding the true meaning of the events in our lives*. Harmony.

Kuofie, M., & Muhammad, N. M. N. (2021). Leaders perspective on post COVID-19 pandemic period: Global business focus. *International Journal of Health and Economic Development, 7*(1), 13–36.

Kuss, D. J., & Griffiths, M. D. (2015). *Internet addiction in psychotherapy*. Palgrave Macmillan.

Loving Kindness Meditation. (2021). *Greater good in action*. https://ggia.berkeley.edu/practice/loving_kindness_meditation

Marques, J. (2009). Awakened leaders: Born or made? *Leadership & Organization Development Journal, 31*(4), 307–323.

Marques, J. F. (2010). Awakened leaders: Who are they and why do we need them? *Development and Learning in Organizations, 24*(2), 7–10.

Ochalla, B., Gall, K., & Casperson, D. M. (2002). Getting it done: Improve your attitude. *Credit Union Management*, Madison, WI.

Pattakos, A. (2008). *Prisoners of our thoughts: Viktor Frankl's principles for discovering meaning in life and work*. Berrett-Koehler.

Potas, N., Açıkalın, Ş. N., Erçetin, Ş. Ş., et al. (2021). Technology addiction of adolescents in the COVID-19 era: Mediating effect of attitude on awareness and behavior. *Current Psychology* (only online published at time of writing this article). https://doi.org/10.1007/s12144-021-01470-8.

Quinn, D. (1992). *Ishmael: An adventure of the mind and spirit*. Bantam Books, Incorporated.

Reeves, A. N. (2018). We think what we see, we see what we think: Recognizing, understanding & interrupting implicit biases: Asset-based financial services industry. *The Secured Lender, 74*(5), 74–76.

Romero, L., Salzman, S. & Folmer, K. (2020, December 13). Kizzmekia Corbett, an African American woman, is praised as key scientist behind COVID-19 vaccine: Dr. Anthony Fauci said Kizzmekia Corbett's involvement is a sign of hope. *ABC News*. https://abcnews.go.com/Health/kizzmekia-corbett-african-american-woman-praised-key-scientist/story?id=74679965

Rutter, M. (2012). Resilience as a dynamic concept. *Development and Psychopathology, 24*, 335–344.

Senge, P. M. (1992). Mental models. *Planning Review, 20*(2), 4.

Steve Jobs'. (2005). *Stanford commencement address (2005)*. Stanford University. https://www.youtube.com/watch?v=UF8uR6Z6KLc

Williamson, V., Murphy, D., & Greenberg, N. (2020). Editorial: COVID-19 and experiences of moral injury in frontline key workers. *Occupational Medicine, 70*(5), 317–319.

Youssef-Morgan, C. M., & Luthans, F. (2013). Positive leadership: Meaning and application across cultures. *Organizational Dynamics, 42*(3), 198–208.

Towards Transformational Leadership Beyond the Covid-19 Pandemic

12

Denis H. J. Caro

This chapter deals with transformational leadership in the face of tectonic changes in the governance of world societies of the future.

Landscape Contours Beyond the Covid-19 Pandemic

The world is reeling from the devastating effects of the Covid-19 pandemic on the health of peoples and national economies. Although this pandemic will be tamed through immunological advances, the repercussions in terms of damaged distribution and supply systems, national debts and deficits, social anarchy, socioeconomic distress, and unemployment will present substantial leadership challenges for the remainder of the decade. As the world focused on controlling the pandemic, the fundamental humanitarian problems of access to basic health care and education, potable water and basic sanitation, and secure food supplies have been sidelined. In the post-Covid-19 era, these challenges cannot be ignored and will require immense and urgent coordinated planetary responses. Across key world nations, such as Brazil, the European Union, India, Indonesia, Mexico, Nigeria, the People's Republic of China, the Russian Federation, and the United States alone, there are well over one billion people who live in acute socioeconomic distress with a lack of access to clean and safe water and adequate sanitation facilities. Billions across Africa, East Asia, and South Asia will continue to suffer from food insecurity, hunger, and malnutrition. Over two billion people will still lack adequate health care and proper education. AIDS, homicides, road trauma, substance abuse, and suicides will continue to plague and claim hundreds of thousands of lives across the planet annually. Toxic air quality will continue to account for millions of deaths each year around the world and environmental deterioration will directly and adversely affect

D. H. J. Caro (✉)
Telfer School of Management, University of Ottawa, Ottawa, ON, Canada

S. K. Dhiman, J. F. Marques (eds.), *Leadership After COVID-19*, Future of Business and Finance, https://doi.org/10.1007/978-3-030-84867-5_12

billions of lives. Premature deaths from all these causes will continue to cost economies over seven trillion dollars annually with the highest losses being across East Asia, Europe, South Asia, and the Americas.

These challenges will compel world communities to coalesce and evolve into an integrated planetary world society. The post-Covid-19 era will witness the rapid disintegration of the world order. The days of twentieth century geopolitical machinations and the dictum that might make right are numbered. The assumption that nations with military power should impose their values on other nations will be bankrupt. The days of political leadership elites that have been ostensibly corrupt, incompetent, self-serving, or unaccountable to people are numbered. Future leaders will be required to become more fully aware of not only national, but also of planetary challenges at hand. For decades corrupt and unethical leaders have too often held political power to the detriment of the health and social development of peoples who are often oppressed through misplaced national priorities. Globalization will become an omnipresent reality with transformations that require more sophisticated forms of governance through dynamic transformational leadership. Increasing international chaos and the decline of sovereign power of nation-states is already in evidence. The alarming socioeconomic disparities and inequities; deteriorating environments; increased corruption, criminality, and terrorism; the proliferation of infectious diseases; and violence point to an increasingly chaotic world community. The ability of the United Nations System to effectively engage in peacebuilding and positive development is stymied in the face of growing international anarchy. The abysmal and miserable living conditions of hundreds of millions feed into the chaotic mass migration and mobility of the global poor. This is clearly not sustainable. The key principle of the international order of non-interference in national affairs is becoming an impediment to dealing with humanity's most pressing common challenges. The resolution of present global problems and the full socio- technological development of humankind may yet take until the end of this century (Turchin, 2007). Ultimately, the leading world nations of tomorrow will be the ones that are on the forefront of knowledge and innovative research in advanced super-intelligence systems, biotechnology, genomics, nanotechnology, nuclear fusion, ocean sciences, renewal energy technologies, robotics, and space technologies (Waslekar & Futehally, 2011). However, the evolution of an integrated world community and planetary governance systems has already started and is inexorable. Transformational leadership will become the lodestar of the emerging planetary governance systems (Caro, 2021).

Planetary Existential Future Threats

Human existential risks are incalculable and remain elusive given the accelerating rate of change in complex planetary systems. The potential for unforeseen and unpleasant shocks is becoming greater. The unfamiliar does not mean improbable. There is a myriad of prognostications for the future of humankind ranging from existential obliteration to a nirvanic technological utopia. The world of the future will no doubt lie between these two extremes. Class exploitation, ecosystem devastation, global and national inequality of income and wealth, pandemics, poverty, racism, and starvation continue to plague humankind (Sachs, 2005). The complex system of global capitalism with its economic uncertainties also contributes to sociopolitical instability (Chaulia, 2013; Piketty, 2014; Soros, 1998). Endless demands of the wealthiest are incompatible with the basic needs of the planet's dispossessed (Torres, 2018; Dartnell, 2015; Wilson, 2006). With 1% of the richest peoples owning more than the remaining 99%, is it any surprise that conflict, crime, and violence are rampant across the world? There are five substantial existential threats that will accentuate the Malthusian problems of food and water scarcity, the destruction of health care systems, the decline of socioeconomic health, and sociopolitical viability of nations. These threaten the Earth's environmental integrity, as well as the physical, mental, spiritual health, and well-being of humankind.

Demographic Threats

By 2050, there will be more than ten billion people on the planet and over four billion will be living in unacceptable conditions. National democratic systems are not effective in dealing with these monumental planetary challenges (Robinson, 1990). American Nobel Physics Laureate Henry W. Kendall asserted: "If we do not halt population growth with justice and compassion, it will be done for us by nature, brutally, and without pity and will leave a ravaged world" (SyamRoy, 2017). Indeed, the severe problems of overpopulation and their consequences cannot persist indefinitely. Diamond (2005) underscored that human history consists of unequal conflicts between the haves and the have-nots, and between the myopic interests of the powerful and the strategic long-term interests of humankind. The noted writer and biochemist Isaac Asimov predicted that the world population explosion, not nuclear warfare, would present the greatest danger to humankind. As he wrote: "To bring about destruction by overcrowding, mass starvation, anarchy, the destruction of cherished values-there is no need to do anything. We need only do nothing, except what comes naturally and breed" (Asimov, 1995, p. 256). Indeed, it is the demographic and population explosive growth that present titanic problems that drive and accentuate the humanitarian and socioeconomic challenges across the planet. It is incumbent on all nations to collaborate and cooperate proactively to redistribute the economic wealth equitably across the planet, even in the face of their own internal economic challenges.

Environmental Threats

Environmental threats include increased atmospheric pollution and toxicity, climatic destabilization, and massive ecosystem degradation (Wagner & Woltzman, 2015; Victor, 2011; Ehlers & Krafft, 2006). Much attention has been drawn to the Anthropocene, the current epoch in which climatic changes result from human development (Viola & Franchini, 2018; Hamilton, 2017; Davies, 2016). The consequences of a projected rise of 2–6 °C will likely be a catastrophic tipping point, resulting in sea level increases of 1–6 m with the inevitable melting of glaciers. This poses a threat to the availability and productivity of agricultural land; the stability of distribution and supply chain systems (Andreoni & Miola, 2015); and the viability of major coastland urban regions. Hundreds of millions of people are at risk of being displaced, especially in low-lying coastal areas of the globe. Tropical cyclones, hurricanes, and tornados are increasing in intensity causing trillions of dollars in damage and losses annually and affecting the lives of billions (Nordhaus, 2013; Therivel, 2010). Climate control through geoengineering and coordinated global proactive strategies to eliminate the dependency on nonrenewable energy remain vital systemic solutions (Morton, 2016). However, the American philosopher Abraham Kaplan (1968) cautions "We can solve some problems in life, but they are usually the less significant ones. Those that are more significant we can only cope with them. We can at best learn to live with them". Indeed, in the face of unrelenting population growth and demands, environmental risks may require coping, rather than preventive strategies, in the short term.

Pandemic Threats

The risk of global pandemics will only increase with time and pressing population growth (Dixon, 2015). This includes viral infections, such as the coronavirus diseases (Covid-19 and SARS-CoV), ebolaviruses, human immunodeficiency viruses, influenza viruses, such as avian and H1N1 flus, and bacterial infections, such as the Methicillin-Resistant *Staphylococcus aureus* (MRSA) Super bug. All pose significant threats to human life across the globe. Often, they are zoonotic in origin and spread quickly in nations with high population densities, poor socioeconomic regions with adverse environmental health conditions, inadequate sanitation, and slow governance response. Integrated globalized markets and transportation systems act as vectors of these diseases that also spread rapidly in nations with high socioeconomic disparities, weak health care infrastructures, and underdeveloped emergency response and management systems. Unchecked these diseases contribute to the impoverishment of economies, societal breakdowns, and sociopolitical anarchy (Diamond, 1997). They carry high mortality and morbidity rates that are propagated rapidly in environments with inadequate public health controls and where antiviral solutions remain unavailable. High-level collaboration and coordination efforts of all world nations are critical in dealing with these insidious and pervasive threats.

Technological Threats

Over the twenty-first century, advanced super-intelligence systems, big-data systems and deep-learning technologies will be instrumental in solving many intractable problems, such as climatic changes and current incurable diseases (Ford, 2018).

However, the proliferation and future ubiquity of these disruptive technologies in themselves pose threats to humankind (Inglehart, 2018; Bostrom, 2014; Bowes & Christensen, 1995). Technological singularity is the tipping point whereby super-intelligence systems will supersede human cognitive capabilities and intelligence (Shanahan, 2015; Kurzweil, 2005). This profound transformation will increasingly manifest as human labour redundancies, massive unemployment, pervasive disruptions of labour markets, profound sociopsychological effects, social anarchy, structural violence, and technostress. The American sociologist Wright C. Mills (1959) predicted a decline of human cognitive and thinking abilities in a society obsessed with technological innovations. Technostress, the ever-increasing anxiety associated with proliferating disruptive technologies that call for constant adaptation and endless systems reengineering, take a significant toll on the human psyche (Caro & Sethi, 1985). The American sociologist Lewis Mumford (1971) warned of the societal dangers of rapidly adopting novel technologies uncritically. Manson (2014) summarizes Mumford's vision as follows:

> The obsolete individual would be entirely de-skilled, reduced to a passive, inert, and trivial accessory to the machine. Technical surveillance and limitless data-collection—an all-seeing eye, or Panopticon—would monitor every individual on the planet. Ultimately, a totalitarian technocracy, centralizing and augmenting its power-complex, ignoring the real needs and values of human life, might produce a world fit only for machines to live in.

Indeed, technological advances are rapid and ubiquitous and give governance systems significant and uncompromising social control and surveillance capabilities over people. Increasingly, the autonomous individual is subject to social conformance to technological norms of controllability and predictability. The omnipresent danger is that humans will become totally alienated and non-sentient automatons (Tegmark, 2017; Hughes, 2004). Moreover, there is a growing philosophical movement of transhumanism that seeks the evolution of intelligent life beyond human form and limitations through human enhancement technologies (Mercer & Trothen, 2014; Ranisch & Sorgner, 2014; More & Vita-More, 2013; Burdett, 2011; Cole-Turner, 2011). Extropianism underscores the need to explicitly recognize cognitive and morphological freedom of individuals to use human enhancement technologies at will (Kaku, 2011). With exponential increases in big-data systems and robotics, super-intelligent systems may command more authority than humans. System algorithms will arbitrate human lives and will be posited as being preferential to human knowledge and wisdom (Mulgan, 2018; Boden, 2016). In this scenario, machines dominate humankind that in turn become subservient to machines. Already, proponents of dataism maintain that the human species is merely a single data processing system and the value of humans is solely defined as their contribution to these systems (Harari, 2017; Lohr, 2015). Dataism presents an existential challenge to the dominant moral ideology of humanism, whereby human sentient feelings and critical independent thinking remain important. These technological threats in the form of a "Homo Technomorphis" would signal the spiritual death of human beings (Manson, 2014). In the face of this threat, it is incumbent on all world nations to reaffirm human dignity and values, as they maturate technological societies, while asserting what it means to be fully human in a planetary community.

War Conflict Threats

War conflict threats are omnipresent and manifest in variegated forms that in their extreme include chemical, biological, radiological, and nuclear (CBRN) weapons of mass destruction (WMD) (Baum, 2015; Falk, 2015; Forest & Howard, 2012; Coyne & Mathers, 2011). Civil and global wars with massive and large-scale deaths, physical and psychological trauma, mass population displacements and upheavals incalculable and unspeakable intergenerational trauma that linger for decades. Wars are the ultimate in horror and obscenity in and of themselves. Massive destruction and disruptions of distribution and supply chains, economies, infrastructures, and telecommunication systems represent collateral damage are significant, but are incomparable to the incalculable assault on the human psyche and humankind. Alas, war conflicts continue as hideous realities today, as they have throughout history. Socioeconomic disparities inflame inherent deep ethnic, ideological, linguistic, racial, and religious differences (Themnér & Wallensteen, 2012). "Us-and-Them" mindsets that cleave the social world into in- and out-groups evoke powerful emotions that breed ethnocentrism and intolerance (Kandel, 2018; Siegel, 2016). Social communities of homogenous peoples promulgate inequalities, polarization, segregation, and xenophobia (Haidt, 2012). Identity politics and populist nationalism that focuses on social inclusivity and power distorts sociopolitical priorities and outcomes (Fukuyama, 2018). Risk factors for and root causes of war are complex and multifaceted. They include disparities in education and health; failing infrastructures; high population densities; inadequate access to water and food resources; low literacy rates; oppression of ethnic and religious minorities and indigenous peoples; overpopulation; poor sociocultural cohesion; significant investments into WMD; socioeconomic distress, including unemployment and poverty; weak governance systems and incompetent leadership (Solar & Irwin, 2010). These in turn amplify extreme ideologies, incite hatreds, and provoke violence through mass and social media outlets that disseminate bias, disinformation, and propaganda. Violent imagery provokes and sanctifies destruction and the horrors of war. Moreover, war conflicts often become conflagrations that transcend national borders. They spread like wildfires that cannot be easily contained nor controlled. Even today, income inequality, inefficient access to key needed survival resources, inequality of opportunities, and ignorance breeds exploitation, extremism, and national disintegration (Levy & Sidel, 2008; Stewart, 2002). This engenders further humanitarian crises, the mass displacements of desperate, impoverished, and unemployed millions; not to mention the biome, ecosystem and environmental damage reeked. All wars have unknown outcomes with untold destruction of human societies and structures and incalculable human suffering. As the Russian writer Vasily S. Grossman expressed in his classic Life and Fate (1960), wars are: "fought by a great evil, struggling to crush a small kernel of human kindness. But if what is human in human beings has not been destroyed even now, then evil will never conquer" (Grossman & Chandler, 2006). Wars are preventable and the risks mitigated, but they require cogent leadership with courage, foresight, great resolve, and vision. It is incumbent all nations to collaborate to eliminate the endemic root causes of war. War remains the common enemy of all humankind and indeed of the future.

There are numerous global hot zones that will compel the world community to prevent and resolve in the twenty-first century (Caro, 2021). Massive and urgent humanitarian assistance, development and significant investments in peacebuilding is essential to avert destructive wars in these regions. Collaboration on urgent humanitarian assistance efforts across international borders remains essential. The exercise of soft power must take precedence over hard power politics of economic and military dominance and war (Nye, 2009). When the noted American architect and systems thinker Buckminster Fuller asserted that: "traditional human power structures and their reign of darkness are about to be rendered obsolete", he was referring to the obsolescence of hard power (Fuller & Kuromiya, 1992). No good will ever come from destructive military interventions and involvement that would be disastrous for the future of all humanity. In the interim, the planet remains highly unstable and volatile with significant regional flashpoints that are potentially conflictual and pose catastrophic risks to humanity and ecosystems. Climatic changes, environmental disasters, ethnic tensions, food shortages, overpopulation, poor income and resource distribution, poverty, and water shortages will be flashpoints of these future conflicts. Unless these planetary issues are addressed, world regions could see the deployment of unspeakably horrific biological and technological weaponry. This must be avoided and mitigated at all costs. Without cogent transformational leadership and concerted peacebuilding efforts to resolve profound humanitarian challenges, regional eco-wars will be inevitable with titanic implications for humankind.

Towards Planetary Consciousness and Integrated Values

Humanity remains resilient and undeterred in the face of planetary challenges and obstacles. Great existential threats also bring new growth, insights, opportunities, and constructive possibilities to overcome adverse conditions. There are countervailing measures to lower and obviate the risks of existential threats, whether they are climatic, environmental, pandemic, technological, or war conflicts. Advancements and development in scientific knowledge and technology have great potential to eliminate and mitigate existential risks. Cognitive abilities, education, knowledge, and understanding remain essential. Cogent transformational leadership with human courage, resolve, strong ethics, and wisdom are critical in navigating through the straits between Scylla and Charybdis. Although world nations face diverse humanitarian challenges and are on different trajectories, they share common human planetary aspirations that transcend national borders. There is an emerging planetary consciousness that binds every human being to a greater world community. Shared international problems require world solutions that will underscore the need for cogent, effective, and ethical planetary governance systems. The ultimate shape of the future will be forged through transformational leaders whose views transcend national borders and paradigms. Cogent and effective planetary governance will require ethical leaders who will reaffirm basic, common, and positive humanitarian values that promote peace, social justice, and reconciliation among diverse peoples.

The Nobel Peace Laureate Lester B. Pearson (1957) asserted: "The best defence of peace is not power, but the removal of the causes of war". The greatest challenge of the twenty-first century is peacebuilding. The primordial prevention of wars is of paramount importance (Legge, 2019; Bretherton & Law, 2015; Cohen & Chehimi, 2010; De Jong, 2010; Hinde, 2008; Lederach, 2005: Schmelzle, 2005; Ackermann, 2003; Galtung, 1969). Ostensibly, root causes of war lie in the massive resource and socioeconomic inequities globally (Stewart, 2002; Thomas et al., 2002). Conflict mediation and prevention, dialogue, nonviolence commitments, reconciliation, and truth are important in peacebuilding (Bergmann, 2019; Philpott & Powers, 2010; Ramírez, 2007). Conflict resolution and peace calls for deep sociocultural engagement and understanding. Fundamentally, peace begins with the understanding of the functioning of the human brain and its cognitive limitations that predispose humans to paranoia and violence (Dietrich, 2018; Koestler, 1967). A planetary, or "us-and-us", mindset countervails ethnocentrism and xenophobia through social behavioural changes that build positive shared identities. A holotropic integration of the conscious and the unconscious lies at the heart of this process (Grof, 2012; Wilber, 2000). Ultimately, a "planetary consciousness", that is rooted in a common identity as humanity is essential. Nations are in effect vast social experiments that forge values and linkages between diverse peoples within communities that are the foundations of humankind values. A planetary community would reaffirm positive human values that transcend cultures and ideologies. Future transformational leaders will affirm and be committed to central human principles and values that include the following.

Human compassion and peace. The reaffirmation of human dignity, duties, and responsibilities are essential to the promulgation of social peace. Caring, compassion, and empathy are essential (Caro, 1993). The moral litmus test of any sociopolitical system is how the most socioeconomically distressed and most socially vulnerable are treated. Transformational leaders have a paramount responsibility to address socioeconomic and sociopolitical inequities, while promoting human dignity and environmental sustainability.

Human dignity and health. Human dignity is inherent and transcendent. Persons have the right to existence, freedom, and respect. As such, they have the right to full human development and health. Health is the full and positive expression of development and growth to become fully human. This focuses on the right to integrated well-being including physical, psychological, and spiritual health in positive, safe, and ecologically sustainable environments.

Human duties and responsibilities. Persons have core obligations towards other human beings, communities, and ecosystems. Individual rights without due diligence to duties and responsibilities leads to the escalation of corruption, demands, and greed that are indiscriminate, unlimited, and ultimately destructive to human communities.

Planetary reverence for life. The world-renowned cosmologist Carl Sagan (1994) asserted: "This pale blue dot is our planetary home". Protecting biodiversity in all its forms and sustaining ecosystems remains a quintessential human duty and responsibility. It begins with each person's reflection of the fundamental principle of what the distinguished humanitarian and theologian Albert Schweitzer (1933) called the "reverence for life", whereby all forms of life and their ecosystems are respected and safeguarded.

Planetary solidarity. Humanity is interconnected and interdependent as a world community. As such, peoples must collaborate in solidarity to strengthen global communities and promote social justice. In the face of economic and political inequities, it is important to confront the destructive effects of blind materialism, corruption and criminality, deleterious substance abuse, forced displacements, human trafficking, unbridled greed, and all forms of violence.

Social engagement and participation. Well-ordered communities require the recognition of mutual rights, duties, and responsibilities to social harmony and order. As instruments that develop and promote the common good through human dignity and rights, social communities need to exercise their collective responsibilities effectively and efficiently. Social engagement reaffirms that all peoples have the duty and the right to proactively engage in the cultural, economic, and political decisions that affect their community.

Social equity. Pope John Paul II affirmed (2000): "There is no true peace without fairness, truth, justice and solidarity". Human communities directly affect individual dignity and social development. Ethical population management policies, gender equality and parity, respect for diverse ethnicities and indigenous peoples, sociocultural harmony and integration, and effective governance are critical to foster social justice.

Social health and integrity. Transformational leaders require a commitment to peace and both economic and social justice that transcend nation-states. This necessitates an understanding of the fundamental human rights to adequate education, employment, food, health care, income, safe environments, and water. This also underscores the need for robust economies and effective infrastructures that include energy systems, technological support, protection and security, and transportation systems.

Socioeconomic justice. Local, national, and global economies must foster and promulgate human and social development. This underscores the right to gainful employment and freedom from socioeconomic distress. These are achieved through responsible fiscal and monetary policies; the equitable distribution of tax revenues;

fair and robust global trade; the avoidance and mitigation of public debt; and zero tolerance of all forms of corruption and crime.

Sociotechnical control and integration. Technological advances and innovations must facilitate, serve, and support the aspirations and needs of humanity. Humankind must never be the servants of technology, but rather always remain its controllers.

Towards Planetary Learning and Governance Systems

Planetary consciousness is not rooted in transcendent values solely. It also emerges and evolves through education and learning and integrated governance systems. One potential instrument in fostering a universal consciousness is through a planetary citizenship charter that would define what it means to be responsible world citizens. This rudimentary learning tool would be educational, informal, and voluntary. It would complement, not supersede, the upholding of national laws and obligations of citizenship. Such a charter would articulate common planetary values that would guide a code of behaviour and conduct that promotes the healthy development of humanity. This might also take the form of a pledge to avoid all forms of ethnic and religious discrimination; to proactively assist in humanitarian efforts to eradicate hunger, illiteracy, poverty, and want; and to consciously and resolutely avoid all forms of corruption, crime, and violence. It would affirm a commitment to healthy living practices and to the protection of biodiversity, ecosystems, and environmental integrity. An international citizenry board would attest to an individual's adherence to basic human values and recognize those who exceed expectations and are model planetary citizens and leaders.

The world community needs greater collaboration and cooperation to tackle planetary systemic challenges. Towards that end, United Nations Systems (UNS) will likely evolve into more cogent and integrated world governance networks by the end of the century. Innovative future networks will crystalize and evolve with specific planetary mandates within innovative world governance systems (Caro, 2021). New holistic governance systems are likely to coopt and engage peoples in ways that challenge the current ontological leadership structures. These network systems will be facilitated, leveraged, and supported through super-intelligent systems far more advanced and potent than conventional ones. For example, the UN General Assembly and the Security Council will likely be superseded through a directly elected World Congress that better represents the planet's peoples and diverse ethnicities. Also, the World Health Organization will likely consolidate and form supra-national governance systems with other international organizations, such as Doctors Without Borders and the International Medical Corps. Future UN systems will likely reflect a truly international systemic base with planetary headquarters and nodal centres more equitably distributed across the planet. Emerging African, East Asian, Islamic, and South Asian nations will play increasingly critical roles in the shape and direction of planetary governance operations with advanced technologically integrated platforms. Transformational leadership will be critical to the creation, enablement, and evolution of future world systems in response to common and pressing planetary challenges. These leaders will be instrumental in assuring that planetary governance systems are effective, efficient, and ethical and benefit humankind and the planet.

Towards Planetary Transformational Leadership

Over the next century, the world community will be inching towards singular and unified planetary governance systems. Nation-states are not fully equipped to deal with planetary systemic problems and national sovereignty will increasingly be ceded to planetary organizations (Rees, 2018). Our small planet with its global existential challenges and threats will compel it. The world's peoples will increasingly demand it. Planetary transformational leadership will articulate and implement it. Planetary governance will not be a panacea, nor will it be dystopian, nor utopian. It will, however, allow for consistent and integrated human and technological development, while fostering greater planetary harmony, justice, and peace. The evolution from nation-state power politics to unified planetary governance systems will be fraught with considerable risks and potential setbacks. The twenty-first century leaders of the constellation of world nations are inexorably setting the foundations of this unified world order, while resolving pressing internal humanitarian, socioeconomic, infrastructure, and governance challenges (Caro, 2021). Many nation-states may collapse and crumble under the weight of herculean problems. Increased human suffering will no doubt form part of the wave of their failures.

The literature on the epistemology of leadership reveals a range of theoretical paradigms, including adaptive leadership (Obolensky, 2014; Moerschell & Lao, 2012) authentic transformational leadership (Bass & Bass, 2009; Avolio & Gardner, 2005; Bommer et al., 2004; Price, 2003); and integral leadership (Larsson & Eid, 2012; Wilber, 2000). All underscore the importance of legitimacy of leadership through ethical behaviours, integrity, openness, and truthfulness. Leadership is a nexus of individual actions, collective behaviours, and system processes in dynamic and evolving sociocultural contexts. The Wu-Shi-Ren (WSR)-li paradigm is a relevant ontological paradigm if one views leadership in the context of complex and dynamic adaptive planetary systems that are constantly evolving (Ma & Osula, 2011; Caro, 2007; Zhu, 2001). Essentially, this model maintains that psychological-cognitive elements (shi-li) and sociopolitical processes (ren-li) that allocate systemic resources (wu-li) are in continuous interplay. The four main components include: relational capital (shi-li), such as authenticity, cognition, ethics, integrity, respect, and trustworthiness; transactional capital (wu-li), such as adaptability, expertise, knowledge, and systemic resources; transactional processes (ren-li), such as collaboration, continuous learning, coordination, knowledge diffusion, negotiation, open communication, resource exchanges, and systems integration; and transformational strategic processes (ren-li). From Zhu's (2002) perspective, "sensing and caring (shi-li)" influence the "knowing (wu-li)" that propel the "doing and transforming" (ren-li). In essence, transformational leaders are change agents that forge these WSR-li components into synergic effective systems that result in positive development and outcomes (Kantur & Iseri-Say, 2012). In so doing, these leaders proactively engage in change management, conflict resolution, environmental and scenario analysis, risk assessment, and strategic analysis (Caro, 2016).

The future leadership competencies required for planetary governance will call for transformational and transcendent skills. Building on relational capital of respect, trust, and understanding of diverse cultures, they will engage in high-level negotiations and strategic processes to direct and influence the evolution of planetary systems. Their perspective will transcend the bounds of nation-states and ecospheres and reflect and integrated planetary paradigm and vision. Planetary leadership will articulate peacebuilding values and inspire and motivate humankind to create a future world community. As change agents, these transformational leaders will be at the nexus of constructive actions, positive collective behaviours, and effective system processes in pursuit of harmony, justice, and peace. Planetary transcendent and transformational leadership competencies and skills will be radically different than those of conventional paradigms. The Weltanschauung of these future leaders will transcend national cultures and will reflect caring and humanitarian values that reflect universal principles of humankind in a planetary eco-sphere. They will enable and foster effective, innovative, and synergistic collaboration across world nations. Super-intelligent systems will be important enablers of future transformational leaders who will be technologically adept and at ease with adaptive systems thinking.

Transformational leadership in an emerging planetary society will require multivariate skill sets, including the ability to prevent and resolve conflicts, and negotiate in the face of complexity and uncertainty (Joiner & Josephs, 2006). It will also call for a profound understanding of diverse sociocultural and sociopolitical systems (Michael & Petito, 2009). Accountability, astuteness, credibility, discipline, emotional intelligence, high personal ethics, and integrity are essential relational capital for effective, harmonious, and stable planetary collaboration. Advanced cognitive and intuitive abilities, courage, decisiveness, and equanimity in the face of pressures and uncertainty are also critical. All these attributes foster, inspire, and motivate trust across diverse world cultures and organizations. The transcendent skills of planetary governance leaders will require foresight and vision, innovative thinking, international coalition building, and negotiation to foster excellence, harmony, and peace. Profound and cogent value commitments and dedication to the service of humankind will be crucial. Most importantly, they will articulate peacebuilding values that inspire and motivate billions of people the world over. These leaders will possess values that preserve and uphold health, well-being, and communal integrity with a holistic understanding of ecosystems, humankind, and technologies (Wilber, 2000). Deep caring values, compassion for humankind, empathy for the human condition, honesty, and humility will be at the heart of future transformational leadership and will inspire others to act ethically, positively, and responsibly.

Global demographic changes and growing sociopolitical chaos and turmoil will likely increase exposure to the range of existential threats in vulnerable environments internationally. Through proactive scenario analysis, leadership that inspires planetary preparedness and collaboration for humanity is crucial. Ultimately, it is the world peoples who will judge whether planetary transformational leaders meet expectations with ethical and moral integrity. They will hold future leaders accountable particularly in time of ultimate tests of catastrophes, disasters, mass emergencies, and pandemics. Leaders must not be found wanting. Planetary threats do not end at the door of national governments. Rather they find closure when communities of the afflicted and dispossessed have been liberated from the economic, humanitarian, and social sufferings and have recovered from the ordeals experienced. What with limited political will, planetary resource constraints, and wavering popular support, future sustainable planetary governance systems will require profound caring values and cogent transcendent and transformational leadership. Cogent and deep commitment and dedication to the service of humankind will be of paramount importance. Indeed, such future leaders of planetary governance systems, will be crucial in the constructive, effective, and peaceful evolution of this "Pale Blue Dot" (Sagan, 1994), that we call our home.

Chapter Lessons

1. The post-Covid-19 world will require transformational leadership to address critical, pressing, and urgent humanitarian, socioeconomic, infrastructure and governance challenges.
2. In the post-Covid-19 era, humankind still faces five existential threats that will compel cogent and integrated leadership responses and the evolution of cogent planetary governance systems.
3. The reaffirmation of key ethical value constructs common to all humankind will be crucial for the emergence of peaceful and stable world community.
4. The post-Covid 19 world will see the emergence and evolution of integrated planetary governance systems.
5. New forms of cogent transformational and transcendental leadership will inevitably be the lodestar in overcoming enormous planetary challenges.

Reflective Questions

1. What are the five existential threats that humankind will continue to face beyond the Covid-19 pandemic? Which are the most pressing and intractable?
2. Why are new planetary governance systems inevitable in the post-Covid-19 era?
3. What are ten key ethical value constructs that will become central to a peaceful world community? Which are the most important?
4. Why is transformational leadership crucial in the emerging planetary governance systems?
5. What are the critical leadership attributes of transformational and transcendent leaders of the future?

References

Ackermann, A. (2003). The idea and practice of conflict prevention. *Journal of Peace Research, 40*(3), 339–347.

Andreoni, V., & Miola, A. (2015). Climate change and supply-chain vulnerability: Methodologies for resilience and impacts quantification. *International Journal of Emergency Systems, 4*(1), 6–26.

Asimov, S. (1995). Letter of February 1, 1966. In *Yours, Isaac Asimov: A lifetime of letters* (p. 256). Doubleday Books.

Avolio, B. J., & Gardner, W. L. (2005). Authentic leadership development: Getting to the root of positive forms of leadership. *Leadership Quarterly, 16*, 315–338.

Bass, B. M., & Bass, R. (2009). *The Bass handbook of leadership: Theory, research, and managerial applications*. The Free Press.

Baum, S. D. (2015). Confronting the threat of nuclear winter. *Futures, 72*, 69–79.

Bergmann, G. (2019). *Co-human harmony: Using our shared humanity to bridge divides*. Barnes and Noble Press.

Boden, M. (2016). *AI: Its nature and future*. Oxford University Press.

Bommer, W. H., Rubin, R. S., & Baldwin, T. T. (2004). Setting the stage for effective leadership: Antecedents of transformational leadership behavior. *Leadership Quarterly, 15*, 195–210.

Bostrom, N. (2014). *Superintelligence: Paths, dangers, and strategies*. Oxford University Press.

Bowes, J. L., & Christensen, C. M. (1995). Disruptive technologies: Catching the wave. *Harvard Business Review, 73*(1), 43–53.

Bretherton, D., & Law, S. F. (Eds.). (2015). *Methodologies in peace psychology* (Peace psychology). Springer International.

Burdett, M. S. (2011). *Transhumanism and transcendence*. Georgetown University Press.

Caro, D. H. J. (Ed.). (1993). *Leadership and caring visions in an environment of constraints*. Canadian College of Health Service Executives.

Caro, D. H. J. (2007). Evolving e-health system symbiosis: Theoretical constructs in international realpolitik space. *International Journal of E-Business Research, 3*(4), 67–78.

Caro, D. H. J. (2016). Towards transformational leadership: The nexus of emergency management systems in Canada. *The International Journal of Emergency Management, 12*(2), 113–135.

Caro, D. H. J. (2021). *Transforming nations after the Covid-19 pandemic: Humanitarian and planetary perspectives*. Springer Nature.

Caro, D. H. J., & Sethi, A. S. (1985). The strategic management of technostress: The chaining of Prometheus. *Journal of Medical Systems, 9*(5–6), 291–304.

Chaulia, S. (2013). *Politics of the global economic crisis: Regulation, responsibility, and radicalism*. Routledge India.

Cohen, V. C., & Chehimi, S. (Eds.). (2010). *Prevention is primary: Strategies for community well-being*. Jossey-Bass Press.

Cole-Turner, R. (Ed.). (2011). *Transhumanism and transcendence: Christian hope in an age of technological enhancement*. Georgetown University Press.

Coyne, C. J., & Rachel, M. (Eds.). (2011). *The handbook on the political economy of war*. Edward Elgar.

Dartnell, L. (2015). *The knowledge: How to rebuild our world from scratch*. Penguin.

Davies, J. (2016). *The birth of the Anthropocene*. University of California Press.

De Jong, J. T. (2010). A public health framework to translate risk factors related to political violence and war into multi-level preventive interventions. *Social Science and Medicine, 70*(1), 71–79.

Diamond, J. (1997). *Guns, germs, and steel: The fates of human societies*. W.W. Norton & Company.

Diamond, J. (2005). *Collapse: How societies choose to fail or succeed*. Penguin.

Dietrich, W. (2018). *Elective conflict mapping*. Palgrave Macmillan.

Dixon, P. (2015). *The future of almost everything: How our world will change over the next 100 years*. Profile Books.

Ehlers, E., & Krafft, T. (Eds.). (2006). *Earth system science in the Anthropocene: Emerging issues and problems*. Springer.
Falk, R. A. (2015). *Humanitarian intervention and legitimacy wars: Seeking peace and justice in the twenty-first century*. Routledge & CRC Press.
Ford, M. (2018). *Architects of intelligence: The truth about AI from the people building it*. Packt Publishing.
Forest, J., & Howard, R. (Eds.). (2012). *Weapons of mass destruction and terrorism*. McGraw-Hill Education.
Fukuyama, F. (2018). *Identity: The demand for dignity and the politics of resentment*. Straus, and Giroux.
Fuller, R. B., & Kuromiya, K. (1992). *Cosmography: A posthumous scenario for the future of humanity*. MacMillan.
Galtung, J. (1969). Violence, peace, and peace research. *Journal of Peace Research, 6*, 167–191.
Grof, S. (2012). *Healing our deepest wounds: The holotropic paradigm shift*. Stream of Experiences Productions.
Grossman, V. S., & Chandler, R. (2006). *Life and fate* (Vintage classic Russians series). New York Review Books Classics.
Haidt, J. (2012). *The righteous mind: Why good people are divided by politics and religion*. Vintage Books.
Hamilton, C. (2017). *Defiant earth: The fate of humans in the Anthropocene*. Polity Press.
Harari, Y. N. (2017). *Homo deus: A brief history of tomorrow*. Signal Books.
Hinde, R. A. (2008). *Ending war: A recipe*. Russell House.
Hughes, J. (2004). *Citizen cyborg: Why democratic societies must respond to the redesigned human of the future*. Westview Press.
Inglehart, R. F. (2018). *Cultural evolution: People's motivations are changing and reshaping the world*. Cambridge University Press.
Joiner, W. B., & Josephs, S. A. (2006). *Leadership agility: Five levels of mastery for anticipating and initiating change*. Jossey-Bass Press.
Kaku, M. (2011). *Physics of the future*. Doubleday.
Kandel, E. R. (2018). *The disordered mind: What unusual brains tell us about ourselves*. Farrar, Straus, and Giroux.
Kantur, D., & Iseri-Say, A. (2012). Organizational resilience: A conceptual integrative framework. *Journal of Management and Organization, 18*(6), 762–773.
Kaplan, A. (1968). Social ethics and sanctity of life: A summary. In D. H. Labby et al. (Eds.), *Life or death: Ethics and options* (p. 154). University of Washington Press.
Koestler, A. (1967). *The ghost in the machine*. Hutchinson.
Kurzweil, R. (2005). *The singularity is near: When humans transcend biology*. Viking Press.
Larsson, G., & Eid, J. (2012). An idea paper on leadership theory integration. *Management Research Review, 35*(3), 177–191.
Lederach, J. P. (2005). *The moral imagination: The art and soul of building peace*. Oxford University Press.
Legge, M. (2019). *Are we done fighting: Building understanding in a world of hate and division*. New Society Publishers.
Levy, B. S., & Sidel, V. W. (Eds.). (2008). *War and public health*. Oxford University Press.
Lohr, S. (2015). *Data-ism: The revolution transforming decision making, consumer behavior, and almost everything else*. Harper Business.
Ma, A. M. J., & Osula, B. (2011). The tao of complex adaptive systems (CAS). *Chinese Management Studies, 5*(1), 94–110.
Manson, W. C. (2014). Homo technomorphis: The relevance of Lewis Mumford. *Counter Punch, 21*(3), 21.
Mercer, C., & Trothen, T. (Eds.). (2014). *Religion and transhumanism: The unknown future of human enhancement*. Praeger.
Michael, M. S., & Petito, F. (Eds.). (2009). *Civilizational dialogue and world order*. Palgrave Macmillan.

Mills, C. W. (1959). *The sociological imagination*. Oxford University Press.
Moerschell, L., & Lao, T. M. (2012). Igniting the leadership spark: An exploration of decision making and punctuated change. *Emergence: Complexity Organizations, 14*(2), 54–68.
More, M., & Vita-More, N. (Eds.). (2013). *The transhumanist reader: Classical and contemporary essays on the science, technology, and philosophy of the human future*. John Wiley & Sons.
Morton, O. (2016). *The planet remade: How geoengineering could change the world*. Princeton University Press.
Mulgan, G. (2018). *Big mind: How collective intelligence can change our good and bad power*. Princeton University Press.
Mumford, L. (1971). *The myth of the machine: Technics and human development*. Mariner Books.
Nordhaus, W. (2013). *The climate casino: Risk, uncertainty, and economics for a warming world*. Yale University Press.
Nye, J. S., Jr. (2009). *Soft power: The means to success in world politics*. Public Affairs.
Obolensky, N. (2014). *Complex adaptive leadership: Embracing paradox and uncertainty*. Gower Publishing.
Pearson, L. B. (1957). The four faces of peace. *Nobel Prize speech*. https://www.nobelprize.org/prizes/peace/1957/pearson/lecture
Philpott, D., & Powers, G. (Eds.). (2010). *Strategies of peace: Transforming conflict in a violent world*. Oxford University Press.
Piketty, T. (2014). *Capital in the twenty-first century*. Harvard University Press.
Pope J. P. II. (2000). *Peace on earth to those who love peace*. Speech January 1, Vatican City. http://www.vatican.va/content/john-paul-ii/en/messages/peace/documents/hf_jp-ii_mes_08121999_xxxiii-world-day-for-peace.html
Price, T. L. (2003). The ethics of authentic transformational leadership. *The Leadership Quarterly, 14*(1), 67–81.
Ramírez, J. M. (2007). Peace through dialogue. *International Journal of World Peace, 24*(1), 65–81.
Ranisch, R., & Sorgner, S. L. (Eds.). (2014). *Post- and transhumanism*. Peter Lang.
Rees, M. (2018). *On the future: Prospects for humanity*. Princeton University Press.
Robinson, J. B. (1990). Futures underglass. A recipe for people who hate to predict. *Futures, 22*, 820–842.
Sachs, J. D. (2005). *The end of poverty: Economic possibilities for our time*. Penguin Press.
Sagan, C. (1994). *The pale blue dot: A vision of a human future in space*. Random House.
Schmelzle, B. (2005). *New trends in peace and conflict impact assessment*. Berghof Foundation.
Schweitzer, A. (1933). *Reverence for life: Sermons 1900-1919*. Irvington Publishers.
Shanahan, M. (2015). *The technological singularity*. MIT Press.
Siegel, D. (2016). *Mind: A journey to the heart of being human*. W.W. Norton & Company.
Solar, O., & Irwin, A. (2010). *A conceptual framework for action on the social determinants of health*. World Health Organization.
Soros, G. (1998). *The crisis of global capitalism: Open society endangered*. Public Affairs.
Stewart, F. (2002). Root causes of violent conflict in developing countries. *British Medical Journal, 324*(7333), 342–345.
SyamRoy, B. (2017). *India's journey towards sustainable populations* (p. 379). Springer International.
Tegmark, M. (2017). *Life 3.0: Being human in the age of artificial intelligence*. Penguin Random House.
Themnér, L., & Wallensteen, P. (2012). Armed conflicts 1946–2011. *Journal of Peace Research, 49*(4), 565–575.
Therivel, R. (2010). *Strategic environmental assessment in action*. Earthscan.
Thomas, J. C., Sage, M., Dillenberg, J., & Guillory, J. V. (2002). A code of ethics for public health. *American Journal of Public Health, 92*(7), 1057–1059.
Torres, P. (2018). *Morality, foresight, and human flourishing: An introduction to existential threats*. Pitchstone Publishing.
Turchin, P. (2007). *War and peace and war: The rise and fall of empires*. Plume Penguin Books.

Victor, D. (2011). *Global warming gridlock: Creating more effective strategies for protecting the planet*. Cambridge University Press.
Viola, E., & Franchini, M. (2018). *Brazil and climate change*. Taylor and Francis.
Wagner, G., & Woltzman, M. (2015). *Climate shock and the economic consequences of a hotter planet*. Princeton University Press.
Waslekar, S., & Futehally, I. (Eds.). (2011). *The big questions of our time*. Strategic Foresight Group.
Wilber, K. (2000). *Integral psychology: Consciousness, spirit, psychology, therapy*. Shambhala Publishers.
Wilson, E. O. (2006). *The creation: An appeal to save life on earth*. W.W. Norton & Company.
Zhu, Z. (2001). Towards an integrating programme for information systems design: An oriental case. *Journal of Information Management, 21*(1), 69–90.
Zhu, Z. (2002). Evaluating contingency approaches to information systems design. *Journal of Information Management, 22*(5), 343–356.

Denis H. J. Caro is a professor emeritus with the Telfer School of Management at the University of Ottawa in Ottawa, Canada. His alma mater is McGill University, and he holds degrees in mathematics, management information systems, and a Doctorate in Hospital and Health Care Administration from the School of Public Health of the University of Minnesota. He has extensive professional and teaching experience across Canada and the United States in emergency management, health care management, and e-health systems. Author of extensive scholarly publications, he is also the recipient of numerous awards in research, teaching, and leadership. He has a passionate love for teaching and students, whom he regards as the "Hope of the 21st Century". Dr. Caro leads a very simple life and admits to being a man of prayer and faith.

Transformational Leadership and Job Crafting

13

Xu Xu and Yuanlu Niu

Faster business cycles produced by COVID-19 accelerate the deviation away from classic authoritarian leadership to more bottom-up designs. How do we build organizational change readiness to take advantage of this transition? We recommend that the mix of transformational leadership, job crafting, and psychological safety can generate a shared vision among stakeholders, which empowers them to craft and update their journey together during this volatile time.

The COVID-19 pandemic changes the way we lead and work, maybe forever. During the process, we might feel like it left us with no choice. We always have a choice, though. We can choose how to treat the crisis and choose to utilize this opportunity to reflect on ways we have been functioning. Instead of waiting to go back to the norm pre-pandemic, we can instead use the time to reflect on the past practice and imagine a brand-new normalcy.

Normalcy brings out a sense of calm and order as we envision work and life after the pandemic. The craving for going back to our routine might reflect how we perceive change. We can be very resistant to change, even for our own good. But truth is, if we don't initiate change, we will have to be changed. Change does not have to be painful, and it does not always involve more work. In fact, the crisis is the perfect time to embrace change, learning to craft through change, realizing that we have more things in control than we thought.

What's the new norm going to be like post-COVID? Will norm even exist? What if one crisis comes after another and crisis is the new norm? We cannot predict the

X. Xu (✉)
School of Business, Henderson State University, Arkadelphia, AR, USA
e-mail: xux@hsu.edu

Y. Niu
Department of Rehabilitation, Human Resources and Communication Disorders, College of Education and Health Professions, University of Arkansas, Fayetteville, AR, USA
e-mail: yn005@uark.edu

S. K. Dhiman, J. F. Marques (eds.), *Leadership After COVID-19*, Future of Business and Finance, https://doi.org/10.1007/978-3-030-84867-5_13

type or the timing of the changes and this cause difficulty in applying management models since theory has boundary conditions. It's hard to predict what models will work in the future given we don't know what the future will be like. For leadership, imagining sailing through the ocean with limited visibility, turbulent water underneath. Employees facing new challenges during the pandemic also seek more self-initiated adjustments to their jobs. Transformational leaders combined with formalization of the job crafting at the organizational level could be the answer to increase organizational change readiness.

Objectives and purposes also update more frequently during crisis. We can use job crafting as a communication tool to help everyone envision the future together. During crisis, we are also more likely to seek meaning in life and work. What are we doing? Why are we doing this? Job crafting throughout the organization can serve as a communication tool to create shared visions among leaders and employees, connecting individual tasks—big or small—to the organization's overarching purpose.

Given the increasing uncertainty brought by the crisis, the visions and challenges are continually evolving and require crafting throughout the organization. Some changes may work, some may not. Perceived and actual job security is low during the crisis. It's crucial to adjust course as needed whenever needed. Employees spotting the trouble will need to speak up without fearing to be fired. Shaping a climate of psychological safety is crucial for the organization to craft and update their journey together during this volatile time.

This chapter examines the implications of job crafting for organizational change readiness in the post COVID-19 era. It concludes that with transformational leadership, organizational-level formalization of the job crafting at a psychological safe workplace would help an organization be change ready. We further offer practical suggestions on integrating job crafting with existing goal setting system to help employees sustain the proactive behaviors.

Changes and Challenges Brought by Crisis

Organizations that are affected heavily by the COVID-19 might need to bring unfavorable organizational changes. Organizational changes during crisis add to the anxiety and fear in employees throughout the organization. People may feel that they are losing control of their life and work. Organizational changes are a shock to the working environment and employees, but they also require individual adjustments. From an evolutionary perspective, there are dynamics between employee behaviors and the organization. How do we help employees to survive and thrive amidst change? Change is inevitable, even though it is often undesirable. During crisis, eliminating the stressors may even seem impossible. What we can change, however, is how we perceive and react to the change. Stress if only harmful if you think it is (Crum et al., 2013).

How do we not let such changes affect employees' morale? Research shows that employees are more positive and proactive about change respond better to it, but then there is the question of how to add positivity to a change that no one wanted at the beginning. Organizational culture, routines, and leaders have the power to affect employees' mindset toward change. Changes are inevitable and are only magnified by COVID-19. When designing post-COVID organizational practices, we are not looking for ways to get back to pre-COVID status. We are proactively changing our perception and protocols toward change. Instead of working on how to deal with changes, we focus on how to grow through changing.

Job crafting is associated with various crucial outcomes, both at individual and organizational levels. For detailed discussions on job crafting, there is a considerable amount of literature reviews and meta-analyses focusing on job crafting (see Lee & Lee, 2018; Lichtenthaler & Fischbach, 2018; Rudolph et al., 2017; and Zhang & Parker, 2019 for example). Their scope, however, does not limit to job crafting during crisis. One paper worth noting is Hulshof et al. (2020), which examined the effects of a job crafting intervention among employees of a Dutch unemployment agency. Overall, their results show that job crafting intervention proved effective in maintaining an employee's well-being during a time of change.

A typical type of job crafting is altering one's tasks boundaries by adjusting the quantity and scope accomplished at work (Wrzesniewski & Dutton, 2001). These self-initiated changes can bring a sense of control back to their daily work. Would job crafting help employees cope with changes better? Will they be more open to changes? In certain areas, this might sound like a chicken and egg problem since maybe people that are more open to changes will also invest in job crafting activities more. Previous research found that proactive personality as a significant predictor of job crafting (Bakker et al., 2012; Plomp et al., 2016), however, few studies explored the relationship between mindset toward change and job crafting. An exception is Demerouti et al. (2017), in which they found that job crafting training and practice help employees be more open to change.

In one shape or another, everyone has been crafting their jobs. The outcomes of job crafting behaviors may not always be desirable from an organizational point of view, and much is to be explored. If something is already happening anyway, change and adaption, why shouldn't we try to understand it and offer some guidance? This chapter summarizes the benefits of job crafting in post-COVID organizational design. It also suggests what is crucial to harnessing the benefits of job crafting, and how it relates to the organization. We also suggest that factors such as transformational leadership and psychological safety are crucial to reap the benefits of job crafting.

Job Crafting to the Rescue

What Is Job Crafting

Job crafting is a type of employee proactive behavior. Proactivity in the workplace has been referred to as "self-starting, change-focused, and future-oriented behaviors"(see Crant et al., 2016; Frese & Fay, 2001; Unsworth & Parker, 2003; Grant & Ashford, 2008). The productivity-enhancing benefits of proactive behaviors have been found both at the individual level and at company level. Seibert et al. (2001) found that proactive employees were more likely to search for innovative solutions.

Wrzesniewski and Dutton (2001) defines job crafting as "the physical and cognitive changes individuals make in the task or relational boundaries of their work." According to Wrzesniewski and Dutton (2001), job crafting helps employees gain meaning in work via three types of crafting: task crafting, relational crafting, and cognitive crafting. Later, Tims and Bakker (2010) and Tims et al. (2012) used job demands-resources (JD-R) theory to further conceptualize job crafting by focusing changes in job characteristics. According to the JD-R framework, all job characteristics can fit into two categories: job demands or job resources. Aspects of the job that take efforts (physical or mental) from the employees are part of the job demands. Job characters that assist employees to meet the demands and grow professionally are job resources. Many empirical studies followed Tims et al. (2012) and operationalized job crafting with four scales: increasing structural job resources (e.g., seeking training opportunities), increasing social job resources (e.g., requesting for feedback from team members), increasing challenging job demands (e.g., starting new projects), and decreasing hindering job demands (e.g., fewer stressful relationships at work). Zhang and Parker (2019) synthesized these two perspectives of job crafting and proposed a hierarchical structure of job crafting integrating the two. They focused on three levels of job crafting: orientation (approach vs. Avoidance), form (cognitive vs. Behavioral), and content (resources vs. Demands). Orientation is the highest order construct, while content is the lowest level one. This hierarchical structure identified eight types of job crafting and brought relevant concepts together nicely. We adopt the integrative framework introduced by Zhang and Parker (2019) in this chapter. One thing worth pointing out is that Zhang and Parker (2019) and most of the research on this topic focus on individual-level job crafting, our discussion extends to team-level and organizational-level crafting.

Outcomes of Job Crafting

Job crafting can influence various important outcomes both at individual and organizational levels. Research has found that job crafting can increase many positive outcomes such as work engagement (Lichtenthaler & Fischbach, 2018), work motivation (Bakker & Demerouti, 2007), job satisfaction (Cheng & Yi, 2018), performance (Lee & Lee, 2018), psychological and subjective well-being (Van Wingerden et al., 2017), career development, and commitment (Kim & Beehr, 2018). Rudolph et al. (2017) conducted a meta-analysis on the relationships of job crafting with different work outcomes. They found that based on the meta-analysis, work engagement is positively linked to overall job crafting. Following the orientation of job crafting: approach (promotion-focused) and avoidance (prevention-focused), existing research indicates that the former type is positively related to various desirable work outcomes as well as benefiting employees' well-being. Additionally, job crafting plays a mediator role for many relationships, transforming practices into positive outcomes. Approach job crafting mediates the positive association between job autonomy and job satisfaction (Zito et al., 2019). Wang et al. (2020) found the relationship between social factors (such as leadership) and beneficial work outcomes is mediated by approach job crafting.

Bakker and Oerlemans (2019) attempted to better understand the underlying mechanism of the relationship between job crafting and work engagement. Following self-determination theory (Deci & Ryan, 2000) they found that the job crafting enhances daily work engagement by satisfying basic psychological needs. More importantly, Bakker and Oerlemans (2019) used self-regulation theories (Bolino et al., 2010) to help explain the negative impacts of job crafting on work engagement in the short run. Future studies are needed to investigate the degree to which organizational support can help reduce the short-run energy depletion caused by job crafting.

Not all the above-mentioned research is directly related to job crafting and organizational change, especially for organizational changes because of crisis. COVID-19 pandemic brings organizational change that can adversely affect the health and well-being of workers, as it induces anxiety and uncertainty. Their work engagement can be negatively affected by having to comply with additional job demands of the crisis introduced with limited resources (Hulshof et al., 2020). Job crafting at both cognitive and behavioral levels can help employees through change. For example, Demerouti et al. (2017) examined the role of job crafting during economic recession to see if it can assist individuals and organizations face austerity-led changes. Interestingly, they did not find a robust impact of job crafting behaviors on work outcomes. Instead, the benefits brought by job crafting training and practice are brought by mindset shift; employees became more open to change after practicing job crafting. If job crafting training could help individuals update their mindset, then the benefits might spill over to other areas not limited to work outcomes. Job crafting can also affect organizational change readiness indirectly through seeking social support since one subdimension of organizational change readiness is "support from the immediate manager" (Cinite et al., 2009).

Most of the research focused on individual-level job crafting and the outcome on the same level. Despite the importance of organizational outcomes, there remains a paucity of evidence on the impact of individual job crafting on a broader, multilevel set of outcomes. Job crafting does not happen in isolation. What are other related effects of individual-level job crafting? For example, if the leader practice job crafting openly, do we expect to see any trickledown effect on the followers? How does the job crafting behavior of a leader affect followers' job outcomes? Can job crafting intervention spread? What are the impacts of employee's job crafting on coworkers and team-level performance? We will review recent research and provide an overview of the levels of job crafting.

Predictors of Job Crafting

Previous literature has investigated many predictors of job crafting including individual difference such as personality, job characteristics, and demographic variables. Wang et al. (2020) integrated socialization literature and argued that two types of social factors will influence employee job crafting: (a) organizational insiders, including leaders, colleagues, and (b) organizational outsiders, such as families and friends. Leadership is a crucial factor that affects employee job crafting.

Leaders could either lead to employee approach or avoidance job crafting. On one hand, leaders can provide valuable job resources which might lead to both behavioral and cognitive crafting that are approach-focused. Some empirical studies found that certain types of leadership such as transformational leadership (Wang et al., 2017; Hetland et al., 2018) and empowering leadership (Kim & Beehr, 2018; Tang et al., 2020) were positively rated to employee promotion-focused job crafting. Leaders also influence organizational culture that affects employees' crafting. On the other hand, avoidance job crafting is positively associated with directive leadership (Esteves & Pereira Lopes, 2017). Leaders that add hindering job demands intentionally or unintentionally would result in employees crafting ways to reduce the related draining.

In the next section, we will focus on a particular set of job crafting predictors that include leaders and team members. We then discuss the importance of formalizing job crafting at the organizational level on reducing uncertainty and increasing clarity of the process. We focus on transformational leadership in this chapter since it can increase job crafting behaviors among their followers (Hetland et al., 2018) and contribute to organizational change readiness (Nordin, 2012).

Leadership, Teams, and Job Crafting

Transformational Leadership and Job Crafting

How do we encourage job crafting? In this section, we explore methods to foster job crafting from the point of leadership, teams, and organizational context. As we mentioned in the previous section, leadership plays an important role in motivating and supporting employee job crafting behaviors. We now explicitly explain the relationship between transformational leadership and job crafting.

Transformational Leadership theory was first labeled by Burns (1978) and further developed by Avolio (1991) and others. Based on the *multifactor leadership questionnaire* developed by (Bass & Avolio, 2000), two key subdimensions of transformational leadership are individual consideration and intellectual stimulation. Offering individual consideration means respecting followers' feelings and preferences, which coincides with the core idea of job crafting. Examples of intellectual stimulation including encouraging followers to update their perception of the tasks and modify methods approaching the work (Podsakoff et al., 1990; Wang et al., 2017), aligning with the cognitive and behavioral part of job crafting respectively.

Comparing to transactional leaders, transformational leaders challenge their followers to take bigger ownership and more autonomy of their job by providing the support needed. According to Avolio and Gibbons (1988), developing followers' self-management and self-development was key objectives of transformational leaders. Having more autonomy and support employees become more motivated to craft their job on both behavioral and cognitive levels. Related literature found that transformational leadership benefits team-level creativity (Kim et al., 2019). Job crafting is a creative process as well; involving employees to "think outside of the box" about their job descriptions. Previous research also shows how employees perceive changes affect their outcome during organizational change (Demerouti et al., 2017). Transformational leaders can motivate followers to view changes as opportunities instead of threat (Burns, 1978). Therefore, transformational leadership can facilitate job crafting by offering motivation both at the cognitive and behavioral levels.

Job Crafting at Individual Vs. Team-Level

Rarely one works alone. One individual behavior impacts others in the team and vice versa. For example, Wang et al. (2020) categorized colleagues as another crucial part of organizational social factors that affect employees' job crafting. Social factors of job crafting also play moderating roles in various job crafting–work outcomes relationship. For example, Shin et al. (2020) suggests that the types of support for coworkers affect the job crafting–work engagement relationship heterogeneously. While emotional support plays a facilitator role, instrumental support might be hindering. Good intention itself is not good enough. How do we design team routines and rituals that can amplify the benefits of job crafting? This topic requires further examination.

Majority of the scholar's attention has focused on job crafting at the individual level. The above-mentioned studies discuss the influences of social factors while treating job crafting as an individual-level construct. The interaction of job crafting and team membership has been studied less extensively. There is no doubt that individual job crafting behaviors would affect other team members given the interdependency exist within a team (Wrzesniewski & Dutton, 2001). Through conducting performance assessments in childcare centers, Leana et al. (2009) found that individual and team-level job crafting are distinct constructs. Collaborative crafting has a positive impact on the quality of care (a collective outcome) while individual crafting does not. Organizational performance is an important outcome but was beyond the scope of Wrzesniewski and Dutton (2001). Tims et al. (2013) proposed that team job crafting is a team-level construct that has theoretical similarity with individual-level job crafting and investigated the influence of team job crafting on individual performance. According to Tims et al. (2013), team crafting means that *"deciding what and how to craft is a team process,"* instead of everyone crafting their jobs the same way. In the future, it will be important to impact of job crafting on team- and organizational-level outcomes.

Job Crafting at Organizational Level

As we have discussed previously, individual job crafting is effortful or even taxing in the short run (Bakker and Oerlemans 2019), and it may not have meaningful impacts on collective outcomes (Leana et al., 2009). In addition to transformational leadership, organizational context could contribute to job crafting. Bakker and

Oerlemans (2019) suggested that a mix of top-down and bottom-up job crafting would produce favorable results for employees and organizations at large. Segarra-Ciprés et al. (2019) also suggested that future studies need to further explore the contextual conditions that facilitate organizations to capture the benefits of employee proactive behavior. According to the interactionist viewpoint (Woodman et al., 1993; Segarra-Ciprés et al., 2019), which suggests that the interaction between the personal factors of employees and the organizational context is central to the understanding of the impact on the organization of employee activities. Therefore, in this chapter, we go one step further by suggesting the formalization of job crafting at the organizational level.

Based on the previous research, we propose that formalization of job crafting at the organizational level is crucial for taking full advantage of its benefits. This might seem counterintuitive since job crafting is defined as the opposite of a top-down job design while formalization brings out impressions such as bureaucratic and rigid. The organizational level at which formalization is applied (Hempel et al., 2012) and what has been formalization will probably to affect the influence it has on job crafting. Existing research has presented both a positive and negative view of formalization. As we have mentioned previously, job crafting involves creativity and innovation. Past innovation literature did not reach a consensus on the impact of formalization on innovation. Segarra-Ciprés et al. (2019) reviewed the related literature and studied the moderating role of innovation process formalization on the relationship between employee proactive behavior and innovation. They found that high level of formalization facilitates both product and process innovation. A major type of formalization that received many criticisms is job formalization—specifications of duties or roles within the team. Job formalization can be the opposite of job crafting, leaving employees little flexibility in the job. Job descriptions formalized in the individual level inhibit reallocation of duties within the team, not to say the organization. It requires certain degrees of freedom to construct an empowered team that is fluid. That does not mean all forms of formalization is harmful and should be disregarded. Adler and Borys (1996) conceptualized two types of bureaucracy: enabling and coercive. They concluded that formalization in the workflow could go either way and enabling formalization can help employees increase their effectiveness. Enabling formalization could provide directions, especially during times of change or crisis.

Organizational formalization of the job crafting process reduces uncertainty within the organization. Formalization also benefits the organization through conveying values and clarifying goals. According to Organ and Greene (1981), "formalization provides a framework for the professional to view his contributions to the organization and the organization's contributions to his professional goals." Organizational formalization could also increase perceived organizational support, which was found to a moderator for the relationships among job crafting, burnout, and satisfaction by Cheng and Yi (2018).

Autonomy through boundaries is a key organizational practice in the empowerment literature (Seibert et al., 2004), which is defined as "organizational structures and practices that encourage autonomous actions, including the development of a clear vision, and clarity regarding goals, work procedures, and areas of responsibility." Applying this concept to job crafting, we propose "crafting through boundaries" under structures of enabling formalization. This organization-wide formalization will help everyone share a common vision for the organization and build the climate together. For both leaders and employees, job crafting practice could involve space of ambiguity and therefore the efforts could be taxing in the short run. Enabling formalization could help reduce the amount of uncertainty and let employees know the boundaries of job crafting: what they can or cannot change. We further explain the practical implications of "crafting through boundaries" in section "Implications for Practice".

Psychological Safety

In the previous section, we focus on the social predictors of job crafting and distinguish job crafting at the individual, team, and organizational level. We further propose the enabling formalization could be beneficial for team job crafting. Besides formalization, psychological safety at the workplace is a crucial factor in motivating individuals to engage in job crafting activities, given the image risks associated with these proactive actions (Grant & Ashford, 2008). Expectancy theory illustrates that individuals weigh the projected benefits and costs of their behaviors before challenging the status quo (Vroom, 1964; Morrison & Phelps, 1999). Psychological safety refers to "employee perceptions regarding the consequences of interpersonal risk-taking" (Edmondson, 1999; Baer & Frese, 2003; Plomp et al., 2019) and is a phenomenon that can be studied across all levels (Edmondson & Lei, 2014).

Edmondson et al. (2004) discussed five team-level outcomes In the previous section, we focus on the social predictors of job crafting and distinguish job crafting at the individual, team, and organizational level. of team psychological safety, which include feedback seeking, help seeking, speaking up about concerns, innovative behavior, and boundary spanning. From a JD-R perspective, Plomp et al. (2019) expected perceived safety increases structural job resources available to employees. For example, one can seek help from leaders regarding professional skills development and then receive new training opportunities. But it's not just the actual level of resources that will be affected. Employees' perceived level of resources will be altered as well. With feedback seeking, expertise from leaders and coworkers In the previous section, we focus on the social predictors of job crafting and distinguish job crafting at the individual, team, and organizational level. Has always been there but were not seen until employees are open to and feel safe about reaching out for feedback. In this sense, formalization of job crafting at the organizational level combined with psychological safety also enable team leaders to provide resources since they have clear expectations to do so.

Plomp et al. (2019) suggested that psychological safety In the previous section, we focus on the social predictors of job crafting and distinguish job crafting at the individual, team, and organizational level. at workplace encourages employees to engage in job crafting since they would have fewer concerns about the reactions receiving from others. Research has also found that psychological safety plays a mediating role in the relationship between leadership styles and team creativity outcome (Kim et al., 2019; Wang et al., 2018; Yin et al., 2019). Kim et al. (2019) explored the importance of transformational leadership on team-level innovation in an organization. They also tested the mediating effect of psychological safety between transformational leadership and group creativity. Yin et al. (2019) examined the relationship between transformational leadership on knowledge sharing. They explored the impact of different leadership dimensions of transformational leadership on knowledge sharing and further explore the mediation effects of psychological safety. Based on these, we also reason that formalization of the job crafting process at a psychological safe workplace In the previous section, we focus on the social predictors of job crafting and distinguish job crafting at the individual, team, and organizational level. Would help lower employees' concerns since the process is supported by the external environment as well.

Shared Visions

Despite the illustrated benefits that come with job crafting, concerns remain, fearing that the practices would lead to a decrease in employee productivity and undesirable outcomes. Another concern is the misalignment between individual preferences and organizational objectives. Two behaviors of transformational leaders closely related to these concerns include: (a) "Fostering the acceptance of group goals" and (b) "Articulating a vision."

We can use job crafting as a communication tool to help true value alignment throughout the organization. Concerns associated with job crafting approach originate from the potential misalignment between individual objectives and organizational goals. We suggest that team-level job crafting could be the tool to help identify such misalignment, which is the first step of creating alignment according to Jim Collins.[1] Specifically, Jim Collins prescribed:

> Working collaboratively with people throughout the organization. Ask each individual to identify something in his or her daily work that is inconsistent with the organization's core values.

How do we find meaning that is consistent with the organization's value? Can we revise the task? What kind of social support will be beneficial? Should we shift our perception? All these are elements of job crafting and answering these questions should help create a shared vision. The process to define this common goal while empowering employees to crafting their own roles requires a collective and open environment in which individuals feel psychologically safe to voice their preferences and concerns.

Objectives of a group require frequent updates during change. Visions and missions are relatively more timeless. Objectives should be more time-variant so we

[1] https://www.jimcollins.com/article_topics/articles/aligning-action.html

can adapt and adjust as external environment changes, especially in this ever-changing context.

Implications for Practice

Job crafting interventions in the format of training sessions have been proved effective even during change or crisis. Running such interventions could be costly and increase perceived workload during stressful times. Our practical recommendation is to integrate job crafting exercises with an organization's existing performance measurement tools.

In particular, one of the most popular goal setting system, OKRs (Objectives Key Results), could work hand in hand with job crafting intervention. Team members can include their self-set job crafting goals as part of the objectives. According to Doerr (2018), OKRs are defined as "a management methodology that helps to ensure that the company focuses efforts on the same important issues throughout the organization." Objectives are defined as "what is to be achieved." Ideally, they would be both operational and inspirational. Goals of an organization are often less visible compared to its mission statement. OKRs helps the goals of everyone to be visible and therefore makes alignment possible. Doerr (2018) explains it as such:

> With OKR transparency, everyone's goals—from the CEO down—are openly shared. Individuals link their objectives to the company's game plan, identify cross-dependencies, and coordinate with other teams. By connecting each contributor to the organization's success, top-down alignment brings meaning to work. By deepening people's sense of ownership, bottom-up OKRs foster engagement and innovation.

Gray (2019) further specifies that "objectives are not written from the top-down or bottom-up in any organization." Every individual in the organization will set their own objectives. Individual objectives, team objectives, organization mission should be consistent but not necessarily identical. One example in Gray (2019) is from Intuit CIO Atticus Tysen and his team members set one or two personal objectives along with three to five business ones every quarter. We can integrate elements of job crafting into one or more objectives while staying focused on the priorities that matter for the organization. Since objectives are often shared across-team or even the whole organization, the visibility makes it easy for one to identify and seek social job resources or support.

Future Directions

The research reported in this chapter shows the potentials of job crafting intervention as well as its limitations. This chapter also explains how transformational leadership and psychological safety play important role for job crafting at the individual, team, and organizational level, and why it is important to formalize job crafting practice at the organizational level. Yet, a number of crucial questions remain unanswered. Mensmann and Frese (2019) found that entrepreneurs' post training personal initiative fade away over time. They argue that "proactive behaviors are not just a set of pre-defined skills that once learned can then be used habitually' instead." In terms of directions for future research, it would be interesting to test whether the effects of job crafting training decrease over time. If so, researchers need to explore maintenance routine that would help sustain the impact without adding workload for employees. During the previous section, we recommend integrating job crafting with goal setting system on the practical level. Therefore, the exercises become part of the organizational routines. According to Feldman and Pentland (2003) and Grant and Ashford (2008), employees also play an active role in shaping organizational routines. Further work is needed to fully understand the interactions between job crafting and work routines in order to find a balance between stability and flexibility.

There are various types of leadership styles and numerous ways of intervention to help us achieve organizational and individual level thriving. Besides investigating which intervention is more effective, future research should also investigate which combinations work better together to enable us to uncover the power of multiple interventions and finding ones that have leveraging effects. The sequence of innervations or trainings could also be important. For example, job crafting training seem to be a promising one to shift people's mindset about change. Once we realize that we can change certain aspects of the job duties, we might be more open to organizational change (Demerouti et al., 2017). If so, such intervention can act as a catalyst for subsequent trainings. For employees working with technology or artificial intelligence, future research should be undertaken to explore how job crafting might have an influence on employees' perception toward new technology.

In this chapter, we use "leaders" and "leadership" interchangeably, linking it to a sense of authority. This simplifies the discussions on "leaders and followers" dynamics, but also has its caveats. Stressed by By (2020) and By et al. (2016), leadership and leaders do not equal to each other. Specifically, leadership is NOT something that official leaders do. Future research should shift the focus toward leadership (what) instead of simply studying the leaders (who). Crevani et al. (2010) emphasized on leadership as a process and we believe the empowering nature of our proposed framework—integrating job crafting with OKRs—can help bring out leadership through team-level crafting.

This chapter was inspired by change and crisis. A natural question to ask is if the discussion would remain relevant post the COVID-19 pandemic. Consider an opposite scenario where organizations are at the peak of the business cycle. To ensure continues growth, it would be the ideal time to update systematically to be change ready, which was described by Charles Handy as "the second curve" (Handy, 2015). In conclusion, it is important to be change ready throughout the system in various stages of business cycles. This does not mean seeking changes for the sake of change. The crafting suggested in this chapter has to support organization visions which can be facilitated by formalization and psychological safety at the workplace.

Five Chapter Takeaways/Lessons

1. Job crafting helps maintain employee work engagement during crisis, but the process is also effortful.
2. Transformational leadership enhances employees' job crafting motivation and provides the support needed.

3. Formalization of job crafting at the organizational level can lower the uncertainty and increase transparency.
4. The impact of transformational leadership on job crafting is strongest when employees have a sense of psychological safety at the workplace.
5. Through job crafting, leaders and followers develop shared visions of the organization, which is crucial for work engagement and other outcomes during turbulent time.

Five Reflection Questions

1. Further work is needed to fully understand the interactions between job crafting and work routines in order to find a balance between stability and flexibility.
2. Researchers need to explore maintenance routine that would help sustain the impact without adding workload for employees.
3. Future research should be undertaken to explore how job crafting might have an influence on employees' perception toward changes.
4. Can we use team-level job crafting training to cultivate transformational leadership?
5. We should explore the possibility of integrating job crafting exercises with an organization's existing performance measurement tools to help goals alignment.

References

Adler, P. S., & Borys, B. (1996). Two types of bureaucracy: Enabling and coercive. *Administrative Science Quarterly, 41*, 61–89. https://doi.org/10.2307/2393986

Avolio, B. J. (1991). *The full range leadership development programs: Basic and advanced manuals*. Bass, Avolio & Associates.

Avolio, B. J., & Gibbons, T. C. (1988). *Developing transformational leaders: A life span approach*. Jossey-Bass.

Baer, M., & Frese, M. (2003). Innovation is not enough: Climates for initiative and psychological safety, process innovations, and firm performance. *Journal of Organizational Behavior: The International Journal of Industrial, Occupational and Organizational Psychology and Behavior, 24*(1), 45–68.

Bakker, A. B., & Demerouti, E. (2007). The job demands-resources model: State of the art. *Journal of Managerial Psychology, 22*(3), 309–328. https://doi.org/10.1108/02683940710733115

Bakker, A. B., & Oerlemans, W. G. M. (2019). Daily job crafting and momentary work engagement: A self-determination and self-regulation perspective. *Journal of Vocational Behavior, 112*, 417–430. https://www.sciencedirect.com/science/article/pii/S000187911830157X

Bakker, A. B., Tims, M., & Derks, D. (2012). Proactive personality and job performance: The role of job crafting and work engagement. *Human Relations, 65*(10), 1359–1378.

Bass, B. M., & Avolio, B. J. (2000). Multifactor leadership questionnaire (2nd ed.). Redwood City, CA: Mind Garden.

Bolino, M., Valcea, S., & Harvey, J. (2010). Employee, manage thyself: The potentially negative implications of expecting employees to behave proactively. *Journal of Occupational and Organizational Psychology, 83*(2), 325–345.

Burns, J. M. (1978). *Leadership*. Harper & Row. https://play.google.com/store/books/details?id=lhrPS_s7EawC&source=gbs_api

By, R. T. (2020). Organizational change and leadership: Out of the quagmire. *Journal of Change Management, 20*(1), 1–6. https://doi.org/10.1080/14697017.2020.1716459

By, R. T., Hughes, M., & Ford, J. (2016). Change leadership: Oxymoron and myths. *Journal of Change Management, 16*(1), 8–17. https://doi.org/10.1080/14697017.2016.1137425

Cheng, J.-C., & Yi, O. (2018). Hotel employee job crafting, burnout, and satisfaction: The moderating role of perceived organizational support. *International Journal of Hospitality Management, 72*, 78–85. https://doi.org/10.1016/j.ijhm.2018.01.005

Cinite, I., Duxbury, L. E., & Higgins, C. (2009). Measurement of perceived organizational readiness for change in the public sector. *British Journal of Management, 20*(2), 265–277. https://doi.org/10.1111/j.1467-8551.2008.00582.x

Crant, J. M., Hu, J., & Jiang, K. (2016). Proactive personality: A twenty-year review. In *Proactivity at work* (pp. 211–243). Routledge.

Crevani, L., Lindgren, M., & Packendorff, J. (2010). Leadership, not leaders: On the study of leadership as practices and interactions. *Scandinavian Journal of Management, 26*(1), 77–86. https://doi.org/10.1016/j.scaman.2009.12.003

Crum, A. J., Salovey, P., & Achor, S. (2013). Rethinking stress: The role of mindsets in determining the stress response. *Journal of Personality and Social Psychology, 104*(4), 716–733. https://doi.org/10.1037/a0031201

Deci, E. L., & Ryan, R. M. (2000). The "what" and "why" of goal pursuits: Human needs and the self-determination of behavior. *Psychological Inquiry, 11*(4), 227–268.

Demerouti, E., Xanthopoulou, D., Petrou, P., & Karagkounis, C. (2017). Does job crafting assist dealing with organizational changes due to austerity measures? Two studies among Greek employees. *European Journal of Work and Organizational Psychology, 26*(4), 574–589. https://doi.org/10.1080/1359432x.2017.1325875

Doerr, J. (2018). *Measure what matters*. Penguin. https://play.google.com/store/books/details?id=u2NDDwAAQBAJ&source=gbs_api

Edmondson, A. (1999). Psychological safety and learning behavior in work teams. *Administrative Science Quarterly, 44*(2), 350–383.

Edmondson, A. C., & Lei, Z. (2014). Psychological safety: The history, renaissance, and future of an interpersonal construct. *Annual Review of Organizational Psychology and Organizational Behavior, 1*, 23–43. https://doi.org/10.1146/annurev-orgpsych-031413-091305

Edmondson, A. C., Kramer, R. M., & Cook, K. S. (2004). Psychological safety, trust, and learning in organizations: A group-level lens. In *Trust and distrust in organizations: Dilemmas and approaches* (Vol. 12, pp. 239–272) https://books.google.com/books?hl=en&lr=&id=l-2FAwAAQBAJ&oi=fnd&pg=PA239&dq=Psychological+safety,+trust,+and+learning+in+organizations&ots=Jcqc8exjL0&sig=Gjx81_9p2S3Pg7QC9huAZcw-LfI

Esteves, T., & Pereira Lopes, M. (2017). Leading to crafting: The relation between leadership perception and nurses' job crafting. *Western Journal of Nursing Research, 39*(6), 763–783. https://doi.org/10.1177/0193945916659507

Feldman, M. S., & Pentland, B. T. (2003). Reconceptualizing organizational routines as a source of flexibility and change. *Administrative Science Quarterly, 48*(1), 94–118. https://doi.org/10.2307/3556620

Frese, M., & Fay, D. (2001). 4. Personal initiative: An active performance concept for work in the 21st century. *Research in Organizational Behavior, 23*, 133–187.

Grant, A. M., & Ashford, S. J. (2008). The dynamics of proactivity at work. *Research in Organizational Behavior, 28*, 3–34. https://www.sciencedirect.com/science/article/pii/S0191308508000038

Gray, D. (2019). Objectives + Key Results (OKR) Leadership. http://books.google.com/books?id=vKRYywEACAAJ&hl=&source=gbs_api

Handy, C. (2015). *The second curve*. Random House. https://play.google.com/store/books/details?id=yztOBQAAQBAJ&source=gbs_api

Hempel, P. S., Zhang, Z.-X., & Han, Y. (2012). Team empowerment and the organizational context: Decentralization and the contrasting effects of formalization. *Journal of Management, 38*(2), 475–501. https://doi.org/10.1177/0149206309342891

Hetland, J., Hetland, H., Bakker, A. B., & Demerouti, E. (2018). Daily transformational leadership and employee job crafting: The role of promotion focus. *European Management Journal, 36*(6), 746–756. https://doi.org/10.1002/job.2375

Hulshof, I. L., Demerouti, E., & Le Blanc, P. M. (2020). Providing services during times of change: Can employees maintain their levels of empowerment, work engagement and service quality through a job crafting intervention. *Frontiers in Psychology, 11*, 87. https://doi.org/10.3389/fpsyg.2020.00087

Kim, M., & Beehr, T. A. (2018). Can empowering leaders affect subordinates' well-being and careers because they encourage subordinates' job crafting behaviors. *Journal of Leadership and Organizational Studies, 25*(2), 184–196. https://doi.org/10.1177/1548051817727702

Kim, B.-J., Park, S., & Kim, T.-H. (2019). The effect of transformational leadership on team creativity: Sequential mediating effect of employee's psychological safety and creativity. *Asian Journal of Technology Innovation, 27*(1), 90–107. https://doi.org/10.1080/19761597.2019.1587304

Leana, C., Appelbaum, E., & Shevchuk, I. (2009). Work process and quality of care in early childhood education: The role of job crafting. *Academy of Management Journal, 52*(6), 1169–1192. https://doi.org/10.5465/AMJ.2009.47084651

Lee, J. Y., & Lee, Y. (2018). Job crafting and performance: Literature review and implications for human resource development. *Human Resource Development Review, 17*(3), 277–313. https://doi.org/10.1177/1534484318788269

Lichtenthaler, P. W., & Fischbach, A. (2018). Leadership, job crafting, and employee health and performance. *Leadership and Organization Development Journal, 39*, 620–632. https://doi.org/10.1108/LODJ-07-2017-0191/full/html

Mensmann, M., & Frese, M. (2019). Who stays proactive after entrepreneurship training? N eed for cognition, personal initiative maintenance, and well-being. *Journal of Organizational Behavior, 40*(1), 20–37. https://doi.org/10.1002/job.2333

Morrison, E. W., & Phelps, C. C. (1999). Taking charge at work: Extrarole efforts to initiate workplace change. *Academy of Management Journal, 42*(4), 403–419. https://doi.org/10.5465/257011

Nordin, N. (2012). The influence of leadership behavior and organizational commitment on organizational readiness for change in a higher learning institution. *Asia Pacific Education Review, 13*(2), 239–249. https://doi.org/10.1007/s12564-011-9200-y

Organ, D. W., & Greene, C. N. (1981). The effects of formalization on professional involvement: A compensatory process approach. *Administrative Science Quarterly, 26*, 237–252. https://doi.org/10.2307/2392471

Plomp, J., Tims, M., Akkermans, J., Khapova, S. N., Jansen, P. G. W., & Bakker, A. B. (2016). Career competencies and job crafting. *Career Development International, 21*(6), 587–602. https://doi.org/10.1108/cdi-08-2016-0145

Plomp, J., Tims, M., Khapova, S. N., Jansen, P. G. W., & Bakker, A. B. (2019). Psychological safety, job crafting, and employability: A comparison between permanent and temporary workers. *Frontiers in Psychology, 10*, 974. https://doi.org/10.3389/fpsyg.2019.00974/full

Podsakoff, P. M., MacKenzie, S. B., Moorman, R. H., & Fetter, R. (1990). Transformational leader behaviors and their effects on followers' trust in leader, satisfaction, and organizational citizenship behaviors. *The Leadership Quarterly, 1*(2), 107–142.

Rudolph, C. W., Katz, I. M., Lavigne, K. N., & Zacher, H. (2017). Job crafting: A meta-analysis of relationships with individual differences, job characteristics, and work outcomes. *Journal of Vocational Behavior, 102*, 112–138. https://doi.org/10.1016/j.jvb.2017.05.008

Segarra-Ciprés, M., Escrig-Tena, A., & García-Juan, B. (2019). Employees' proactive behavior and innovation performance. *European Journal of Innovation Management, 22*, 866–888. https://doi.org/10.1108/EJIM-02-2019-0041/full/html

Seibert, S. E., Kraimer, M. L., & Crant, J. M. (2001). What do proactive people do? A longitudinal model linking proactive personality and career success. *Personnel Psychology, 54*(4), 845–874. https://doi.org/10.1111/j.1744-6570.2001.tb00234.x

Seibert, S. E., Silver, S. R., & Randolph, W. A. (2004). Taking empowerment to the next level: A multiple-level model of empowerment, performance, and satisfaction. *Academy of Management Journal, 47*(3), 332–349. https://doi.org/10.2307/20159585

Shin, Y., Hur, W.-M., & Choi, W.-H. (2020). Coworker support as a double-edged sword: A moderated mediation model of job crafting, work engagement, and job performance. *The International Journal of Human Resource Management, 31*(11), 1417–1438. https://doi.org/10.1080/09585192.2017.1407352

Tang, S., Zhang, G., & Wang, H.-J. (2020). Daily empowering leadership and job crafting: Examining moderators. *International Journal of Environmental Research and Public Health, 17*(16), 5756. https://doi.org/10.3390/ijerph17165756

Tims, M., & Bakker, A. B. (2010). Job crafting: Towards a new model of individual job redesign. *SA Journal of Industrial Psychology, 36*(2), 1–9.

Tims, M., Bakker, A. B., & Derks, D. (2012). Development and validation of the job crafting scale. *Journal of Vocational Behavior, 80*(1), 173–186.

Tims, M., Bakker, A. B., Derks, D., & van Rhenen, W. (2013). Job crafting at the team and individual level. *Group & Organization Management, 38*(4), 427–454. https://doi.org/10.1177/1059601113492421

Unsworth, K. L., & Parker, S. K. (2003). Proactivity and innovation: Promoting a new workforce for the new workplace. In *The new workplace: A guide to the human impact of modern working practices* (pp. 175–196).

Van Wingerden, J., Bakker, A. B., & Derks, D. (2017). Fostering employee Well-being via a job crafting intervention. *Journal of Vocational Behavior, 100*, 164–174. https://www.sciencedirect.com/science/article/pii/S000187911730026X

Vroom, V. H. (1964). *Work and motivation*. Wiley. https://psycnet.apa.org/record/1964-35027-000

Wang, H.-J., Demerouti, E., & Le Blanc, P. (2017). Transformational leadership, adaptability, and job crafting: The moderating role of organizational identification. *Journal of Vocational Behavior, 100*, 185–195. https://doi.org/10.1016/j.jvb.2017.03.009

Wang, Y., Liu, J., & Zhu, Y. (2018). Humble leadership, psychological safety, knowledge sharing, and follower creativity: A cross-level investigation. *Frontiers in Psychology, 9*, 1727. https://doi.org/10.3389/fpsyg.2018.01727/full

Wang, H., Li, P., & Chen, S. (2020). The impact of social factors on job crafting: a meta-analysis and review. *International Journal of Environmental Research and Public Health, 17*(21), 8016. https://www.preprints.org/manuscript/202008.0522/download/final_file

Woodman, R. W., Sawyer, J. E., & Griffin, R. W. (1993). Toward a theory of organizational creativity. *Academy of Management Review, 18*(2), 293–321.

Wrzesniewski, A., & Dutton, J. E. (2001). Crafting a job: Revisioning employees as active crafters of their work. *Academy of Management Review, 26*(2), 179–201.

Yin, J., Ma, Z., Yu, H., Jia, M., & Liao, G. (2019). Transformational leadership and employee knowledge sharing: Explore the mediating roles of psychological safety and team efficacy. *Journal of Knowledge Management, 24*(2), 150–171. https://doi.org/10.1108/jkm-12-2018-0776

Zhang, F., & Parker, S. K. (2019). Reorienting job crafting research: A hierarchical structure of job crafting concepts and integrative review. *Journal of Organizational Behavior, 40*(2), 126–146. https://espace.curtin.edu.au/bitstream/handle/20.500.11937/76998/77220.pdf?sequence=2

Zito, M., Colombo, L., Borgogni, L., Callea, A., Cenciotti, R., Ingusci, E., & Cortese, C. G. (2019). The nature of job crafting: Positive and negative relations with job satisfaction and work-family conflict. *International Journal of Environmental Research and Public Health, 16*(7), 1176.

Xu Xu is an associate professor of Economics and Data Analytics in the School of Business at Henderson State University. She received her PhD in economics from Southern Illinois University Carbondale. Her research focuses on the impact of perception on various social, economic outcomes such as migration, education, and tourism. Her papers have appeared in *Growth and Change*, the *Journal of Continuing Higher Education, Kyklos, Economic Modelling, Economic Inquiry, Tourism Management Perspectives*, etc.

Yuanlu Niu is an assistant professor of Human Resource and Workforce Development at University of Arkansas. She holds a PhD in Education with a concentration in the Workforce Education and Development and an MBA from Southern Illinois University Carbondale. Her research focuses on discrimination in the workplace, career development, human resource development, and workforce diversity. Her papers have been published in *Asia Pacific Business Review, International Journal of Chinese Culture and Management, Journal of Education, International Journal of Chinese Culture and Management,* etc.

Fostering Sustainable Change: Building on the Lessons from the COVID-19 Pandemic

14

Elizabeth F. R. Gingerich

Introduction

Annual global GHG has been on a trajectory of rapid rise, heating up the atmosphere perilously. The world came together in 2015, acknowledging the dangers of unmitigated climate change, collectively vowing to keep the climate to below 2 °C even though at the time of the Paris climate agreement, global temperatures were already registered at 1.5 °C. At that time, the largest contributors to anthropogenic releases of heat-trapping gases included transportation, fossil-fuel-based energy for heating and electricity generation, and livestock or factory farming. The largest GHG emitters were identified as China (the most populous with over 1.3 billion people) and the USA (highest per capita rate of emissions), with India and the European Union included in the top 5 (UCS, 2019).

The hope was with all nations on board, understanding the enormity of the situation and the firm imperative of working together to stave off the dire consequences of climate change, releases could be curbed and rising temperatures forestalled. But with the US withdrawal from the accord in June of 2017 (which formally took effect on November 4, 2020), the numbers worldwide were left stagnant as traveling and energy-use routines largely remained unchanged. In early 2020, however, COVID-19 shut down the world economy, forcing departures from living and doing business as usual. Was this the precipitating event that could actually force the alteration of habits on a permanent basis to ultimately check emissions and protect the planet?

E. F. R. Gingerich (✉)
Valparaiso University, Valparaiso, IN, USA
e-mail: elizabeth.gingerich@valpo.edu

S. K. Dhiman, J. F. Marques (eds.), *Leadership After COVID-19*, Future of Business and Finance, https://doi.org/10.1007/978-3-030-84867-5_14

Pre-Pandemic Collective Action

The *United Nations Intergovernmental Panel on Climate Change* (IPCC) concluded in its 2013 *Fifth Assessment Report* (AR5) that the emissions of carbon and methane—the most predominant sources of anthropologically caused, heat-trapping gases—emanate from energy production and usage, transportation, human consumption levels, livestock farming, rising populations, and landfills—all contributing to the overall warming of the planet, rising sea levels, and catastrophic weather events (IPCC, 2013). The AR5 found that in the last 200 years, GHG levels had risen by over 30% and that this dramatic rise had led to the most deleterious changes in the atmosphere's composition in 650,000 years (IPCC, 2013). Without urgent and concerted international action to mitigate this phenomenon, irreversible harm to the planet would inevitably occur with the death and displacement of millions of people across the globe, the spread of abject poverty, prolonged famine and drought, rising ocean levels, massive food insecurities, and accelerated loss of plant and animal species.

This universal call to recognize the severity of the problem and commence remediating actions to reverse or halt CO_2 increases culminated in nearly every country in the world joining the Paris Agreement (a/k/a Conference of Parties (COP)21), executed in December of 2015. This alignment of nations additionally involved a joinder of prominent business leaders—all essential players needed to effectuate policies and implement actions to reduce carbon levels and draw down on the use of nonrenewable energy sources. But, as of the beginning of 2020, energy consumption continued to remain particularly problematic in North America, China, the European Union countries, India, and Brazil (IEA, 2020). Response to this problem has varied on both a nationwide and regional basis. Although energy demands were generally depressed during the initial stages of the various COVID lockdowns imposed worldwide at different times and at varying levels of restrictions, electricity demand quickly recovered in most countries by September and October 2020. Resumption of normal demand was largely driven by industrial and commercial sectors and often exceeded usage from the prior year. However, renewables represented a more significant portion of the energy mix used (IEA, 2020).

Given the dire predictions of unmitigated climate change, both public and private stakeholders agreed to join together to craft climate action plans in a historic display of international cooperation at the 2015 COP21. This level of collaboration between signatory countries, intergovernmental agencies, and private actors was unprecedented. Bill Gates (*Microsoft*), Mark Zuckerburg (*Facebook*), Richard Branson (*Virgin Group*), Jeff Bezos (*Amazon*), and other business leaders comprising the *Breakthrough Energy Coalition* announced an initial pledge of $7 billion toward the advancement of clean energy, transportation, and agriculture. The initiative was announced in conjunction with *Mission Innovation*—a joint effort launched by 21 governments, including the USA, Britain, Australia, Germany, China, and Brazil—to double the amount of public money invested in clean energy innovation (Climate Initiatives Platform, 2020).

According to the *United Nations Framework Convention on Climate Change* (UNFCCC), the primary objectives of the Paris Agreement were established to:

1. Hold the increase in the global average temperature to below 2 °C above pre-industrial levels and to pursue efforts to limit the temperature increase to 1.5 °C above pre-industrial levels;
2. Increase the ability to adapt to the adverse impact of climate change and support climate adaptation and low greenhouse gas emissions development; and.
3. Make financing consistent with a pathway toward low greenhouse gas emissions and climate-resilient innovation (UNFCCC, 2020).

The Paris Agreement's original signatories (excepting Syria and Nicaragua—the latter opting out for the express reason that the carbon control limitations had not gone far enough), left with a commitment to expedite efforts to move to lower-carbon economies. Emerging economies were not expected to design and deploy similar strategies at coordinated timetables as many such poorer nations find themselves the greatest victims of climate change and face the multi-faceted challenges of controlling greenhouse gas emissions, reducing dependence on foreign sources of energy, growing their respective economies, and solidifying national security interests. For all participants, however, the sustainable use of a nation's resources to satisfy a rising demand for energy without causing further environmental degradation remained the optimal goal.

The Agreement provides a clear pathway for its signatories to follow to wean off fossil fuels and track progress of climate action undertaken through an enhanced transparency framework (ETF). Beginning in 2024, participating countries using these tools must report on actions taken in furtherance of the Paris goals to show any progress or deficiencies in climate mitigation and adaptation (UNFCCC, 2020). Full transparency in this endeavor is predicted to pinpoint where neglect remains in forming and launching climate action policies and where more ambitious targets should be undertaken. With global CO_2 levels actually rising on an annual basis since the entry of the Paris Agreement, the efficacy of the Agreement's directives is questionable. But have the worldwide pandemic and resulting decrease of certain types of emissions fortuitously strengthened these objectives? Government and business leaders appear to be answering the clarion call to engage in more effective collective action by opening up new and more sustainable opportunities for investment while keeping planetary preservation as the guiding directive.

Enter COVID-19

On December 31, 2019, the *World Health Organization's* (WHO) Country Office in the People's Republic of China intercepted a media statement issued by the Wuhan Municipal Health Commission from its website on cases of "viral pneumonia" in Wuhan, China. A year later, after witnessing the virus's impact on nearly every nation, lockdowns have been implemented, unemployment levels increased, and economies severely harmed. The WHO currently reports that in the USA alone, there have been 18,648,989 confirmed COVID-19 cases with over 328,000 deaths registered, while in the world there have been 79,232,555 confirmed cases of the virus with 1,754,493 deaths reported (WHO, 2020).

In early 2020, just before the declaration of the world pandemic, the effect of climate action efforts revealed mixed results. Yearly GHG emissions remained high with carbon emissions rising from 53 billion tons in 2015 to 55 billion tons over 4 years later—barely helped by the COVID-driven contraction of the economy. Stoppage of air flights and the curtailing of automobile combustion showed that the world was still not on track to avoid irreversible climate change. But yet there had been signs of progress. Since the signing of the Paris Agreement, the emergence of low-carbon solutions and establishment of new carbon-neutrality targets were evident in an increasing number of countries, regions, cities, and businesses. By the end of December 2020, low-carbon solutions had been shown to be competitive in commercial and industrial sectors representing approximately 25% of emissions. By 2030, these same solutions are forecasted to be competitive in business sectors representing 70% of all global emissions (IEA, 2020).

The combination of the climate action urgency generated by the Paris Agreement and the temporary economic and social stranglehold created by the pandemic have pushed the world toward embracing a zero carbon, digitally dominant future. Such transition is slated to add over 35 million net jobs (offset by the smaller loss of positions in declining industries) globally by 2030, with unprecedented growth in the renewable energy, energy-efficient building, organic agriculture, and land restoration sectors (*Systemiq*, Turner et al., 2020). In essence, the world economy is being reshaped by a combination of low-carbon solutions and accelerated digitization, fostering renewed competitiveness and attracting alternate sources of investment.

While defining the full impact of the COVID-19 pandemic would be premature until vaccinations have controlled the spread worldwide, it is acutely clear that the road to recovery for all nations will command unprecedented investment to produce more sustainable and resilient economies. This objective has already been taken up by the European Council and European Commission through the EU Recovery Fund (Lamy et al., 2020) as well as by the UK Government's £100 billion national infrastructure strategy plan to invest in green infrastructure to create a net-zero economy by 2050, with up to 68% emission cuts achieved by 2030 (*Systemiq*, Turner et al., 2020). And in the USA, clean technology has been allocated a prime role in the country's economic recovery, with the potential to drive $1–2 trillion of green infrastructure investments, primarily in renewable power—creating 15–20 million new jobs in the process. This surge is forecasted to surpass oil and gas investment for the first time in history as rising capital markets are eclipsing fossil fuel project development (Goldman Sachs Research Group, 2020).

"Build Back Better"—the campaign slogan adopted by then-presidential-candidate Joe Biden in 2020 — might prove to be prescient in both its nomenclature and literal meaning. This anticipated reformation refers to changes in energy supply grids, transportation hubs, communication systems, and national infrastructure networks—many in need of an extreme makeover—and ripe for sustainable transition.

Many jobs losses—including those in the fossil fuel industry—will inevitably become permanent. There is a "blank slate" of sorts. Rebuilding an economy from its core foundation upwards is somewhat reminiscent of Japan's post-war transformation after the conclusion of World War II: Japan unexpectedly attained a position of economic superiority in the wake of the bombings in Hiroshima and Nagasaki. The devastation lay waste to several key metropolitan areas but shortly thereafter, a massive rebuilding commenced. New opportunities were created in burgeoning technical and manufacturing fields. Japan literally transitioned from ashes to economic superpower status by the 1970s and remains an economic powerhouse to the present day (Smith, 1995). Such a dramatic change in economic re-structuring might be an example for other countries to emulate in the quest to produce more sustainable and resilient economies.

Rising to the Challenge

The science is uncontroverted. Since 2015, emissions have risen and irreversible climate tipping points have been triggered. Loss of life and property are already unparalleled. Climate action plans must be deployed *en masse* in order to establish meaningful change and economic transformation. Many countries are beginning to listen to their constituents who are prioritizing the implementation of climate protection policies and legislation and support those commercial players who are calling for zero-carbon solutions. Representatives must stay attuned as the vast majority of people unequivocally feel that their own actions in purchasing ethically, donating, and recycling can effect meaningful change and that governments and businesses should reflect this behavior (Townsend, 2018).

The restlessness and isolation created by COVID lockdowns have allowed individuals to reflect on a more sustainable reconfiguration of products, services, and supply chains. There is greater awareness of the dire consequences of a warming planet and growing governmental and private business response thereto. Companies have more closely aligned with key sustainability objectives as demonstrated by changing technologies, training methods, and procurement schemes. Laws, rules, and regulations have been issued that incorporate sustainability objectives. A more circular economy has emerged replacing a destructive lineal system which ignores the accumulation of waste and the exhaustion of finite resources.

Governments

Youth climate engagement and those becoming more attuned to their natural surroundings appear to be translating their concerns into state climate action. Since the beginning of the outbreak in late 2019, elections in the EU, UK, New Zealand, and the USA have all been won by leaders championing strong climate platforms. Countries acknowledging both the problem of rapid planetary demise and the concomitant opportunity for correction are taking steps to harness the necessary capital to establish globally competitive players in more sustainable industries. A growing number of net-zero-carbon commitments and laws have been adopted by an increasing number of countries. In particular, as of the end of 2020:

- Countries, cities, and regions comprising over 50% of GDP now have net-zero targets in place.
- Over 100 countries and the EU have net-zero commitments and more than 100 others are considering adopting one.
- 18 US states and regions are committed to keeping temperature rise to well below 2 degrees Celsius, with efforts to reach 1.5 degree Celsius. Many of these are increasingly setting net-zero targets for 2050 or earlier.
- China has committed to carbon neutrality by 2060 and has reported surprising carbon uptakes in forestation while so much of the world's forests are being removed either unintentionally or via catastrophic weather events.
- US President Joe Biden has committed to re-engage on climate issues.
- The two global superpowers (USA and China) account for around 40% of global emissions.
- The EU, UK, and US President Joe Biden are considering carbon border tax adjustments in jurisdictions which account for 30% of global imports by value (*Systemiq*, Turner et al., 2020).
- France, the UK, and New Zealand have each made climate risk disclosure mandatory or committed to do so (Henley, 2020).
- In 2020, the Bank of England announced that it would be conducting climate stress tests on lenders and insurers beginning in 2021.
- South Korea's New Deal has already directed $95 billion into green and digital technology fields (*Systemiq*, Turner et al., 2020).

Businesses

Although the USA was no longer part of the global compact from 2017 through the end of 2020 to limit the global temperature rise to 2 degrees Celsius (3.6 degrees Fahrenheit)—which is the acknowledged threshold for avoiding dangerous global warming—the private sector has stepped up significantly to help develop clean energy solutions. Thousands of corporations and governmental units have pledged to meet or exceed the Paris objectives. *Apple, Google, Facebook, Amazon, Virgin Air, Dow Chemical, Hewlett Packard Enterprise, Starbucks, Walmart*, and *Johnson & Johnson* have committed to generating 100% of their energy from renewable resources to help mitigate climate change. Several have already met their goals while over 1500 companies with combined revenues of $12.5 trillion have set net-zero targets (Liu, 2020).

A 2017 US survey of 153 major corporations with combined revenues in excess of $250 million indicated that 84% were "actively pursuing or considering purchasing renewable energy over the next 5-10 years" (Energy Boom, 2017). Over 87% of these entities stated that the 2016 election had no impact on their decisions to actively pursue renewable energy purchases. Additionally, 22 Fortune 500 companies committed to powering 100% of their operations with renewable energy including *Walmart* and *General Motors*, with *Google* already meeting its renewable energy target in 2017 (Energy Boom, 2017). While benevolence in protecting the planet is presumptively a driving motivation, the change in corporate paradigm is no doubt intrinsically tied to the economy and lower prices in renewable energy fields. Now, envisioning a fully functional, post-COVID era, large companies will most likely continue to constitute the strongest advocates for further clean energy development at state, national, and global levels. In fact, a growing number of Fortune 100 and 500 companies have committed their businesses to corporate sustainable goals, driving small and medium entities (SMEs) to follow suit.

Countries are not the only entities embracing the net-zero pledge. Since 2018:

- *One World Alliance* and others representing >15% global air passengers have issued net-zero commitments.
- European steelmakers representing 13% of global production have set 2030–50 net-zero targets.
- 40 companies representing one-third of global cement production capacity have committed to be carbon neutral by 2050.
- *General Mills*, *Cargill*, and *Walmart* have each committed to regenerative agriculture.
- 200 companies, covering 20% of the global plastics packaging market, have transformative circularity commitments, up from just one in 2015 (*Systemiq*, Turner et al., 2020).
- *General Electric Co.* aims to be carbon neutral at its more than 1000 factories and other facilities worldwide by 2030, leaving aside emissions from the fossil fuel burning products that have defined much of the company's recent history (Beene, 2020).

Investment

Paris-aligned and post-pandemic-looking governments and businesses have the potential to adopt low-carbon policies to effect widespread, sustainable, global impact. In fact, regions accounting for over 50% of GDP now have embraced net-zero targets as have over 1500 businesses holding combined revenues exceeding $12.5 trillion. The imposition of carbon border tax adjustments—especially in the steel, aluminum, and food industries—is gaining wider acceptance in EU, UK, and US markets (*Systemiq*, Turner et al., 2020). Greater demand for more sustainably made products is changing the "business as usual" approach and general consumer behavior. And this fact is reverberating in investment activity. The value of Environmental, Social, and Corporate Governance (ESG) assets worldwide has almost doubled over the four years, hitting $40.5 trillion in 2020: "Institutional investors representing $5 trillion assets under management have now committed to align portfolios with a 1.5°C scenario by 2050 via the Net-Zero Asset Owner Alliance" (*Systemiq*, Turner et al., 2020).

New sources of wealth creation and destruction are emerging as existing financial markets can now discern the shifting of priorities favoring clean technologies and solutions. Fossil fuel production is losing capital support and industries tied to it are in decline with coal hit the hardest. In the USA, coal stocks have lost over half their value in 2019 alone and the industry has been on the rapid decline globally since 2015 (*Systemiq*, Turner et al., 2020). Even before the pandemic hit full force and while still under a Trump presidency, US coal production and consumption fell 16% and 40% between 2016 and 2020. In fact, since 2014, the average lifetime of major oil and gas industry projects has declined from 50 to 30 years (*Systemiq*, Turner et al., 2020).

The financial sector has already begun to integrate climate as a meaningful factor into mainstream business investment in the anticipated post-COVID era. Investment funds have been pouring into assets regarded as *green* or *sustainable*. In fact, by the beginning of 2020, green finance had already surpassed $31 trillion. According to the *Global Sustainable Investment Alliance*—a group of organizations tracking financial movements in five regions from the USA to Australia—such green investments have moved up 34% since the signing of the Paris Agreement. Understanding that installing a solar farm, constructing renewable-energy-based power plants, or transitioning to a network of electric buses all require concentrated investment, the bond market has been booming with respect to supporting environmentally friendly projects. To date, nearly 200 countries have committed to embracing green finance strategies pursuant to the terms of the 2015 Agreement (Global Sustainable Investment Alliance, 2019).

In January 2020, the *World Economic Forum* held its annual flagship meeting in Davos, Switzerland, headed by government and business leaders. At this event, the top risks to the global economy were all identified as climate-related—even before massive pandemic-related lockdowns were announced. With respect to green or sustainable financing, several of the countries and businesses leading the summit all advocated a transition to a low-carbon investment strategy, emphasizing that such a move could lead to an economic boost of $26 trillion before 2030 as well as the creation of more than 65 million new jobs (EDIE, 2020).

On December 15, 2020, the U.S. Federal Reserve announced that it had joined a group of approximately 75 other central banks focused on identifying and eliminating the general risk global warming poses to the global financial system. This move came after the US central bank's five-member governing board voted unanimously to become a formal member of the *Network of Central Banks and Supervisors for Greening the Financial System* (NSGS). Begun in 2017, the international coalition was formed to exchange "ideas, research, and best practices on the development of environment and climate risk management for the financial sector" (Smialek, 2020). Within the same timeframe, the *New York State Common Retirement Fund*, the third-largest public pension fund in the USA, completed a systematic review of its fossil fuel holdings, and announced its decision to withdraw investment from the "riskiest" companies by 2025, additionally committing to totally transitioning its entire $226 billion fund to a net-zero emissions portfolio by 2040 (Gardner & Podder, 2020).

Transportation

Transportation in the USA—and throughout the world—is changing dramatically. Before the outbreak of COVID, calendar year 2019 set records in aviation travel, advancements in groundbreaking-vehicle technologies, and significant increases in freight traffic as online commerce continued to escalate. The movement from gas-powered cars to electric vehicles (EVs) has only accelerated during the time of COVID. *Bloomberg Business* projects that 50% of all new vehicles will be EVs by 2030. EVs are being touted as a way to better ensure access to high-quality transport, improve system efficiency, dramatically reduce injuries and fatalities from road-traffic accidents, and lower the environmental footprint of the industry. This transition also emphasizes the role that technology and digital platforms can play in the further development of sustainable transportation and more shared-mobility innovations. Already more than ten automakers (including *Volvo*, *Renault*, and *Fiat*) have committed to EV sales targets for the period between 2020 and 2025 while the *VW Group* has announced plans to invest $66 billion in EV technology by 2024 (*Systemiq*, Turner et al., 2020).

In the USA, transportation is the number one source of greenhouse gas emissions. To help curb fossil-fuel-based emissions, *Ford Motor Co.* announced in June of 2020—after the first wave of COVID—that it would become a carbon neutral company by 2050, the first US automaker to do so (Ford, 2020). *General Motors* released its own EV supertruck—the 2022 Hummer EV Edition in late 2020—as a testament to that company's commitment to forge new paths with zero emissions (GMC, 2020).

Forecasting to 2021, *Tesla, Inc.* announced that its electric vehicle business would exceed 500,000 deliveries during that year. Its key projects—a Chinese factory (Shanghai Gigafactory) and its Model Y SUV—were both ahead of schedule and *Tesla, Inc.'s* plans to operate a fourth Gigafactory in Germany and a fifth outside of Austin, Texas are underway (Dans, 2020). *Tesla* introduced its Cybertruck in the US market in late 2019 while beginning to take truck reservations in China on July 3, 2020. Despite temporary lockdown production delays due to the lockdown, *Tesla* still managed to produce total 82,272 vehicles and ship over 90,650, just a 4.8% decline from the previous quarter—a historical record for the company. A growing number of US Cybertruck reservation holders served as the catalyst to *Tesla* accelerating the construction of Gigafactory Texas by shifting to 24/7 operations (Merano, 2020). Even during the height of the outbreak, Tesla's successful push toward mass electrification earned it the title of the most valuable automotive company in the world. Challenging Tesla pickups is Plymouth, Michigan-headquartered *Rivian Automotive*, which began building its battery-powered pickup trucks and SUVs in late 2020. *Rivian* has already raised over one billion US dollars, mainly through *Ford* and *Amazon* purchases and investments—the latter placing an order for 100,000 electric delivery vehicles.

Mass Transit In 2018, the US transportation sector contributed more greenhouse gas emissions—primarily from personal automobiles and trucks—than any other economic sector. With the significant curbing of travel-associated emissions came the inevitable realization that when affairs are "normalized" upon wresting control of the pandemic, those emissions will most likely rise precipitously. However, one should not discount the pre-COVID successes in sustainability measures with respect to public transportation. Pro-transit ballot referenda have been recently passed in several US cities and states. For example, residents of Fairfax, Virginia, approved the issuance of $160 million in bonds for the maintenance and improvement of the *Washington Metropolitan Area Transit Authority* and in Denver, Colorado, a majority of citizens voted in the affirmative to a climate change sales tax, calculated to fund sustainable initiatives, including public transit. On November 3, 2020, the citizens of Austin, Texas helped to pass Propositions A and B which were designed to develop the city's first light rail system—a downtown tunnel system—and to fund the construction of additional transportation infrastructure, including sidewalks and bikeways, throughout the city (Winters, 2020).

High-Speed Rail (HSR) High-speed rail is a form of transportation that is used to connect certain major cities throughout the world. With more than 15,000 miles of track, China was the first country to have attained the most miles of high-speed rail globally. By 2021, it is expected to have over 18,000 miles of high-speed rail tracks. With that goal, China would have high-speed rail connecting 80% of its major cities. High-speed rail is particularly popular there because of its speed, its ability to serve densely populated cities, and the convenience offered to its passengers (Lawrence et al., 2019).

Cycling and Walking Paths Within the first several months of the global lockdown, and shortly after Prime Minister Boris Johnson had been released from the hospital after contracted COVID himself, the UK announced new measures to combat the nation's worsening traffic congestion and rising pollution levels in an attempt to reshape public perception of transport generally. On July 28, 2020, Johnson officially launched the "cycling and walking revolution" supported by a £2 billion investment allocated for the construction of thousands of miles of cycle lanes (Ballinger, 2020). A similar network had already been installed throughout EU member nations and is readily expanding.

Energy

Already before the full effect of COVID was realized, the US had experienced a combined decline in coal and an increase in natural gas and renewable energy generation, resulting in an almost 3% drop in energy-related CO_2 emissions. In addition to the USA, over two-thirds of all Organization for Economic Co-operation and Development (OECD) countries had witnessed a decrease in emissions, including Germany (5%), South Korea (3%), the UK, Italy (4%), France (3%), Poland (4%), and Spain (8%) (IEA, 2020). Electricity generation—responsible for one-third of total OECD emissions, decreased by almost 200 TWh in 2019, the most significant drop of the decade and renewable energy output overtook coal in the same year for the first time ever, generating nearly 3000 TWh of energy (IEA, 2020).

With the signing of the Paris Agreement by nearly every country in the world, the dual commitments to lower-carbon emissions and invigorate the clean energy sector (i.e., hydroelectric, wind, solar, geothermal, and biofuels) were galvanized. Before 2015, many nations and business sectors had already engaged in emissions trading, subsidized renewable energy (RE) development, or used a carbon tax—or had adopted a combination thereof. Other entities were deterred by the historical high cost of RE manufacture and the inability to store any surplus. Within the last decade, however, two phenomena have occurred worldwide: (1) clean energy generation and storage technologies have rapidly advanced and (2) the cost of constructing and installing renewable energy projects had sharply declined. For the first time ever, solar energy alone has become cheaper to produce than natural gas (IEA, 2020).

According to a joint *CNN Business* and a Paris-based *International Energy Agency* (IEA) report, offshore wind turbines have been predicted to generate enough energy to power every home and business on the planet. The report further states that $1 trillion could be invested in the industry by 2040 as lower costs and government financial and administrative support have successfully encouraged the installation of larger turbines and floating foundations that allow for deep-water operations (Riley, 2019). According to the IEA, Chinese government sustainable energy policies will help the country overtake the UK as maintaining the largest offshore wind fleet by 2025 (IEA, 2020). The USA has the potential to enlarge this market, especially along the coasts of California, Oregon, and Washington.

Another blow to continued reliance on fossil-fueled based energy production occurred after COVID was fully entrenched in American society. In June 2020, the Office of Washington D.C. Attorney General (OAG) sued four of the world's largest oil companies—BP, Royal Dutch Shell, Chevron, and Exxon Mobil—asserting that these companies had been aware for more than half a century of the harm caused by their fossil fuel production. Regardless, they embarked on a multi-decade, multi-million-dollar public relations campaign to create doubt about the existence and/or seriousness of climate change caused by use of their products. Specifically, the OAG's lawsuit alleges that these fossil fuel companies knew as early as the 1950s that burning gas and oil could accumulate carbon emissions to a point where planetary existence was threatened. However, as alleged in the complaints, they obfuscated the truth to protect their profit margins, purportedly exaggerating their commitments to environmental preservation and intentionally concealing their products' harmful consequences in the process (OAG, 2020). This legal maneuver was replicated by several other states just 3 months later, this time requesting monetary damages sustained by impacted consumers and investors.

With plummeting solar PV costs and an extension of solar credits through 2021, America's business tycoons are expanding their roles in the market. Most noteworthy in early 2020 was the formal announcement of the construction on 7100 of federal land in Southern Nevada of the largest solar power plant in the US owned and financed by billionaire Warren Buffet/Berkshire Hathaway Energy (BHE) through its subsidiary, Nevada Energy, the amount of electricity projected to be generated by this solar energy plant is estimated at a whopping 690 megawatts (Dlouhy, 2020).

Agriculture, Forestry, and Land Restoration

According to the U.S. Environmental Protection Agency (EPA), approximately 24% of global greenhouse gas emissions stem from the agricultural and land management sectors, largely as a consequence of crop cultivation and livestock farming as well as from land-clearing (deforestation) activities. Of the three predominant greenhouse gases, *carbon dioxide* is generated directly from fossil fuel usage by farming methods and machinery; *methane* is typically a byproduct of agricultural waste and livestock operations; and nitrous oxide is derived from fertilizer use (EPA, 2020).

The onset of COVID-19 and commensurate lockdowns put a new spotlight on food deliveries, drive-throughs, and the overall safety of food distribution. Also, during this time, plant-based meats and the alternative-protein industries have come forward, growing to $5 billion over the last two years. Major fast-food chains including *Burger King*, *Starbuck's*, and *Wendy's* are now offering meat-free burgers, bringing this trend into mainstream food services. By 2030, the market is projected to grow more than 18fold to $85 billion (*Systemiq*, Turner et al., 2020).

The UK's Environmental Land Management program is set to reward farmers for undertaking environmental measures on their properties. Prior to 2019, the market for forestry and land use credits doubled in value to $160 million. With proper governance, it is anticipated that terrestrial carbon investments could evolve into a $50 billion market by 2030, setting an example for tropical-forested nations to invest in their own natural capital while improving the livelihoods for their indigenous communities (*Systemiq*, Turner et al., 2020).

"Doughnut Economics" During a Time of COVID

There may never be a time like this, while the world is still suffering from the effects of COVID-19, to implement leadership models necessary to reset the world economy. "Doughnut economics" may very well represent the model to follow as it pertains to revamping the way economies are structured in a time of climate and pandemic crisis (Raworth, 2020). Kate Raworth's economic model, positing an ecological boundary outer core, a social boundary inner core, and basic life essentials at the center, supplies a visual framework of sustainable development for a better functioning world society. Individuals and businesses have already learned how to reinvent the way they live their lives and conduct business, both locally and globally, as lockdowns and recommendations force a "business *not* as usual" scenario. Vast unemployment as well as climate and economic inequalities must be addressed. World economies came to a standstill with millions made jobless while the *Black Lives Matter* movement spawned mass worldwide protests focusing on racial inequalities. With social awakening evidenced in the streets, exposing deep-rooted social and economic conflict, perhaps a more sustainable type of capitalism could be fashioned at this time. A new world order guided by the *World Trade Organization* (WTO) was established after the end of WWII, marked by unprecedented economic growth and manufacturing, seismic global trade, and heightened interconnectivity between populations and societies. The proliferation of goods and services ostensibly lifted many people out of poverty worldwide. Jobs shifted from rich to poorer countries, widening the income gap exponentially. However, this largely unconstrained pursuit of economic growth and corporate profits has come at a cost to the environment. The world is suffering from a shrinking of natural resources, causing the climate to radically change, and dangerously compromising air, water, and land. Landfills and oceans are the receptacles of an inordinate amount of largely unregulated waste—particularly of plastics—in the wake of this unprecedented growth.

At this time in history, many now have the chance to actually *witness* and *analyze* what is occurring around them and how humans are interacting with nature. The world can absorb and reflect on the forces of climate change which has been borne out by the uncontrolled wildfires in the American West, parts of Europe, and Australia, while hurricanes and typhoons have ravaged the shorelines of East Asia and the Gulf of Mexico coastline. In so doing, the virus could represent a significant opportunity to reconfigure consumption behaviors. The urgency is apparent; humanity can change its relationship with the planet under proper leadership and motivation. Trafficking in wild animals and depositing them in markets has transferred the virus and ignited the current pandemic. This contamination is indicative of how people are abusing the natural world. Governments and businesses—and the people they serve—cannot view this episode as temporary after which a return to the old ways is expected. Returning to full employment and kick-starting the economy should not signal the re-entrenchment of former harmful ways. Rather, the time is here to create new jobs with new purposes and goals. In so doing, a more sustainable existence can be created.

Enhancement of a Shared Economy

Rising companies like *Airbnb* and *Uber* have already shown how assets can be shared between individuals pre-COVID. Pandemic-driven isolation has temporarily put much of that economic movement on hold but has also demonstrated just how far it can rebound and flourish. In calling for an overhaul of the global economy, social and economic theorist Jeremy Rifkin has seized upon this growing "shared economy," highlighting a declining productivity rate commensurate with the exponential exhaustion of natural resources, rising unemployment, and disparate treatment of individuals. Rifkin explains that a Third Industrial Revolution is unfolding with the convergence of three pivotal technologies: an ultra-fast 5G communication internet, a renewable energy internet, and a driverless mobility internet (Rifkin, 2020). This twenty-first century smart, digitalized infrastructure is giving rise to a radical new sharing economy that is transforming the way we manage, power, and move economic life. But with climate change now ravaging the planet, it will need to happen quickly.

Conclusion

On a world stage in December 2020, United Nations Secretary General António Guterres declared that humanity's survival would be impossible without the USA—the world's largest cumulative source of heat-trapping emissions and the planet's largest military and economic power—rejoining the Paris Agreement and achieving net-zero-carbon emissions by 2050. It was the USA, after all, that helped to craft the Paris Agreement in 2015, putting signatory nations on a collective trajectory to begin cutting greenhouse gas emissions. But in the 5 years since the Agreement's execution, the US withdrew its participation and GHG emissions worldwide continued to rise.

And, then, the coronavirus began to devastate communities and shock the world economy—all the while giving its citizenry time to pause and consider the consequences of its unchecked growth.

A relaxing of carbon output during the time of COVID lockdown shows the possibilities of transformative, sustainable renovation and signals the ramping up of zero-carbon solutions, including clean energy generation and storage, alternative plant-based food sources, electric vehicles, and more sustainable aviation fuels. The 2015 Paris Agreement lay the groundwork for global transformation and the pandemic, while decimating both populations and economies, has allowed for regrouping—accelerating sustainable climate action. A post-COVID world needs to recover the economy and at the same time, transition to a green future—two inseparable tasks.

Discussion Questions

1. How would you advise national and business leaders with respect to creating ways of meeting the Paris Agreement primary objective of keeping the climate below 2 °C?
2. What does "Build Back Better" mean to you in the context of environmental policy-making?
3. What can you do locally to be part of the solution to stopping further environmental degradation?
4. Do you think that a comprehensive national strategy can be adopted by governments to combat COVID-19 and the climate crisis simultaneously? Why or why not?
5. What positive changes have you personally witnessed that the science of climate change is being taken seriously?

References

Ballinger, A. (2020, July 28). Boris Johnson's cycling revolution. *Cycling Weekly*. https://www.cyclingweekly.com/news/latest-news/boris-johnsons-2-billion-cycling-revolution-heres-what-you-need-to-know-460776#:~:text=Boris%20Johnson's%20cycling%20announcement,improving%20the%20National%20Cycle%20Network

Beene, R. (2020, October 15). GE targets carbon neutrality for its own operations by 2030. *Bloomberg News*. https://www.bloomberg.com/news/articles/2020-10-15/ge-targets-carbon-neutrality-for-its-own-operations-by-2030

Climate Initiatives Platform. (2020). *Breakthrough energy coalition and mission innovation*. climateinitiativesplatform.org.

Dans, E. (2020, July 6). Tesla's success is good news for everyone. *Forbes*. https://www.forbes.com/sites/enriquedans/2020/07/06/teslas-success-is-good-news-foreveryone/?sh=67ea038e5ceb

Dlouhy, J. A. (2020, May 11). Buffett-backed giant solar project near Las Vegas wins Trump's blessing, *L.A. Times*. https://www.latimes.com/business/story/2020-05-11/buffett-solar-trump

Emergency Department Information Exchange (EDIE). (2020, January 26). *Davos 2020: Calls to climate action*. https://www.edie.net/news/7/Davos-2020%2D%2DCalls-to-climate-action-and-everything-else-you-may-have-missed/

Energy Boom. (2017). *Corporate investment in clean energy*. https://energyboom.com/corporate-investment-in-clean-energy/

Environmental Protection Agency (EPA). (2020, December). World Agricultural Emission Statistics. *EPA Publications*. https://www.epa.gov/ghg emissions/global-greenhouse-gas-emissions-data

Ford Motor Co. (2020, June 24). Ford expands climate change goals, sets target to become carbon neutral by 2050. *Ford's Annual Sustainability Report*. https://media.ford.com/content/fordmedia/fna/us/en/news/2020/06/24/ford-expands-climate-c hange-goals.html

Gardner, T., & Podder, S. (2020, December 9). New York State Pension Fund Sets 2040 goal of net zero carbon emissions. *Reuters*. https://www.reuters.com/article/new-york-state-pension-fund-energy/new-york-state-pension-fund-sets-2040-goal-of-net-zero-carbon-emissions-idUSKBN28J223

General Motors Corporation. (2020, October 20). GM Announces Its 2022 EV Hummer. *GM Media*. https://media.gm.com/media/us/en/gm/home.detail; html/content/Pages/news/us/en/2020/oct/1020-hummer.html

Global Sustainable Investment Alliance. (2019, April 16). *GSIA report finds increase in sustainable investing*. https://sdg.iisd.org/news/gsia-report-finds-increase-in-sustainable-investing/

Goldman Sachs Research Group. (2020, June 17). Carbonomics: The Green Engine of Economic Recovery. *Goldman Sachs*. https://www.goldmansachs.com/insights/pages/gsresearch/carbonomics-green-engine-of-economicrecovery-f/report.pdf

Henley, J. (2020). France's "big green recovery plan" not big enough for campaigners. *The Guardian*. https://www.theguardian.com/world/2020/sep/03/france-launches-big-green-recovery-plan-part-100bnstimulus-covid

International Energy Agency (IEA). (2020, December). COVID-19 impact on electricity. Statistics report. iea.org

International Panel on Climate Change (IPCC). (2013). Climate change 2013: the physical science basis. In T. F. Stocker, D. Qin, G.-K. Plattner, M. Tignor, S. K. Allen, J. Boschung, A. Nauels, Y. Xia, V. Bex, & P. M. Midgley (Eds.), *Fifth Assessment Report of the Intergovernmental Panel on Climate Change*. Cambridge University Press. https://www.ipcc.ch/site/assets/uploads/2018/02/WG1AR5_all_final.pdf; https://www.ipcc.ch/report/ar5/wg1/

Lamy, P., Pons, G., Borchers-Gasnier, A., Leturcq, P., Delair, M., Magdalinski, E., & Pellerin-Carlin, T. (2020). Greener after—A Green Recovery Stimulus for a post-COVID-19 Europe. *Notre Europe, Institut Jacques Delors*. https://institutdelors.eu/wp-content/uploads/2020/05/GreenerAfter_Lamy-et-al_200514.pdf

Lawrence, M., Bullock, R., & Liu, Z. (2019). China's high-speed rail development. *International Bank for Reconstruction and Development/the World Bank*. http://documents1.worldbank.org/curated/en/933411559841476316/pdf/Chinas-high-speed-rail-development.pdf

Liu, E. (2020, June 28). The 100 most sustainable companies, reranked by social factors. *Barron's*. https://www.barrons.com/articles/these-companies-rank-best-on-social-criteriaand-could-reward-investors-51593215993

Merano, M. (2020, November 14). Tesla Cybertruck production edges closer. *Teslarati*. https://www.teslarati.com/tesla-cybertruck-production-giga-texas-24-7-night-construction-video/

Office of Attorney General of D.C. (2020, June 25). *AG Racine Sues Exxon Mobil, BP, Chevron, and Shell for misleading consumers about the role fossil fuels play in climate change*. https://oag.dc.gov/release/ag-racine-sues-exxon-mobil-bp-chevron-and-shell

Raworth, K. (2020, October 27). Could circular economics fix the planet? *BBC HARDtalk Interview*. https://www.bbc.co.uk/ideas/videos/could-circular-economics-fix-the-planet/p06j8f32

Rifkin, J. (2020). The Third Industrial Revolution: A radical new sharing economy by Jeremy Rifkin. *Bergensia*. https://bergensia.com/the-third-industrial-revolution-a-radical-new-sharing-economy-by-jeremy-rifkin/

Riley, C. (2019, October 25). Offshore wind could power the world. *CNN Business*. https://www.cnn.com/2019/10/25/business/offshore-wind-energy/index.html

Smialek, J. (2020, December 15). Fed Joins Climate Network, to Applause from the left. *The New York Times*. https://www.nytimes.com/2020/12/15/business/economy/fed-climate-network.html

Smith, D. B. (1995). *Japan since 1945 the rise of an economic superpower*. St. Martin's Press.

Townsend, S. (2018, November 21). 88% of consumers want you to help them make a difference. *Forbes*. https://www.forbes.com/sites/solitairetownsend/2018/11/21/consumers-want-you-to-help-them-make-a-difference/?sh=1563754c6954

Turner, J., Meldrum, M., Oppenheim, J., Kick, M., & Duplat, A.-C. (2020, December). *The Paris effect—How the climate agreement is REshaping the global economy executive summary* [informed by international energy agency, energy transitions commission, food and land use coalition, world resources institute, and climate watch]. https://www.systemiq.earth/wp-content/uploads/2020/12/The-Paris-Effect-SYSTEMIQ-Executive-SummaryDecember-2020.pdf

Union of Concerned Scientists (UCS). (2019). *Earth Systems Science Data*. https://www.ucsusa.org/resources/each-countrys-share-co2-emissions

United Nations Framework Convention on Climate Change (UNFCCC). (2020). *Paris agreement*. https://unfccc.int/process-and-meetings/the-paris-agreem ent/the-paris-agreement

Winters, J. (2020, November 4). Last night's winner? Public transit. *The Beacon*. https://grist.org/beacon/public-transit-steals-the-election/

World Health Organization COVID-19 Statistics. (2020, December). https://covid19.who.int/; https://www.who.int/emergencies/diseases/novel-coronavirus-2019/interactive-timeline?gclid=Cj0KCQiA_qD_BRDiARIsANjZ2LD9iqD2VCQW-tew_s92SzQjg3amNf9QVsCvd6ps5wWZBO9EYzOUA2kaAn2oEALw_wcB#

Elizabeth F. R. Gingerich teaches graduate and undergraduate courses in business law and is editor-in-chief of Valpo's Journal of Values-Based Leadership. She completed her J.D. from Indiana University, Indianapolis. She brings nearly three decades of law experience into the classroom, most recently as a law partner with the Terrell & Thrall LLP. She has lectured at national and international conferences on intellectual property, and her work has been published in The Indiana Law Review, Res Gestae, and Employee Relations Law Journal. She is a member of both the Indiana and Virginia State Bar Associations and maintains a limited practice in corporate law.

Leading Through VUCA Times for a Sustainable Future of Work: Expert Views on the Global Automotive Industry

15

Claude-Hélène Mayer and Katharina Wilke

Introduction

Not only since the outbreak of COVID-19, leaders and organizations have already been dealing with speedy changes across industries and global economies (Maar, 2020). COVID-19 has itself ushered a new era into the business world which calls for a complete reset, and a mindset that moves from disruption towards transformation (McKinsey & Company, 2021). Leaders need to restructure the organizations, guide and monitor change, manage retrenchments and job loss in an industry which finds itself between global competition and closure (ILO, 2020a). To be able to adjust to the changes, the new complexities, and adversities and deal with them effectively, managers and leaders have to be agile and smart (Morieux, 2011). This is particularly the case when the world is being perceived as volatile, uncertain, complex, and ambiguous [VUCA] (Sarkar, 2015). The VUCA environment is mainly characterized by post-modernist strategic dilemmas which require new orientation, new sets of skills and interdisciplinary and international attempts to solve problems (Kumar Das & Ara, 2014). As Betof et al. (2014) point out, the identifiable boundaries of global marketplaces and industries have become permeable and shift continuously. Leaders, managers, and organizations realize that they have to adapt, make sense of, and respond to change speedily so that they can progress within and in partnership with the organizations in an evolving environment.

C.-H. Mayer (✉)
Department of Industrial Psychology and People Management, University of Johannesburg, Johannesburg, South Africa

Institut für Therapeutische Kommunikation, Europa-Universität Viadrina, Frankfurt (Oder), Germany

K. Wilke
Institut für Therapeutische Kommunikation, Europa-Universität Viadrina, Frankfurt (Oder), Germany

S. K. Dhiman, J. F. Marques (eds.), *Leadership After COVID-19*, Future of Business and Finance, https://doi.org/10.1007/978-3-030-84867-5_15

According to Raghuramapatruni and Kosuri (2017), leaders need to focus on the following aspects of leadership in VUCA situations:

- creating an environment of openness that values discovery, diverse perspectives, and experimentation;
- detecting the weak signals that foretell shifts in customer loyalty, or opportunities enabled by new technology;
- conducting iterative dialogues that put new ideas into the context of the company's work and translate new information into differentiating capabilities;
- unpacking business challenges to reveal the learning gaps for individuals, teams, and the organization's practices, processes, and systems;
- strengthening thoughtful decision-making in the organization.

The automotive industry is one of the biggest industries globally and finds itself in a highly competitive realm; however, for many business and IT/engineering students, the most attractive employers are based in the tech and IT business industry rather than in the automotive industry (Universum, 2019). Not only does the complex context of the global automotive industry face the challenge of talent management and of regaining its attractiveness as a future-driven employer, but it is also challenged by changes within the organization, the Fourth Industrial Revolution (4IR), competition from various industries and global environmental factors (Wilke, 2020). This chapter will present insights into VUCA times and into the context of the global automotive industry with a specific focus on experts' views on the challenges and their suggestions on how to deal with them effectively.

Leading in VUCA Times

Already at the beginning of the century, Drucker (2001, 2007) highlighted that humankind is moving into a new kind of society which is driven by knowledge, large datasets, protectionism, and an aging society—trends that he expected to have a major influence on the society and the global economy.

The term VUCA was coined in 1985 by Bennis and Nanus in describing the new situation in the 1990s with regard to the collapse of the USSR (Bennis & Nanus, 1985). Perceptions changed dramatically at that time in the USA from having to fight only one cold war enemy (the USSR) to having a highly diverse and ambiguous world with various enemies. Later, the term was used by Barber (1992) who described the environment of the early 1990s as turbulent, uncertain in terms of geopolitics, and driven by complex, uncertain technological advancement.

In this context, the concept of VUCA has gained attention in industrial and organizational research and management practice (Bennett & Lemoine, 2014; Elkington et al., 2017; Kok & van den Heuvel, 2019; VUCA, 2020). It deals with disruptive changes in workplaces which are volatile, uncertain, complex, and ambiguous.

One of the major aspects leaders have to consider in today's world of work is that standards have to give way to individuality and that the leaders themselves need to invent new orientations, worldviews, skills, and practices (VUCA, 2020). Kok and van den Heuvel (2019) point out that leaders and organizations need to develop interdisciplinary approaches and perspectives on processes of leadership, spirituality, and discernment. Mack et al. (2016) have highlighted that VUCA times and VUCA management need to move into a new era while integrating tools and approaches which are anchored in systemic structural approaches, tetralemma logics (referring to logical systems originated from Indian cultures), as well as synthetic and simultaneous thinking styles.

From organizational and employee perspectives, Deloitte (2019) explains that ethics have become a very important part of business and that ethical considerations and values are usually embedded in corporate social responsibility programs. These programs focus on doing business ethically and sustainably, thereby highlighting the positive impact on environment, social and human relations and economic impact not only in organizations, but also in societies (Deloitte, 2019). The societal impact is mentioned as an outstanding motivator for employees and leaders in recent times, shifting industry and business organizations towards social enterprises. Deloitte Insights (2019, p. 2) states:

> A social enterprise is an organization whose mission combines revenue growth and profit-making with the need to respect and support its environment and stakeholder network. This includes listening to, investing in, and actively managing the trends that are shaping today's world. It is an organization that shoulders its responsibility to be a good citizen (both inside and outside the organization), serving as a role model for its peers and promoting a high degree of collaboration at every level of the organization.

Having an impact at societal levels might be experienced as providing a countermovement against VUCA trends, which can often be perceived as being uncontrollable and beyond the influence of leaders and employees. By developing business towards social enterprises, leaders and employees might increasingly experience their own impact in counteracting volatile, uncertain, complex, and ambiguous experiences in a specifically defined area of their life.

The change in organizations towards social enterprises and experiences of changing societal and global environments clearly affects leadership. Deloitte Insights (2019, p. 2) mentions that leadership and leaders need to constantly learn, rethink, change, and adjust:

> Faced with the relentless acceleration of artificial intelligence (AI), cognitive technologies, and automation, 86 percent of respondents to this year's Global Human Capital Trends survey believe they must reinvent their ability to learn. After nearly 10 years of economic growth, and despite a pervasive corporate focus on digital transformation, 84 percent of respondents told us they need to rethink their workforce experience to improve productivity. And in the face of new pressures to move faster and adapt to a far more diverse workforce, 80 percent believe they need to develop leaders differently.

This statement highlights that the focus needs to be on human potential, human resources, and principles to move through VUCA times. A stable and certain environment can be built on reliable human cooperation and collaboration which moves towards a positive outcome for a global context based on human values and needs. Further, employees need a reliable communication between leaders and themselves, referring to constant check-ups and feedback and acknowledgement of their work as well as their impact. Cheng (2019) describes the following phenomenon in manager/leader and employee interaction:

> In studying departing workers, Gallup found that more than half said that in the three months prior to their leaving neither their manager nor other company leader had spoken with them about their job satisfaction or their future. Effective managers who are good communicators can boost a company's retention – and its bottom line.

In their book, Elkington et al. (2017) present different ideas on VUCA leadership and emphasize that leadership in VUCA times needs ethics, but also resilience in terms of foundational mindsets, in addition to a new kind of skillset, such as change management, innovation, and collaboration skills. The authors Chawla and Lenka (2018) assert that a positive, creative, courageous, and confident mindset is needed to adjust to a VUCA world. The authors also emphasize for the Indian context that both the transformational and the resonance leadership style are impactful in the VUCA world (Chawla & Lenka, 2018).

The Context of the Global Automotive Industry

In the automotive industry, the changes of the past years are particularly reflected in products, technologies, distribution channels, new competitors, and customer profiles (Wilke, 2020). Berret et al. (2017) confirm that traditional automotive companies need to adapt their leadership strategies on how to embrace the change in the automotive ecology to survive in the future mobility landscape. The world is changing at a dramatic pace; the change affects society and education and also politics, economy, and industries. The automotive industry in particular is expecting more changes within the next few years (Berret et al., 2017). These changes will have strong impacts on societies and humankind, particularly since 1.1 billion vehicles are used on global levels and more than 50 million people work across the automotive industry's value chain (Sumantran et al., 2017).

To lead through the changes successfully, future-oriented leadership is a crucial factor (Clifton & Harter, 2019). Sumantran et al. (2017) emphasize that the automotive industry is no longer a single player, but needs to acquire a systemic view which shapes the industry in the context of newly evolving urban designs and landscapes. These future work changes need new leadership which acts competently regarding automation and augmentation, machine-driven and data-powered environments, problem-solving and increasing analytical skills, cross-functional teamwork, and remote working skills as their new requirements. Gissler et al. (2016, p. 3) have recently highlighted that the high levels of competition are a challenge for the automotive industry from the industry itself and also from organizations based in other industries. They are becoming a threat to the original equipment manufacturers (OEMs) in the following way:

> Swift, agile digital disruptors – many from outside the industry, and particularly from the technology sector – are already eating into all areas of the auto value chain with offers that give them direct access to customers and their data. Their incursions directly threaten the profitability of the established OEM business domains (Gissler et al., 2016, p. 3).

Besides the usual competition, COVID-19 has put a lot of strain onto the automotive industry, mainly with regard to a sharp drop in demand and investment, a "struggle with an abrupt and widespread stoppage of economic activity," disrupted supply chains and closing factories (ILO, 2020a, p. 1). To stay successful throughout the COVID-19 crisis and post-COVID-19, leadership needs to be agile, optimized, and strategic and social business objectives need to align with the expectations and needs of the workforce. Adaptations in human resources (HR) operations and strategies need to be prioritized. Since management seems to be challenged to deal with the workforce effectively, experts are needed to support managers in this regard. Human principles are benchmarks for reinventing the future world of work, moving leaders forward with transparency and openness, collaboration and personal relationships, growth and passion, ethics and fairness, purpose and meaning (Deloitte Insights, 2019).

Purpose, Aim, and Research Focus

For managers and leaders, new models and guidance are needed on how to manage in an effective and agile, complex, and uncomplicated manner (Morieux, 2018). The purpose of this study is to present expert views on how to lead in VUCA times with specific regard to the global automotive industry. The study aims at providing insight, a deeper understanding, and increased guidance for leaders in the global automotive industries on how to lead in VUCA times, based on the research conducted with experts in the field. The findings will respond to the research question: *What do experts suggest that leaders and organizations in the automotive industry should do to create successful and sustainable organizations?*

Research Methodology

The research design used is empirical and qualitative in nature and refers to a phenomenological research paradigm which aims to generate an in-depth understanding of complex social environments (Flick et al., 2004) and, based on the study, to provide problem-solving solutions (Cheldelin et al., 2003) which can improve management practice (Bennett, 1991).

The Sample and Sampling Procedure

The survey was conducted with 30 experts across five different categories: automotive experts, automotive HR experts, previous automotive industry interns who worked in a different industry, previous automotive industry interns about to enter the workforce, and participants who had not worked in the automotive industry. Twenty-nine participants were selected through convenience sampling and one participant through snowball sampling (Etikan et al., 2016). The sample included experts from Generation X, Generation Y, and Generation Z. In terms of education, participants had apprenticeships, Bachelor and Master's degrees. They had different areas of expertise in the automotive industry, such as manufacturers, retailers, suppliers; they were based in Asia, Europe, and the USA and worked in research and development, production, procurement, finance, HR, sales, marketing and public relations, business development, and after-sales. Furthermore, the experts held different positions such as manager, industry expert, employee, specialist, or working/research student.

Data Collection and Analysis

Data were collected through a qualitative survey which was applied online and in two steps. To ensure the feasibility of the study, a pre-test was conducted with selected HR specialists, automotive experts, and participants from different industries. Based on the pre-test, the survey was further developed and adjusted. In a second step, data were collected through a qualitative survey. The survey consisted of 11 pages in PDF format, with questions on demographics, professional experiences, the future of work, international work experience, anticipated future challenges, leadership, change management, dealing with the workforce, talent management, career development, engagement, and motivation to develop smart future work contexts.

The surveys were distributed via email, and on completion, were thoroughly analyzed, summarized, and evaluated, following the qualitative content analysis of Mayring (2008). The content analysis system used was systematic and analytical in nature (Mayring, 1994, pp. 159–162).

The researchers mainly followed five steps in the data analysis process, as described by Clarke and Hoggett (2018), namely (1) the data were subjected to an initial, preliminary, and holistic assessment, (2) themes were generated, (3) data were coded, (4) the body of the text was broken down into meaningful pieces that were labeled, and (5) closer attention was paid to the subtleties and nuances of the meaning inherent in the data, through the hermeneutical processes that were applied by the researchers.

During the analysis process, inductive content analysis was used in order to create categories from the data and to gain insight into the social reality of the participants, to reduce the data to its essential content, and to develop categories from the data. However, since the selected survey categories created a framework for the analysis, the content analysis was also deductive in nature. An integrated inductive–deductive process of content analysis is known as an "abductive" approach (see Mayer, 2011).

Quality Criteria and Ethical Considerations

Triangulation of data, methods, and theories was used to ensure the quality of the research study (Collis & Hussey, 2003; Creswell & Miller, 2000; Creswell & Plano Clark, 2011; Creswell, 2013). The researchers triangulated the methods, as well as the primary and secondary resources used, to establish credibility. Qualitative quality criteria were used, such as credibility, transferability, dependability (Lincoln & Guba, 1985); confirmability and ethical considerations were adhered to (Creswell & Plano Clark, 2011; Creswell, 2013). Credibility and transferability were established through detailed descriptions of the research processes and settings. To ensure dependability in terms of consistency and stability of the findings, data were categorized in a transparent and easy-to-follow way (Patton, 2002). Confirmability was further used as a quality criterion through applied internal consistency (Lincoln & Guba, 1985; Mayring, 2008). Confirmability of data and document trail (Creswell, 2013) was promoted through inter-subjective validation processes (Yin, 2009).

Ethical considerations were followed, including voluntary participation, information about research purpose and practice, and informed consent (Patton, 2002). Personal privacy and anonymity were ensured throughout the entire research process (Schurink, 1998). Participants provided written consent and were informed about confidentiality and possibilities of withdrawal from the research participation.

Limitations of the Study

The study is limited to the described methodological research design, paradigm, and approach. Subjective insights were gained and explored from 30 experts across different organizations, countries, and areas of expertise within the global and international automotive industry. The insights might not be generalizable and they might not be representative for the global international industry. The research might provide very specific insights. The study is limited in terms of the sampling procedures and the defined aim without proclaiming generalizations.

Findings

In the following, findings will be presented first, with regard to significant expected changes. Second, the findings will examine global organizational trends for leading in VUCA times, in terms of organizational changes and changes in leadership values and actions.

Expected Changes in Future Work Environment

Findings show that rapid and highly significant changes on different levels are not only already perceived but also expected for the near future, at manufacturer, workforce, and customer levels. Experts highlight that on manufacturer level, changes have and will affect product technology, product development, and organization and business models.

In terms of product technology, the main change is and will be seen in engine electrification, smart cars, sustainable mobility, the use of artificial intelligence, and the connection of digitalization and urbanization in automotive manufacturing (P2, P4).[1] Regarding product development, competitors have been challenging the

[1] P means participant. P2 is, for example, Participant 2.

industry by developing smart and environmentally friendly solutions and big data solutions. Product developers will need further qualifications and skills to survive in the automotive industry and drive it forward (P5).

Finally, changes will be experienced in the ways in which organizations and businesses are led: hierarchies need to flatten to attend quickly to the changes, inter- and cross-functional networks are needed, and new forms of agile working are required. The automotive industry needs to change from an automotive producer to become a mobility service provider (P2) which offers a convenient and smooth customer experience. P2, for example, points out:

> Electrification is the change with perhaps the most visibility right now but also I believe there will be a significant shift toward business models offering more convenience and less hassle when purchasing and servicing vehicles (taking the lead from Amazon, for example).

Additionally, these new business models impact retail and ownership models. New retail channels are expected to replace dealerships; customers are not striving to own a car, but rather, to being mobile in the future. Furthermore, talent management needs to be reinvented, since the new generation shows a tendency to prefer working in the fast-moving, dynamic tech environment, which promises diverse employee benefits and a reasonably quick career progression.

At the workforce level, changes are expected in terms of integration of robots in the workplaces, increased human–machine interaction, and increasing automation. P5 emphasizes: "More and more jobs are being replaced by machines." Employees will need to undergo advanced training in technological changes, and employees who become redundant need occupational redeployment offers. An increase in IT jobs in the automotive industry is also expected. P1 points out that employees need a mindset shift towards electric vehicle technology. Owing to the costs related to this shift, employees are likely to expect fewer investments in training and development, but also general hiring freezing and reduction of employee benefits. Further on, the expectations of the workforce are changing: members of the generations from the year 2000 enjoy working in organizations which have flat hierarchies, flexible working hours, and which are needs-based, according to the experts such as P3.

In terms of changes regarding customers, it is assumed that face-to-face interaction will transition to remote and online interaction and more customers will use car-sharing options. The car as a status symbol changes towards mobility as a status symbol (P1) and for the younger generation, holding a driver's license does not even seem to be desirable or necessary (P5).

General Trends for Leading in VUCA Times: The Social Enterprise as a Foundation

Generally, findings show that the experts experience leaders in the automotive industry as being very aware and conscious of the changes and uncertainties in the industry. However, they are not yet sufficiently action-driven and need to increasingly develop agile and flexible leadership skills to build social enterprises that focus on human experience, provide a mission which employees identify with, and build meaningful and purposeful tasks, as well as a sustainable holistic approach with societal impact. Experts suggest that despite technological advancements, human interaction and needs, relationships, networks, and meaning-making will support the organization to stay sustainable while focusing on employee acquisition, development, and retention.

In order to lead through complex and uncertain times, one overall finding is that leaders need to transform their organizations into "social enterprises" which move beyond corporate social responsibility, revenue, and profit orientation (see Fig. 15.1.) Experts highlight that organizations as social enterprises need to work primarily towards building positive human interactions with a meaningful environmental impact, in order to be sustainable in a volatile and uncertain world. They need to actively support the environment and stakeholders, acting respectfully as role models and supporting each other through collaboration. To gain influence and drive the change, leaders need to cooperate with HR and increase human interaction while digitalizing the world of work, focusing on purpose and meaning, ethics, and transparency as foundational skills. In terms of the values of leaders, faith and passion, individual and personal solutions, the definition of career goals and personal preferences, as well as ethical and action-driven leadership are core to post-COVID-19 leadership.

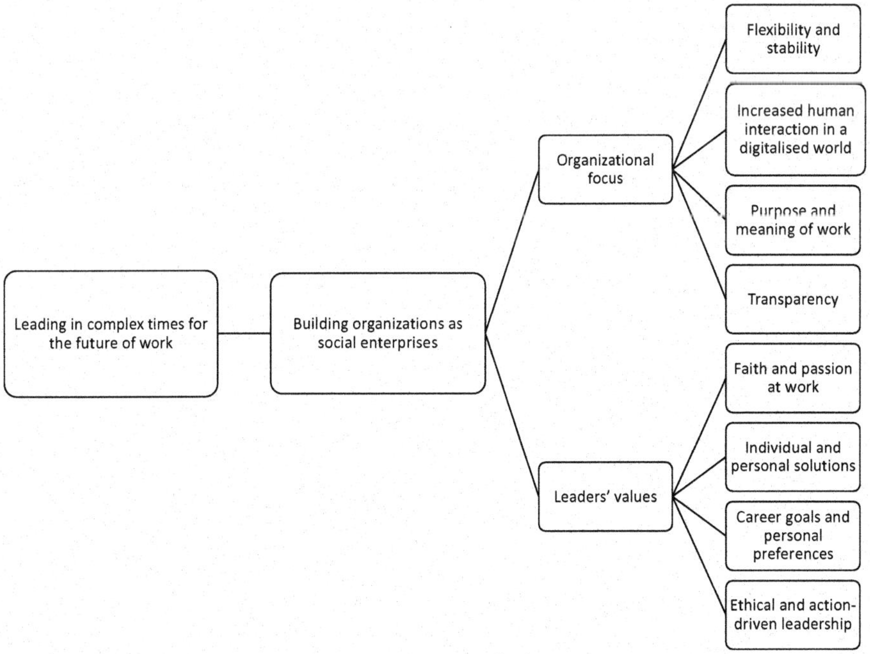

Fig. 15.1 Leading in complex times

Organizational Focus

Leading in complex and VUCA times in the automotive industry, anticipating the changes of the future and the uncertainties, new organizational foci will have to be defined and promoted to be sustainable and successful in the future automotive industry. Experts emphasize that organizations need to become more flexible and organizational cultures need to adjust and progress. Additionally, organizations are required to balance the need for creating flexibility with the need to create stability in organizations. Since organizational cultures will change towards remote working concepts, employees will have to increase (digitalized) human interaction on all levels. This interaction will be based on a proper IT infrastructure within the organizations—but in order to make the best use of it, employees must be trained on and develop skills in that regard. They further have to be rapid in terms of their adaptation and response rate to changes in the organizational and work culture and environment. This means that employees will need an increase in adaptability, creativity, flexibility, and auto-didactical competences to deal with occurring challenges by themselves and in the context of their employee networks.

Organizations need to further develop and communicate purpose and meaning as part of their organizational culture, since the creation of individual purpose and meaning might not be strong enough to keep employees motivated and engaged. The creation of purpose and meaning will connect to the expectations of the new workforce which has an increasing need to engage in a workplace that is meaningful and purposeful. To counteract the uncertainties of volatile work environment trends further, organizations need to be transparent in their processes, their plans, and the way they address the challenges which lie ahead in terms of required skillsets for top- and medium-level jobs. However, organizations in the automotive industry also need to focus on the gender gap, according to the participants. Since this industry sector is traditionally a male-dominated place of work, organizations are to focus on the gender gap in terms of current and future employees for more inclusive and diverse perspectives.

Leaders' Values

Findings show that the view on leadership, how it should be defined, and what it entails is relating to a transformational, ethical, and action-driven leadership style (P5, P8). Experts highlight that leadership needs to be team-oriented and empowering the workforce (P4). It should be based on ethics, values, and needs and therefore should have a clear mission statement and purpose, enabling collaboration, team spirit, success, and aligning diverse interests.

Based on the leadership, employees should be able to be creative, innovative, critical thinking, motivated, and encouraged to think out of the box (P2). Leaders should apply a systemic mindset to address VUCA experiences in management and organizations and challenge the status quo constantly (P11). Several of the experts criticize the fact that often the described leadership is valued theoretically, but not implemented practically within the organization. They speak of an obvious skill gap that needs to be addressed through educational systems, advanced adult and employee education, training and development, and intrinsic motivated self-learning opportunities.

Leaders need to value faith and passion on the job—which is strongly related to meaning and purpose for the individual employee as well as for the organization. Passion is seen as being strongly connected to motivation and meaning that can be derived from the job. Passion is often related to intrinsic motivation and not to externally motivating factors, such as monetary rewards or recognition. Experts highlight that employees need leaders and organizations which are passionate about meaning and purpose and about the employee's and organizational contribution to the bigger picture, such as the environment, the market, the society, the organization, and the product itself. The passion of working for the organization is surely also connected to collaboration with HR and its positive contribution to the development of humankind.

Organizations and leadership need to focus on the individual, his/her impact and personal solutions, work styles, and application of theory into practice. Employees enjoy leaders who are empathetic and relatable, and who value, appreciate, and recognize their employees. Leaders therefore need to find ways to value every single employee, provide individual feedback and career development plans on an individual basis.

Since employees have a need for work–life balance and secure and stable jobs, it is of utmost importance for leaders to develop impactful jobs within the organization which can adjust to changing environments and organizations quickly, which are inclusive and dynamic. Careers are valued in terms of impact and personal development and progression, not necessarily according to status or position. Experts further highlight that leaders need to support building a good and positive reputation of the organization which is based on ethical values, transparency, and action-orientation so that employees are recognized as working for a reputable organization.

Discussion

The findings regarding the research question show that experts in the field of the global automotive industry agree with many aspects described in the literature regarding how to sustain in VUCA times. The challenges highlighted by the ILO (2020a, b) are visible to experts in the automotive industry and, on the one hand, are viewed as a threat. But on the other hand, challenges are viewed as a push towards new levels of transformation (McKinsey & Company, 2021). Experts agree that in VUCA times, agile and smart actions specifically addressing the contextual challenges are crucial (Morieux, 2011). Experts described the challenges on different levels of the global industry and thereby contribute to the corpus of the literature which emphasizes that problem-solving for contemporary and future complexities is necessary (Kumar Das & Ara, 2014). While Raghuramapatruni and Kosuri (2017) point out certain leadership shifts that are needed, the experts in the field highlight similar leadership aspects, which are presented in Table 15.1.

Table 15.1 Leadership challenges in VUCA times

	Leadership challenges		
	Raghuramapatruni and Kosuri (2017)	Experts in the field of the automotive industry	Specific aspects by experts
Environment and culture	Creating an environment of openness that values discovery, diverse perspectives, and experimentation	Transform the automotive environment and organizational culture actively	Organizational changes and new leadership values (i.e. transparency, openness, fairness, purpose-driven, creating meaning and purpose, appreciation)
Understanding the complexity of changes	Detecting the weak signals that foretell shifts in customer loyalty, or opportunities enabled by new technology	Understanding challenges on: – Manufacturer – Workforce – Customer levels	Manufacturer: – Product technology – Product development and organization – New business models
			Workforce: – Human–machine interaction – Automation – Remote and digitalized working – Changing expectations of the workforce itself
			Customer: – Increased direct interaction with customers through online channels – Change of the meaning of mobility and product for customers
Communication and collaboration	Conducting iterative dialogues that put new ideas into the context of the company's work and translate new information into differentiating capabilities	Increase collaboration within and across organizations in the industry and with competitors	Action-driven and open, transparent communication between leaders and the different levels of the organizational environment, and regular feedback
Learning organizations and lifelong learning	Unpacking business challenges to reveal the learning gaps for individuals, teams, and the organization's practices, processes, and systems	Challenges not viewed as threat, but as transformative potential	Potential to transform organizations into social enterprises
			Potential to value and develop each employee individually
Decision-making	Strengthening thoughtful decision-making in the organization	Changes in ways of decision-making	Based on human values, supported by technology, and a neat collaboration in the leadership network (vertical and horizontal)

The findings confirm Drucker's (2001, 2007) view on the VUCA world at the beginning of the twenty-first century. However, while the literature often focuses on the aspect of disruptiveness of VUCA times (Bennett & Lemoine, 2014; Elkington et al., 2017; Kok & van den Heuvel, 2019; VUCA, 2020), experts in the field seem to keep a more positive view which points out the challenges, but also provides practical advice on how to deal with them. Leaders need to become active players, as findings show, to shift the boundaries of complex challenges, work through complex issues by using all the (human) resources and capital they have, and focus on the communication with the individual and its specific impact towards a more comprehensible, manageable, and meaningful world of work.

While some of the new literature on VUCA offers suggestions on exactly how to intervene in leadership and organizations for transformation (see Kok & van den Heuvel, 2019; Mack et al., 2016), experts in the field rather describe more broadly the changes required and the aspects which need to be addressed at organizational and leadership levels. The social enterprises mentioned by Deloitte Insights (2019) are also reflected upon by automotive industry experts who highlight a needed shift in the industry to focus on HR and reinvented leadership models with focus on ethics and informed, collaborative actions, based on constructive human values which foster communication, constant check-ups, and feedback (as in Cheng, 2019) with positive, creative, innovative, and constructive mindsets (Elkington et al., 2017; Chawla & Lenka, 2018). As pointed out in the literature (see Gissler et al., 2016; Sumantran et al., 2017; ILO, 2020a, b), the experts confirm that the complexity of the automotive industry is extraordinary in its technological, system-integration, design, and system thinking levels.

Finally, the study findings match the emphasis in the literature that employees in the automotive industry have to gear up in terms of training, flexibility, and human interaction. At the same time, leaders' values such as faith and passion, their individual and personal solutions, and definitions of career goals and personal preferences, are core to ethical and action-driven post-COVID-19 leadership.

Conclusions and Recommendations for Future Research and Leadership Practice

As described in the beginning of this chapter, the purpose of the study was to present expert views on how to lead in VUCA times with specific regard to the global automotive industry. The study aimed at providing insight, a deeper understanding, and increased guidance for leaders in the global automotive industries on leadership in VUCA times. The research question explored the views of experts in the field of how to maintain successful and sustainable organizations.

Findings show that organizational and leadership changes are required to happen rapidly and in an informed way on organizational, as well as leadership levels. Individuals working in the global automotive industry have to adapt quickly and need to anticipate the future trends of the industry which may be defined by volatile, uncertain, complex, and ambiguous trends and challenges. Generally, and contrary to a large amount of literature which focuses on the disruptiveness of VUCA times, the views of the experts are neutral to positive, value- and action-driven, highlighting the challenges and providing guidance on how to deal with them effectively through applied leadership.

Findings show that organizations need to transform in the direction of social enterprises which value the human factor over all other aspects of the organizations. Organizations, transformed towards social enterprises, need to change with regard to their own foci and need to be prepared to change rapidly, adjust quickly to environmental and organizational trends in terms of structures, processes, and culture based on network collaboration. The organization as well as the leadership of the future needs to be flexible, adjustable, but also creative, innovative, and broadly skilled with specific skills in IT and new technologies and abilities to anticipate the future trends occurring at individual leadership and organizational levels. Leadership values and actions need to be strong, systemic, knowledge-driven, and person-centered. Accordingly, leaders' actions need to have a strong, purpose, and meaning-oriented focus, which may filter into the organizations and vice versa, to motivate and engage the current and new generations of employees striving in the industry. Action-driven leadership will be informed through transparency on all levels of the organization and needs to be implemented on all levels of the organization, in cooperation with the organizational environment and in organizational processes and the organizational culture.

For future research, it is recommended that empirical mixed-method studies need to be conducted in the global automotive industry with focus on the impact of organizational changes and leadership within the social enterprise realm. The effects of changes on the automotive organization as a social enterprise on different organizational levels, in terms of employees, manufacturers, customers, and future trends need to be further researched. It is also recommended, particularly focusing on the impact of VUCA trends, to explore the role of women leaders in the automotive environment post-coronavirus. COVID-19 research has shown which important roles women leaders play during VUCA times; however, traditionally male-dominated organizations might not have realized the potential positive impact of closing the gender gap (Johnson & Williams, 2020; Mayer & May, 2020 in review).

Further research will be needed with regard to the impact of meaning-making and purpose construction of automotive companies in the context of leadership. With this in mind, the influence of spiritual aspects in new technology-led automotive organizations needs to be explored further. It is also a question of which, how, and what kind of talent needs to be recruited in the future for creating automotive organizations which have to become systemically led, sustainable social enterprises. Finally, another research focus could be on how different global networks in the automotive industry can increase a remote, but human-based interaction which is informed by regional and cultural aspects on the one hand and works for a globalized, sustainable, and eco-friendly industry on the other hand.

On an organizational level, the automotive industry needs to focus on leadership which is prepared to take on the challenges of VUCA times from a positive organizational perspective. At different levels, the industry needs to be transformed into a social enterprise which is shaped by meaning and purpose. This needs a value shift and a recruitment of leaders who work with meaning and purpose, for the good of humankind (besides profit) and who are able and willing to integrate technological advances with their employees' and customers' values. Leadership needs to head in a more ethical, transparent, and action-driven direction, which is prepared to develop and focus on the needs of employees, the organization, and its customers. In terms of closing the gender gap, automotive organizations need to attract women leaders in order to reflect inclusive and diverse values. Finally, leaders must have strong personalities, healthy mindsets, and resilience to withstand the volatile, uncertain, complex, and ambiguous promoted threats of the times and transform them into challenges which can be met through the development of new structures, processes, strong, creative, and innovative mindsets, and transformed leadership values.

Acknowledgement We thank all experts who invested time to participate in this global research project.

References

Barber, H. F. (1992). Developing strategic leadership: The US Army war college experience. *Journal of Management Development, 11*(6), 4–12. https://doi.org/10.1108/02621719210018208

Bennett, R. (1991). How is management research carried out? In N. Smith & P. Dainty (Eds.), *The management research handbook*. Routledge.

Bennett, N., & Lemoine, G. J. (2014). What a difference a word makes: Understanding threats to performance in a VUCA world. *Business Horizons, 57*(3), 311–317.

Bennis, W. G., & Nanus, B. (1985). *Leaders: The strategies for taking charge*. Harper & Row.

Berret, M., Bernhart, W., Winterhoff, M., Seyger, R., Kirstetter, E., & Riederle, S. (2017). Automotive disruption radar. Issue #1. *Tracking disruption signals in the automotive industry*. https://www.rolandberger.com/de/Publications/pub_automotive_disruptio n_radar.html

Betof, E., Ownes, L. M. D., & Todd, S. (2014). *Leaders as teachers. Action guide*. Association for Talent Development. American Association for Training & Development.

Chawla, S., & Lenka, U. (2018). Leadership in VUCA environment. In S. Dhir & Sushil (Eds.), *Flexible strategies in VUCA markets. Flexible systems management*. Springer.

Cheldelin, S., Druckman, D., & Fast, L. (2003). *Conflict: From analysis to intervention*. Continuum.

Cheng, C. (2019). 3 Factors Strongly Linked to Better Employee Retention, According to 32 Million LinkedIn Profiles. Retrieved (03.12.2019) from: https://business.linkedin.com/talent-solutions/blog/trends-andresearch/2019/3-factors-linked-to-better-employee-retention?_lrsc=3d7e24fe-78d7-4dee-93ecb08c6f686168&utm_source=social&utm_medium=leap&utm_campaign=linkedin&src=li-leap.

Clarke, S., & Hoggett, P. (2018). *Researching beneath the surface: Psycho-social research methods in practice*. Routledge.

Clifton, J., & Harter, J. (2019). *It's the manager*. Gallup Press.

Collis, J., & Hussey, R. (2003). *Business research: A practical guide for undergraduate and postgraduate students* (2nd ed.). Palgrave Macmillan.

Creswell, J. W. (2013). *Qualitative inquiry & research: Choosing among five approaches* (3rd ed.).

Creswell, J., & Miller, D. (2000). Determining validity in qualitative inquiry. *Theory Into Practice*, 124–130.

Creswell, J. W., & Plano Clark, V. I. (2011). *Designing and conducting mixed methods research* (2nd ed.). Sage.

Deloitte Insights. (2019). Leading the social enterprise: Reinvent with a human focus. *2019 Deloitte global human capital trends*. https://www2.deloitte.com/content/dam/insights/us/articles/5136_HC-Trends-2019/DI_HC-Trends-2019.Pdf

Drucker, P. F. (2001). *The essential Drucker*. Harper Business.
Drucker, P. F. (2007). *The essential Drucker: Selections from management works*. Butterworth-Heinemann.
Elkington, R., van der Steege, M., Glick-Smith, J., & Moos Breen, J. (2017). *Visionary leadership in a turbulent world. Thriving in the new VUCA context*. Emerald.
Etikan, I., Musa, S., & Alkassim, R. (2016). Comparison of convenience sampling and purposive sampling. *American Journal of Theoretical and Applied Statistics, 5*(1), 1–4.
Flick, U., von Kardoff, E., & Steinke, I. (2004). *A companion to qualitative research*. Sage.
Gissler, A., Oertel, C., Knackfuss, C., & Kupferschmidt, F. (2016). Are you ready for pole position? Driving digitization in the auto industry. https://docplayer.net/53962174-Are-you-ready-for-pole-position.Html
ILO. (2020a). *Monitor: COVID-19 and the world of work* (6th ed.). https://www.ilo.org/global/topics/coronavirus/impacts-and-responses/WCMS_755910/lang%2D%2Dde/index.htm
ILO. (2020b). ILO sectorial brief. *Covid-19 and the automotive industry*. https://www.ilo.org/sector/Resources/publications/WCMS_741343/lang%2D%2Den/index.htm
Johnson, C., & Williams, B. (2020). Gender and political leadership in a time of COVID. *Politics & Gender*, 1–8. https://doi.org/10.1017/S1743923X2000029X
Kok, J., & van den Heuvel, S. (2019). Leading in a Vuca world. In *Integrating leadership, discernment and spirituality*. Springer.
Kumar Das, K., & Ara, A. (2014). Leadership in VUCA WORLD: A case of Lenovo. *International Journal of Current Research, 6*(04), 6410–6419.
Lincoln, Y. S., & Guba, E. G. (1985). *Naturalistic inquiry*. Sage.
Maar, B. (2020). How the Covid-19 pandemic is fast-tracking digital transformation in companies. *Forbes*. https://www.forbes.com/sites/bernardmarr/2020/03/17/how-the-covid-19-pandemic-is-fast-tracking-digital-transformation-in-companies/?sh=6a859ff2a8ee
Mack, O., Khare, A., Kramer, A., & Burgartz, T. (2016). *Managing in a Vuca world*. Springer.
Mayer, C.-H. (2011). *The meaning of sense of coherence in transcultural management*. Waxmann.
Mayer, C.-H., & May, M. (2020). Women leaders transcending the demands of Covid-19: A positive psychology 2.0 perspective. *Frontiers of Psychology*. (in Review).
Mayring, P. (1994). Qualitative Inhaltsanalyse. In A. Böhm, A. Mengel, & T. Muhr (Eds.), *Texte verstehen: Konzepte, Methoden, Werkzeuge* (pp. 159–176). Universitätsverlag.
Mayring, P. (2008). *Qualitative Inhaltsanalyse. Grundlagen und Techniken*. Beltz.
McKinsey & Company. (2021). *Covid-19: implications for business. Executive Briefing*. https://www.mckinsey.com/business-functions/risk/our-insights/covid-19-implications-for-business#
Morieux, Y. (2011). Smart rules: Six ways to get people to solve problems without you. *Harvard Business Review, 89*(9), 78–86.
Morieux, Y. (2018). *Bringing managers back to work*. Boston Consulting Group. https://www.bcg.com/en-in/publications/2018/bringing-managers-back-to-work
Patton, M. (2002). *Qualitative evaluation and research methods* (3rd ed.). Sage.
Raghuramapatruni, R., & Kosuri, S. R. (2017). The straits of success in a VUCA world. *Journal of Business and Management, 1*, 16–22.
Sarkar, A. (2015). *We live in a VUCA World: the importance of responsible leadership* (Vol. 30(3), pp. 9–1). Emerald Group Publishing, Development and Learning in Organizations.
Schurink, E. (1998). Designing qualitative research. In A. de Vos (Ed.), *Research on grass roots: A primer for the caring professions*. JL van Schaik Publishers.
Sumantran, V., Fine, C., & Gonsalvez, D. (2017). *Fast, Smarter, Greener. The future of the car and urban mobility*. MIT Press.
Universum. (2019). World's most attractive employers 2019. *Global insights on how students currently view companies*. https://universumglobal.com/wmae-2019/
VUCA. (2020). *Vuca-World*. https://www.vuca-world.org/
Wilke, K. (2020). *Managing talent in the automotive industry. Gaining competitive advantage in times of change*. Doctoral dissertation. Europa Universität Viadrina.
Yin, R. K. (2009). *Case study research: Design and methods* (4th ed.). Sage.

Leading Through Crisis: The Role of Mindfulness

16

Alisha Gupta and Christopher S. Reina

Leading Through Crisis: The Role of Mindfulness

The important role that leadership plays during times of crisis is well documented (Halverson et al., 2004; James & Wooten, 2005; James et al., 2011; Mumford et al., 2007). With regulations like mask-wearing, reduced in-person work interactions, more virtual meetings, and increased time at home, the COVID-19 pandemic simultaneously presents physical, social, emotional, and cognitive challenges for leaders to manage. COVID-19 has dramatically changed the way we work, and there is no doubt that COVID-19 continues to impact relationship dynamics, both personal and in the workplace (Pietromonaco & Overall, 2020). One reason that crisis situations such as COVID-19 represent an important leadership challenge is that leaders must manage their followers' emotional responses, which are often negative due to the stress and uncertainty brought upon by novel or ambiguous situations (Mumford et al., 2007). Interestingly, however, we have a limited understanding of how leaders can best manage others' emotions specifically during such crisis situations.

While the impact of leader emotions during crisis situations has been studied previously (i.e., Madera & Smith, 2009), researchers have overlooked the importance of understanding follower emotions during times of change. Understanding the negative emotional implications of crisis situations for followers is crucial because of its impact on individual work outcomes such as job performance (Shockley et al., 2012), job satisfaction (Niklas & Dormann, 2005), interpersonal workplace behaviors (Lee & Allen, 2002), and subjective well-being (Busseri, 2018). Crises bring about abrupt changes which contribute to high levels of stress and fear (Anicich et al., 2020; Kiefer, 2002; Hogan & Overmyer-Day, 1994; Marks

A. Gupta (✉) · C. S. Reina
Department of Management and Entrepreneurship, Virginia Commonwealth University, Richmond, VA, USA
e-mail: guptaa26@vcu.edu; csreina@vcu.edu

S. K. Dhiman, J. F. Marques (eds.), *Leadership After COVID-19*, Future of Business and Finance, https://doi.org/10.1007/978-3-030-84867-5_16

& Mirvis, 1992), and leaders have a key role in shaping how followers perceive these changes and associated emotions.

In this chapter, we contribute to the leadership literature in three primary ways. First, we develop a model of mindful leadership in crisis. To underscore the importance of leaders managing the emotional space for their employees during times of crisis, we build on previous work that reinforces the importance of workplace emotions during change (Kiefer, 2002). Our model extends previous work by considering how leader behaviors such as empathy, active listening, and empowerment may aid in managing followers' negative emotional responses, which ultimately impact their levels of job satisfaction, satisfaction with their leader, relationship quality, and job performance.

Second, we contribute to mindfulness theory by articulating the relational effects of mindfulness. To date, much of the research on mindfulness within the organizational sciences has focused on its effects for the mindful individual him/herself, with little work addressing how mindfulness of a focal individual impacts those with whom they interact. We suggest that mindfulness plays a vital role in helping leaders effectively manage follower emotions, and in doing so, we answer calls to further expand our understanding of the mechanisms by which leader mindfulness operates at work (Reb et al., 2020). We also build on and extend Kiefer's work (2002) by integrating leader mindfulness as a predictor of follower affective states in order to help leaders better guide followers through crisis situations. To the best of our knowledge, this represents one of the first integrations of leader mindfulness with crisis leadership.

Finally, we aim to contribute to the high-quality connections and positive work relationships literatures. Research on high-quality connections is entrenched within the positive organizational scholarship (POS) literature, which considers the processes and outcomes of positive workplace phenomena (Cameron & Caza, 2004; Ragins & Button, 2007). Nested within POS, extant research on high-quality connections suggests that empathy and active listening are vital for the development of high-quality connections (Stephens et al., 2012), but does not yet expand upon the role of empowerment. We suggest that leader mindfulness plays a key role in ensuring that leaders exhibit these three behaviors to followers during crisis situations.

The remaining portion of the chapter is as follows: first, we briefly review the importance of negative affect in a crisis situation and review the crisis leadership literature. Following this, we propose a conceptual framework of leader mindfulness by building on Kiefer (2002) to construct a framework of positive leadership behaviors during a time of crisis (Bell & Hall, 1954; Conger et al., 2000; Dutton & Ragins, 2007; Gooty et al., 2010). We theorize that if leaders are mindful, they exhibit more empathy, active listening, and empowering behaviors toward followers. These relational mechanisms then serve to improve follower affect and influence outcomes such as job satisfaction, satisfaction with the leader, leader–follower relationship quality, and job performance during a time of crisis. A visualization of our model is presented in Fig. 16.1. Finally, we conclude by discussing limitations and suggestions for future research.

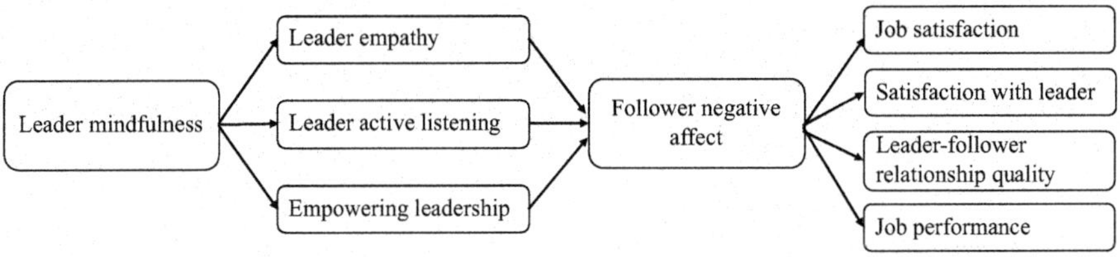

Fig. 16.1 Proposed model

Negative Affect During a Crisis

Negative affect, characterized by "a general dimension of subjective distress and unpleasurable engagement that subsumes a variety of aversive mood states, including anger, contempt, disgust, guilt, fear, and nervousness" (Watson et al., 1988, p. 1063), is especially important to manage during a crisis situation. Considerable management research has shown the direct impact of negative affect on individual outcomes at work like counterproductive work behaviors (Lee & Allen, 2002), subjective well-being (Busseri, 2018), and its spillover effect into an individual's home life and even the next day (Sonnentag & Binnewies, 2013). Despite the workplace implications of negative affect and the potentially heightened negative affect during a crisis, crisis management researchers have not yet focused on the role of leader management of follower affect.

To emphasize why leaders should focus on managing follower emotions, we should first understand why emotions in the workplace during change are important. Kiefer's (2002) framework implies that we should not dismiss the significance of emotions, but instead recognize that emotions provide valuable insight to change processes. More specifically, emotions are triggered when events are pertinent to life and identity—so radical, organizational change is bound to lead to emotional reactions. Second, Kiefer argues we must more fully understand emotions at work in order to learn about individuals' goals and needs in the workplace. Kiefer (2002) proposes that perceptions of change and the emotions induced are likely to vary according to what is at stake for a particular stakeholder. Lastly, emotions are not the product of a specific individual, but more of a result of interactions with the social environment, and thus it is important to recognize the relational context of emotions and the history of the social environment when leading an organization through change (Kiefer, 2002).

Considering these reasons for the importance of emotions in the workplace, we follow Kiefer's perspective in that leaders should aim to manage follower affect during change. In order to manage organizational change effectively, we need to know "what emotions are experienced, what they are about, and what the consequences are" (Kiefer, 2002, p. 52). While Kiefer emphasizes the importance of understanding emotions during change, the framework offers a limited understanding of how leaders can help manage emotions for followers. We extend Kiefer's framework by developing a model of leadership in crisis in which mindfulness plays a focal role in aiding leaders in managing follower emotions.

Leadership in Crisis

Crisis is "a low-probability, high-impact event [which threatens] the viability of the organization and is characterized by ambiguity of cause, effect, and means of resolution, as well as by a belief that decisions must be made swiftly" (Pearson & Clair, 1998, p. 59). Leading during crisis requires skills of grasping the significance of the crisis for the organization and responding quickly to an ambiguous situation (Garcia, 2006). Leaders play a major role in influencing both follower and organizational performance during a crisis as studies show that followers turn to their leaders in crisis (Hunt et al., 1999). Further, leaders' influence on follower perceptions and performance is higher in a crisis situation than in non-crisis situations (Mumford et al., 2007), and research suggests that leadership plays an important role in determining organizational performance during crisis conditions (Tushman & O'Reilly, 1996).

Researchers have previously studied the influence of leadership styles and qualities during crises including charismatic leadership (Pillai, 1996; Bligh et al., 2004; Halverson et al., 2004), transformational leadership (Pillai, 2013), communication (Jin et al., 2017), leaders' emotional expressions (Madera & Smith, 2009), and leaders' perceptions and sensemaking skills (Combe & Carrington, 2015; Weick, 1988). Consideration of mindfulness and how it can inform how individuals work through crisis situations has been slow to develop. To this end, we suggest that leading during a crisis requires leaders to be intentional and present with followers. Being present with followers requires an understanding of the emotions followers may be feeling during a crisis and adjusting their behaviors in order to help followers manage their emotions. In our framework, we suggest that mindful leaders exhibit three sets of leadership behaviors which can reduce the amount of negative affect experienced by their followers.

Mindfulness Theory

With its core roots in Buddhism, mindfulness has largely emerged in the Western world as a treatment for stress within the mindfulness-based stress reduction framework (MBSR; Kabat-Zinn, 2003). Kabat-Zinn notably defined mindfulness as "paying attention in a particular way: on purpose, in the present moment, and nonjudgmentally" (1994, p. 4). Mindfulness has also found its way into the business realm to help address the fast-pace, demanding lifestyle that the working population faces (Good et al., 2016). Recently, researchers have characterized mindfulness as a state which involves both attentional and metacognitive components (Kudesia, 2019; Reina & Kudesia, 2020; Bishop et al., 2004; Glomb et al., 2011; Hafenbrack, 2017). When an individual exhibits a high level of mindfulness, they experience focused attention which is directed toward the present moment rather than past or future-oriented thoughts or feelings. Additionally, they are aware of and able to monitor their attention in a metacognitively detached way such that they are able to observe the thoughts and emotions that occur without getting caught up in them (Reina &

Kudesia, 2020). Put simply, mindfulness involves intentionally paying attention to the present moment which reduces reliance on "autopilot" and brings about a state of being which is less weighed down by emotional and cognitive baggage.

This reduction in autopilot has been suggested to lead to intrapersonal outcomes such as improved emotional regulation (Glomb et al., 2011; Hülsheger et al., 2013), decreased emotional exhaustion (Hülsheger et al., 2013), and decreased rumination (Glomb et al., 2011), but empirical studies addressing the interpersonal outcomes of mindfulness have been slower to accumulate. However, there are some recent examples of research addressing the impact of leader mindfulness on follower outcomes including follower well-being (Pinck & Sonnentag, 2017), follower performance (Reb et al., 2014, 2019), follower attitudes and behaviors (Reb et al., 2014), and follower satisfaction with their leader (Arendt et al., 2019). While this recent literature has begun to study leader mindfulness in relation to follower outcomes, more work is still needed to further explicate the specific interpersonal behaviors of mindful leaders when it comes to helping followers work through difficult emotions. In this chapter, we aim to focus on the interpersonal effects of mindfulness and discuss the specific mechanisms by which leader mindfulness may impact follower affect when dealing with crisis situations.

Theoretical Background

Leader Behaviors: Empathy, Active Listening, and Empowering Leadership

We aim to contribute to the evolving literature on leader mindfulness by proposing a framework of the specific behaviors that leader mindfulness predicts which help leaders more effectively manage follower affect, and we ground our selection of leader behaviors by integrating mindfulness at work theory and research on high-quality connections.

We believe that mindfulness plays a unique role in helping leaders manage follower affect during crisis for three important reasons. First, previous mindfulness research suggests that mindfulness may have a particularly strong influence when employees are going through organizational or work role transitions or challenges (Glomb et al., 2011). For example, COVID-19 presents a transition for many working professionals whether that is virtual work, simultaneously working and caring for children at home, or adjusting to a less social, more isolating work atmosphere. Second, during a radical organizational change, leaders have to manage their own emotions as well as those of their followers, and mindfulness is well-suited in such environments because it increases an individual's tolerance of his or her own negative emotions, as well as others' negative emotions (Glomb et al., 2011).

Finally, mindfulness has been suggested to facilitate interpersonal connections (Glomb et al., 2011) and has important interpersonal effects (Hafenbrack et al., 2020; Jones et al., 2019; Reb et al., 2014, 2018). Though there are many interpersonal mechanisms that may transmit the effects of leader mindfulness to follower outcomes, we first suggest that empathy and active listening are especially valuable. As we detail in the upcoming sections, both empathy and active listening involve nonjudgment and an orientation toward being present with followers which represent core aspects of mindfulness. Empathy requires individuals to take the perspective of another individual (Bar-On & Parker, 2000; Gentry et al., 2016; George, 2000; Goleman, 1995; Salovey & Mayer, 1990), and active listening requires an individual to listen nonjudgmentally to another individual, which complements the notion that mindfulness also involves a sense of nonjudgment towards others. In short, mindfulness allows leaders to detach from their own thoughts and observe others' thoughts, feelings, or behaviors nonjudgmentally to be present with others during challenging times. For these reasons, we suggest that mindfulness with its present-moment and metacognitive components may lead to positive leader behaviors which are especially helpful in managing follower affect during times of crisis.

In addition to mindfulness theory, our framework extends current theorizing on high-quality connections which represent the "cognitive, emotional, and behavioral mechanisms and aspects of the context that build and strength high-quality connections in organizations" (Stephens et al., 2012, p. 1). Researchers have suggested that both empathy and active listening, a form of respectful engagement, are important mechanisms that contribute to high-quality workplace connections (Bernstein, 2003; Dutton, 2003; Dutton & Heaphy, 2003; Stephens et al., 2012). Along with empathy and active listening, we suggest empowering leader behaviors are also important in times of crisis. While the high-quality connections literature has briefly mentioned the importance of empowerment (Dutton & Heaphy, 2003), we suggest that empowering leadership behaviors play a critical role in the development of the leader–follower connection. Together, these three mechanisms (empathy, active listening, and empowerment) have independently been associated with effective leadership and follower outcomes as we discuss in detail below, and we further suggest that each of these behaviors can help increase the quality of interpersonal connection between leaders and followers during a crisis as well.

Leader Empathy

Empathy is defined as the "ability to perceive accurately how another person is feeling" (Levenson & Ruef, 1992, p. 234) and fundamentally contributes to the management of relationships (Khodabakhsh, 2012). Put simply, empathy is the ability to put yourself in someone else's shoes. Due to the notion that effective leadership stems from a strong understanding of follower needs, emotions, and perspectives (Bar-On & Parker, 2000; Gentry et al., 2016; George, 2000; Goleman, 1995; Salovey & Mayer, 1990), leader empathy is a crucial quality in effective leadership. A growing body of literature explores the impact of leader empathy on follower outcomes like performance (Kock et al., 2019) and perceptions of leaders (Bell & Hall, 1954; Kellett et al., 2002, 2006; Meinecke & Kauffeld, 2019; Wolff et al., 2002).

Not only is empathy important in day-to-day leader behavior, but empathy is particularly vital in the context of leadership during a crisis. In line with relevant work by Sergent and Stajkovic (2020), who found that female governors expressed more empathy when addressing the COVID-19 pandemic, we suggest that expressing empathy plays a role in managing follower negative affect induced by COVID-19. To understand followers' crisis-related negative affect, effective leaders should have an understanding of followers' needs, emotions, and perspectives. Leaders who empathize, or intentionally take the perspective of their followers, will then be able to understand the source of the crisis-related negative affect. As a result of empathizing with followers, effective leaders should express behaviors that exhibit concern or acknowledgement of follower emotions to manage followers' negative emotions and ultimately, improve follower work outcomes.

As an example, the abrupt change to virtual work and schooling as a result of COVID-19 may have employees with children feeling particularly stressed in attempts to simultaneously work and care for children at home. If empathizing deeply with followers, leaders may give their followers more flexibility in their working hours due to an understanding of follower stress. As followers perceive higher levels of empathy from their leader, we suggest it will reduce the negative affect experienced by followers and lead to the improvement of follower outcomes such as satisfaction with their leader.

Leader Active Listening

Rogers (1959) characterized active listening as an accepting and nonjudgmental way of attending to another individual. Nonjudgmentally listening to another person allows that person to feel accepted and cared for, which allows for the creation of understanding and trust, two key components of building a relationship (Lloyd et al., 2017; Rogers, 1959). Importantly, active listening involves an emotional support aspect (Jones, 2011). That is, active listening is a "central dyadic mechanism of providing, perceiving, and receiving beneficial emotional support" (Jones, 2011, p. 85). Leader active listening is an approach to respectful engagement by being accepting of, or at least trying to be accepting of, employees' opinions and ideas (Bass & Avolio, 1994; Dutton, 2003; Spears, 1995).

Active listening has important implications for employee outcomes like perceived leadership effectiveness (Johnson & Bechler, 1998), employee commitment (Lobdell et al., 1993), organizational trust and performance (Stine et al., 1995), and fostering leader–member exchange (LMX), job satisfaction, and satisfaction with the leader (Bodie, 2012; Lloyd et al., 2017; Steil & Bommelje, 2004). Leader active listening has yet to receive much empirical or theoretical attention, while more practical leadership handbooks and popular press leadership treatments have suggested that active listening represents a key management skill (Drucker, 2004; Ewing & Banks, 1980). A theoretical basis of leader active listening is crucial to ground these claims (Lloyd et al., 2017). In addition, Fessell et al. (2020) posit that mentors should expect to hear about grief, anxiety, and fear during a crisis, and that the skill of active listening may be an opportunity to develop meaningful connections or to revitalize dormant connections. In line with Lloyd et al. (2017) and Fessell et al.

(2020), we posit that active listening is a valuable way leaders can support followers emotionally (Jones, 2011).

It is important to note that with the COVID-19 crisis, leaders and followers are increasingly communicating via digital platforms, so leader active listening may look different in comparison to face-to-face active listening. The nature of leader active listening on digital platforms has been examined and findings indicate that employees feel heard when they are able to ask questions, that the ability to give anonymous input is an important way to further give employees an opportunity to voice their views, and that employees tend to gauge the quality of leader active listening by the quantity and quality of follow up (or a lack thereof) by their leaders (Cardon et al., 2019). We suggest that leader active listening is an especially effective behavior that allows leaders to emotionally support their followers during the COVID-19 crisis by reducing the negative affect followers experience. In turn, the opportunity for followers to express their voice results in positive follower outcomes like increased engagement (Rees et al., 2013), retention (Spencer, 1986), and organizational commitment (Farndale et al., 2011).

Empowering Leadership

At its core, psychological empowerment reflects individuals' orientations to their work role and reflects four main ideas (Spreitzer, 1995; Thomas & Velthouse, 1990). First, psychological empowerment involves the notion of fit between the requirements of a work role and individuals' values. Second, empowerment involves individuals' self-efficacy, or sense of competence in their work role. Third, the degree to which individuals feel they are able to make their own decisions and regulate their actions informs their level of perceived empowerment. Finally, psychological empowerment reflects individuals' ability to make an impact on their work outcomes. Researchers have empirically studied empowering leader behaviors and linked them to employee job performance (Hill et al., 2014; Liden et al., 2000), job satisfaction (Hill et al., 2014; Seibert et al., 2011), and decreased strain (Seibert et al., 2011).

Within the context of COVID-19, we consider the common case that followers may feel stressed due to lower productivity levels. Data show that "62% of workers reported losing at least one hour of productivity due to COVID-19 related stress, with 32% losing more than two hours per day" (Kathryn, 2020). Leading during a crisis requires that leaders empower followers to remain productive during COVID-19 despite the increased distractions, levels of stress, and shift in communication medium. Further, given that previous research shows that leaders play a vital role in ensuring follower empowerment when there is a high need for electronic communication (Hill et al., 2014), we posit that COVID-19 is a crisis scenario in which empowering leadership behaviors will be especially beneficial for followers. We suggest that leaders who engage in a high degree of communication expressing empowering behaviors will amplify follower psychological empowerment and thus reduce negative affect and improve positive follower outcomes (Hill et al., 2014).

Discussion

We expect leader mindfulness to play a unique role during a crisis by encouraging the three positive leader behaviors of empathy, active listening, and empowering leadership. While some research has previously considered these relationships (mindfulness and empathy: Jones et al., 2019; Walsh, 2008; Winning & Boag, 2015; and mindfulness and active listening: Jones et al., 2019), exploring these relationships empirically within the context of crisis situations is an important area for future work.

Leader mindfulness should enhance leaders' abilities to express empathy. In doing so, mindfulness operates by encouraging leaders to step back from their own perspective and judgment. By removing oneself from their thoughts, feelings, and actions, mindful leaders are better able to step into the position of their followers. Only then will leaders be able to express empathy, by exhibiting concern and acknowledgement of followers' crisis-related affect nonjudgmentally. Leader mindfulness will also support the management of follower emotions through the process of active listening. If leaders are mindful, they will detach from their own thoughts and feelings and take a nonjudgmental, intentional approach to actively listening to their followers. Leaders can then immerse themselves in their follower's experience, thoughts, and feelings to understand the crisis-related negative affect. Active listening is a way of providing emotional support to followers and is a crucial leader behavior in managing affect. Finally, mindfulness will encourage leaders to psychologically empower their followers. Mindful leaders will better understand the heightened affect than non-mindful leaders that comes while working during a crisis. Mindful leaders will also better manage follower affect by intentionally expressing empowering behaviors in order to increase follower psychological empowerment. If followers are psychologically empowered, they will feel a higher sense of competence in their job and in their abilities to impact their own work outcomes which will reduce feelings of negative affect.

It is important to note that the degree of negative affect felt among followers is likely to vary. Mindful leaders will recognize that not all followers require the same amount of empathy, active listening, or empowerment. Rather, it depends on the severity of each follower's negative affect. Mindfulness will allow leaders to make this distinction between followers because leaders can detach from their own thoughts and feelings and attend to each follower individually. In addition, mindful leaders will also recognize that follower negative affect is likely to vary between phases of change in response to a crisis. Some followers may feel the highest amount of negative emotions immediately after a crisis or change event occurs, whereas other followers may experience higher levels of negative affect as the crisis situation continues to emerge. Because more mindful leaders are able to put themselves in their followers' shoes over time and across changing situations, they will have an understanding of the degree of negative affect being experienced by each follower and can thus accordingly express the necessary amount of empathy, active listening, and empowering leadership appropriate to best help each follower.

It is also important to remember that because mindfulness is a state of being that can vary moment to moment, it may be challenging for leaders to maintain high levels of mindfulness, in general, and especially as they themselves navigate the stress and strain associated with living through a crisis event. It follows that leaders' ability to express positive behaviors to support their followers will be dependent on their level of mindfulness in a given moment. In other words, as leaders' mindfulness varies, their positive interpersonal behaviors expressed to followers may vary as well. However, we suggest that more mindful leaders as opposed to those leaders who exhibit lower levels of mindfulness will be better able to attend to each interaction with their followers in order to best support them and help them manage their negative emotions associated with the crisis scenario.

Limitations and Suggestions for Future Research

Our framework advances a conceptual understanding of the relationship of leader mindfulness and follower outcomes as it pertains to a crisis situation. It is our goal to reinforce and begin the conversation in this space, and it is our hope that researchers continue to contribute to this space. As scholars have recently noted, a comprehensive mindfulness theory is still needed in order to ground empirical research on leader mindfulness (Reb et al., 2020), and we suggest that an overarching theory of mindful leadership in crisis would also further contribute to important work in this area. In this paper, we integrate crisis leadership with mindfulness theory utilizing the literature on high-quality connections to holistically ground our framework. Although we believe that empathy, active listening, and empowerment represent three key outcomes of mindful leadership which are especially useful in allowing managers to help employees deal with crisis situations, there are other leader behaviors that could also manage follower affect that future researchers could explore. Examples of other potentially relevant mediators include psychological flexibility and paradoxical leader behaviors. Furthermore, beyond the indirect effects of leader mindfulness on follower outcomes via leader empathy, active listening, and empowering leadership, future researchers could explore the possibility of leader mindfulness also directly impacting follower outcomes. However, to further our understanding of the impacts of leader mindfulness, more work is needed to empirically test these indirect and direct relationships of leader mindfulness on follower outcomes.

In addition, Kiefer (2002) further suggested that rather than categorizing emotions as good or bad, which is an overly simplistic approach to understanding emotions, that it would be more beneficial to understand discrete emotions such as fear or joy (Gooty et al., 2010) because specific emotions arise from various aspects of change and are likely to result in different behaviors on the change process. Although out of the scope of our current manuscript, we recommend researchers in the future to explore the leader's role of managing the various types of negative affect (stress, fear, anger) in times of a crisis.

Future researchers should consider the challenge of empirically testing this framework considering the rare frequency and unexpected nature of crises. Accurately capturing follower affect during crisis situations ideally would include data from before the crisis occurs, include multiple data points during the crisis, and also include data points after the crisis period had concluded, which often may not be feasible. Alternatively, researchers can further test these relationships in a laboratory setting or work with organizations to gather data before, during, and after an anticipated period of change. Future researchers should also account for follower affect and leader mindfulness fluctuations. We suggest that future researchers consider longitudinal and/or an experience sampling methodologies to reduce recall bias and to best capture the fluctuations of the variables of interest over time. Our framework assumes that crisis situations induce negative follower affect, and we also suggest that follower affect demonstrates considerable between and within-person variance over time. Future researchers should design studies which collect both within and between-person data, as well as consider follower positive and negative affectivity in tandem to better understand how affect unfolds during a crisis. These study designs will also be beneficial to further develop our understanding of fluctuations in leader mindfulness and leader behaviors according to their understanding of follower emotions over time. Finally, to reduce the likelihood of common method bias, leaders should self-report their own levels of mindfulness and followers should report leader behaviors. A combination of objective measurements as well as subjective measurements (both leader and follower-rated) would further help strengthen further empirical studies considering these variables of interest.

Practical Implications

Many organizations have begun to offer mindfulness training for employees as a result of the intrapersonal effects of mindfulness (Hafenbrack et al., 2020), but the current chapter reinforces the need to further consider the relational effects of mindfulness. As research continues to develop in this space, organizations should consider investing further in leader mindfulness training. In addition, organizations should consider developing and implementing training which reinforces behaviors associated with empathy, active listening, and empowerment in general, as well as during crisis situations in particular.

Conclusion

Our framework serves to advance mindfulness theory as it pertains to leader mindfulness. We proposed that leaders who are more mindful will exhibit more empathy, active listening, and empowering leadership and we explored these relationships within the context of the COVID-19 crisis. When followers receive higher amount of these three leader behaviors, we suggest that their perceptions of negative affect will decrease and thus lead to positive outcomes such as job satisfaction, satisfaction with the leader, higher leader–follower relationship quality, and job performance. We hope that research considering how leaders can help followers manage affect during a crisis continues to gain research traction, as leading effectively during crises is vital to organization well-being and performance.

Chapter Takeaways

1. Past scholars have acknowledged the consequences of negative affect in the workplace but have not explained how exactly leaders can more effectively manage follower negative affect. We build a model of mindful leadership in a crisis that aims to explain the underlying mechanisms by which a leader's mindfulness may impact follower outcomes.
2. Leader mindfulness contributes to leaders exhibiting higher levels of empathy, active listening, and empowering leadership. This occurs because mindfulness encourages leaders not to get caught up in their own mind and emotions, allowing leaders to be more present and connected with their followers.
3. The far-reaching implications of the COVID-19 pandemic have presented an opportunity for leaders to help followers manage negative emotions more effectively and represent an especially instructive example of how leader mindfulness can benefit organizational employees.
4. Negative affect experienced during a crisis will likely vary over time and mindful leaders will be especially able to recognize and adapt their behaviors to meet followers' needs throughout the duration of a crisis event.
5. Future researchers should consider longitudinal and/or an experience sampling method (ESM) designs that capture data from both followers and leaders. These designs will reduce recall bias and capture fluctuations in leader mindfulness and behaviors over time in order to more rigorously link these fluctuations to follower emotional states and outcomes ideally before, during, and after crisis situations.

Reflection Questions

1. Why is follower negative affect important for leaders to address during a crisis?
2. Why is leader mindfulness particularly important in the context of crisis leadership?
3. What are some strengths and weaknesses of the proposed framework?
4. How does the proposed framework advance extant mindfulness theory? How does it advance the high-quality relationships and positive organizational behavior literatures?
5. How could management consultants and leaders utilize the proposed model in guiding an organization through change?

References

Anicich, E. M., Foulk, T. A., Osborne, M. R., Gale, J., & Schaerer, M. (2020). Getting back to the "new normal": Autonomy restoration during a global pandemic. *Journal of Applied Psychology, 105*(9), 931–943. https://doi.org/10.1037/apl0000655

Arendt, J. F. W., Pircher Verdorfer, A., & Kugler, K. G. (2019). Mindfulness and leadership: Communication as a behavioral correlate of leader mindfulness and its effect on follower satisfaction. *Frontiers in Psychology, 10*, 667. https://doi.org/10.3389/fpsyg.2019.00667

Bar-On, R., & Parker, J. D. A. (2000). *The handbook of emotional intelligence: Theory, development, assessment, and application at home, school, and in the workplace* (pp. xv, 528). Jossey-Bass.

Bass, B. M., & Avolio, B. J. (Eds.). (1994). *Improving organizational effectiveness through transformational leadership*. Sage.

Bell, G. B., & Hall, H. E., Jr. (1954). The relationship between leadership and empathy. *The Journal of Abnormal and Social Psychology, 49*(1), 156–157. https://doi.org/10.1037/h0053927

Bernstein, S. D. (2003). Positive organizational scholarship: Meet the movement: An interview with Kim Cameron, Jane Dutton, and Robert Quinn. *Journal of Management Inquiry, 12*(3), 266–271. https://doi.org/10.1177/1056492603256341

Bishop, S. R., Lau, M., Shapiro, S., Carlson, L., Anderson, N. D., Carmody, J., Segal, Z. V., Abbey, S., Speca, M., Velting, D., & Devins, G. (2004). Mindfulness: A proposed operational definition. *Clinical Psychology: Science and Practice, 11*(3), 230–241. https://doi.org/10.1093/clipsy.bph077

Bligh, M. C., Kohles, J. C., & Meindl, J. R. (2004). Charisma under crisis: Presidential leadership, rhetoric, and media responses before and after the September 11th terrorist attacks. *The Leadership Quarterly, 15*(2), 211–239. https://doi.org/10.1016/j.leaqua.2004.02.005

Bodie, G. D. (2012). Listening as positive communication. In *The positive side of interpersonal communication* (pp. 109–125).

Busseri, M. A. (2018). Examining the structure of subjective well-being through meta-analysis of the associations among positive affect, negative affect, and life satisfaction. *Personality and Individual Differences, 122*, 68–71. https://doi.org/10.1016/j.paid.2017.10.003

Cameron, K. S., & Caza, A. (2004). Introduction: Contributions to the discipline of positive organizational scholarship. *American Behavioral Scientist, 47*(6), 731–739.

Cardon, P. W., Huang, Y., & Power, G. (2019). Leadership communication on internal digital platforms, emotional capital, and corporate performance: The case for leader-centric listening. *International Journal of Business Communication*. https://doi.org/10.1177/2329488419828808

Combe, I. A., & Carrington, D. J. (2015). Leaders' sensemaking under crises: Emerging cognitive consensus over time within management teams. *The Leadership Quarterly, 26*(3), 307–322. https://doi.org/10.1016/j.leaqua.2015.02.002

Conger, J. A., Kanungo, R. N., & Menon, S. T. (2000). Charismatic leadership and follower effects. *Journal of Organizational Behavior, 21*(7), 747–767. https://doi.org/10.1002/1099-1379(200011)21:7<747::AID-JOB46>3.0.CO;2-J

Drucker, P. F. (2004). What makes an effective executive? *Harvard Business Review, 82*(6), 58–63.

Dutton, J. E. (2003). *Energize your workplace: How to create and sustain high-quality connections at work* (Vol. 50). Wiley.

Dutton, J. E., & Heaphy, E. D. (2003). The power of high-quality connections. *Positive organizational scholarship: Foundations of a new discipline, 3*, 263–278.

Dutton, J. E., & Ragins, B. R. (2007). Moving forward: Positive relationships at work as a research frontier. In J. E. Dutton & B. R. Ragins (Eds.), *Exploring positive relationships at work: Building a theoretical and research foundation* (pp. 387–400). Lawrence Erlbaum.

Ewing, D., & Banks, P. (1980). Listening and responding to employees' concerns. *Harvard Business Review, 58*(1), 101–114.

Farndale, E., Van Ruiten, J., Kelliher, C., & Hope-Hailey, V. (2011). The influence of perceived employee voice on organizational commitment: An exchange perspective. *Human Resource Management, 50*(1), 113–129.

Fessell, D. P., Chopra, V., & Saint, S. (2020, October 29). Mentoring during a crisis. *Harvard Business Review*. https://hbr.org/2020/10/mentoring-during-a-crisis

Garcia, H. F. (2006). Effective leadership response to crisis. *Strategy & Leadership, 34*, 4–10. https://doi.org/10.1108/10878570610637849

Gentry, W., Weber, T., Center for Creative Leadership, Golnaz, S., & Teachers College. (2016). *Empathy in the workplace: A tool for effective leadership*. Center for Creative Leadership. https://doi.org/10.35613/ccl.2016.1070

George, J. M. (2000). Emotions and leadership: The role of emotional intelligence. *Human Relations, 53*(8), 1027–1055. https://doi.org/10.1177/0018726700538001
Glomb, T. M., Duffy, M. K., Bono, J. E., & Yang, T. (2011). Mindfulness at work. In A. Joshi, H. Liao, & J. J. Martocchio (Eds.), *Research in personnel and human resources management* (Vol. 30, pp. 115–157). Emerald Group. https://doi.org/10.1108/S0742-7301(2011)0000030005
Goleman, D. (1995). *Emotional intelligence*. Bantam Books.
Good, D. J., Lyddy, C. J., Glomb, T. M., Bono, J. E., Brown, K. W., Duffy, M. K., … Lazar, S. W. (2016). Contemplating mindfulness at work: An integrative review. *Journal of Management, 42*(1), 114–142. https://doi.org/10.1177/0149206315617003
Gooty, J., Connelly, S., Griffith, J., & Gupta, A. (2010). Leadership, affect and emotions: A state of the science review. *The Leadership Quarterly, 21*(6), 979–1004. https://doi.org/10.1016/j.leaqua.2010.10.005
Hafenbrack, A. C. (2017). Mindfulness meditation as an on-the-spot workplace intervention. *Journal of Business Research, 75*, 118–129. https://doi.org/10.1016/j.jbusres.2017.01.017
Hafenbrack, A. C., Cameron, L. D., Spreitzer, G. M., Zhang, C., Noval, L. J., & Shaffakat, S. (2020). Helping people by being in the present: Mindfulness increases prosocial behavior. *Organizational Behavior and Human Decision Processes, 159*, 21–38. https://doi.org/10.1016/j.obhdp.2019.08.005
Halverson, S. K., Murphy, S. E., & Riggio, R. E. (2004). Charismatic leadership in crisis situations: A laboratory investigation of stress and crisis. *Small Group Research, 35*(5), 495–514.
Hill, N. S., Kang, J. H., & Seo, M. G. (2014). The interactive effect of leader–member exchange and electronic communication on employee psychological empowerment and work outcomes. *The Leadership Quarterly, 25*(4), 772–783. https://doi.org/10.1016/j.leaqua.2014.04.006
Hogan, E. A., & Overmyer-Day, L. (1994). The psychology of mergers and acquisitions. *International Review of Industrial and Organizational Psychology, 9*, 247–247.
Hülsheger, U., Alberts, H., Feinholdt, A., & Lang, J. (2013). Benefits of mindfulness at work: The role of mindfulness in emotion regulation, emotional exhaustion, and job satisfaction. *The Journal of Applied Psychology, 98*(2), 310. https://doi.org/10.1037/a0031313
Hunt, J. G., Boal, K. B., & Dodge, G. E. (1999). The effects of visionary and crisis-responsive charisma on followers: An experimental examination of two kinds of charismatic leadership. *The Leadership Quarterly, 10*(3), 423–448. https://doi.org/10.1016/S1048-9843(99)00027-2
James, E. H., & Wooten, L. P. (2005). Leadership as (un)usual. *Organizational Dynamics, 34*(2), 141–152. https://doi.org/10.1016/j.orgdyn.2005.03.005
James, E. H., Wooten, L. P., & Dushek, K. (2011). Crisis management: Informing a new leadership research agenda. *Academy of Management Annals, 5*(1), 455–493. https://doi.org/10.5465/19416520.2011.589594
Jin, Y., Meng, J., & Berger, B. (2017). The influence of communication leadership qualities on effective crisis preparedness strategy implementation: Insights from a global study. *Communication Management Review, 02*(01), 8–29. https://doi.org/10.22522/cmr20170118
Johnson, S. D., & Bechler, C. (1998). Examining the relationship between listening effectiveness and leadership emergence: Perceptions, behaviors, and recall. *Small Group Research, 29*(4), 452–471. https://doi.org/10.1177/1046496498294003
Jones, S. M. (2011). Supportive listening. *International Journal of Listening, 25*(1–2), 85–103. https://doi.org/10.1080/10904018.2011.536475
Jones, S. M., Bodie, G. D., & Hughes, S. D. (2019). The impact of mindfulness on empathy, active listening, and perceived provisions of emotional support. *Communication Research, 46*(6), 838–865. https://doi.org/10.1177/0093650215626983
Kabat-Zinn, J. (2003). Mindfulness-based stress reduction (MBSR). *Constructivism in the Human Sciences, 8*(2), 73.
Kabat-Zinn, J. (1994). *Wherever you go, there you are: Mindfulness meditation in everyday life*. Hachette Books.
Kathryn, M. (2020, April 14). *Employee stress levels caused by COVID19*. Human Resource Executive. https://hrexecutive.com/hres-number-of-the-day-coronavirus-stress/

Kellett, J. B., Humphrey, R. H., & Sleeth, R. G. (2002). Empathy and complex task performance: Two routes to leadership. *The Leadership Quarterly, 13*(5), 523–544. https://doi.org/10.1016/S1048-9843(02)00142-X

Kellett, J. B., Humphrey, R. H., & Sleeth, R. G. (2006). Empathy and the emergence of task and relations leaders. *The Leadership Quarterly, 17*(2), 146–162. https://doi.org/10.1016/j.leaqua.2005.12.003

Khodabakhsh, M. (2012). Attachment styles as predictors of empathy in nursing students. *Journal of Medical Ethics and History of Medicine, 5*, 8.

Kiefer, T. (2002). Analyzing emotions for a better understanding of organizational change: Fear, joy, and anger during a merger. In N. M. Ashkanasy, W. J. Zerbe, & C. E. Härtel (Eds.), *Managing emotions in the workplace* (pp. 45–69). ME Sharpe.

Kock, N., Mayfield, M., Mayfield, J., Sexton, S., & De La Garza, L. M. (2019). Empathetic leadership: How leader emotional support and understanding influences follower performance. *Journal of Leadership & Organizational Studies, 26*(2), 217–236. https://doi.org/10.1177/1548051818806290

Kudesia, R. S. (2019). Mindfulness as metacognitive practice. *Academy of Management Review, 44*(2), 405–423. https://doi.org/10.5465/amr.2015.0333

Lee, K., & Allen, N. J. (2002). Organizational citizenship behavior and workplace deviance: The role of affect and cognitions. *Journal of Applied Psychology, 87*(1), 131–142. https://doi.org/10.1037/0021-9010.87.1.131

Levenson, R. W., & Ruef, A. M. (1992). Empathy: A physiological substrate. *Journal of Personality and Social Psychology, 63*(2), 234–246. https://doi.org/10.1037/0022-3514.63.2.234

Liden, R., Wayne, S., & Sparrowe, R. (2000). An examination of the mediating role of psychological empowerment on the relations between the job, interpersonal relationships, and work outcomes. *The Journal of Applied Psychology, 85*, 407–416. https://doi.org/10.1037/0021-9010.85.3.407

Lloyd, K. J., Boer, D., & Voelpel, S. C. (2017). From listening to leading: Toward an understanding of supervisor listening within the framework of leader-member exchange theory. *International Journal of Business Communication, 54*(4), 431–451. https://doi.org/10.1177/2329488415572778

Lobdell, C. L., Sonoda, K. T., & Arnold, W. E. (1993). The influence of perceived supervisor listening behavior on employee commitment. *International Listening Association Journal, 7*(1), 92–110. https://doi.org/10.1080/10904018.1993.10499116

Madera, J. M., & Smith, D. B. (2009). The effects of leader negative emotions on evaluations of leadership in a crisis situation: The role of anger and sadness. *The Leadership Quarterly, 20*(2), 103–114. https://doi.org/10.1016/j.leaqua.2009.01.007

Marks, M. L., & Mirvis, P. H. (1992). Rebuilding after the Merger: Dealing with "survivor sickness". *Organizational Dynamics, 21*(2), 18–32. https://doi.org/10.1016/0090-2616(92)90061-Q

Meinecke, A. L., & Kauffeld, S. (2019). Engaging the hearts and minds of followers: Leader empathy and language style matching during appraisal interviews. *Journal of Business and Psychology, 34*(4), 485–501. https://doi.org/10.1007/s10869-018-9554-9

Mumford, M. D., Friedrich, T. L., Caughron, J. J., & Byrne, C. L. (2007). Leader cognition in real-world settings: How do leaders think about crises? *The Leadership Quarterly, 18*(6), 515–543. https://doi.org/10.1016/j.leaqua.2007.09.002

Niklas, C. D., & Dormann, C. (2005). The impact of state affect on job satisfaction. *European Journal of Work and Organizational Psychology, 14*(4), 367–388. https://doi.org/10.1080/13594320500348880

Pearson, C. M., & Clair, J. A. (1998). Reframing crisis management. *The Academy of Management Review, 23*(1), 59–76. https://doi.org/10.2307/259099

Pietromonaco, P. R., & Overall, N. C. (2020). Applying relationship science to evaluate how the COVID-19 pandemic may impact couples' relationships. *American Psychologist, 76*, 438–450. https://doi.org/10.1037/amp0000714

Pillai, R. (1996). Crisis and the emergence of charismatic leadership in groups: An experimental investigation. *Journal of Applied Social Psychology, 26*(6), 543–562. https://doi.org/10.1111/j.1559-1816.1996.tb02730.x

Pillai, R. (2013). Transformational leadership for crisis management. In *Handbook of research on crisis leadership in organizations*. https://www.elgaronline.com/view/edcoll/9781781006399/9781781006399.00011.xml

Pinck, A., & Sonnentag, S. (2017). Leader mindfulness and employee well-being: The mediating role of transformational leadership. *Mindfulness, 9*, 884–896. https://doi.org/10.1007/s12671-017-0828-5

Ragins, B. R., & Button, J. E. (2007). Positive relationships at work: An introduction and invitation. In *In exploring positive relationships at work: Building a theoretical and research foundation* (pp. 3–25). Lawrence Erlbaum.

Reb, J., Narayanan, J., & Chaturvedi, S. (2014). Leading mindfully: Two studies on the influence of supervisor trait mindfulness on employee well-being and performance. *Mindfulness, 5*(1), 36–45. https://doi.org/10.1007/s12671-012-0144-z

Reb, J., Chaturvedi, S., Narayanan, J., & Kudesia, R. S. (2018). Leader mindfulness and employee performance: A sequential mediation model of LMX quality, interpersonal justice, and employee stress. *Journal of Business Ethics, 160*(3), 745–763. https://doi.org/10.1007/s10551-018-3927-x

Reb, J., Allen, T., & Vogus, T. J. (2020). Mindfulness arrives at work: Deepening our understanding of mindfulness in organizations. *Organizational Behavior and Human Decision Processes, 159*, 1–7. https://doi.org/10.1016/j.obhdp.2020.04.001

Reb, J., Chaturvedi, S., Narayanan, J., & Kudesia, R. S. (2019). Leader mindfulness and employee performance: A sequential mediation model of LMX quality, interpersonal justice, and employee stress. Journal of Business Ethics, 160(3), 745–763.

Rees, C., Alfes, K., & Gatenby, M. (2013). Employee voice and engagement: Connections and consequences. *The International Journal of Human Resource Management, 24*(14), 2780–2798.

Reina, C. S., & Kudesia, R. S. (2020). Wherever you go, there you become: How mindfulness arises in everyday situations. *Organizational Behavior and Human Decision Processes, 159*, 78–96. https://doi.org/10.1016/j.obhdp.2019.11.008

Rogers, C. R. (1959). *A theory of therapy, personality, and interpersonal relationships: As developed in the client-centered framework* (Vol. 3, pp. 184–256). McGraw-Hill.

Salovey, P., & Mayer, J. D. (1990). Emotional intelligence. *Imagination, Cognition and Personality, 9*(3), 185–211. https://doi.org/10.2190/DUGG-P24E-52WK-6CDG

Seibert, S., Wang, G., & Courtright, S. (2011). Antecedents and consequences of psychological and team empowerment in organizations: A meta-analytic review. *The Journal of Applied Psychology, 96*, 981–1003. https://doi.org/10.1037/a0022676

Sergent, K., & Stajkovic, A. D. (2020). Women's leadership is associated with fewer deaths during the COVID-19 crisis: Quantitative and qualitative analyses of United States governors. *Journal of Applied Psychology, 105*(8), 771. https://doi.org/10.1037/apl0000577

Shockley, K. M., Ispas, D., Rossi, M. E., & Levine, E. L. (2012). A meta-analytic investigation of the relationship between state affect, discrete emotions, and job performance. *Human Performance, 25*(5), 377–411. https://doi.org/10.1080/08959285.2012.721832

Sonnentag, S., & Binnewies, C. (2013). Daily affect spillover from work to home: Detachment from work and sleep as moderators. *Journal of Vocational Behavior, 83*(2), 198–208. https://doi.org/10.1016/j.jvb.2013.03.008

Spears, L. C. (1995). *Reflections on leadership: How Robert K. Greenleaf's theory of servant-leadership influenced today's top management thinkers (no. 658.4092 R333r)*. Wiley.

Spencer, D. G. (1986). Employee voice and employee retention. *Academy of Management Journal, 29*(3), 488–502.

Spreitzer, G. M. (1995). Psychological empowerment in the workplace: Dimensions, measurement, and validation. *Academy of Management Journal, 38*(5), 1442–1465. https://doi.org/10.5465/256865

Spreitzer, G. M., Janasz, S. C. D., & Quinn, R. E. (1999). Empowered to lead: The role of psychological empowerment in leadership. *Journal of Organizational Behavior, 20*(4), 511–526. https://doi.org/10.1002/(SICI)1099-1379(199907)20:4<511::AID-JOB900>3.0.CO;2-L

Steil, L. K., & Bommelje, R. K. (2004). *Listening leaders: The ten golden rules to listen, lead & succeed.* Beaver's Pond Press.

Stephens, J. P., Heaphy, E., & Dutton, J. E. (2012). High-quality connections. In *The Oxford handbook of positive organizational scholarship* (pp. 385–399). Oxford University Press.

Stine, M., Thompson, T., & Cusella, L. (1995). The impact of organizational structure and supervisory listening indicators on subordinate support, trust, intrinsic motivation, and performance. *International Journal of Listening, 9*(1), 84–105. https://doi.org/10.1080/10904018.1995.10499143

Thomas, K. W., & Velthouse, B. A. (1990). Cognitive elements of empowerment: An "interpretive" model of intrinsic task motivation. *Academy of Management Review, 15*(4), 666–681. https://doi.org/10.5465/amr.1990.4310926

Tushman, M. L., & O'Reilly, C. A. (1996). Ambidextrous organizations: Managing evolutionary and revolutionary change. *California Management Review, 38*(4), 8–29. https://doi.org/10.2307/41165852

Walsh, R. A. (2008). Mindfulness and empathy. In *Mindfulness and the therapeutic relationship* (pp. 72–86).

Watson, D., Clark, L. A., & Tellegen, A. (1988). Development and validation of brief measures of positive and negative affect: The PANAS scales. *Journal of Personality and Social Psychology, 54*(6), 1063–1070. https://doi.org/10.1037/0022-3514.54.6.1063

Weick, K. E. (1988). Enacted sensemaking in crisis situations. *Journal of Management Studies, 25*(4), 305–317. https://doi.org/10.1111/j.1467-6486.1988.tb00039.x

Winning, A. P., & Boag, S. (2015). Does brief mindfulness training increase empathy? The role of personality. *Personality and Individual Differences, 86*, 492–498. https://doi.org/10.1016/j.paid.2015.07.011

Wolff, S. B., Pescosolido, A. T., & Druskat, V. U. (2002). Emotional intelligence as the basis of leadership emergence in self-managing teams. *The Leadership Quarterly, 13*(5), 505–522. https://doi.org/10.1016/S1048-9843(02)00141-8

Alisha Gupta is a doctoral student at Virginia Commonwealth University (VCU) where she is pursuing a PhD in Business with a concentration in Management. Her research interests are mindfulness and emotions in the workplace.

Christopher S. Reina is an Associate Professor in the Department of Management and Entrepreneurship at VCU and the Founder and President of Leading Without Ego, LLC. He consults and leads trainings on mindfulness and mindful leadership. His research focuses on the intersection of leadership, mindfulness, and emotions in the workplace and how they bring about employee and organizational well-being. Christopher received his Ph.D. in Business Administration from the W. P. Carey School of Business at Arizona State University and he has extensive industry experience in leadership training and development as well as sales and marketing in the healthcare and food industries. His research has been featured in such outlets as *Harvard Business Review, Leadership Quarterly, Organizational Behavior and Human Decision Processes, Journal of Applied Psychology, Organization Science,* and he is an author of several book chapters on the topics of mindfulness, emotions, and neuroscience.

Post-Pandemic Crisis: Global Leadership and Our New Food Emergency

17

H. Eric Schockman and Anita Ravani

Introduction

This chapter is written in the hopeful twilight of the COVID-19 pandemic, with several highly effective vaccines in the pipeline being readied to release worldwide. Simultaneously, we witness the cruelty and injustice of "vaccine nationalism"transpiring where rich countries (Britain, European Union, USA) are putting the emerging countries at the back of the line for distribution, potentially costing further untold global carnage. COVID-19 has represented an exogenous shock to every institution and system worldwide, especially the already under threat of food systems before the pandemic. Let us be clear: there is no vaccine for global hunger and food insecurity. Hunger and malnutrition (even before COVID-19) have been increasing due to degradation of natural resources, overall climate change, conflicts and wars, rising inequality, producing an estimated total of 842 million individuals suffering from chronic hunger (FAO, 2013) and in developing countries almost five million children under the age of five dying from malnutrition-related causes every year (FAO, 2012). Global food prices and inflation for essential commodities have been rising over the past 5 years. While conflicts and environmental destabilization are major contributing causes, the pandemic has exposed glaring holes in our food supply chain. Public expenditure on agriculture has been stagnant. UN data suggests that relative spending on agriculture compared with the sector's contribution to the GDP of many countries has declined globally since the early 2000s (Economist, 2019). The pandemic has made our food systems more

H. E. Schockman (✉)
Woodbury University, Burbank, CA, USA
e-mail: eric.schockman@woodbury.edu

A. Ravani
Pepperdine University, Malibu, CA, USA
e-mail: anita.ravani@pepperdine.edu

S. K. Dhiman, J. F. Marques (eds.), *Leadership After COVID-19*, Future of Business and Finance, https://doi.org/10.1007/978-3-030-84867-5_17

vulnerable and has provided a wake-up call for how global leaders should be thinking about how future food chain supply systems should be constructed.

The question begs itself for an answer: if people around the globe are dying not only of the coronavirus but also hunger/food insecurity, what does the future of global leadership look like? We know from past global disasters that crisis leadership has manifested itself, at least for short-term fixes. However, we need to explore what internal elements sustain crisis leaders and how can these skills/traits/competencies translate into tangible solutions in solving the worsening global food emergency in both the developed and the developing worlds. The conundrum we believe can be unraveled by bifurcating our analysis into two dimensions: a deep-dive into crisis leadership competencies and then determining how these may or not apply to more equitable global food distribution. We see this imbroglio situation creating greater opacity in what composites the global agricultural food supply chain (AFSC) and its two main variables: food availability (production) and food accessibility (price and inflation). We will examine two diametrically opposite country case studies: India (primarily) and the USA (more cursory) and identify the systemic system flaws in the existing AFSC and recommendations for holistic policy solutions of crisis leadership competencies for the future governance in both the private and public sectors.

Crisis Global Leader Competencies

Crisis global leader (CGL) competencies are immediately available and established traits practical and actively usable in an agile global business and public sector environment. CGLs possess the ability to successfully manage change, maintain and build relationships with stakeholders, and implement strategies on the global stage (Caligiuri, 2006; Caligiuri & Cascio, 1998; Petrick et al., 1999; Pless et al., 2011). A wide-ranging agile skillset must be fully developed in the CGL's cache to fight a wide array of abstruse and crisis laden environments. CGL competencies are a leader's skillsets to enact and facilitate positive results (Anderson, 2005; Mendenhall & Stevens, 2017). Effective CGLs have intelligent relationship aptitude, which is the ability to understand diverse cultures (and micro-cultures) and the talent to build trusting relationships through social acumen.

The ambiguity in global business and government creates an extremely challenging environment for leaders during times of crisis. The cyclical and magnitude increase in terrorism, natural disasters, and ethical and moral violations have been a serious concern to manage. Crisis management has become a critical component for success in both the private and public sectors. The skillsets of a CGL consist of several wide-ranging competencies. Chaudhuri and Alagaraja (2014) posit that global leaders have to perform in a complex and unpredictable global environment. Adaptation to new cultural values, proactive learning, intellect, charisma, and the ability to build social relationships are important competency skills needed for global leaders to be successful. In the private sector, crisis management has become a part of the business landscape due to widespread events such as recalls, corporate fraud, and natural disasters (Thomas et al., 2013). Historically firms have experienced long-term reputational and profitability risks when the crisis is not managed well. Crisis management requires the integration of skills, abilities, and leadership traits to plan, respond, and learn from crisis events, even when under high levels of security and ambiguity. Crisis leadership competencies (Ivy, 2017; Caligiuri, 2006; Maznevski & DiStefano, 2000; Twomey & Twomey, 2008; Kim & McLean, 2015) encompass: personal competencies (*adaptation; emotional awareness; resilience);* professional competencies (*ambiguity; collaboration; communication; conflict management; innovation);* and social competencies (*cultural acceptance; cultural integration; cultural intelligence (CQ)).*

The Global AFSC and COVID-19

COVID-19 has been a major unprecedented disruptor in food supply chains: it has been both global in scope and lasted longer than past disruptions (for example, in the global financial collapse in 2008, food price spikes in 2007–2008, and the SARS pandemic in 2003). Its impact has been disproportional as well: in both developing and developed countries, the poorer, marginal classes have seen dramatic spikes in securing nutritious food (as well as suffering disproportionately higher COVID-19 case infections and deaths). Food supply chains, especially in the developing world (India), have been impacted severely since their traditional infrastructural food systems depend on labor-intensive (vs. capital-intensive) arrangements meaning that rural migrants, day-laborers, small farmers, women have less capacity to cope and remain afloat. Compound to this is a lack of demand as global trade patterns have been altered, and there are also logistical challenges, access to markets, finance, etc. India, for the record, has the largest malnourished and hungry population on the planet (India Food Bank, 2020). Whereas in the more developed world, the pandemic has caused less dislocation on the (food availability) production side (with minor shortage inconveniences of such non-food commodities as toilet paper and cleaning supplies or an occasional meat disruption as workers in slaughter plants became infected). However, there has been massive angst on the food accessibility-side. In contrast, in the USA, nearly 26 million adults—12% of all adults in the country reported struggling to put food on their tables (CBPP, 2010). The pandemic's food insecurity impact in the USA has fallen disproportionately among poor, Black, Latinx, Indigenous, and immigrant households.

The confluence of a global pandemic, crisis leadership (or lack thereof), and rising global hunger are essentially the variables that impact the global AFSC. This might raise another existential question: haven't we been here before? Can history shed any light on how previous pandemics were handled and how previous societies and their leaders responded? Most scholars would reach back to the Bubonic Plague or the Spanish Influenza of 1918 for some guidance. We instead decided to reach back even further during the Western civilized world's formation to: The Plague of Athens (around 430 BC.)

Ancient Greek Plagues: Back to the Future

According to Thompson (2020), reports of the Plague of Athens were local and concentrated within a single city-state, but it was nonetheless a global pandemic. The Peloponnesian War was winding down, as was Sparta's late victory over the neophyte Athenian democracy. In the Plays of Aristophanes produced during or in the aftermath of the Peloponnesian War, plentiful food and gluttonous feasting symbolized peace as contrasted to wartime's hungry hardship. In his *History of the Peloponnesian War,* Thucydides tells us that the plague originated in Ethiopia and spreads across the Aegean Sea (Littman, 2009). Initial symptoms of the plague initially sounded like COVID-19: fever, sneezing, violent cough, hoarseness of the throat. It then moved down to the lungs and stomach: people spewing bile, reddish skin with pustules and ulcers, liquid diarrhea, gangrene of the toes, and genitals. On the moral plane, egotism and self-centeredness reigned supreme among the elite and ruling establishment of Athens. Thucydides wrote about some 26% of the hoplites (military-aged males) were killed by the disease. It eventually killed 25–30% of Athens' citizens over a 3-year duration (Bellemore et al., 1994). In Thucydides own words:

> *It was generally agreed that no season had ever been so healthy in respect of other ailments. Previous diseases all turned off into the plague; the rest of the people were attacked without exciting cause, and* ***without warning, in perfect health.*** *It began with violent sensations of heat in the head, and* ***redness and burning in the eyes;*** *internally, the* ***throat and tongue were blood-red from the start****, emitting an abnormal and* ***malodorous breath****. These symptoms developed* ***into sneezing and hoarseness****, and before long the trouble descended into the chest, attended by* ***violent coughing.*** *Whenever it settled in the heart, it upset it, and evacuations of bile ensued, of every kind for which the doctors have a name; these also together with great distress. Most patients suffered an attack of* ***empty retching, inducing violent convulsions****, in some cases soon after the abatement of the previous symptoms, in others much later. The* ***body was neither unduly hot externally to the touch, nor yellowish in colour, but flushed and livid****, with an efflorescence of* ***small blisters and sores. Internally, the heat was so intense that the victims could not endure the laying-on of even the lightest wraps and linens****; indeed nothing would suffice, but they must go naked,* ***and a plunge into cold water would give the greatest relief. Many who were left unattended actually did this, jumping into wells****, so unquenchable was the* ***thirst*** *which possessed them; but it was all the same, whether they drank much or little. The victims were attacked throughout by inability to rest and by* ***sleeplessness. Throughout the height of the disease, the body would not waste away*** *but would hold out against the distress beyond all expectation. The* ***majority succumbed to the internal heat before their strength was entirely exhausted, on the seventh or ninth day****. Or else,* ***if they survived, the plague would descend to the bowels****, where severe lesions would form,* ***together with an attack of uniformly fluid diarrhoea*** *which in most cases ended in* ***death through exhaustion****. Thus the malady which* ***first settle in the head passed through the whole body, starting at the top****. And if the patient recovered from the worst effects, symptoms appeared in the form of a seizure of the extremities: the* ***privy parts and the tips of the fingers and toes were attacked,*** *and many survived with the loss of these, others with the* ***loss of their eyes.*** *Some rose from their beds with a total and* ***immediate loss of memory****, unable to recall their own names or to recognize their next of kin* (Page, 1953, pp. 97–119 emphasis original)

The public health response was to offer sacrifices to the gods because Apollo's arrows carried epidemic diseases. The Plague of Athens was an initial shot-over-the-bow. Early globalization, trade networks, and global supply chains had great benefits, and severe risks as fractured supply chains could stultify a world global power. Epidemiologists tell us that toxigenic fungi and mycotoxins entered the human food supplies over 10,000 years ago. Homer's poems revealed the close union between food, religion, and the ritualistic social contract as early as the Late Bronze Age. Some historians suggested that the outbreak of this fifth century BCE plague was caused by moldy food as well as mass migrations of people due to the Peloponnesian War to Athens, where food supply was very scared forcing the over-crowded Athenian population to consume any food, even when moldy (Target Health, 2019). Others suggest it could have been typhus, smallpox, measles, avian flu, or even an early version of Ebola. Thucydides was not an urban planner nor a medical expert but knew that poor housing conditions, poor sanitation, problematic clean drinking water, dense conditions added to the causalities among his country-men. His astute observations also noted that diseases were an equal-opportunity killer: attaching the pious, the impious, the poor, and the rich. Given that the disease might have mutated over time, the exact nature of the Athenian plague may never be known. Katherine Kelaidis's elegant summation crystalizes what the Great Plague meant for Athens and the future of Western civilization, "Thucydides and his contemporaries did not believe that we are born good. We become good by choosing to do good. We become brave by choosing courage… The ancient Athenians failed to do this in the face of a plague and lost their democracy" (Kelaidis, 2020).

What "lessons" can we learn reflecting back to this historical period that might be applicable to the impact of today's pandemic on food insecurity/supply chains/ CGLs? With or without the plague, the Mediterranean world lived with a constant threat of food shortages and not eating enough. Food supply was impacted greatly by countless events such as climate, distribution, trade, transportation, and demographic pressures (Fenn, 1996). The ancient, more primitive version of the AFSC was around, and plagues/pandemics greatly impacted humanity's established food systems. Socrates, Plato, and Aristotle's moral teachings could be conflated as antecedents of CGL competencies in their exploration of the "soul" and what constitutes living a virtuous life. At this juncture, to further ground our thesis, we shall examine more closely the conditions in India and the USA and how the food and leadership crises have developed differently (yet similar) as the underbelly of the COVID-19 pandemic.

Major Focus on India and the AFSC

India's history is riddled with conquests, empires that have shaped the staunch traditional values that have been passed on for thousands of years. India's cultural and economic repository has been challenged through many past pandemics. The Cholera pandemic (1817–1824) that was believed to have originated in Jessore's small Indian town was a source of contagion that has been traced back to contaminated rice and claimed the lives of hundreds of thousands of Indians. The Bombay plague of 1896 is said to have originated in China and made its way back to Bombay through naval routes. Wild rats spread the Bombay plague, and if the disease was not caught in an early stage would lead to death in 48 h. Spanish flu (1918–1920) has been traced back to a military base in Kansas, US. British rule in India dominated slave labor. As the Britishers got infected, the low caste workers serving the Britishers as servants spread this disease among the lower caste poor whose immunity and nutrition were already compromised. Smallpox pandemic in the early 1960s went largely unreported because of social stigma and isolation associated with the disease and is believed to have accounted for nearly 60% of all worldwide cases ever reported. Cultural and educational reluctance played a role in many Indian's refusing to get vaccinated for smallpox, and it was not until a decade later that strong campaigns from the World Health Organization (WHO) played a critical role in vaccinating the Indian public to eradicate the smallpox pandemic.

As the world has evolved and global boundaries are less visible, the transference of disease has become common. In 2019, it was reported that a new virus has developed in China surrounding the controversy of food delivery in the wet markets of Wuhan, China. Supposedly the combination of all animal groups sold for human consumption combined with the unhygienic delivery space of the market crossbred an unlikely and highly contagious biological weapon known as coronavirus disease and dubbed COVID-19 for the year that it was detected. WHO reports that globally (as a marker) as of 12:12 p.m., CEST, September 29, 2020, 33,206,004 confirmed cases of COVID-19 had been reported resulted in 999,239 deaths. No doubt, as the world continues to operate in a global environment, future pandemics will come with more frequency, magnitude, and complexity. A clear narrative is being told from past pandemics experienced in India, and there is as well a lack of structure, leadership, and consensus that have hindered quick action for the country. In India, as far as pandemics are concerned, history seems to be repeating itself as the Indian economy has sustained an irrefutable decline that has farmworkers, laborers, and transportation at the center of it. In India, the data suggests that there are some 40–50 million seasonal migrants, and the majority of migrants work in micro and small enterprises without formal employment contracts and unemployment benefits.

Demand for food supply is a perpetual need that is evolving into more demand than supply can handle. As the world population steadily increases, this demand will be increased exponentially. The relationship between supply and demand of food is a direct positive linear relationship from an economic perspective. Therefore, the existing short supply of food will also exponentially increase in response to higher demands creating severe food shortages (Govindan et al., 2017). According to the Indian Food Bank's *Hunger in India* (2020), India has the largest malnourished population globally, citing that approximately 15% of the entire population is undernourished.

Furthermore, the breakdown includes 20% of children under the age of 5 who are underweight, 37.9% of children under the age of 5 who are stunted, and 51.4% of women between the ages of 15 and 49 (reproductive age) who are anemic. These statistics posit that India's underbelly is severely poor and starving from lack of food availability. This lack of food availability is caused by inadequacies in the food supply chain system. Supply chain quality is supposed to be the continuous process of improvement to enhanced performance and achieve customer satisfaction (Siddh et al., 2017). The main cause of lack of food availability in India is poor leadership, food loss and waste, and high prices, which is exacerbated due to an inadequate supply chain system.

India, pre-COVID, had the largest population of hungry people and was incapable of providing adequate food for everyone. Now, in the midst of COVID, India's shattered food supply chain system is screaming for a remedy. Tortajada and Biswas (2020) conjecture that COVID-19 has critically damaged India's capacity to produce and sustain food availability by disrupting the local, regional, and national supply chain. The pandemic amplified interruption has impacted the food waste problem as well, which already accounts for 40% of India's food each year (Thomas et al., 2020). India is grossly falling short of providing essential and much-needed food to its citizens. Furthermore, India grapples with how to correct a flawed supply chain system, production efficiency, lack of appropriate refrigeration, and misguided management and leadership practices (Ritchie et al., 2018; Krishnan et al., 2020). As a resolution to balance food needs and increase food availability at the household level, food distribution losses must be minimized, and a more robust and agile agricultural supply change management system needs to be established.

Bush et al. (2015) posit that globally corporate social responsibility, sustainability practices, standards and certification schemes, private interest governance schemes, and public and private auditing have created global commodity chains that are successful. There are two broad sets of questions for theorizing about private governance structures. This includes the credibility, authority, and economic power of the actors who control the financial, material, and human resources allocation. And second, the design, content, and execution of quality standards and certification schemes. There is a need for transparent private governance and corporate accountability in India. Private governance is the concept of creating an economically viable solution where advanced contracts are utilized to mobilize collaborators that would be better off working together, thereby creating an external market free from traditional government and corporate structures in India. The political corruption, malfeasance, bribery, etc., and the fact that Indian citizens have little to no help from the government suggest that intervention is immediately needed. The empowerment of marginalized workers and producers must be incorporated into the supply chain (MacDonald, 2007). This means that marginalized individuals and groups exercise a meaningful level of control in the system as valuable stakeholders. A typical Indian farmer is a small producer who must contend with low and unstable prices and income. The Indian farmer is also forced to accept a lack of access to social infrastructure and services and frequently deals with the insecurity of crop production and lack of financial feasibility. Women (overall) and women small farmers (in particular) are at the bottom of the feeding chain.

To meet the increasing demand for food, leadership needs to focus on the sustainability of food production, quality, distribution, and food safety of the food supply chain. A supply chain system allows the movement of food products from producer to user. Several underlying factors underscore the robustness of an adequate food supply chain system that is rooted in quality and time-consciousness. The efficiency of the food supply chain system ensures that food is transported, delivered, and ready for sale in a timely manner and ensure good quality and timely market delivery to avoid food waste and expiration (Govindan et al., 2017; Kamble et al., 2020; Kashyap & Agarwal, 2020). The micro factors that exert external and internal forces on the food processing industry must be examined to ensure environmental sustainability, such as cost, quality, energy, cost of labor, and safety regulations. Green supply chain management (GSCM) incorporates green purchasing, green production, green presentation, and inverse logistics to reduce and prevent waste and pollution. Green purchasing considers the macro and micro impacts of cost, quality, and performance as factors of decision-making by the purchaser and the supplier. GSCM aims to minimize the impact of energy consumption and pollutants by incorporating a business model of implementing environmental protection and low carbon footprint from raw to delivered product and upholds procurement of socially responsible and sustainable consumption practice.

Supplier sourcing is dependent upon quality, price, and location. Based on these criteria, GSCM encourages an organization to engage its supplier in green projects to ensure better, environmentally friendly performance in the supply chain. By providing an objective environmental criterion, the performance is a collaborative supply chain activity that incorporates green decision management. Food waste produces air and water emissions as well as creates food safety concerns that are directly impacted by the environment. Global Food Security Index 2019 (2019) reported that food wastage and loss totaled 10.10% as a factor of total domestic supply quantity in low-income countries. India's food procession sector faces an acute environmental problem with the existing supply chain and food safety caused by pollution, infrastructure failure, and policy failure. Lack of cold storage and transportation facilities in India has caused a major challenge in the food supply infrastructure. These two main culprits behind the food supply chain system's failure led to a lack of food availability and food accessibility. In the following sections, an outline is provided to identify the missing components of the existing food supply chain system and then provide further solutions and policy implementation ideas.

Food Availability (Production)

Food availability (production) and food accessibility (price and inflation) are two major systemic food systems weaknesses in the global agriculture food supply chain (AFSC) of the food chain supply that has severely impacted the marginalized poor in India. Apart from creating food deserts (defined as regions where people have limited access to healthy and affordable food), the massive amounts of food loss and waste in India have created a considerable carbon footprint. The AFSC has both upstream and downstream factors that have added to poverty and food scarcity by increasing prices and promoting widespread food insecurity for the indigenous population. Government intervention (or lack thereof) has added further burden to developing a solution to this severe and immediate food shortage problem. Although food systems are deteriorating worldwide, innovation such as blockchain technology, a systematic approach to improving local organic farming, and nonprofit organizations' involvement at all levels of society is needed to regulate this massive break in the food supply system of India.

The demand for food supply is a constant variable. Furthermore, this constant need for food demand is on the rise yielding to a massive shortage of food supply in India. Food supply chain management is a vertically integrated structure that incorporates joint ventures and strategic alliances among supply chain players and retailers to provide food supplies to the public. A traditional logistics model cannot meet the market's full demands (Dellino et al., 2018). In India, inadequacies in the supply chain have led different stakeholders to seek solutions in a value-added logistics system that provides services and supports the increasing operational complexity of the food retail chain by incorporating adequate logistics and information technology solutions.

India is among the world's largest producers of agricultural products that are traded globally. Surveys by the FAO and USDA estimated that 40% of the Indian population is believed to be vegetarian. India's vegetarian population is the largest dairy product consumer to supplement protein needs (Chandra, 2020). Dairy food products are highly susceptible to spoilage and therefore require proper refrigeration. Furthermore, India has an enormous consumption of perishable dairy products. Perishable products have a short shelf-life, and the main concern surrounding them is product safety and quality standards in the developing world's climate uncertainty environment.

Moreover, the perishable food products contribute to a high level of food waste because the demand and information transparency of perishable food supply chain trading are inefficient (Siddh et al., 2017). Cold chain management is part of the supply chain that encompasses the delivery of food supplies that are perishable or prone to microbial spoilage. Food safety is an immediate need. Thus, a cold chain management system is urgently required to stop waste and support demand.

Additionally, since the government currently lacks a food safety system, there are opportunities for a new or existing NGO to assist with regulating the product's health and safety. For example, the Global FoodBanking Network does ensure food product safety of its global partners, which in India includes entities such as the Bangalore Food Bank, No Food Waste, Feeding India, and the India FoodBanking Network. However, more is still needed.

At the same time, we see hope in the technological revolutions that the pandemic has fostered, which could be applied to the tattered agricultural sector and in feeding more people. For example, we look to the new cold storage massive global undertaking to deliver the early vaccines to desperate populations as India still struggles to improve its ability to store and move vaccines in a temperature-controlled environment. This unprecedented logistical effort involving private-public cooperation is like a neo-Marshal Plan for getting the vaccines from the manufacturing plants injected into people's arms. This cold supply chain could be adapted to saving the massive food waste, especially in low-income countries, that would allow fresh fruits, vegetables, dairy, and other perishable produce to reach remote villages around the globe. As global warming continues to wreck-havoc the food production side, cold food storage will be critical to capture the almost one-third of food produced for human consumption that is lost to waste. The hemorrhaging of nutritional food loss through a determined global political-will supplemented via technological innovations could yield more accessible and cost-saving necessities to reach the most vulnerable. The pandemic has taught humanity that science, technology, and the positive side of globalism should be harnessed to solve global hunger and food insecurity.

During the current COVID-19 outbreak, the shortage of farmworkers has already created huge negative yields. This has driven India's market economy to integrate a sustainable food supply that is fueled both by fast-moving consumer goods buttressed by mega-corporations and policymakers. The agri-food supply chain's sustainability principle and management are strategically challenged in today's environment by society's expectations and measures stakeholders' performance as key performance indexes. Therefore, the adoption of sustainable practices in India is slow-moving (Joshi et al., 2020) and currently fails to provide acceptable performance. Although India's agri-food industry is slow to adopt practices towards sustainable development, India is increasingly integrating the development of competitiveness and the strategy of sustainability. Again, this is where there are more opportunities and gaps to fill and for NGOs to participate, and for alternatives like locally grown organic sustainable crops with a locally derivative supply chain.

The world population is on the rise and is expected to reach 9.6 billion by 2050 (Krishnan et al., 2020). Although COVID has wreaked its havoc on the world population, farming has been severely impacted both globally and in India. Farmers in India are in a daily fight for survival as production has tremendously decreased. This means that the demand for food will increase, and the supply will decrease. There has also been documented a substantial fall in producer prices and rising urban consumer prices in India and some African countries (Minten & Reardon, 2008). More than one-third of global food production is wasted or lost annually (Thomas et al., 2020). Consumers and policymakers are continuously demanding better management of environmental resources. The consumer also desires essential information about quality, safety, sustainability, and consumer products' origin.

Lack of sustainable supply chain system is a key factor to be considered for massive food loss in India. Kashyap and Agarwal (2020) state that food loss generates greenhouse gas emissions; therefore, the loss is like a double-edged sword. The loss of good consumable food and the generation of dangerous greenhouse emissions are harmful to human health. Kashyap and Agarwal (2020) conducted a study of food loss and greenhouse emissions for India's food waste for 2013. They reported that the total food loss was approximately 58.3 million tons (Mt) mass losses in sugar cane and rice. This correlated to approximatey 115 bill m3 of water loss and land footprint and carbon footprint of approximately 9.58+ million hectares (Mha). Food loss and waste in India's-carbon footprint, loss of resources such as water, land, greenhouse emissions related to food loss—the opportunity cost (Man et al., 2017). Therefore, environmental change is driven by food production lost to waste in the downstream process of the supply chain. We know from the medical community that unhealthy diets are a leading cause of global diseases (Aleksandrowicz et al., 2019; Gupta, 2019; Verma et al., 2020). In India, under-nutrition is prevalent. The pandemic data suggest poor people are switching to lower quality diets with fewer nutrients. Affluent diets are consumption patterns of sophisticated consumers that demand a high-quality product consumed by households' wealthiest. Unfortunately, COVID-19 has created more anger, and the Indian population's resentment is fueling food hoarding by the affluent and not leaving much for the poor to consume.

Food Accessibility (Price and Inflation)

The inclusion of blockchain technology (BT) utilizing technology to incorporate transparent and straightforward contracts between users can revolutionize India's agricultural supply chain by removing trust-related factors and improving performance (Kamble et al., 2020). Food safety, supply, and availability in India remain an enigma. Although historically a rich agrarian powerhouse, India struggles to feed its own. In India, non-farm income now accounts for 61% of rural incomes, up from 28% four decades earlier (Trebbin, 2014; Chand et al., 2018). Compounding the reduced importance of farm income is the sector's substantial mechanization during the past few decades (Thomas et al., 2020). This time around (post-COVID-19), agriculture will play less of a buffering role for those who have lost employment in other sectors, both because it is smaller in relative size and because its very structure has changed. Agricultural buffering capacity will be further constrained if supply chains are not functioning correctly (Andotra & Pooja, 2009). Nearly all governments in the region have responded with a range of social protection measures. Relief has included cash transfers and unemployment benefits, food provision in kind (e.g., school feeding) or through vouchers, wage subsidies, and waiver or postponement of utility bills. There should be expanded social protections against the vacillations of the market, such as: strengthening land tenure security, improving access to finance, facilitating better risk management for small landholders, and promoting inclusive agribusiness models that would help smallholders adapt to changing food demand and higher quality standards of modern supply chains.

In the face of the global panacea of COVID-19, many world leaders have responded with basic Keynesian economic principles of government intervention to infuse capital spending. The pandemic caused turmoil that threatens both financial stability and food access. Furthermore, the steep decline in employment, demise of businesses caused by closure, and the general micro- and macro-economic impact parlays into less availability and affordability of nutritious food, especially to the underserved. The disruptions experienced in the distribution and infrastructure breakdown of the food supply chain will magnify hunger and malnutrition in India.

Blockchain technology provides a source of enhanced transparency and accountability in the supply chain management system by eliminating trust-related issues. BT creates an environment of transparency and traceability that allows broader participation of stakeholders and will facilitate lower transaction costs, increase time efficacy, and reduce lead times to develop a highly secure and relevant environment for the agri-supply chain system. Another suggestion would be to subsidize mobile cells for the poor to allow contactless mobile payments and access to the banking and credit systems.

Food prices and inflation have taken an enormous toll on India's food supply chain system credited to food waste and government control of food distribution. Food waste is a compound problem that involves all efforts from soil erosion, depletion of water resources, air pollution that adds to the carbon footprint and eventually leads to global warming. Generally, food waste in the supply chain system refers to the loss that occurred during either distribution, industrial processing, or consumption due to throwing away food due to consumer negligence (Ghosh et al., 2015). Food waste leads to food loss, especially for the poor. In purely economic terms, the opportunity cost of food wasted means food loss for human consumption. Food waste is a global problem that required intervention by CGL policymakers at the international and local levels to create key policy initiatives that remedy and lessen food waste.

There is a lack of access to organized markets in India that create unintended price fluctuations borne by the consumer. Both formal and informal buyers offer most products in India to set a competitive price (Joshi et al., 2020). Since there is no consensus on pricing or price stability, price gouging is prevalent. To visualize the problem's magnitude, the open-air markets or bazaars where most of Indian's shops are a daily façade. It is expected that one may not be able to purchase a pound of tomatoes for the same price tomorrow. How, then, does a nation that does not practice price stabilization create a regular market for consumers? Adding to information asymmetry is India's government, which currently rations grains and sugar (Chandra, 2020). Each person is only allowed to purchase the preset quota; however, the government does not set or stabilize the grains and sugar ration distribution prices.

Food availability (production) and food accessibility (price and inflation) are both critical factors directly impacted by a supply chain system's robustness. India has some missed opportunities to regain control during the COVID-19 pandemic to provide essential food needs for its population. In the absence of a government structure, there is a massive opportunity for entrepreneurs, nonprofit, small, and large business owners who fit within the food supply chain to create a remarkable positive change. Supply chain participants can incorporate criteria defined by GSCM that promotes organizations to collaborate with green projects and embody social responsibility and sustainability. Private governance that facilitates economically viable alternative solutions by enforcing advanced contracts that utilize collaboration free from traditional government intrusion and supports an agile supply chain system is a possible solution. Also, leadership that focuses on the quality of food safety distribution to minimize food waste, which creates efficiencies and increases food availability for many hungry Indian citizens, is another viable option. For food loss and waste (FLW), we need to set up innovations at the community level for sharing food, better innovations in technology and e-commerce, and innovations in the green policy. Furthermore, incorporating a fair, transparent, and confident transaction network using blockchain technology to create a smart contract between small farmers and suppliers will provide much-needed agility to the supply chain system. Add to that open, transparent, and fair trade agreements that eliminate harmful tariffs and even create future global and regional grain reserves (modeled after the US strategic oil reserve program).

Minor Focus on the USA and the AFSC

The coronavirus has revealed the true nature of hunger in America. In reality, the USA has never had a coherent food policy ever since the Great Depression. Its food emergency security blanket has been delegated as an after-thought to the nonprofit sector and relegated to the Department of Agriculture (whose mission is to tie rural agricultural development, farmers, and the nutrition-needy under one rubric).The pandemic has precipitated in the farming sector, tons of unharvested crops that are being plowed under, and livestock in the millions that are being euthanized. On the nonprofit side, the largest and most tenuous entities are the nation's 250+ food banks that receive some government subsidies and private donations but mostly relieve the largess of the corporate food industry's discarded product. About 1 in 6 have borrowed money to eat from friends or have gotten food from a food bank through one of the agencies they distribute to (Pew Research Center, 2020). The pandemic and high unemployment in America today have caused an explosion of demand from hungry families with children, the elderly, and the hard-hit lower-middle class. The most developed and sophisticated food system and supply chain in the world is on serious life support. Supply (food production) has never been a problem: purchasing power is. Since the pandemic hit, 17.4% of mothers with children under 12 report they cannot afford food. During the pandemic, job loss is over 27 million people, many of which no longer have employer-health benefits. Without steady income, insurance, and a true government-provided safety net, families are falling into a state of food insecurity and without the proper nutritional intake, leaving themselves and their children more susceptible to disease (Offenheiser, 2020).

Healthy food accessibility in America presented significant challenges even before the pandemic took a foot-hole. The USDA's Food Pyramid has guided for years on what types of food Americans should eat for a healthy diet. Data has shown adult obesity rates in 2017–2018 stood at 42.4% for the general population, while obesity-related health conditions like heart disease, stroke, type 2 diabetes, certain types of cancers were the leading causes of preventable, premature death (CDC, 2020a). A profit-driven, meat-centered food system is making us sick as (2013) data shows the USA (and other developed countries) consume yearly 100 kg per person, equivalent to about 50 chickens or half a cow (BBC, 2019). Remember that epidemiologists think that COVID-19 probably came from some zoonotic cross-over, as did SARS in 2004 and MERS in 2012. Scientists estimate that more than 6 out of every ten known infectious diseases in people spread from animals (CDC, 2020b).

Food accessibility is also tied to food prices. The import and export supply chains have been seriously impacted by the pandemic reflecting higher consumer prices in the USA, especially for fish, dairy, eggs, and meat (US Bureau of Labor Statistics, 2020). Food purchases are a major part of the public's household budgets (estimates are roughly around 20%), so when food prices spike, either consumer shift their dietary habits to less nutritious foods or cut back on consumption to pay for other pressing monthly expenses like heating, rent, and gasoline. Market conditions are fluid targets but have been pinching the budgets of millions of Americans who live on the cusp of hunger, thus reinforcing the adage "it is expensive to eat healthy and providing food is our common ground."

Conclusion and Recommendations

The global COVID-19 pandemic has demonstrated missteps from leaders of both India and the USA through the lens of global crisis leader competencies. Prime Minister Narendra Modi has been widely criticized for lack of transparency, poor management (the pandemic has devastated the economy and disrupted the educational system), spewing public disinformation like India is managing the coronavirus pandemic better than many developed countries (the country is number two in confirmed infections behind the USA), and shifting blame to the United Nations for overall ineffectiveness in fighting the pandemic. President Donald Trump has blamed China for the deadly contagion that originated in Wuhan, politicized the country's public health response through errors of commission, omission, and complacency, relegated science to the alter of his reelection, demonstrated little empathy or emotional awareness to soaring death tolls, nor the cultural intelligence to the devastating disparities the pandemic brought upon communities of color and native tribes. These two global leaders are prime examples of CGL competencies squandered.

Homo-sapiens have indeed evolved into the sophistication of human-designed, made, and programmed computer AI and algorithms that accomplished the fastest trains, computer devices, and even the far reaches of space travel. However, systemic structures needed to feed humans have not progressed at this hyper speed. World hunger continues to be a real ongoing, slow-moving pandemic for which no vaccine is being created, unlike those that will eventually eradicate COVID-19. Considering COVID-19 and its remedies, several current vaccines require the subzero temperature to store and distribute the vaccine. This is problematic because globally, there is a shortage of cold supply chain systems. Similarly, for food distribution and containment of spoilage, the cold supply chain is a missing and weak link of the global agriculture food supply chain (AFSC) that needs immediate remedy, especially in the developing world. AFSC, as we argue in this essay, will be critical in managing the world food supplies in the future.

Investment in the cold supply chain system is necessary to end the COVID-19 pandemic and make headway into ending the massive amounts of food waste that is currently occurring worldwide. Food distribution needs an agile, robust, and effective form of delivery that is possible if the AFSC is repurposed to meet the demand by providing a medium that yields less food spoilage. Although this is not an exhaustive list, we recommend including AI, such as blockchain technology in AFSC, ramping up cold supply chain system, and inclusion of various NGOs that can participate at different levels of the AFSC to provide transparency and efficacy. Food availability and accessibility need to come together not just in India or in the USA, but globally if we ever will sanctify the notion that "food as a right, not as a privilege." As documented by our review, history has shown us that dangerous illnesses will wreak havoc on societies time and time again. Learning invaluable lessons from history to contain these harmful contagions starts with healthy, sustainable food systems and inculcating proper competencies in our future CGLs. Building resilient food systems locally (farmer-to-consumer) may become a method of managing the global market's vacillations.

Imagine that we can manage the AFSC delivery system's sanctity and build the competency skills in our next generation of global leaders. In that case, we can not only lessen the chances of harmful and deadly viruses in the future but find an effective way to feed humanity.

Five Chapter Takeaways

1. Leadership in times of crisis defines the future. In the face of a serious pandemic that has exacerbated chronic hunger and food insecurity for millions of people, equipping the next generation of crisis global leaders (CGL)'s with proven personal, professional, and social competencies/skillsets can make a difference.
2. The global agriculture food supply chain (AFSC) two components: food availability (production) and food accessibility (price and inflation) are both needed to successfully address hunger and food insecurity, especially in a pandemic.
3. We can draw important lessons from past global pandemics like the Plague of Athens in regard to globalized food sourcing and leadership development.
4. The chapter offers two empirical cases: India's example of the beak-down of the AFSC's food production and accessibility for the developing world and the United States' example of the failure to provide food accessibility (purchasing power) for the developing world both happening in the midst of global pandemic.
5. Recommendations for solving the global hunger/food insecurity problem include but are not limited to: investment in cold supply chain systems, building sustainable resilient food systems, implementing blockchain technology for agriculture, and constructing green supply chain management.

Five Reflection Questions

1. Integration of smart technology: In the wake of the global crisis of COVID-19, future panaceas are going to continue to get more complex. How can leaders integrate smart technologies that have autonomous functioning to avoid some of the costly mistakes that have been made in the past?
2. Inclusion of the private sector and to what extent: How can the private sector be involved as a part of the solution to combat future pandemics and food disruptions?
3. Government intervention and to what extent: How can global governments deploy/maintain resources in preparation for future disruptions? Should the United Nations declare "food as a right"?

4. Public education of food waste: Should the public be educated to avoid/lessen the burden of food waste and loss? And should the public be provided incentives for involvement and to be part of the solution?
5. Leadership focus on innovation: As we head into more complexities in the future, how can leaders focus on innovative solutions to lessen the impact of a complete economic shut-down and a scarcity of food?

References

Aleksandrowicz, L., Green, R., Joy, E. J. M., Harris, F., Hillier, J., Vetter, S. H., Smith, P., Kulkarni, B., Dangour, A. D., & Haines, A. (2019). Environmental impacts of dietary shifts in India: A modelling study using nationally representative data. *Environment International, 126*, 207–215. https://doi.org/10.1016/j.envint.2019.02.004

Anderson, B. A. (2005). Expatriate selection: Good management or good luck? *The International Journal of Human Resource Management, 16*(4), 567–583. https://doi.org/10.1080/09585190500051647

Andotra, N., & Pooja. (2009). TOC supply chain management solution for food processing industries. *Journal of Small Business and Entrepreneurship, 22*(3), 239–251. http://www.tandfonline.com/loi/rsbe20

BBC. (2019, February 4). *Which countries eat the most meat?* https://www.bbc.com/news/health-47057341

Bellemore, J., Plant, I., & Cunningham, L. (1994, October). Plague of Athens—Fungal poison? *Journal of the History of Medicine and Allied Sciences, 49*(4), 521–545.

Bush, S. R., Oosterveer, P., Bailey, M., & Mol, A. P. J. (2015). Sustainability governance of chains and networks: A review and future outlook. *Journal of Cleaner Production, 107*, 8–19. https://doi.org/10.1016/j.jclepro.2014.10.019

Caligiuri, P. (2006). Developing global leaders. *Human Resource Management Review, 16*(2), 219–228. https://doi.org/10.1016/j.hrmr.2006.03.009

Caligiuri, P., & Cascio, W. (1998). Can we send her there? Maximizing the success of western women on global assignments. *Journal of World Business, 33*, 394–416.

CBPP, Center for Budget and Policy Priorities. (2010, December 10). https://www.cbpp.org/research/poverty-and-inequality/tracking-the-covid-19-recessions-effects-on-food-housing-and

CDC. (2020a). *Adult obesity facts*. https://www.cdc.gov/obesity/data/adult.html

CDC. (2020b). *Zoonotic diseases*. https://www.cdc.gov/onehealth/basics/zoonotic-diseases.htm

Chand, P., Thakkar, J. J., & Ghosh, K. K. (2018). Analysis of supply chain complexity drivers for Indian mining equipment manufacturing companies combining SAP-LAP and AHP. *Resources Policy, 59*, 389–410. https://doi.org/10.1016/j.resourpol.2018.08.011

Chandra, A. (2020, April 27). *India: COVID-19 impact on the Indian sugar industry*. https://apps.fas.usda.gov/newgainapi/api/Report/DownloadReportByFileName?fileName=Covid-19%20Impact%20on%20the%20Indian%20Sugar%20Industry_New%20Delhi_India_04-19-2020; https://www.fas.usda.gov/data/india-covid-19-impact-indian-sugar-industry

Chaudhuri, S., & Alagaraja, M. (2014). An expatriate's perspective on leadership and leading (a global organization) in India: Interview with Matt Barney. *Human Resource Development International, 17*(3), 358–365. https://doi.org/10.1080/13678868.2014.896125

Dellino, G., Laudadio, T., Mari, R., Mastronardi, N., & Meloni, C. (2018). A reliable decision support system for fresh food supply chain management. *International Journal of Production Research, 56*(4), 1458–1485. https://doi.org/10.1080/00207543.2017.1367106

Economist, Intelligence Unit Limited. (2019). *Global food security index 2019*.

FAO. (2012). *100 days to Rio +20, 100 facts: Making the link between people, food and the environment*. Food and Agriculture Organization of the United Nations.

FAO. (2013). *The state of food and agriculture, food systems for better nutrition*. Food and Agriculture Organization of the United Nations.

Fenn, R. (1996). *Keeping the balance: Ancient Greek philosophical concerns with population and environment*. https://www.jstor.org/stable/27503492

Ghosh, P. R., Sharma, S. B., Haigh, Y. T., Evers, A. L. B., & Ho, G. (2015). An overview of food loss and waste: Why does it matter? *Cosmos, 11*(1), 89–103. https://pepperdine.on.worldcat.org/oclc/5948768006

Global Food Security Index 2019. (2019). https://www.economist.com/. https://foodsecurityindex.eiu.com/

Govindan, K., Kadziński, M., & Sivakumar, R. (2017). Application of a novel PROMETHEE-based method for construction of a group compromise ranking to prioritization of green suppliers in food supply chain. *Omega, 71*, 129–145. https://doi.org/10.1016/j.omega.2016.10.004

Gupta, D. (2019). An urge of rural entrepreneurial development in India-one step ahead for economic development. *Global Journal of Enterprise Information System, 10*(3), 124–130. https://doi.org/10.18311/gjeis/2019

India Food Bank. (2020, October 27). *Hunger in India*. India Food Banking Network. https://www.indiafoodbanking.org/hunger

Ivy, K. L. (2017). Developing global leaders: Building effective global inter-cultural collaborative online learning environments. *International Journal on E-Learning, 16*(1), 33–46. https://lib.pepperdine.edu/login?url=https://search.ebscohost.com/login.aspx?direct=true&db=eft&AN=121382931&login.asp%3fcustid%3ds8480238&site=ehost-live&scope=site

Joshi, S., Singh, R. K., & Sharma, M. (2020). Sustainable Agri-food supply chain practices: Few empirical evidence from a developing economy. *Global Business Review*. https://doi.org/10.1177/0972150920907014

Kamble, S. S., Gunasekaran, A., & Sharma, R. (2020). Modeling the blockchain enabled traceability in agriculture supply chain. *International Journal of Information Management, 52*, 101967. https://doi.org/10.1016/j.ijinfomgt.2019.05.023

Kashyap, D., & Agarwal, T. (2020). Food loss in India: Water footprint, land footprint and GHG emissions. *Environment, Development and Sustainability, 22*(4), 2905–2918. https://doi.org/10.1007/s10668-019-00325-4

Kelaidis, K. (2020, March 23). *What the Great Plague of Athens can teach us now*. https://www.theatlantic.com/ideas/archive/2020/03/great-plague-athens-has-eerie-parallels-today/608545/

Kim, J., & McLean, G. N. (2015). An integrative framework for global competency: Levels and dimensions. *Human Resource Development International, 18*(3), 235–258.

Krishnan, R., Agarwal, R., Bajada, C., & Arshinder, K. (2020). Redesigning a food supply chain for environmental sustainability—An analysis of resource use and recovery. *Journal of Cleaner Production, 242*, 118374. https://doi.org/10.1016/j.jclepro.2019.118374

Littman, R. J. (2009). The plague of Athens: Epidemiology and paleopathology. Mount Sinai journal of medicine. *A Journal of Translational and Personalized Medicine, 76*(5), 456–467.

MacDonald, K. (2007). Globalizing justice within coffee supply chains? Fair trade, Starbucks and the transformation of supply chain governance. *Third World Quarterly, 28*(4), 793–812. https://doi.org/10.1080/01436590701336663

Man, M. S., Soni, G., Jain, R., Sharma, M. K., & Yadav, V. (2017). Agri-fresh food supply chain quality (AFSCQ): A literature review. *Industrial Management & Data Systems, 117*(9), 2015–2044. https://doi.org/10.1108/IMDS-10-2016-0427

Maznevski, M. L., & DiStefano, J. J. (2000). Global leaders are team players: Developing global leaders through membership on global teams. *Human Resource Management, 39*(2), 185. https://doi.org/10.1002/1099-050X(200022/23)39:2/3<195:AID-HRM9>3.0.CO;2-I

Mendenhall, M. E., & Stevens, M. J. (2017). *Global leadership: Research, practice, and development*. Routledge.

Minten, B., & Reardon, T. (2008). Food prices, quality, and quality's pricing in supermarkets versus traditional markets in developing countries. *Review of Agricultural Economics, 30*(3), 480–490.

Offenheiser, R. (2020, June 19). The coronavirus has revealed the true nature of hunger in America. *The Chronicle of Philanthropy*. https://www.philanthropy.com/article/the-coronavirus-has-revealed-the-true-nature-of-hunger-in-america

Page, D. (1953). Thucydides description of the plague. *The Classical Quarterly, 3*, 97–119.

Petrick, J. A., Scherer, R. F., Brodzinski, J. D., Quinn, J. F., & Ainina, M. F. (1999). Global leadership skills and reputational capital: Intangible resources for sustainable competitive advantage. *Academy of Management Perspectives, 13*(1), 58–69.

Pew Research Center. (2020, September 24). *Economic fallout from COVID-19 continues to hit lower-income Americans the hardest*. https://www.pewsocialtrends.org/2020/09/24/economic-fallout-from-covid-19-continues-to-hit-lower-income-americans-the-hardest/

Pless, N. M., Maak, T., & Stahl, G. K. (2011). Developing responsible global leaders through international service-learning programs: The Ulysses experience. *Academy of Management Learning & Education, 10*(2), 237–260. https://doi.org/10.5465/amle.10.2.zqr237

Ritchie, H., Reay, D., & Higgins, P. (2018). Sustainable food security in India—Domestic production and macronutrient availability. *PLoS One, 13*(3), 1–17. https://doi.org/10.1371/journal.pone.0193766

Siddh, M. M., Soni, G., Jain, R., Sharma, M. K., & Yadav, V. (2017). Agri-fresh food supply chain quality (AFSCQ): A literature review. *Industrial Management & Data Systems, 117*(9), 2015–2044. https://doi.org/10.1108/IMDS-10-2016-0427

Target Health Blog. (2019, April 15). *The plague of Athens leading to the fall of the golden age of Greece*. https://www.targethealth.com/post/the-plague-of-athens-leading-to-the-fall-of-the-golden-age-of-greece

Thomas, R. J., Bellin, J., Jules, C., & Lynton, N. (2013). Developing tomorrow's global leaders. *MIT Sloan Management Review, 55*(1), 12–13. https://lib.pepperdine.edu/login?url=https://search.ebscohost.com/login.aspx?direct=true&db=buh&AN=90320397&login.asp%3fcustid%3ds8480238&site=ehost-live&scope=site

Thomas, S. N., Edwin, L., Chinnadurai, S., Harsha, K., Salagrama, V., Prakash, R., Prajith, K. K., Die-Quadi, Y., He, P., & Ward, A. (2020). Document card | FAO | Food and agriculture organization of the United Nations. Home | Food and Agriculture Organization of the United Nations. https://www.fao.org/documents/card/en/c/CA8382EN

Thompson, C. (2020). *Post-COVID leadership and followership landscape*. Unpublished paper. Pepperdine University.

Tortajada, C., & Biswas, A. K. (2020). Water management in post-2020 world. *International Journal of Water Resources Development, 36*(6), 874–878. https://doi.org/10.1080/07900627.2020.1837451

Trebbin, A. (2014). Linking small farmers to modern retail through producer organizations—Experiences with producer companies in India. *Food Policy, 45*, 35–44. https://doi.org/10.1016/j.foodpol.2013.12.007

Twomey, R. F., & Twomey, D. F. (2008). Developing business leaders for global competitiveness. *Competition Forum, 6*(1), 109–115. https://lib.pepperdine.edu/login?url=https://search.ebscohost.com/login.aspx?direct=true&db=s3h&AN=35637566&login.asp%3fcustid%3ds8480238&site=ehost-live&scope=site

US Bureau of Labor Statistics. (2020). *The Impact of the COVID-19 Pandemic on food price indexes and data collection*. https://www.bls.gov/opub/mlr/2020/article/the-impact-of-the-covid-19-pandemic-on-food-price-indexes-and-data-collection.htm

Verma, M. v. d. B., de Vreede, L., Achterbosch, T., & Rutten, M. M. (2020). Consumers discard a lot more food than widely believed: Estimates of global food waste using an energy gap approach and affluence elasticity of food waste. *PLoS One, 15*(2), 1–14. https://doi.org/10.1371/journal.pone.0228369

H. Eric Schockman is a Professor of Political Science and International Relations and Director of the Center for Leadership, Equity and Diversity at Woodbury University. He also teaches in the Ph.D. program in Global Leadership and Change at Pepperdine University. A public policy expert, Dr. Schockman previously served as Associate Dean and Associate Adjunct Professor at the Sol Price School of Public Policy at the University of Southern California. He is President and founder of the Global Hunger Foundation, dedicated to helping women in the developing world break the chains of poverty by funding projects designed to provide sustainable development and organic farming. He has also written several books and edited many articles on leadership and politics in California, the nation, and international affairs and presented on panels on these same topics. Dr. Schockman holds a Ph.D. in Political Science and International Relations from the University of California.

Anita Ravani is the founder of APR Investment and Management, a leading management and consulting firm based out of Los Angeles, California that specializes in finance and accounting to drive consumer decision-making. She is a member of senior management at a Global Financial Frim and has more than 20 years of finance and accounting experience working with Fortune 500 companies to solve their most important financial challenges. Anita is a two-time inductee of the prestigious Beta Gamma Sigma Honor Society and holds a Ph.D. in Global Leadership and Change from the Graduate School of Education and Psychology at Pepperdine University.

18 School Leadership and Information Literacy: Leading in Crisis and Beyond COVID-19

Nicola Sum

School, Leadership, and Crisis

"Knowledge is dead; the school, however, serves the living" (Einstein et al., 1954)

While the school has continued to serve, the state of school life reflects its exhaustion under the pressure of global accountability and policymaking (Ball, 2017; Lingard et al., 2013) and ambitious expectations for knowledge driven economies (Ball, 2004; Cogburn, 1998). Discourses of school improvement, twenty-first century teaching and learning, buildings and technology have driven multiple agendas seeking to transform schools, while the purpose and impact have remained contentious points of debate in an increasingly globalised forum (Anderson-Levitt, 2003; World Bank, 2011). Buried in the depths of the data, frequent misinformation and conflicted perspectives, are school leaders seeking to ensure that the support for students and their families remains consistent and of value. Increasingly, unforeseen events over the past two decades such as localised political unrest, regional health epidemics such as the SARS outbreak, and most recently the COVID-19 global pandemic, continue to shift many schooling intentions in unexpected ways by challenging the purpose and nature of the day-to-day aspects of school life. This chapter proposes that one aspect of leading through such challenges is the information literacy of school leaders. Information literacy, an evolving and equally debated concept, reflects the need for access, understanding, evaluation, and actions informed by available information. This is critical to the challenge faced by school leaders both during crisis and across everyday decision-making. Therefore, two key questions are raised for exploration in this chapter:

N. Sum (✉)
Monash University, VIC, Australia
e-mail: nicola.sum@monash.edu

S. K. Dhiman, J. F. Marques (eds.), *Leadership After COVID-19*, Future of Business and Finance, https://doi.org/10.1007/978-3-030-84867-5_18

- How do school leaders perceive their own information literacy in their leadership practice?
- What are the implications of these information literate practices in times of crisis?

In exploring these questions, this chapter draws on findings from two different case studies of school leaders, to explore the significance of information literacy within leadership practice in schools. The two case studies are presented as illustrative examples of how leaders perceive information literacy in their work in schools. The first illustrates a case in Bangladesh, of school leaders immersed in a crisis of political unrest, while the second illustrates the perceptions and experiences of a case in Australia, during the most recent COVID-19 pandemic. Through these illustrations, this chapter seeks to outline the significance of information literacy for school leadership and the opportunities to develop sustainable practice beyond crisis.

In structuring this discussion, the chapter begins with a review of literature mapping the changing conceptualisation of information literacy, its relationship to fields beyond library science and writing instruction, and specifically to educational leadership practice. The literature leads to the theoretical framing, using ideas of information literacy as a catalyst for educational change in leadership, from the work of Bruce (2004). This frames the exploration of the two illustrative case studies of school leaders' perceptions of their work in relation to information literacy. The examples are followed by a discussion of key themes across the case studies. The chapter concludes with reflective questions and points of further consideration for both educational leadership researchers and practitioners in the field of school leadership.

Information Literacy: Conceptualisations, Relationship to Education and Educational Leadership

Information literacy is most widely documented in the scholarship related to library science, with its origins in instructional approaches to writing, frequently within the context of higher educational institutions (Rader, 2002; Weiner, 2012). In their literature review of information literacy spanning almost 30 years to 2002, Rader (2002) noted that much of the extant literature focused on information literacy within academic library contexts. Generally, this was with the aim of developing the information skills of students. This often separated the development of information literacy from the curriculum specific programs delivered to students. It also enacted a separation of specialisations, with librarians overseeing the development of information skills, while other classroom teachers or university academics delivered curriculum concepts (Rader, 2002). A further literature review by Pinto et al. (2010) also highlighted the initial developments in information literacy as largely the domain of higher educational institutions. Over time, the emphasis has shifted from a user-training lens, to a broader collaborative educational approach, which involves a growing number of educational stakeholders alongside librarians (McKeever et al., 2017; Norgaard, 2003). Such shifts, in considerations of the who and the how, led to information literacy becoming a new skillset which included "knowing how to locate and use the information necessary to solve problems and to take decisions efficiently and effectively" (Pinto et al., 2010, p. 4). This later literature review on information literacy identified the shift towards criticality (Pinto et al., 2010).

The need for criticality in the conceptualisation of information literacy became increasingly significant through developments in information technologies. Scholarship on the nature of digital natives (Selwyn, 2009), globalisation and technology infrastructure (Çoklar et al., 2017; Selwyn & Brown, 2000) meant that the original scale of information, and scope of information literacy, was rapidly changed. In some instances this shift has been identified as an informatics global civilisation (Tehranian, 2001). Where Rader's (2002) literature review shared a common starting point with information technology developments in the 1970s, by the end of those 30 years, the impact of information technologies, as it reverberated through globalised aspects of culture, society, and politics, resulted in an information literacy that was more dynamic, context driven, critical, and discerning. Increasingly, scholars have identified that "being information literate requires more than the ability to work analytically with information. It also demands that we know how to manage information in more creative and meaningful ways" (Ward, 2006, p. 396). Across the last 20 years, tension between the speed of technology and its relationship to information literacy has continued to build. Scholars have questioned the relationships between developing infrastructures for information technology and the role of government (Selwyn & Brown, 2000), the way in which policy is developed (Weiner, 2011, 2012), and most recently, the challenges of addressing the inter-connected nature of online information and disinformation challenges for policy makers (Montgomery, 2020).

Within an educational context, matters of equity, inclusion, and organisational change management amplify these tensions. Consider these issues from a global to a local scale. One of the most significant drivers for organisational change stems from the nature of globalised education policy. Global policymakers have focused on education as a pathway to economic development through a sequence of agendas including the Education for All initiative (EFA), millennium development goals (MDGs), and the sustainable development goals focused on Education 2030 (UNESCO, 1990, 2000, 2015, 2018). While these agendas were not always explicit in all educational contexts at national level, the increased use of standardised testing and international comparative analysis has changed the ways in which nation-states make decisions about investment in education (Ball, 1998; Lingard et al., 2013). The increasingly global-local dynamic of educational decision-making generates a very different maze of information, which schools and school leaders must navigate. Information circulates from a diverse number of sources, be it in regard to financial planning for schools, curriculum development, national and other standardised testing priorities and protocols, staffing and the associated professional development, student well-being and academic outcomes, and a myriad of broader community engagement initiatives. More recent scholarship on information literacy has sought to address this intersection of information, technology, and education, as a broader consideration of schooling and specifically, related to concepts such as skills for twenty-first century learning and lifelong learning. Therefore, information literacy becomes a critical skill in "knowing when and why you need information, where to find it, and how to use and communicate it in an ethical manner" (McKeever et al., 2017, p. 51). Through such conceptualisations, information literacy exists across multiple levels of school life. The levels relate to students' experiences of learning in individual classrooms, teachers' practice of designing and delivering curriculum, school leadership approaches to facilitating and enabling such practices and experiences within school, but also within leaders' own day-to-day approaches to leadership. Furthermore, as part of leadership practice, information literacy is critical within the broader community expectations of school decision-making and home-school engagement.

Several key features of information literacy emerge in education and for school leadership. Firstly, information literacy is more effective through collaboration and inherently requires the sharing of practice and approaches (Norgaard, 2003). Secondly, information literacy needs to be extended across fields and disciplines because "the domain of knowledge and skill involved in information literacy is much larger than previously imagined. When we begin to consider not only success in life and career, but also the dual goals of personal and world transformation as the benchmarks of the information literate individual, we are no longer talking about discrete critical thinking skills or database searching skills" (Ward, 2006, p. 400). Lastly, the experiential demands of information literacy reflect the importance of context and technology, because specific localised challenges and technological advancements require critically informed approaches to decision-making (Carlsson & Sundin, 2020; Çoklar et al., 2017). What does this mean for the work of school leaders? What happens to these challenges when they are compounded by events of crisis and unexpected change?

Researchers in educational leadership have long identified that the impact of school leaders on school effectiveness is second only to that of the classroom teacher (Hallinger & Heck, 1996; Heck & Hallinger, 2005). More recently, the work of school leaders has also evolved within the changing context of school life, and empirical studies of the global and local, or glocal, dimensions of such contexts (Sum, 2020). Leading schools involves navigating both the global and the local, so that effective leadership requires the negotiation of multiple domains such as the political, economic, and cultural (Brooks & Normore, 2010). In negotiating the global and the local, Brooks and Normore (2010) identify information literacy as a necessary component of leadership practice. School leaders are required to access and process information using the digital platforms and devices used by various stakeholders while applying a critical lens towards interpreting and making judgements as required for their work (Brooks & Normore, 2010). In this way, the evolving conceptualisation of information literacy from information studies across to broader education, and within the context of globalised technological advancements, aligns to the challenge facing school leaders. It is for the school leader to navigate the information, be that suggested directions, policies, strategic priorities, staff feedback, or parental concerns. The global or national change agenda is not always the agenda that best meets the needs of those living closest to school life.

School leaders are at the epicentre of an information tornado. It is a commonplace practice for principals, but little addressed or understood phenomenon about their leadership. Complex and conflicting information must be accessed, identified, analysed, and evaluated, then measured against priorities from within the eye of an ever-powerful storm. School leaders must do all this in a calm, outwardly reassuring and empathetic manner, for it is their leadership which must transform any crisis into a safe journey onwards.

Theoretical Framework: Information Literacy for Educational Change and Leadership

Given the challenge for school leaders, and the contemporary idea of information literacy as dynamic and situated, the two illustrative case studies which follow are explored using the framework of information literacy as a catalyst for educational change as proposed by Bruce (2004). Bruce argues that information literacy is transformational for the school as an organisation, and as a setting for students' learning. The four key principles of this proposition are outlined in this section. Given that information literacy is evident at multiple levels within schools, for the purpose of this chapter, the principles are also transposed and explored with a focus on school leadership practice. School leaders who can enact best practice which integrates information literacy in their own work and throughout the school, create an environment that fosters lifelong learning approaches (Brooks & Normore, 2010). In times of rapid technological development, or unexpected crisis, the learning organisation will be able to both adapt and pivot most effectively. Four key factors proposed by Bruce (2004) for facilitating information literacy are:

1. Partnerships between key personnel.
2. Teacher education and staff development.
3. Establishing policy and guidelines.
4. Cultural change and change in educational values.

Partnerships between key personnel are consistent with the way in which scholars have shown the conceptualisation of information literacy to have shifted from the singular domain of library science to a global experience of collaborative co-construction (Pinto et al., 2010; Ward, 2006). Information literacy cannot occur in isolation. For school leaders, this points to the need to be immersed in professional networks and associations, multiple stakeholder relationships, and a lived experience of distributed leadership (Harris & Spillane, 2008). Leadership practice must enact partnership across school work on curriculum design, staff training and professional development, professional learning communities, and policy work (Bruce, 2004).

Given the rich practice of partnerships, professional learning and development are essential to embedding a culture of continuous critical self-reflection and learning. Bruce (2004) identifies hurdles to such development programs, in particular, the need to adapt designs for learning to create new and more authentic experiences for students, the risk of emphasising content at the expense of process in a learning context, and the gap in technological skills to be able to support learning. For school leaders, these are aspects to address within school, but are as relevant to consider within the scope of their own leadership work. For example, hurdles may arise from struggles to adapt existing approaches due to limited experiences or lack of leadership preparation, pressure to secure the "what" without addressing changes in the "how" or "why", and limitations arising from a gap in skills to utilise the technology and platforms available to school leaders.

The need to establish policies and guidelines is self-evident in the global forums on information literacy, which have been referenced in preceding discussion of the literature. For the purposes of this chapter, policies at institutional level enable school leaders to lay clear foundations for partnerships, approaches to learning, and ongoing staff professional development. Enacting clear policies helps frame the nature of collaboration between teachers, the learning opportunities and resources made available to students, and the protocols for communicating within and across the school community. School leaders will also face an obligatory component of managing policies from top-down authoritative bodies and mediating these policies for their staff and their communities.

Cultural change reflects the progress made in the preceding three aspects: policy, staff development, and partnerships. Bruce (2004) identifies cultural change as the paradigm shift to student-centred pedagogies and process orientation to teaching. Such a shift must be built on changes in educational values. It requires policies and guidelines that facilitate the adoption of information literacy education. While this is constructed in regard to students, it can also be extended to the consideration of teachers and school leaders—their adoption of information literacy practices and engagement with information specialists. Such collaboration, and shifts towards an information literate approach, will require staff development that highlights the challenges of modifying or developing new learning experiences, the focus on process rather than voluminous content, and the effective use of technology. Therefore, by its collaborative prerequisite, information literacy requires partnerships across all stakeholders in the teaching and learning context, with shared responsibility underlined by clear objectives.

Illustrative Example A: School Leaders in Political Crisis

The first illustrative example is set in Bangladesh. All names and identities expressed here are pseudonyms. This example is a case study of school leadership in English Medium Schools (EMSs) in Bangladesh. This section begins with a brief outline of the context, before exploring the role of EMSs within the broader education system of Bangladesh. The backdrop informs the discussion of key findings in relation to how school leaders in EMSs in Bangladesh approached the crisis in student safety created by local political unrest. The findings will then discuss the school leaders' perceptions of information literacy as it related to their everyday work.

As a relatively smaller nation, neighboured by India and China, Bangladesh has driven its own sustained economic growth and positioned itself as a part of the rising South. Bangladesh also made considerable progress towards the MDGs, specifically in relation to improving primary school level enrolments (UNESCO, 2015). The sustained economic growth has given rise to an increased proportion of upper-class families within the local community. This, coupled with a public education system that is already stretched to accommodate goals such as increased enrolment targets, has led to a demand for alternative and better quality schools for local children. An already established group of EMSs in Dhaka city has found themselves inundated with aspiring families.

Originally, EMSs were formed in the settling of people following partition and the war of independence fought by the people of Bangladesh in 1971. School leaders in this group of EMSs work at this intersection of global economic, social and cultural changes, and local family aspirations. Data from the case study showed that these schools differentiated themselves from the government run schools by providing a foreign curriculum to local students and using English as the medium of instruction. Originally, the imported curriculum was primarily from the UK system, delivered via a local partnership with the British Council. However, over time, some schools have moved to other curriculum models such as that of the International Baccalaureate (IBO), individual states of Australia or Canada, or districts of North America. At the time of the study, local communities and the government were witness to an increasing voice of fundamentalist Islamic groups, heightened by the tension of an upcoming general election. While such political tension was not an altogether new experience for the schools and their local communities, the situation was exacerbated by an act of terrorism carried out on foreign nationals living in the city of Dhaka. These elements, amongst a number of other politico-religious uncertainties, resulted in a time of operational crisis for EMSs. At times all schools were expected to remain open and continue to operate as everyday practice, with the risk of violence ever-present. At other times, schools would need to close without much notice, throwing school bus transportation, student and staff safety, and organisational planning into complete upheaval. Through it all, students remained enrolled in their programs of study, and those with examinations faced the task ahead of completing terminal examinations as a means of securing their university studies (usually overseas).

Information literacy for these school leaders, and during this crisis, was tied to the safety and welfare of all staff and students while ensuring the ongoing learning for students. One of the key aspects for school leaders was the widespread engagement in both formal and informal encounters, and the information that these encounters generated for school leaders within their local community. School leaders across the EMSs referred to multiple examples of formal and informal communication and sources of information. For example, many parents were very comfortable with making appointments directly with Principals. Parents would raise their concerns, and offer suggestions, as to how the school might tackle logistical issues related to the transportation of students in a sudden school shutdown. Similarly, school leaders themselves were engaged in regular staff meetings, and emergency meetings, which they used to share concerns and clarify expectations within and across different teaching teams. These formal opportunities to identify, gather, analyse, and evaluate information were second nature to the school leaders. However, parents would also seek out school leaders informally beyond the context of day-to-day school life. Such informal conversations could happen at wider social gatherings, during everyday personal activities such as grocery shopping, or in spaces such as social clubs or art and music events. In such informal settings, parents sought out school leaders as a sign of respect, but also as an opportunity to clarify the operational and academic decisions being made within the schools. Often such informal opportunities could also provide school leaders the chance to network with representatives of government agencies, or others with similar policymaking roles, who might be willing to share possible insights into the challenge at hand. School leaders themselves discussed how they created informal opportunities to engage with teachers, other professional staff and students during school time by being visible across the campus or within playgrounds and classrooms. By creating these opportunities, school leaders were able to discuss staff concerns or listen to student queries directly from the source. These examples of formal and informal encounters, within and beyond school settings, demonstrate the high level of partnership between key stakeholders—school leaders, students, teachers, parents, policymakers. While the direct relationship to government agencies was not as strong in this context, the partnerships with parents were highly visible. This school–home partnership provided support for school leaders in negotiating and securing strategies for school shutdown, safe transportation routes, and shared cultural expectations about when, why, and how such decisions would be made.

Beyond collaboration with parents, school leaders in EMSs ensured that their access to information and approach to analysing and enacting decisions were co-constructed with their own staff. This was expressed in multiple ways. In addition to the formal and informal communication shared above, school leaders were consistent in identifying that they did not make decisions in isolation. Instead, they viewed their leadership practice as a joint endeavour, meaning that they were comfortable redirecting certain information and associated tasks to others in their team. This willingness, to delegate and distribute, demonstrated the level of trust present within school. The desire to be transparent amongst staff also reflected the cultural value of authentic leadership within schools. Leaders who were willing to share information, and delegate decisions and actions, signified a school culture which strengthened its people. This was evident in the access and use of professional networks across the EMSs. Many educators shared their experiences of belonging to local professional learning communities in Dhaka. They were simultaneously connected to international learning communities through online networks and forums. These networks provided opportunities for teachers to complete new professional development courses, share best practice, and engage in self-reflection related to their classroom approaches. Similarly, school leaders were involved in local leadership associations, meeting monthly to share challenges and strategies for addressing the most pressing matters at hand. At such network meetings, school leaders would share information acquired through both formal and informal communications as a way of generating solutions with fellow school principals. While some of these professional networks occurred locally, the international networks would occur remotely via online platforms. It was interesting to note that the use of online facilities for teacher training and professional networks was sound and well-established.

However, the integration of technology, social media, and broader online platforms was not as clear in relation to the teaching and learning experiences of students. Here the data showed that formal classroom interactions paid little heed to online platforms beyond the early notions of information literacy—that is, to search and find answers to a fixed concept. In this realm, it was the students who initiated the informal interaction by raising questions about issues such as the political challenges, the refugee crisis of the Rohingya people, and the global tensions related to Muslim identity and Islamic fundamentalism. Teachers and school leaders expressed that it was students who brought these questions into the classroom. The educators themselves rarely used online media platforms as sources for classroom activities. Online media and social media platforms were deemed unreliable for school activities. Leaders expressed stronger reliance on information gathered directly from their community rather than what was available via media outlets. By contrast, educators were comfortable engaging with social media platforms for their personal use, but they were emphatic that such platforms did not belong in the classroom. The challenge here is that while teachers and school leaders utilise technology for their own professional learning and networks, the related practices were not being demonstrated in the way learning opportunities were being created for and with students. It was clear that EMSs were open to student debate and rich discussions were part of the learning culture, but there did appear to be a gap in protocols in this respect.

Illustrative Example B: School Leaders' Practice During COVID-19

The second illustrative example is based on a case study of school leadership in Australia during the most recent crisis of COVID-19. This case study brought together school principals from public schools in the South East region of Victoria, Australia. The principals met regularly throughout the second half of the school year of 2020, sharing their most recent challenges, strategies, outcomes, and aspirations. Unlike the EMSs in Bangladesh, the principals worked in government schools, and so their practice was situated within a state-wide education system, and part of a national framework. Inherently, state run schools exist within an extended chain of command from centralised policymakers, out through regional offices, to the school principals. School leaders within these schools are supported by leadership teams, and in this case, serve communities of diverse socio-economic and cultural backgrounds in the south-eastern part of the state of Victoria. The academic year begins each January in Australia, meaning schools were in full swing as COVID-19 unfurled itself on the local community. Information was rapid, though not always accurate, while decisions were time compressed and of the highest priority for school principals. The health and well-being of staff, students, and families within the community remained tied to the ways in which educators responded to the challenges they faced. The preliminary findings of this case study are shared here as an illustration of what happened to leadership practice in the maddening deluge of information which circulated and continues to circulate regarding COVID-19 and its implications.

Across the meetings shared with principals, two key themes oscillated in tension with each other. Firstly, there was the self-reflection of how the practice of school leadership was being shaped by the crisis of a global pandemic. This generated internalised ideas of leading and being a leader. When sharing their ideas on how school leadership was being shaped by COVID-19, the term trust and the idea that school leaders had become community leaders were significant. Trust referred to the need for school leaders to present their confident and professional "face". This trust put school leaders in a position of accountability for the well-being of all those within school, but by extension, to all those within the immediate school community. In being a school leader, the level of trust placed on principals meant that they worked as leaders across the whole community. Information that school leaders received was then being shared in ways that the members of school could digest and process. This information was perceived as reliable, because the school leaders embodied the role of "village elder" and therefore were trusted. Within school settings, school leaders understood the nuances of non-verbal cues when communicating with staff, and the ways in which staff members or students may perceive the information being delivered. This added pressure to the information, and delivery of information, to help manage the rapidly changing situation. What school leaders shared was the realisation of the need to become the role of community leader. This was not a negotiated process, but an internalised self-reflection related to securing the trust of all those who found themselves reliant on the school leader to also lead where gaps in information appeared. In order to internalise these expectations, school leaders relied on their own networks of colleagues. Often the leaders were part of formal networks based on geographical area and regional offices. However, most also called upon informal networks, with past mentors and other colleagues, who provided significant support in processing the necessary shift from school to community leadership. The ways in which the school leaders experienced the change in the leadership profile were one of the most strongly expressed responses shared in the case study.

Secondly, there was a sense of expected leadership, shaped by national coverage and the broader media perceptions of schools and schooling. While the challenge of internalising a shifting sense of self as leader, and the imbued trust which accompanied this, was met with positions of strength amongst leaders, it remained at tension with the broader expectations of schools within the general community. In particular, there was a perception that the discourse in the mainstream media was not always consistent in regard to the work being done in school and by school leaders. Furthermore, media coverage was not consistently supportive of the work of schools. Some principals shared that the climate in the media had reached saturation points, in particular with references to school leaders. Consequently, leaders expressed a sense of schools seemingly at risk of being "caught out" for perceived mistakes. This implied risk in any decisions being taken at school level, and a challenge in the timing and manner of communication for school leaders. The balancing act was particularly difficult during the earlier part of school shutdowns, and online learning, because principals found themselves at the end of an information chain. Policy statements and positions were being communicated at state level to the media, and time constraints increasingly resulted in schools leaders becoming the final destination for such information rather than the first. To the local community this sometimes meant that parents were hearing decisions through television press updates before school leaders were able to formally circulate the information. The chain of information, and access to higher level decisions, highlight the potential disruption of the media. This applied to both the portrayal of school leadership work and the effective communication between policy makers and school leaders. It was most apparent and impactful in the first weeks of facing COVID-19 challenges.

As school leaders collaborated within their networks, and engaged more informally with their regional office teams, their sense of agency and the shared expertise of other colleagues seemed to empower them in their work. Several principals spoke of the shift to planning beyond the immediacy of online learning, trusting their curriculum leaders and teachers to follow through with instructional expertise, and looking ahead to planning for what school might look like in a COVID-normal time. Schools had experienced two instances of lockdown and accompanying phased returns of students to school. However, the last of the four terms for the academic year enabled all students to return to school for a full timetable of classes and events. By this stage, school leaders were reflective about the impact that the time away from school had on students. However, this was not driven by academic concerns, but rather, the social-emotional aspects of students' well-being, the changes in the friendship groups, and some of the key events which may have previously served as a form of rite of passage through either primary or the secondary schooling years. This relational focus of their work as school leaders also extended to parents. Many parents made the time to communicate their appreciation for the work of teachers and school leaders. Such feedback from parents enabled the school leaders to acknowledge the challenge of the journey they had completed by the end of the year. Until this endpoint, school leaders had sustained a very focused outlook on the work that needed to be done, the people in their care, and the ways in which they could continue to reach out to students and parents at home. It seemed that the acknowledgement from parents consolidated the partnership which had been facilitating the shifts in schooling—from on site, to online, and back again.

Discussion

Based on the conceptualisations of information literacy, the theoretical framing of the four key elements proposed by Bruce (2004), and the illustrative examples, this discussion explores two themes. Firstly, the opportunities for information literacy pursued by school leaders in both crises, and the gaps which emerge for the dynamic and situated practice of information literacy that is needed in education, are considered. Secondly, the implications of expectations of school leaders within the wider community, as discourses of the next normal, reimagining education, and learning gaps take hold, are identified.

Two different examples of crises have been used to illustrate school leaders' perceptions of information literacy within their leadership practice. Both examples demonstrate the different ways in which school leaders build and rely on partnership across key personnel as proposed by Bruce (2004). In the case of school leaders in EMSs, the cultural backdrop contributed to the much wider informal partnerships between school, home, and the broader community. These collaborations enabled the school leaders to co-construct meaningful interpretations of the challenges and to build strategies based on the information available to them for the welfare of students and staff. In a different context, of Australian principals in state schools, the response to crisis began with information sharing and communication through formal interactions and positional authority. While parents expressed support for educators, school leaders spent considerable time negotiating the manner in which parents came to know of certain strategies and approaches for school closures or changes to learning approaches. In both examples, the level of teacher education and professional development showed commitment from school leaders to empower their teams, and furthermore, to practice distributed approaches to leadership where possible (Bruce, 2004; Harris & Spillane, 2008). The term trust was explicit in both cases, and this is critical as we look ahead to how schooling may change in the continued challenges of COVID-19 and beyond. In a meeting following the global celebration of World Teachers Day 2020, UNESCO identified the need to acknowledge the social value of teachers' work, and the significance of human interaction (UNESCO, 2021). As educators globally experienced gaps and challenges in the rapid shift to online learning, this technological transition and hurdle highlights a key gap in the four factors Bruce (2004) identified for information literacy. There is a gap in the policies and implementation guidelines with regard to a more holistic integration of technology with learning. Over the last two decades, scholars have been anticipating that "by opening schools up to the 'world' and thereby reducing the inequalities of time and space, educational superhighways are, in many cases, being presented as `great levellers' for schools, students and teaching staff" (Selwyn & Brown, 2000, p. 670). However, the pandemic has shown technology to be a factor of inequity. In practice, school cultures and policies were still evolving to a fully integrated process for information literacy within the student experience. It is significant to note that school leaders themselves were fluent and confident with technology as it fitted their own development, and most teachers were confident in participating in various professional development and network activities through technology. Enabling the same level of integration for students and for learning has shown itself to be a gap, and one critical in any crisis where schools shut down (Harris, 2020; Hooge & Pont, 2020).

Throughout the COVID-19 disruption, the focus has remained sharply on leadership. For school leaders, there has been a rush to publications and guidance which advocate and recommend a host of changes that promise better positioning in the "next normal". These have included leadership that needs to act across various stages of resilience, reimagination, and reform (Sneader & Singhal, 2020), pause for reimagining schooling (Zhao, 2020), principles to protect organisational performance and leverage opportunities to become "market shapers" (Renjen, 2020), and calls for increased investment and adoption of online learning or hybrid approaches (Hooge & Pont, 2020). Any one of these agendas brings forth a major educational change that is not only organisational, but requires systemic uptake and follow through. In championing for change, there is a risk of minimising the work that is being done by school leaders and their teams. In order to argue for bigger and better things, we fail to acknowledge both the vastness of systemic changes that have been led and delivered by school teams at the source of the challenges, and the condensed timelines within which such change was undertaken. That is not to say change is not necessary. Rather that there is a possibility that the speed and voracity of the information tornado which has accompanied COVID-19, and the potential damage which may lie in the wake of misinformation, present school leaders with tough decisions. Leaders are facing compounded challenges and physical and mental exhaustion (Hatami et al., 2020). There are many expectations which we as a society have of our institutions, and that enthusiasm brings forth many possibilities. However, while it may be "possible to speculate, hope and imagine what the future of education will be, right now the jury is still out. This is unprecedented territory with few education signposts, clues or markers" (Harris, 2020, p. 322). Sifting through the possibilities, trying to identify ways to reimagine, and considering what may be the best investment to make for serving their community will require information literacy in new and nuanced ways.

Conclusion

As COVID-19 continues to impact upon the nature of educational provision across the globe, many challenges have emerged, leading to a flurry of publications intended to guide educators and policymakers with oversight of education systems. This chapter has explored the need for information literacy that enables school leaders to know when, why, and where they need input, and how to critically evaluate and process the many forms and sources of information in order to enact meaningful change in schools (McKeever et al., 2017). Some takeaways from this discussion to consider begin with the fact that school leaders continue to work at the core of their community, and alongside their teams, because schools have never stopped providing learning opportunities. Secondly, school leaders continue to be inundated with information deemed necessary for their role, even when their health and well-being need further consideration. Thirdly, as highlighted in the illustrative examples, school leaders find themselves as community leaders—a role they are assigned as an expression of trust amongst families and community members. This role as community leader is another dimension of information literate practice they are expected to fulfil. Second to last, principals do not lead in a vacuum. Likewise, they are currently relying on the strength of informal networks to supplement the demands of formal expectations of their role. Lastly, while such tensions may not be entirely new, the role of school leaders has been elevated to political football in the media coverage of schooling during this most recent time of COVID-19. With these closing remarks, the following questions are presented for further reflection:

- What is the role of educational policymakers in regard to potential misinformation about schools and school leaders?
- How could school leaders be supported to address the gap of technological integration?
- Who are the key personnel to provide partnership and support for school leaders?
- How can strengthening information literacy of aspiring school leaders sustain their time as school principals?
- While there are calls to reimagine education, where will information for such re-imagining come from?

References

Anderson-Levitt, K. M. (2003). A world culture of schooling? In *Local meanings, global schooling* (pp. 1–26). Springer.

Ball, S. J. (1998). Big policies/small world: An introduction to international perspectives in education policy. *Comparative Education, 34*(2), 119–130. https://doi.org/10.1080/03050069828225

Ball, S. J. (2004, June 17). Education for sale! The commodification of everything? In *King Annual Education Lecture 2004*, London.

Ball, S. J. (2017). *The education debate*. Policy Press.

Brooks, J. S., & Normore, A. H. (2010, January 1). Educational leadership and globalization: Literacy for a glocal perspective. *Educational Policy, 24*(1), 52–82. https://doi.org/10.1177/0895904809354070

Bruce, C. (2004). Information literacy as a catalyst for educational change. A background paper. In P. A. Danaher (Ed.), *Proceedings "Lifelong Learning: Whose responsibility and what is your contribution?", the 3rd International Lifelong Learning Conference* (pp. 8–19). Yeppoon.

Carlsson, H., & Sundin, O. (2020, March). Educating for democracy? The role of media and information literacy education for pupils in Swedish compulsory school. In *International conference on information* (pp. 307–326). Springer.

Cogburn, D. L. (1998). Globalisation, knowledge, education and training in the information age. *International Forum on Information and Documentation, 23*, 23–29.

Çoklar, A. N., Yaman, N. D., & Yurdakul, I. K. (2017). Information literacy and digital nativity as determinants of online information search strategies. *Computers in Human Behavior, 70*, 1–9. https://doi.org/10.1016/j.chb.2016.12.050

Einstein, A., Seelig, C., Bargmann, S., Unna, I., & Wolff, B. (1954). Ideas and opinions (p. 384). New York: Wings Books.

Hallinger, P., & Heck, R. H. (1996, February 1). Reassessing the Principal's role in school effectiveness: A review of empirical research, 1980–1995. *Educational Administration Quarterly, 32*(1), 5–44. https://doi.org/10.1177/0013161x96032001002

Harris, A. (2020). COVID-19—School leadership in crisis? *Journal of Professional Capital and Community, 5*(3/4), 321–326. https://doi.org/10.1108/JPCC-06-2020-0045

Harris, A., & Spillane, J. (2008). Distributed leadership through the looking glass. *Management in Education, 22*(1), 31–34. https://doi.org/10.1177/0892020607085623

Hatami, H., Sjatil, P., & Sneader, K. (2020). https://www.mckinsey.com/featured-insights/leadership/the-toughest-leadership-test

Heck, R. H., & Hallinger, P. (2005). The study of educational leadership and management: Where does the field stand today? *Educational Management Administration & Leadership, 33*(2), 229–244.

Hooge, E., & Pont, B. (2020). School leadership in unpredictable times. *European Journal of Education, 55*(2), 135–138. https://doi.org/10.1111/ejed.12397

Lingard, B., Martino, W., & Rezai-Rashti, G. (2013). Testing regimes, accountabilities and education policy: Commensurate global and national developments. *Journal of Education Policy, 28*(5), 539–556. https://doi.org/10.1080/02680939.2013.820042

McKeever, C., Bates, J., & Reilly, J. (2017). School library staff perspectives on teacher information literacy and collaboration. *The Journal of Information Literacy, 11*(2), 51–68. https://doi.org/10.11645/11.2.2187

Montgomery, M. (2020). *Disinformation as a wicked problem: Why we need co-regulatory frameworks*. T. B. Institution. https://www.brookings.edu/wp-content/uploads/2020/08/Montgomery_Disinformation-Regulation_PDF.pdf

Norgaard, R. (2003). Writing information literacy: Contributions to a concept. *Reference and User Services Quarterly, 43*(2), 124–130.

Pinto, M., Cordón, J. A., & Gómez Díaz, R. (2010). Thirty years of information literacy (1977—2007): A terminological, conceptual and statistical analysis. *Journal of Librarianship and Information Science, 42*(1), 3–19. https://doi.org/10.1177/0961000609345091

Rader, H. B. (2002). Information literacy 1973–2002: A selected literature review. *Library Trends, 51*(2), 242–259.

Renjen, P. (2020). *The heart of resilient leadership: Responding to COVID-19*. https://www2.deloitte.com/us/en/insights/economy/covid-19/heart-of-resilient-leadership-responding-to-covid-19.html

Selwyn, N. (2009). The digital native—Myth and reality. *ASLIB Proceedings, 61*(4), 364–379. https://doi.org/10.1108/00012530910973776

Selwyn, N., & Brown, P. (2000). Education, nation states and the globalization of information networks. *Journal of Education Policy, 15*(6), 661–682. https://doi.org/10.1080/02680930010000245

Sneader, K., & Singhal, S. (2020). *Beyond coronavirus: The path to the next normal*. McKinsey. https://www.mckinsey.com/industries/healthcare-systems-and-services/our-insights/beyond-coronavirus-thepath-to-the-next-normal

Sum, N. (2020). Glocalisation: Issues and strategies for school leadership. In J. S. Brooks & A. Heffernan (Eds.), *The school leadership survival guide: What to do when things go wrong, how to learn from mistakes, and why you should prepare for the worst*. Information Age.

Tehranian, M. (2001). Towards a fourth civilisation: The dawning of the informatic age. *Global Dialogue, 3*(1), 112–123.

UNESCO. (1990). *World conference on EFA, Jomtien, 1990—background document* world conference on EFA, Jomtien, 1990, Thailand.

UNESCO. (2000). *The Dakar framework for action: Education for all: Meeting our collective commitments: Including six regional frameworks for action*. The Dakar framework for action, Dakar

UNESCO. (2015). Education for All 2000–2015: Achievements and challenges. In *EFA global monitoring report 2015* (p. 516).

UNESCO. (2018). *Accountability in education: meeting our commitments* (Global Education Monitoring Report 2017/8, Issue. https://apo.org.au/node/143391

UNESCO. (2021). GEM2020: *Addressing the future of teaching and learning*. https://en.unesco.org/news/gem-2020-addressing-future-teaching-and-learning

Ward, D. (2006). Revisioning information literacy for lifelong meaning. *The Journal of Academic Librarianship, 32*(4), 396–402. https://doi.org/10.1016/j.acalib.2006.03.006

Weiner, S. (2011). How information literacy becomes policy: An analysis using the multiple streams framework. *Library Trends, 60*(2), 297–311. https://doi.org/10.1353/lib.2011.0037

Weiner, S. A. (2012). Institutionalizing information literacy. *The Journal of Academic Librarianship, 38*(5), 287–293. https://doi.org/10.1016/j.acalib.2012.05.004

World Bank. (2011). "Learning for All : Investing in People's Knowledge and Skills to Promote Development". Washington, DC. © World Bank. https://openknowledge.worldbank.org/handle/10986/27790 License: CC BY 3.0 IGO

Zhao, Y. (2020). COVID-19 as a catalyst for educational change. *Prospects, 49*(1), 29–33. https://doi.org/10.1007/s11125-020-09477-y

Nicola Sum, PhD, is a lecturer in educational leadership within the Faculty of Education at Monash University. Her work in the faculty draws on over 20 years of school experience, having worked in the Victorian, UK and international school systems. Following her work as a school principal, Nicola completed her doctoral studies on the inter-connected nature of glocalisation (global-local) and educational leadership practice. She teaches in post-graduate programs of principal preparation, educational leadership, educational research and globalisation, alongside undergraduate studies in teaching and learning and teacher leadership. Her research interests include school leadership, principal preparation, international education, education systems, and global education policy.

Supporting Leadership Success in Times of Global Disruption: Best Practices for Transformational Executive Coaching

19

Noushin Bayat and Kerri Cissna

Introduction

The COVID-19 pandemic continues to require organizations across every industry, large or small, national or multinational, local or global, to quickly change the way they work, make decisions, deliver services and products, and collaborate to ensure survival. Almost overnight, leaders had to make tough decisions about their talent management practices, incorporating remote workforces, providing support and capabilities training to their teams, and addressing supply chain challenges where the very presence of their employees could be a health threat. Facing COVID-19 continues to impact the very fabric of many organizations that are based on hierarchical structures characterized by slow decision-making and silos. The urgency of needing to make quick decisions in the face of COVID-19 revealed many weak points in our current state of organizational and societal leadership, where indecisiveness, lack of collaboration, and mistrust add to the already heavy burden and health toll on every sector of society and economy (De Smet et al., 2021; Kaiser, 2020; Worley & Jules, 2020).

The events of 2020 brought immediate and heightened attention to what researchers had coined since the late 1990s as "VUCA," referring to conditions where volatility, unpredictability, complexity, and ambiguity change the very nature of decision-making and leadership best practices (Bayat, 2018). Whereas a top-down hierarchical leadership model proves effective in addressing challenges that have a clear cause and effect; leadership within VUCA environments requires agile and adaptive decision-making and collaborative facilitation to iterate through a series of innovative solutions on an ongoing basis. The COVID-19 pandemic has amplified

N. Bayat
Texas A&M, Master of Engineering Technical Management, College Station Texas, TX, USA

K. Cissna (✉)
Miami University Farmer School of Business, Oxford, OH, USA

S. K. Dhiman, J. F. Marques (eds.), *Leadership After COVID-19*, Future of Business and Finance, https://doi.org/10.1007/978-3-030-84867-5_19

this need astronomically. As Worley and Jules (2020) contend, not only were the characteristics of the virus a big unknown to leaders, but also their organizations—no matter how agile—were completely unprepared for such a crisis.

Leading researchers provide evidence of the need for exploratory and collaborative leadership skills, often referred to as Vertical Development, to complement the more linear top-down (horizontal) authoritative approach to leadership (Arena & Uhl-Bien, 2016; Cavanagh & Lane, 2012; Collinson & Tourish, 2015; Grint, 2010; Holman, 2010; Scharmer, 2010). Vertical skill-sets are typically not in the wheelhouse of executive leaders who are often required to come up with a solution to "fix" things fast (top-down model). As leaders confront the realities of a post-COVID-19 world, executive coaches will continue to find themselves as trusted advisors to leaders who are managing challenges and crises that have no precedent or blueprint for clear action. As such, understanding the nature of today's complex environments and its impact on leadership behavior and coaching best practices is critical for coaches and the leaders they support (Bayat, 2018). This chapter summarizes a qualitative research study conducted in 2017–2018 that examined best practices for executive coaching in the years prior to the COVID-19 pandemic—an era where increasingly diversified and interconnected global networks of production created a disruptive world for all organizations. The findings are extremely relevant today, as society demonstrates a growing hunger for trust and confidence in leadership.

Background

Leading in a world of nearly 7.5 billion people (U.S. Census Bureau, 2017), global leaders in public and private sectors face unprecedented change often characterized by the term VUCA – volatile, uncertain, complex and ambiguous (Johansen, 2012; Stiehm & Townsend, 2002). First introduced at the U.S. Army War College, VUCA reflected the changing dynamics of a post-Cold War environment where a strategic focus on "Russia, Russia, Russia" shifted to "VUCA, VUCA, VUCA" (Barber, 1992; Steihm & Townsend, 2022, pp. 5–6). VUCA conditions heightened by COVID-19 continue to surface at alarming rates, making leadership agility and innovative problem solving a requirement. Researchers continue to site VUCA conditions as key to understanding the nature of dramatic changes global leaders face today (Bennett & Lemoine, 2014; Gandhi, 2017; Hall & Rowland, 2016; Kauffman & Hodgetts, 2016; Petrie, 2014; Rodriguez & Rodriguez, 2015; Wilson & Lawton-Smith, 2016).

Scholars envisioned the first decades of the twenty-first century as a threshold where old systems reach their tipping points, leading to new opportunities to engage a globally connected world (Johansen, 2012). The COVID-19 pandemic continues to reveal this threshold of our healthcare, political, education, technological and economic systems which stand fragile and often immobile in the face of changing demands. Global leaders are needed, across every industry, who have a wide scope and perspective to create a common cause for success among the larger interdependent systems (Arthur, 1996; Harari, 2020; Johansen, 2012). As these predictions continue to unfold, leadership will look very different than it did in the past.

Problem Statement

Change is the only constant, but what happens when *constant disruptive change* becomes the norm? Ambiguous conditions can diminish predictability which negatively impacts the ease of mind that comes from clearly identifiable cause and effect. Research in neuroscience reveals that our brain constantly delivers predictions about our environment based on past experience or memories (Barrett, 2018). When predictions do not match the reality of a situation, then an intense learning process kicks into gear that often creates feelings of anxiety and discomfort. Thus, our current state of constant change, chaos, and distraction causes people to experience confusion, anxiety, and a sense of diminishing trust and doubt in our abilities to problem-solve. Given our need for cognitive stability, people often "grasp at any story that holds potential to ameliorate the discomfort" (Cavanagh & Lane, 2012, p. 82). So often, people prefer a sense of false certainty, instead of the discomfort that often accompanies not knowing. Leaders now have to recognize and help manage the intense emotions that people are experiencing as a result of COVID-19, in addition to establishing trust and credibility for leading under duress.

COVID-19 has led to a significant amount of public distrust, as leaders mishandled the pandemic in a variety of ways leading to high records of deaths and the worst recession that has been recorded (Warden, 2020). The absences or incapacities of leadership, lack of direction, and leadership incompetence are responsible for contributing to what health experts are calling the greatest policy failure for a generation (Horton, 2020). The COVID-19 outbreak blind-sided many policymakers, leading to restrictions on human activity. There were six key drivers that influenced the severity of COVID-19: the exponential pace of transmission, global interconnectedness, health-sector capacity, wider state capacity, the economic impact of suppression measures, and fragilities caused by the 2008 financial crisis (Collins et al., 2020). There were five key challenges that leaders had to confront as a result: technical assessment, risk perception, evaluation, management, and communication (Collins et al., 2020). Leadership decisions are not always clear or intuitive, and each choice has a downside which makes leading quite difficult during a pandemic like COVID-19 (Fischhoff, 2020).

Although the COVID-19 pandemic highlighted the need for new leadership approaches, surveys revealed a crisis of leadership years before, with research showing that over 80% of organizations doubted their leadership pipeline's competency to meet current challenges (Kaiser & Curphy, 2013; Sinar, Wellins, Ray, Abel & Neal, 2015). An IBM global survey of over 1500 global leaders revealed that more than half of all senior officers struggled with confidence in their own ability to manage complexity and nearly 80% foresee the complexity becoming greater, noting that they have "never faced a learning curve so steep" (IBM Global CEO Study, 2012, p. 18). A survey of over 13,000 global leaders revealed <20% of leaders are viewed as capable of effectively managing their organizations (Sinar et al., 2015). Harvard Kennedy School of Public Policy (Rosenthal, 2012) found that 70% of the USA believe that there is a leadership crisis in our country and that we are at a risk of declining as a nation if our leadership does not improve (as cited in, Kaiser & Curphy, 2013, p. 295). The costs associated with lackluster leadership are estimated to be around \$1.5–\$2.7 million per senior executive who fails to provide effective leadership (Gaddis & Foster, 2015; Kaiser & Hogan, 2011), in addition to costs resulting from severance packages and lost work opportunities (Gaddis & Foster, 2015).

Literature Review

VUCA frequently appears in scholarly literature as conditions that are volatile, unpredictable/uncertain, complex, and ambiguous. Volatility refers to the frequency and stability of change; uncertainty refers to the lack of understanding for the "meaningful ramifications" of change; complexity refers to intricate interconnections that diminish the capacity to determine linear causality of change; and ambiguity refers to not knowing the "rules of the game" (Bennett & Lemoine, 2014, p. 313). Scholars use a variety of terms or labels to explain the escalating pace, volume, and complexity of change facing global leaders, including: super-industrialism (Toffler, 1971), third wave (Toffler, 1980), permanent white water (Vaill, 1996), power shift (Toffler, 1990), new economy (Scharmer, 2000), VUCA (Steihm & Townsend, 2002), liquid modernity (Bauman, 2007), and a general crisis of industrialism (Toffler, 2007), among others. These terms are used to describe a world of disruptive change where unpredictability and heightened complexity blur decisive decision-making (Bauman, 2007; Scharmer, 2001; Toffler, 1990; Vaill, 1996). This seems like it could be a leadership nightmare, but it is actually an opportunity for leaders who are ready to embrace change and leverage diverse teams for creative solutions and innovations. Leaders can prepare for this VUCA environment by further understanding the impact of complexity.

Impact of Complexity on Global Leaders

Paradox is a symptom of the VUCA environment, which is known to defy linear rationality and challenges leaders both emotionally and cognitively (Cavanagh & Lane, 2012; Lewis, 2000; Smith, 2015; Vince & Broussine, 1996). There are four dimensions that have been identified to describe this complexity as: multiplicity, interdependence, ambiguity, and flux (Lane et al., 2004). These complexities create business challenges that executives cannot predict (Mendenhall et al., 2013). This means that modern global leaders are confronted with multiple competing goals and strategies such as collaboration vs. control, individuality vs. group loyalty, flexibility vs. efficiency, profit vs. social contribution (Fiol, 2002; Jarzabkowski & Sillince, 2007; O'Reilly & Tushman, 2011; Smith, 2015; Smith & Lewis, 2011; Smith & Tushman, 2005). These competing goals and strategies are described as paradoxical and "contradictory yet interrelated elements that exist simultaneously and persist over time" (Smith & Lewis, 2011, p. 382).

These paradoxes can cause difficult emotions for global leaders who rely on consistency between attitude/behavior and cognition/action (Smith, 2015; Smith &

Lewis, 2011). Without this type of consistency, leaders cope with defense mechanisms such as denial, repression, humor, or decision-making paralysis to deal with the emotional discomforts inherent in contradictory situations (Cavanagh & Lane, 2012; Smith & Berg, 1987; Smith & Lewis, 2011; Vince & Broussine, 1996). These intense situations can trigger experiences which some scholars refer to as crucible, demanding that global leaders acquire new worldviews, mental models, and perspectives (Thomas, 2008).

Executive coaches are needed to help global leaders adjust to the new demands that accompany such paradoxical situations. Scholars suggest that this can be done with the acquisition of emotional and behavioral skills that help cope with this intense work situation (Fugate et al., 2008; Gilley et al., 2009; Goleman, 2000; Grant, 2014; Jamali et al., 2009). Other researchers have revealed that challenges of a VUCA world are adaptive instead of technical (Heifetz, 1994, 2002; Heifetz & Linsky, 2004; Helsing, Howell, Kegan, & Lahey, 2009; Kegan & Lahey, 2016; Petrie, 2014). Technical challenges demand a leader's vision and expertise to find a solution, while adaptive challenges require the participation of an interdisciplinary team in order to identify the best path forward (Heifetz, 1994; Heifetz & Linsky, 2004; Helsing et al., 2008; Kegan & Lahey, 2016). Adaptive challenges are also more complicated because they require leaders to examine their own underlying beliefs, assumptions, biases, and values in order to chart a breakthrough solution (Heifetz & Linsky, 2004; Helsing et al., 2008). This is where the role of a modern executive coach becomes extremely important, as it is difficult for a leader to do this type of complex work in isolation. Leaders must learn to manage emotions that are tied to complexity while also learning adaptive leadership skills and helping team members to manage emotions/behaviors that are typically not discussed in the workplace.

Impact of Complexity on Leadership Development

Conventional models of leadership development often focus on developing specific individual traits for successful leadership. A VUCA environment challenges the core principles of hierarchical management practices and leadership programs that focus on decisive control and predictable outcomes (Collinson & Tourish, 2015; Grint & Jackson, 2010; Sinclair, 2008; Wilson, 2016). A new type of leadership is emerging as a collaborative process, anchored and sustained within the organization's social capital instead of its human capital (Arena & Uhl-Bien, 2016; Collinson & Tourish, 2015; Grint, 2010; Holman, 2010; Sinclair, 2008). Scholars use the terms horizontal and vertical to point to the differing approaches for developing technical skills (McGuire & Rhodes, 2009; Petrie, 2014). Technical challenges are addressed by horizontal development, and adaptive skills are needed for vertical development to deal with adaptive challenges.

The behavioral competencies referred to as horizontal development (technical learning) focus on skills, abilities, and behaviors that are most useful in the face of clearly defined problems that have clear solutions (Petrie, 2014). The competencies that leaders need in times of complexity are referred to as vertical development. These competencies are more nuanced and complex in terms of learning, and reflect an individual's core assumptions and mental models of how they view the world and their relationships, their presence with themselves and others around them. The process of developing thinking competencies which reflect mental models is a developmental process that often requires specific stages of development over extended periods of time (Helsing, Howell, Kegan & Lahey, 2009; Petrie, 2014).

The Founder of Paypal, Peter Thiel, describes horizontal and vertical processes as the two ways that we make progress towards future goals (2014). The horizontal or extensive progress happens when leaders "copy and paste" the things that worked in the past with a few adjustments, while the vertical progress is made by doing/trying new things (Thiel, 2014). Vertical progress is obviously more difficult because it cannot rely on pattern recognition or imagining things that have already been experienced. If horizontal development refers to the size of cup which holds knowledge and skills, vertical development refers to expanding the size of the cup to hold more complex scenarios. .

Global leaders in a VUCA world require a more collective exploratory approach, instead of a linear approach based on a leader's decisive authority and expertise (Arena & Uhl-Bien, 2016; Cavanagh & Lane, 2012; Collinson & Tourish, 2015; Grint, 2010; Holman, 2010). Systems scholars contend that the missing link in leadership development programs is the collaboration with all stakeholders from start to finish in identifying clear intentions and charting innovative implementations across the system as a whole (Arena & Uhl-Bien, 2016; Cavanagh & Lane, 2012; Holman, 2010; Scharmer, 2010). Executive coaches can guide leaders through this process of vertical thinking by leveraging the talent on diverse teams to create innovative solutions through deep listening, facilitation and collaboration, but it will take a commitment to doing things differently.

Impact of Complexity on Executive Coaching

The complex problems that global leaders face in a modern VUCA world challenge the evidence-based models of executive coaching which assume a predictable context with linear causation (Cavanagh & Lane, 2012). Executive coaches no longer have a privileged position of prediction and control as part of their profession; therefore, they cannot rely on the stories and anecdotes from the past. Coaching programs need to shift away from a linear and stable playing field which focuses on predictable cause and effect scenarios, and move towards placing emphasis on supporting individual team members through constant uncertainty and change (Cavanagh & Lane, 2012; Susing & Cavanagh, 2013). An executive coach must now support leaders as they navigate the complex and paradoxical landscape of today's business world. However, scholars point to a lack of consistency in coaching practice—in terms of assessments and philosophical approaches (Bono et al., 2009)—and a general disagreement about how to impact behavior change (Nieminen et al., 2013, p. 179). As a result, a study was conducted to explore ways that executive coaches can better prepare leaders (and themselves) for this type of complexity. This chapter will describe the qualitative research study which identifies best practices for executive coaches to employ in a VUCA environment. These practices have become essential for leading through the uncertainties of a COVID-19 pandemic and beyond.

Theoretical Foundations

This research study is grounded in complexity systems theory, which helps us understand how human behavior changes when environments change from predictability, control, and linear causation to unpredictability and lack of control without a clear sense of causation. In this theory, mechanisms of engaging within complex systems have to change in order to become more adaptive, flexible, collaborative and capable of being open to the emergence of innovative solutions. A system is brought together to achieve something and is always more than the sum of its parts (Cavanagh & Lane, 2012; Meadows, 2008). System refers to "a set of things—people, cells, molecules, or whatever—interconnected in such a way that they produce their own pattern of behavior over time" (Meadows, 2008, p. 2). Something new emerges as a result of the *interaction* of the parts which is different than each of the separate parts (Cavanagh & Lane, 2012). This product is an *emergence* of the system's connectivity and interrelations between all of its parts (Cavanagh & Lane, 2012; Holman, 2010; Meadows, 2008).

There is a difference between simple, complex, and chaotic systems. In a simple system, the relationship between its parts are linear, repetitive, predictable, and understandable. A complex system's response to change is unpredictable in nature because its parts adapt in iterative ways, and a chaotic system deals with change that is so highly unstable and unpredictable that it appears as chaos (Cavanagh & Lane, 2012). The space between the rational linear system and the chaotic unstable system is referred to as the "edge of chaos" (p. 77). This is where human systems reside in ways that are self-organizing and adaptive to change. Stacey (1999, 2001, 2007) defines this complex response mechanism as similar to an ongoing conversation which changes in response to the shifting context (as cited in Cavanagh & Lane, 2012). What emerges from human systems are certain self-organizing behaviors, roles, processes, and outcomes in ways that help humans manage external conditions (Morrison, 2000).

Methodology

A qualitative study was utilized for this study to gain a deeper understanding of: (a) the strategies and practices that successful executive coaches utilize in supporting senior executives of global teams or organization, (b) the challenges they face in implementing these strategies, (c) the ways in which they measure the success of executive coaching, and (d) recommendations they have for other executive coaches.

Data collection was conducted through semi-structured interviews lasting about 60-min each. The majority of the interviews were conducted via Zoom online conference platform during the months of January to March 2017. Participants responded to 14 interview questions drawing on personal reflections from their years of executive coaching experience with senior executives at global organizations.

Sample

A total of 39 executive coaches participated in this study, all regarded as successful executive coaches by their years of practice, referral base, client roster, and testimonials. The majority were Caucasian, with the exception of one African American male and one Malaysian-Australian (Asian) female. The sample had an average age of 57 years old, with a range in age from 47 to 75 years of age. There were 14 (37%) women and 24 (63%) men, all with university degrees, including five with doctoral degrees, 18 with masters degrees, and 14 with bachelor degrees. Their experience providing full-time executive coaching support to global leaders ranged from a low of 5 years, to a high of 30 years, with an average yielding 17 years. The majority resided in the USA, with others living in Norway, Netherlands, Mexico, France, Poland, Malaysia, South Africa, and the UK. Nineteen participants held a coaching certification from an International Coach Federation (ICF) approved coaching program. Participants noted they obtain clients mostly through referrals and word of mouth.

Key Findings

This study was designed to help provide a roadmap for leaders in a VUCA environment but the findings are now critical for preparing global leaders in a post-COVID-19 world. Through conversations with 39 global executive coaching practitioners, this study generated nine strategies for highly successful executive coaches who are supporting senior level executives of global teams or organizations. These nine strategies are summarized as follows:

The Secret: Psychological Safety

> The secret to effectively coaching a senior level global executive is to create a psychologically safe space for the executive to reveal tightly held vulnerabilities and fear-based defense mechanisms.

Executive leaders are very guarded and cautious in their willingness to open up and trust a coach to facilitate their inner work. The key, therefore, to creating a fully trusting relationship goes beyond cognitive expertise in coaching and psychology. Findings from this study indicate that the key to coaching success is the ability to create a trusting environment. Over 70% of participants noted the executive coach's ability to support their client in becoming aware of their "inner work life" and helping them to shift to a more healthy belief system is the secret for effectively coaching a global executive.

An executive coach has the responsibility of helping their clients to recognize first and foremost that leadership is not a position, it is a state of being. The psychological safety helps create the space for leaders to recognize that the greatest journey they are on is an "inward" path that takes time to cultivate. From this place, they can begin to see that every person on their team has the opportunity to become a leader as well, which decentralizes decision-making and distributes power in a way that is needed for a VUCA environment. From this place, leadership becomes about connecting to people, not about the task at hand.

Respondents in this study also noted the factors that strongly impact a trusting coaching engagement are the coach's credibility, reliability, and authenticity. They explained that they would never be able to outsmart their clients, and never should. However, the credibility that coaches bring is in their relational and psychological expertise—to know the client's psychology and their own psychology. This is indicative in the respondent's strong conviction that the secret to effectively coaching a global executive is in their ability to facilitate their own psychological process or "inner work." Global executives look to executive coaches who are psychologically stable and safe, which takes time to cultivate.

As executive coaches help leaders to experience psychological safety, they will be more prepared to transfer this to the entire organizational composition. In 2012, the people analytics team at Google discovered that psychological safety was one of the key identifiers of a high performing team (Rozovsky, 2015). The six ways to create psychological safety in the workplace are: approach conflict as a collaborator (not adversary), speak human to human, anticipate reactions and countermoves, replace blame with curiosity, ask for feedback on delivery, and gauge the emotions related to feeling safe (Delizonna, 2017). The psychological safety that is created on teams will result in the risk-taking that is essential for innovation and creativity in a VUCA world (Schockman & Cissna, 2019).

The Best Strategy: Presence

> The best strategy is to facilitate a state of presence in yourself and the client. This has less to do with the technical skills of coaching and much more to do with an attitude of compassion, respect, and present-moment awareness.

Findings from this study reveal that the ability of an executive coach to "be presence" and to "facilitate presence" are key ingredients to having an executive leader open up to the transformational aspect of coaching. Respondents define presence in terms of the coach's ability to be fully present in the moment. A coach with this ability can help to slow down the client enough so that they are able to experience presence as well. Even with the diversity of expertise in the sample of executive coaches who were interviewed, there was uniformity about the notion of presence—a shared conviction that the quality of presence each coach cultivates in their own life and within the coaching engagement is perhaps the differentiating quality of a successful coaching engagement. While there is an insistent drive in bringing standardization and empirical efficacy to executive coaching in order to claim its professional status, there is not much effort placed on examining this notion of presence and how to cultivate it within coach training programs, executive leadership programs, or graduate business school education.

Wasylyshyn (2015) explores the importance of presence as it specifically relates to the evolving role of an executive coach as a Trusted Leadership Adviser (TLA). She describes three states of presence in a TLA relationship as: (a) crucible: where the TLA supports the client to meet the challenges of their business world, (b) sanctuary: where the TLA affirms and reinforces the client's strengths, and (c) personal harmony: where the TLA supports the client's psychological preparedness for life (Wasylyshyn, 2015, p. 289).

Scharmer (2009) coined "Theory U" as the process with which leaders can move through the various dimensions of responding to change in order to get to the emerging complexity of their future: from reacting, to re-designing, to reframing, and finally to presencing (p. 50). Scharmer (2009) notes that modern learning efforts focus on the first three levels of confronting change: reacting, re-designing (learning), and reframing assumptions (double-loop learning) which are based on learning from past experiences. Yet in today's world, leaders are dealing with challenges that cannot be easily addressed by reflecting on past experiences and must therefore be able to face situations as dynamic complexity. This type of complexity is recognized by three characteristics (Scharmer, 2010, p. 21): unclarity around what the solution(s) might be, unclarity around delineating the problem itself, and unclarity in identifying all the stakeholders involved. In facing such a dynamic complexity, Scharmer (2001, 2009, 2010) introduces the concept of presencing as the mechanism that allows individuals to come into full awareness of the present moment and thus access the future that is emerging. This capacity for presencing, according to Senge and Jaworski (2005), requires individuals to cultivate their "capacity to suspend" habitual streams of thought (p. 400). He thus upholds the values of mindfulness based practices in allowing the individual the ability to cultivate stillness so that past conditioning can fall away and make room for the emergence of new patterns and possibilities. Mindfulness practices strengthen the ability of the practitioner to observe feelings and thoughts without judgment. This ability depends upon the strength of the practitioner's emotional intelligence (EI), which is shown to have a significant impact on anxiety and stress reduction (Johnson & Blanchard, 2016).

Dr. Ellen Langer (2014) is a psychology professor at Harvard University, who describes a flexible state that is government by being actively present in each moment, noticing new things by becoming sensitive to contexts and perspectives, as mindfulness. Mindless leaders will govern with rules and regulations, but the mindful leaders who are taught to be "present" will be guided by rules but not determined by them (Langer, 2014). Mindless people act like robots who evaluate things in a rigid way, while mindful leaders are open to surprise, sensitive to context, and liberated from the tyranny of old mindsets (Langer, 1989). Practicing mindfulness and "presence" has been a strong determinant of coaching success, as it provides the coach with an awareness of what is happening in the moment which cultivates a human response of compassion, empathy, and care as opposed to automation.

The Winning Skill: Equanimity, Open-Mindedness (Non-judgmental)

> The skill that sets a highly successful executive coach apart is the coach's open-mindedness—an ability to listen deeply, be compassionate, open, non-judgmental, agenda-free, and hold the client in high regard.

Observation without judgment for self and the client was shared most frequently in terms of contributing to a trusting environment. Research studies examining equanimity note its potential in supporting global executives to be able to observe unpleasant experience with neutrality and compassion (Desbordes et al., 2015; Grabovac et al., 2011). Respondents also noted that executive coaches must bring an expertise on relational and facilitative skills to their coaching engagements with global leaders.

Given the executive leader's very busy schedule, many coaches noted a focus on helping the executive shift from "doing" to "being." This state of presence was described as coming from a place of observation without judgment, a state of being which is coined as "equanimity" in the Buddhist mindfulness tradition. Equanimity, in this tradition, arises from the power of observation, to be able to see things that are happening without getting emotionally invested in them. This ability to observe without judgment allows leaders not to take anything personally and to react to situations with balance and centeredness. "Equanimity is a protection from what are called the Eight Worldly Winds: praise and blame, success and failure, pleasure and pain, fame and disrepute" (Fronsdal & Pandita, 2005). This allows awareness to be unbiased by facilitating an attitude of non-attachment/resistance.

Respondents in this study note that the coach's ability to create psychological safety is key to supporting executives in becoming aware of their own underlying beliefs and assumptions and being open to feedback. Observation without judgment for self and the client was shared most frequently in terms of contributing to a trusting environment. Research studies examining equanimity note its potential in supporting global executives to be able to observe unpleasant experiences with neutrality and compassion (Desbordes et al., 2015; Grabovac et al., 2011). Respondents also noted that executive coaches must bring an expertise on relational and facilitative skills to their coaching engagements with global leaders.

In a VUCA environment, the power of equanimity becomes invaluable for leadership. It enables leaders to remain grounded in the midst of extremes, without reactivity. The mind is steady and responsive, accepting the moment for what it is.

By training the mind to see things without judgment and self-interest, leaders can choose to make small choices that show great care rather than reacting without much forethought.

The Toughest Part: Ego

> The toughest part about coaching a global executive is the coach's insecurities, manifested in their desires to be liked or to be right, inability to speak truth to power, and inability to be patient for real transformation to occur.

With VUCA conditions continuing to increase the rate of change and disruption, global executives feel added pressure if they do not know how to respond or how to come up with a winning solution on their own. These insecurities are shared by executive coaches who also have a desire to provide clear solutions. As leaders and coaches share the same struggles with ego and insecurities, scholars describe the importance of drawing upon the collective capacity of teams within an organization to address their key challenges and overcome individual egoic needs/demands.

Respondents in this study note that most global executives rose to the top of the organization not because of their relational expertise, but because of their often ambitious and singularly focused and competitive desire to "be the best." This is the positive side of ego which drives a leader towards success, yet capabilities of individual achievement can also feed the negative side of ego which can negatively impact executive leadership success. This is especially true at the c-suite, where leaders are never solely prepared to deal with the enormity of pressures from key stakeholders, shareholders, board members, media outlets, consumers, and employees. As such, respondents noted the importance of executive coaches bringing not only their psychological expertise to the coaching engagement, but also their keen abilities and skills to support the executive towards managing the ego and recognizing their need for teams and other stakeholders.

Most respondents noted that coaches might be intimidated when working with a senior level executive. When this type of fear sets in, they might resort to people pleasing or wanting to prove their worth and value. The most typical challenges faced by executive coaches were cited as the desire for the coach to be liked, to be right, to have the solutions, an attempt to outsmart the leader, and/or fix the executive's challenges. In addressing these challenges, respondents noted the importance of the coach to develop their own internal sense of confidence, self-awareness, and presence so that they can be calm in challenging situations and not feel the need to fix things.

In addition, coaches may bring their own personal biases to the situation. Therefore, respondents noted the importance of remaining neutral and supporting the client to achieve their goals, instead of imposing some sort of personal or professional agenda on the client. In fact, one high level senior coach explained that after a 1–2 year engagement, he often needs to recuse himself from the client because he often feels he has become too vested in the outcome and in his own interventions.

The second type of challenge that arises is client willingness/ability to be coached. Given that most of the coaching is about supporting the client in transforming underlying beliefs and assumptions, the client must be willing to participate in the process. Respondents noted that habits are tough to break and explained how the global executive wants quick solutions and to impose their will on the coach to "fix it." Therefore, the coach's self-awareness is key in determining whether to say no to the coaching engagement or to support the client in continuing to engage in the coaching process. One respondent who supervises executive coaches internationally said that a client's resistance is a sign that the coach needs to have a different approach and noted that he never blames the client when they show resistance. Instead, he brainstorms with his executive coaching team to determine in what ways they are not meeting the needs of the client and thus experiencing his or her resistance.

In this study, respondents noted that the toughest part of coaching a global executive is their own capacity to speak truth to power and bring a strong empathetic yet courageous coaching presence. Respondents explained that executive clients are busy to an inhuman degree. They are often overwhelmed and stretched beyond human capacity. Two respondents explained that these busy executives often engage in a form of transference where they want to overwhelm their coach so that their coach can experience the same emotion. As such, the respondents noted the importance of the coach practicing presence and being strong and aware enough to feel the overwhelm but not resort to judgment or blame or withdrawal—that by sharing the emotion and experience with their client, they are modeling to the client what it is like to deal with overwhelm with a sense of grounded presence.

The Typical Constraint: Organizational Mandates

> The most frequent constraint that interferes with providing executive coaching to global executives was reported as mandates from the organization in terms of reporting, the use of specific coaching models, or sharing of confidential information.

Organizational mandates on executive coaching practices were reported as the most common constraint. The unique role of the executive coach requires autonomy in addressing the vertical needs of clients, while mandates that come from organizations are typically limited to horizontal thinking. Scholars discuss the importance of developing vertical capabilities in leaders (relational and wisdom-based), as an addition to their already horizontal knowledge base (technical and information-based). Such relational skills are developmental and require a longer steady state of engagement with the executive. While most suggest a 6 month engagement, other coaches suggest a year or longer to ensure that they are supporting the executive to meet their work challenges by continuing to practice new relational skills that allow them to reduce their often controlling managerial style and step into a more influencing leadership style. However, mandates from an organization can interfere with the executive coaches ability to create the right program for each client.

Respondents noted that such transformational capabilities require both an inside/out and outside/in approach to learning which cannot be controlled by organizational mandates. For example, an inside/out approach to coaching an executive focuses on helping them shift their underlying beliefs and assumptions first, and then allowing this internal shift to impact their external environment. But respondents also noted the importance of an outside/in approach where executive leaders did not have to wait for their inner habits to shift. Instead, they would be guided by their coach to do certain tasks which impacted their internal landscape. For example, one respondent explained how he instructed his executive client who was perceived as harsh, uncaring, and controlling to walk around his company for 15 min each day and compliment his employees on the good job they are doing. The coach explained that at first the global executive felt this was fake but after this exercise, he noted that he felt compassion and enjoyed the kindness others showed him.

The Ethical Dilemma: Loyalty/Transparency Polarity

> Confidentiality is a tricky part of coaching a global executive, because of the magnitude and implications of what is shared by the client and the sponsoring agency. The best way to address this dilemma is by having loyalty and transparency with the client.

Respondents noted various interferences by either the hiring department (often HR) or colleagues/peers in either wanting to direct the course of the coaching engagement, to gain access to confidential content, or impose specific coaching methodologies or outcomes. All respondents noted the importance of 100% confidentiality in their coaching engagements and their full intent in protecting their client. However, some respondents noted that if they are pressed to share specific information, they bring transparency to clients and inform them of the information they are being asked to share. In cases where they cannot bring transparency to their client, the respondents noted they would recuse themselves of the coaching engagement. This polarity between loyalty to the client and confidentiality with the organization was reported as ethically challenging.

Participants in this study were noted that facing and dealing with ethical dilemmas is a natural part of the job as an executive coach to a global executive. They noted that given the position of the global executive, they often speak about gray areas in terms of sales or production or certain ways of dealing with other executives or employees. The respondents noted that it is their job to bring their client to a state of empowerment and clarity so that they can deal effectively with the enormity of issues and challenges they are dealing with on a daily basis. However, they noted that it is also very important to be working with individuals who have strong positive visions. These individuals are good but may be caught in bad situations.

The Outer Success Metric: Compassionate Leadership

> The frequent measure of success is agreeing on key outcomes and conducting pre/post assessments—but the executive's informal assessment of the improved quality of human interaction whether the coach helped shift their perspective from fear to love is the most powerful.

Responses from the study regarding the measurements of success reflect this "unmeasurable" impact of successful coaching engagements, with most coaches noting that their personal measure of success is when the client calls them a few years later and tells them how important their coaching was for them. Given that transformational change takes time, developmental coaching scholars point to the longer term 4-step process (rejection, understanding, using, and integration) that is usually associated with transformational learning, and the typical oversight of organizations to ensure that the fourth step—integration—is allotted the appropriate time frame (Heorhiadi et al., 2014).

Aside from personal anecdotes, the success criteria that most respondents are held accountable to is mostly perceived behavior change based on goals and objectives that they jointly create together with their client and sometimes the client's peers or boss. Often, respondents noted that their client's satisfaction or their increased presence and wellness is all they are held accountable for, and if they can reach that through subjective informal feedback then they know they have succeeded. Most respondents also use some form of pre- and post-assessment, often a 360 feedback or another assessment or tool which the organization uses. When asked about their organization's measurement of the coaching success, respondents either identified assessments or they said they did not know how the organization measures the coaching success. Most noted that informal assessments of perceived behavior change or client satisfaction are mostly used by organizations to informally measure coaching success.

Measuring the success of executive coaching engagements often runs the gamut of informal and formal perceptions of behavior change, and often the expectation of measurable business results. Scholars explain the usual goal of executive coaching, across all methodologies, is "some behavior change on the part of the senior executive ... [and] that executive coaching work is often focused on the interpersonal sphere" (Brotman et al., 1998, p. 41).

The Inner Success Metric: Transformative Coaching

> The most frequent way that coaches measure their own sense of success is whether they facilitated the expansion of their client's awareness from fear and doubt to love and possibility.

In terms of their own measure of success, most respondents noted their client's satisfaction and sense of overall wellness are their own measure of personal success.

Respondents also noted that getting referrals from the client or renewing their contract is their own personal measure of success. Scholars contend that regardless of empirical measures of success, clients report the positive impact of executive coaching engagements (Bono et al., 2009); a strong perceived value in investing in executive coaching (ICF, 1998); and the strong satisfaction of stakeholders (such as HR directors) with the results (McGovern et al., 2001).

The Advice: Tune-in to Yourself and Your Clients

> The most frequent advice for aspiring executive coaches of global leaders is to continue their own self-transformation, followed by: become a relational/leadership expert, continue to receive coaching and supervision, and develop professionally.

Executive coaches need to be engaged in a continual process of learning and growth which develops new mental models. Mental models are deeply rooted cognitive constructs which determine how we see and interpret the world based on years of acculturation and socialization, and changing them often requires the provision of new alternative cognitive structures (Dhanaraj & Khanna, 2011). Changing mental models thus depends upon utilizing transformational learning (Mezirow, 2000; Mezirow & Taylor, 2009; Taylor, 1998, 2009) and understanding its difference with informative learning which "allows people to learn more about the things that fit their mental models … transformative learning is the process of changing mental models" (Heorhiadi et al., 2014, p. 5). Scholars (Argyris, 2008; Mezirow, 2000; Mezirow & Taylor, 2009) refer to this dimension of learning as double-loop (or transformational) learning as a way to discern it from single-loop learning. While in single-loop learning, individuals look at a problem and choose a plan of action; in double-loop learning, individuals look internally and reflect on their underlying assumptions that caused them to choose that specific action and how they might change their underlying assumptions. This type of reflection is quite challenging and often brings out strong defense mechanisms, especially in leaders who view themselves as highly educated, skillful, and competitive (Argyris, 2008). In fact, scholars note that this internal turn, this self-reflection, is an anxiety-provoking proposition for many individuals because it challenges our sense of cognitive stability (Schein, 2010).

While organizations usually attempt to resolve issues of defensiveness by focusing on improving employee motivation or engagement through new compensation programs or corporate culture initiatives, these programs do not work because a defensive attitude typically blocks learning despite high individual commitment (Argyris, 2008). In fact, Perry (2006) notes that when individuals feel threatened or fearful, they become less capable of learning and retrieving cognitive signals. "In essence, fear destroys the capacity to learn" (p. 23). These fear-based reactions occur because transformational learning is a process that includes four phases: rejection, understanding, using, and integration (Heorhiadi et al., 2014). Organizations usually stop at the understanding or using level, without the necessary infrastructures to ensure that employees also experience the fourth step of transformational learning: integration. At the integration level, mental models include the best of both the old way of doing things and the new. Learning new mental models therefore includes four steps which include: (a) critical self-reflection, (b) identification of underlying assumptions and values, (c) changing underlying assumptions or values, and (d) changing behavior (Heorhiadi et al., 2014).

Scholars note that individuals are capable of adapting to new challenges because of the brain's ability to be malleable (Buonomano & Merzenich, 1998; Cozolino & Sprokay, 2006; Trojan & Pokorny, 1999). The required ingredient is the inclusion of environments that promote transformational learning by ensuring safe and trusting relationships, maintenance of moderate arousal levels, activating thinking and feeling, self-reflective languaging, and co-creating positive self-narratives (Cozolino & Sprokay, 2006).

Conclusion

Leadership is a state of being, not a position or a process. Whether you are currently an executive coach or a global executive leader or not, the findings from this study provide insights into the competencies that are needed for leadership in a vastly changing world. Trends from the past are no longer useful when predicting future innovation, thus necessitating that "we must deal with situations as they evolve" (Scharmer, 2009, p. 61). Executive coaches must now support leaders in becoming present to their current challenges, instead of being swept into stories, judgments, or over-analysis of past experiences so that they can engage with and learn from their emerging future.

Coaching legend Tim Gallwey (1974), in his forward to John Passmore's book, *Leadership Coaching* (2010), explains that in essence, coaching is "facilitating learning and unlearning... in a territory that belongs to another person... a sacred territory precisely because it is inner... the unique human gifts of compassion, kindness, and clarity are required in greater degrees" (p. xxi–xxii). This study's findings corroborate Gallwey's convictions in that most respondents identified the coach's presence of empathy, non-judgment, and compassion as key to driving an effective coaching engagement. In fact, respondents regard this quality of the coach's presence as even more important than the coach's business acumen or global/cultural awareness.

Yet more importantly, this study's findings brought to the forefront the aspect of "coach as instrument"—the necessity of the coach to continually strive for self-awareness and transformation in their own lives, stating that you can only take the client as far as you have gone yourself. The esteemed coaching scholar, Karol Wasylyshyn (2015), predicts that in the decades to come, business historians will describe the twenty-first century development of leaders as one where "the *behavior* of executives—*how* they lead people—assumed prominence on a par with other essential leadership competencies" (p. 279). Those drawn to the fields of behavioral sciences and executive coaching will "have urgent and myriad opportunities to influence how twenty-first century business executives are selected, developed and supported as they grapple with the magnitude of the leadership issues before them" (Wasylyshy, Shorey & Chafin, 2012, p. 84). The COVID-19 pandemic highlights these opportunities across every industry, for coaches to empower executive leaders to slow down their reactive thinking, listen deeply, become aware of their own mental models (beliefs, assumptions and blindspots) in order to facilitate the emergence of innovative solutions for the complex challenges facing humanity.

Key Takeaways

1. The secret to effectively coaching a senior level global executive is to be credible and compassionate enough to create a psychologically safe space for the executive to reveal tightly held vulnerabilities and fear-based defense mechanisms.
2. The best strategy is to facilitate a state of presence in yourself and the client, which has less to do with the technical skills of coaching and much more to do with an attitude of compassion, respect, and present-moment awareness.
3. The skill that sets a highly successful executive coach apart from the rest is the coach's presence—the ability to listen deeply, be compassionate, open minded, non-judgmental, agenda-free, and hold the client in high regard.
4. The toughest parts about coaching are insecurities, inability to speak truth to power, and inability to be patient for real transformation to occur. The most frequent constraints are the mandates from the organization.
5. The most frequent advice for aspiring executive coaches of global leaders is to continue their own self-transformation, followed by: become a relational/leadership expert, continue to receive coaching and supervision, and develop professionally.

Reflection Questions

1. An executive coach can only take clients as deep as they have gone themselves. What vulnerabilities are you aware of in yourself that often trigger your defense mechanisms?
2. As an executive coach, what are some ways that you can create psychological safety for your clients to reveal vulnerabilities?
3. How can you show your client that you are deeply listening to them?
4. Make a list of all the insecurities that you face as an executive coach. Now read it as if it came from one of your clients. How would you respond to them?
5. What is the most difficult part of the confidentiality constraints that you have as an executive coach, and how might those be different in a global context?
6. Describe three things that you have done recently to leave your comfort zone and try something new?
7. What are the types of lifelong learning activities that you enjoy and find challenging?

References

Arena, M., & Uhl-Bien, M. (2016). Complexity leadership theory: Shifting from human capital to social capital. *People Strategy, 39*(2), 22–27. Business Source Premier. (Accession No. 114282989).

Argyris, C. (2008). *Teaching smart people how to learn* [Kindle version]. www.amazon.com

Arthur, B. (1996). Increasing returns and the new world of business. *Harvard Business Review, July-Aug*, 1–10. Business Source Premier. (Accession No. 9607100436).

Barber, H. F. (1992). Developing strategic leadership: The US Army War College Experience. *Journal of Management Development, 11*(6), 4–12.

Barrett, L. F. (2018). *How emotions are made: The secret life of the brain*. First Mariner Books.

Bauman, Z. (2007). *Liquid times: Living in an age of uncertainty* [Kindle version]. www.amazon.com

Bayat, N. (2018). Supporting leadership success in a complex global economy: Best practices in executive coaching. Unpublished doctoral dissertation, Pepperdine University.

Bennett, J. M., Bennett, M. J., & Allen, W. (2003). Developing intercultural competence in the language classroom. In D. L. Lange & R. M. Paige (Eds.), *Culture as the core: Perspectives on culture in second language learning* (pp. 237–270). Information Age Publishing.

Bennett, N., & Lemoine, G. (2014). What a difference a word makes: Understanding threats to performance in a VUCA world. *Business Horizons, 57*, 311–317. https://doi.org/10.1016/j.bushor.2014.01.001

Bono, J., Purvanova, R., Towler, A., & Peterson, D. (2009). A survey of executive coaching practices. *Personnel Psychology, 62*, 361–404. https://doi.org/10.1111/j.1744-6570.2009.01142.x

Brotman, L. E., Liberi, W. P., & Wasylyshyn, K. M. (1998). Executive coaching: The need for standards of competence. *Consulting Psychology Journal: Practice and Research, 50*, 40–46.

Bruce, J. (2020). The leader's guide to managing Covid-19 panic. *Forbes*. https://www.forbes.com/sites/janbruce/2020/03/05/the-leaders-guide-to-managing-covid-19-panic/?sh=2b3b15c659ea

Buonomano, D. V., & Merzenich, M. M. (1998). Cortical plasticity: From synapses to maps. *Annual Review of Neuroscience, 21*(1), 149–186.

Cavanagh, M., & Lane, D. (2012). Coaching psychology coming of age: The challenges we face in the messy world of complexity. *International Coaching Psychology Review, 7*(1), 75–90. Retrieved from Academic Search Complete Database. (Accession No. 72336613).

Cissna, K., & Schockman, H. E. (2020a). The role of mindfulness in leadership, followership, and organizations. In S. K. Dhiman (Ed.), *The Routledge companion to mindfulness at work*. Taylor & Francis.

Cissna, K., & Schockman, H. E. (2020b). Finding the key to positive leadership: Applying virtue ethics and inclusivity. In *New horizons in positive leadership and change*. Springer.

Collins, A., Florin, M., & Renn, O. (2020). COVID-19 risk governance: Drivers, responses and lessons to be learned. *Journal of Risk Research, 23*, 1073–1082. https://doi.org/10.1080/13669877.2020.1760332

Collinson, D., & Tourish, D. (2015). Teaching leadership critically: New directions for leadership pedagogy. *Academy of Management Learning and Education, 14*(4), 576–594. https://doi.org/10.5465/amle.2014.0079

Cozolino, L., & Sprokay, S. (2006). Neuroscience and adult learning. *New Directions for Adult and Continuing Education, 110*, 11–19.

De Smet, A, Gagnon, C., & Mygatt, E. (2021). *Organizing for the future: Nine keys to becoming a future-ready company*. McKinsey and Company. https://www.mckinsey.com/business-functions/organization/our-insights/organizing-for-the-future-nine-keys-to-becoming-a-future-ready-company

Delizonna, L. (2017). High-performing teams need psychological safety. Here's how to create it. *Harvard Business Review*, 24. https://hbr.org/2017/08/high-performing-teams-need-psychological-safetyheres-how-to-create-it

Desbordes, G., Gard, T., Hoge, E., Holzel, B., Kerr, C., Lazar, S., Olendzki, A., & Vago, D. (2015). Moving beyond mindfulness: Defining equanimity as an outcome measure in meditation 345 and contemplative research. *Mindfulness, 6*, 356–372. https://doi.org/10.1007/s12671-013-0269-8

Dhanaraj, C., & Khanna, T. (2011). Transforming mental models on emerging markets. *Academy of Management Learning & Education, 10*(4), 684–701. https://doi.org/10.5465/amle.2011.0511

Edelman (2010). *2019 Edelman trust barometer reveals "my employer" is the most trust institution.* https://www.edelman.com/news-awards/2019-edelman-trust-barometer-reveals-my-employer-most-trusted-institution

Feldman, D., & Lawrence, J. (Eds.). (2011). *Structures and transformations in modern British history*. Cambridge University Press.

Fiol, C. (2002). Capitalizing on paradox: The role of language in transforming organizational identities. *Organizational Science, 13*(6), 653–666. Retrieved from Business Source Premier Database. (Accession No. 8681197).

Fischhoff, B. (2020). Making decisions in a COVID-19 world. *JAMA, 324*(2), 139. https://doi.org/10.1001/jama.2020.10178

Fronsdal, G., & Pandita, S. (2005). A perfect balance: Cultivating equanimity. *Tricycle: The Buddhist Review*. https://tricycle.org/magazine/perfect-balance/

Fugate, M. E. L., Kinicki, A. J., & Prussia, G. E. (2008). Employee coping with organizational change: An examination of alternative theoretical perspectives and models. *Personnel Psychology, 61*(1), 1–36. https://doi.org/10.1111/j.1744-6570.2008.00104.x

Gaddis, B., & Foster, J. (2015). Meta-analysis of dark side personality characteristics and critical work behaviors among leaders across the globe: Findings and implications for leadership development and executive coaching. *Applied Psychology: An International Review, 64*(1), 25–54. https://doi.org/10.1111/apps.12017

Gallwey, W. T. (1974). *The inner game of tennis*. Random House.

Gandhi, L. (2017). Human resource challenges in VUCA and SMAC business environments. *ASBM Journal and Management, 10*(1), 1–5. Business Source Premier Database. (accession no. 120832170).

Gilley, A., McMillan, H. S., & Gilley, J. W. (2009). Organizational change and characteristics of leadership effectiveness. *Journal of Leadership & Organizational Studies, 16*(1), 38–47. Business Source Premier Database. (Accession No. 43630518).

Goleman, D. (2000). Leadership that gets results. *Harvard Business Review, 78*(2), 78–90. https://hbr.org/2000/03/leadership-that-gets-results

Grabovac, A., Lau, M., & Willett, B. (2011). Mechanisms of mindfulness: A Buddhist psychological model. *Mindfulness, 2*(3), 154–166. https://doi.org/10.1007/s12671-011-0054-5

Grant, A. (2014). The efficacy of executive coaching in times of organizational change. *Journal of Change Management, 14*(2), 258–280. https://doi.org/10.1080/14697017.2013.805159

Grint, K. (2010). Leadership: A very short introduction. Oxford: Oxford University Press.

Grint, K., & Jackson, B. (2010). Toward "socially constructive" social constructions of leadership. *Management Communication Quarterly, 24*(2), 348–355.

Hall, R., & Rowland, C. (2016). Leadership development for managers in turbulent times. *Journal of Management Development, 35*(8), 942–955. https://doi.org/10.1108/JMD-09-2015-0121

Harari, Y. (2020). *How to survive the 21st century.* Davos Economic Forum. https://www.weforum.org/agenda/2020/01/yuval-hararis-warning-davos-speech-future-predications/

Heifetz, R. A. (1994). *Leadership without easy answers*. Harvard University Press.

Heifetz, R. A., & Linsky, M. (2004). When leadership spells danger. *Educational Leadership, 61*(7), 33–37. Education Full Text Database. (Accession No. 507898931).

Heifetz, R. A. (2002). Bringing the spirit of invention to leadership. *Journal of Staff Development, 23*(2), 44–46. Retrieved from Education Full Text Database. (Accession No. 507757609).

Helsing, D., Howell, A., Kegan, R., & Lahey, L. (2008). Putting the development into professional development: Understanding and overturning educational leaders' immunities to change. *Harvard Educational Review, 78*(3), 437–465. http://hepgjournals.org.lib.pepperdine.edu/doi/pdf/10.17763/haer.78.3.888l759g1qm54660?code=hepg-site

Heorhiadi, A., La Venture, K., & Conbere, J. (2014). What do organizations need to learn to become a learning organization. *OD Practitioner, 46*(2), 5–9. Academic Search Complete Database. (Accession No. 95420732).

Holman, P. (2010). *Engaging emergence: Turning upheaval into opportunity*. Berrett-Koehler.

Horton, R. (2020). *The covid-19 catastrophe: What's gone wrong and how to stop it happening again*. Wiley.

IBM Global CEO Study. (2012). *Capitalizing on complexity: Insights from the global chief executive officer study*. http://www-01.ibm.com/common/ssi/cgibin/ssialias?htmlfid=GBE03297USEN

ICF. (2014). *International coaching federation competencies*. Retrieved from https://coachfederation.org/core-competencies

Jamali, D., Sidani, Y., & Zouein, C. (2009). The learning organization: Tracking progress in a developing country. *The Learning Organization, 16*(2), 103–121. Business Source Premier Database. (Accession No. 36610178).

Jarzabkowski, P., & Sillince, J. (2007). A rhetoric-in- context approach to building commitment to multiple strategic goals. *Organization Studies, 28*, 1639–1665. https://doi.org/10.1177/0170840607075266

Johansen, B. (2012). *Leaders make the future: Ten new leadership skills for an uncertain world*. Berrett-Koehler.

Johnson, S., & Blanchard, A. (2016). Emotional intelligence and mental health: Stress and symptom reporting pathways. *Journal of Mental Health Counseling, 38*(1), 79–92. https://doi.org/10.17744/mehc.38.1.06

Kaiser, R., & Curphy, G. (2013). Leadership development: The failure of an industry and the opportunity for consulting psychologists. *Consulting Psychology Journal: Practice and Research, 65*(4), 294–302. https://doi.org/10.1037/a0035460

Kaiser, R. B. (2020). Leading in an unprecedented global crisis: The heightened importance of versatility. *Consulting Psychology Journal: Practice and Research, 72*, 135–154.

Kaiser, R. B., & Hogan, J. (2011). Personality, leader behavior, and overdoing it. *Consulting Psychology Journal: Practice and Research, 63*, 219–242. https://doi.org/10.1037/a0026795

Kauffman, C., & Hodgetts, W. (2016). Model agility: Coaching effectiveness and four perspectives on a case study. *Consulting Psychology Journal: Practice and Research, 68*(2), 157–176. https://doi.org/10.1037/cpb0000062

Kegan, R., & Lahey, L. L. (2016). *An everyone culture: Becoming a deliberately developmental organization*. Harvard Business Review Press.

Lane, H. W., Maznevski, M. L., Mendenhall, M. E., & McNett, J. (2004). *The Blackwell handbook of global management: A guide to managing complexity*. Blackwell.

Langer, E. (1989). *Mindfulness*. Addison-Wesley.

Langer, E. J. (2014). Mindfulness forward and back. In *The Wiley Blackwell handbook of mindfulness* (Vol. 1, pp. 7–20). Wiley.

Lewis, M. (2000). Exploring paradox: Toward a more comprehensive guide. *Academy of Management Review, 25*, 760–776. https://doi.org/10.5465/AMR.2000.3707712

McGovern, J., Lindemann, M., Vergara, M., Murphy, S., Barker, L., & Warrenfeltz, R. (2001). Maximizing the impact of executive coaching: Behavioral change, organizational outcomes, and return on investment. *The Manchester Review, 6*, 1–9. https://www.performanceconsultants.com/wp-content/uploads/maximizing-the-impactof-executive-coaching.pdf

McGuire, C., & Rhodes, G. (2009). *Transforming your leadership culture*. Jossey-Bass.

Meadows, D. (2008). *Thinking in systems: A primer*. Chelsea Green Publishing.

Mendenhall, M., Osland, J., Bird, A., Oddou, G., Maznevski, M., Stevens, M., & Stahl, G. (2013). *Global leadership: Research, practice, and development* [Kindle version]. www.amazon.com

Mezirow, J. (2000). *Learning as transformation: Critical perspectives on a theory in progress*. Wiley.

Mezirow, J., & Taylor, E. W. (Eds.). (2009). *Transformative learning in practice: Insights from community, workplace, and higher education*. Wiley.

Morrison, A. (2000). Developing a global leadership model. *Human Resource Management, 39*(2), 117–131. https://doi.org/10.1002/1099-050X(200022/23)39:2/3<117::AID-HRM3>3.0.CO;2-1

Nieminen, L., Biermeier-Hanson, B., & Denison, D. (2013). Aligning leadership and organizational culture: The leader-culture fit framework for coaching organizational leaders. *Consulting Psychology Journal: Practice and Research, 65*(3), 177–198. https://doi.org/10.1037/a0034385

O'Reilly, C., & Tushman, M. (2011). Organizational ambidexterity in action: How managers explore and exploit. *California Management Review, 53*(4), 5–22. Retrieved from Business Source Premier Database. (Accession No. 65087784).

Passmore, J. (2016). *Excellence in coaching: The industry guide*. Kogan Page.

Perry, B. (2006). Fear and learning: Trauma-related factors in the adult education process. In S. Johnson & K. Taylor (Eds.), *The neuroscience of adult learning* (pp. 21–27). Jossey-Bass.

Petrie, N. (2014). *Future trends in leadership development*. http://insights.ccl.org/wp-content/uploads/2015/04/futureTrends.pdf

Rodriguez, A., & Rodriguez, Y. (2015). Metaphors for today's leadership: VUCA world, millennial and "cloud leaders". *Journal of Management Development, 34*(7), 854–866. https://doi.org/10.1108/JMD-09-2013-0110

Rosenthal, S. (2012). *National leadership index 2011: A national study of confidence in leadership*. http://web.archive.org/web/20130605125029/; http://www.centerforpublicleadership.org/index.php?option=com_k2&view=item&id=886

Rozovsky, J. (2015). *The five keys to a successful Google team*. https://rework.withgoogle.com/blog/five-keys-to-a-successful-google-team/

Scharmer, C. (2000, 25–26 May). *Presencing: Learning from the future as it emerges – On the tacit dimension of leading revolutionary change*. Paper presented at the Conference on Knowledge and Innovation. Helsinki School of Economics. http://www.ottoscharmer.com/sites/default/files/2000_Presencing.pdf

Scharmer, C. (2001). Self-transcending knowledge: Sensing and organizing around emerging opportunities. *Journal of Knowledge Management, 5*(2), 137–151. https://doi.org/10.1108/13673270110393185

Scharmer, C. (2009). Theory u: Leading from the future as it emerges. SF, CA: Behrett-Koehler.

Scharmer, O. (2010). *The blind spot of institutional leadership: How to create deep innovation through moving from egosystem to ecosystem awareness*. Paper presented at the World Economic Forum Annual Meeting of the New Champions 2010. http://www.ottoscharmer.com/docs/articles/2010_DeepInnovation_Tianjin.pdf

Schein, E. (2010). *Organizational culture and leadership*. Jossey-Bass.

Schockman, H.E. & Cissna, K. (2019). Mindfulness companion: The role of mindful leaders, followers and organizations. Routledge Handbook of Mindfulness, Flow and Creativity in the Workplace. Taylor and Francis Publishing: Oxfordshire, United Kingdom.

Schockman, H.E. & Cissna, K. (2019). Finding the key to positive leadership: Applying inclusivity and virtue ethics: Applying inclusivity and irtue ethics. Positive leadership and change: Exemplary approaches and new directions. Springer: New York.

Senge, P., & Jaworski, J. (2005). Presence: An exploration of profound change in people, organizations, and society [Kindle version]. Retrieved from https://www.amazon.com.

Sinar, E., Wellins, R. S., Ray, R., Abel, A. L., & Neal, S. N. (2015). *Global leadership forecast 2014/2015*. Development Dimensions International. http://www.ddiworld.com/ddi/media/trend-research/global-leadership-forecast-2014-2015_tr_ddi.pdf?ext=.pdf

Sinclair, A. (2008). *Leadership for the disillusioned: Moving beyond myths and heroes to leading that liberates* [Kindle version]. www.amazon.com

Smith, K., & Berg, D. (1987). *Paradoxes of group life*. Jossey-Bass.

Smith, W. (2015). Dynamic decision making: A model of senior leaders managing strategic paradoxes. *Academy of Management Journal, 1015*(1), 58–89. https://doi.org/10.5465/amj.2011.0932

Smith, W., & Lewis, M. (2011). Toward a theory of paradox: A dynamic equilibrium model of organizing. *Academy of Management Review, 36*(2), 381–403. https://doi.org/10.5465/AMR.2011.59330958

Smith, W., & Tushman, M. (2005). Managing strategic contradictions: A top management model for managing innovation streams. *Organization Science, 16*(5), 522–536. https://doi.org/10.1287/orsc.1050.0134

Stacey, R. (1999). *Strategic management and organizational dynamics: The challenge of complexity*. Financial Times.

Stacey, R. (2001). *Complex responsive processes in organizations: Learning and knowledge creation*. Routledge.

Stacey, R. (2007). *Strategic management and organizational dynamics: The challenge of complexity*. Financial Times.

Steihm, J. H., & Townsend, N. W. (2002). *The U.S. army war college: Military education in a democracy*. Temple University Press.

Susing, I., & Cavanagh, M. (2013). At the intersection of performance: Personality and adult development in coaching. *International Coaching Psychology Review, 8*(2), 58–69. Academic Search Complete Database. (Accession No. 93728930).

Swift, A. (2016). *Americans' trust in mass media sinks to new low (Gallup, 2016)*. www.gallup.com/poll/195542/americans-trust-mass-media-sinks-new-low.aspx

Taylor, E. (1998). *The theory and practice of transformative learning: A critical review*. ERIC Clearinghouse. https://eric.ed.gov/?id=ED423422

Taylor, E. (2009). Fostering transformative learning. In J. Mezirow & E. Taylor (Eds.), *Transformative learning in practice*. Jossey-Bass.

Thiel, P. (2014). *Zero to one*. Penguin Random House.

Thomas, R. (2008). *Crucibles of leadership: How to learn from experience to become a great lleader*. Harvard Business Review Press.

Toffler, A. (1971). *Future shock*. Bantam Books.

Toffler, A. (1980). *The third wave*. Bantam Books.

Toffler, A. (1990). *Power shift*. Bantam Books.

Toffler, A. (2007). The perspective of the future. *Confrontation, 100*, 35–37.

Trojan, S., & Pokorny, J. (1999). Theoretical aspects of neuroplasticity. *Physiological Research, 48*, 87–98.

Vaill, P. (1996). *Learning as a way of being: Strategies for survival in a world of permanent white water* [Kindle version]. www.amazon.com

Vince, R., & Broussine, M. (1996). Paradox, defense and attachment: Accessing and working with emotions and relations underlying organizational change. *Organization Studies, 17*(1), 1–21. Business Source Premier Database. (Accession No. 6497025).

Wasylyshyn, K. M. (2015). The trusted leadership advisor: Another view from the bridge between business and psychology. *Consulting Psychology Journal: Practice and Research, 67*(4), 279.

Wiese, C., & Ricci, R. (2010). *10 characteristics of high-performing teams*. www.huffingtonpost.com/carl-wiese/10-characteristics-of-hig_b_1536155.html#

Wilson, S. (2016). *Thinking differently about leadership: A critical history of leadership studies*. Edward Elgar.

Wasylyshyn, K. M., Shorey, H. S., & Chaffin, J. S. (2012). Patterns of leadership behaviour: Implications for successful executive coaching outcomes. *The Coaching Psychologist, 8*(2), 74–85.

Wilson, W., & Lawton-Smith, C. (2016). Spot-coaching: A new approach to coaching for organisations operating in the VUCA environment. *International Coaching Psychology Review, 11*(1), 24–38. Academic Search Complete Database. (Accession No. 113283164).

Worley, C. G., & Jules, C. (2020). COVID-19's uncomfortable revelations about Agile and Sustainable Organizations in a VUCA world. *The Journal of Applied Behavioral Science, 56*(3), 279–283. https://doi.org/10.1177/0021886320936263

Noushin Bayat is Visiting Professor of Practice in Personal Leadership Coaching, Master of Engineering Technical Management Program at Texas A&M University. She is Director of Digital Transformation at Executive Leadership Consulting, and founder of Engaging Wisdom, Inc, a consultancy organization that provides change management, leadership development, and executive coaching services within agile organizational environments that require stakeholder management and engagement across all business functions. Dr. Bayat is passionate about mental wellness and strives to create healthy work cultures and operational strategies that empower individuals and teams to thrive. Dr. Bayat's client list includes: Children's Hospital Los Angeles, University of Southern California (USC), Gap USA, Nestle Globe, Nestle USA, Dreyers Grand Ice Cream, Kaiser Permanente, Tesco's Fresh & Easy Markets, and Deloitte & Touche, among others. Dr. Bayat has a doctorate in organizational leadership from Pepperdine University where her research focused on how complex global systems impact not only leaders, but also operational and decision-making systems and how coaching best practices need to adapt to support leaders to thrive within this web of complexity. Findings point to "presence" as a key factor in thriving through VUCA conditions.

Kerri Cissna is a Visiting Assistant Professor in Entrepreneurship and Creativity at the John W. Altman Institute for Entrepreneurship in Miami University's Farmer School of Business. She was a Postdoctoral Fellow with the Program for Leadership and Character at Wake Forest University where she teaches entrepreneurship. Dr. Cissna earned a Ph.D. in global leadership and change from Pepperdine University where she also teaches Leading the Philanthropic Enterprise. Dr. Cissna is also a lecturer at California State University Long Beach. She formerly served as Executive Director of Leadership Long Beach and as Assistant Vice-Chancellor, Director of Housing and Residence Life, and the Leadership Development Coordinator at Pepperdine University.

Everything Gonna Be Alright: Antecedents to Nurses' Change Adaptability in the COVID-19 Era

20

Simona Leonelli and Emanuele Primavera

Background

The spread of COVID-19 infection resulted in the World Health Organization declaring the global pandemic. This public health emergency led governments to make significant economic investments aimed at reorganizing hospital staff, which has consequently upset the ordinary routine of healthcare workers. The COVID-19 pandemic has caused a second-order episodic change. According to Verhaeghe et al. (2006), changes can be distinguished in first-order and second-order changes. The first-order changes are related to normal operational changes (e.g., tasks, working hours), while the second-order changes are related to internal system changes (e.g., changes in the ward type, such as a transition from internal medicine ward into COVID-19 ward). Changes can be also episodic or continuous (Weick & Quinn, 1999). Episodic changes are related to infrequent and discontinuous changes occurring on a macro-environmental level (i.e., downsizing or enlarging wards). In contrast, continuous changes are often recurrent and cumulative, and they occur on a micro-environmental level (i.e., changing colleagues, tasks, and working hours).

Implementing both episodic or continuous change in the healthcare industry is hard and challenging. Its results are generally short-lived since healthcare workers tend to behave differently and to show more "resistance to change" than the personnel operating in other industries (e.g., manufacturing) (Amarantou et al., 2018). These difficulties depend on the industry characteristics and the services provided by healthcare workers. The provision of healthcare services, in fact, takes place in a complex and dynamic environment, where groups of individuals act in diverse and

S. Leonelli (✉)
Department of Economics and Management "M. Fanno", University of Padova, Padova, Italy
e-mail: simona.leonelli@unipd.it

E. Primavera
AUSL Pescara, "Santo Spirito" Hospital, Pescara, Italy

S. K. Dhiman, J. F. Marques (eds.), *Leadership After COVID-19*, Future of Business and Finance, https://doi.org/10.1007/978-3-030-84867-5_20

unpredictable ways, where tensions arise due to opposing forces of competition (and/or cooperation), and where decisions are influenced by the contexts, priorities, and backgrounds of healthcare professionals (Amarantou et al., 2018; Plsek & Greenhalgh, 2001).

A large body of literature investigates the causes and consequences of organizational change (see Armenakis & Bedeian, 1999; Bordia et al., 2004a), and instruments to make changes that would be accepted and implemented by employees (see Folger & Skarlicki, 1999; Piderit, 2000). Other studies investigate the impact of change on employees' psychological well-being, evoking stress reactions, and other negative consequences such as absenteeism, turnover intention, job performance, and organizational citizenship behavior (Bordia et al., 2004b; Bourbonnais et al., 2005; Verhaeghe et al., 2006). However, the antecedents to change adaptability are less understood. Management literature and practice do not put enough emphasis on the personal and emotional aspects of change management (Oreg, 2006; Shanley, 2007). Previous studies about adaptability to change focus on how individuals react to organizational change (Armenakis & Bedeian, 1999; Ployhart & Bliese, 2006). Judge et al. (1999), for example, examine how some personality traits (i.e., locus of control, self-efficacy, self-esteem, positive affectivity, openness to experience, tolerance for ambiguity, and risk aversion) influence the ability to cope with organizational change. Similarly, Wanberg and Banas (2000) show that individual personality traits (i.e., self-esteem, optimism, perceived control) and contextual factors (i.e., information, participation, change self-efficacy, social support, personal impact) impact openness to organizational change. However, there are still many challenges to understanding change process and employee change adaptability (Pettigrew et al., 2001).

Drawing on the change management theory, the present study aims to identify the personal abilities and behaviors affecting adaptability to change in healthcare organizations in a crisis period (i.e., COVID-19 pandemic), analyzing the difference in perception between nurses involved directly in the crisis emergence (i.e., working in COVID-19 wards) and those indirectly involved (i.e., not working in COVID-19 wards).

Adaptability to Change Through the Lens of the Change Management Theory

Change management requires relational, operational, and strategic competencies (Yukl & Becker, 2006). In the first part of this paragraph, we review the more important theories that laid the foundations for creating various models relating to change management. Lewin (1951) is considered the precursor of change management models and believed that changes are composed of three stages: unfreezing—which arises when the change is needed; moving—when change is started; and refreezing—when equilibrium is established. He also postulated some assumptions to make effective change. In detail: (1) he underlined the importance of a change motivator and employees in order to make the change occurs in organizations; (2) he showed that in order to change, there is a need to adapt, integrate the new processes in the routines, and cease past practices; finally (3) he revealed that resistance to change is common.

Subsequently, Lippitt et al. (1958) have expanded Lewin's three-stage model. They have focused more on the role and responsibility of the change agents (i.e., persons, groups, organizations, and communities), and then they have analyzed the evolution of the change, identifying seven steps. Summarizing, they underlined the importance of the clarification of the problem, then focused on the examination of alternative routes and the establishment of the intentions for action, finally, they implemented the transformation of intentions in actual change. In order to effectively implement the change, they also argued that managers should develop and maintain relationships with those involved in or affected by the change highlighting the importance of sharing information throughout the process (Spear, 2016).

Egan (1988) starting from Lewin's model focused mainly on the unfreezing and moving phases, underling the importance of the assessment of problems and opportunities of the current scenario (i.e., diagnosis), the creation of a preferred scenario evaluating alternative possibilities to establish a viable agenda for change (i.e., visioning), and the design of plans that move the system from the current to the preferred scenario—such as making the plan realizable (i.e., planning for a change). Finally, Harris and Beckhard (1987) developed the "change equation" in order to assess the likelihood of change being successful. The model analyses the current organizational environment and employee attitude toward the change, as these are the most common change barriers. The equation's left side is composed of the sum of the current levels of dissatisfaction, the shared vision of a better future, and the first steps toward a new vision. The equation's right side includes the resistance to change. In order to make the change initiative successful, the sum on the left side should be bigger than the variable on the right side.

However, among the many different change management theories and models, the most widely used in health care settings to address the adoption of innovations and changes is Kotter's process for transformational change (Campbell, 2008). Kotter's model (1996) is a dynamic model comprised of eight stages that can be organized into three phases: creating a climate for change, engaging and enabling the organization, and implementing and sustaining the change. The present study aims to examine the antecedents to nurses' adaptability to change through the lens of the change management theory. To do so, individual nurses' abilities and behaviors are linked at the three stages of Kotter's model.

Positive Behaviors to Create a Right Climate for Change

The "creating a climate for change" phase consists of three stages that are establishing a sense of urgency, creating a guiding coalition, and developing a vision and strategy. Kotter (1996) argues that, when seeking change, the greatest mistake is to permit complacency. Creating urgency involves helping people see and feel firsthand why a change needs to occur, thus avoiding their resistance to change

(Campbell, 2008). Implementing a guiding coalition and developing a vision and strategy promote the facilitation of change mobilization (Clark, 2010).

We hypothesize that individual positive behavior can help create a right climate to improve adaptability to change. Positive behavior allows positive outcomes to be expected even in crises and permits individuals to deal with daily life actively (Cohn & Fredrickson, 2010; Scheier & Carver, 1985). Moreover, individual positive behavior enables individuals to persist when tasks become difficult or when they should face adversities. Finally, individuals having a positive behavior show higher levels of motivation, persistence, and performance (Luthans et al., 2008). This implies that nurses showing positive behaviors will easily and rapidly adapt to changing compared to nurses having negative behavior.

Hypothesis 1: Nurses' positive behavior positively affects their adaptability to change.

Coping Ability to Engage and Enable the Organization for Change

The "engaging and enabling the organization for change" phase is composed of three stages that are communicating the vision, enabling action, and creating short-term wins. According to Kotter (1996), once the vision is defined, it should be communicated frequently and convincingly to all employees. In order to implement this vision, activity to promote the changes should be carried out, such as providing incentives or asking for feedback on how to benefit from such changes (Campbell, 2008). Allowing workers to participate in the change enables the facilitation of change mobilization (Clark, 2010).

We hypothesize that the coping ability can help to manage changes and improve the individual adaptability to change. Coping is defined as the cognitive and behavioral efforts made to master, tolerate, or reduce external and internal demands and conflicts (Folkman & Lazarus, 1980; Lim et al., 2010). This means that nurses with higher coping abilities react and manage difficulties better than those with lower coping abilities. Moreover, their ability to develop a strategy to prepare themselves to cope with changes can be considered as the most effective strategy to deal with changes (Bowman, 2013). Thus, we state that the greater nurses' coping abilities, the higher their adaptability to change.

Hypothesis 2: Nurses' coping ability positively affects their adaptability to change.

Leadership/Authority Ability to Implement and Sustain Change

The "implementing and sustaining changes" phase comprises two stages: consolidating gains to produce more change and anchoring new approaches in the organizational culture. According to Kotter (1996), success in implementing change should not be declared prematurely. There is a high likelihood of returning to the status quo if changes are not firmly anchored. In this phase, it is necessary to maintain the focus on the desired vision, as well as the strategic steps required to accomplish it, until the change permanently becomes an essential part of the organization's culture, thus being clearly reflected in the shared set of norms and values (Clark, 2010).

We hypothesize that leadership/authority ability influences adaptability to change and allows the easy implementation and sustainment of changes. Leadership/authority ability is recognized as a significant factor influencing how the relations with/between employees are managed within an organization (Shanley, 2007). According to Kiffin-Petersen and Cordery (2003), the quality of leadership/authority is fundamental during major organizational change. In the health care setting, nurses generally cover informal leadership/authority roles (Gustafsson et al., 2010). Consider, for example, the relationship between old tenured nurses and the young ones or the relationship between nurses and nurse assistants. Nurses generally serve the informal function of a superior having an overall nursing responsibility. This leadership/authority ability is useful when the other team members need competence and authority to solve problems or cope with changes. However, this ability is useful in team dynamics and fundamental at the individual level. Nurses' leadership/authority role makes them stronger and self-confident about uncertainty provoked by changes, increasing their adaptability to change. Thus, we affirm:

Hypothesis 3: Nurses' leadership/authority ability positively affects nurses' change adaptability.

Method

Sample and Data Collection Procedure

A descriptive cross-sectional design was employed in the present study, based on a sample of nurses who voluntarily answered an online questionnaire in April and May 2020. The nurses enrolled met the following inclusion criteria: being Italian and being employed as professionals in care services promoting direct contact with patients. The questionnaire was administered online, by using Facebook, due to the national restrictions and social distancing rules in place at the time. First, we found three Facebook pages where many nurses were registered. Thereafter, we posted a short study introduction there, along with the link to our questionnaire, which was in Italian. The administration of online questionnaires poses several challenges to the identification of a starting sample. Therefore, following Houser's (2016) recommendations, the total initial sample was calculated by taking into account the number of people who actually viewed our post. In order to monitor our social network post views, we used the Brand24 tool. The post had 956 views in total. The questionnaire received 258 answers (29.4% response rate) from the nurses, with 281 answers being complete and eligible, due to missing data and bias.

Ethical Consideration

The local research ethics committee approval was not required for this study. Participants were made aware of the study objective and were asked to sign an informed consent form. They did not receive nor were they offered any remuneration for completing the questionnaire. During the course of the study, the ethical principles stated in the Declaration of Helsinki were followed at all times. The investigators further provided their email addresses in case of questions and doubts.

Measures

To measure *adaptability to change*, *positive behavior*, and *coping ability* we asked "Are you able to adapt to change?" "How often have you felt that things were going your way?" and "How often have you felt that, even if difficulties were piling up, you could overcome them?" respectively. Answers follow the 5-point Likert scale rules where 1 means "never" and 5 "always." To measure the *leadership/authority* attitude, however, we used four items of the Narcissistic Personality Inventory scale (Gentile et al., 2013). Also, in this case, answers followed the Likert 5-point rules, although 1 means "totally disagree" and 5 "fully agree."

Consistently with the extant literature, we have included some control variables that have been found by prior studies to be correlated with our variables of interest. Specifically, at individual level, we controlled for nurses' age and gender, and at the environmental level, for ward type and geographical area. Nurse age was measured as a 4-point ordinal scale taking the value 1 if the nurse was under 30 years old, 2 if the nurse was between 30 and 39 years old, 3 if the nurse was between 40 and 49 years old, and 4 if the nurse was over 50 years old. Nurse gender and ward type were dummy variables that were assigned the value 1 if nurses were man or if the ward was a COVID-19 ward, and zero otherwise. Ultimately, a 4-point ordinal scale based on the 4 macro-areas identified by the Italian National Institute of Statistics (ISTAT) (i.e., 1 = Northeast, 2 = Northwest, 3 = Center, and 4 = South and Islands) was employed to measure the geographical area.

Statistical Analyses

The data was analyzed using quantitative techniques employing Stata 16 as the statistical software. We examined the eigenvalue graph (not reported) and conducted the confirmatory factor analysis (CFA) to check if the four items pertaining to *leadership/authority* measured a unique construct (Table 20.1). The eigenvalue graph confirmed that only one factor should be retained, while factors loadings and the Cronbach's alpha (0.88) indicated a high degree of reliability. Descriptive statistics are also shown to present the main sample characteristics. Finally, linear regression models are employed to test our hypotheses.

Table 20.1 Factor loadings for exploratory factor analysis of the leadership/authority items

Leadership/authority	*M*	SD	Factor loading	α
1. I like having authority over other people	2.08	1.10	0.84	0.88
2. I have a strong will to power	1.84	1.07	0.83	
3. People always seem to recognize my authority	2.40	1.14	0.73	
4. I am a born leader	2.02	1.10	0.82	

Table 20.2 Participant demographic data ($n = 281$)

Full sample characteristics	*n*	%
Gender		
Female	237	84.3
Male	44	15.7
Age		
<30 years old	47	16.7
30–39 years old	92	32.8
40–49 years old	86	30.6
>50 years old	56	19.9
COVID-19 ward		
COVID-19	192	68.3
No-COVID-19	89	31.7
Geographical area		
Northeast	83	29.5
Northwest	92	32.7
Center	49	17.5
South and islands	57	20.3

Results

The characteristics of the sample examined are set forth in Table 20.2. The nurses included in the sample are mainly female (84.3%), aged between 30 and 39 (32.8%), working for the most part in COVID wards (71.2%), in hospitals situated in Northwest Italy (32.7%).

Descriptive statistics and Spearman's correlations of the variables are presented in Table 20.3. Since all the correlation values are below 0.50, we can state that there is a small correlation between the variables. The Variance Inflation Factor (VIF) was employed to control for multicollinearity and common method variance. All the variable values are shown to be close to 1, indicating that almost no correlation exists between them (Hair et al., 2011), and that our model has not been affected by any common method variance (Kock, 2015)—not reported here.

Table 20.4 presents our linear model results. We investigated the results for the full sample, and through cross-sectional analysis, by dividing our sample into COVID-19 wards and no-COVID-19 ones. For the entire sample and the two subsamples, we performed two linear regressions, respectively. The first linear regression (i.e., Step 1) only includes the control variables, while the second (i.e., Step 2) includes the

Table 20.3 Descriptive statistics and correlations for study variables

Variable	n	M	SD	1	2	3	4	5	6	7	8
1. Nurse adaptability to change	281	3.65	0.97	–							
2. Nurse positive behavior	281	3.15	0.83	0.28***	–						
3. Nurse coping ability	281	3.08	0.98	0.11	0.09	–					
4. Nurse leadership/ authority	281	−0.01	0.94	0.36***	0.16**	−0.02	–				
5. Nurse age	281	2.54	0.99	−0.10	0.07	0.12	0.01	–			
6. Nurse gender[a]	281	0.16	0.36	0.11	0.07	0.04	0.12*	−0.04	–		
7. COVID-19 ward[b]	281	0.68	0.47	−0.01	0.04	−0.05	−0.10	−0.13	−0.09	–	
8. Geographical area	281	2.25	1.12	0.10	0.09	0.04	0.03	−0.06	0.07	0.03	–

*$p < 0.05$, **$p < 0.01$, ***$p < 0.001$
[a]0 = Woman and 1 = Man
[b]0 = No-COVID-19 ward and 1 = COVID-19 ward

independent variables. Hypothesis 1 suggests that nurses' positive behavior positively affects nurses' adaptability to change. Our results support this hypothesis, given the existence of a positive and significant relationship between positive behavior and adaptability to change ($\beta = 0.29$, $p < 0.001$). An interesting point emerges when we focus on the differences between nurses working in COVID-19 wards and those not working in COVID-19 wards. The positive behavior of nurses working in COVID-19 wards exerts a less positive role on the relationship with adaptability to change ($\beta = 0.28$, $p < 0.001$) compared to the positive behavior of nurses not working in COVID-19 wards ($\beta = 0.24$, $p < 0.05$). Hypothesis 2 states that nurses' coping ability positively affects their adaptability to change. Our results confirm this hypothesis; in fact, there is a positive and significant relationship between coping ability and adaptability to change ($\beta = 0.12$, $p < 0.05$). The coping ability of nurses working in No-COVID-19 wards exerts a more positive role on the relationship with adaptability to change ($\beta = 0.24$, $p < 0.05$); however, the results of the coping ability of nurses working in COVID-19 wards are not significant even though they are always positive ($\beta = 0.06$, $p > 0.1$). Hypothesis 3 suggests that nurses' leadership/authority ability positively affects nurses' adaptability to change. Our results support this hypothesis, given the existence of a positive and significant relationship between leadership/authority ability and adaptability to change ($\beta = 0.29$, $p < 0.001$). When considering the differences between nurses working in COVID-19 wards and those not working in COVID-19 wards a relevant aspect is brought to light. The leadership/authority ability of nurses working in COVID-19 wards exerts a more positive role on the relationship with adaptability to change ($\beta = 0.31$, $p < 0.001$) compared to the leadership/authority ability of nurses not working in COVID-19 wards ($\beta = 0.25$, $p < 0.05$). Finally, the

Table 20.4 Regression analysis: focus on the differences between COVID-19 and No-COVID-19 wards

	Full sample		COVID-19 wards		No-COVID-19 wards	
Variables	Step 1	Step 2	Step 1	Step 2	Step 1	Step 2
DV: Nurse adaptability to change						
Intercept	3.66*** (3.21, 4.10)	2.52*** (1.93, 3.12)	3.57*** (3.11, 4.02)	2.76*** (2.11, 3.42)	3.77*** (2.95, 4.58)	2.01*** (0.83, 3.20)
Control variables						
Nurse age	−0.10 (−0.22, 0.01)	−0.13* (−0.24, −0.03)	−0.07 (−0.20, 0.07)	−0.12* (−0.25, 0.00)	−0.14 (−0.37, 0.08)	−0.14 (−0.34, 0.07)
Nurse gender	0.25 (−0.06, 0.57)	0.09 (−0.19, 0.38)	0.07 (−0.32, 0.46)	−0.05 (−0.41, 0.31)	0.50 (−0.05, 1.04)	0.32 (−0.17, 0.81)
COVID-19 ward	0.00 (−0.25, 0.24)	0.02 (−0.20, 0.25)	–	–	–	–
Geographical area	0.09 (−0.01, 0.20)	0.06 (−0.03, 0.15)	0.10 (−0.02, 0.23)	0.07 (−0.04, 0.18)	0.07 (−0.11, 0.26)	0.06 (−0.10, 0.22)
Independent variables						
Nurse positive behavior		0.29*** (0.17, 0.42)		0.28*** (0.13, 0.42)		0.34* (0.06, 0.61)
Nurse coping ability		0.12* (0.01, 0.23)		0.06 (−0.07, 0.19)		0.24* (0.04, 0.42)
Nurse leadership/ authority		0.29*** (0.18, 0.41)		0.31*** (0.18, 0.44)		0.25* (0.02, 0.48)
N	281	281	192	192	89	89
R-squared	0.03*	0.21***	0.02	0.19***	0.08	0.29***
Root MSE	0.97	0.88	0.94	0.86	1.02	0.92

$^{*}p < 0.05$, $^{**}p < 0.01$, $^{***}p < 0.001$
Confidence interval in parenthesis

nurses' age variable plays an interesting role. Results show that nurses' age has a negative and significant relationship with adaptability to change ($\beta = -0.13, p < 0.05$), while this effect is slightly less negative for nurses working in COVID-19 wards ($\beta = -0.12, p < 0.05$).

Discussions and Conclusions

The aim of this study was to identify how nurses' abilities and behaviors affect their adaptability to change in crisis periods. Our results provided strong support for our hypotheses. Findings indicate that nurses' positive behavior, coping, and leadership/authority abilities positively affect their adaptability to change. Therefore, we contribute to the change management and nursing management literatures underlining the importance of individual antecedents in change adaptability. Paying attention and favoring employees' positive behavior and abilities can increase their change adaptability, and consequently, their organizational commitment to change. Investing in the commitment to change allows nurses to better support or adapt to change initiatives because they believe that changes are valuable (Herscovitch & Meyer, 2002).

Considering the COVID-19 pandemic as an environmental setting for our study, we further push the knowledge in the fields of change management and nursing management. In fact, interesting results emerge when we consider nurses involved directly in the crisis emergence (i.e., those who work in COVID-19 wards) and those indirectly involved (i.e., those who do not work in COVID-19 wards). Specifically, results show that nurses' positive behavior and coping ability have a stronger effect on the relationship with change adaptability in nurses working in no-COVID-19 wards compared to those working in COVID-19 ones. Conversely, nurses' leadership/authority ability has a stronger effect on the relationship with change adaptability in nurses working in COVID-19 wards compared to those working in no-COVID-19 wards. These results explain that the antecedents to change adaptability act differently based on the involvement in the crisis. Leadership/authority ability is an antecedent that could be linked to feelings of rigor. Our results show that it is stronger when nurses are directly involved in the crisis emergence. Nurses can implement this ability to avoid making errors in the procedures to be followed, to avoid expanding the contagion, and finally to enridge a barrier between them and everything that happens in the ward. Positive behavior and coping ability, however, are antecedents related to feelings of hope. Our results show that they are stronger in nurses indirectly involved in the crisis emergence. Thus, nurses in an indirect context show hope in order to support themselves and the patients (just consider the motto "everything will be alright") and indirectly support their colleagues who work in COVID-19 wards.

Practical Implications

The present study reveals that it is important to invest in the development and management of nurses' abilities and behavior because they have a strong impact on their change adaptability. The paper's practical implications are important for head nurse and nurse managers, underlining the necessity of two types of interventions at the individual and group levels. At the individual level, we underline the need to take care of nurses' psychological well-being because it impacts their behavior and ward performance. We suggest that the head nurse takes the time to look at his/her workers and talk with them to understand whether they are physically and psychologically sane or they are feeling stressed. In collaboration with the nurse managers, the head nurse can promote the presence in the hospital of a psychologist to periodically follow the nurses. This is important, particularly in a crisis period, because a psychologist would help nurses recognize which individual factors (i.e., background, fears, etc.) hinder the change and work together to increase change adaptability. Moreover, the head nurse and nurse managers should be more present in nurses' daily lives because they are often perceived as detached figures. Creating a more significant relationship between them will help increase their adaptability to change. Additionally, effective communication processes and practical participation in the ideation and implementation of change will promote affective commitment to change and facilitate change adaptability. At the group level, we propose to implement some activities to improve and stimulate nurses' adaptability to change, such as team building and focus groups (DiMeglio et al., 2005). Team building improves the relationships between people, enabling the development of coping and leadership/authority abilities. Similarly, focus groups are multidisciplinary meetings that help the working group establish a common thought through members' interactions. This context could give rise to food for thought to improve the propensity and adaptability to change. Lastly, we call for a major application of change management elements in the healthcare environment, combined with the above interventions, to improve health care workers' propensity and adaptability to change.

Five-Chapter Takeaways/Lessons

1. Nurses' positive behavior positively affects their adaptability to change.
2. Nurses' coping ability positively affects their adaptability to change.
3. Nurses' leadership/authority ability positively affects nurses' change adaptability.
4. Results explain that the antecedents to change adaptability act differently based on the involvement in the crisis, showing that nurses' abilities and behavior of those directly involved in the crisis emergence have lower benefit in their adaptability to change.
5. This paper invites head nurses and nurse managers to take care of nurses' personality factors that affect their abilities and behaviors.

Five Reflection Questions

1. In which way other individual abilities and behaviors might affect nurses' adaptability to change?
2. Does the mentor's figure in health care organizations can help in implement the adaptability to change?
3. Do nurse managers really take care of their team considering physical and psychological well-being?
4. In which way the national and international politics can improve nurses' well-being and adaptability to change?
5. Could providing better economic and financial conditions for nurses lead to their greater well-being?

References

Amarantou, V., Kazakopoulou, S., Chatzoudes, D., & Chatzoglou, P. (2018). Resistance to change: An empirical investigation of its antecedents. *Journal of Organizational Change Management, 31*(2), 426–450.

Armenakis, A. A., & Bedeian, A. G. (1999). Organizational change: A review of theory and research in the 1990s. *Journal of Management, 25*(3), 293–315.

Bordia, P., Hobman, E., Jones, E., Gallois, C., & Callan, V. J. (2004a). Uncertainty during organizational change: Types, consequences, and management strategies. *Journal of Business and Psychology, 18*(4), 507–532.
Bordia, P., Hunt, E., Paulsen, N., Tourish, D., & DiFonzo, N. (2004b). Uncertainty during organizational change: Is it all about control? *European Journal of Work and Organizational Psychology, 13*(3), 345–365.
Bourbonnais, R., Brisson, C., Malenfant, R., & Vézina, M. (2005). Health care restructuring, work environment, and health of nurses. *American Journal of Industrial Medicine, 47*(1), 54–64.
Bowman, M. (2013). *The professional nurse: Coping with change, now and the future*. Springer.
Campbell, R. J. (2008). Change management in health care. *The Health Care Manager, 27*(1), 23–39.
Clark, C. (2010). From incivility to civility: Transforming the culture. *Reflections on Nursing Leadership, 36*(3), 98–102.
Cohn, M. A., & Fredrickson, B. L. (2010). In search of durable positive psychology interventions: Predictors and consequences of long-term positive behavior change. *The Journal of Positive Psychology, 5*(5), 355–366.
DiMeglio, K., Padula, C., Piatek, C., Korber, S., Barrett, A., Ducharme, M., Lucas, S., Piermont, N., Joyal, E., & DeNicola, V. (2005). Group cohesion and nurse satisfaction: Examination of a team-building approach. *JONA: The Journal of Nursing Administration, 35*(3), 110–120.
Egan, G. (1988). *Change agent skills B: Managing innovation and change*. Prentice Hall.
Folger, R., & Skarlicki, D. P. (1999). Unfairness and resistance to change: Hardship as mistreatment. *Journal of Organizational Change Management, 12*(1), 35–50.
Folkman, S., & Lazarus, R. S. (1980). An analysis of coping in a middle-aged community sample. *Journal of Health and Social Behavior, 21*(3), 219–239.
Gentile, B., Miller, J. D., Hoffman, B. J., Reidy, D. E., Zeichner, A., & Campbell, W. K. (2013). A test of two brief measures of grandiose narcissism: The Narcissistic Personality Inventory–13 and the Narcissistic Personality Inventory-16. *Psychological Assessment, 25*(4), 1120–1136.
Gustafsson, C., Fagerberg, I., & Asp, M. (2010). Supportive leadership in Swedish community night nursing. *Journal of Nursing Management, 18*(7), 822–831.
Hair, J. F., Christian, M. R., & Marko, S. (2011). "PLS-SEM: Indeed a silver bullet." *Journal of Marketing theory and Practice, 19*(2), 139–152.
Harris, R. T., & Beckhard, R. (1987). *Organizational transitions: Managing complex change*. Addison-Wesley.
Herscovitch, L., & Meyer, J. P. (2002). Commitment to organizational change: Extension of a three-component model. *Journal of Applied Psychology, 87*(3), 474–487.
Houser, J. (2016). Nursing research: Reading, using and creating evidence. Sudbury, MA: Jones & Bartlett Learning.
Judge, T. A., Thoresen, C. J., Pucik, V., & Welbourne, T. M. (1999). Managerial coping with organizational change: A dispositional perspective. *Journal of Applied Psychology, 84*(1), 107–122.
Kiffin-Petersen, S., & Cordery, J. (2003). Trust, individualism and job characteristics as predictors of employee preference for teamwork. *International Journal of Human Resource Management, 14*(1), 93–116.
Kock, N. (2015). Common method bias in PLS-SEM: A full collinearity assessment approach. *International Journal of e-Collaboration (IJeC), 11*(4), 1–10.
Kotter, J. P. (1996). *Leading change*. Harvard Business Press.
Lewin, K. (1951). *Field theory in social science*. Harper & Row.
Lim, J., Bogossian, F., & Ahern, K. (2010). Stress and coping in Australian nurses: A systematic review. *International Nursing Review, 57*(1), 22–31.
Lippitt, R., Watson, J., & Wesley, B. (1958). *The dynamics of planned change*. Harcourt Brace.
Luthans, F., Avey, J. B., & Patera, J. L. (2008). Experimental analysis of a web-based training intervention to develop positive psychological capital. *Academy of Management Learning & Education, 7*(2), 209–221.
Oreg, S. (2006). Personality, context, and resistance to organizational change. *European Journal of Work and Organizational Psychology, 15*(1), 73–101.

Pettigrew, A. M., Woodman, R. W., & Cameron, K. S. (2001). Studying organizational change and development: Challenges for future research. *Academy of Management Journal, 44*(4), 697–713.

Piderit, S. K. (2000). Rethinking resistance and recognizing ambivalence: A multidimensional view of attitudes toward an organizational change. *Academy of Management Review, 25*(4), 783–794.

Ployhart, R. E., & Bliese, P. D. (2006). Individual adaptability (I-ADAPT) theory: Conceptualizing the antecedents, consequences, and measurement of individual differences in adaptability. In *Understanding adaptability: A prerequisite for effective performance within complex environments*. Emerald Group Publishing.

Plsek, P. E., & Greenhalgh, T. (2001). The challenge of complexity in health care. *BMJ, 323*(7313), 625–628.

Scheier, M. F., & Carver, C. S. (1985). Optimism, coping, and health: Assessment and implications of generalized outcome expectancies. *Health Psychology, 4*(3), 219–247.

Shanley, C. (2007). Management of change for nurses: Lessons from the discipline of organizational studies. *Journal of Nursing Management, 15*(5), 538–546.

Spear, M. (2016). How to facilitate change. *Plastic Surgical Nursing, 36*(2), 58–61.

Verhaeghe, R., Vlerick, P., Gemmel, P., Maele, G. V., & Backer, G. D. (2006). Impact of recurrent changes in the work environment on nurses' psychological Well-being and sickness absence. *Journal of Advanced Nursing, 56*(6), 646–656.

Wanberg, C. R., & Banas, J. T. (2000). Predictors and outcomes of openness to changes in a reorganizing workplace. *Journal of Applied Psychology, 85*(1), 132–142.

Weick, K. E., & Quinn, R. E. (1999). Organizational change and development. *Annual Review of Psychology, 50*(1), 361–386.

Yukl, G. A., & Becker, W. S. (2006). Effective empowerment in organizations. *Organization Management Journal, 3*(3), 210–231.

Simona Leonelli is Research Fellow at the University of Padova (Italy). Previously, she was Postdoctoral Research Fellow at the University G. d'Annunzio Chieti-Pescara (Italy) where she received her Ph.D. in Accounting, Management, and Finance in 2017. She was visiting researcher at Skema Business School (Nice—France). Her main research interest lies in the area of Entrepreneurship and Business Organization. She focuses on the existing relationship between entrepreneurs' personality traits (e.g., narcissism) and innovative performance, survival, and growth of start-ups and SMEs. She published in Journal of Small Business and Entrepreneurship, Journal of Entrepreneurship and Small Business, Sinergie, and Prospettive in Organizzazione. She has also published two books: one with Edward Elgard Publishing entitled "Entrepreneurial Personality and Small Business Management" and one with Emerald Publishing entitled "Sustainable entrepreneurship." She is Adjunct Professor of Business Organization, Behavior in Organization, and Organization Design and Governance of Human Capital at the University of Padova.

Emanuele Primavera is a Registered Nurse of the AUSL Pescara (Italy). He has a master's degree in management for health professions. He published several papers in national and international journals. His research interests are nurses' fundamental care, workload, and stress perception. In collaboration with Simona Leonelli, he has created a model to organize geriatric units following the positive aging culture. During the pandemic period, he worked in a COVID-19 medical ward.

21 The Post-Pandemic Workplace: Challenges and Prospects

Dinyar M. Pestonjee and Taronish A. Pastakia

It is no secret that the COVID-19 pandemic has brought about a major emphasis on the slogan "Work from Home!" in never before imagined magnitudes. A few MNCs have even optimistically announced that the "work-from-home" option shall be made available to most of their employees even after the pandemic is over. Some countries like Germany have contemplated legislature to make the "Right to Work-from-Home" a legal right for all their citizens. While these developments may seem optimistically revolutionary in nature, we must however ask ourselves, "Are our homes truly designed to act as our workplaces?"

It is true that a handful of companies with progressive HR policies have over the past couple of decades, on and off experimented with allowing small segments of their workforce to meet their deadlines in the comfort of their homes. However, most of these in-house HR experiments have implemented protocols in controlled settings, allowing for smooth and gradual transitions of their employees, thereby giving them not just time to adapt and reorient their schemas but also allowing for ample opportunity to modify their home/workplace ergonomically.

Most "lockdowns" or "shelter-in-place" directives enforced by governments the world over in the spring of 2019 did not provide enough advance warnings for the workforce and HR professionals to even contemplate about reimagining their home as their office. There are a few notable exceptions like New Zealand wherein ample notice was given prior to enforcement of a lockdown. However, in countries like India, due to the sheer suddenness of said restrictions, for most employees, the anxiety of hoarding food and provisions took precedence during that epoch between the

D. M. Pestonjee (✉)
School of Petroleum Management (SPM), Pandit Deendayal Petroleum University (PDPU), Gandhinagar, Gujarat, India

T. A. Pastakia
Department of Psychology, St. Xavier's College (Autonomous) Ahmedabad, Ahmedabad, Gujarat, India

S. K. Dhiman, J. F. Marques (eds.), *Leadership After COVID-19*, Future of Business and Finance, https://doi.org/10.1007/978-3-030-84867-5_21

announcement and the enforcement of the first lockdown. Moreover, the unprecedented nature of the calamity was such that most employees truly believed (or rather, hoped against hope) that these restricted measures will be transient in nature and not persist beyond a few weeks.

All of the above mentioned and many more unforeseen circumstances have acted as uncontrolled variables which have thrown this transition from the pre-COVID "office" to the new "home-office" into disarray, thereby making the adaptation a living nightmare for many. Since those companies which do have experiential knowledge of experimentation with various alterations of work-from-home protocols are only a handful and hailing from just a few industries like the IT sector, there is indeed a huge dearth of empirical evidence in the existing OB/HR literature to deal with this mighty cannonball of never before seen workplace adaptation problems which the pandemic has thrust upon the planet.

Apart from an in-depth exploration of novel workplace adaptation methods for the OB/HR profession stemming from the above explained causal factors, this review article shall also explore, in conjunction, other impacts relevant to these novel workplace adaptations, which the lockdown restrictions have had (and are likely to have in the near future) on the sudden brakes put on excessively materialistic lifestyles of the urban populace, the likely disruptions in population density, changes in labor migration patterns, the likely geopolitical shifts in focus of infrastructure development for various governments, etc.

It is no secret to the world of HR professionals that workplace design tremendously impacts job performance, specifically, the workplace layout, ventilation, lighting, thermal comfort, and other office equipment/infrastructure (Mendis, 2016). Traditionally (i.e. in pre-pandemic times) interior designers and architects most often focused on applying the principles of ergonomics with the principal aim to balance the optimization of job performance versus space utilization depending on space availability, costing, etc. The inclusion of health-related factors has majorly been observed in designers who favor experimentation. The COVID-19 pandemic, however, has rapidly brought into focus, the significance of epidemiological variables on all of the above mentioned (but not limited to) fundamental elements of workplace design (Cita & Budiyanti, 2020). Whether it is the conventional "office" or the fast becoming popular "home-office," these fundamentals of ergonomics shall henceforth need to have a fourfold focus on maximizing job performance, minimizing cost, maximizing space utilization, and most-importantly, minimizing the probability of transmission of infection. Some of these are explored below in relative detail.

Masks, social distancing, and sanitization have become the ABCs of the new "normal" socially approved behavior in most public places the world over. Most workplaces have already made essential modifications (usually government-mandated) such as installing hand-sanitizers, increasing restricted-access zones, and temporarily blocking alternate seats in conference rooms, transport vehicles, etc. However, most global experts have time and again cautioned the general public against assuming that COVID-19 vaccines will be a silver bullet and also against assuming that this will be the first and last pandemic of the century. In fact multiple agencies including the WHO have issued public statements warning governments and people globally to take COVID-19 as a wake-up call. That wake-up call is not restricted in its applicability to the health infrastructure of a country, but is directed towards almost every industry, service, organization, or individual that directly or indirectly indulges in public dealings, both at the micro and macro levels.

Therefore, transient and temporary modifications to the workplace would be extremely myopic for an organization. It is in the evolutionary nature of viruses and pathogens to undergo relatively rapid mutations. It is also in their nature to become endemic and/or seasonal in specific geographical regions depending on climate, ethnicity, population density, socio-economic activity, etc. Governments are thereby (and will be in the immediate future) forced to rapidly modify restrictions on public movement and workplace access based on the epidemiological waveforms which are also in part dependent on lockdown fatigue, burnout, isolation, and public behavior in general. Therefore, architects, interior designers, HR professionals, IT experts, epidemiologists, and mental health professionals, all need to come together to envision a new future of workplace layout wherein the one-size-fits-all approach will definitely not work.

Automated or no-contact sanitizer dispensers should henceforth become a permanent fixture in any building. Automated or no-contact doors and windows must also become the norm. If sensor-based electronics are out of the budget for more humble establishments, the more "*jugaadu*" and innovative foot-based dispensers and door/window handles can be used. Cloistered desks and claustrophobic cubicles must necessarily become a thing of the past.

Since the regular 6-ft. distance rule is not enough to prevent transmission in closed and artificially ventilated environs, the focus on ventilation is most crucial. For quite a few decades, and more so in the twenty-first century, there is a growing perception among business managers that buildings with glass facades and centrally air-conditioned rooms/hallways increase the respectability of an organization but flaunting a more "modern" look in front of potential clients. However, more and more health agencies (government or otherwise) are cautioning people to choose natural ventilation as much as possible, whether in public transport or in stationary buildings. This needs to be reincorporated as a way of life. Open spaces and amphitheaters (as opposed to enclosed halls and theaters) should be the accepted venues for meetings where online participation is not conducive. Seating arrangement should include social distancing as a part of the layout rather than a temporary modification. More importantly, alternatives to centralized (or even de-centralized) air-conditioning must be applied in extremely hot, extremely frigid, and/or extremely humid climates.

An aspect of ergonomic design that must go hand-in-hand with (but often is in contravention to) ventilation is thermal comfort. Certain educational campuses like the Indian Institute of Technology (IIT) Gandhinagar have already incorporated a centralized "passive cooling system" in their buildings, utilizing an innovative and intricate combination of recycled water and naturally occurring wind-patterns to replace centralized air-conditioning, taking inspiration from the traditional engineering technology of the world-famous "*pol-architecture*" a world-heritage site in the eastern part of Ahmedabad, Gujarat. If being environment-friendly is not enough incentive for other organizations to follow suit, the threat of having their offices frequently shut-down and labeled as "containment zones" by local authorities should be incentive enough to take inspiration and incorporate such changes for the long-term.

It can be argued that while many educational campuses tend to be located away from cities and have the luxury of some semblance of green-cover, it is often not the case for most offices which tend to be located in urban corporate districts in the middle of a concrete jungle where the vegetation is largely decorative and ornamental. Hence, natural ventilation may not be a feasible option where the petroleum-addled industries have a relatively greater detrimental impact on air quality. Cities which have introduced carefully planned "lungs" or patches of green-cover in strategic locations would be better suited to incorporate such open-ventilation based designs in their workplaces.

Natural ventilation may also not be a very feasible option in extremely frigid climates where closed spaces become an existential necessity. In such cases, to compensate for thermal comfort, the workplace layout will necessitate incorporation of workstations with increased isolation and minimal physical contact with colleagues. This isolation is especially likely to be compounded with the necessity to introduce staggered working hours, staggered lunch-times, closure of communal sitting places like cafeterias, smoking rooms, etc. which will even disallow the few minutes of small-talk and camaraderie which most employees look forward to in a work-day. All of this becomes especially demanding on the HR professionals to find innovative ways and means to manage a parallel pandemic of rapidly declining mental health, which will surely have an adverse effect on the overall worker output. More importantly, the dearth of existing research in developing online training exercises and employee enhancement programmers (to replace the traditional offline ones which require a lot of physical contact especially in exercises aimed at improving group cohesion and leadership skills) is also a major challenge pending before most if not all industries and sectors.

Although high-tech air purifiers which filter out pathogens and viruses have been developed at the prototype level, the probability of mass-scale use (whether domestic or industrial) is still quite low for the near future. Until then, the focus on optimal and innovative ventilation as a primary tool to combat workplace transmission will remain.

Another very crucial element of ergonomic design that must not be overlooked is lighting. It is commonsensical to think that lighting may not be an aspect that requires any modification in workplace design due to the pandemic. It is well-known among OB/HR professionals and industrial psychologists that based on the famous Hawthorne experiments, lighting may not always have an adverse impact on job performance. It must be remembered, however, that the physical proximity of group members was crucial for the findings of the Hawthorne experiments to be valid. If the workplace design cannot prevent physical distancing from exacerbating into psychological isolation, then the impact of lighting and exploring its optimal levels must be investigated in a renewed manner.

The placement of office equipment (including but not limited to furniture, electronics, dividers/partitions, etc.) is also an aspect to be rethought of especially in areas of a workplace not restricted to potential clients, brokers, and consumers/customers. Remodeling of waiting areas, one-way walking corridors/hallways, as well as policies on reasonable restrictions on and precautionary measures pertaining to the access of commonly used equipment like water-dispensers, washrooms, chairs/sofas, cafeterias, etc. need to be hashed out at the top management level in a manner that is not in contravention to existing fire codes and other emergency evacuation laws implemented by local government bodies.

Apart from major ergonomic adaptations, the need of the hour is also to incorporate HR policies to maintain a balance between the ease of performing one's job role versus neutralizing the risk of transmission. Minimizing offline face-to-face interactions (even with social distancing and among employees in the same building) must become a matter of written policy to avoid complacency especially from top management. Moreover, the use of technology for tracking and tracing purposes should also become a norm (Basu et al., 2020). Some countries have already mandated the use of certain applications/software to facilitate this (e.g. the "*Aarogya Setu*" app in India). Similar software are likely to be developed to track one's vaccination status as well in the very near future. However, an amalgamation of this data with employee attendance at the grassroots level can make the system more robust and disciplined. A few innovators have also developed prototypes of clothing which can warn when social distancing is not maintained. This can be incorporated in the uniforms or dress codes of most employees.

Another major risk of transmission of air-borne pathogens (especially asymptomatic) is the use of outdated masks due to complacency or thrifty behavior, in spite of strict adherence to wearing them. Certain prototypes of masks which change color on becoming redundant/expired have already been developed which can also possibly be incorporated into uniforms or dress codes. While thermal guns have become quite common-place in entry/exit points of public places, the use of CCTV cameras equipped with thermal imaging can have wider coverage and accuracy with relatively less human error. The technology was first popularized by a few international airports to screen potential swine-flu carriers almost a decade ago. However, domestic usage of the same has not become widespread yet although it clearly has the potential to. Similarly, the use of sniffer dogs as a screening test for COVID-19 at strategic points of entry is also an underutilized resource. Dogs are commonly trained to sniff out narcotics, explosives, and even to some extent, detect cancer. Recently, Finland became the first country to deploy sniffer dogs trained to detect COVID-19. It would be more efficient for organizations in the long run to invest in this service.

It is not only a matter of business ethics and civic sense, but rather in the self-interest of establishments and organizations to take all of the above discussed measures seriously and invest in them long-term rather than transiently. The lesser the rate of transmission of infection in your workplace, the less likely is it to be forcefully closed-down and/or sealed by the competent authority.

The above detailed recommendations of workplace adaptation are mainly discussed in the context of the traditional "office" in the post-pandemic context. However, the fundamental elements of workplace design also need to be applied in equal parts to the newly evolving concept of the "home-office." This process becomes especially challenging since the conventional office has the luxury of availing the expertise of HR, ergonomic, and mental health professionals on its payroll.

On the face of it, the idea of long-term and relatively permanent "work-from-home" policies seem to be an attractive concept for both the employees and employers alike. The prospect of avoiding long hours of commute in dusty urban jungles, not having to migrate from one city to another, relatively flexible working hours, etc. are not only a boon for a prospective employee but also for recruiters since they can justify offering lower salaries if their employees do not necessarily need to relocate to dense urban metros with sky-rocketing rents and costs of living. In pre-pandemic times, the work-from-home option was severely limited and mostly observed in a few select MNCs. The "new normal" however can even have small traders and MSMEs potentially employing white-collar workers from across the globe if the vast majority of their work can be accomplished simply with a desktop/laptop and a smartphone. No longer will an employer feel unable to hire someone simply due to geographical constraints. The possibilities seem varied and optimistic.

However, without careful consideration of the applications of workplace design in the home environment with competent policies aiding to facilitate the process, the entire concept can become potentially disastrous. Since the commencement of "shelter-in-place" or "lockdown" measures which were so suddenly imposed by various governments across the planet, the initial feedback of employees in most sectors has overall not been very encouraging. Even disregarding extraneous factors like feelings of job insecurity due to the global economic slowdown, lockdown fatigue, unforeseen restrictions on social life, etc. the impact on job performance has been detrimental especially with respect to job roles wherein considerable teamwork and coordination is required which is cumbersome to sustain online in the long run. Prima facie, the core hindrance seems twofold.

The first is the lack of adequate online infrastructure that most organizations faced. Even though the fast-evolving and freely available video-conferencing, cloud storage, and communication software did exist before the pandemic, most organizations (public as well as private) have only recently introduced to specialized and customized e-office platforms. With the added pressures of adjusting to rapidly evolving social norms, the learning curve became too steep and thereby too stressful. If future "work-from-home" policies are to be sustainable, HR professionals need to come up with modified training protocols as a fundamental part of their recruitment policy.

The second is the fast-disappearing demarcation between personal and professional life due to the same geographical location and ergonomic surroundings for work and home. While the flexibility of dealing with household chores and job requirements at the same time seems inviting at first, it rapidly becomes a distractor. Similarly, while flexible working hours may seem enticing on the surface, the lack of coordination that results from it (especially in the pursuit of superordinate goals) makes the concept of work-life boundaries redundant. Subordinates especially have to bear the brunt of supervisors emailing work and holding online meetings at all hours of the day. Once again, if work-from-home policies are to be successful and sustainable, sustainable HR policies need to be enforced along with finding alternatives to traditional team-building activities.

It is for these reasons that each prospective "work-from-home" employee will need to individually rethink his/her home environment as a work environment and develop the ability to successfully switch between the two as and when required. With the advent of nuclear families, very few households have segregated and relatively noise-proof "work rooms" or "study rooms" (Kaushik & Guleria, 2020). HR, ergonomic, and mental health professionals need to actively guide and facilitate this transformation of the home into a workplace at an individual level with each employee since the average employee does not comprehend without specialized knowledge, the nuances of how workplace designs impact job performance and mental health. While handholding each employee in this task is of course not pragmatic, training workshops in this regard must be a matter of regular HR activity over and above having ergonomic and mental health experts permanently on the payroll which is the need of the hour, if the world of work is to be reimagined at the most fundamental level (Bryan, 2020). Until virtual reality (VR) technology and hologram technology become advanced enough to be wholly immersive as well as accessible in retail to the common masses, the above discussed work-from-home experience (and the hindrances that come with it) will be prevalent.

It must be noted that all of the above points of workplace adaptation discussed are majorly applicable in industries or services wherein most of the work can be accomplished with a personal computer. Many other white-collar jobs which necessitate physical interaction with customers and other stakeholders and almost all blue-collar jobs will require a variety of different workplace adaptations, each one fundamentally different from the next. Some of these are discussed below.

The hospitality management industry (including but not restricted to hotels, restaurants, tourism, etc.) has come up with quite a few innovative ways to sustain and adapt to the pandemic in spite of being an industry which necessitates physical contact with the general masses on a huge scale. While many hotels have offered services as quarantine centers, restaurants have adapted by increasing curb-side and open-air seating, improving take-away services, introducing no-contact food deliveries, redesigning indoor seating, redesigning kitchens with separate workstations, and even converting buffets into other formats of dining. In tourism, some companies have introduced the concept of "virtual tours" in a desperate attempt to stay afloat, the long-term viability of which remains to be seen.

The logistics industry has also rapidly evolved. While the men and women of the delivery and courier services have often had the misfortune of becoming "super-spreaders" until drone-delivery services become common-place in the future, the HR professionals will have to work on finding ways and means to minimize their physical contact at the collection centers and improve the quality of the "no-contact" delivery service.

Similarly, the transportation industry has also modified its workplace drastically whether it's at a mass transportation level (air, rail, and sea) or at a domestic level (buses, cab-services, etc.). Although the airline industry has been severely impacted due to drastically deserted airports, they have adapted by increasing cargo services and are likely to be in higher demand when dedicated vaccination air corridors become a regular phenomenon. At a domestic level, while the indigenous auto-rickshaws were fortunately designed to be open-air in the first place, their contemporary cab-drivers and bus-drivers have also modified their vehicles to minimize physical contact using simple means like partitions, frequent sanitization, open windows wherever possible, online bookings, and online payments. Moreover, driverless metro trains and local trains seem likely to become the norm in the near future. Hyperloop technology which uses smaller transportation pods than railway carriages will also revolutionize long-distance transportation in the not-so-distant future. If work-from-home policies become more and more popular among the white-collar populace and the population densities of metro cities reduce as a result, the lowered demand for daily transport services combined with increased restrictions on overcrowding is also likely to make the workplace relatively safer for the blue-collar employees of this industry.

The entertainment industry is one of the hardest hit by the pandemic. Cinema houses were already losing audiences to OTT platforms and YouTubers prior to the pandemic; personalized devices were fast replacing the cinematic experience which has only been hastened by the pandemic and is likely to continue. However, at the grassroots level, creating safe workplaces has been a monumental challenge for production houses since shooting movies and TV-series/web-series requires excessive traveling and managing a multitude of professionals at different locations, thereby redesigning the workplace each day. The theater and stand-up comedy industry have attempted to adapt by conducting more online shows with video-conferencing facility and fewer offline ones. While live shows with social distancing may still survive, large-scale tightly packed concerts are likely to be a thing of the past at least in the immediate future. Event managers have similarly attempted to adapt their work environments, especially weddings and receptions, whereas other corporate and academic events like seminars, conferences, and workshops have had relatively greater success in transitioning almost completely online by facilitating the advent of the "webinar."

An allied industry which has also severely suffered is sports. While the postponement of the Tokyo Olympics may seem transient for now, sports competitions are not likely to be the same as before. Contact sports especially have greater risks of transmission. While a few contactless sports like tennis and cricket have commenced internationally with no audience, the rigidness of the elaborate safety protocols are not only cost-intensive, but are also taking a toll on the mental health of the players. Moreover, conducting competitions at local, state, and national levels with similarly rigid protocols does not seem to be conducive and pragmatic. While a few niche sports like shooting and archery may survive by conducting online competitions, the vast majority need to redesign their training and competition protocols at a very fundamental level for long-term sustainability.

Since public servants in government offices need to deal with the public by nature of their job requirements, combined with bureaucratic sluggishness, the adaptation of the workplace has been relatively slower than in the private sector. Most jobs which require only a personal computer have introduced work-from-home policies and staggered working hours along with introducing and training employees on new e-office platforms. While many public dealings have attempted to be avoided (like online grievance portals, online processing of government documentation, online payment of taxes, etc.) here too, at the grassroots level, certain work-protocols are not amenable to much modification such as in law enforcement, correctional and military services wherein physical contact with nefarious elements is necessary for law and order and national security. While the executive branch may have been slower to adapt, the legislative and judicial branches have started experimenting with online assembly sessions, online court hearings, etc. In fact, some of the workplace modifications by the judiciary may likely be permanent even post-pandemic such as allowing witnesses and lawyers to appear before the court online and present arguments, thereby reducing the backlog of cases that the Indian judiciary always seems to have.

Like most frontline workers, journalists have also attempted to modify their workplaces by exceedingly preferring online interviews and even in some cases, anchoring their news telecasts from home instead of their high-tech studios. At the grassroots level however, since journalists on the field require to travel at a moment's notice, social distancing often takes a backseat while chasing a story. Printing presses, however, have adapted better by making simple ergonomic modifications for their blue-collar workers.

While that may be the case, not all factories are designed to facilitate modifications for social distancing. With modernization, factories in all industries have become larger in size and increasingly automated. In spite of this, factory workers often have to work in close proximity out of necessity, due to the design of the machines. While office spaces may be relatively easy to redesign, factory spaces seem too cost-intensive to redesign for the short-term. However, with technological innovation and creativity, for the long-term it is a crucial measure to take so as to prevent mass transmission. Ironically, some industries where factory workers need to work in closer proximity have actually seen fewer outbreaks of COVID-19 due to the nature of their work gear, such as food processing units, chemical factories, etc. where the workers need to wear protective gear from head-to-toe as part of their job description. Other industries can learn from this serendipitous experience. Cottage industries and MSMEs which are also prominent for highly congested work environments also need to rapidly evolve and redesign their workplaces in order to survive in the long-term. Not only factory spaces, but the cloistered residential quarters of most blue-collar workers also need redesigning if the manufacturing sector aims to be sustainable in the future.

Factories and wholesale units have control over their work environments at the organizational level. However, the retail sector is an amalgamation of a multitude of small traders each having his/her own conceptualization of an ideal workplace, thereby facilitating adaptation with a lot more difficulty. Shopping malls and stand-alone shops in most parts of India have learnt rapidly to modify their workplaces due to frequent shut-downs by local authorities, especially during the lockdown periods. Most of them have figured out various protocols and systems for controlling the influx of customers, designating shiftwork for employees, etc. in a manner that is in sync with COVID guidelines. Conversely, the traditional "*mandi*" system and other open marketplaces in India tend to be unnecessarily congested due to conflicts over "prime locations" by the multitude of stakeholders that participate. In such cases, local authorities at the municipal and panchayat levels need to take a leadership role in redesigning and allocating public spaces for such markets without bias or prejudice. While some attempts have been made in this direction (e.g. temporarily relocating the famous Kalupur market of Ahmedabad to the riverfront area to facilitate social distancing), modifications like these need to be made long-term via appropriate legislation in order to make them immune from socio-political pressures.

The banking sector has also been an essential service during the pandemic. They have the highest potential of converting almost all of their functions and public dealings online. This is impeded in part due to lack of internet connectivity in many parts of the country and in part due to a cultural overemphasis on a predominantly cash economy. In spite of this, the pace and volume of online transactions has increased manifold in the past few years and is likely to increase even more in the immediate future, thereby allowing more and more employees to potentially opt for a "work-from-home" setup.

The pandemic may not have severely permeated rural India yet. However, it is likely to do so with time, just like previous pandemics in recorded history. Therefore, workplace modifications need to be contemplated for the primary sector as well. While social distancing is relatively easier to accommodate (given proper awareness at the grassroots level) during sowing or harvesting in an open field, the congested environs of APMC markets and other mandis need to be redesigned since the vast majority of the Indian populace is still employed in agriculture. In animal husbandry, the milk cooperatives of India have taken rapid and impressive steps to redesign their milk collection centers during the lockdown period, thereby ensuring a steady and uninterrupted supply for the country in the midst of an epoch of panic buying and hoarding. Certain other primary sector activities like fishing and meatpacking are relatively difficult to reimagine due to the nature of their work requiring close proximity.

The education sector has probably undergone the highest degree of workplace adaptation. Not only have teachers and examiners had to reimagine the workplace ergonomically and technologically, but the nature of the work has also drastically changed since, in spite of technological infrastructure available freely and widely, the nature of online teaching has necessitated a fundamental change in pedagogy and assessment as well. Moreover, this has been drastically different for primary schooling, high schools, and higher education. Until completely immersive VR technology does not become common-place, the teaching-learning experience will never have the same richness as that of a physical classroom or laboratory. Skill-based learning is especially non-conducive through online teaching (AbuMezied,

2017). Despite all these hindrances, certain modifications that this sector has undergone are likely to remain post-pandemic as well. For one, education has become more inclusive with geographical boundaries being less of a hindrance for both students and faculty. Webinars have replaced seminars and conferences due to which their volume has also increased since they are extremely cost-effective. More and more creativity is demanded from the faculty to produce application-based questions for open-book exams and viva voce due to which the traditional emphasis on rote-learning which has plagued the Indian education system since decades is on a rapid decline. Although overcrowded classrooms of the pre-pandemic era may not come back in a hurry, completely online education is also not a sustainable option. Hybrid classes (a mixture of both offline and online participants in a class), however, may slowly become the norm with increase in vaccinations. Offline examinations on paper are proving to be great sources of transmission of COVID-19 in spite of strict adherence to social distancing, especially for exam officers who handle multiple answer sheets from hundreds of students. This will likely hasten the transformation of paper-based examinations to electronic examinations which was already underway on a massive scale in India with the establishment of the National Testing Agency, a couple of years prior to the pandemic.

Last but not the least, the sector which has been the first line of defense against the pandemic is the healthcare industry. In spite of having the most nuanced knowledge to deal with this novel virus, workplace adaptations in this sector have been relatively few, not because of lack of will or ignorance, but rather due to the nature of the work itself. Working from home is not an option for most employees of this industry, except for some mental health workers. Overflowing hospitals in the past year have necessitated longer shifts. Fatigue and burnout have become the norm. Governments across the globe (both developing and developed countries) have had a rude shock by suddenly becoming woefully aware of the shortcomings of their healthcare infrastructure. Only those workplace adaptations which aid in managing the overflow of patients have been focused upon until now and implemented on a war-footing such as more efficient *triage* systems, better bio-waste management protocols, normalizing the use of PPE kits, technological innovation in ventilator and oxygen supply, alternative *intubation* protocols, assembly line systems for mass testing and vaccination drives, etc. (Jaffle, 2020). There is still an acute need for massive changes in the approach towards workplaces in the healthcare system, both for physical and mental health since the current manner in which corona warriors are grappling with managing the pandemic is clearly not sustainable in the long run.

Regardless of one's profession, there are unmistakably certain common trends (positive as well as negative) revolving around the general mental health of the populace, based on prima facie observations and preliminary reports.

The first positive trend is a novel *sense of togetherness*. Nothing brings people together better than the threat of existence especially from another species. During the various staggered phases of lockdown, most countries saw an unprecedented number of NGOs, civil society workers, and private citizens making a spontaneous effort to help fellow citizens in need, with food, shelter, and transport. Those who were fortunate enough to not have to worry about paying the bills reported better quality time spent with family members. To prevent social distancing from turning into social isolation, people utilized telecom and video-conferencing services more frequently, not just for business, but also to reach out to friends and family. Apart from the isolated cases of discrimination against COVID patients and corona warriors, the majority of the populace came together to offer help to fellow neighbors in quarantine to boost morale as well as other kinds of assistance. On the international front, a great number of wars and conflicts saw ceasefires, at least temporarily.

The second positive trend is the *search for new meaning in life*. Existential crises often compel people to put aside their day-to-day petty squabbles and daily anxieties of career growth, workplace politics, etc. and attempt to contemplate on reprioritizing their overall motives and goals in life. The lockdown phases of 2020 did just that to many if not all by applying sudden brakes to the regular fast-paced urban life which was characteristic of our "old normal."

The third positive trend was *testing one's inner strength* in unprecedented and never before imagined ways. This strength was both at a physical/immunological level, as well as at a mental/emotional level. In personal, professional, and social lives, individuals showed resilience to counter the varied ramifications and trickle-down effects of the pandemic, the major ones being adapting to curfews, adjusting to new home environments and finding creative ways to relearn/retrain oneself with new skills for better employment prospects.

The fourth positive trend was a newfound *creativity in daily chores*. For those who were fortunate enough to not lose the roof over their heads due to unemployment, there was a unique challenge of balancing their work-from-home duties with their household duties. The unavailability of domestic help for the majority not only imbibed a newfound appreciation for domestic labor, but also necessitated constant adaptation to come up with novel procedures/protocols to enable optimization of household chores while upholding basic standards of hygiene.

In pre-pandemic times, mental health was largely considered a personal issue. In times of riots and/or natural calamities, these problems were transiently addressed on a community level. The fifth positive trend is *counteracting anxiety and depression*, not just at the individual or community level, but on a global scale. Electronic media (both the traditional mainstream media as well as the recently emerged social media) have played a huge role by conducting awareness programs, offering online mental health services and facilitating morale boosting online events.

Complementing the above five positive trends are five major negative trends regarding general mental health based on prima facie observations and reports.

The first negative trend is an exponential *rise in general anxiety*. Depression was fast becoming a major cause of death globally even in pre-pandemic times. The series of lockdowns and shelter-in-place protocols only exacerbated the process by leaving few opportunities for venting out frustrations, resulting in a rise in domestic violence, substance-addiction abuse and withdrawal, suicide attempts, etc.

The second negative trend (closely related to the first) is a proportionate *rise in death anxiety*. In pre-pandemic times, death anxiety was an issue believed to be relevant only to patients (and their families) suffering from terminal illnesses, or individuals whose jobs put them at mortal risk every single day. Very few times in history does there come a point when every common man/woman/other on the street is unsure about his/her/their physical existence.

The third negative trend (following logically from the first and second) is a collective *rise in existential anxiety*. While death anxiety pertains to the anxiety about one's well-being and physical existence at an individual or family level, the anxiety about the existence of one's community, country, or the entire human species as we know it is applicable at a global level. Mass paranoia, panic buying, hoarding, building bunkers, end-of-the-world conspiracies, organizing independent armed militias, etc. are all characteristic of existential anxiety.

The fourth negative trend, especially in places with very severe lockdown restrictions is a tumultuous *rise in claustrophobic reactions* to daily stressors. While the above three trends have been observed before in history during World Wars, the Cold War, tsunamis, earthquakes, volcanic eruptions, etc., this particular trend is extremely peculiar to the COVID-19 pandemic wherein concepts like "stay apart to stay safe," "stay home and fight the war," "stay home and be a hero," etc. are extremely counterintuitive for the general public.

The fifth negative trend, directly in contravention to the second positive trend discussed above, is the *inability to find new meaning in life*. For many people, the sudden "pause" on regular life, rather than encouraging contemplation of their life choices, placed them in limbo. Individuals who had especially come to believe their work life to be the entirety and sole purpose of their existence had especially greater trouble in reconciling with the new era so suddenly thrust upon them by the pandemic and could not find new meaning of life without professional help, the lack of which has had ripple effects on the organizational health of their workplace.

In conclusion, all white-collar professionals (both HR and non-HR alike) must now come to terms with the realization that regardless of how long the pandemic is likely to last, a complete return to the old "normal" is woefully unlikely. Therefore, a certain willingness or an open-minded attitude towards welcoming a "new normal" in their work-lives (whatever the nature of that may turn out to be) will be most essential in order for the OB/HR profession to empirically explore the merits and demerits of these novel workplace adaptations, let alone enforce them in the near future.

Chapter Takeaways

1. While there are certain common adaptations that most workplaces are likely to require in the post-pandemic world, the one-size-fits-all approach is clearly not conducive. Every industry/service/sector is different and requires a creative manner of tackling the balance between health safety, job productivity, and cost-effectiveness.
2. Workplace adaptations cannot simply be left to the ergonomic experts. Technological innovation needs to be expedited for sustainable and long-term change.
3. An utter disregard for the significance of mental health impacts of workplace design has been the bane of both the public and private sectors. The pandemic is a rude wake-up call for all of humanity in this regard.

4. In order for "work-from-home" policies to be successful in the long run, the knowledge of basic principles of ergonomics now needs to become a matter of general knowledge for all white-collar professionals irrespective of their specialization.
5. The world has fundamentally changed and highly unlikely to revert to the old normal. Any organization that stays in denial of this realization is likely to perish.

Reflection Questions

1. What are the fundamental changes that need to be incorporated in the OB/HR curriculum of all MBA/PGDM post-graduate programs?
2. What are the new "accepted practices" in HR likely to be in the post-pandemic world?
3. What is the nature of "package negotiations" with potential recruiters likely to be in the post-pandemic world during campus placements, especially if work-from-home policies become the norm rather than the exception?
4. What are the fundamental elements that an HR executive should bear in mind while designing recruitment and training policies for newly hired recruits of the post-pandemic world?
5. How should day-to-day HR functions like employee appraisal, team-building exercises, leadership training, etc. be fundamentally different or similar for "on-site" versus "work-from-home" employees in the post-pandemic world?

References

AbuMezied, A. (2017). What role will education play in the fourth industrial revolution? *World economic forum*. agenda/2016/01.

Basu, D. S., Verma, P., & Malviya, S. (2020). India Inc. resets workspaces for life after COVID-19 lockdown. *The Economic Times*, articleshow/75286800.

Bryan, L. (2020). *Companies around the globe have rolled out mandatory remote work, whether you're a newbie or WFH veteran, here's what you need to do stay productive*. British Broadcasting Corporation, worklife/article/20200312.

Cita, S. U., & Budiyanti, R. (2020). Workplace requirements in new normal era due to Covid-19 pandemic: Design criteria and health environment perspectives. *Journal of Public Health for Tropical and Coastal Region, 3*(2), 8–14.

Jaffle, E. (2020). The role of emergency medical services in containing COVID-19. *The American Journal of Emergency Medicine*. https://doi.org/10.1016/2020.04.023

Kaushik, M., & Guleira, N. (2020). The impact of pandemic Covid-19 in workplace. *European Journal of Business and Management, 12*(15), 10.

Mendis, M. S. (2016). Workplace design and job performance: A study of operational level employees in the apparel industry of Sri Lanka. *International Journal of Scientific and Research Publications, 6*(12), 148–153.

Dinyar M. Pestonjee served the Indian Institute of Management (IIM), Ahmedabad, Gujarat, India for over two decades (1979–2001) as Professor of Organizational Behavior. In November, 2000, he was conferred the title of Honorary Professor of the Albert Schweitzer International University, Geneva (Switzerland). He was Chairman, Organizational Behavior Area for three terms and also L&T Chair Professor of Organizational Behavior (1992–1999). He is a Psychologist by training having obtained his M.A. in Psychology with First Class First, and Ph.D. in Industrial Psychology from the Aligarh Muslim University. He has been conferred a Doctor of Letters (Honoris Causa) by the Banaras Hindu University in April 2003 before serving there as a Professor of Psychology for 15 years (1964–1979). A year later, he was also awarded the Albert Schweitzer Medal for Science and Peace in April 2004 at the 50th Anniversary of the Nobel Peace Prize. He has over five decades of teaching experience. He is author/co-author of fifteen books and over 150 research articles. He was Founder Dean, Faculty of Applied Management, CEPT University, Ahmedabad. Since 2009, he is the GSPL Chair Professor at School of Petroleum Management, Pandit Deendayal Petroleum University, Gandhinagar, Gujarat, India. He was conferred, in the year 2001, the Life-Time Achievement Award by his alma mater the Department of Psychology, the Aligarh Muslim University (AMU). Recently, the Indian Academy of Management (INDAM) conferred the Life-Time Achievement Award (December 2017) for his contributions to research in the field of Management.

Taronish A. Pastakia is currently serving as Assistant Professor in the Department of Psychology at St. Xavier's College (Autonomous) Ahmedabad, Gujarat, India having obtained his M.Sc. in Cognitive Science from the Indian Institute of Technology (IIT) Gandhinagar and B.A. in Psychology from St. Xavier's College, Ahmedabad. He has qualified the UGC-NET examination in the subjects of Psychology (with JRF), Criminology, Sociology, and Anthropology.

22 Motivating Remote Workers During COVID-19 Outbreak: Job Demands-Resources Perspective

Sevgi Emirza

Introduction

The COVID-19 outbreak has introduced unprecedented and sharp disruptions to societies and global economies. Many countries have had to take severe control measures to manage the risk of spread of the virus, including social distancing, lockdown, and quarantine. From an individual perspective, millions of employees have shifted to remote working overnight (Kniffin et al., 2020). This shift meant a radical change in the way people work given that workers were forced to working from home rather than making a voluntary choice (Waizenegger et al., 2020). Moreover, having limited experiences with remote working, organizations, organizational members, and managers were not prepared to perform in a remote working setting (Desilver, 2020).

Getting through these exceptional times requires collective efforts, dedication, and commitment of all organizational members. Hence, motivating remote workers and gaining their full support is of great importance for accomplishing organizational goals. Literature on remote work provides insightful understanding on how to design effective remote working programs that motivate employees for enhanced commitment and higher performance (Allen et al., 2015; Kowalski & Swanson, 2005; Sardeshmukh et al., 2012). These prior studies were conducted in a setting where employees voluntarily chose working from home as it served their best interest (Shockley & Allen, 2012). However, in the current context employees have been forced to work from home regardless of their preferences and the suitability of their jobs for remote working. As a result, the extant knowledge on remote working might not effectively apply to a mandatory working from home situation. Hence, it is crucial to examine the dynamics of employee motivation and understand how to better motivate remote-working employees in a context of forced remote working (Wang et al., 2020).

S. Emirza (✉)
Faculty of Business, Dokuz Eylül University, İzmir, Turkey
e-mail: sevgi.bakar@deu.edu.tr

S. K. Dhiman, J. F. Marques (eds.), *Leadership After COVID-19*, Future of Business and Finance, https://doi.org/10.1007/978-3-030-84867-5_22

Remote working might result in unfavorable outcomes such as higher turnover intention, increased stress, and more work family conflict, when it is mandatory rather than voluntary (Kaduk et al., 2019; Lapierre et al., 2016). These findings indicate that the extent to which remote working has a voluntary basis significantly determines the benefits and outcomes associated with it. Hence, given that the majority of prior literature on the motivating and demotivating characteristics of remote work is predicated on the assumption of discretionary remote work (Lapierre et al., 2016), they might not provide a thorough and complete explanation of how to support and motivate employees who switch to a forced remote working plan. As such, the current study aims to explore if and how leaders have managed to motivate and support their subordinates who have been forced to work from home during the COVID-19 outbreak.

The current study adopts job demands-resources (JD-R) theory as a theoretical framework. Differing from other motivation theories, JD-R considers both the unique and interactive effects of demanding (i.e., job demands) and supportive (i.e., job resources) job characteristics to explain motivational outcomes. JD-R theory maps well onto the involuntary nature of remote working during the pandemic. It is because the involuntary nature of remote working during the pandemic is likely to result in taxing and demanding outcomes for those who have never desired to work from home, while proding beneficial and positive outcomes for those who have always wanted but never had the chance or approval to work from home.

Drawing on JD-R theory, the current study expects to reveal job characteristics over which supervisors exercise discretion and thus are able to influence the motivation of employees working from home. This study is organized as follows: first literature review on JD-R theory is presented. Next, methodology and findings of the current research are described. Lastly, implications and limitations of the current study are discussed in the discussion section.

Literature Review

JD-R theory postulates that all working environments (i.e., virtual and physical) could be represented by two main aspects which are job demands and job resources (Bakker & Demerouti, 2014). Job demands refer to the taxing physical, psychological, mental, social, and organizational characteristics of the job that necessitate workers to put continuous physical and psychological effort to accomplish work goals. Job demands include aspects such as work overload, time pressure, work-home conflict, emotionally demanding interactions, role ambiguity, and conflict, etc. Job demands are negatively valued because they come with psychological and physical costs. Job resources refer to psychological, physical, social, and organizational features of the job that support workers in the achievement of work goals, mitigate negative effects of job demands, and contribute to the growth and development of workers (Bakker & Demerouti, 2007). Job resources include features such as autonomy and job control, social support, supervisory coaching, performance feedback, etc. Job demands positively contribute to the well-being and motivation of employees by assisting in task accomplishment.

The theory proposes two distinct but related processes to explain motivational outcomes (Bakker & Demerouti, 2007). The first process is called the stress or health-impairment process and it relates negatively to well-being such as burnout and psychosomatic health complaints (Bakker et al., 2003). This process is the result of prolonged excessive job demands that tax the psychological and physical energy of employees and lead to strain and exhaustion.

The second process is called the motivational process and it is associated with motivation, engagement, and enjoyment (Bakker et al., 2010). In the motivational process, job resources facilitate goal accomplishment by increasing the willingness of employees to exert further effort. Job resources also help employees to satisfy basic needs of autonomy, relatedness, and competence and by doing so, promote a mental state of mind qualified by energy and enthusiasm (Fernet et al., 2013). Prior studies provided empirical evidence on the main effects of job demands and job resources in which job demands are the most important predictors of exhaustion and job resources are the most important predictors of engagement (Hakanen et al., 2008).

In addition to these main effects, job demands and job resources also interactively predict motivational outcomes. This interaction works in two ways. The first interaction, called the buffering effect, occurs when job resources mitigate undesired effects of job demands on exhaustion and motivation. This suggests that job resources (social support, autonomy, and feedback) alleviate the effect of job demands (workload, emotional, and physical demand) on exhaustion (Xanthopoulou et al., 2007). Moreover, job resources also lessen the negative effect of job demands on motivation (Bakker et al., 2007). In the same way, the negative effect of job demands on exhaustion is stronger when job resources are lacking (Bakker et al., 2003).

The second interaction is that job resources influence motivation more strongly when job demands are high. In other words, job demands intensify the positive impact of job resources on motivation. For example, a study demonstrated that job resources are most useful and beneficial, especially when job demands are high. In other words, job resources influence motivation more positively when job demands are also high (Hakanen et al., 2005).

The Role of Leaders in Motivating Employees from the JD-R Perspective

In JD-R literature, leader behaviors and characteristics such as supervisory support and coaching are considered job resources (Breevaart et al., 2014). Beyond being a job resource, leaders also have an indirect effect on motivation by influencing the way demands and resources are allocated across employees. Accordingly, leaders might stimulate employee motivation by maintaining a balanced distribution among job demands and resources. For instance, one study showed that transformational leaders promote employee engagement by providing employees with enhanced job resources such as autonomy and support (Breevaart et al., 2014).

This proposition is related to leaders' capability to create work environments that are conducive for employee engagement (Shuck & Herd, 2012). In other words, leaders have the capacity to influence aspects of a job in such a way that employee engagement flourishes. From the JD-R perspective, this denotes that leaders control job demands and job resources in a balanced manner so that employees could successfully accomplish task goals, and at the same time, satisfy their needs, which in turn promotes employees' involvement and engagement in the job (Kahn, 2010). Accordingly, leaders could foster employee motivation by providing work resources (e.g., job control, empowerment, more opportunities to use skills and development resources) and development resources (e.g., performance feedback, opportunities for growth and development) whereas controlling job demands (e.g., work overload, work pressure, and cognitive demands) (Schaufeli, 2015).

The presence of job resources offered by leaders could help employees accomplish work goals effectively and also fulfill the requirements of job demands. Yet, the absence of those job resources would have the opposite effect by draining emotional energy against job demands and thwarting successful goal attainment. Hence, leaders' supply of job resources could activate the buffer effect and mitigate the negative effect of job demands. Moreover, presenting more job resources might be particularly motivating and useful when job demands are high (Hakanen et al., 2005). Assuming that the sudden shift to remote work might complicate conducting work for employees less experienced with remote working and/or disfavoring remote working, some employees might perceive their jobs as more demanding and challenging when working from home during the pandemic. For example, some employees cohabiting with others might lack appropriate working space, or those with caring responsibilities (Nash & Churchill, 2020) might experience more struggle and burden and perceive higher demands. Under these unfavorable conditions of job demands, job resources become more salient and have a stronger effect on motivation and engagement. In other words, leaders' supply of job resources encourages more employee dedication and motivation against this backdrop of increased demands and burdens, that is when those resources are particularly needed.

Even though JD-R literature posits that job resources are conducive to employee motivation and well-being, it assumes that all resources have similar positive effects. However, as mentioned before, the mandatory nature of remote working, coupled with the emotional challenges of isolation and quarantine (Kawohl & Nordt, 2020) further complicates the issue of motivation. For example, employees who used to fulfill their relatedness needs through social resources at work such as coworker support, team atmosphere, or appreciation of those served (e.g., customers or citizens) are likely to fail to address these needs during remote working given the social distancing and isolation measures. Considering the scarcity of social resources during remote working, offering or creating opportunities for social support by leaders, thus, could make a larger positive impact on employee motivation and well-being compared to providing coaching or support in physical work setting. Hence, it is crucial to explore which specific job resources are more valued by and beneficial to employees working remotely during the pandemic.

Management scholars propose that the COVID-19 outbreak has caused and probably will continue to cause long-lasting organizational changes. One of these changes includes an increasing trend towards working from home. Results of a survey revealed that more than 80% of business leaders intend to apply flexible working arrangements after employees return to offices (Gartner, 2020). Moreover, some scholars even expect more occupations to be performed permanently through remote working (Sytch & Greer, 2020). This accelerated trend increases the need for future work on remote workers' motivation, performance, and well-being. Moreover, health authorities warn about the possibility of future outbreaks similar to or more serious than the COVID-19 pandemic (Tollefson, 2020). This increases the likelihood that this global experiment of mandatory remote working (Kramer & Kramer, 2020) could be repeated to protect the health of employees as well as maintain business as usual. Hence, even though the COVID-19 virus disappears one day, and many involuntary remote workers go back to their offices, organizations and leaders should still be prepared against such disruptive and challenging situations. Hence, it is both necessary and functional to understand how supervisors could promote the motivation and dedication of employees forced to work remotely during the pandemic.

Methodology

A qualitative study was conducted to understand whether and how supervisors have managed to encourage motivation and engagement of remote subordinates during the pandemic. Using a convenience sampling, semi-structured interviews with 12 employees were conducted in October 2020. All interviews were conducted online, via Zoom. The number of interviewees was determined based on the saturation level, until when no new data or information emerged (Strauss & Corbin, 1998).

Interviewees were selected based on convenience sampling. Yet, they all have two common characteristics. First, they all used to work in a physical office before the COVID-19 pandemic but were forced to work from home following the preventive measures taken by their organizations. The second common characteristic is that all interviewees are white-collar workers working in a finance-related job or field in Turkey. Other characteristics of the participants are shown in Table 22.1.

Table 22.1 Attributes of the participants

Participant number	Gender	Previous remote working experience	Supervisory roles	Industry	Department
P1	Female	X		Banking	Financial regulation
P2	Female		X	Banking	Strategy and planning
P3	Male	X		Energy	Financial advisory
P4	Female			Banking	Auditing
P5	Female	X	X	Auditing	Auditing
P6	Female	X		Pharmaceutical	Financial analysis
P7	Female	X	X	Auditing	Auditing
P8	Female			Banking	Strategy and planning
P9	Female		X	Textile	Investment
P10	Female	X		Logistics	Financial reporting
P11	Male		X	NGO	Financial analysis
P12	Male	X	X	Auditing	Auditing

The interview questions aimed to explore which job demands and job resources are related to the ways in which supervisors have motivated their subordinates who happened to work from home after the COVID-19 outbreak. For this purpose, one main question was asked.

> *From the beginning of the pandemic until now, how do you view and assess the efforts of your direct supervisor in keeping and maintaining the motivation of subordinates (you and your peers in the same department) while working from home?*

Considering that JD-R theory is the theoretical framework of this study, participants were expected to specify job demands and job resources in relation to their supervisors' motivating attempts. Some interviewees readily elaborated on job demands and job resources that influenced their motivations while working from home and the role of supervisors in managing these factors. Yet, some interviewees evaluated their supervisors' attempts with a limited focus on job demands and resources and did not provide sufficient details about the supervisors' role in managing job demands and resources for motivating them. When this was the case, the following secondary questions were directed at the interviewees to help them focus more on the job demands and resources supervisors managed to motivate them:

- *Could you please talk about your working hours? Do you work the same hours as when you were working at the office?*
- *Could you please compare your current workload with the one you had prior to working from home? Is it the same or different? If it is different, why has it changed?*
- *How has your supervisor been in distributing the work tasks across the team/ department while working from home?*
- *How has been your supervisors' communication with you and your peers while working from home? Has he/she been available whenever you and others have needed him/her?*
- *Could you please tell me about the training and development processes during the pandemic? Have they been disrupted, or have you and your peers been able to continue receiving training throughout this period?*

All interviewees were asked to respond to these questions in order to assess their own supervisor by taking a subordinate's viewpoint. Yet, some participants who have supervisory roles were also asked to assess their own efforts to motivate their subordinates by taking a supervisory viewpoint. Hence, those interviewees with supervisory roles presented both a self-evaluation with regard to their own practices for motivating their team members, as well as their perception regarding the attempts that their supervisor has undertaken to motivate those interviewees.

Data analysis was based on a theoretical or deductive thematic analysis (Braun & Clarke, 2006). Theoretical thematic analysis adopts a top-down approach in which the analyst probes into the data to uncover theoretically driven themes and categorization. Hence, using a JD-R lens, data was expected to have two common themes. One theme was based around job demands, the presence of which might hinder the motivation of employees. Another theme related to job resources, the presence of which might create favorable results for motivation and the lack of thereof might impair motivation. However, firstly data was coded based on the narratives described by interviewees. This process focused on generating initial codes based on words and sentences with an aim of revealing common themes for first-order categorizations. Then first-order categorizations were organized based on common themes and patterns based on JD-R theory.

Findings

All of the participants stated that in March 2020 they adopted a working from home plan. At the time of the interviews, a majority of participants (10 out of 12) stated that they continue working remotely, rarely visiting the office for very specific purposes and for a very short-time. Two interviewees have started a hybrid working routine after June 2020. One visits the office two or sometimes 3 days a week and works from home for the rest of the week, and the other interviewee works from home for a whole week every 3 weeks.

A majority of interviewees (8 out of 12) stated that before mandatory remote during the pandemic, their company had already been practicing a kind of flexible working arrangement in which employees were allowed to work one day away from the office each week.

When explaining their supervisors' attempts at motivating them, many interviewees readily called their current work environment and job characteristics into play. In other words, they assessed their supervisors' motivating attempts in relation to changes occurred in working conditions and job characteristics while working from home. This suggests that work–life during the pandemic has its own outcomes that lead organizational members to perceive their supervisors' efforts in the light of these outcomes.

Job Demands

The thematic analysis of responses revealed that the most prominent job demands that influenced their motivation negatively in this period were longer working hours and work overload. At first sight, this might seem surprising because the majority of interviewees expressed that before the pandemic, they had been working from home 1 or 2 days a week and their companies had had appropriate infrastructure for remote working. However, even though previous experience and appropriate IT structure might be helpful with adapting to working from home during the pandemic, analysis revealed that they were not able to prevent increasing job demands during constant working from home. It is because, as the analysis revealed, the increase in job demands is a natural outcome of the fact that the the majority of tasks were initially designed to be performed through physical interaction and fully in-person and are not feasible for remote working.

Working Hours

One of the challenges of remote working is the lack of boundaries between work and personal time. For example, one industry report revealed that employees working from home have difficulty ending the work day and work longer than they are supposed to (Avast Business, 2018). However, the presence of boundaries between work and personal time is essential for recovery and mental disengagement from work because high after-hours availability and low boundary control are associated with reduced psychological detachment (Mellner, 2016). Similarly, studies have shown that (Clinton et al., 2017; Ropponen et al., 2018) longer working hours are associated with diminished psychological detachment in the evenings, reduced sleep quality, and decreased morning vigor, an important dimension of motivation (Schaufeli et al., 2006). In other words, when employees experience adequate relaxation during off-job time, they work with higher motivation and enthusiasm the next day (ten Brummelhuis & Bakker, 2012).

Referring to JD-R theory, long working hours have been closely related to job demands. One study regarded prolonged work hours as a job demand (Kinnunen et al., 2011) and another reported that working overtime is more prevalent in jobs with high demands (Van der Hulst et al., 2006). The study by Amagasa and Nakayama (2012) found that in jobs with long work hours, employees perceive higher job demands.

In the current study, working longer hours was also reported in relation to job demands. A majority of interviewees (9 out of 12) expressed that during the pandemic their working days have started to stretch and they have begun to work during what is supposed to be off-job time. This negative change in the work schedule was reported to create both physical and psychological strain on interviewees.

Consistent with the finding of Van der Hulst et al. (2006) that overtime is the result of increased job demand, some interviewees stated that they have to work longer hours because they now have more workload compared to pre-pandemic levels.

P4: Our working hours before switching to remote work were standard... We now have 24/7 access to the system... That's why the workload has increased in this sense as well, because we have constant access and for our continuous development... They do not tell you directly to turn on your computer after 6 o'clock. But because you cannot finish your tasks within normal working hours, they indirectly expect us to turn on the computer...In other words, the deadline is the same, yet the workload is too much... So, they say indirectly that you already have access. You can take it whenever you want, you can finish this job.

P6: Your computer is always at home, you are always in front of the computer, the job never ends. When you work from home, sometimes you do not eat lunch. Or you can still continue from five to seven in the evening. So, we had a little difficulty in managing it.

P2: The boundaries were very clear while we were working at the office... Even if my director had called at eight o'clock when I had come home, I wouldn't have had a tool, I would have had nothing to do. Now, there is a feeling that you can work endlessly.

Moreover, supervisors' approach is another factor that influences working hours of employees. While some supervisors respect traditional working hours and refrain from enforcing subordinates to work after hours, others do not show enough consideration for personal time.

P1: For example, there were cases when he called after a 2.5-hour meeting lasting from morning to noon, as soon as the meeting was over without considering whether you needed the toilet or water. Or, in the same vein, he does not care about the lunch break and does not respect the working hours. But actually, we can say that the demotivating things were greater. I think he could do things like paying more attention to normal working hours, that is, paying more attention to the time periods where people can meet their basic needs, or not to have meetings in the evenings or to call while eating and so on.

P6: Frankly, we have heard about some managers exploiting this. Here, they are sending e-mails in the evening, asking for or expecting something. Working from home can sometimes allow for such abuses.

Supervisors' role in prolonged work hours is consistent with previous findings. Research shows that when supervisors tend to continue working during off-job time, this leads to intrusion into employees' nonwork lives, which results in reduced relaxation and detachment and increased exhaustion (Park et al., 2011; Sonnentag & Schiffner, 2018).

Lastly, prolonged work hours could be the result of the characteristics of employees. Some participants reported that even there is no explicit instruction to do so, they feel under pressure to be available and accessible all the time when working from home, which causes huge stress and anxiety.

P2: You feel an incredible press at home. When I see a text 10 minutes later, no matter who send it, I feel very nervous. So, I don't even have an hour break I give myself, you know? This is incredibly demotivating. Actually, maybe people don't expect it from you... But I do not know what its name is, maybe self-discipline. It is really tiring. I was taking a lot more breaks at the office. I work incredibly hard from home... You feel like you are being watched and I should always be online.

The pressure expressed by P2 represents a reaction to the always-on-culture (Derks et al., 2015), indicating the expectation of supervisors and group norms that subordinates should be constantly accessible and available. Such a pressure might hamper employees' detachment from work and thus result in increased stress (Lee et al., 2017; Suh & Lee, 2017) and poorer well-being (Kompier et al., 2012). According to Matusik and Mickel (2011), the person or the self is mostly the source of this expectation to be available and responsive.

One reason for feeling pressure to be constantly available while working might be related to employees' overcommitment. Prior research showed that workload is positively related to employees' overcommitment. Overcommitment refers to "a set of attitudes, behaviors and emotions that reflect excessive striving in combination with a strong desire of being approved and esteemed" (Siegrist, 2001, p. 55). Overcommitted individuals tend to show excessive levels of commitment to work and perform at a level beyond what is expected of them. Hence, overcommitted individuals might find it more difficult to detach from work and subject to higher job demands and higher workload (Huyghebaert et al., 2018; Van Vegchel et al., 2005).

Overall, a majority of participants reported that they have been working for longer hours since they have switched to remote working. Even though the apparent reason of extended working time seems to be the alteration in the working mode, the analysis of responses revealed that the underlying reasons of increasing working hours are increased workload, supervisors' expectations, and characteristics of employees.

Workload

Workload is one of the most prominent job demands. Karasek Jr (1979) equates psychological job demands with workload that is based on the extent to which an employee is required to perform excessive work within a limited time. Psychological workload is a function of the mental effort required by tasks, the number of tasks, and strict time limits (Karasek et al., 1998).

A majority of interviewees (9 out of 12) reported that they have experienced work overload since they started working from home. The underlying reasons described by interviewees for increased workload could be examined under four groups:

Spending More Time and Effort on Communicating with Others. Interviewees reported that one reason for increased workload is that it takes more time to connect and communicate with others in remote working. Because online meetings take more time compared to causal gatherings, employees spend more time on communication. Despite the increased number of meetings and calls, participants reported that they are not as effective as meeting in-person. This factor has been cited by scholars suggesting that reaching what might be simple information in a physical work setting becomes a challenge when working remotely (Larson et al., 2020).

> *P3: When you work remotely, you have more meetings unavoidably. So instead of just saying something to your friend sitting next to you, you start to think about if it is right now or not, or shall I call him? Or you are setting up meetings, even such little things take your time… It is much more difficult to understand a topic in an online meeting. Because the voices overlap, the connection is broken,* etc., *so it is not very healthy…Nothing can replace sitting side by side, drinking tea and drawing things on paper. Something is always missing.*

> *P6: For a job that you would normally do with another employee in 5 minutes when we were at the office, we now continuously have meetings for even the slightest thing, an online conversation. That's why there were times when we worked much more than we normally do in the first place. This slightly lowered our motivation, frankly. We had a little difficulty until the whole company got used to it.*

> *P7: My workload has increased because of this. We are constantly on the phone or meeting online to solve anything. We are in a constant conversation. There are days when my phone never stops, I talk on the phone until the evening. You have to call 30 people for even a simple signature.*

For the same reason of difficulties in communicating and transferring knowledge, some supervisors find taking on others' work more convenient and easier. Hence, some supervisors purposely prefer taking over more work when they think actually doing the task might take less time and hence be less demanding compared to explaining it to the subordinate in an online setting by sharing screen, etc.

> *P1: My manager said that "Instead of telling you, it is easier for me to do it myself." In other words, people can continue with those jobs they already know and actually take the burden more and do not have too many delegations down… This is because training and teaching are very difficult in remote working. For example, even if I want to share a screen, you actually get very obsessed with technical details. I mean, even the speech quality is getting weaker, the internet gets poor.*

P11: When I send them a report, they send it back to me asking "what is this and what is that, how can I get this here?". Then I tell myself that it's best to do it myself, because I find it more difficult to connect and share screenshots and give them instructions. I say "write your questions clearly and send me an e-mail. I will collect them all, do it collectively and send it back to you." This is how I do it.Does it increase my workload? Yes, it does...

Difficulties in Coordinating Team Members. Another reason for the increased workload relates to the problem of coordinating and organizing others in the team. It is mostly those with supervisory roles that have such difficulty monitoring subordinates and keeping them focused on the job. Spending more time on observing and coordinating others was reported to contribute to the workload of supervisors. Moreover, after failing to reach others several times, supervisors have conceded to perform what other team members are supposed to do. Even though undertaking subordinates' duties does not seem appropriate and sustainable, interviewees acknowledged that, as supervisors, they are the ones who are accountable for the accomplishment of tasks; hence, they have no choice but to pick up where subordinates leave off.

P4: When we were one-to-one, I could make him do a task over and over until he got it right. However, now I cannot even make contact with him. It is very difficult for me to teach my subordinates and get work done. For example, I call but am unable to reach, and I send e-mails, but receive no response. When we want to give feedback about these, we cannot reach the person to whom we will give the feedback... As there are always such disconnections, after a while something like this occurred in us, in the upper levels like me. Instead of trying to get him to do the job, I should leave him alone. I will be doing that job at the end of the day anyway, so I should do it now, instead of working overtime...

P7: We have had a hard time keeping track of the teams. We cannot track the teams, they are not online, we call them but cannot reach... We had trouble getting work done remotely. Obviously, this caused a decrease in our motivation at our levels... They are not online; this is the difficulty of working remotely. I am writing, for example, are you okay? What are you doing? A reply comes after 2 hours, or no reaction... If someone in your team does not do his/her task, you have to take the time for that task because you have the responsibility for that task. When the team does not complete a task, I make that effort myself, unfortunately.

However, coordination problems reported to occur mostly with those who are new to rules, procedures and work practices.

P4: There is a communicator that we use within the company. Normally, if we are not in front of the computer, we lock our account so that when someone writes to us, they do not expect an urgent response. You know, it is very important in our corporate culture. He (i.e., *the subordinate) seems online, I write, but he replies after half an hour.*

Moreover, coordination of remote members is also influenced by how much supervisors and team members know each other. One interviewee expressed that ensuring coordination is much easier and more efficient when team members have mutual acquittance.

P5: I had a project this March, my team was very familiar. The job was not a new job, the work done was obvious. We had a very productive time. I mean, we finished the project in two and a half weeks even we had one and a half months to complete it. But now I am entering a new project, it is a new one. I don't know the team, I don't know the client. I definitely do not know the person I talked to 24 times. But in this process, I had a hard time managing the team.

Overall, analysis of responses revealed maintaining coordination across teams that consist of newcomers who are not familiar with the group norms and rules required team leaders to exert higher effort to keep them focused on the work and maintain coordination. This is consistent with the work of McCarter and Sheremeta (2013), which demonstrates the decrease in group coordination and functioning following the entry of a newcomer. Even though their study explains this decrease in coordination with a reduction in trust among group members after the arrival of a newcomer, interviewees did not refer to anything about trust when talking about coordination problems. The coordination problems expressed by interviewees might have more to do with the socialization and adaptation process of newcomers, because work teams, especially in the auditing industry, do not exist long enough to live through all stages of team building. Hence, four stages of socialization, task mastery, role clarification, acculturation, and social integration (Fisher, 1990), are essential for newcomers to learn organizational norms and values and perform accordingly. As expressed by interviewees, most of the newcomers had been recruited almost 7 months before shifting to remote working, which suggests that they might not have enough time to go through all four stages of socialization and complete the adaptation process.

Coordination across members is central to the accomplishment of group goals, particularly for jobs with task interdependence (Hertel et al., 2004). In jobs with high task interdependence, interaction across members is of great importance because even a single action by one member could have significant impacts on work processes conducted by other members. This task interdependence for some jobs was expressed by the following statements:

P7: You are nothing without team, you cannot do anything alone. But if the team does nothing, you will be unable to complete that task on your own, you will be unable to keep up.

P12: Consequently, a logjam on one side affects all other sides. If a subordinate cannot do his task on time, then I cannot review it on time. The report cannot be completed on time because I cannot review on time. When the report is not finished on time, my manager cannot read it in time. It is not complete when he cannot read in that time, and his senior manager cannot look at it in time. The workload of the senior manager also increases.... With this pandemic, there is a bottleneck at the bottom, so when you say to the manager, "I'm sorry, I couldn't finish this Tuesday, I will give you this Friday," you mess up the entire work of the manager... As such, everyone's work started to stall and everyone was influenced in the same way.

Literature on team work and coordination suggests that in temporary or newly established teams, as is the case expressed by the interviewees, the personalities of newcomers are of substantive importance for conformity and hence coordination. For example, newcomers with collective orientation (Hagemann et al., 2020) or highly interdependent self-construal experience higher alignment with group goals and better coordination within their team.

Disruption in the Training of New Recruits. The third reason for the increased workload is associated with the training of newcomers. More precisely, the disruption of the informal and on-the-job training of newcomers precludes them from developing the competencies and skills required for them to perform efficiently.

The interruption of on-the-job training of new recruits has brought about new burdens for supervisors who are responsible for training them. Interviewees expressed that training subordinates online demands more time and energy; it is also less effective compared to in-person training.

> *P5: Although the cameras are open, I do not understand whether I can convey things at that moment. For example, I cover a task, maybe in 2 hours. Then I turn off the headset and microphone and I see that I have no energy left. And I do not know if he really understands. Because when we were side by side, I could understand what he did not understand even from his groaning.*
>
> *P7: You are sharing a screen, saying "look at this cell, look here, it does this." You are trying to explain your logic. I know that I have told the simplest subject 5 times to even a senior, who thinks he is the smartest. You know, telling this 5 times means 15 minutes and 20 minutes for one person. Imagine you spend 1 hour on this job. You know, if you work with 5 seniors at the same time, you are already telling them all day long. It was more difficult to train remotely. The convenience of physical and face-to-face communication didn't happen on the camera, so we couldn't do it.*

This problem is particularly the case in those jobs that are designed to be trained through on-the-job training. It appears that the shift to remote working that occurred abruptly left no time to think about how to redesign on-the-job training of the new recruits. Experiencing difficulty in training others might be a product of how these jobs were designed. As one interviewee stated, on-the-job training requires occupants to see, experience, and come across all components of the job, which cannot be achieved with remote training.

> *P12: These friends do not only have technical development. These friends experience changes and developments in terms of behavior. We provide this with social communication. So, when he goes there, he sees the manager meeting with the client. This is actually a behavioral role model for them... When we get there, we generally work on problem solving. We just solve problems. The teams have started to fail to see how we overcome these problems. Because everything started to happen over the phone. When I do not meet face-to-face, I do not think that these types of skills are well-developed ... Even this is very important, how you sit by a client, how you stand up. You (implying subordinates) can't even see that. Because you work at home with your pajamas. When he meets the clients, he wears shorts under his shirt. This is lacking seriousness.*

Besides being less convenient, less efficient, and more demanding, compared to on-the-job training, remote training results in higher workload for everyone involved in the process. The lack of on-the-job training opportunities impacted the workloads of supervisors and seniors in two ways. First, it forced supervisors and senior members of the team to put in more time to train newcomers.

> *P7: This is the hardest part of not being able to be side by side, for us actually not being able to train newcomers on-the-job... A newcomer doesn't know the analysis he is supposed to do. The senior has to explain but it takes longer to explain remotely. Therefore, everyone's work was disrupted. Everyone's computer had to be turned on full-time from morning to night. Certainly, our workload has increased a lot.*

Disruption of on-the-job training of newcomers has increased the workload of other team members in a second way. Accordingly, interviewees reported that more experienced and competent members have started to undertake the tasks that are normally supposed to be performed by newcomers. This is because newcomers could not gain the required competencies and skills they need to perform their job thoroughly.

P4: Before they (i.e., *newcomers) could learn the job completely, we switched to remote working. Since they do not know the job well, we are doing what they are supposed to do. That's why our load has never actually decreased, on the contrary, it has increased exponentially… Generally, more work is assigned to those who do the job better. That is why there have been very few days since March when I have not overworked. I was a person who normally never worked before working remotely.*

P8: Since the new staff could not be trained, the workload of the experienced staff has increased, it has an impact on me, as well. Because I am the most experienced person, I have to do the majority of the work when I work together with them, when we are working from home.

P11: We had a hard time during the orientation process of a new friend. And I still think there is more difficulty… But if we were at the computer, for example, I could hand over the documents to him and see how he entered them. Since I cannot do such a thing right now, I could not delegate the task to him.

Overall, on-the-job training of newcomers has been interrupted following the shift to remote working. Because the training was originally designed to be delivered in-person, remote training attempts fail to yield the same benefits as the original ones. This problem creates a situation where newcomers have started to fall behind in their otherwise professional development and seniors and supervisors have to take on more workload.

Importantly, one supervisor acknowledged that slowing down in professional development creates disappointment and demotivation for the newcomer.

P11: That's why I can say that this education process was quite undermined. That person (i.e., *the newcomer) is falling behind. He feels like he's doing worthless work… Because he keeps asking me "is there another job? Do I do this? Can you give me another job? Can you give me an extra job?"*

Hence, the adverse effects of disruption of newcomer training are not limited to bringing more workload to senior employees. It also negatively influences newcomers' self-evaluations and their attitudes to the job itself. One study showed that effective remote work experiences and training positively relate to remote work self-efficacy, which refers to beliefs about one's capability to perform tasks effectively in the domain of remote working. Moreover, remote work self-efficacy, in turn, positively influences attitudes like job satisfaction and organizational commitment and also individuals' ability to cope with difficulties (Staples et al., 1999). Given that training of newcomers is far from being effective as stated by interviewees, newcomers are less likely to develop strong remote working self-efficacy related to their jobs. As explained by one participant above, one newcomer feels that he does worthless and insignificant work, which probably influences his self-confidence and motivation negatively (Barrick et al., 2013; Gagné et al., 1997).

Acting as A Bridge Between Higher and Lower Levels. The last reason for increased workload is the need to serve as a bridge conveying information figures and instructions between levels. Interviewees with supervisory roles acknowledged that they have started to work more to transmit messages between upper levels and lower levels. This is because while managers used to communicate directly with team members at the office, now during remote working they prefer to contact only the team leader asking him/her to maintain the flow of information, demands, directives, and any material. In the following account this situation is described by an interviewee from a team leader's point of view:

> P2: *My director used to work more one-on-one with the team. Now everything is filtered out of me. That's why I've been a constant buffer. You know, he used to work with the team about the things he could do quickly. But right now, for example, he doesn't prefer this at all because otherwise he would put in more effort.*
>
> P4: *When he* (i.e., *the manager) sees an error, he tells the team leader instead of directly contacting the person who makes the error. The manager contacts the team leader. There is always a hierarchy. Before the pandemic, he used to directly call us and ask for corrections.*

Interviewees with supervisory roles also acknowledged that they have to reduce their interaction with other team members and instead contact mostly with team leaders or experienced subordinates due to heavy workload and time limitations. They reported that they ask seniors to serve as a bridge to transmit information and materials between them and other team members.

> P2: *I have had to contact my friends who have been in the team for 1 year, much less during this period. Normally, I used to work with everyone in the team. But this time, I need to work in a very hierarchical manner in this process. Because otherwise, I have to explain everything all over again. Now, I ask them* (i.e., *seniors) to explain other members by saying, "Could you explain this to your friends, do it with them." Because I don't really have that much time.*
>
> P7: *You have to remotely manage a team of 6–7 people. You know, I gave a lot of responsibility to the team leader at first. I should have shared some of his responsibility. I always communicated with him because he was the team leader. But maybe I should have communicated with the whole team, from juniors to seniors. You know, it was easy for me, but it didn't work very well either. The important thing is to communicate with the full team and understand what they all do. Because that's when they own the job.*

Contacting only the team leader or the most experienced subordinate in the team might unburden managers from the duties of tracking each subordinate in the team and save them time and effort to invest in other jobs. Yet, an interviewee acting as a bridge expressed that this role has brought in too much workload that it has hindered her from doing her own tasks.

> P5: *When the day is over, especially like 5 o'clock in the evening, I am worn-out, but I still have unfinished jobs which I have to do at night by overworking. Because during the day, I tell my supervisor what I get from the client, convey what I get from the manager to the team... I feel like tasks have been offloaded onto the middle level. They* (i.e., *supervisors) think like she solves it anyway, she meets with the client, she is always there together with the team, she will tell me anything. We are almost dead while transferring it from one to another or taking it from one and transmitting it to another,* etc. *It was difficult to serve that bridge function... I think the time of the lower levels was expended so that they* (i.e., *supervisors) make better use of their own time.*

Other than increasing the workload of team leaders as bridges, managers' contacting only one person has led to disappointment and negatively influenced the motivation and job involvement of other team members who are deprived of managers' contact and communication.

P7: I received a comment from one of my friends. He said "You have never talked to us, you have always talked to the Senior. Why did you never talk to us? We were very sorry." Team members are expecting us to communicate.

P5: For example, our manager in the last project was changed. My team wouldn't have known this, if I hadn't told them. This is the lack of communication. The manager told me, "you will let the team know". Well, what happens then? Team members feel worthless and demotivated. And unity in the team can be lost.

As a remedy, interviewees reported that they have started to spend more time and communicate with other team members, as well.

P2: My team is only with me in meetings. That is why you feel that the bond starts to weaken, and it reduces the commitment. To overcome this, I try to arrange meetings in which we gather all together and our director also attends.

P7: So, I realized my mistake, frankly. In the subsequent projects, for example, on the first day of the week, we have meetings with the whole team. I ask them "Are you doing that task, right? Are you okay, do you understand?" I communicate this way.

Job Resources

Based on the thematic analysis of responses, the most effective job resources provided by supervisors that influenced employee motivation positively in this period were based on five categories: supervisory communication, supervisory technical support, supervisory social support, reward and recognition, and flexibility and job control.

JD-R theory proposes that while the presence of job resources is helpful for maintaining employee motivation and engagement, the lack of such resources has an adverse effect on motivation (Bakker & Demerouti, 2014). Hence, responses that indicated both the presence and absence of the same job resource were taken into account while forming common categories.

Supervisory Communication

Supervisory communication and supervisory coaching are significant job resources which might serveas a proxy for feedback and relationship quality (Bakker et al., 2005). Accordingly, employees benefit improved communication with supervisor because accurate task-related information provided by supervisor could help employees to accomplish task goals increasing the odds of being rewarded. Similarly, coaching behaviors like communicating clear directions and expectations (Tanskanen et al., 2019) and high-quality relationships (Breevaart et al., 2015) that are associated with more frequent and better communication are considered as job resources that enhance motivation of employees.

According to the analysis, supervisor communication emerged as an important job resource category. Accordingly, while some supervisors might effortlessly acclimatize themselves to the new virtual environment, some others might fall short of aligning daily leadership behaviors to the remote working setting. Subordinates assessed the lack of supervisor communication as a problem that influenced their motivation negatively during working from home.

> *P4: Since March, we have not communicated by phone in any way, but rarely, he replies to our e-mails... So, our communication is completely broken at this point... He could not manage this process well, I mean, as a manager, because he did not communicate with the team*
>
> *P12: I wish we could talk at least once a week. I have a manager that I haven't spoken to for a month... But I really can't call my manager so easily. Something must happen if I am going to call him.*

This outcome is not surprising because previous studies have found that communication (Ozimek, 2020; Wang et al., 2020) and lack of face-to-face supervision (Golden, 2006; Larson et al., 2020) are important challenges of remote working Moreover, management scholars and practitioners recommend leaders to maintain frequent, transparent, and consistent communication with subordinates to facilitate their transition to remote work (Sull et al., 2020).

Interviewees reported the lack of supervisory communication as an important aspect of their motivation during working from home. Accordingly, supervisors who have failed to reach out to subordinates or refrain from any communication were assessed negatively. Subordinates felt lonely and stressed when they did not have sufficient communication with their supervisors.

> *P5: Frankly, I would have felt better if he had been calling me rather than me reaching out to him. We have been left alone.*
>
> *P8: My supervisor has completely withdrawn himself. For example, I have a question. He directs me to the director, which actually lowered my motivation. Because I am constantly dealing with the director because he personally does not want to deal with director...This has obviously been a stress factor for us. I also do not want to stay in constant contact with the director*

Supervisory Technical Support

One important leadership behavior relates to day-to-day management and organization of tasks to be accomplished by subordinates. This behavior is described as task-oriented leadership and includes practices such as setting directions by defining group goals and objectives, identifying subordinate roles by assigning tasks, emphasizing performance and efficiency standards (Fleishman, 1973). Task-oriented leadership behaviors are essential for employee performance and effectiveness, given that subordinates need an optimal level of task-oriented leadership to perform well (Lambert et al., 2012). Research has shown that task-related leadership behaviors contribute positively to the job performance of subordinates (Judge et al., 2004).

Interviewees who stated that they received task-related direction from their supervisor expressed that they feel motivated, encouraged, and supported.

> *P7: When they see that I cannot catch up, they take some of my responsibilities and do it themselves. Even this is something that increases my motivation... He (i.e., one manager) says, "tell me if you cannot catch up, let me step in when you have difficulties with the teams" ... My managers have been very supportive about how tasks are performed.*

P10: Because I was a newcomer, my manager showed interest by calling me "You just started, do you have anything missing, is there anything we can help," whether from teams or by phone. It is a good thing for me to even do that.

One interviewee with supervisory roles reported that he regularly meets with his subordinates every morning to make sure that he provides them with every task-related support. He added that this is particularly important for subordinates with less experience and professional knowledge.

P12: I think this is very important to increase their motivation. Every morning I say that at half past eight, everyone will turn on the computer. First, we will sit down and, have a cup of coffee. Then let's plan how to do our job, then let's do it. Of course, I talk to all of them during the day, but at least once in the morning, let's find the way we will go... By doing this, I draw their direction, and I give them a lot of support.

When such task-related assistance is not provided, it leaves employees without any necessary guidance and direction for the accomplishment of work tasks. Lack of task-related assistance not only causes subordinates to perform badly, but also makes them feel unvalued and incompetent (Lambert et al., 2012). As one interviewee reported, she could not benefit from such assistance while working from home, which resulted in difficulty and anxiety for her.

P5: I am working in a new project where there are a lot of things I could not solve. But at the end of a whole month, we will have the chance to look together for the first time tomorrow. Because he has had a lot of work (i.e., *the manager) to deal with... Of course, this makes me anxious, I am still nervous. What will we face tomorrow, how will we solve it? You know, this created a little difficulty.*

Supervisory Social Support

The COVID-19 pandemic has caused unprecedented social distancing in order to better manage the risk of spreading the virus. However, this has led to feelings of loneliness and isolation for many people, which has adverse impacts on mental and psychological well-being (Killgore et al., 2020). This raises the importance of maintaining social connectedness and social networks to help with problems associated with isolation.

All of the interviewees had been working at offices before the pandemic, except 1- or 2-days of flexible working schedules. Following the lockdown and the shift to remote working interviewees have experienced that physical distance from others has led to a decline in social bonds, which itself has become a demotivating factor.

P2: Remote working initially was an incredibly demotivating factor. For example, I used to have small talks about anything with people in the team. I used to ask things like, "How are you doing today? You were at the concert yesterday, right? How was it?" Such instances are lost now. This was a tremendous unifying and motivating force in the work life. Remote working has weakened the personal bonds I established with team members... We understood that physical contact adds a very different value.

One important leadership behavior is called people or relationship-oriented leadership. This type of leadership refers to how much a leader cares for and nurtures subordinates, is concerned about their well-being and welfare, and shows supportive and appreciative behaviors (Bass, 1990). These types of behaviors contribute to the employees' satisfaction with the leader, job satisfaction, and motivation (Judge et al., 2004).

Considering the negative consequences of working from home accompanied by the forced lockdown, some supervisors attempt to address the social needs of subordinates by holding social meetings where team members can meet and socialize.

> *P2: We are doing bi-weekly meetings all together online. But we never talked about business at the meetings. Or we celebrated the classic office birthdays all together online, we always met at every birthday. So, I can say that these have increased some motivation.*
>
> *P10: We hold a department meeting over the Teams platform every two weeks. We organize such meetings in order not to feel disconnected from each other in social terms.*

But it may have also had an effect. It was already an established team before, and its foundation was solid. Satin had been working together for 2 years. Of course, it may have had an effect. Frankly, I did not feel any deficiency in this regard.

Some others have preferred to make directive calls to each subordinate and ask after their health and well-being.

> *P9: I call them every other day, if not every day, and ask them about their health, even though we have no work-related things to talk about.*
>
> *P12: I like to form some emotional bonds with them... I usually call them one at a time and chitchat like "do you have an issue, how is it going?" I create chitchat groups and I write there every morning saying "good morning diamonds." Then, we all get to work.*

Similarly, less formal and unstructured communication tools also help team members stay in touch and maintain social bonds and a sense of connectivity, as noted by an interviewee:

> *P6: We are working with Microsoft Teams. We have a chitchat group; we also have a group where we do regular work... We are still always in communication with each other. Be it online or remotely, from chat, from WhatsApp. That's why I can't say that we have lost much of the team spirit.*

While receiving the required level of relationship-oriented and supportive leadership contributes to the motivation of subordinates and helps address their social needs, the lack of such leadership leaves subordinates feeling undervalued, causing them to think that their supervisor does not care about their problems. When subordinates are deprived of such supervisory support, then they lack psychological need fulfillment, which results in a decrease in motivation (Lambert et al., 2012).

One interviewee lamented the fact that they have lost even the smallest and slightest moments of social connection that they used to have before working from home. She stated that her supervisors have failed to address her social needs and motivate her.

> *P5: We used to get coffee, and chat outside. Now we are unable to do anything other than the work. Frankly, I cannot say that they (i.e., managers) did socially motivating things. Because they themselves are not motivated... It is very valuable for us to be able to talk to people for two minutes because we work really hard, but we lost this. We have started to lose our motivation and contact, we started to get bored... I haven't had the opportunity to talk about anything with my managers and team outside of work for 6 months.*

Reward and Recognition

A key aspect of effective leadership includes motivating subordinates to promote high-quality performance and optimal efficacy. Cascio (2000) considers performance management as the biggest challenge of managing remote working. He suggests supervisors define performance expectations and objectives and facilitate successful performance by providing necessary resources. He also proposes that managers encourage high performance and effective goal attainment. For this purpose, he recommends that supervisors provide timely, fair, and value rewards to remote workers to ensure achievement of assigned goals. Managers basically can use financial and non-financial rewards to motivate employees for high performance.

Analysis revealed that some supervisors while working from home during the pandemic use recognition and attention as a rewarding tool to motivate employees. Interviewees stated that some supervisors reward high employee performance by appreciating and recognizing how hard subordinates work and how much effort they have put forth.

> P2: *I think being appreciated and having your efforts seen motivate a lot. I think I tried to do this a lot and it has a positive effect. Because it is very important to make someone feel that "you are doing this task despite these conditions" ... We have a reward awarded to high performers... My manager gave it to me. I was really happy with this. Oh, I felt like "so, he has seen it." I think it motivates me that he sees my effort.*
>
> P12: *We do not have the freedom to plan the weekend. A freedom that is difficult to come by during the busy season. I tell them that "We will do this, and if it ends, nobody will call anyone over the weekend after 2 weeks." They are actually a little more motivated this way.*

Providing financial rewards and monetary incentives are another option that leaders could use to motivate employees and promote high performance. Accordingly, pay for performance systems reward high employee performance based on the employees' contribution to accomplishments. One interviewee stated that her efforts and contributions she has made throughout pandemic were rewarded by a higher rise in salary.

> P7: *I cannot say that my manager did things like "you are very good at work, we reward you for this" in this process. But in October, they called and told me that "you got a higher pay raise because you contributed, and we think there will be big responsibilities in the future." Fortunately, a peformance-based system is now being used in which those who perform well are promoted, while those who do not work get no promotion.*

Overall, supervisors have used both financial and non-financial rewarding tools to encourage employee performance and keep employees motivated during these times.

While appreciating and rewarding hard work and effort during these difficult times help motivate employees, failure to do so might have an adverse effect on motivation. As expressed by one interviewee, subordinates expected their supervisors to be more supportive and helpful when they have performance and adaptation problems during the pandemic. But the interviewee reproached that their managers do not show any concern and understanding and instead hold employees responsible for problems.

> *P12: When we suddenly retreated to homes, we had a problem of adaptation... Everyone was distracted... Managers should have tolerated it. However, some managers have had expectations as if I was still working full performance. And when their expectations were not met, they found it easier to say "your performance plummeted" ... When your performance suffers, there is no one to investigate the reasons... Frankly, nobody is making an extra effort to improve your performance.*

However, in the presence of uncertainty, it is only natural that employees might feel psychological strain, anxiety, and lower morale (DiFonzo & Bordia, 1998), which might influence their performance negatively (Cullen et al., 2014). Hence, effective strategies in such circumstances might include adopting open and effective communication and engaging in supportive actions that facilitate trust of employees in the organization (Allen et al., 2007).

Flexibility and Job Control

In JD-R literature, job autonomy orcontrol is considered an important job resource that influences the motivation of employees (Fernet et al., 2013). Flexibility refers to the autonomy to choose the time and location of work. Remote working bestows upon employees the freedom to schedule their work hours based on family demands (Golden et al., 2006; Kossek et al., 2006) and this flexibility has been described as one of the leading motivations for remote work (Mann et al., 2000).

Job control or job autonomy refers to the discretion about how to perform one's job and the freedom to take personal initiative when deciding on the pace and phases of the work. Employees working remotely perceive having higher autonomy (Delanoeije et al., 2019), which positively contributes to their motivation (Sardeshmukh et al., 2012).

Importantly job control is a significant job resource that positively impacts employee motivation by acting as a buffer against job demands (Bakker et al., 2005). Job autonomy is crucial to the management of stressful situations that are associated with poor well-being and lower motivation. Given that employees have faced with work overload and increased job demands during the mandaroty remote work, job control and flexibility might help them not only to shield against associated strain but also to maintain motivation and engagement.

One interviewee with supervisory roles reported that she has taken a lax approach to deadlines and work scheduling in order to make employees feel more capable of dealing with the stresses of remote working and thus feel more motivated.

> *P2: My motivation tool in the pandemic is more like not being too tight on anything, not giving tight deadlines, a little more, "we will do that anyway no worries; it doesn't matter if it is not finished, you stay at home today."*

Half of the interviewees (6 out of 12) reported that their supervisor provided them with the required discretion to have flexibility and/or control over their job during remote working. They assessed this job resource and their supervisors positively.

P10: So, for example, if an employee with a child is unable to work in the morning, she is given the choice to work at night to compensate... Our manager was very flexible in this regard. When we started working from home, the first day he said, "We are going through a difficult period, I do not expect anyone to perform as well as they do in the office, I just want everyone to feel comfortable". That's why I think it was a nice act.

P11: My director tells me "You don't need to get permission right now. You can even sleep at home as long as you're done with the job, I don't care." In this respect, I can say that I am working with a very positive director who supports everyone and supports in all circumstances.

Management scholars suggest that allowing flexibility might help promote work–life balance (Sull et al., 2020). Having the flexibility to adjust the schedule and control over the timing of the work is especially crucial for those with domestic roles and caring responsibilities.

One interviewee reported that as a mother, the most motivating factor was her supervisor's encouraging to have a break for looking after her child during the day and having the flexibility of performing work duties when it works best for her, which is in the evenings.

P2: Since I am a mother and also an employee, working from home has been very difficult for me. I felt very motivated when my manager said to me "first take care of your daughter." I felt bad at first, but then I saw that because I was shown this understanding, I was more motivated and tried to compensate in the evenings.

One interviewee works for a company that adopted a partial remote working plan during the pandemic, which required employees to work at the office for half-month. She asked for permission to work remotely for the whole month due to her health issues. She expressed her appreciation for having the flexibility to choose between working from home and going to the office only when she feels like.

P9: I have an allergic condition. That's why I said I wouldn't come to work for a while, I won't be able to come. They definitely understood it. Nobody said, "you should come, or you have to come to work", until I said, "I am coming"... But my manager went to work every day.

These responses indicate that not all remote employees have similar flexibility during the pandemic. However, employees provided with flexibility by their supervisors found this resource motivating and also evaluated their supervisor positively. This finding is consistent with previous studies suggesting that enabling employees to schedule their work to fit their needs improves the remote working experience and results in better outcomes such as increased satisfaction and productivity (Baltes et al., 1999).

Discussion

Drawing on JD-R theory, the current study aimed to understand whether and how supervisors have motivated their subordinates who were forced to work from home during the COVID-19 pandemic. Results of the thematic analysis revealed that there are specific job aspects within the reach of supervisors that positively influence the motivation of employees in mandatory remote working. Five job resources, supervisory communication, supervisory technical support, supervisory social support, reward and recognition, flexibility and control emerged as important factors that supervisors have utilized to promote employee motivation. In other words, these five job resources provided by supervisors help employees to overcome job demands and satisfy basic psychological needs (autonomy, competence, and affiliation, Van den Broeck et al., 2008), which in turn enhance their well-being and motivation. Moreover, results revealed two important job demands, which are long work hours and work overload, that negatively effect employee motivation. Even though a few interviewees referred to the role of supervisors in increasing job demands, most of the reasons for increased job demands during the pandemic were reported to be related to the nature of remote work, such as interdependency of work tasks.

Job resources that were found motivating generally overlap with prior findings. However, some unique aspects of job resources were also identified. For example, rewards and recognition of performance by the supervisor were specified as characteristics that influence employee motivation. Accordingly, participants stated that they expect their performance to be appreciated and recognized by their supervisor while working remotely. Moreover, being rewarded for high performance was reported to be another sign that employees' efforts are seen, and that supervisors are able to distinguish those working hard while working from home. This factor relates to how remote performance is monitored, measured, and appraised, which represents a challenge from a supervisory perspective (Kurland & Bailey, 1999). Performance of remote workers might not be easily seen even though they work really hard and maybe longer hours than non-remote workers. This precludes supervisors from observing the strengths and weaknesses of employees, measuring productivity, and delivering relevant feedback unless the job yields easily measurable outcomes such as sales targets. Hence, organizations might adopt appraisal systems with result-focused assessments rather than process-focused assessments (Kniffin et al., 2020). However, the concern with this practice might be that remote workers miss the opportunity to receive feedback on the accuracy of their behaviors and learn how to improve their performance.

Job resources enhance the motivation and engagement of employees, yet the absence of such resources curtails motivation and dedication. Communication, or more accurately the lack of supervisory communication is another job resource that interviewees reported to be related to their motivation. Despite subordinates' desire for more frequent communication with supervisors, supervisors were reported to be unavailable or inaccessible to subordinates during the remote work. One of the greatest challenges of remote working is the lack of face-to-face communication and associated benefits (e.g., exchange of information, feedback) (Greer & Payne, 2014). Much of the face-to-face communication depends on physical proximity and increased spatial distance as a result of remote working disrupts traditional communication channels used in physical settings. Given that satisfaction with supervisory communication greatly improves employee motivation and engagement (Karanges et al., 2015), maintaining effective communication with remote workers is crucial. Studies suggest that training of organizational members helps improve adaptation of employees to use remote communication channels effectively and exhibit a better virtual presence (Akkirman & Harris, 2005; Venkatesh & Johnson,

2002). Moreover, establishing more formalized and well-planned communication procedures between supervisors and remote workers and providing relevant training might help enhance satisfaction with communication (Duxbury & Neufeld, 1999).

Another significant challenge of remote working during the pandemic is the adaptation and training of newcomers. Supervisors expressed that the major problem is related to new recruits, especially those with little or no job experience. The underlying reason for this challenge is that training in many finance-related jobs depends on on-the-job training. Interviewees with supervisory roles expressed their concerns over the lack of physical proximity during remote work, which impaired the exchange of specific information and technical information and also the opportunity to monitor and check newcomers' practice of newly learned skills. Disruption of on-the-job training due to a sudden shift to a remote work plan has resulted in increased workload for experienced members and supervisors. Moreover, socialization, adaptation, and assimilation of newcomers have been negatively influenced, such that newcomers feel like outsiders and less integrated into the team. This is reasonable given that socialization happens as a newcomer gains the essential knowledge, values, and behavior patterns required to perform task roles and assignments. Future studies are recommended to explore how to design on-the-job training in an online setting so that newcomers joining remote teams can be trained effectively.

One strength of the current study is that it examined supervisors' attempts at motivating employees with a dual perspective. The employee perspective identified how subordinates perceive their supervisors in motivating and encouraging them while working remotely during the pandemic. Conversely, the leader perspective specified how supervisors self-evaluate their own supervisory performance in motivating their subordinates. Importantly, the analysis revealed that these two perspectives are generally compatible with each other. For example, some subordinates specified that supervisors' preference to contact one person in the team, mostly the team leader or a senior, increases the workload of that contact person. Similarly, those with supervisory roles supported this view by stating that they indeed communicated hierarchically with others in their team by asking one subordinate to maintain communication between themselves and with others in the team. Therefore, providing both the supervisor and the employee perspectives adds to the comprehensiveness and generality of the findings.

An important limitation of the current study is associated with the generalizability of its findings. The interviews were conducted with a sample of white-collar employees whose jobs mostly related to finance. The characteristics of the jobs, such as on-the-job-training and interdependency across team members might have influenced perceptions of participants about remote working.

Chapter Takeaways/Lessons

1. Employees forced to work from home during the pandemic experience unique challenges such as working longer hours and dealing with work overload. Increase in such demands curtails motivation and dedication of employees in this period.

2. Employees who are provided with specific job resources by supervisors find it easier to deal with job demands, thus have higher motivation during difficult times.
3. Unlike prior studies on remote work, this study suggests that recognizing and rewarding hard work have motivate remote workers during a forced remote working plan.
4. The greatest challenge of remote working for teams with high interdependency is to maintain collaboration and coordination. Communication and exchange of information are disrupted during the mandatory remote work.
5. Leaders' technical and social support help maintain the motivation of employees.

Reflection Questions

1. According to job demands-resources theory, which aspects of a job are considered job demands and how do job sources influence employee motivation and well-being?
2. According to job demands-resources theory, which aspects of a job are considered job resources and how do job demands contribute to employee motivation?
3. What is the role of leaders in influencing job characteristics and also employee motivation?
4. According to the results of the study, which factors influenced employee motivation negatively?
5. According to the results of the study, which factors promoted employee motivation?

References

Akkirman, A. D., & Harris, D. L. (2005). Organizational communication satisfaction in the virtual workplace. *Journal of Management Development, 24*(5), 397–409. https://doi.org/10.1108/02621710510598427

Allen, J., Jimmieson, N. L., Bordia, P., & Irmer, B. E. (2007). Uncertainty during organizational change: Managing perceptions through communication. *Journal of Change Management, 7*(2), 187–210. https://doi.org/10.1080/14697010701563379

Allen, T. D., Golden, T. D., & Shockley, K. M. (2015). How effective is telecommuting? Assessing the status of our scientific findings. *Psychological Science in the Public Interest, 16*(2), 40–68. https://doi.org/10.1177/1529100615593273

Amagasa, T., & Nakayama, T. (2012). Relationship between long working hours and depression in two working populations: A structural equation model approach. *Journal of Occupational and Environmental Medicine, 54*(7), 868–874. https://doi.org/10.1097/JOM.0b013e318250ca00

Avast Business. (2018). *2018 mobile workforce report.* https://blog.avast.com/hubfs/blog-files/Mobile-Workforce-Report-Master.pdf

Bakker, A. B., & Demerouti, E. (2007). The job demands-resources model: State of the art. *Journal of Managerial Psychology, 22*(3), 309–328. https://doi.org/10.1108/02683940710733115

Bakker, A. B., & Demerouti, E. (2014). Job demands–resources theory. In P. Y. Chen & C. L. Cooper (Eds.), *Wellbeing: A complete reference guide* (Vol. III, pp. 1–28). Wiley. https://doi.org/10.1002/9781118539415.wbwell019

Bakker, A. B., Demerouti, E., & Euwema, M. C. (2005). Job resources buffer the impact of job demands on burnout. *Journal of Occupational Health Psychology, 10*(2), 170–180. https://doi.org/10.1037/1076-8998.10.2.170

Bakker, A. B., Demerouti, E., & Schaufeli, W. B. (2003). Dual processes at work in a call center: An application of the job demands–resources model. *European Journal of Work and Organizational Psychology, 12*, 393–417. https://doi.org/10.1080/13594320344000165

Bakker, A. B., Demerouti, E., Taris, T. W., Schaufeli, W. B., & Schreurs, P. J. G. (2003). A multigroup analysis of the job demands-resources model in four home care organizations. *International Journal of Stress Management, 10*, 16–38. https://doi.org/10.1037/1072-5245.10.1.16

Bakker, A. B., Hakanen, J. J., Demerouti, E., & Xanthopoulou, D. (2007). Job resources boost work engagement, particularly when job demands are high. *Journal of Educational Psychology, 99*(2), 274–284. https://doi.org/10.1037/0022-0663.99.2.274

Bakker, A. B., Van Veldhoven, M. J. P. M., & Xanthopoulou, D. (2010). Beyond the demand-control model: Thriving on high job demands and resources. *Journal of Personnel Psychology, 9*, 3–16. https://doi.org/10.1027/1866-5888/a000006

Baltes, B. B., Briggs, T. E., Huff, J. W., Wright, J. A., & Neuman, G. A. (1999). Flexible and compressed workweek schedules: A meta-analysis of their effects on work-related criteria. *Journal of Applied Psychology, 84*(4), 496–513. https://doi.org/10.1037/0021-9010.84.4.496

Barrick, M. R., Mount, M. K., & Li, N. (2013). The theory of purposeful work behavior: The role of personality, higher-order goals, and job characteristics. *Academy of Management Review, 38*(1), 132–153. https://doi.org/10.5465/amr.2010.0479

Bass, B. M. (1990). *Bass and Stogdill's handbook of leadership*. Free Press.

Braun, V., & Clarke, V. (2006). Using thematic analysis in psychology. *Qualitative Research in Psychology, 3*(2), 77–101. https://doi.org/10.1191/1478088706qp063oa

Breevaart, K., Bakker, A. B., Demerouti, E., & van den Heuvel, M. (2015). Leader-member exchange, work engagement, and job performance. *Journal of Managerial Psychology, 30*(7), 754–770. https://doi.org/10.1108/JMP-03-2013-0088

Breevaart, K., Bakker, A. B., Hetland, J., Demerouti, E., Olsen, O. K., & Espevik, R. (2014). Daily transactional and transformational leadership and daily employee engagement. *Journal of Occupational and Organizational Psychology, 87*(1), 138–157. https://doi.org/10.1111/joop.12041

Breevaart, K., Bakker, A. B., Hetland, J., & Hetland, H. (2014). The influence of constructive and destructive leadership behaviors on follower burnout. In M. P. Leiter, A. B. Bakker, & C. Maslach (Eds.), *Burnout at work: A psychological perspective* (pp. 102–121). Psychology Press.

Cascio, W. F. (2000). Managing a virtual workplace. *Academy of Management Executive, 14*(3), 81–90. https://doi.org/10.5465/ame.2000.4468068

Clinton, M. E., Conway, N., & Sturges, J. (2017). "It's tough hanging-up a call": The relationships between calling and work hours, psychological detachment, sleep quality, and morning vigor. *Journal of Occupational Health Psychology, 22*(1), 28–39. https://doi.org/10.1037/ocp0000025

Cullen, K. L., Edwards, B. D., Casper, W. C., & Gue, K. R. (2014). Employees' adaptability and perceptions of change-related uncertainty: Implications for perceived organizational support, job satisfaction, and performance. *Journal of Business and Psychology, 29*(2), 269–280. https://doi.org/10.1007/s10869-013-9312-y

Delanoeije, J., Verbruggen, M., & Germeys, L. (2019). Boundary role transitions: A day-to-day approach to explain the effects of home-based telework on work-to-home conflict and home-to-work conflict. *Human Relations, 72*(12), 1843–1868. https://doi.org/10.1177/0018726718823071

Derks, D., van Duin, D., Tims, M., & Bakker, A. B. (2015). Smartphone use and work–home interference: The moderating role of social norms and employee work engagement. *Journal of Occupational and Organizational Psychology, 88*(1), 155–177. https://doi.org/10.1111/joop.12083

Desilver, D. (2020). *Working from home was a luxury for the relatively affluent before coronavirus—Not any more*. World Economic Forum. https://www.weforum.org/agenda/2020/03/working-from-home-coronavirus-workers-future-of-work/

DiFonzo, N., & Bordia, R. (1998). A tale of two corporations: Managing uncertainty during organizational change. *Human Resource Management, 37*(3–4), 295–303. https://doi.org/10.1002/(SICI)1099-050X(199823/24)37:3/4<295::AID-HRM10>3.0.CO;2-3

Duxbury, L., & Neufeld, D. (1999). An empirical evaluation of the impacts of telecommuting on intra-organizational communication. *Journal of Engineering and Technology Management, 16*(1), 1–28. https://doi.org/10.1016/S0923-4748(98)00026-5

Fernet, C., Austin, S., Trépanier, S. G., & Dussault, M. (2013). How do job characteristics contribute to burnout? Exploring the distinct mediating roles of perceived autonomy, competence, and relatedness. *European Journal of Work and Organizational Psychology, 22*(2), 123–137. https://doi.org/10.1080/1359432X.2011.632161

Fisher, C. D. (1990). Organizational socialization: An integrative review. In G. R. Ferris & K. M. Rowland (Eds.), *Career and human resources development* (pp. 163–207). JAI Press.

Fleishman, E. A. (1973). Twenty years of consideration and structure. In E. A. Fleishman & J. G. Hunt (Eds.), *Current developments in the study of leadership* (pp. 1–40). Southern Illinois University Press.

Gagné, M., Senecal, C. B., & Koestner, R. (1997). Proximal job characteristics, feelings of empowerment, and intrinsic motivation: A multidimensional model 1. *Journal of Applied Social Psychology, 27*(14), 1222–1240. https://doi.org/10.1111/j.1559-1816.1997.tb01803.x

Gartner. (2020). *Gartner survey reveals 82% of company leaders plan to allow employees to work remotely some of the time*. News Release, July 2020. https://www.gartner.com/en/newsroom/press-releases/2020-07-14-gartner-survey-reveals-82-percent-of-company-leaders-plan-to-allow-employees-to-work-remotely-some-of-the-time

Golden, T., Veiga, J., & Simsek, Z. (2006). Telecommuting's differential impact on work-home conflict: Is there no place like home? *Journal of Applied Psychology, 91*(6), 1340–1350. https://doi.org/10.1037/0021-9010.91.6.1340

Golden, T. D. (2006). The role of relationships in understanding telecommuter satisfaction. *Journal of Organizational Behavior, 27*(3), 319–340. https://doi.org/10.1002/job.369

Greer, T. W., & Payne, S. C. (2014). Overcoming telework challenges: Outcomes of successful telework strategies. *The Psychologist-Manager Journal, 17*(2), 87–111. https://doi.org/10.1037/mgr0000014

Hagemann, V., Ontrup, G., & Kluge, A. (2020). Collective orientation and its implications for coordination and team performance in interdependent work contexts. *Team Performance Management: An International Journal*. https://doi.org/10.1108/TPM-03-2020-0020

Hakanen, J. J., Bakker, A. B., & Demerouti, E. (2005). How dentists cope with their job demands and stay engaged: The moderating role of job resources. *European Journal of Oral Sciences, 113*(6), 479–487. https://doi.org/10.1111/j.1600-0722.2005.00250.x

Hakanen, J. J., Schaufeli, W. B., & Ahola, K. (2008). The job demands-resources model: A three-year cross-lagged study of burnout, depression, commitment, and work engagement. *Work & Stress, 22*(3), 224–241. https://doi.org/10.1080/02678370802379432

Hertel, G., Konradt, U., & Orlikowski, B. (2004). Managing distance by interdependence: Goal setting, task interdependence, and team-based rewards in virtual teams. *European Journal of Work and Organizational Psychology, 13*(1), 1–28. https://doi.org/10.1080/13594320344000228

Huyghebaert, T., Gillet, N., Beltou, N., Tellier, F., & Fouquereau, E. (2018). Effects of workload on teachers' functioning: A moderated mediation model including sleeping problems and over-commitment. *Stress and Health, 34*(5), 601–611. https://doi.org/10.1002/smi.2820

Judge, T. A., Piccolo, R. F., & Ilies, R. (2004). The forgotten ones? The validity of consideration and initiating structure in leadership research. *Journal of Applied Psychology, 89*(1), 36–51. https://doi.org/10.1037/0021-9010.89.1.36

Kaduk, A., Genadek, K., Kelly, E. L., & Moen, P. (2019). Involuntary vs. voluntary flexible work: Insights for scholars and stakeholders. *Community, Work and Family, 22*(4), 412–442. https://doi.org/10.1080/13668803.2019.1616532

Kahn, W. (2010). The essence of employee engagement: Lessons from the field. In S. Albrecht (Ed.), *Handbook of employee engagement* (pp. 20–30). Edward Elgar.

Karanges, E., Johnston, K., Beatson, A., & Lings, I. (2015). The influence of internal communication on employee engagement: A pilot study. *Public Relations Review, 41*(1), 129–131. https://doi.org/10.1016/j.pubrev.2014.12.003

Karasek, R. A., Jr. (1979). Job demands, job decision latitude, and mental strain: Implications for job redesign. *Administrative Science Quarterly, 24*, 285–308. https://doi.org/10.2307/2392498

Karasek, R., Brisson, C., Kawakami, N., Houtman, I., Bongers, P., & Amick, B. (1998). The Job Content Questionnaire (JCQ): An instrument for internationally comparative assessments of psychosocial job characteristics. *Journal of Occupational Health Psychology, 3*(4), 322–355. https://doi.org/10.1037/1076-8998.3.4.322

Kawohl, W., & Nordt, C. (2020). COVID-19, unemployment, and suicide. *The Lancet Psychiatry, 7*(5), 389–390. https://doi.org/10.1016/S2215-0366(20)30141-3

Killgore, W. D., Cloonen, S. A., Taylor, E. C., & Dailey, N. S. (2020). Loneliness: A signature mental health concern in the era of COVID-19. *Psychiatry Research, 290*, 113117. https://doi.org/10.1016/j.psychres.2020.113117

Kinnunen, U., Feldt, T., Siltaloppi, M., & Sonnentag, S. (2011). Job demands–resources model in the context of recovery: Testing recovery experiences as mediators. *European Journal of Work and Organizational Psychology, 20*(6), 805–832. https://doi.org/10.1080/1359432X.2010.524411

Kniffin, K. M., Narayanan, J., Anseel, F., Antonakis, J., Ashford, S. P., Bakker, A. B., et al. (2020). COVID-19 and the workplace: Implications, issues, and insights for future research and action. *American Psychologist*. https://doi.org/10.1037/amp0000716

Kompier, M. A., Taris, T. W., & Van Veldhoven, M. (2012). Tossing and turning-insomnia in relation to occupational stress, rumination, fatigue, and well-being. *Scandinavian Journal of Work, Environment & Health, 38*(3), 238–246. https://www.jstor.org/stable/41508889

Kossek, E., Lautsch, B., & Eaton, S. (2006). Telecommuting, control, and boundary management: Correlates of policy use and practice, job control, and work-family effectiveness. *Journal of Vocational Behavior, 68*(2), 347–367. https://doi.org/10.1016/j.jvb.2005.07.002

Kowalski, K., & Swanson, J. A. (2005). Critical success factors in developing teleworking programs. *Benchmarking: An International Journal, 12*(3), 236–249. https://doi.org/10.1108/14635770510600357

Kramer, A., & Kramer, K. Z. (2020). The potential impact of the Covid-19 pandemic on occupational status, work from home, and occupational mobility. *Journal of Vocational Behavior, 119*. https://doi.org/10.1016/j.jvb.2020.103442

Kurland, N. B., & Bailey, D. E. (1999). Telework: The advantages and challenges of working here, there, anywhere, and anytime. *Organizational Dynamics, 28*(2), 53–68.

Lambert, L. S., Tepper, B. J., Carr, J. C., Holt, D. T., & Barelka, A. J. (2012). Forgotten but not gone: An examination of fit between leader consideration and initiating structure needed and received. *Journal of Applied Psychology, 97*(5), 913–930. https://doi.org/10.1037/a0028970

Lapierre, L. M., Van Steenbergen, E. F., Peeters, M. C., & Kluwer, E. S. (2016). Juggling work and family responsibilities when involuntarily working more from home: A multiwave study of financial sales professionals. *Journal of Organizational Behavior, 37*(6), 804–822. https://doi.org/10.1002/job.2075

Larson, B. Z., Vroman, S. R., & Makarius, E. E. (2020). A guide to managing your (newly) remote workers. *Harvard Business Review, 18*.

Lee, K., Suh, C., Kim, J. E., & Park, J. O. (2017). The impact of long working hours on psychosocial stress response among white-collar workers. *Industrial Health, 55*(1), 46–53.

Mann, S., Varey, R., & Button, W. (2000). An exploration of the emotional impact of tele-working via computer-mediated communication. *Journal of Managerial Psychology, 15*(7), 668–690. https://doi.org/10.1108/02683940010378054

Matusik, S. M., & Mickel, A. M. (2011). Embracing or embattled by converged mobile devices? Users experiences with a contemporary connectivity technology. *Human Relations, 64*(8), 1001–1030. https://doi.org/10.1177/0018726711405552

McCarter, M. W., & Sheremeta, R. M. (2013). You can't put old wine in new bottles: The effect of newcomers on coordination in groups. *PLoS One, 8*(1), e55058. https://doi.org/10.1371/journal.pone.0055058

Mellner, C. (2016). After-hours availability expectations, work-related smartphone use during leisure, and psychological detachment: The moderating role of boundary control. *International Journal of Workplace Health Management, 9*(2), 146–164. https://doi.org/10.1108/IJWHM-07-2015-0050

Nash, M., & Churchill, B. (2020). Caring during COVID-19: A gendered analysis of Australian university responses to managing remote working and caring responsibilities. *Gender, Work and Organization, 27*(5), 833–846. https://doi.org/10.1111/gwao.12484

Ozimek, A. (2020). The future of remote work. *SSRN*. https://ssrn.com/abstract=3638597. https://doi.org/10.2139/ssrn.3638597

Park, Y., Fritz, C., & Jex, S. M. (2011). Relationships between work-home segmentation and psychological detachment from work: The role of communication technology use at home. *Journal of Occupational Health Psychology, 16*(4), 457–467. https://doi.org/10.1037/a0023594

Ropponen, A., Härmä, M., Bergbom, B., Nätti, J., & Sallinen, M. (2018). The vicious circle of working hours, sleep, and recovery in expert work. *International Journal of Environmental Research and Public Health, 15*(7), 1361–1372. https://doi.org/10.3390/ijerph15071361

Sardeshmukh, S. R., Sharma, D., & Golden, T. D. (2012). Impact of telework on exhaustion and job engagement: A job demands and job resources model. *New Technology, Work and Employment, 27*, 193–207. https://doi.org/10.1111/j.1468-005X.2012.00284.x

Schaufeli, W. B. (2015). Engaging leadership in the job demands-resources model. *Career Development International, 20*(5), 446–463. https://doi.org/10.1108/CDI-02-2015-0025

Schaufeli, W. B., Bakker, A. B., & Salanova, M. (2006). The measurement of work engagement with a short questionnaire: A cross-national study. *Educational and Psychological Measurement, 66*(4), 701–716. https://doi.org/10.1177/0013164405282471

Shockley, K. M., & Allen, T. D. (2012). Motives for flexible work arrangement use. *Community, Work & Family, 15*(2), 217–231. https://doi.org/10.1080/13668803.2011.609661

Shuck, B., & Herd, A. M. (2012). Employee engagement and leadership: Exploring the convergence of two frameworks and implications for leadership development in HRD. *Human Resource Development Review, 11*(2), 156–181. https://doi.org/10.1177/1534484312438211

Siegrist, J. (2001). A theory of occupational stress. In J. Dunham (Ed.), *Stress in the workplace: Past, present and future* (pp. 52–66). Whurr Publishers.

Sonnentag, S., & Schiffner, C. (2018). Psychological detachment from work during nonwork time and employee well-being: The role of leader's detachment. *The Spanish Journal of Psychology, 22*(e3), 204. https://doi.org/10.1017/sjp.2019.2

Staples, D. S., Hulland, J. S., & Higgins, C. A. (1999). A self-efficacy theory explanation for the management of remote workers in virtual organizations. *Organization Science, 10*(6), 758–776. https://doi.org/10.1287/orsc.10.6.758

Strauss, A., & Corbin, J. (1998). *Basics of qualitative research techniques*. Sage.

Suh, A., & Lee, J. (2017). Understanding teleworkers' technostress and its influence on job satisfaction. *Internet Research, 27*(1), 140–159. https://doi.org/10.1108/IntR-06-2015-0181

Sull, D., Sull, C., & Bersin, J. (2020). Five ways leaders can support remote work. *MIT Sloan Management Review, 61*(4), 1–10.

Sytch, M., & Greer, L. I. (2020). Is your organization ready for permanent WFH? *Harvard Business Review*. https://hbr.org/2020/08/is-your-organizationready-for-permanent-wfh

Tanskanen, J., Mäkelä, L., & Viitala, R. (2019). Linking managerial coaching and leader–member exchange on work engagement and performance. *Journal of Happiness Studies, 20*(4), 1217–1240. https://doi.org/10.1007/s10902-018-9996-9

ten Brummelhuis, L. L., & Bakker, A. B. (2012). Staying engaged during the week: The effect of off-job activities on next day work engagement. *Journal of Occupational Health Psychology, 17*(4), 445–455. https://doi.org/10.1037/a0029213

Tollefson, J. (2020). Why deforestation and extinctions make pandemics more likely. *Nature, 584*(7820), 398–402. https://doi.org/10.1038/d41586-020-02341-1

Van den Broeck, A., Vansteenkiste, M., De Witte, H., & Lens, W. (2008). Explaining the relationships between job characteristics, burnout, and engagement: The role of basic psychological need satisfaction. *Work & Stress, 22*(3), 277–294. https://doi.org/10.1080/02678370802393672

Van der Hulst, M., Van Veldhoven, M., & Beckers, D. (2006). Overtime and need for recovery in relation to job demands and job control. *Journal of Occupational Health, 48*(1), 11–19. https://doi.org/10.1539/joh.48.11

Van Vegchel, N., De Jonge, J., Bosma, H., & Schaufeli, W. (2005). Reviewing the effort–reward imbalance model: Drawing up the balance of 45 empirical studies. *Social Science & Medicine, 60*(5), 1117–1131. https://doi.org/10.1016/j.socscimed.2004.06.043

Venkatesh, V., & Johnson, P. (2002). Telecommuting technology implementations: A within-and between-subjects longitudinal field study. *Personnel Psychology, 55*(3), 661–687. https://doi.org/10.1111/j.1744-6570.2002.tb00125.x

Waizenegger, L., McKenna, B., Cai, W., & Bendz, T. (2020). An affordance perspective of team collaboration and enforced working from home during COVID-19. *European Journal of Information Systems, 29*(4), 429–442. https://doi.org/10.1080/0960085X.2020.1800417

Wang, B., Liu, Y., Qian, J., & Parker, S. K. (2020). Achieving effective remote working during the COVID-19 pandemic: A work design perspective. *Applied Psychology.* https://doi.org/10.1111/apps.12290

Xanthopoulou, D., Bakker, A. B., Dollard, M. F., Demerouti, E., Schaufeli, W. B., Taris, T. W., & Schreurs, P. J. G. (2007). When do job demands particularly predict burnout? The moderating role of job resources. *Journal of Managerial Psychology, 22*, 766–786. https://doi.org/10.1108/02683940710837714

Sevgi Emirza , Ph.D. is a research assistant at Dokuz Eylül University Faculty of Business. Her work focuses mainly on leadership studies, person-supervisor fit, and job attitudes and behaviors.

Sustainable Leadership After COVID-19: Distributing Leadership Using an Integrated Framework of Leader-Personality Profiles

23

Courtney E. Owens

Introduction

To be a successful leader in today's turbulent and uncertain environment, organizations need a wide variety of characteristics within their leadership. The range of characteristics is so wide in fact that no one person can be the perfect leader. The good news is, no one needs to be. Leaders can choose to modify their own behavior as the situation demands, or instead, bring in others who have strengths in the areas where the current leadership feels weak. Identifying their own leader-personality profile enables leaders to recognize their own individual strengths and weaknesses.

I present herein a new integrated framework of leader-personality profiles. These profiles are particularly relevant to the current global environment as we emerge from COVID-19, and we realize afresh the importance of distributed leadership. Now more than ever we must recognize our interdependence on one another. If all seven leader-personality profiles are represented and contributing, then organizations can be assured that the necessary perspectives are present to enable a successful way forward.

This chapter begins with an overview of what leadership looks like in a post-COVID-19 environment. Next is a brief description of distributive leadership and why this is particularly relevant to leaders after COVID-19. Then we move into a discussion of personality, with a brief review of personality traits and profiles. Then follows the principal focus of this chapter—a presentation of a new integrated framework of leader-personality profiles. Seven profiles are presented and described. The chapter closes with a brief conclusion, chapter takeaways, and reflection questions.

C. E. Owens (✉)
Alliance Manchester Business School, University of Manchester, Manchester, UK
e-mail: courtneyelizabeth.owens@manchester.ac.uk

S. K. Dhiman, J. F. Marques (eds.), *Leadership After COVID-19*, Future of Business and Finance, https://doi.org/10.1007/978-3-030-84867-5_23

Leadership After COVID-19

One of the great lessons of the COVID-19 pandemic is just how complex and unpredictable the future is. We cannot eliminate the uncertainty, so leaders need new ways to deal with it. We must learn to live with uncertainty, acknowledging that any one person cannot foresee the impact of every event. Volatility is the new normal, evidenced by frequent and rapid change. With globalization and more employees working from home, business continues to become increasingly complex; there are many moving parts that are positioned in disparate locations. Moreover, the ambiguity of the global situation makes it difficult to comprehend the entire state of affairs; there can be several—and sometimes conflicting—interpretations of the same event.

This combination of uncertainty, volatility, complexity, and ambiguity presents unique challenges for the leader in a post-COVID-19 environment. There is an extremely wide range of leadership characteristics that are required in order to be agile enough to adapt to the demanding complexity and volatility of these times. In fact, the range of necessary characteristics needed is so wide that no one person can be the perfect leader.

This recognition that not one person can be all things perfectly has been described as the death of the hero leader. The hero leader was that mythical perfect person, like Superman, who swooped in with their superpowers to save the day. There is an implicit assumption about the hero leader that the successful outcome depended on the decisions and actions of a single person (Meindl et al., 1985). This assumption is unrealistic because most organizations have multiple people who influence decisions and the implementation of those decisions. Hero leadership may have been something that leaders used to strive for, but after learning our lessons from COVID-19, we must acknowledge that this strategy is no longer effective. There are too many moving parts, too many uncertainties and ambiguities that no one person can imagine all the possible scenarios and simultaneously implement and execute the appropriate responses. Instead, we must be honest and authentic, recognize we are not able to do it all ourselves, and that we require the combined strengths of those around us in order to succeed. We must recognize that individually, we are "incomplete" (Ancona et al., 2007).

The incomplete leader has been described as someone who hones their own strengths while finding others who can make up for their limitations. We start with ourselves, identifying our own set of strengths and weaknesses. Then, we can look to others who can complement us and supplement the things we are missing. In this way, we can create an environment where leadership is distributed across multiple people.

Ancona et al. (2007) stated it this way: "Only when leaders come to see themselves as incomplete—as having both strengths and weaknesses—will they be able to make up for their missing skills by relying on others" (p. 94). First, we must acknowledge that we are incomplete leaders. Then we can address the question, "how do we become complete?" The answer can be found in distributed leadership. Distributed leadership is a process in an organization that involves multiple leaders with overlapping but different responsibilities (Gronn, 2002; Yukl, 2013). It is something that does not require a single individual to perform all of the essential leadership functions, but rather a set of people who can perform them collectively (Yukl, 1999). Not only can responsibilities be shared with team members and peers, but could also be pushed down to lower levels or up to superiors. Yukl (1999) brings further clarity to what distributive leadership might look like: "some leadership functions (e.g., making important decisions) may be shared by several members of a group, some leadership functions may be allocated to individual members, and a particular leadership function may be performed by different people at different times" (pp. 292–293). This is a logical and pragmatic solution of how to approach leadership in today's uncertain and complex environment.

As evidenced throughout this volume on leadership, the term *leadership* can carry various connotations of meaning, so it is useful to define how the term will be used in this chapter. Leadership can be defined as a role, trait, behavior, or process. Even so, many definitions over the years reflected the assumption that leadership is a process whereby the leader exerts influence over others to guide or facilitate people and or activities (e.g. Drath & Palus, 1994; Hemphill & Coons, 1957; Katz & Kahn, 1978; Rauch & Behling, 1984). I agree with this assumption. I take the view that leadership is not limited to just the few in a specialized role, but also includes a social process of influencing others. In his classic textbook on leadership, Northouse (2010) provides an excellent synopsis of the leadership literature which can be summarized with the following definition: "Leadership is a process by which an individual influences a group of individuals to achieve a common goal" (p. 3). Leadership can be shown by many more people than just a few at the top; any person who influences a group of people to work together can be a leader in the group. Thus for this chapter, leadership is defined as the ability of an individual to "influence, motivate and enable others to contribute toward the effectiveness and success of the organizations of which they are members" (House et al., 1999, p. 184). To understand how leaders can influence, enable, or motivate the performance of others, it is helpful to examine the processes used by leaders. Here I suggest that our leader-personality profile is one way to describe the natural inclination for the processes we choose to utilize.

A variety of leadership models have been published, albeit primarily in the area of leadership behaviors. There has been a proliferation of taxonomies on leadership behaviors (see Bass, 1990; Yukl, 2013), but there is yet to be published an integrated framework of leader-personality profiles as is presented here. As we emerge from COVID-19, now is the time to build on lessons learned and create distributed leadership processes based on the seven leader-personality profiles.

Personality Profiles

We all have a personality and we can easily identify the personality traits of those we know well. We might use words such as shy, outgoing, introverted, or extraverted. Personality is defined as "consistent and enduring individual differences in ways of thinking, feeling, and acting" (Costa & McCrae, 2008, p. 180). This contemporary definition is supported by ancient texts including Greek philosophers, the Torah, and the Bible. Circa 370 BC, Plato suggested that our soul was a tripartite personality and could be divided into three parts: intellect, needs, and will. The earlier Torah text, also known as the Old Testament in the Bible, written circa 1470 BC, also refers to our personality as our soul and references three parts: mind, heart, and strength (Deuteronomy 6:5, New International Version). In Biblical texts, the three-part personality of mind, heart, and strength appears three times in the New Testament and was written circa 70 AD (Luke 10:27, Mark 12:30, Matt 22:37). All these definitions can be understood as describing the same concepts. The mind is our intellect, where our thoughts reside. The heart is the seat of our emotions, feelings, and felt needs. Strength is the strength of will to act, which is evidenced as behaviors. It is the unique combination of these three parts—the mind, heart, and will—that determines our personalities.

Personality *traits* are the indicators that measure our different ways of thinking, feeling, and acting. The Five Factor Model (FFM; Costa & McCrae, 1992a), colloquially called "the Big Five," is arguably the most extensively researched model of personality traits in the field of personality psychology. The FFM's five factors (neuroticism, extraversion, openness, agreeableness, and conscientiousness) are well-known, but often incorrectly described as traits, rather than categories of traits. Factors are not personality traits per se, but rather groupings of similar traits (Costa & McCrae, 1992a). When structured in a hierarchical manner, personality psychologists use the terms *factors* and *facets*. The term *facet* designates the lower-level, narrower traits that are located within each of the higher level, broader *factors*. Figure 23.1 shows the five factors and their facets as represented in the FFM (Costa & McCrae, 1992a).

The factors and facets of the FFMFive Factor Model (FFM) (Costa & McCrae, 1992a, b).

The factor of neuroticism is concerned with levels of self-confidence, self-esteem, and composure under pressure. Someone who scores highly on neuroticism would tend to be self-critical, may be moody, or approach life with a "glass half-empty" perspective. Alternatively, someone with a low score on neuroticism would be confident, resilient, and steady in the face of pressure. As shown in Figure 23.1, the neuroticism factor includes facets such as angry-hostility, depression, self-consciousness, and vulnerability.

The factor of extraversion concerns sociability and measures the need for social interaction. Someone who scores highly on extraversion would tend to be outgoing, optimistic, and dislike working by themselves. Someone who scores low on extraversion would appear quiet and reserved and does not mind working alone. Extraversion includes traits such as gregariousness, activity, and positive emotions.

Openness concerns levels of imagination, curiosity, and creative potential. Someone who scores highly on openness would tend to be imaginative, quick-witted; they may be easily bored and not pay attention to the details. Someone who scores low on openness is likely more practical and focused, showing an affinity for routine work. The factor of openness includes the facets of imagination, feelings, and intellect.

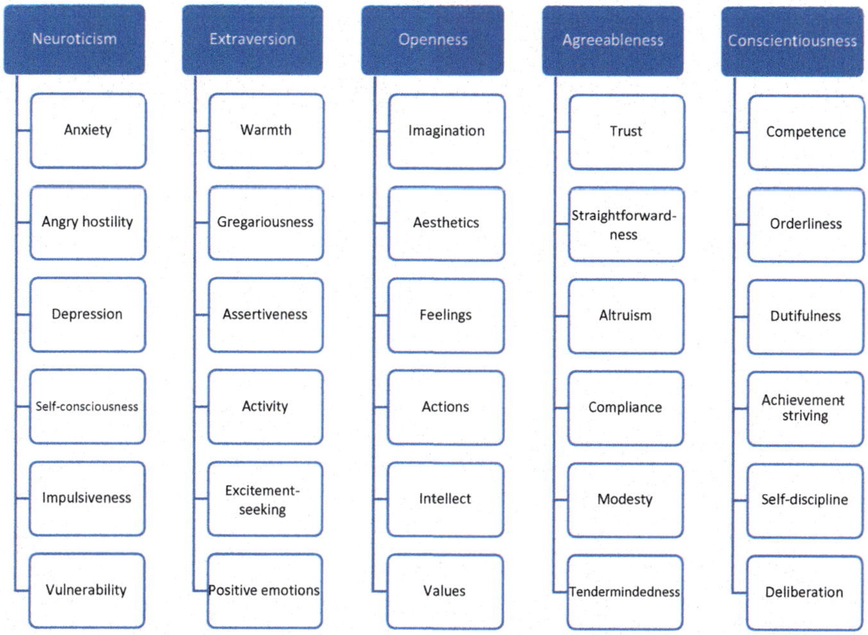

Fig. 23.1 The factors and facets of the FFM (Costa & McCrae, 1992a, b)

Agreeableness is the degree with which a person seems socially sensitive, tactful, and altruistic. A high score on agreeableness indicates someone who is friendly, compliant, and quickly engenders trust. A low score indicates someone who is independent, frank, and direct. The factor of agreeableness includes the traits of altruism, compliance, modesty, and tender mindedness.

Conscientiousness is the level to which a person seems self-controlled and responsible. A high score on conscientiousness indicates someone who is dependable, organized, and thorough; they are easy to supervise, but may be inflexible with rules. A low score on conscientiousness indicates someone who is spontaneous and adaptable, but may tend to resist rules and close supervision. The factor of conscientiousness includes the facets of competence, orderliness, and dutifulness.

One of the strengths of the trait approach is the ability to produce psychometrically sound instruments for measurement, as evidenced in the well-documented psychometric properties of the NEO Personality Inventory (Costa & McCrae, 1992b), the official test of the FFM. Thousands of empirical studies have been published using the FFM traits as predictors for a variety of outcomes allowing further investigation with meta-analytic methods. Results of meta-analyses show personality is a significant predictor of important outcomes such as job performance (Barrick & Mount, 1991), job satisfaction (Judge et al., 2002), and leadership styles (Bono & Judge, 2004).

In contrast to traits, personality *types* are focused on the organization of multiple traits within an individual, and how the arrangement of these traits might define particular types of people (Sava & Popa, 2011). Early theorists, such as Hippocrates,

Table 23.1 Four personality profiles identified by FFM factors (Gerlach et al., 2018)

Type	N	E	O	A	C
Average	Avg	Avg	Avg	Avg	Avg
Self-centered	Avg	+	–	–	–
Reserved	–	Avg	–	Avg	Avg
Role model	–	+	+	+	+

N neuroticism, *E* extraversion, *O* openness, *A* agreeableness, *C* conscientiousness, + above average score, *Avg* average score, – below average score

Freud, and Jung studied personality by identifying types; at the time, these individual differences were sometimes called temperaments. Today, we often see consultants and practitioners readily embracing types, as it is a practical and pragmatic way to group individuals. But the measurement of types is highly controversial in the research community. Take the Myers Briggs Type Indicator (MBTI; Myers & McCaulley, 1985), for example: a contemporary personality assessment which is built entirely on Jung's typology, the MBTI is widely utilized by consultants and highly criticized by personality researchers. The MBTI is a personality test that identifies 16 personality types from a combination of four dichotomies: introversion versus extraversion, sensing versus intuition, thinking versus feeling, and judging versus perception. Although the MBTI has a very large commercial base, it is criticized by researchers due to concerns around its psychometric properties and scientific validity (Pittenger, 2005). Studies have shown participants received different type profiles when retested (Howes & Carskadon, 1979; McCaulley & Carskadon, 1983); in one particular study, researchers found nearly 70% of the participants' MBTI profiles changed after three administrations of the test (Salter et al., 2005). Furthermore, a comprehensive review revealed few consistent relationships between MBTI type and managerial effectiveness (Gardner & Martinko, 1996).

Historically, traits and types have each been studied in isolation. Nevertheless, a contemporary perspective is emerging that traits and types need not be mutually exclusive; personality profiles could be considered as a prototypical configuration of traits (Asendorpf et al., 2001). More recently, studies have started taking this approach of building personality profiles empirically from traits. Early seminal work (Asendorpf et al., 2001; Caspi & Silva, 1995; Robins et al., 1996) was refined and extended (Gerlach et al., 2018) with empirical evidence to support the existence of at least four profiles: average, self-centered, reserved, and role model. As shown in Table 23.1, the average profile is characterized by average scores on all five factors. The self-centered profile shows a high score on extraversion, an average score on neuroticism, and low scores on the remaining factors. The reserved profile is characterized by average scores in extraversion, agreeableness, and conscientiousness, with low scores in neuroticism and openness. The role model profile displays socially desirable traits and is marked by high scores on all factors apart from neuroticism. Table 23.1 summarizes each of the four profiles and their differing scores on the FFM factors.

While this approach to integrate traits into profiles reflects a significant start to establishing a psychometrically sound instrument for measurement, there is still more to gain by researching the finer grained distinction of facets. For example, consider the traits of gregariousness and excitement-seeking, facets of the extraversion factor. In a study of police officer and firefighter recruits, both groups of recruits generally scored higher than a normative sample on the excitement-seeking facet, while police recruits scored higher than firefighters on the gregariousness facet (Salters-Pedneault et al., 2010). When measuring at the facet level, more nuanced and meaningful differences can be discerned. If personality is only measured at the level of factors, the distinctions afforded by study at the facet level will be missed, which can have a significant impact on the prediction of important outcomes such as job performance or leadership styles.

Research that integrates traits into profiles will help to address some of the methodological concerns of typology research. Finer distinctions that include the measurement of facets will improve nuanced prediction of leadership and job performance. Future models of personality profiles should integrate such an approach, as I do here.

Leader-Personality Profiles

Why then develop personality profiles specific to the context of leadership? And why especially now, as we emerge from COVID-19? When conducting personality research, recognizing the context in which the personality traits are exhibited has consistently proven to be important in understanding personality psychology. Also called *situational strength*, it has been found to be an important moderator in the examination of individual difference variables (Bem & Allen, 1974; Hattrup & Jackson, 1996; Judge & Zapata, 2015; Murphy & Dzieweczynski, 2005). When using personality traits to predict job performance, researchers suggested the variance in job performance attributable to situational strength was "far from trivial" (Judge & Zapata, 2015, p. 1167). For example, in a study comparing overall-personality, home-personality and work-personality, results showed that work-personality was a better predictor of job satisfaction than either overall-personality or home-personality (Heller et al., 2009). Work-personality has also been found to be a better predictor of work-related criteria than overall personality (Bowling & Burns, 2010).

Most personality assessments measure overall personality, as they are capturing who you are overall and are not specific to a certain context. The tests usually ask questions such as who you are when you are at a party or how you spend your personal time. However, what I advocate here is to recognize the importance of context in the personality test itself. For example, when Heller et al. (2009) measured work-personality, it was defined as the "characteristic patterns of thoughts, feelings and behaviors at work" (p. 1055). I suggest taking a step further and considering personality within the specific context of leadership. Building on the definitions of leadership and personality mentioned earlier in this chapter, I therefore define leader-personality as the consistent ways of thinking, feeling, and acting when influencing, motivating, or enabling others to contribute toward the success of their organization.

As the focus here is to describe the characteristic traits of the individual, I have chosen the title of leader-personality rather than leadership-personality. Yet this does not diminish the importance of acknowledging that leadership is in the context of working with others and having followers. The term leadership is often used when focusing on a process that involves the relationship of leaders and their followers, whereas the term leader is more focused on the characteristics of the individual (Day, 2000). Keeping with our definition of leaders as possibly anyone and not necessarily specified by a job role, leader-personality profiles identify the traits of anyone who acts in the context of influencing, motivating, or enabling others to contribute toward the success of their organization.

Leader-personality profiles are based on the definitions of personality presented earlier in this chapter. Thus it is the unique combination of three parts—the mind (thoughts), heart (feelings), and will (actions or behaviors)—that determines our leader-personalities. To integrate these three parts of personality into leader-personality profiles, first consider the design of a Venn diagram, as shown in Fig. 23.2.

When these three parts of personality are set into a Venn diagram, it displays how they combine to create seven profiles. One profile is primarily driven by the mind, one by the heart, and one by the will. Another profile is driven equally by both their mind and will, one by both their will and heart, and another equally by their heart and mind. And one profile is equally driven by all three parts: the mind, heart, and will. While much empirical work has been done to suggest the existence of at least four personality profiles (Gerlach et al., 2018), there remains very little theoretical understanding behind those findings. I suggest a biblical text can provide the theoretical grounding of how many personality profiles exist and the purpose of each profile. In this text, the word "gift" is used to describe each profile:

Fig. 23.2 Three-part personality

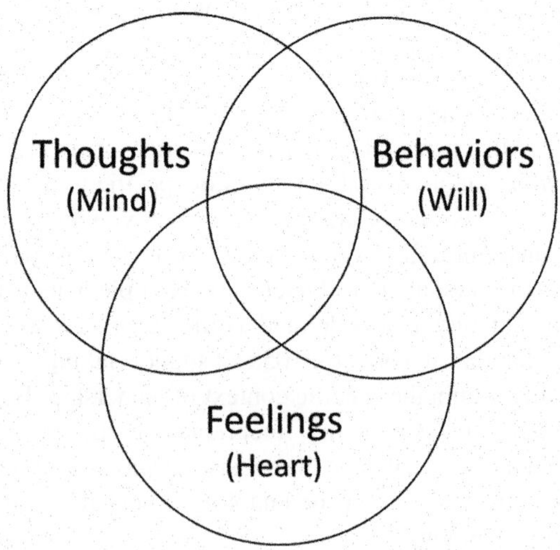

> We have different gifts, according to the grace given to each of us. If your gift is *prophesying*, then prophesy in accordance with your faith; if it is *serving*, then serve; if it is *teaching*, then teach; if it is to *encourage*, then give encouragement; if it is *giving*, then give generously; if it is to *lead*, do it diligently; if it is to *show mercy*, do it cheerfully. (Romans 12: 6–8)

These seven gifts were given to individuals by God and have been described as "inherent tendencies that characterize each different person" (Walker, 1991, p. 2023). Walker's (1991) description of "inherent tendencies" noticeably aligns with Costa and McCrae's (2008) definition of personality as "enduring individual differences." Since both cases are describing personality, this biblical text is therefore used as the inspiration for the labels for each of the seven leader-personality profiles: Prophet, Server, Teacher, Encourager, Giver, Administrator, and Sympathizer. Two labels (Administrator and Sympathizer) have been modified slightly from the biblical text which will be further described herein. I have placed the seven profiles into the Venn diagram (see Fig. 23.3) and use their locations to assist in developing the understanding of each profile.

Even though the seven labels are drawn from biblical text, this is not to imply that these seven profiles are for Christians only. The context of the passage reveals that the gifts are for "all people" (Romans 12:3). The original Greek word used is ανθρωποσ *(anthropos)*, meaning "every man" in a gender-neutral way. The gifts were given by God for all people, whether Christian or not (Winston, 2009).

We all have a mind, heart, and will, and it is the unique combination of these three parts that make our leader-personality. We tend to be most comfortable in one or two areas and lead from there (e.g., someone who leads with their heart, or someone who leads with their mind). The seven profiles are not roles nor job descriptions, but rather personality descriptors. The Teacher tends to be most comfortable leading with their mind, as opposed to the Sympathizer, who leads with their heart. The Prophet leads with their will and tends to act before thinking. The Administrator

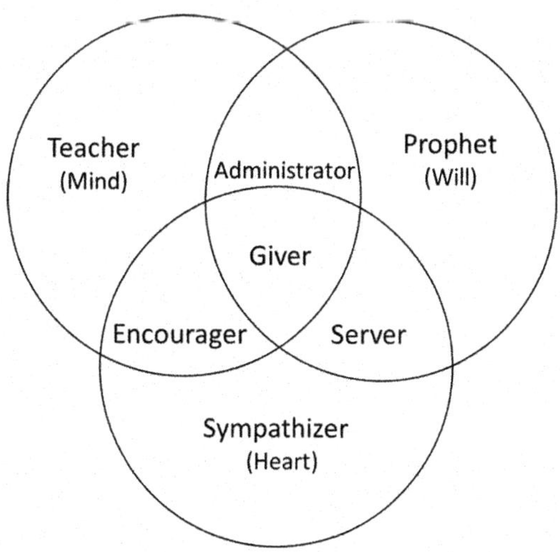

Fig. 23.3 Seven leader-personality profiles

integrates both mind and strength of will, showing excellence in supervising people and processes. The Encourager is like a coach, who leads with both the heart and mind, encouraging others to obtain their best as well as communicating the logic of why it is best. The Server combines both heart and will, causing them to take up efforts in which they can serve others by their actions. The Giver integrates all three areas of the mind, heart, and will and is someone who leads by being generous and resourceful; a natural networker, they know who needs to connect in order to get things done.

The remainder of this chapter provides a description of each leader-personality profile, integrating theoretically related personality and leadership research. Also included are the original Koine Greek words and their definitions, as suggested by the context of the biblical book of Romans, on which the labels for the profiles were based. The seven biblical gifts have been extensively researched by DellaVecchio and Winston (2015), Fortune and Fortune (2009), and Winston (2009), so while their research lacks a focus on personality or leadership, their interpretations of the seven profiles bring a rich contribution to this discussion. Descriptions start with the profiles of Teacher, Sympathizer, and Prophet because each of these profiles is focused primarily on one of the three parts of personality. Presented next are the profiles that overlap into two areas of personality: the Administrator, Encourager, and Server. Lastly the profile of Giver will be described, which equally combines all three areas of personality.

As you read through the various profiles, think about your own leadership style and see which profiles resonate with you. You will likely find at least one, and maybe even two or three, that you feel describe you well. Moreover, you will likely find at least one, maybe more, that you know do not describe you well—this is to be expected as we are all incomplete leaders. It has been argued that people have some combination of all profiles (Winston, 2009), but even this argument supports the idea that we are stronger in some areas more than others. Thus the conclusion remains the same that we are all incomplete. Recognizing our incompleteness is the first step to improving ourselves so we might be successful leaders in a post-COVID environment.

Teacher

As revealed in Fig. 23.3, the Teacher is one who leads with their mind. They lack a strong inclination in the areas of the heart and will to act. Thus, they tend to be most comfortable leading with in a logical, rational way, which may appear non-emotional and slow to respond. They tend toward intellectual discussions, which may appear unfeeling or cold in their approach while taking a long time to decide before they act. They may also find themselves "teaching" in their approach to others—they will research and deliberate what they determine is best, then communicate that in a logical and systematic way, either in writing or verbally. They may not currently be in the job role of a teacher, but might find they enjoy that particular role. Another good description of this profile is someone who is a researcher, because they are highly analytical, wanting to validate any facts or arguments that are presented to them. They are intellectually sharp and enjoy problem-solving—anything that stretches the mind. The original Greek word for teaching is διδασκων *(didaskon)* which means to instruct, clarify, illustrate, or simplify for the sake of communication and understanding (Bryant, 1991). DellaVecchio and Winston (2015) suggested that a Teacher profile has an extraordinary ability to discern, analyze, and deliver information so that others will learn. Fortune and Fortune (2009) suggested this profile is one who loves to research and communicate truth. Taken together, this indicates a person who is a strong communicator, whether it be written or oral, and with a strong ability to help others grasp the important concepts. For a leadership context, the Teacher profile is thus defined as someone who exhibits strong ability to analyze and deliver information so that others will understand.

Theoretically, this profile is likely to score high on most of the openness personality facets, particularly intellect and imagination. Intellect describes someone who is intellectually curious, often questioning, and desires stimulation that comes from new ideas. Imagination is the level of creativity and innovation. A low score would be expected on agreeableness, particularly the facet of tender mindedness. Tender mindedness describes one who can be swayed by emotions or feelings over rational judgment—this is the very opposite of a Teacher, who prefers logic and rational judgment over emotions. The Teacher can also be slow to accept the perspectives of others, as they first want to check the source or validate the facts. Because of this, they may appear reserved or distant, but this cold logic can bring an important perspective and is necessary to bring balance to leadership.

Moreover, the leadership literature also suggests there are leaders who lead naturally with their mind. Daniel Kahneman's (2011) book, titled "Thinking, Fast and Slow," explored the thinking processes of the human mind and noted two different systems of thinking: System 1 thinking is "fast"—it is quick, reactive, and automatic. Good fast decisions come from those who have many years of specific experience in a particular area. System 2 thinking is "slow," deliberate, and effortful; this is the normal process used for problem-solving. Not everyone naturally engages in System 2 thinking, but those with a Teacher profile would likely be naturally inclined to it. The ability to perform System 2 thinking is an important aspect of leadership and can be naturally provided by someone with a Teacher leader-personality profile.

Sympathizer

The Sympathizer profile, as shown in Fig. 23.3, is one who leads with their heart. They also lack a strong inclination in the areas of the mind and will. Thus, the Sympathizer is relationally focused and strongly desires to see harmony among relationships. They are likely high on emotional intelligence and will be known for showing care and kindness to others.

The Greek word used here, ελεων *(eleon),* is translated as "mercy" in the New International Version of the Bible (Romans 12:8). This word is derived from ελεοσ *(eleos)*, which means to have compassion on (Bryant, 1991). DellaVecchio and Winston (2015) and Winston (2009) labeled this profile as "Showing mercy," while Fortune and Fortune (2009) used the title "Compassion person." While compassion and mercy are close to the biblical context, Sympathizer is a more suitable title for this leader-personality profile which can encompass a broad range of caring leadership behaviors.

DellaVecchio and Winston (2015) suggested that this profile has the extraordinary ability to feel and act upon genuine empathy for others who are in pain. Fortune and Fortune (2009) suggested this person is one who shows compassion, love, and care to those in need. Taken together, this indicates that a Sympathizer will respond with empathy to those around them and will score exceptionally high on emotional intelligence. Thus, this leader-personality profile is defined as one who genuinely feels empathy for others and cares deeply for the well-being of people.

The Sympathizer profile is likely to score highly on the factor of agreeableness, particularly the facets of compliance and tender mindedness. Compliance is the desire to get along with others, being cooperative to the point of not wanting to express disagreement. Tender mindedness is being sympathetic and caring about humanitarian causes; one who is often swayed by feelings rather than rational judgment—this particularly aligns with the idea of making decisions with the heart rather than the head. It is also reasonable to expect low scores on neuroticism traits, especially the facet of angry-hostility. Angry-hostility describes someone who is quick to take offense, which is opposite to someone who is patient and kind, like those with a Sympathizer profile.

Supporting leadership literature can be found in Goleman's (1995) work on emotional intelligence that described the importance of leading with the heart. He defined the components of emotional intelligence as self-awareness, self-regulation, motivation, empathy, and social skill (Goleman, 1998). The component of empathy was defined as the ability to understand the emotional make-up of other people and shows skill in treating people according to their emotional reactions. He recognized the distinction between intelligence quotient and emotional quotient, stating that they have little to do with each other, which further supports the distinction between the mind and the heart as shown in this framework.

When in leadership positions, Sympathizer profiles may show a tendency to make decisions that please others due to their high scores on empathy and compliance. This may lead to behaviors that appear non-confrontational or indecisive, which are potential weaknesses for leadership. The Sympathizer profile should be aware of these weaknesses, but feel secure knowing that emotional intelligence is an important element of leadership.

Prophet

Figure 23.3 shows the Prophet is one whose will to act is the primary focus in their leader-personality style. They also lack a strong inclination in the areas of the heart and mind. Thus, the Prophet profile might not take the time to think before they act and will likely show little care for the feelings of others. The Prophet leads primarily with strength of will, so often their first response is to act; they want to see things get done. The Greek word for this profile is προφητεια (*propheteia*) which is defined in the biblical context as making known or divulging vital information necessary for spiritual living and development (Bryant, 1991). The label of Prophet is appropriate because like spiritual prophets, the person with this profile will frequently offer warnings on why something might go wrong. Just as the marketing and management literature has adopted the term *evangelist* to describe a zealous advocate, so also can the term *prophet* be applied to a non-religious context to mean one who speaks in a visionary way, is able to make predictions, or foresees potential doom. Due to the tendency to set aside feelings or thoughtful deliberations, they may seem blunt or confrontational in an effort to just get things done.

According to DellaVecchio and Winston (2015), people with these profiles have the ability to quickly discern good and evil. Fortune and Fortune (2009) suggested this profile is one who clearly perceives the will of God. Both of these definitions have a strongly spiritual perspective, which is not necessarily warranted by the context (Winston, 2009). When applied to a leadership context, I suggest this person can foresee when there might be trouble ahead; they are often good at envisioning a better future and identifying potential trouble spots along the way. Thus, the definition for this profile is one who exhibits a strong ability to communicate warning and vital information necessary for proceeding rightly.

The personality traits of this profile are likely to score highly on many of the facets of neuroticism, such as depression and angry-hostility, and low on particular agreeableness facets such as compliance. Depression is feeling frequently discouraged or discontented; this discontentment becomes an important motivator for speaking out with a new vision. Angry-hostility is being quick to take offense; they may feel easily insulted when others are unwilling to trust what they "see" so clearly. Compliance is one who shows a desire to get along with others and is unwilling to express disagreement—this is the opposite of a Prophet who will willingly and frequently raise objections. From a leadership standpoint, criticality and disagreement are important to making good decisions so, within reason, these objections should be welcomed.

The concept of grit in the leadership literature is theoretically relevant here; grit is a combination of passion and perseverance (Duckworth, 2017). Those with grit are deeply passionate about what they believe. They can persevere in their belief so strongly that it can construed as either determination or stubbornness. This determination comes naturally to those with a Prophet profile. This is needed in leadership, as we need leaders who bring vision, direction, and determination. Because of their strong conscience and desire to see things done right, their warnings should be thoughtfully considered in order to prevent future problems.

Administrator

Figure 23.3 shows the Administrator is one who leads equally with both their mind and will. They also lack a strong inclination in the area of the heart. Thus, in their efforts to think things through and get things done, they may leave other people's feelings and opinions out of the process. Even so, the Administrator is an excellent overseer who enables people and processes to function effectively. According to DellaVecchio and Winston (2015), Administrators have a strong ability to identify the appropriate goals, communicate those goals to others, and help others work harmoniously to achieve those goals. Fortune and Fortune (2009) suggested this profile is one who loves to organize or direct others.

The Greek word used here is προισταμενοσ *(proistamenous)* which means to stand over or place over (Bryant, 1991). The Greek word is translated by the New International Version of the Bible as "to lead" (Romans 12:8). As evidenced in this volume on leadership, "to lead" can be understood in a plethora of ways. As the original Greek means "to stand over," I have chosen to use the label of Administrator, as it indicates this person is a strong supervisor or manager, one who oversees or monitors people and processes. DellaVecchio and Winston (2015) and Winston (2009) labeled this profile as "Ruler," while Fortune and Fortune (2009) chose "Administrator." Using the label of Administrator incorporates the ideas of management and oversight without confounding other definitions of leadership. Management and leadership are distinct, albeit related, concepts (Yukl, 2013). A strong Administrator naturally brings the management qualities of monitoring and oversight as their strength in leadership.

As a natural manager, those with the Administrator profile are good at making plans and implementing them. They enjoy the challenge of establishing new procedures and are excellent at creating order out of chaos. They are often capable and responsible. Thus, the definition for this profile is someone who naturally sees the need for new procedures, then establishes and oversees procedures and/or people, in order to achieve organizational goals.

As evidenced by the well-researched personality traits of managers (e.g., Barrick & Mount, 1991; Barrick et al., 2001; Hurtz & Donovan, 2000), the Administrator profile is likely to score highly on most conscientiousness facets, especially competence, orderliness, and dutifulness. Competence is the trait of being confident and well-prepared, one who takes pride in common sense and prudence. Orderliness is one who is well-organized, tidy, and methodical. Dutifulness is one who sticks to the rules and keeps their promises. As Fig. 23.3 shows the Administrator does not include an overlap into the heart, it is reasonable to expect a low score on agreeableness, particularly modesty. A high score on modesty is someone who dislikes being the center of attention or has a low opinion of themselves—this is the opposite of what would be expected from a competent overseer who believes in their abilities and is able to run meetings as they supervise others. This becomes both a strength and weakness in leadership. Their strength is the ability to establish and monitor processes to help others achieve the organization's goals, but the weakness is the potential lack of heart and care for the relational aspects of those they work with.

Encourager

The Encourager leads with a combination of their heart and mind (Fig. 23.3). They are known for having a positive, cheerful attitude and being able to find the silver lining in any situation. Another good description for this profile might be a coach, as they enjoy challenging others to grow and are excellent at motivating others.

DellaVecchio and Winston (2015) described this profile as someone who has the ability to call forth the best in others through encouragement and motivation. Fortune and Fortune (2009) suggested this profile loves to encourage others to live a victorious life. The word encourager comes from the Greek word παρακαλων *(parakalon)*. This word has two parts—a "call" and "companionship"—which together they mean to be with and for another (Bryant, 1991). Taken together, this indicates this profile is willing to walk with others on their journey while calling forth their best along the way. The definition for the Encourager profile is someone who walks alongside others and encourages them to accomplish their best for the organization.

Because of the overlap of heart and mind (Fig. 23.3), the Encourager profile would likely score highly on agreeableness and openness facets. Feelings, a facet of openness, describe someone who is sensitive to the feelings of others. The cheerful attitude and ability to motivate others lead us to expect this profile would also score highly on the facets of gregariousness and positive emotions. Gregariousness describes someone who likes to be around people and is highly sociable. Someone who scores high on positive emotions is cheerful, high-spirited, and buoyant in mood. Because of the overall cheerful and positive attitude, it would be expected this profile would score low on depression. Depression has been described earlier under the Prophet profile; as shown in Fig. 23.3, the Prophet profile is situated exactly opposite to the Encourager (see Fig. 23.3), so it is reasonable to expect these two profiles might have some opposing qualities. Moreover, depression is a facet of neuroticism, which those who lead with their will may be more prone to. The area of the will is the only area with which the Encourager profile does not overlap.

The leadership literature around executive coaching is relevant to the Encourager profile. Executive coaching has been defined as practical, goal-focused, one-on-one learning for the purpose of behavioral change (Hall et al., 1999; Peterson, 1996). The objective of executive coaching is to encourage behavioral change and improve individual performance, which is expected to enhance organizational effectiveness (Day, 2000). Someone with an Encourager leader-personality profile might find themselves naturally drawn to this literature and might already play the role of coach or mentor within their field. Thus, the strength an Encourager profile brings to leadership lies in their ability to motivate others to contribute to the success of the organization.

Server

The Server profile leads with both their heart and will (Fig. 23.3); they are a do-er who rolls up their sleeves to get things done in a way that serves those around them. They are focused on the emotional and practical aspects of enabling others to best serve the organization but might not take the time to think before they act. According to DellaVecchio and Winston (2015), Server profiles have the desire to free others to work more effectively and will elevate the needs of the other person without concern for their own rank or recognition. Fortune and Fortune (2009) suggested this profile loves to serve others. The Greek word for serving is διακονια *(diakonia)* which means to aid and can be interpreted as the ability to identify unmet needs and then make use of available resources to accomplish the desired goals (Bryant, 1991). Taken together, this indicates that this person is a helper who cares for the needs of others. Thus, the definition of a Server leader-personality profile is someone who will serve others, without regard for themselves, in the best interest of the other person and the organization.

Because of this profile's emphasis on heart and will, and lack of influence of the mind (see Fig. 23.3), this profile would be expected to score highly on agreeableness and neuroticism facets, and low on openness facets. Because of the focus on the other person rather than themselves, this profile will likely score highly on self-consciousness, which is someone who is uncomfortable in drawing attention to themselves. A high score is expected on modesty, which is related to humility and deference to others—this particularly aligns well with the academic literature around servant leadership. As do-ers, this profile would be expected to score highly on activity, which is someone who enjoys a high energy level and may find sedentary work unappealing. Lastly, it would be reasonable to expect a low score on intellect, which is focused on being intellectually curious—this profile would rather be getting something done than investigating theoretical questions.

The leadership literature related to the Server profile can be found in the substantial amount of published research on servant leadership. Greenleaf's (1977) book "Servant Leadership" was a seminal work that sparked much discussion and research. He defined the servant leader as one who has a natural feeling that they want to serve, and the servant leader will be a servant first (Greenleaf, 1977). Further research investigating servant leadership described it is as leading others by serving them instead of serving self and suggested six aspects: voluntary subordination, authentic self, covenantal relationship, responsible morality, transcendental spirituality, and transforming influence (Sendjaya & Cooper, 2011).

Those with a Server profile exhibit a readiness to renounce their superior status if it prevents them from helping others in a practical way. Contrary to many leaders who crave the spotlight, Servers who put the interests of the organization and others above their own naturally bring this important component of leadership to the table.

Giver

As evidenced in Fig. 23.3, the Giver distinctively combines the mind, heart, and will to bring a unique leader-personality profile to the table. This is not to imply that the Giver is perfect in all three areas. Rather the three areas of mind, heart and will integrate to create a profile that creates different strengths but also lacks the unique strengths provided by the other profiles. A Giver is a natural networker who seeks to enable others behind the scenes. They may also be good with money or a natural entrepreneur.

DellaVecchio and Winston (2015) suggested that a Giver profile may give of their income, time, or energy in ways that exceed a normal standard. Fortune and Fortune (2009) suggested the Giver profile is one who loves to give time, talent, energy, and means to benefit others. The Greek word for giving is μεταδιδουσ *(metadidous)* which means to give over, share, or transfer (Bryant, 1991). Taken together, this indicates this profile is a strong resourcer, who can share or transfer resources to ensure the effective use of time, money, energy, or skill. For a leadership context, the Giver profile is defined as someone who exhibits the ability to allocate and share resources to enable attainment of the organization's goals.

Because of the combination of mind, heart, and will, the personality traits are more difficult to theoretically predict in this case. A natural networker, it is reasonable to expect some level of extraversion, yet they may also be happy to work behind the scenes to get things done, thus an average level of extraversion is proposed. Because of their tendency to be good with financial resources, a high level of detail-conscientiousness is expected, which is reflected in the trait of orderliness, a facet of conscientiousness. Most likely this profile would score highly on altruism, a facet of agreeableness, which is described as being generous and giving. Because of their balanced combination of mind, heart, and will, this profile might be especially resilient, dealing well with stress, thus it would be reasonable to expect a low score on the trait of vulnerability (a facet of neuroticism). Vulnerability is defined as not coping well with stress or crises.

This description of the Giver profile corresponds with Adam Grant's (2013) concept of Givers in his book "Give and Take." Grant stated that Givers focus on the interests of others, share credit, and make connections with others. He provides a list of values usually evident in Givers, including helpfulness, dependability, and responding to the needs of others. He also mentions altruism as a trait often seen in Givers (and is found lacking in those who are Takers). The leadership strengths of those with a Giver profile lie in their ability to manage resources for the benefit of all.

Table 23.2 provides a summary of the leader-personality profiles I have proposed, including their theoretically suggested personality traits, based on the overlaps of the three personality areas of mind, heart, and will.

Conclusion

As we emerge from the COVID-19 pandemic, now is the time to recognize our lessons learned and implement a distributive leadership strategy. Leader-personality profiles are one way of discerning the different personalities and perspectives that should be included in organizational leadership. The seven profiles, based on biblical "gifts," are particularly relevant to the context of distributive leadership because the wider context of Romans 12 asserts that the gifts are intended to be utilized together. Two verses (Romans 12:4–5) just prior to the list of gifts (Romans 12:6–8) give an analogy of the body to show how different parts are meant to be used together and not in isolation. The analogy describes different body parts working together: "For just as each of us has one body with many members, and these members do not all have the same function, so in Christ we, though many, form one body, and each member belongs to all the others" (Romans 12: 4–5, NIV). Each part cannot work alone successfully, but rather they need each other.

The idea of the body working together is further expounded by the same author (the apostle Paul) in another letter where he wrote:

Table 23.2 Summary of leader-personality profiles and personality traits

Profile	Leads with their…	Definition	Personality factors	Personality facets
Teacher	Mind	Analyzes and delivers information so that others will understand	−N, +O, −A	+Intellect +Imagination −Tender mindedness
Sympathizer	Heart	Genuinely feels empathy for others and cares deeply for the well-being of people	−N, −O, +A	+Tender mindedness +Compliance −Angry-hostility
Prophet	Will	Communicates warning and vital information necessary for proceeding rightly	+N, −O, −A	+Angry-hostility +Depression −Compliance
Administrator	Mind and will	Establishes and oversees people and/or procedures, in order to achieve organizational goals	+N, +O, −A	+Competence +Orderliness +Dutifulness −Modesty
Encourager	Mind and heart	Walks alongside others and encourages them to accomplish their best for the organization	−N, +O, +A	+Feelings +Gregariousness +Positive emotions −Depression
Server	Heart and will	Serves others in practical ways in the best interest of getting tasks done	+N, −O, +A	+Self-consciousness +Modesty +Activity −Intellect
Giver	Mind, heart, and will	Allocates and shares resources to enable attainment of the organization's goals	Avg N, Avg O, Avg A	+Altruism +Orderliness −Vulnerability

N neuroticism, *O* openness, *A* agreeableness, *(+)* high score, *(−)* low score, *Avg* average score

> Even so the body is not made up of one part but of many. Now if the foot should say, "because I am not a hand, I do not belong to the body," it would not for that reason stop being part of the body. And if the ear should say, "because I am not an eye, I do not belong to the body," it would not for that reason stop being part of the body. If the whole body were an eye, where would the sense of hearing be? If the whole body were an ear, where would the sense of smell be? But in fact, God has placed the parts in the body, every one of them, just as he wanted them to be. If they were all one part, where would the body be? As it is, there are many parts, but one body. The eye cannot say to the hand, "I don't need you!" And the head cannot say to the feet, "I don't need you!" (1 Corinthians 12:14–21)

Here the analogy is applied to the concept of distributed leadership, where it can be acknowledged that no one person is meant to work alone, but we must work together by relying on the strengths of each other. While a variety of leadership models have been published over the years, they have predominantly focused on leadership behaviors. Leadership behavior taxonomies provide useful lists of leadership skills, but speak nothing to the way we naturally lead. Herein I presented a model of leader-personality profiles that suggests your natural leader-personality, helping you to identify your characteristic strengths and weaknesses. This enables you to be your best when able and ask others for assistance where needed. Uniquely relevant for today's environment as we emerge from COVID-19, this framework of leader-personality profiles introduces a model of distributive leadership that is appropriate and sustainable for our uncertain world.

Chapter Takeaways

1. As we emerge from COVID-19, we must find leadership strategies that are effective in an uncertain and complex world. Appropriate and sustainable leadership can be found through a distributive leadership approach.
2. The strategy of trying to be the hero leader is no longer adequate. We must acknowledge that we are incomplete. We can address our incompleteness by identifying our strengths and weaknesses and legitimately depending on others in the areas where we are weak.
3. There are seven leader-personality profiles, each based on a combination of the three personality areas of mind, heart, and will.
4. The seven leader-personality profiles are Teacher, Sympathizer, Prophet, Administrator, Encourager, Server, and Giver.
5. Of the seven leader-personality profiles, several are likely to describe you, and several are likely to not describe you. This framework can help you identify your natural leadership strengths and weaknesses.

Reflection Questions

1. This chapter suggests hero leadership is no longer sustainable after COVID-19 and the best strategy is distributed leadership. To what extent do you agree? Why?
2. Consider each of the seven leader-personality profiles. Identify a situation where each leadership profile would be especially appropriate and effective.
3. Which leader-personality profiles do you identify with?
4. With a work colleague, discuss the profiles you identify with. Does your colleague agree with your assessment?
5. Identify a work colleague who is strong in the leader-personality areas you are weak. Develop a plan on how you might lead together.

References

Ancona, D., Malone, T. W., Orlikowski, W. J., & Senge, P. M. (2007). In praise of the incomplete leader. Harvard Business Review, *February*, pp 92–100.

Asendorpf, J. B., Borkenau, P., Ostendorf, F., & van Aken, M. A. G. (2001). Carving personality description at its joints: Confirmation of three replicable personality prototypes for both children and adults. *European Journal of Personality, 15*, 169–198.

Barrick, M. R., & Mount, M. K. (1991). The Big Five personality dimensions and job performance: A meta-analysis [Article]. *Personnel Psychology, 44*(1), 1–26. https://doi.org/10.1111/j.1744-6570.1991.tb00688.x

Barrick, M. R., Mount, M. K., & Judge, T. A. (2001). Personality and performance at the beginning of the new millennium: What do we know and where do we go next? *Personality and Performance, 9*(1/2), 9–30.

Bass, B. M. (1990). *Handbook of leadership: A survey of theory and research*. Free Press.

Bem, D. J., & Allen, A. (1974). On predicting some of the people some of the time - Search for cross-situational consistencies in behavior. *Psychological Review, 81*(6), 506–520. https://doi.org/10.1037/h0037130

Bono, J. E., & Judge, T. A. (2004). Personality and transformational and transactional leadership: A meta-analysis. *Journal of Applied Psychology, 89*(5), 901–910. https://doi.org/10.1037/0021-9010.89.5.901

Bowling, N. A., & Burns, G. N. (2010). A comparison of work-specific and general personality measures as predictors of work and non-work criteria. *Personality and Individual Differences, 49*, 95–101.

Bryant, C. (1991). *Rediscovering our spiritual gifts*. Upper Room Books.

Caspi, A., & Silva, P. A. (1995). Temperamental qualities at age three predict personality traits in young adulthood: Longitudinal evidence from a birth cohort. *Child Development, 66*, 486–498.

Costa, P. T., & McCrae, R. R. (1992a). Four ways five factors are basic. *Personality and Individual Differences, 13*(6), 653–665.

Costa, P. T., & McCrae, R. R. (1992b). *Revised NEO Personality Inventory (NEO-PI-R) and NEO Five-Factor Inventory (NEO-FFI) professional manual*. Psychological Assessment Resources.

Costa, P. T., & McCrae, R. R. (2008). The revised NEO personality inventory (NEO-PI-R). In G. J. Boyle, G. Matthews, & D. H. Saklofske (Eds.), *The SAGE handbook of personality theory and assessment*. Sage.

Day, D. V. (2000). Leadership development: A review in context. *Leadership Quarterly, 11*(4), 591–613.

DellaVecchio, D., & Winston, B. E. (2015). A seven-scale instrument to measure the Romans 12 motivational gifts and a proposition that the Romans 12 gift profiles might apply to person-job fit analysis. *International Journal of Leadership Studies, 9*(1), 1–22.

Drath, W. H., & Palus, C. J. (1994). *Making common sense: Leadership as meaning-making in a community of practice*. Center for Creative Leadership.

Duckworth, A. (2017). *Grit: Why passion and resilience are the secrets to success*. Vermilion.

Fortune, D., & Fortune, K. (2009). *Discover your God-given gifts*. Chosen Books.

Gardner, W. L., & Martinko, M. J. (1996). Using the Myers-Briggs type indicator to study managers: A literature review and research agenda. *Journal of Management, 22*(1), 45–83. https://doi.org/10.1177/014920639602200103

Gerlach, M., Farb, B., Revelle, W., & Amaral, L. A. N. (2018). A robust data-driven approach identifies four personality types across four large data sets. *Nature Human Behaviour, 2*(10), 735–742. https://doi.org/10.1038/s41562-018-0419-z

Goleman, D. (1995). *Emotional intelligence*. Bloomsbury.

Goleman, D. (1998). What makes a leader? *Harvard Business Review, 76*(6), 93–102.

Grant, A. (2013). *Give and Take: Why helping others drives our success*. Penguin Books.

Greenleaf, R. K. (1977). *Servant leadership*. Paulist Press.

Gronn, P. (2002). Distributed leadership as a unit of analysis. *The Leadership Quarterly, 13*, 423–451.

Hall, D. T., Otazo, K. L., & Hollenbeck, G. P. (1999). Behind closed doors: What really happens in executive coaching. *Organizational Dynamics, 29*(Winter), 39–53.

Hattrup, K., & Jackson, S. E. (1996). Learning about individual differences by taking situations seriously. In K. R. Murphy (Ed.), *Individual differences and behavior in organizations*. Jossey-Bass.

Heller, D., Ferris, D., Brown, D., & Watson, D. (2009). The influence of work personality on job satisfaction: Incremental validity and mediation effects. *Journal of Personality, 77*(4), 1051–1084.

Hemphill, J. K., & Coons, A. E. (1957). Development of the leader behavior description questionnaire. In R. M. Stogdill & A. E. Coons (Eds.), *Leader behavior: Its description and measurement* (pp. 6–38). Bureau of Business Research, Ohio State University.

House, R. J., Hanges, P. J., Ruiz-Quintanilla, S. A., Dorfman, P. W., Javidan, M., Dickson, M., & Associates. (1999). Cultural influences on leadership and organizations: Project GLOBE. In W. H. Mobley, M. J. Gessner, & V. Arnold (Eds.), *Advances in global leadership* (pp. 131–233). JAI Press.

Howes, R. J., & Carskadon, T. G. (1979). Test-retest reliabilities of the Myers-Briggs Type Indicator as a function of mood changes. *Research in Psychological Type, 2*, 67–72.

Hurtz, G. M., & Donovan, J. J. (2000). Personality and job performance: The Big Five revisited. *Journal of Applied Psychology, 85*(6), 869–879.

Judge, T. A., Heller, D., & Mount, M. K. (2002). Five-factor model of personality and job satisfaction: A meta-analysis. *Journal of Applied Psychology, 87*(3), 530–541. https://doi.org/10.1037/0021.9010.87.3.530

Judge, T. A., & Zapata, C. P. (2015). The person-situation debate revisited: Effect of situation strength and trait activation on the validity of the Big Five personality traits in predicting job performance. *Academy of Management Journal, 58*(4), 1149–1179. https://doi.org/10.5465/amj.2010.0837

Kahneman, D. (2011). *Thinking, fast and slow*. Penguin Books.

Katz, D., & Kahn, R. L. (1978). *The social psychology of organizations* (2nd ed.). Wiley.

McCaulley, M. H., & Carskadon, T. G. (1983). Test-retest reliabilities of scales and subscales of the Myers-Briggs Type Indicator and of criteria for clinical interpretive hypotheses involving them. *Research in Psychological Type, 6*, 24–36.

Meindl, J. R., Erlich, S. B., & Dukerich, J. M. (1985). The romance of leadership. *Administrative Science Quarterly, 30*, 78–102.

Murphy, K. R., & Dzieweczynski, J. L. (2005). Why don't measures of broad dimensions of personality perform better as predictors of job performance? *Human Performance, 18*(4), 343–359.

Myers, I. B., & McCaulley, M. H. (1985). *Manual: A guide to the development and use of the Myers-Briggs type indicator*. Consulting Psychologists Press.

Northouse, P. G. (2010). *Leadership: Theory and practice* (5th ed.). Sage.

Peterson, D. B. (1996). Executive coaching at work: The art of one-on-one change. *Consulting Psychology Journal: Practice and Research, 48*, 78–86.

Pittenger, D. J. (2005). Cautionary comments regarding the Myers-Briggs Type Indicator. *Consulting Psychology Journal: Practice and Research, 57*(3), 210–221.

Rauch, C. F., & Behling, O. (1984). Functionalism: Basis for an alternate approach to the study of leadership. In J. G. Hunt, D. M. Hosking, C. A. Schriesheim, & R. Stewart (Eds.), *Leaders and managers: International perspectives on managerial behavior and leadership* (pp. 45–62). Pergamon Press.

Robins, R. W., John, O. P., Caspi, A., Moffitt, T. E., & StouthamerLoeber, M. (1996). Resilient, overcontrolled, and undercontrolled boys: Three replicable personality types. *Journal of Personality and Social Psychology, 70*(1), 157–171. https://doi.org/10.1037/0022-3514.70.1.157

Salter, D. W., Forney, D. S., & Evans, N. J. (2005). Two approaches to examining the stability of Myers-Briggs type indicator scores. *Measurement & Evaluation in Counseling & Development, 37*(4), 208–219.

Salters-Pedneault, K., Ruef, A. M., & Orr, S. P. (2010). Personality and psychophysiological profiles of police officer and firefighter recruits. *Personality and Individual Differences, 49*(3), 210–215. https://doi.org/10.1016/j.paid.2010.03.037

Sava, F. A., & Popa, R. I. (2011). Personality types based on the Big Five Model: A cluster analysis over the Romanian population. *Cognition, Brain, Behaviour, 15*(3), 359–384.

Sendjaya, S., & Cooper, B. (2011). Servant Leadership Behaviour Scale: A hierarchical model and test of construct validity. *European Journal of Work and Organizational Psychology, 20*(3), 416–436. Article Pii 924954904.. https://doi.org/10.1080/13594321003590549

Walker, P. (1991). Holy spirit gifts and power. In J. W. Hayford & J. Horner (Eds.), *Spirit filled life Bible*. Thomas Nelson Publishers.

Winston, B. E. (2009). The Romans 12 gifts: Useful for person-job fit. *Journal of Biblical Perspectives in Leadership, 2*(2), 114–134.

Yukl, G. (1999). An evaluation of conceptual weaknesses in transformational and charismatic leadership theories. *Leadership Quarterly, 10*(2), 285–305.
Yukl, G. (2013). *Leadership in organizations* (8th ed.). Pearson.

Courtney E. Owens, PhD, MBA, CPsychol is a Chartered Organizational Psychologist and serves as the Deputy Director of the Engineering Leadership Development Program and Lecturer in Leadership and Organization at Alliance Manager Business School, University of Manchester, UK. She holds a PhD in Organizational Psychology from the University of Manchester, UK and an MBA from the University of Washington, WA, USA. She teaches and presents work-personality, leader-personality, leadership, and self-awareness. Her research interests focus on personality traits in the context of the workplace, biblical psychology, and leader development.

Leadership After COVID-19: Can Food Banks, Food Pantries Help Serve Diverse Populations? 24

Sonya Sharififard

Introduction

Food insecurity refers to a condition in which an individual has insufficient or reduced intake, reduced or less quality, limited or no variety, or desirability in their diet, and disrupted eating patterns because of limited or no access to nutritious and safe foods (Barrett, 2010). According to the United States Department of Agriculture (USDA), food insecurity is categorized as either "low food security" or "very low food security." Low food security occurs when an individual obtains enough calories in their respective diets, but is inclusive of a diet that has less quality and variety. Very low food security is defined as eating less or not at all because of limited resources (USDA, 2018). The most common forms of food insecurity include either the inability to afford balanced and nutritional meals, the reduction in the size of meals, the conserving of available food, or the avoidance of eating regular meals because of a lack of funds. If one requires a specific food item, it is likely that the food environment of their neighborhood is in an area that might not always be personally and economically acceptable.

Food insecurity issues cannot be framed from a food scarcity lens or the lens of food marketing. Recurring disparities in food environments contribute to the lack of healthful, nutritious, and specialized foods. The lack of grocery stores, coupled with a lack of specialized food stores, each contributed to the problems of food insecurity differently. While individuals are perpetually changing their diets, food insecurity has been linked to structural deficiencies in the local food system, unpredictable circumstances, natural disasters, and chronic poverty (Clay & Ross, 2020; Clay et al., 2018; Hendriks, 2015; Richterman et al., 2019). The COVID-19 pandemic currently poses several concerns and threats to the nutritional health of individuals

S. Sharififard (✉)
Pepperdine University, Malibu, CA, USA
e-mail: Sonya.Sharififard@pepperdine.edu

S. K. Dhiman, J. F. Marques (eds.), *Leadership After COVID-19*, Future of Business and Finance, https://doi.org/10.1007/978-3-030-84867-5_24

(Fitzpatrick et al., 2020). The COVID-19 pandemic has disproportionately affected communities and individuals experiencing food insecurity.

Food systems policies have generally affected the food supply and have contributed to low food security among individuals and disproportionately influenced domestic and global food prices (Neff et al., 2009). While such aspects of food insecurity can be a combination of social, physical, traditional, and cultural factors, the complex nature of the food supply chain evolves, and the availability of food affects the food environment's characteristics. While food insecurity can be attributed to specific populations and geographic inequities, it has primarily been a public health issue (Leddy et al., 2020; Murthy, 2016).

Food delivery to consumers involves many actors, including individuals and agencies (National Research Council, 2015). Within the food and agriculture systems, supply chains, market segmentation, and regulations across states and cities affect the composition of regional and local food systems (Nesheim et al., 2015). On average, the variety of convenience foods, easy-to-prepare foods, ready-to-go snacks, and consumption has increased, while the time spent on food preparation has decreased. Genetic engineering techniques also have affected the overall food system. Of all corn and soybean crops, 90% have been genetically engineered (Fernandez-Cornejo et al., 2014). The genetic engineering of such crops has affected the rate of food quality, food preferences, and food marketing.

Alston et al. (2008) argued that improving the quality of foods might increase food waste, leading to subsequent environmental problems (Alston et al., 2008). Different food products and the product assortment at food stores and retailers can affect consumer interests. Social influences and food behaviors of a community affect grocery shopping behaviors of residents in that same area and their nutritional decisions (Leonard et al., 2014). The demand for fresh and nutritious meals and the ease of disposing of food items have increased food waste. Policies that subsidize fewer goods can lead to lower micronutrient intake in response to having dietary diversity in the food system (Pingali, 2010). The policies that support dietary diversity but fail to consider micro- and macronutrient food quality can begin to restart a cycle of food insecurity. Diets vary from person to person especially among dietary adherences, food customs, and other food diets.

Race and Nutritional Access

Geographic, racial, and class disparities and health discrepancies can persist if the interplay between food preferences, social networks, and the shift of neighborhood characteristics over time do not align with specific or recommended dietary preferences, food choices, and the availability of markets and food products. According to Helling and Sawicki (2010), when African-American/Black neighborhoods are primarily poor, the insufficient availability of retail stores affects the lack of grocers and businesses offering quality produce in these neighborhoods. The researchers also indicate that such disadvantaged neighborhoods provide less access to nutritious foods with smaller grocers. Residents have a longer commute to larger supermarkets with fresh produce than predominantly White neighborhoods. Neighborhoods with higher proportions of African-American/Black residents have more fast-food restaurants and fewer supermarkets than neighborhoods with higher proportions of White residents (Hilmers et al., 2012). Non-fast food restaurants are more prevalent in racially mixed and White neighborhoods than in African-American/Black or Hispanic neighborhoods (Dimitri & Rogus, 2014), which influences the diet and food quality of individuals residing in those neighborhoods. Other researchers have found no difference in diet quality because of living closer to a supermarket (Larson et al., 2009; Moore & Diez Roux, 2006; Morland et al., 2002; Raja et al., 2008;), but have considered food environment measures for neighborhood characteristics. Other missing analyses included the prevalence of public transportation, which would affect safety and neighborhood behaviors practiced by residents in large cities who are newly acquainted with the public transit system and the neighborhood with a traditional market presence.

Further, low-income, minority, and immigrant communities that are disparately affected by food production and restrictions particular to their diets and religious accordance (Neff et al., 2009) may also encounter challenges with commuting to an accessible grocer. The zip codes of such communities and their proximity to a variety of foods are of critical importance to the types of barriers that may exist in those sectors and their relationships to diet quality and neighborhood safety (Bader et al., 2010).

Kamarulzaman et al. (2016) implicate that only several large urban cities in the USA have adequate food choices for individuals following a Halal diet. As international populations assimilate to their host country's customs and culture, they are also more likely to change their practices as well as the nutritional content of their food choices. Further, traditional stores are likely to be in larger cities. Residents who reside in these cities rely on public transportation, which may be limited to some geographic areas and municipalities. These barriers also affect rural areas and consist of similar barriers that other communities in differing geographic areas have in terms of food provision (Mirabitur et al., 2016; Waters-Bailey et al., 2019).

Ethnic markets and similar specialty stores are likely to be more important to specific communities and populations. A group of people who are hesitant and unwilling to make purchases at large traditional markets might feel excluded or uncomfortable because their preferred items are superseded by unfamiliar food choices and ingredients (Joassart-Marcelli et al., 2017). Such food practices may also be met with perceived stigmas within a community that makes ethnic groups feel uncomfortable and unsafe in the environments and neighborhoods in which they reside.

The Interconnectedness of Food Systems

The food supply chain in the modern U.S. food system is overly complex and involves multiple actors and processes. The food system has direct effects on individual health and food consumption. Food consumption, as determined by food quality, quantity, and safety affects the food system indirectly. A sustainable food system is one that provides foods that are accessible, acceptable, adequate, and available (Shannon et al., 2015). Some of the changes that are shaped by the local food context include environmental shifts, such as pollution. These changes can, in turn, create indirect and unintended consequences on the overall food system.

Food prices and food insecurity rely on several assumptions about the relationship between costs and consumption, as well as consumption and food security. Food production and productivity respond to technology and the availability of land for irrigation. Consumer income and food preferences influence the demand for specific foods. According to the National Research Council (2015), as incomes rise, consumers demand more animal protein sources, which generally require higher prices of production. External forces such as weather, transportation, agricultural policies, food processing, food marketing, food packaging, and restrictions of various retail sectors have also impacted consumer food prices in the food supply chain (Nesheim et al., 2015). However, food consumption patterns are not more likely to significantly differ or change among populations.

Small changes in food prices can significantly affect food consumption patterns (Alston et al., 2008). Focusing individually on specific consumer behaviors and consumption patterns to the changes in food prices can be problematic, as suggested by Farnese, 2010. Food production and consumption vary across regions and populations. Differences in price, food preferences, and income are all part of the ways in which consumers change their food consumption and make decisions about their purchases. The per capita consumption of the same or different foods also varies among populations across the USA. Consumers continually make different dietary choices, whether conscious, about food consumption within a broader context of available, affordable, and acceptable foods (Nesheim et al., 2015; Tom et al., 2016).

Additionally, the core aspects of the US food system, as it relates specifically to fruits and vegetables, include several environmental outcomes and external processes that affect the agencies involved in the supply chain. To follow the USDA dietary and nutritional recommendations, one would have to significantly increase their overall fruit and vegetable consumption (Krebs-Smith & Kantor, 2001). The individual quantity of such consumption would affect the entire food supply chain and potentially cause threats to the food system over time. Further, prolonged dietary intake consistent with similar nutritional recommendations would ultimately affect the relationship between the environment and dietary patterns (Tom et al., 2016).

Food Retailers, Food Banks, and Food Pantries

As suggested by Bazerghi et al., 2016, food banks may not be able to resolve all client needs and meet all nutritional requirements. Patrons might have specific food and dietary needs. A food bank might encounter several challenges in attempting to consistently meet the demands of providing every food product type that might be requested or desired in the community served. Further, a food bank could not trace every type of dietary preference, custom or desired food rule. It is common to find foods with lower nutritional contents, less variety, and even items that would make patrons desire additional food as a result from a lack of essential nutrients. Offering foods of a lower nutritional value and foods with no dietary or cultural contents was not perceived as a direct barrier to overall food access. Instead, the types of food items currently available inside the pantries are necessary for maintaining operations and follow specific guidelines and regulations.

Multiethnic representation in the USA varies significantly from region to region. Food pantries consist of limited food options overall. Individuals could potentially visit their local food bank that is either entirely or partially devoid of dietary foods, which can be more difficult when deciding to visit their food pantry. However, the food pantry can differentiate itself from the local or community food bank, making it more connected to individual and community needs to be most inclusive as possible. Further, one cannot assert that individuals would choose healthful, nutrient-rich foods if provided with adequate access. Also, the availability of specific foods in a neighborhood does not necessarily infer an increased or decreased consumption of healthful food items. However, there are further implications for considering the population's health disparities. As it relates to the spatial complexity of food insecurity, neighborhoods with a lower variety of foods would not be as important for individuals experiencing food insecurity if there is no access to the specific food item(s) they need.

Overall, the food banks and food pantries play a specific role in reducing the impact of food insecurity where there is a growing demand for food sources and modern food retailing in influencing consumers' food choices and dietary patterns. However, if a local food bank serves as one of the only providers to supply food items in times of need, those same individuals might feel cultural, spiritual, or social isolation. In turn, they might consume smaller portions of food that are not a part of their regular dietary intake or use food items that are not available. If the requirements for maintaining a balanced and healthy level of dietary intake are excluded from an individual's respective dietary intake, they might not have the opportunity to seek food from other food retailers or community services.

Further, the more that food pantries and food banks begin to further rely on services related mostly to donations and external sourcing, the more likely it is for some issues surrounding food insecurity to persist. Food donations can often limit the types of food items that might be requested or preferred by members of a community. The limitations and policies required for operating a food bank can also affect the quantity and quality of foods available. Also, the unpredictability of donations poses additional barriers to food assistance. Many essential foods necessary will also be more challenging to acquire as the supply of adequate, nutritious, multiethnic, and healthy foods becomes less accessible and more difficult to find in the neighborhood. The overall impact of the food pantry does not help reinforce detailed discussions necessary for preparing foods per dietary rules.

Economically, if convenience stores were to offer more food items, including specialized and healthy food containing essential nutrients, they would likely charge more for those items, which would not necessarily be affordable for the individual members of a community. Yet, the factors that differentiate the food environment include the importance of the design of cities and neighborhoods. A group of individuals who might express an unwillingness to make purchases at large traditional markets might feel excluded or uncomfortable because their preferred items are superseded by unfamiliar food choices and ingredients (Joassart-Marcelli et al., 2017). Such food practices may also be met with perceived stigmas within a community that makes ethnic groups feel uncomfortable and unsafe in the environments and neighborhoods in which they reside, making the design of the communities more important to the food environment. If individual members of a community continue to feel cultural and social isolation because of food consumption patterns, the effectiveness of food banks and community food services could be challenged in some communities.

Areas with a larger concentration of several convenience stores may not necessarily be places where developers choose to invest. In that same respect, future developers could evaluate implications of the values that a public institution of higher education serves, bridging public–private sector partnerships. Additionally, high start-up costs and the availability of attractive land for developers to build grocery stores with more product offerings are also considerations for professionals, such as realtors. In areas where longer travel would be required to reach a food retailer or food bank, individuals would need to consider their dietary needs among the impacts of traveling longer distances. The same would apply for food sources located in communities that typically lack safe and accessible crosswalks and traffic lights. Individuals who continue to use community food services, such as food banks, could consider how another service would better meet their basic needs if transportation and accessibility are of greater significance to their transportation needs.

The lack of transportation also affects individuals who cannot travel longer distances from their place of residence. In many cases, the food banks help solve transportation barriers in limited capacities for those who require immediate and short-term basic needs. Also, those with limited or no reliable transportation might opt to use food services and shop from food retailers which are more geographically convenient. Concerning spatial complexity and the effects on food accessibility, community food services must continue to meet the demands required of their communities with how their cities are designed. While it is challenging to determine how diverse populations would benefit from a variety of food stores and food products within the neighborhoods of their residence, a lack of multiethnic food products in the food banks would not necessarily help to improve the food environment overall; but it would be necessary to understand the quality of foods in low-income, high-poverty neighborhoods.

If food banks were to introduce more food products derived from dietary laws or cultural and customary contents, economic, political, and social changes might occur and affect some community preferences, behaviors, and practices. Food distributors and foodservice providers would also see the effects of their business models and individual contracts with institutions in providing a variety of foods that would also be affordable. As such, public institutions, such as institutes of higher education, that would prefer to keep foods of a religious or cultural purpose separate from the food pantry or community's culture generally, could find other viable solutions to providing relevant and inclusive food products for the populations they serve.

The food system changes in response to consumer demands and is affected by individuals who follow specific food customs over time. One cannot find what they are looking for in terms of food, without compromising the other, especially regarding dietary customs and food preparation. The spatial complexity of the food environment can, in many ways, inform how the community food environment contributes to better and preferable consumer interests over time. Dietary preferences and food laws might be more conducive to secular food rules or preferences when operating food banks that serve a diverse population. It is additional consideration to infer what happens when religious/secular relationships begin to cause shifts in public institutions. The mix between secular and religious providers varies among communities (Minow, 2003). Food providers also vary across states and municipalities concerning the global food system.

Recommendations

The quality of foods at food pantries and throughout the overall food environment will continue to affect individuals who encounter barriers to food access. Additionally, it can help with introducing new ways of approaching food insecurity and the changing food environments across communities and cross-cultural neighborhoods. The study can further help residents identify their consistent mode(s) of transportation and how they select their food expenditures and necessities and basic needs. While the researcher did not assess shopping behaviors and personal accessibility to specific food stores, this study's findings could help understand the relationship between the ethnic composition of specific neighborhoods and the overall diverse dietary and food preferences of various populations in the USA.

While diverse populations might not collectively follow religious or dietary food customs, irrespective of a background that is related to faith-based institutions, athletic performance, physical training, or medical necessities, it is beneficial to understand how all members of a community access and consume food. It is also as important to be able to determine how food is acquired, prepared, stored, and handled. Food banks could work to help with developing culturally relevant partnerships with their communities while also influencing communities where individuals requiring such services are valued and respected emotionally, socially, and culturally. Further, volunteers and staff can promote leading opportunities that support a culture of inclusion and well-being as part of their services. These events can further open the opportunity to address other community concerns and communicate ideas for promoting wellness and well-being.

To comply with food and dietary rules/customs, the staff could possibly work to ensure appropriate restrictions of cross-exposure of certain food items available. In that same respect, food distributions should not stigmatize any member of a community, volunteers, or staff. If there is also a growing interest in selecting categories from additional choices of foods, it would be beneficial to identify the variety of foods that would be necessary and requested by patrons. If specific food retailers or other grocers are not available in the community, individuals might challenge how their community meets their personal and social needs. Future research has the potential to explore the relationships between the types of food preferences and food laws affecting communities as well as the varying forms of food insecurity emerging in some areas. Researchers can work to understand the perceptions of food access introduced in this study and consider other solutions for increasing access to healthful and sustainable foods among some of the populations experiencing food insecurity.

It would also be beneficial for researchers to address systemic inequalities and ethnic preferences of food consumption. If there are adequate resources for individuals following a diet consistent with religious, cultural, athletic, or other personal/dietary preferences, it would be important to understand how food banks supplement shortfalls, if any, of food supply for clients they serve. Other researchers could consider identifying concentrations of food deserts and the types of food retailers commonly found in those same areas. Dietary food laws and food security policies in the USA could also be used to infer quantitative and qualitative understandings of the local food environment. Direct changes of the retail food environment in neighborhoods and the convergence of public health concerns can also assist policymakers and researchers in identifying immediate risks associated with disparities and the identification of areas which can become food deserts. By further studying dietary quality changes because of a pandemic, researchers, practitioners, and academicians can obtain an overview of current community food practices and food bank systems to align with the convergence of the broader food systems. Additionally, the types of food products available in specific regions or the neighborhoods of similarly situated populations can help inform public health outcomes.

For individual communities, it is important to better understand the types of examples set forth by local academic institutions, and public entities, broadly defined and the importance of how public institutions work to support and sustain cultural, faith-based, and secular values in an environment that promotes respectful discourse, dialog, and decision-making is important to the advancement of leadership in local communities. These can help inform institutional policy decisions at the state and local level while advancing future development in public health and leadership studies. Emerging basic needs for children and adults could also be used to help with providing the relevant and appropriate resources necessary for nutritional support.

Understanding some of the systemic, legal, physical, and attitudinal barriers or restrictions that populations face in making food choices is an important aspect of learning about food-related and dietary consumption. It is also important to consider the best needs for patrons, such as how individuals with specific dietary needs or restrictions continue to alter or improve some aspects of their regular diets without risking the quality of the foods they are used to consuming. Building a pantry or food bank that continues to reflect such individual and communal needs is important for various reasons, including improving services, creating a place where others feel safe to share in the benefits of community wellness and individual growth, and preparing for better public health outcomes beyond the food environment. Individuals can also learn more about the global food system and its impact on individual and local communities. At an organizational level, leaders could better understand the need for systems thinking (Senge & Sterman, 1992) in their services related to food to benefit their respective institutions. The importance of local and regional food banks understanding the global food system and the diverse needs of the populations they serve can impact the types of donations and foods available, as well as the frequency of certain food items.

Chapter Takeaways/Lessons

- An integrated understanding of the social, economic, cultural, spiritual, and geographic aspects of the global food system and their implications for agricultural production and efficiency is helpful in managing food policies systemically and globally.
- Food production, food marketing, and food distribution systems can help to contribute to meeting the goals of protecting food security and public health.
- After the pandemic, immediate developments about the local-to-global connections affecting the interconnected food systems, food laws, and sustainable food consumption became critical to the relationships between agricultural efficiency and food marketing and food marketing and nutrient security.
- Collaboration between international partners in the food supply chain should work toward promoting societal growth.
- Food banks will continue to cultivate broader conversations about food security, poverty, global health, and hunger.

Reflection Questions

- To what extent do food industry leaders who serve in multiple jurisdictions respond to cultural food preferences and transcend the various types of food systems?
- What are the benefits of a structurally, economically, and geographically diverse food system?
- How can food retailers help to improve the local food environment in a post-pandemic world?
- What educative practices can help support agricultural production and procurement in the future?
- How can technologies drive more inclusive, culturally relevant food networks and food environments?

References

Alston, J. M., Sumner, D. A., & Vosti, S. A. (2008). Farm subsidies and obesity in the United States: National evidence and international comparisons. *Food Policy, 33*(6), 470–479. https://doi.org/10.1016/j.foodpol.2008.05.008

Bader, M. D., Purciel, M., Yousefzadeh, P., & Neckerman, K. M. (2010). Disparities in neighborhood food environments: Implications of measurement strategies. *Economic Geography, 86*(4), 409–430. https://doi.org/10.1111/j.1944-8287.2010.01084.x

Barrett, C. B. (2010). Measuring food insecurity. *Science, 327*(5967), 825–828. https://doi.org/10.1126/science.1182768

Bazerghi, C., McKay, F. H., & Dunn, M. (2016). The role of food banks in addressing food insecurity: A systematic review. *Journal of Community Health, 41*(4), 732–740. https://doi.org/10.1007/s10900-015-0147-5

Clay, L. A., Papas, M. A., Gill, K. B., & Abramson, D. M. (2018). Factors associated with continued food insecurity among households recovering from hurricane Katrina. *International Journal of Environmental Research and Public Health, 15*(8), 1647. https://doi.org/10.3390/ijerph15081647

Clay, L. A., & Ross, A. D. (2020). Factors associated with food insecurity following hurricane Harvey in Texas. *International Journal of Environmental Research and Public Health, 17*(3), 762. https://doi.org/10.3390/ijerph17030762

Dimitri, C., & Rogus, S. (2014). Food choices, food security, and food policy. *Journal of International Affairs, 67*(2), 19–31. https://www.jstor.org/stable/24461733

Farnese, P. L. (2010). Remembering the farmer in the agriculture policy and obesity debate. *Food & Drug Law Journal, 65*, 391. https://heinonline.org/HOL/P?h=hein.journals/foodlj65&i=403

Fernandez-Cornejo, J., Wechsler, S., Livingston, M., & Mitchell, L. (2014). Genetically engineered crops in the United States. United States Department of Agriculture (Report No. ERR-162). https://www.ers.usda.gov/publications/pub-details/?pubid=45182

Fitzpatrick, K. M., Harris, C., Drawve, G., & Willis, D. E. (2020). Assessing food insecurity among US adults during the COVID-19 pandemic. *Journal of Hunger & Environmental Nutrition, 16*, 1–18. https://doi.org/10.1080/19320248.2020.1830221

Helling, A., & Sawicki, D. S. (2010). Race and residential accessibility to shopping and services. *Housing Policy Debate, 14*(1–2), 69–101. https://doi.org/10.1080/10511482.2003.9521469

Hendriks, S. L. (2015). The food security continuum: A novel tool for understanding food insecurity as a range of experiences. *Food Security, 7*(3), 609–619. https://doi.org/10.1007/s12571-015-0457-6

Hilmers, A., Hilmers, D. C., & Dave, J. (2012). Neighborhood disparities in access to healthy foods and their effects on environmental justice. *American Journal of Public Health, 102*(9), 1644–1654. https://doi.org/10.2105/AJPH.2012.300865

Joassart-Marcelli, P., Rossiter, J. S., & Bosco, F. J. (2017). Ethnic markets and community food security in an urban "food desert". *Environment and Planning A: Economy and Space, 49*(7), 1642–1663. https://doi.org/10.1177/0308518X17700394

Kamarulzaman, Y., Veeck, A., Mumuni, A. G., Luqmani, M., & Quraeshi, Z. A. (2016). Religion, markets, and digital media: Seeking halal food in the US. *Journal of Macromarketing, 36*(4), 400–411. https://doi.org/10.1177/0276146715622243

Krebs-Smith, S. M., & Kantor, L. S. (2001). Choose a variety of fruits and vegetables daily: Understanding the complexities. *The Journal of Nutrition, 131*(2), 487S–501S. https://doi.org/10.1093/jn/131.2.487S

Larson, N. I., Story, M. T., & Nelson, M. C. (2009). Neighborhood environments: Disparities in access to healthy foods in the U.S. *American Journal of Preventive Medicine, 36*(1), 74–81. https://doi.org/10.1016/j.amepre.2008.09.025

Leddy, A. M., Weiser, S. D., Palar, K., & Seligman, H. (2020). A conceptual model for understanding the rapid COVID-19–related increase in food insecurity and its impact on health and healthcare. *The American Journal of Clinical Nutrition, 112*(5), 1162–1169. https://doi.org/10.1093/ajcn/nqaa226

Leonard, T., McKillop, C., Carson, J. A., & Shuval, K. (2014). Neighborhood effects on food consumption. *Journal of Behavioral and Experimental Economics, 51*, 99–113. https://doi.org/10.1016/j.socec.2014.04.002

Minow, M. (2003). *Partners, not rivals: Privatization and the public good.* Beacon Press.

Mirabitur, E., Peterson, K. E., Rathz, C., Matlen, S., & Kasper, N. (2016). Predictors of college student food security and fruit and vegetable intake differ by housing type. *Journal ofAmerican College Health, 64*(7), 555–564. https://doi.org/10.1080/07448481.2016.1192543

Moore, L. V., & Diez Roux, A. V. (2006). Associations of neighborhood characteristics with the location and type of food stores. *American Journal of Public Health, 96*(2), 325–331. https://doi.org/10.2105/AJPH.2004.058040

Morland, K., Wing, S., Roux, A. D., & Poole, C. (2002). Neighborhood characteristics associated with the location of food stores and food service places. *American Journal of Preventive Medicine, 22*(1), 23–29. https://doi.org/10.1016/S0749-3797(01)00403-2

Murthy, V. H. (2016). Food insecurity: A public health issue. *Public Health Reports, 131*(5), 655–657. https://doi.org/10.1177/0033354916664154

National Research Council. (2015). *A framework for assessing effects of the food system.* National Academies Press.

Neff, R. A., Palmer, A. M., McKenzie, S. E., & Lawrence, R. S. (2009). Food systems and public health disparities. *Journal of Hunger & Environmental Nutrition, 4*(3–4), 282–314. https://doi.org/10.1080/19320240903337041

Nesheim, M. C., Oria, M., & Yih, P. T. (2015). *A framework for assessing effects of the food system.* National Academies Press.

Pingali, P. (2010). Changing food systems in the developing world. In *Obesity Prevention* (pp. 511–520). Academic Press.

Raja, S., Ma, C., & Yadav, P. (2008). Beyond food deserts: Measuring and mapping racial disparities in neighborhood food environments. *Journal of Planning Education and Research, 27*(4), 469–482. https://doi.org/10.1177/0739456X08317461

Richterman, A., Franke, M. F., Constant, G., Jerome, G., Ternier, R., & Ivers, L. C. (2019). Food insecurity and self-reported cholera in Haitian households: An analysis of the 2012 demographic and health survey. *PLoS Neglected Tropical Diseases, 13*(1). https://doi.org/10.1371/journal.pntd.0007134

Senge, P. M., & Sterman, J. D. (1992). Systems thinking and organizational learning: Acting locally and thinking globally in the organization of the future. *European Journal of Operational Research, 59*(1), 137–150. https://doi.org/10.1016/0377-2217(92)90011-W

Shannon, K. L., Kim, B. F., McKenzie, S. E., & Lawrence, R. S. (2015). Food system policy, public health, and human rights in the United States. *Annual Review of Public Health, 36*, 151–173. https://doi.org/10.1146/annurev-publhealth-031914-122621

Tom, M. S., Fischbeck, P. S., & Hendrickson, C. T. (2016). Energy use, blue water footprint, and greenhouse gas emissions for current food consumption patterns and dietary recommendations in the US. *Environment Systems and Decisions, 36*(1), 92–103. https://doi.org/10.1007/s10669-015-9577-y

United States Department of Agriculture. (2018). Definitions of Food Security. https://www.ers.usda.gov/topics/food-nutrition-assistance/food-security-in-theus/definitions-of-food-security.aspx

Waters-Bailey, S., McGraw, M. S., & Barr, J. (2019). Serving the whole student: Addressing non-academic barriers facing rural community college students. *New Directions for Community Colleges, 2019*(187), 83–93. https://doi.org/10.1002/cc.20372

Sonya Sharififard, PhD has co-authored: New Horizons in Positive Leadership and Change (Springer 2020) and Workplace Spirituality and Fulfillment (Palgrave 2018). She has presented research at major international conferences. Her research focuses on advancing student success, workplace well-being, and law and policy in higher education.

25

Surviving During Post COVID-19 Pandemic: A Practical Guide to Plan for the Uncertain Times

Debra J. Dean

Introduction

Elliott, Swartz, and Herbane (2010) referred to the boiled frog syndrome in their book on Business Continuity Management. They explained that placing a frog into boiling water will cause it to jump out and save its own life. However, placing a frog in lukewarm water and slowly raising the temperature will not alert the frog to any harm. In essence, the frog placed directly in the boiling water quickly becomes uncomfortable, perceives danger, and takes action. However, slow changes in the temperature do not alert the frog to the impending danger. The frog may be slightly uncomfortable but will adjust and remain in the pot of hot water until they are too weak to take action.

This analogy of the frog to the human can be seen in many ways. In domestic violence situations, the spouse does not start the relationship with violence and anger. Instead, it gradually occurs and escalates over time causing the victim to adjust and make excuses for the behavior. In the workplace, there may be red flags that gradually pop up over time that if attended to early could avoid disasters, catastrophes, or mitigate risk. If those red flags that pop up gradually are not attended to, the people involved may not recognize the danger and they could be blindsided by the imminent danger. Creating a disaster preparation plan, a business continuity plan, or a strategic plan to ward off such dangers or be prepared for future events can save lives and save businesses, schools, and more.

In organizations, complacency with the status quo equals missed opportunities. If not vigilant, they fail to adapt and fall to their demise. Kodak film missed the chance to capitalize on the digital imaging revolution. It was not out of fear; however, but lack of competitive perception as Kodak invented the first digital camera in

D. J. Dean (✉)
Regent University, Colorado Springs, CO, USA
e-mail: debrdea@regent.edu

S. K. Dhiman, J. F. Marques (eds.), *Leadership After COVID-19*, Future of Business and Finance, https://doi.org/10.1007/978-3-030-84867-5_25

1975, but never marketed it. Another company that failed to adapt is Blackberry. They were once a noticeable and desirable communication competitor in the marketplace; however, their slow market reaction left their walkie talkie keyboard phones to boil with the frogs as smartphones became popular.

In 2020, it was easy to see where a company landed on the business continuity spectrum. Some companies found themselves scrambling when rapid change needed to take place as a result of the worldwide pandemic of COVID-19. If not prepared, businesses of all size lost precious time, money, and energy as they tried to figure things out. Without the proper planning in place, employees were furloughed, customers were frustrated, reputations were damaged, and companies failed to exist. It did not matter if it was the local grocery store that could not adapt to online ordering, the local restaurants that could not switch from in-seat dining to curbside pickup, or the United States Postal Service that announced it may shut down as the COVID-19 pandemic is financially crippling them (Pecorin, 2020).

On the other end of the spectrum, some companies had plans in place and were able to easily and quickly notice the need for change and adapt. For companies that had a well-thought-out plan in place, they may have caught flack for the years of preparing the plan; however, the cost of business continuity planning has never been more valued than now. Those companies and schools were able to pivot quickly to move to online learning or remote workplaces. They had the infrastructure in place to allow students and employees to connect virtually. All involved were well trained, documents were already in electronic formats, and policies and procedures were written to keep the business moving with little or no loss of time and money.

This chapter walks through a successful and ongoing business continuity planning strategy that is provided as a checks and balance opportunity for companies that "did this well" and as a planning guide for those that have yet to figure it out. In reality, every single company, school, and even household should consider the "what if" scenarios for possible disruptions.

Business Continuity Planning

Filipović, Krišto, and Podrug (2018) wrote of possibly the "oldest recognized continuity plan" as Noah building the Ark documented in the book of Genesis. Noah was told to build the Ark and was provided with specifics as to the expectations of materials to use (cypress wood) and size (300 cubits long, 50 cubits wide, 30 cubits high). Noah was to include a roof, leaving room below the roof, and a door to cover the upper, middle, and lower decks. The plan included who and what was to be included in the Ark. In modern times, we might call them essential personnel. If visiting the Ark Encounter in Williamstown, Kentucky it will be clear to see the level of detail that went into the Ark and the forethought of what was needed to survive for 40 days and nights in a boat that would encounter violent winds and rain. A similar approach is needed in modern times as we try to prepare for the worst and plan for the best.

In 1999, I had never heard of business continuity. However, I was young and eager to volunteer for almost any new project. It was March 11, 1999 and I had my first meeting for the Year 2000 (Y2K) Business Continuity Plan (BCP) plan. It was invigorating, creative, and a bit frightful all at the same time. Up until that point in my life, I had never considered the world not working as it had in the past. The fear with Y2K was that electronics might shut down, cars may not work, computers may break, phones may be unavailable, banking machines may breakdown, and anything that relied on computer programming could potentially faulter because the computers, up until that point in time, were programmed with 2-digit years instead of 4-digit years. The big question was, what would happen when the clock rolled from 12/31/99 to 01/01/00?

The creative brainstorming that continued throughout the year was impressive. Notice, this was a lengthy process. It was not one that happened overnight. We pondered what would happen if our cars did not work, how could we talk to one another, who were essential employees and how could we get them to work, and so much more. In the end, a large document was put together with phone trees for every employee, their address in case we needed to pick them up, lists of employees with vehicles that did not rely on electronics, and phone numbers of friends and families in different states in case we needed to bounce phones from state-to-state to try and contact one another. The BCP plan was distributed to every employee and they were to take a copy home with them.

After Y2K happened, the planning did not stop. Each year, several times a year, planning committees gathered to brainstorm new risks to the company and build on the existing strategic plan. It was a multi-national company and each geographical location had their own set of risks including natural disasters.

Having a BCP plan on paper is not enough. There must be annual training with key personnel. Each person must know if they are a day 1, day 2, or day 3 responder. And, they need to know where to go. At one point, a boiler exploded in the basement of the large building and employees knew where to meet and who to call right away. Other events occurred with hurricanes, blizzards, and monumental floods. With each year and each event, the BCP plan was strengthened as lessons learned were documented and the plan was altered as necessary. This role was not taken lightly. I was on the BCP committee and over the years my role changed as I promoted to different departments in the company. The one role that remained the same was that one person (sometimes more than one) was always at the helm and it was their job to manage the BCP plan. For many of the rest of us, it was a role we managed alongside our other tasks in customer service, operations, accounting, legal, etc. There must be someone with the job title and job description to manage the plan year after year, month after month, and day after day; especially when the plan is activated, and all eyes turn to them for direction.

BCP Plans: Getting Started

Burtles and Noakes-Fry (2016) wrote about getting started with the creation of the Business Continuity Plan. They explained that "by looking at the main roles in the typical organizational structure, you can see how individual actions in these roles are likely to change when the organization, or its activities, is threatened or disturbed" (p.14). In the early days of 1999, the main idea was to start brainstorming.

Identifying key personnel throughout the organization to attend workshops allowed a natural flow of ideas to take place. As one person thought about their work and the impact that may take place should an event occur, another person spoke to their concern for the expectations of their team. In reality, there is not a specific set of rules or formality that needs to take place to get started. The main idea is to start sooner rather than later. And, considering the fallout of 2020, the conversation can easily start with a reflection of what went well and what did not work well. The BCP plan should document the ways in which 2020 ran smoothly. Perhaps the employees were already set up with work from home capability. Or, perhaps students already knew how to log in to their virtual campus. Also, list the ways 2020 was not smooth and start to brainstorm ways to fix those disruptions for future events. In one legal firm, it was found that employees did not have a way to work from home, their files were all in paper, and employees literally and physically needed to be in the office. As a result, they lost at least 2 weeks of production time, encountered months of frustration, and furloughed many employees because the infrastructure and planning were not properly in place. Now, months after the initial work-from-home directive, employees are still battling with technology issues and pondering over how to file their documents and retrieve physical mail.

Business Disruption

There are many business disruption reasons to consider. At the same time, it is impossible to consider all possible scenarios. Who would have ever imagined a virus could be released from China in 2020 that would shut down the world and cause people to lose their jobs, schools to shut down, and millions of deaths. McDonough (2019) explained that causes could include business opportunities, economy, personnel and customer issues, legal and/or legislative regulation, technology, weather, and seasonality. This section of the chapter should help with brainstorming as you consider the "what if" scenarios. In other words, what if the building is shut down because of a fire, flood, or snowstorm? And, what if the phone lines and Internet go down because of a terrorist attack?

Pandemics

The COVID-19 pandemic is just one of many pandemics that have plagued the earth over the years; however, it is the biggest in our lifetime as it has had worldwide reach and impacted nearly every human on the planet. As of January 2021, more than 88 M people have died as a result of COVID-19. Prior to COVID-19, there were plenty of other pandemics that plagued the world, or parts of it. Since the 1918 flu, there have been many circumstances that caused disruption in the world. The top three flu pandemics were in 1918, 1957, and 1968 (Rogers, 2020). It is estimated that the 1918 pandemic caused an estimated 50 M deaths worldwide (Redfield, 2019a). The 1957 Asian flu pandemic resulted in an estimated 1–2 M deaths (Rogers, 2020). And, it is estimated that 1 M deaths resulted from the 1968 pandemic (Redfield, 2019b). When people die or are in fear of dying, work and school will usually not take priority. It is important to recognize this fear and help employees or students know that you empathize with them. We cannot expect our top performers to perform at all if they are concerned about their basic needs of food, water, safety, shelter.

In 2020, the effect of COVID-19 on businesses was devastating as many lost their business, most employees were forced to either work from home, be furloughed, or lose their jobs entirely. Essential business workers were identified as food service workers and grocery store staff. And, schools shut down or went virtual for the majority of the year. Such disruptions cannot be avoided; however, they can be planned for if planning takes place ahead of time. In an effort to help you make the best plan for the future, it is wise to seek advice from schools and businesses that did this well. Some schools already had their students, teachers, and staff trained to do school online. For some, it was no different from what they had done in the past. For some businesses, working from home was an option anyway and employees were already trained with the virtual private network (VPN) process. They were already equipped with the tools they needed to succeed. But it is challenging to take into account all possible interruptions that could happen in the future.

Natural Disasters

In addition to pandemics, natural disasters are on the rise and can disrupt the normal way of life. Natural disasters may include blizzards, cyclones, droughts, earthquakes, famine, floods, hurricanes, landslides, lightning, tornadoes, tsunamis, volcanoes, wildfires, winter storms, etc. The largest hurricane on record in the USA is the Great Galveston hurricane of 1900 where 6000–12,000 people lost their lives and more than 3600 buildings were lost (Little, 2017). According to Broach (2019), the costliest hurricane was in 2005 when Category 5 Hurricane Katrina breached levees causing more than $160.2B in damage.

Roos (2018) wrote of the "mind boggling destruction" from the 2004 tsunami in Thailand, Sri Lanka, and Indonesia. It was the day after Christmas when a 9.1 magnitude earthquake in the Indian Ocean caused the tsunami to rip through the sleepy coastal city killing an estimated 230,000 people. Oskin (2017) stated that the Japanese 9.0 earthquake and tsunami in 2011 caused an estimated $199B in damage and killed at least 15,894 people. It is considered the "most costly natural disaster ever" (Parry, 2017). Additionally, the earthquake and tsunami caused a nuclear meltdown at the Fukushima Daiichi Nuclear Power Plant, "the world's worst nuclear accident since Chernobyl" (Parry, 2017). The business continuity planning or disaster preparation aspect of Parry's article that caught my eye was of children having readily accessible hard plastic helmets in their locker at Okawa elementary school. This same event taught valuable lessons as Toyota was impacted greatly causing a ripple down effect to all of their suppliers worldwide.

If you are reading this and thinking "I'm Safe" because you don't live near a fault line or an ocean, think again. The 2020 Derecho "was the most costly thunderstorm disaster in U.S. history" (Henson, 2020). The storm appeared out of nowhere and is estimated to have damages at $7.5B, "higher than many hurricanes" (Henson, 2020). On August 10, 2020, the Derecho "at least 60 miles wide and 400 miles long"… "raced from Iowa to Indiana" (Henson, 2020). The estimated wind speed in Cedar Rapids was 140 mph (Kopelman, 2020). As a point of reference, a Category 4 hurricane is 130–156 mph and a Category 5 hurricane is more than 157 mph. From a disruption perspective, this storm has caused businesses and schools to shut down permanently or close temporarily for months. Chase, Murray, and Rynard (2020) warned of the destruction to those that had not seen it saying it is, "unimaginable." They wrote

> There are simply no words, photos or videos sufficient to describe the full extent of the carnage. A land hurricane. A bomb. An apocalypse. A 40-mile wide tornado. An artillery barrage. Not even those descriptions suffice as we simply haven't seen something like this before, we have no frame of reference. Local reporters have covered it extensively under impossible conditions, but unless you see it in person, it's impossible to fully visualize.

The National Centers for Environmental Information documents billion-dollar weather and climate disasters (Jacobs, 2020). Topping the list at $16.5B is the Western Wildfires that burned more than 10.2 million acres in 2020. Tornadoes in the Southeast, Ohio Valley, and Midwest caused an estimated $12.1B in damage in 2011. The California Freeze of 1990 cost an estimated $6.9B. Midwest Flooding in the summer of 1993 cost an estimated $38.1B. And, the US Drought in the Summer of 1988 cost an estimated $45B.

The East Coast Blizzard and Severe Weather of 1993 cost $10.1B (Jacobs, 2020). This storm is called the Storm of the Century as it impacted much of Canada and at least 26 US states. The largest snow accumulation was 60+ inches on Mt. LeConte. The Florida Panhandle reported "4" of snow. Snow was even seen in Jacksonville, Florida. The superstorm dropped 6–30 inches of snow in Kentucky, shut down interstates, and stranded motorists from Lexington Kentucky to the Tennessee and West Virginia borders. As precautions in 1993, workplaces told their employees they could stay in a hotel close to work and the company would pay for it in fear that the road conditions would be too treacherous to commute.

The following year, the 1994 snowstorm dropped nearly 16 inches on Louisville, Kentucky shutting down interstates, closing schools and businesses, and activating 4-wheel drive clubs to rescue people stranded throughout the state. The UPS hub estimated their loss at $110 M as their employees were unable to get to work for days (Glowicki, 2019). As a result of the 1994 snowstorm, snow removal plans were reviewed and additional funding was provided for snow removal efforts, something that had not been done since 1978.

Catastrophic Events

In addition to pandemics and natural disasters, catastrophic events have caused disruptions over the years too and planning for them in the future could mean life or death. Terrorist attacks, school shootings, and workplace violence have caused numerous deaths and disruptions in over the years. While it is nearly impossible to predict if and when something tragic like this will happen, it is something to consider with business continuity plans and strategic plans to primarily protect human life and secondly mitigate risk.

When relocating from one state to another, I found myself uneasy about the school security in our new location and voiced my concerns to the principal, superintendent, school board, and eventually the police department. The small town thought they were "fine" with their unlocked doors, lack of video monitoring, and office on the second floor. This school was "not okay" from my perspective as we had been in previous schools that were well prepared to mitigate the risk of school violence and school shootings. At one point, I asked our previous school to provide me with a copy of their emergency protocol so I could share. Unfortunately, years past and the school did not do anything. The final straw for me was when my daughter called with her friends huddled in a classroom saying there was a shooter in the building. I rushed to the school, entered the front door (unlocked), walked up the stairs (as children were walking freely through the hallways), and found my child and her friends. There was clearly no lack of urgency and no plan to keep the children safe. I was able to walk right in and get my child.

The following lists some, but unfortunately not all, of the terrorist attacks, mass shootings, and bombings in America. The list includes the 1949 Camden in New Jersey; 1966 University of Texas; 1975 Easter Sunday in Hamilton, Ohio; 1982 Wilkes-Barre, Pennsylvania; 1983 Wah Mee in Seattle, Washington; 1984 Palm Sunday in Brooklyn, New York; 1984 San Ysidro McDonalds in California; 1986 Edmond Post Office in Oklahoma; 1991 Luby's in Kileen, Texas; 1995 Oklahoma City Federal Building; 1996 Atlanta Olympics; 1999 Atlanta; 1999 Columbine High School; 2001 terrorist attacks of September 11th; 2005 Red Lake Senior High School; 2006 West Nickel Mines School; 2007 Virginia Tech; 2009 Binghamton; 2009 Fort Hood; 2009 Geneva County; 2012 Aurora Theater; 2012 Sandy Hook Elementary School; 2012 Oikos University; 2013 Washington Navy Yard; 2013 Santa Monica College; 2014 Marysville Pilchuck High School; 2015 Umpqua Community College; 2015 San Bernardino; 2016 Orlando nightclub; 2017 Sutherland Springs Church; 2018 Pittsburgh Synagogue; 2018 Stoneman Douglas High School; 2018 Thousand Oaks; 2019 El Paso Walmart; 2019 STEM School Highlands Ranch in Colorado; and 2019 Virginia Beach.

An exhaustive list could provide a committee with information of what has happened in history so the BCP committee could prepare for as many scenarios as possible. For example, in 1989, Joseph Wesbecker walked into his former workplace and killed eight people, injuring 13 others (Garr and Muhammad, 2019). And, Rosenblatt (2018) wrote of the deadliest shooting in modern US history as the 2017 Las Vegas shooting that killed 60 and wounded 867 people at the Jason Aldean concert. These acts of violence are different, yet similar. One was in a workplace and the other at a concert. A committee charged with preventing such tragedies can come up with plans to prevent such disasters and plans to act if something happens.

Strategic Planning

It may appear overwhelming to consider all of the possible disruptions that could occur; however, without a plan things could go from bad to worse very quickly. Parry (2017) wrote of the "generic wording of the template" referring to the Educational Plan that was to provide instructions on emergency situations. The plan was vague and left the readers puzzled. They needed more clarity about what to do in specific situations. It is essential to have a plan; however, the plan should be easy to access, easy to read, easy to comprehend, and easy to implement quickly. Strategically planning for the future can make the difference between life or death, profit or loss, and a thriving business or shutting down and closing the doors forever.

Leadership and Followership Theory

There are a plethora of leadership theories including, but not limited to, Authentic Leadership Theory, Charismatic Leadership Theory, Servant Leadership Theory, Situational Leadership Theory, Spiritual Leadership Theory, Transactional Leadership Theory, and Transformational Leadership Theory. To date, no one theory of leadership has been deemed better or worse at dealing with business continuity planning, disaster management, or recovery efforts. One can assume that the laissez-faire approach would not be best and in talking with emergency room personnel about this topic, some think an autocratic or direct approach is necessary to ensure clear communication and directives are known and easy to understand.

Behera (2016) documented that "no theory so far has been able to fully fit the behaviors required for emergency management leadership" and wrote that "leadership is key to response efforts at a time when responders are faced with incomplete information, poor communications, and high levels of stress and fatigue." In her study of the United States Coast Guard, she found that the four main principles of authentic leadership theory could extend to emergency preparation and response. Those principles include balanced processing, relational transparency, internalized moral perspective, and self-awareness (Behera, 2016, p. 125). Although a specific theory has not yet been matched as the best predictive style, it is important to note that leaders must take action to develop the BCP plan, ensure the plan is managed at least annually, if not quarterly or monthly, and safeguard their human capital as best possible. With that in mind, perhaps a leadership style or leadership theory is not what is needed so much as a leader—period. In other words, any person can stand up and say we need a plan. Any person can make the plan happen. They do not even need the formal title of leader.

Followership theory is a newer effort; whereas leadership theory has been around much longer. King (1990) wrote that "leader" was a term noted in the 1300s, the word "leadership" emerged in the 1700s, and research on the topic began in the twentieth century. Uhl-Bien, Riggio, Lowe, and Carsten (2014) explain that without followers, there would be no need for leaders; however, "followers are often left out of the leadership research equation" (p. 83). The pioneers of followership theory include Kelley (1992), Chaleff (1997), and Kellerman (2008). Each scholar developed their own followership types. Kelley has five including (a) the sheep, (b) the yes-people, (c) the alienated, (d) the pragmatics, and (e) the star followers. Chaleff uses four quadrants of support including (a) Partner: high support, high challenge; (b) Implementer: high support, low challenge; (c) Individualist: low support, high challenge; and (d) Resource: low support, low challenge. And, Kellerman's five types of followership are (a) isolate, (b) bystander, (c) participant, (d) activist, and (e) diehard. With any strategic plan such as a crisis management plan, disaster recovery plan, or business continuity plan leaders and followers are needed. The key to success is that all parties involved know what the expectations are, and they have a written plan that is easily accessible and easy to understand and implement.

When developing a plan, albeit strategic for the sake of making money or business continuity for the sake of mitigating risk, leaders and followers go hand-in-hand. It is essential that the two work together to ensure the plan is Specific, Measurable, Attainable, Relevant, and Timebound (SMART). Moynihan (2012) described the "Failure of Initiative" pertaining to Hurricane Katrina and the slow response time. As the hurricane, and all that comes with it such as winds, rain, storm surges, and debris, pounded the Gulf Coast, the Department of Defense (DOD) was slow to respond because of all the red tape they, themselves, had created in the process. Moynihan presented the case of Hurricane Katrina where red tape reduced performance and organizational culture enhances effectiveness. In learning from this catastrophe, current and future business continuity plans should include a culture of preparedness and common sense that includes input from leaders and followers alike.

Change Management

Change management often refers to changes in the organization such as downsizing, offshoring, or mergers and acquisitions. Those events definitely require change as the employees are often left with managing the day-to-day business in a somewhat different, possibly even a chaotic state. The same is true with sudden disasters or pandemics as the day-to-day routine is interrupted and things must change. In 2020, human resources and technology services departments probably felt more demand in their services as change was happening throughout the organization. Employees and students managed change as they were accustomed to waking up, getting ready for their day, commuting somewhere, and interacting with people face-to-face. Instead, their routine changed, and they were left with waking up, walking to their computer, and turning it on to maybe see someone virtually on occasion. In addition to their work or school routine that had previously been blocked off by their homelife, they now integrate working, helping children with homeschool, and managing the daily affairs in one place instead of leaving and compartmentalizing their activities. All of this requires change and adaptation to a different way of life.

Lewin developed the Change Management Model with three steps: unfreezing, changing, and refreezing. Cummings, Bridgman, and Brown (2015) examined Lewin's 1947 model and wrote of the "fundamental assumptions underlying *any* change in a human system" (p. 34). While the concern of some over Lewin and the development of the simple three step change model is debatable, the premise remains that the model is ingenious as it simply demonstrates change in three steps and is considered the foundation of all change theories (Cummings, et al., 2015).

One such theory is by Myer and Moore (2006). Their Crisis in Context Theory (CCT) proposes that the impact of change felt by an individual or a group of people will depend on their proximity to the event/situation, the individual and social reactions to the event/situation, the relationship one has to the event/situation, and the changes formed by the event/situation. This can be seen with the aftermath of such events. In 2020, many people suffered greatly because of the virus itself, the loss of a loved one, the loss of a job, or the disruption to their life in one way or another. For others, 2020 was a blessing as they had been wanting to spend more time at home anyway. As you can see, the same event/situation can trigger responses in people differently depending on their circumstances. This offers a great reminder for us to not assume that all people are okay because we are okay, or that all people are not okay because we are not okay. As a leader, it is critical to check on your followers to make sure they are adapting well and that their basic needs are met.

Crisis Management

Zhong and Pheng Low (2009) observed the increase in crisis incidents along with their severity and restated that a "crisis can happen to any organization" (p. 271). With this in mind, the need for preparation is more important now than in previous decades of our lifetime. Zhong and Pheng Low (2009) documented ways in which an organization may experience crisis as the threat could be external, such as a natural disaster or internal, such as a structural change. The emphasis on crisis management preparation involves the role of communication. Zhong and Pheng Low (2009) note that in a crisis, people need to consider the "short decision time, stress, complexity and uncertainty, immediate and appropriate communication" that will directly impact the affect and recovery from the crisis.

The phrases may be similar, but different. We may call it business continuity planning, disaster management planning, strategic planning, crisis management, or something else, but the end result should be the same. The goal is to reduce risk and take care of people first. Without people, the business will not matter. It is critical to take the time sooner, rather than later, to establish a plan, revisit the plan if there is already one written, and update the plan to make sure it is Specific, Measurable, Attainable, Relevant, and Timebound (SMART). The plan should be accessible and easy to understand. After all, when the plan is needed, emotions will be high, fear and uncertainty will be high, and stress levels will be high. The plan should address those concerns and be easy.

Social Responsibility

Corporate social responsibility (CSR) is defined as "actions that appear to further some social good, beyond the interests of the firm and that which is required by law" (McWilliams and Siegel, 2001). The corporate aspect applies to business. Thus, corporate social responsibility was seen in 2020 when schools quickly pivoted to provide meals for students that would otherwise go hungry without their school lunch. We also saw where some teachers went above and beyond to meet their students at home and show them how to do a math problem through the protection of their glass window or door. And, we saw where some business leaders provided their employees with basic needs such as milk, bread, eggs, and even toilet paper. These actions went above and beyond the normal business regimen to care for the employees; to love people.

Outside of the workplace and schools, we saw where countless volunteers provided food and other basic necessities to families and individuals in need. And, where groups collected offerings to provide personal protection equipment (PPE) and support for first responders. Overall, the idea of social responsibility is that we, as human beings, do good deeds. It is the actions of doing unto others as you would like to have them do unto you; the Golden Rule.

Chapter Takeaways

The main takeaway from this chapter is to have a business continuity plan sooner rather than later. If you have one, update it on a routine basis to make sure it is up-to-date, accessible, and easy to implement. With this in mind the following takeaways are proposed:

1. Every person should have a strategic continuity, crisis management, or disaster recovery plan. Families can benefit from such a plan as they will need to know how to get ahold of people in case of an emergency. They will need to know what to do and where to go in the event of certain circumstances. In the event of the Christmas 2020 Nashville bombing outside of the AT&T building, families in many states found it difficult or impossible to use the Internet or cellphones to connect with one another. Ask yourself, what the plan is if this situation happens again and what the plan is if other situations happen that will impact you as an individual, your family, your business, and your community.
2. Once you have a plan in place, consider if the plan is Specific, Measurable, Attainable, Relevant, and Timebound (SMART). The goal is to have enough information in the plan, so it is not confusing and to make it easy to implement.
3. Once the plan is in place, ensure each person has a copy of the plan in a place they will be able to access it. An electronic version is great; however, a paper copy is also needed in case electronic devices are not working. Distribute the plan and put reminders on the calendar to update the plan at least annually, if not quarterly or monthly.
4. Once the plan is written and distributed, schedule a mock drill. This is similar to a fire drill you might have at work or at school. Assume an emergency has

occurred and activate the plan to see if the parties involved can (a) find the plan, (b) know how to read it and implement it, and (c) respond accordingly. After the drill, bring all parties together to discuss the strengths, weaknesses, opportunities, and threats (SWOT) of the plan. Then, update the plan as necessary.

5. Schedule time on the calendar to have mock drills at least annually, if not quarterly or monthly. This is important to ensure all essential personnel know what is expected of them. And, it gives you a chance to re-evaluate the plan and know if the right people are involved and if additional items should be added or updated in the plan.

Reflective Questions

The big question to ask is "what if." By continually asking this question to those around you, a culture of preparedness will begin. Cultivate this culture with ongoing questions of "what if" and continuously update your BCP plan accordingly. The following questions will help you get started:

1. Do we have a crisis management plan, disaster recovery plan, or business continuity plan? If so, where is it and when was the last time it was updated or practiced?
2. If we do not have a crisis management plan, disaster recovery plan, or business continuity plan when will we schedule time to bring the right people together to develop such a plan (why not sooner rather than later)?
3. What disruption will we start with first? It is not possible to account for all probable disruptions; however, start with one and move forward. A good one to start with may be reflection of how you and your team responded to the COVID-19 pandemic, then review some of the other crises listed in this chapter to consider how you would respond to natural disasters and catastrophic events.
4. Who should be involved in the planning process? Remember to include members of the team from various viewpoints. More often than not, senior level leaders make plans that are not practical for other employees to follow. Make sure all employees have a chance to speak into the plan.
5. How will we strategically manage the plan going forward? Will one person be in charge to make sure it is updated on a routine basis at least annually, if not quarterly or monthly. When, where, and how often will the mock drills happen?
6. How will we define success?

References

Behera, J. (2016). *Authentic leadership in disaster: Leader and employee viewpoints in disaster preparation and response* (Order No. 10252862). Available from ProQuest Central; ProQuest Dissertations & Theses Global; ProQuest One Academic. (1873089698). http://eres.regent.edu/login?url=https://www-proquest-com.ezproxy.regent.edu/dissertations-theses/authentic-leadership-disaster-leader-employee/docview/1873089698/se-2?accountid=13479

Broach, D. (2019). *The most expensive hurricanes in U.S. history: Where do the 2018 storms rank?* https://www.nola.com/news/weather/article_99ac151d-aa22-57a9-802e-45413efc9c1c.html

Burtles, J., & Noakes-Fry, K. (2016). *The manager's guide to business continuity exercises: Testing your plan*. Rothstein Associates, Incorporated.

Chaleff, I. (1997). The courageous follower: Standing up to and for our leaders. *NASSP Bulletin, 81*(586), 119–119. https://doi.org/10.1177/019263659708158616

Chase, R., Murray, I., & Rynard, P. (2020). *It's even worse than you think in cedar rapids*. https://iowastartingline.com/2020/08/16/cedar-rapids-is-even-worse-than-you-think/

Cummings, S., Bridgman, T., & Brown, K. G. (2015). Unfreezing change as three steps: Rethinking Kurt Lewin's legacy for change management. *Human Relations, 69*(1), 33–60. https://doi.org/10.1177/0018726715577707

Elliott, D., Swartz, E., & Herbane, B. (2010). *Business continuity management: A crisis management approach*. Routledge. https://doi.org/10.4324/9780203866337

Filipović, D., Krišto, M., & Podrug, N. (2018). Impact of crisis situations on development of business continuity management in Croatia. *Management (Split, Croatia), 23*(1), 99–122. https://doi.org/10.30924/mjcmi/2018.23.1.99

Garr, R., & Muhammad, L. (2019). *Standard Gravure remembered: Here are all the victims from the 1989 mass shooting*. https://www.courier-journal.com/in-depth/news/local/2019/09/12/louisvilles-standard-gravure-shooting-anniversary-all-victims/2284348001/

Glowicki, M. (2019, January 16). *The storm of 1994: Here's how the blizzard led to better snow response*. https://www.courier-journal.com/story/news/local/2019/01/16/kentucky-1994-blizzard-storm-led-better-snow-response/2594574002/

Henson, B. (2020). *Iowa derecho in August was most costly thunderstorm disaster in U.S. history*. https://www.washingtonpost.com/weather/2020/10/17/iowa-derecho-damage-cost/

Jacobs, N. (2020). *Billion-dollar weather and climate disasters: Events*. https://www.ncdc.noaa.gov/billions/events/US/1980-2020

Kellerman, B. (2008). *Followership: How followers are creating change and changing leaders*. Harvard Business School Press.

Kelley, R. (1992). *The power of followership. How to create leaders people want to follow, and followers who lead themselves*. Doubleday/Currency.

King, A. (1990). Evolution of leadership theory. *Vikalpa: The Journal for Decision Makers, 15*(2), 43–56. https://doi.org/10.1177/0256090919900205

Kopelman, R. (2020). *Top wind speeds in Iowa Derecho estimated at 140 mph in Cedar Rapids*. https://cbs2iowa.com/news/local/top-wind-speeds-in-iowa-derecho-estimated-at-140-mph-in-cedar-rapids

Little, B. (2017). *How the Galveston hurricane of 1900 became the deadliest U.S. natural disaster*. https://www.history.com/news/how-the-galveston-hurricane-of-1900-became-the-deadliest-u-sb-natural-disaster

McDonough, D. (2019). *Business Disruption & Preparation for Long-term Success*. CCG. https://www.commercialcreditgroup.com/blog/business-disruption

McWilliams, A., & Siegel, D. (2001). Corporate social responsibility: A theory of the firm perspective. *The Academy of Management Review, 26*(1), 117–127. https://doi.org/10.2307/259398

Moynihan, D. P. (2012). A theory of culture-switching: Leadership and red-tape during hurricane katrina. *Public Administration (London), 90*(4), 851–868. https://doi.org/10.1111/j.1467-9299.2011.02017.x

Myer, R. A., & Moore, H. B. (2006). Crisis in context theory: An ecological model. *Journal of Counseling and Development, 84*(2), 139–147. https://doi.org/10.1002/j.1556-6678.2006.tb00389.x

Oskin, B. (2017). *Japan earthquake & tsunami of 2011: Facts and information*. https://www.livescience.com/39110-japan-2011-earthquake-tsunami-facts.html

Parry, R. (2017). *The school beneath the wave: The unimaginable tragedy of Japan's tsunami*. https://www.theguardian.com/world/2017/aug/24/the-school-beneath-the-wave-the-unimaginable-tragedy-of-japans-tsunami

Pecorin, A. (2020). Postal service says it's going broke due to pandemic. In *Trump flatly opposes emergency aid*. https://abcnews.go.com/Politics/postal-service-broke-due-pandemic-trump-flatly-opposes/story?id=70119153

Redfield, R. (2019a). *1918 Pandemic (H1N1 virus).* https://www.cdc.gov/flu/pandemic-resources/1918-pandemic-h1n1.html
Redfield, R. (2019b). *1968 Pandemic (H3N2 virus).* https://www.cdc.gov/flu/pandemic-resources/1968-pandemic.html#:~:text=It%20was%20first%20noted%20in,a%20seasonal%20influenza%20A%20virus.
Rogers, K. (2020). 1957 flu pandemic. https://www.britannica.com/event/1957-flu-pandemic
Roos, D. (2018, October 02). *The 2004 Tsunami wiped away towns with 'Mind-Boggling' destruction.* https://www.history.com/news/deadliest-tsunami-2004-indian-ocean
Rosenblatt, K. (2018). *Las Vegas shooting is deadliest in modern U.S. history.* https://www.nbcnews.com/storyline/las-vegas-shooting/las-vegas-shooting-deadliest-modern-u-s-history-n806486
Uhl-Bien, M., Riggio, R. E., Lowe, K. B., & Carsten, M. K. (2014). Followership theory: A review and research agenda. *The Leadership Quarterly, 25*(1), 83–104. https://doi.org/10.1016/j.leaqua.2013.11.007
Zhong, Y., & Pheng Low, S. (2009). Managing crisis response communication in construction projects - from a complexity perspective. *Disaster Prevention and Management, 18*(3), 270–282. https://doi.org/10.1108/09653560910965637

Debra J. Dean is an adjunct professor at Regent University. She has 25+ years of experience in corporate with responsibilities including, but not limited to, business continuity plans, business transformation, quality control, and operations excellence. She is a published researcher and sought-after speaker with topics related to faith at work, followership, organizational metaphors, respectful pluralism, and social responsibility. She holds a Ph.D. in organizational leadership from Regent University. Dean holds many titles including the 2020 Woman of Influence, Most Influential Business Consultancy CEO, Operational Excellence Leader of the Year, and Top Female Leader of the Year.

Towards Developing a Framework of Emergency Leadership

26

Mohammed Aboramadan and Yasir Mansoor Kundi

Introduction

A wide range of leadership and management skills are required to deal with both emergencies and major catastrophic events. Emergency management seek to formulate policy and ensure programs are in place in order to mitigate vulnerability, and loss of lives and property when disasters occur, as well as to promote environmental protection and inter-agency coordination (McEntire & Dawson, 2007). Leadership can be honed and promoted by dealing with emergencies and crises, as a leader is required to react to and effectively manage all the risks and uncertainties that crises bring in their wake and, ultimately, to reinstate normality (Kearns et al., 2019). Hence, despite the acknowledged damage that crises can cause, they also present opportunity, in that they can be leveraged by leaders to reform structural and policy landscapes.

We are currently navigating our way through an unprecedented crisis, namely the COVID-19 pandemic (Wilson, 2020). Not only has COVID-19 struck with greater force than any pandemic since the Spanish Flu of the early 20th century, but it is striking a world characterized by a greater degree of interconnection than ever seen in human history. In any public health crisis, including the present one, effective

The original version of this chapter was revised. The correction to this chapter is available at https://doi.org/10.1007/978-3-030-84867-5_33

M. Aboramadan (✉)
Department of Economics, University of Insubria, Varese, Italy
e-mail: mohammed.aboramadan@uninsubria.it

Y. M. Kundi
Institute of Business Administration (IBA) Karachi, Karachi, Pakistan
e-mail: ymkundi@iba.edu.pk

S. K. Dhiman, J. F. Marques (eds.), *Leadership After COVID-19*, Future of Business and Finance, https://doi.org/10.1007/978-3-030-84867-5_26

leadership is crucial. In a fast-moving crisis environment, swift and high-quality decision-making is vital, whatever the challenges to be met (Hannah et al., 2010; Pearson & Clair, 1998). Moreover, assessments of rapidly changing data and decisions taken accordingly must be owned by all stakeholders in the crisis response, from the managers of a command center through personnel on the ground (Gorge, 2006; Mitroff, 2004).

Generally speaking, multiple scholars have emphasized the key role of leadership in managing emergencies (Demiroz & Kapucu, 2012; Kapucu & Van Wart, 2008; Rubin, 1985; Waugh & Streib, 2006). However, stating that leaders' matter, on the one hand, and offering two-dimensional portraits of them, on the other, are of little help in understanding the vital question of how real people lead in the management of crises and the enormous range of variables which impact their efficacy (Trainor & Velotti, 2013). Given the expanding remit of emergency management, there is a strong need to review and discuss how leaders should lead in emergency times.

Most research on emergency leadership is mixed (e.g., Hannah et al., 2009, 2010; Mitroff & Alpaslan, 2003; Sweeny, 2008; Wilson, 2020), focusing on certain single trait such as leaders' efficacy (Hadley et al., 2011), or comprises case studies of one-off crisis events (Caulfield, 2018; Littlefield & Quenette, 2007). Examples of case studies of this type are Vaughan's (1996) and Bateman's (2008) examinations of leadership in the face of the Challenger explosion and during the Iraq war, respectively. Other case studies were on crisis leadership during the Katerina hurricane (Littlefield & Quenette, 2007) and pandemic leadership in New Zealand (Wilson, 2020). A small number of researchers have also conducted crisis studies either in the field (e.g., Pillai & Meindl, 1998) or the laboratory (e.g., Halverson et al., 2004; Hunt et al., 1999). On another note, research has generally stressed the value of charisma and the transformational leader beloved of fiction (e.g., Halverson et al., 2004; Pearson & Clair, 1998), while few studies have drilled down into the detail of what makes an effective leader in the context of emergency events (e.g., Dückers et al., 2017; Wilson, 2020; Sweeny, 2008; Wooten & James, 2008).

Instead, we need to examine how should leadership operates throughout an emergency management process to propose a framework which can be empirically tested and utilized for future research. Thereafter, we must ensure a particular focus on the important but less glamorous dimensions of leadership which the mass media—and sometimes academic studies—do not portray, including communication and the ability to think strategically, as well as a flexible but vital toolkit comprising rapid but thorough data assessment, decision-making, sense-making, and creativity skills (Boin et al., 2005; Hershkovich et al., 2016; Wilson, 2020).

Moreover, although the value of effective leaders in times of crisis is well understood and documented, the literature offers limited numbers of operational metric or a roadmap to explain leaders' ability to assess information and make effective decisions in an emergency context (Tourish, 2020). Therefore, the aim of the current study is to devise and propose an assessment tool to enhance our ability to recognize, train, and make use of current and potential leaders who may be effective decision-makers in emergency settings.

Emergency and Crisis Situations

A crisis has been defined as a significant risk to the social system's basic institutions or fundamental principles and standards that demand crucial decisions under time constraint and exceedingly unpredictable circumstances (Rosenthal et al., 1989). Crisis leaders must overcome obstacles under conditions of severe stress, including: understanding the crisis; making decisions quickly despite insufficient and scattered information; communicating effectively; and sharing power and authority (Rosenthal et al., 1989)

Five basic characteristics underpin the concept of emergency management (Farazmand, 2007). First, responders must reject anything already known; second, they must be prepared and ready for constant change; third, for events to be characterized as in the need of "emergency management," certain preconditions must be fulfilled; fourth, the knowledge, abilities, and mindsets required fall outside the competence of most personnel involved in the fields of administration and governance; and fifth, to be successful, there must be no limit on the resources on which emergency management can draw and it must be led by an outstanding but disciplined leadership entity (Farazmand, 2007).

On another hand, Boin et al. (2016) have highlighted a set of tasks to be focused on in order to successfully manage a crisis. These are sensemaking, decision-making, coordination, making a meaning, account giving, and learning. These tasks should go in harmony in order to manage a crisis in an effective manner. Sensemaking is related to diagnosing a crisis situation in an adequate manner (Dückers et al., 2017); decision-making is about identifying crucial factors which can help the leader to decide at the strategic levels (Dückers et al., 2017); coordination is a task of gathering multiple stakeholders to act in a network or system pattern during the crisis (Boin & Bynander, 2015) and allocating the limited resources; making a meaning includes that the leader provides an explanation of the crisis, consequences, response, and the roles which should be played by different stakeholders; account giving refers to assuming responsibility (Dückers et al., 2017); and learning is focused on critically evaluating the stakeholders' role in a crisis and draw useful conclusions during and after a crisis to ensure better future performance (Smith & Elliott, 2007; Stern, 1997).

A Review of Emergency Leadership Skills

Today's leaders must be perceived as legitimate by the people they command and must have their trust, otherwise the system will not operate and chaotic, even anarchic, outcomes will ensue, with long-term and wide-ranging consequences (Bhaduri, 2019; Bowers et al., 2017). They must have the skills and the personality traits necessary to take effective command to ensure that all actors effectively carry out their part in coordinated response efforts. In administrative terms, leadership must be exercised not only publicly and during the active response phase but also during the backstage operations to ensure effective mitigation, preparedness, and recovery (Kapucu & Van Wart, 2008; Wilson, 2020).

Although existing emergency leadership studies predominantly focus on how emergencies produce charismatic or transformational leaders, and the benefits such people bring (e.g., Bass, 1998; Halverson et al., 2004), Aguilera (1990) suggests that effective crisis resolution can be more prosaically framed as a sequence of decisions taken and judgments made.

On top of the need to identify, collect, and evaluate data, both theoretical (e.g., Boin et al., 2005) and empirical research (Hale et al., 2006; Mintzberg et al., 1976) have identified decision-making as a crucial leadership task within crisis management (Aguilera, 1990; Smart & Vertinsky, 1977; Wooten & James, 2008). To make accurate and effective decisions during a crisis, leaders must elicit and consider all possible modes of response, evaluate them, and recommend actions accordingly (Mintzberg et al., 1976; Sweeny, 2008).

When responding to an extreme crisis event, collecting and analyzing data on number of casualties, and extent and type of damage, is fundamental because leaders will take decisions on how to distribute personnel and other resources accordingly. Hence, the skills to assess data, make swift, informed decisions, and think divergently also lie at the heart of effective leadership in times of crisis (Boin et al., 2005; Kearns et al., 2019; Klann, 2003; Useem et al., 2005; Wooten & James, 2008).

Fiedler (2002) has also identified key variables in leader–follower interactions in crisis situations. Fiedler's (2002) important finding was that the value of a leader's experience rests on their ability to communicate with their followers. Moreover, the ability of leaders to perform higher cognitive tasks, such as decision-making and judgment is a predictor of effective leadership in stressful situations (Fiedler, 2002).

On another note, leaders may be more confident about their ability to make good judgments and decisions in challenging circumstances if they feel they can draw on a record of previous behaviors and experiences demonstrating a high level of intelligence (Anderson et al., 2008). Therefore, it has been argued that training simulations offer an environment in which individuals can control several situational variables and therefore are more likely to identify direct relationships between the accuracy of decisions taken by leaders during crisis management and their efficacy as leaders (Hadley et al., 2011).

In the same line of inquiry, the ability to think creatively and solve problems flexibly, according to situational criteria, largely rests on an aptitude for divergent thinking (Gibson et al., 2009; Mumford et al., 1998) and is very much needed in handling emergencies (Anderson, 2018). An individual capable of divergent thinking will generate many alternative solutions to a given problem (Gibson et al., 2009; Hadley et al., 2011; Mumford et al., 1998). People who have a history of divergent thinking are likely to be confident in their ability to transfer the skills which underpin on the fluid and difficult context of crisis management.

Successful emergency leaders must carry out certain key tasks following the assertions of Boin et al. (2005). Firstly, they must be constantly on the alert for potential crises and ensure everything necessary is done in the preparation phase to mitigate the risk that will occur. Secondly, they must be willing to accept responsibility for taking decisions and persuading their followers to accept them. Next, they must continually motivate and inspire followers, maintain group morale, and ensure everyone is willing to work the best of their ability toward the same goal, as well as prepare them practically and psychologically to accept the outcome, achieve closure, and leave the crisis behind. Lastly, the leader must be able to critically assess every stage of a situation and draw lessons about how future response efforts can benefit from failures and successes.

Other studies of emergency management indicate that transformational leadership characteristics such as self-confidence and decisiveness are valuable in achieving adaptation through collaboration (Waugh & Streib, 2006; Wise, 2006). Others (see. Caro, 2015, 2016a, b; Karaca et al., 2012; Kapucu & Van Wart, 2006, 2008; Zhang et al., 2012) have identified effectiveness of transformational leadership in managing emergencies. In addition to the large focus on transformational leadership, attention has been paid also to the servant leadership (Wankhade et al., 2015). Despite these studies, we focus instead on a roadmap to emergency leadership in managing emergencies and crisis situations instead of focusing on a single trait or a single leadership style. Instead of focusing on the leadership style, we shed light on what leaders need to do in an emergency situation.

Toward a Framework of Emergency Leadership

Component 1: Early Recognition of the Problem

The starting point of effective emergency management is that all stakeholders acknowledge that a threat has arisen which demands urgent attention (Anderson, 2018; Wilson, 2020). In a crisis situation, leaders and managers need to determine what is the crisis and how to define the conditions of the crisis (Deitchman, 2013; Mikušová & Horváthová, 2019). In reality, many leaders don't have the tools to overcome the complexity of a crisis situation (Ansell & Boin, 2019). Boin et al.

(2013) have identified problem recognition as the early step in dealing with a crisis. In fact, we argue that early recognition of the crisis is half the solution to manage it. In a crisis situation, where there is no recognition of the problem, conflicts, lack of trust, and intolerance with mistakes are going to be consequences with the absence of the early recognition of the problem. Given the previous discussion, the following can be advanced:

In an emergency situation, leaders need to early recognize the crisis and identify processes of dealing with uncertainty.

Component 2: Operating with Clear Vision and Objectives

In crisis times, leaders must have the flexibility to undertake more strategic thinking, leverage institutional norms and knowhow, and develop a collective vision and goals (Hershkovich et al., 2016; Mikušová & Horváthová, 2019). All leaders need to make an active contribution to the operation, direction, and objectives of the employing organization (Boin & Renaud, 2013). When emergencies arise, leaders should be able to automatically recall organizational norms and values and utilize the necessary mindset and skills to achieve them (Mikušová & Horváthová, 2019; Kearns et al., 2019). Leaders and individuals who can call on a clear vision and deeply-held values are better prepared to behave in a better way even when lives are in imminent danger, for example, during extreme weather events, pandemics, terrorist attacks, or wars (Hershkovich et al., 2016). Therefore, we posit the following:

In an emergency situation, leaders need to operate according to a clear vision and set out clear objectives.

Component 3: Thinking and Acting Strategically

One vital element of emergency leadership is the creation and implementation of strategic planning (Hershkovich et al., 2016). By their nature, emergency events tend to occur in problematic environments in which allocating scarce resources is key to success, particularly during the response phase (Deitchman, 2013; Hick et al., 2012; Klann, 2003; Hershkovich et al., 2016). The process of planning must adhere to three values: It should be continuous, integrative, and adaptable (Hershkovich et al., 2016). In addition to the strategic level, emergency management leaders must able to act at the operational level (Boin & Renaud, 2013). These roles may include organizational restructuring and applying creativity in the search for solutions (Anderson, 2018; Hershkovich et al., 2016; Kearns et al., 2019). Hence, the following is proposed:

In an emergency situation, leaders need to act strategically and undertake planning which is creative, flexible, and integrative.

Component 4: Making Innovative Decisions

Crisis management is often conceptualized as the ability to make accurate and effective decisions in circumstances of extreme stress and confusion, and this is clearly a vital element of the role at strategic level (Boin et al., 2013). Researchers generally agree that emergency leaders must focus on decision making (Boin et al., 2005; Hershkovich et al., 2016). Previous research has identified the role of decision-making in emergency management (Boin et al., 2013; Hale et al., 2006; Bakker et al., 2019). Decision-making during a crisis environment needs to encourage group-thinking, creativity, and finding innovative techniques instead of the classical ones (Schraagen & van de Ven, 2008). Furthermore, the role of involving employees is of utmost attention during crisis situations as this will help in generating feedback and innovative solutions. Therefore, a robust innovative-oriented decision-making needs to be implemented during crisis times. Based on the above, we propose the following:

In an emergency situation, leaders need to follow innovative decision-making and involve followers in decision making.

Component 5: Ethics-Based Decision-Making

Emergency management calls on both leaders and individuals to take decisions of multiple different types. However, ethical complexities can pose some of the greatest challenges for leaders during emergencies (Wilson, 2020). Under such circumstances, leaders need to encourage decision-making process which does not make physical, social, and psychological harm for their followers even at minimum levels. In a crisis situation, solidarity must be a top propriety for emergency leaders. This would also yield significant effect in activating the role reciprocity. When followers perceive their leaders as ethical in decision-making, they will be more likely to reciprocate their leaders and the organization with positive behaviors despite the presence of the crisis. Given the previous discussion, the following is proposed:

In an emergency situation, leaders need to prioritize ethics in decision-making.

Component 6: Demonstrating Empathy: Prioritize Dealing with Human Tragedy

The immediate reaction of people affected by largescale crisis is to think about how they and their loved ones are going to survive and meet their basic needs, rather than about community or wider outcomes (Anderson, 2018). One fundamental part of leadership is the responsibility to make a positive difference in the lives of followers and other stakeholders, and in times of crisis, leaders must shoulder this responsibility by taking time to acknowledge the fear and suffering experienced by employees and their families (Anderson, 2018). As a crisis has consequences on daily lives of people and affects their psychological and physical well-being, leaders need to consider that a crisis can be a human tragedy for employees. Therefore, the following can be advanced:

In an emergency situation, leaders need to emphasize with others.

Component 7: Enhancing People' Endurance and Stimulating Spirituality

Another important element in leadership is to keep a careful watch on, and continuously enhance employees' endurance during and after a crisis (Hershkovich et al., 2016). According to Hershkovich et al. (2016), within chaotic settings, endurance building requires leaders to identify followers' needs even before they are voiced, follow-up on the welfare of team members, and understand the complicated emotional, personal, and professional reactions to an emergency.

As part of this process, leaders must leverage the value of symbols and ceremonies to create a team from disparate individuals and ensure schedules are strictly adhered to within a highly-disciplined environment, if necessary, intervening to encourage or correct (Hershkovich et al., 2016).

Scholars have, moreover, found that spirituality can have multiple positive impacts on workplace health and well-being, including boosting employee morale, and reducing work-related stress and burnout (Aboramadan and Dahleez, 2021). One recent study found a positive correlation between psychological, physical, and mental well-being and the practice of workplace spirituality (Pawar, 2016). Weick and Sutcliffe (2007) draw on elements of mindfulness to conceptualize the management of unforeseen events, stressing the value of "preoccupation with failure, reluctance to simplify interpretations, and sensitivity to operations" (p. 45) in anticipating and recognizing surprise events, and commitment to resilience and deference to expertise when they happen. Given the above, it seems that emergency leaders should work towards inculcating spiritual values during emergencies to foster well-being among organizational members. Based on this, we propose the following:

In an emergency situation, leaders need to enhance people's endurance and promote spirituality to enhance their wellbeing.

Component 8: Communication

Ensuring clear communication between and among organizational members including leaders in crisis situations is a vital part of crisis management (Anderson, 2018; Boin et al., 2005, 2013; Deitchman, 2013; Hadley et al., 2011; Wilson, 2020). Mishandling communications can put the safety of employees and other actors at risk and has a severely adverse impact on how operations are perceived (Boin et al., 2013).

Routine communication may be ineffective in the enormously different context of an emergency situation. Effective communication must explain the nature of the emergency and its possible consequences, as well as outlining what action is being taken to mitigate these (Boin et al., 2013; Craig & Amernic, 2020; Kearns et al., 2019). Moreover, it must include "actionable advice," so all parties are aware what is expected of them, and why (Hershkovich et al., 2016). Crisis communication must, instead, be flexible enough to convey fast-moving, and unpredictable information (Boin et al., 2013). Given the above, the following can be advanced:

In an emergency situation, leaders need to utilize communications in a meaningful manner.

Component 9: Sensemaking

Sensemaking of a is a fundamental component for leaders both operationally and strategically (Boin & Renaud, 2013; Boin et al., 2013). Sensemaking theory explains how individuals gain an interpretation of an unpredictable or uncertain situation through making observations, analyzing these observations, and taking action (Maitlis & Christianson, 2014). Hence, clear and effective sensemaking is an essential part of emergency management if informed decisions are to be taken. For sensemaking to have a value, suggestions have to be made on analysis capabilities, decisions support systems, communication channels, and upgrading detection systems (Ansell et al., 2010). Tried-and-tested data-processing procedures must be in place so that information reaches the right people, feedback is facilitated, returned, and reviewed, and all individuals are involved in creating a constant and dynamic information flow to enable overall understanding, encourage the best analysis of potential outcomes and consequences, and identify which data are lacking and how to obtain them (Comfort & Okada, 2013). Wilson (2020) similarly suggests emergency leaders to benefit from leveraging a pool of shared knowledge, systems, and norms in order to facilitate managing a crisis. Given the previous discussion, we advance the following:

In an emergency situation, leaders need to create, support, and test sensemaking techniques.

Component 10: Emergency-Based Learning

Learning at the organizational level in crisis times has been considered as one of the most important challenges in crisis management (Broekema et al., 2017). Organizations can, through learning, enhance their abilities to manage crisis in an effective manner (Crichton et al., 2009). Organizations are called on to show that

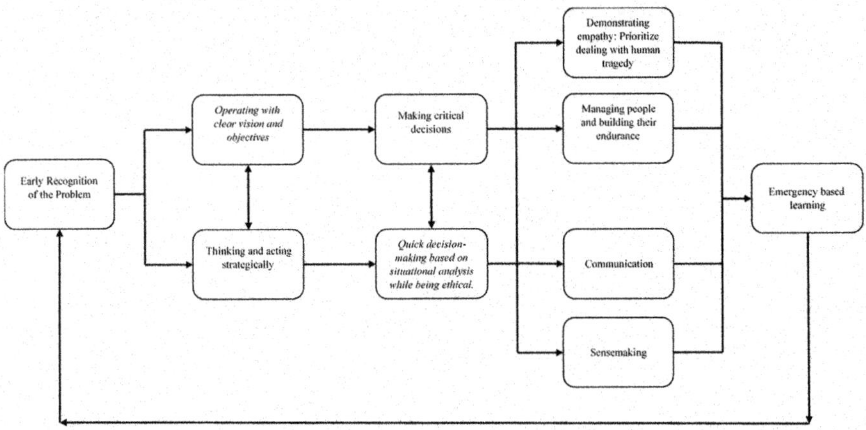

Fig. 26.1 Proposed Framework of Emergency Leadership

they wish, and are able, to learn from failures (Boin et al., 2013). Antonacopoulou and Sheaffer (2014) have highlighted that learning in a crisis is characterized by "engaging dynamically with the unknown and developing new understandings, by experimenting with existing knowledge to improve actions and negotiations with emotions, attitudes, and behaviors in response to forces shaping learning and crisis"

Therefore, leaders must be able and willing to learn (Wilson, 2020), both while the crisis is ongoing, to assess what is working and what is not, as well as when it has ended, to evaluate what worked and what did not. Without learning, adaptation is impossible and without the ability to adapt, managers will continue to rely on processes which do not meet needs and be unable to derive innovative and situation-specific solutions (Boin et al., 2013; Hadley et al., 2011; Hershkovich et al., 2016). Based on the previous arguments, we advance the following (Fig. 26.1):

In an emergency situation, leaders need to document events during a crisis to enable organizational members to learn from them.

Conclusion, Lessons, and Future Research

Scholarly research into emergency management frequently states that traditional bureaucratic models increasingly struggle to meet the challenges posed by today's crises (Light, 2008; Lagadec, 2009). Recently, leadership has been seen among the most crucial aspects of crisis management and can have an enormous impact on successfully managing it (Boin & Bynander, 2015). Despite the variation in leadership requirements across emergencies, a detailed framework to assess leadership tasks in crisis management is very much needed. It is important that all societies in our globalized world share an understanding of how leaders in times of emergencies can act more effectively. If such a shared understanding is lacking, leaders have to endure in a painful, critical, and unfair process.

Therefore, the current paper represented an attempt to develop a framework to evaluate the tasks associated with emergency leadership. It paves the way for policy makers and organizations to look carefully at all the tasks which comprise emergency leadership. By breaking down leadership tasks and setting them against the context of the chaotic and challenging conditions in which they must be carried out, this framework will enable fairer and more nuanced evaluations of leadership performance during emergencies. From this paper, five lessons can be learnt. First, the early recognition of the emergency is half the way to handle the emergency. Second, decision-making is a key in handling any emergency. Third, although decision-making is essential, leaders in emergency situations, should recognize the human tragedy of the emergency or the crisis. Fourth, communication, sensemaking, and strategic thinking are key to successful emergency management. Fifth, emergency-based learning would provide insights and lessons for organizations on how to deal with crises and emergencies.

Although this paper provides a good step to understand the skills and tasks related with a leader in an emergency, the proposed framework should be held for empirical validation across sectors and countries to check for its universality. Therefore, we suggest future research to validate this framework through collecting data across countries and sectors alike.

Key Takeaways

1. In an emergency situation, traditional models of leadership seem not to be effective.
2. Leadership is critical for managing emergency and crisis situations.
3. Leadership needs to follow an effective roadmap to guarantee effective crisis management.
4. Decision-making, sensemaking, innovation, and strategic thinking are keys to successfully manage a crisis.
5. Leaders should enhance followers' wellbeing and promote a climate of spirituality during emergencies.

Reflective Questions

1. What does the literature tell us about effective leadership in emergencies?
2. Why do we need a framework for leadership during emergencies?
3. Is it true that we need more a general framework to be adopted for emergency management rather than a specific leadership style?
4. What characterizes effective leadership during emergencies?
5. What should a leader do in an emergency or a crisis situation starting from early recognition of the problem to learning?

References

Aboramadan, M., & Dahleez, K. (2021). Workplace Spirituality and Job Performance in Higher Education. *Journal of Management, Spirituality & Religion, 18*(2), 128–150(23). https://www.ingentaconnect.com/content/jmsr/rmsr20;jsessionid=bhisfnh4bfedo.x-ic-live-03

Aguilera, D. (1990). *Crisis intervention theory and methodology*. Mosby.

Craig, R,. & Amernic, J. (2020). The language of leadership in a deadly pandemic. *Strategy & Leadership, 48*(5), 41–47. https://doi.org/10.1108/SL-05-2020-0068.

Anderson, L. (2018). Leadership during crisis: Navigating complexity and uncertainty. *Leader to Leader, 2018*(90), 49–54.

Anderson, D. W., Krajewski, H. T., Goffin, R. D., & Jackson, D. N. (2008). A leadership self-efficacy taxonomy and its relation to effective leadership. *The Leadership Quarterly, 19*(5), 595–608.

Ansell, C., & Boin, A. (2019). Taming deep uncertainty: The potential of pragmatist principles for understanding and improving strategic crisis management. *Administration and Society, 51*(7), 1079–1112.

Ansell, C., Boin, A., & Keller, A. (2010). Managing transboundary crises: Identifying the building blocks of an effective response system. *Journal of Contingencies & Crisis Management, 18*(4), 195–207.

Antonacopoulou, E. P., & Sheaffer, Z. (2014). Learning in crisis: Rethinking the relationship between organizational learning and crisis management. *Journal of Management Inquiry, 23*, 5–21.

Bakker, M. H., Kerstholt, J. H., van Bommel, M., & Giebels, E. (2019). Decision-making during a crisis: the interplay of narratives and statistical information before and after crisis communication. *Journal of Risk Research, 22*(11), 1409–1429.

Bass, B. M. (1998). *Transformational leadership: Industrial, military and educational impact*. Erlbaum.

Bateman, T. O. M. (2008). Leading for results: Brief-but-powerful lessons from Katrina and Iraq. *Organizational Dynamics, 37*(4), 301–312.

Bhaduri, R. M. (2019). Leveraging culture and leadership in crisis management. *European Journal of Training and Development, 43*(6), 554–569.

Boin, A., & F. Bynander. (2015). Explaining success and failure in crisis coordination." Geografiska Annaler: Series A, Physical Geography 97 (1): 123–135.

Boin, A., & Renaud, C. (2013). Orchestrating joint sensemaking across government levels: Challenges and requirements for crisis leadership. *Journal of Leadership Studies, 7*, 41–46.

Boin, A., t'Hart, P., Stern, E., & Sundelius, B. (2005). *The politics of crisis management: Understanding public leadership when it matters most*. Cambridge University Press.

Boin, A., Kuipers, S., & Overdijk, W. (2013). Leadership in times of crisis: A framework for assessment. *International Review of Public Administration, 18*, 79–91.

Boin, A., t'Hart, P., Stern, E., & Sundelius, B. (2016). *The politics of crisis management: Public leadership under pressure* (2nd ed.). Cambridge University Press.

Bowers, M. R., Hall, J. R., & Srinivasan, M. M. (2017). Organizational culture and leadership style: The missing combination for selecting the right leader for effective crisis management. *Business Horizons, 60*(4), 551–563.

Broekema, W., Van Kleef, D., & Steen, T. (2017). What factors drive organizational learning from crises? Insights from the Dutch Food Safety Services' response to four veterinary crises. *Journal of Contingencies & Crisis Management, 25*(4), 326–340.

Caro, D. H. (2015). Code orange: Towards transformational leadership of emergency management systems. *Healthcare Management Forum, 28*, 195–201.

Caro, D. (2016a). The nexus of transformational leadership of emergency services systems: Beyond the Wu-Shi-Ren (WSR)-Li paradigm. *International Journal of Emergency Services, 5*(1), 18–33.

Caro, D. H. J. (2016b). Towards transformational leadership: The nexus of emergency management systems in Canada. *International Journal of Emergency Management, 12*(2), 113–135.

Caulfield, J. L. (2018). Using case work as a pretest to measure crisis leadership Preparedness. *Journal of Management Education, 42*(6), 704–730.

Comfort, L. K., & Okada, A. (2013). Emergent leadership in extreme events: A knowledge commons for sustainable communities. *International Review of Public Administration, 18*(1), 61–77.

Crichton, M. T., et al. (2009). Enhancing organizational resilience through emergency planning: Learnings from cross-sectoral lessons. *Journal of Contingencies & Crisis Management, 17*(1), 24–37.

Deitchman, S. (2013). Enhancing crisis leadership in public health emergencies. *Disaster Medicine and Public Health Preparedness, 7*(5), 534–540.

Demiroz, F., & Kapucu, N. (2012). The role of leadership in managing emergencies and disasters. *European Journal of Economic & Political Studies, 5*(1), 91–101.

Dückers, M. L. A., Yzermans, C. J., Jong, W., & Boin, A. (2017). Psychosocial Crisis Management: The Unexplored Intersection of Crisis Leadership and Psychosocial Support. *Risk, Hazards & Crisis in Public Policy, 8*(2), 94–112.

Farazmand, A. (2007). Learning from the Katrina crisis: A global and international perspective with implications for future crisis management. *Public Administration Review, 67*, 149–159.

Fiedler, F. E. (2002). Proactive ways to improve leadership performance. In R. L. Lowman (Ed.), *Handbook of organizational consulting psychology* (pp. 76–105). Jossey-Bass.

Gibson, C., Folley, B. S., & Park, S. (2009). Enhanced divergent thinking and creativity in musicians: A behavioral and near-infrared spectroscopy study. *Brain and Cognition, 69*(1), 162–169.

Gorge, M. (2006). Crisis management best practice–where do we start from? *Computer Fraud & Security, 2006*(6), 10–13.

Hadley, C. N., Pittinsky, T. L., Sommer, S. A., & Zhu, W. (2011). Measuring the efficacy of leaders to assess information and make decisions in a crisis: The C-LEAD scale. *The Leadership Quarterly, 22*(4), 633–648.

Hale, J. E., Hale, D. P., & Dulek, R. E. (2006). Decision processes during crisis response: An exploratory investigation. *Journal of Managerial Issues, 18*, 301–320.

Halverson, S. K., Murphy, S. E., & Riggio, R. E. (2004). Charismatic leadership in crisis situations: A laboratory investigation of stress and crisis. *Small Group Research, 35*(5), 495–514.

Hannah, S. T., Uhl-Bien, M., Avolio, B. J., & Cavarretta, F. L. (2009). A framework for examining leadership in extreme contexts. *The Leadership Quarterly, 20*(6), 897–919.

Hannah, S. T., Campbell, D. J., & Matthews, M. D. (2010). Advancing a research agenda for leadership in dangerous contexts. *Military Psychology, 22*(supl), S157–S189.

Hershkovich, O., Gilad, D., Zimlichman, E., & Kreiss, Y. (2016). Effective medical leadership in times of emergency: A perspective. *Disaster and Military Medicine, 2*(1), 1–5.

Hick, J. L., Hanfling, D., & Cantrill, S. V. (2012). Allocating scarce resources in disasters: Emergency department principles. *Annals of Emergency Medicine, 59*(3), 177–187.

Hunt, J. G., Boal, K. B., & Dodge, G. E. (1999). The effects of visionary and crisis-responsive charisma on followers: An experimental examination of two kinds of charismatic leadership. *The Leadership Quarterly, 10*(3), 423–448.

Kapucu, N., & Van Wart, M. (2006). The evolving role of the public sector in managing catastrophic disasters: Lessons learned. *Administration and Society, 38*(3), 279–308.

Kapucu, N., & Van Wart, M. (2008). Making matters worse: An anatomy of leadership failures in managing catastrophic events. *Administration and Society, 40*(7), 711–740.

Karaca, H., Kapucu, N., & Van Wart, M. (2012). Examining the Role of Transformational Leadership in Emergency Management: The Case of FEMA. *Risk, Hazards & Crisis in Public Policy, 3*(3), 19–37.

Kearns, K., Alexander, C., Duane, M., Gardner, E., Morse, E., & McShane, L. (2019). Leadership in a crisis. *Journal of Public Affairs Education, 25*(4), 542–557.

Klann, G. (2003). *Crisis leadership: Using military lessons, organizational experiences, and the power of influence to lessen the impact of chaos on the people you lead.* Center for Creative Leadership.

Lagadec, P. (2009). A new cosmology of risks and crises: Time for a radical shift in paradigm and practice. *Review of Policy Research, 26*(4), 473–486.

Light, P. C. (2008). *Predicting organizational crisis readiness: Perspectives and practices toward a pathway to preparedness*. New York University.

Littlefield, R. S., & Quenette, A. M. (2007). Crisis leadership and Hurricane Katrina: The portrayal of authority by the media in natural disasters. *Journal of Applied Communication Research, 35*(1), 26–47.

Maitlis, S., & Christianson, M. (2014). Sensemaking in Organizations: Taking stock and moving forward. *Academy of Management Annals, 8*(1), 57–125.

McEntire, D. A., & Dawson, G. (2007). The intergovernmental context. In W. L. Waugh & K. Tierney (Eds.), *Emergency management: Principles and practice for local government.* County Management Association.

Mikušová, M., & Horváthová, P. (2019). Prepared for a crisis? Basic elements of crisis management in an organisation. *Economic Research-Ekonomska Istrazivanja, 32*(1), 1844–1868.

Mintzberg, H., Raisinghani, D., & Theoret, A. (1976). The structure of "unstructured" decision processes. *Administrative Science Quarterly, 21*, 246–275.

Mitroff, I. (2004). *Crisis leadership: Planning for the unthinkable.* Wiley.

Mitroff, I. I., & Alpaslan, M. C. (2003). Preparing for evil. *Harvard Business Review, 81*, 109–115.

Mumford, M. D., Marks, M. A., Connelly, M. S., Zaccaro, S. J., & Johnson, J. F. (1998). Domain-based scoring in divergent-thinking tests: Validation evidence in an occupational sample. *Creativity Research Journal, 11*(2), 151–163.

Pawar, B. S. (2016). Workplace spirituality and employee well-being: An empirical examination. *Employee Relations, 38*(6), 975–994.

Pearson, C. M., & Clair, J. A. (1998). Reframing crisis management. *Academy of Management Review, 23*(1), 59–76.

Pillai, R., & Meindl, J. R. (1998). Context and charisma: A "meso" level examination of the relationship of organic structure, collectivism, and crisis to charismatic leadership. *Journal of Management, 24*(5), 643–671.

Rosenthal, U., Charles, M. T., & t'Hart, P. (1989). The world of crises and crisis management. In U. Rosenthal, M. T. Charles, & P. t'Hart (Eds.), *Coping with crises: The management of disasters, riots, and terrorism.* Charles C. Thomas.

Rubin, C. B. (1985). The community recovery process in the United States after a major natural disaster. *International Journal of Mass Emergencies and Disasters, 3*(2), 9–28.

Schraagen, J. M., & van de Ven, J. G. M. (2008). Improving Decision Making in Crisis Response through Critical Thinking Support. *Journal of Cognitive Engineering and Decision Making, 2*(4), 311–327.

Smart, C., & Vertinsky, I. (1977). Designs for crisis decision units. *Administrative Science Quarterly, 22*, 640–657.

Smith, D., & Elliott, D. (2007). Exploring the barriers to learning from crisis: Organizational learning and crisis. *Management Learning, 38*(5), 519–538.

Stern, E. K. (1997). Crisis and learning: A conceptual balance sheet. *Journal of Contingencies & Crisis Management, 5*(2), 69–86.

Sweeny, K. (2008). Crisis decision theory: Decisions in the face of negative events. *Psychological Bulletin, 134*(1), 61.

Tourish, D. (2020). Introduction to the special issue: Why the coronavirus crisis is also a crisis of leadership. *Leadership, 16*(3), 261–272.

Trainor, J. E., & Velotti, L. (2013). Leadership in crises, disasters and catastrophes. *Journal of Leadership Studies, 7*(3), 38–40.

Useem, M., Cook, J. R., & Sutton, L. (2005). Developing leaders for decision making under stress: Wildland firefighters in the South Canyon Fire and its aftermath. *Academy of Management Learning & Education, 4*(4), 461–485.

Vaughan, D. (1996). *The Challenger launch decision: Risky technology, culture and deviance at NASA*. University of Chicago Press.

Wankhade, P., van Weir, D., & Bunt, S. (2015). Servant-leadership in times of crises and emergen cies and disasters: A critical perspective. In *European Academy of Management Proceedings*.

Waugh, W. L., & Streib, G. (2006). Collaboration and leadership for effective emergency management. *Public Administration Review, 66*, 131–140.

Weick, K. E., & Sutcliffe, K. M. (2007). *Managing the unexpected: Resilient performance in the age of uncertainty* (2nd ed.). Jossey-Bass.

Wilson, S. (2020). Pandemic leadership: Lessons from New Zealand's approach to COVID-19. *Leadership, 16*(3), 279–293.

Wise, C. R. (2006). Organizing for homeland security after Katrina: Is adaptive management what's missing? *Public Administration Review, 66*(3), 302–318.

Wooten, L. P., & James, E. H. (2008). Linking crisis management and leadership competencies: The role of human resource development. *Advances in Developing Human Resources, 10*(3), 352–379.

Zhang, Z., Jia, M., & Gu, L. (2012). Transformational leadership in crisis situations: Evidence from the People's Republic of China. *International Journal of Human Resource Management, 23*, 4085–4109.

Dr. Mohammed Aboramadan received his PhD in Economics and Management (Major: Management) from the university of Pavia, Italy. Currently, Dr. Aboramadan works as a research fellow at the department of economics of Insubria University, Italy. His areas of research are focused on HRM, Leadership, employee performance, organizational performance. Dr. Aboramadan has published at the international journal of contemporary hospitality management, journal of hospitality marketing and management, personnel review, journal of management development, Voluntas, academy of management proceedings, international journal of organizational analysis, Evidence Based-HRM, international journal of educational management, journal for higher education policy and management, international journal of public administration, journal for global business advancement, journal of islamic accounting and business research, journal of enterprise information systems, benchmarking: international journal, journal of management spirituality and religion.

Yasir Mansoor Kundi received his PhD in Organizational Behavior from IAE-Aix Marseille University, France. His research interests revolve around leadership and employee careers and work-related behaviors. He has published his research in recent years in outlets including: Personnel Review, Management Decision, Journal of Career Assessment, and International Journal of Conflict Management.

Internal–External Leadership Model in the Post-COVID-19, Digital VUCA World

27

Sonja Lang and Michael J. D. Sutton

Introduction

In this chapter the author will present an innovative leadership model that builds on a framework for repackaging a proven Swiss Army Knife of tools to approach digitized workplaces affected by COVID-19 and the VUCA (volatility, uncertainty, complexity, and ambiguity) ecosystem our world has been thrust into. Today our organizations are challenged to improve creativity, originality, initiative, innovation, critical thinking, and complex problem-solving. We will trigger new insights into how to foster these competencies and flourish in a world undergoing dramatic transformations. Humankind has entered a period comprising the Fourth Industrial Revolution (Centre for the New Economy and Society, 2018). Activities taking place in our multinational, multicultural, and multilingual workforces require new business models and leadership strategies to cope with the fundamental pace and dramatic impact of change. Humankind has the choice to create individual and institutional opportunities that will shape the transformation and mold this Fourth Industrial Revolution (Schwab, 2015, par. 1):

> The First Industrial Revolution used water and steam power to mechanize production. The Second used electric power to create mass production. The Third used electronics and information technology to automate production. Now a Fourth Industrial Revolution is building on the Third, the digital revolution that has been occurring since the middle of the last century. It is characterized by a fusion of technologies that is blurring the lines between the physical, digital, and biological spheres.

S. Lang (✉)
Mindful Clarity, Frankfurt, Germany
e-mail: sonja.lang@mindfulclarity.org

M. J. D. Sutton
FUNIFICATION, Apache Junction, AZ, USA
e-mail: michaeljdsutton@funification.biz

S. K. Dhiman, J. F. Marques (eds.), *Leadership After COVID-19*, Future of Business and Finance, https://doi.org/10.1007/978-3-030-84867-5_27

A gap in research exists to successfully navigate the journey humankind is making from the Third to the Fourth Industrial Revolutions. Our complex, inter-related global workplaces and living spaces are the new foundations for the emotional, cognitive, and behavioral changes we will experience as individuals and organizations. The emergent VUCA (volatility, uncertainty, complexity, and ambiguity) world, which has been compounded and fast forwarded by the COVID-19 pandemic, will be depicted in terms of our potential to sustain, survive, and thrive in the chaos enveloping many of us.

Consequently, a conceptual leadership framework will be described that encompasses a range of existing leadership models important for the construction of new methods for interaction and leadership. Two leadership models, the Authentic and Servant Leadership Models, surfaced as highly relevant to the VUCA world. Those models will be synthesized into a new prototypical model for coping and personally improving within the midst of the struggle triggered by the surrounding VUCA ecosystem. Finally, the reader will develop a familiarity with several tools for pragmatic application of the synthesized leadership model.

Problem Statement

The digital revolution is a term sometimes used to describe the effects of the reduction prices and the rationalization of costs associated with information and computer technologies (ICT). However, the real issue is the availability of a wealth of information, updated in real time, recyclable, and potentially used to create innovation in a unique manner. The digital revolution (digitalization) is intricately linked to the latter stages of the Third Industrial Revolution and can also be described as prominent within the current, Fourth Industrial Revolution. Digitalization is often felt as a threat, i.e., being made redundant at work, which is how people often define their own value. Many workers feel they are being pushed into a void. Employees, managers, and executives experience an increased fear of the future and even self. Those feelings have been exacerbated by the COVID-19 pandemic and the VUCA ecosystem surrounding our everyday actions. This sensation is driving individuals to intuitively look to increase control, look to hold on to status quo, and fight change. Thus, their fear becomes a reality.

Individuals, facilitated by ICT, pass from digital domains to a physical reality that is offline from the telecommunications networks. The interconnected ICT has the potential to empower, enable, surveil, and govern the lives of humans. But this new environment will challenge us all (Schwab, 2017, p. 50–51):

> ...the deluge of information available today, the velocity of disruption and the acceleration of innovation are hard to comprehend or anticipate. They constitute a source of constant surprise. In such a context, it is the leader's ability to continually learn, adapt and challenge his or her own conceptual and operating models of success that will distinguish the next generation of business leaders.

Thus, the research literature continually alludes to the problem this chapter will investigate (Brynjolfsson & McAfee, 2011; Peters, 2017): "How can humankind muster the new and innovative leadership capabilities to cope and excel in these emergent workspaces and living spaces?" The thesis of this chapter is that leaders initially need to work on the self to cope with the changes. The transformation is a massive opportunity for humankind to leave the hamster wheel behind—leaving it to machines—and focus on being human, i.e., building relationships, making valuable connections with others, collaborating on unique methods for social change. One day the majority of humankind could wake up in the morning knowing who they are, what they want to achieve, and having the tools to action and improve their lives and those around them. We are proposing a unique approach for social transformation.

Gap Analysis

The Third Industrial Revolution required organizations to apply an operating style that responded to more and more complex situations (Jandrić et al., 2018). Now, since we are in the beginning of the of the Fourth Industrial Revolution, we have discovered ourselves enraptured and enveloped by a hyper-complex world that demands success through clarity, simplicity, and excellence (Negroponte, 1998, par. 4):

> Face it—the digital revolution is over…Its literal form, the technology, is already beginning to be taken for granted, and its connotation will become tomorrow's commercial and cultural compost for new ideas. Like air and drinking water, being digital will be noticed only by its absence, not its presence.

We have witnessed the emergence of a unique epoch suggesting a profound transformation of business, the economy, lifestyles, society, and education. The constructs of change are based upon our concepts of the speed of light, velocity of systems, single and double loop feedback cycles, and artificial intelligence control (Peters & Jandrić, 2018). The most significant difference between the Third and Fourth Industrial Revolutions is how fast information and change occur and how the available information is processed. The increased speed of change and the pace of interaction has brought about VUCA (volatility, uncertainty, complexity, and ambiguity) (Hilbert, 2012, p. 9):

> Information technologies help us transmit information not only through space – which is communication – but also through time – which is storage. Our global technological memory has roughly doubled every 3 years over recent decades, from less than 3 exabytes in 1986 to about 300 in 2007. ... *Our numbers also indicate that the year 2002 marked the beginning of the digital age, since this was the year that humankind started to store more information on digital than on analogue storage devices* [emphasis added]. This transition happened in the blink of an eye in historical terms. Just 1% of the world's capacity to store information was in digital format in 1986; our digital memory represented 25% of the total in the year 2000 and exploded to 97% of the world's storage capacity by 2007.

VUCA intersects leadership within a range of levels. For example, Bawany (2014, p. 46) described the interconnection as:

> In essence, the heart of the leadership challenge that confronts today's leaders is learning how to lead in situations of ever greater volatility and uncertainty in a globalized business environment, allied with the needs to deal with scale, complexity and new organizational forms that often break with the traditional organizational models and structures within which many have learned their 'leadership trade'. So, the basic assumption that past experience is the key to future leadership success is more open to scrutiny than ever.

VUCA also has been intersected by the pandemic (COVID-19). Many researchers are trying to grapple with how this intersection will impact the workplace. Strack et al. (2020, p. 1) interconnected VUCA and COVID-19 with the speed of time:

> During the crisis, we communicate openly with empathy. In the new now, leadership will come from the head, heart, and hands—the focus of our discussion here. ... During the crisis, organizations endeavor to stand together with employees and society. In the new now, this momentum will lead to a purpose driven culture. ...Successful organizations will depend on leaders who are as empathetic as they are capable. Technological change makes our world a fast-paced one on any given day, and unexpected circumstances (like a pandemic) force companies and teams to adapt at lightning speed.

The next section will describe that VUCA world, accelerated by COVID-19, and how it impacts leadership approaches in more detail.

Global Context for VUCA

VUCA was a term coined by the U.S. Army War College and first applied in 1987 to the concept of leadership theories (Bennis & Nanus, 1985). Originally from military parlance (McChrystal et al., 2015), VUCA described four dimensions that have been adapted recently in the economy (Lenz, 2019; Petry, 2018) Humans are obligated to constantly adapt and respond to new situations because of the accelerated changes. The question is: "How we adapt as humans and particularly as leaders?" Mengel (2020 p. 75) introduced the assertion by Avanessian and Malik (2016) that we exist in a:

> 'speculative time structure' where 'future happens before the present.' They proposed a concept of the 'post-contemporary' in which they conceptualized transformative, speculative, poetic actions and pragmatics towards an 'open future' instead of an 'automated future.'

Subsequently, Mengel (2020, p. 73) proposed that "[m]eaningful leadership paradigms need to go beyond reestablishing the alleged stability of the past by 'paddling backwards' or 'muddling through' the challenges of the present" (Scharmer, 2016). In our present and the future, our VUCA context urgently demands unique long-term approaches to leadership.

Short-term changes tend to be rejected as the unconscious mind (Bargh & Morsella, 2008) undermines the acceptance of change—resisting while holding on to the status quo. In the longer term, however, humans are most capable of adapting to new situations and changes (Lamm & Gordon, 2010). Therefore, leaders of the future will need to address and inspire their subordinates and with a clearly developed and communicated vision (Klewes & Langen, 2008). Being focused and present in the situation and being authentic will have growing importance. Leaders will neglect the role of communication at their own peril (Gerkhardt et al., 2008, p. 19):

> The objective is defined by means of a vision and concrete subordinate targets. A clear and comprehensible picture of the future creates clarity and indicates the direction in which the journey is going. The vision must be easy to communicate and should be an appeal to stakeholders, staff and customers. The objectives should be as tangible as possible and suitably challenging for the individuals concerned. Furthermore, it is essential to present the objectives in a positive light in view of the imminent change, so that the people affected are motivated and have an interest in supporting and implementing the vision.

The transition between Third Industrial Revolution and the Fourth Industrial Revolution effected by VUCA and the pandemic is aptly illustrated by Lowe (2016) where he described the transition in worldviews from the Pig Face Model to the Holonic Model (Fig. 27.1). In the Pig Face Model, the economy is at the center of focus. Ecology and society are aberrations, (minor and almost afterthoughts), on the "face" of the economy. After the transition, the economy still plays a central focus and is the bullseye of the Holonic Model but is reduced in size and impact, while society envelopes the economy and ecology encompass both society and the economy. We propose a further extension of this change in worldview to include the Internal-External worldview. In this current extended transition from the Holonic Model, we propose that the economy is no longer the bullseye, and in fact, ecology is the new bullseye. For a brief transition period, society had initially moved into the center. Yet, a renewed awareness of nature as a whole has moved ecology into the center, (e.g., Fridays for Future). Ecology is now enveloped by society and both are now enveloped by the economy. The economy and ecology support humankind from each side.

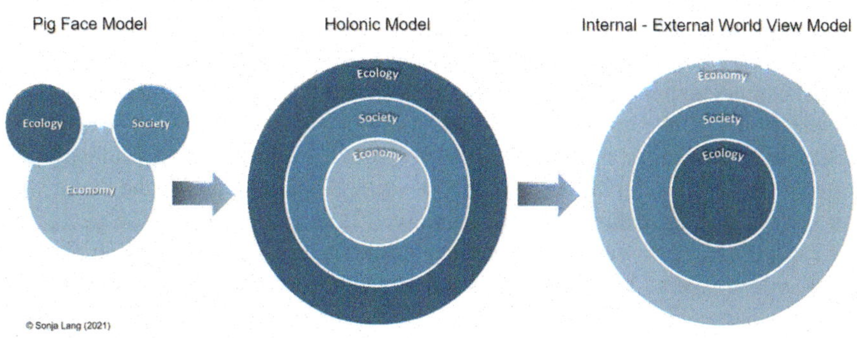

Fig. 27.1 Adapted from Lowe (2016, p. 230). The lucky country? Reinventing Australia. University of Queensland Press. © 2016 Ian Lowe, with permission

We suggest that to function in the VUCA world, the leader needs a mindset different from what was applicable in earlier epochs. A cyclic macro-historian, Khaldun, proposed an historical concept for why city-states eventually lose their luster and collapse (Galtung et al., 1997). Khaldun called it "*asibiya* - the collective purpose, unity and memory that binds a group" (Daffara, 2004, p. 25). When *asibiya* is absent, our social ecosystem breaks down. The global combination of COVID-19 and VUCA suggests that our social ecosystem (workplaces and living spaces) have been significantly and negatively influenced. The outcomes appear to be demand one or more new leadership model to fill the vacuum. However, when *asibiya* is fostered and sustained, "a post COVID-19 world and cultural paradigm or zeitgeist, requires the bottom-up co-design of a collective purpose and vision to [enroll] the peoples of this planet into a resilient social-ecological system." *Asibiya* could furnish the foundation for a clear, shared vision of collective purpose for an organization's leaders, internal stakeholders, and external stakeholders. We have an opportunity to move from fragmentation to unification, but only courage to change will motive humankind to take the steps necessary for transformation.

Later in this chapter, we will provide a detailed description of proposed factors that influence the roles of communication in a leader's decision-making. We will also elucidate methods that could effectively enhance the understanding of leaders into the hyper-complex interdependencies as well as their authenticity and credibility in communicating their visions.

Conceptual Framework for Leadership Models

Management styles came into vogue in the industrial era and were driven by the need for increased efficiency of machines and human tasks under pinned by a Command-and-Control approach. With the emergence of the digital VUCA world, these old leadership practices were no longer maintainable. We will describe and define the characteristics of the two models.

We propose that leadership is a phenomenon that acts through the process of influencing and providing subordinates with purposes targeted at collective effort to ensure that the team/organization will achieve its goal (Jones et al., 2011). Regardless of the several contexts and methods in which the term leadership was defined during the last century, experts generally agree that leadership significantly influenced both organizational results and organizational atmosphere (Chen & Silverthorne, 2005; Alvesson & Sveningsson, 2003; Northouse, 2021); Furthermore, specialists suggested that useful leadership involved influence and common goals, and that it was a process occurring within groups (Northouse, 2021).

Leadership styles essentially expressed how a leader could influence employees and how leaders could influence their activities in order to achieve organizational goals (Gyoker et al., 2014). According to Berde (2013), leadership style was a way of exercising power and encompassed a set of all the tools and methods by which managers influenced their employees. Leadership behavior, in turn, prevailed through the leadership style used, that is, style-reflective behavior that stemmed from the personality of the leader, which is often less conscious and therefore difficult to regulate. Müller et al. (2007) suggested that leadership depended upon the situation and circumstances. Furthermore, Blanchard et al. (1993) introduced the idea that certain leadership styles were more effective and appropriate in certain situations than in others. Northouse (2021) compiled a comprehensive, but not all inclusive, text on the most common and accepted leadership models, which included:

- Adaptive Leadership,
- Authentic Leadership,
- Behavioral Approach,
- Culture and Leadership,
- Ethical Leadership,
- Followership,
- Gender and Leadership,
- Leader–Member Exchange Theory,
- Path–Goal Theory,
- Servant Leadership,
- Situational Approach,
- Skills Approach,
- Team Leadership,
- Trait Approach,
- Transformational Leadership.

Many of these approaches, models, and theories were based upon the transition in leadership styles that emerged from the Third Industrial Revolution and some may prove applicable to the Fourth Industrial Revolution. Other models have emerged recently proposed by a number of different sources. For example, Baldoni (2020, par. 9–10) proposed a virtual/invisible leadership approach where:

> Virtual leadership comes down to presence. Since we cannot be there, we must be *felt* there. Presence for leaders means being accessible to others—letting people know that you are available to listen as well as to support. A fully present leader is one who is engaged in the work and conversant with the people who do the job.

Mengel (2020) furnished an exhausting list of new leadership models spawned by researchers who discerned that the current models were just no longer working:

- Elkington et al. (2017) proposed a *Visionary Leadership in a Turbulent World*, claiming it could induce success in the VUCA 2.0 worldview.
- Piel and Johnson (2015) proposed a *Quantum Leadership model*, founded upon the formulation of empirical paradigms stemming from chaos and complexity theories. The quantum leadership model purported that the lack of certainty and coherence could be incorporated into a leadership model.
- Suderman and Foster (2015) offered the *Murmuration Leadership model* to provide a focal point for humanizing the workplace through what the authors labeled *we-leadership*.

- Finally, Mengel (2020, p. 76) promulgated his new trans-disciplinary model: *Post-Contemporary Leadership (PoCo)*. The model merged a "complex and highly adaptive system floating in the multi-dimensional time-space (dis-) continuum."

Let's explore the Command-and-Control Approach and plumb why it is broken in the context of VUCA, and more specifically because of the COVID-19 pandemic.

Command-and-Control Approach

New approaches in leadership due to technological changes initially emerged in the military context. However, as businesses also faced increasing challenges in terms of leadership and management, similarities between the two environments became obvious (Wittmann, 2017). Acknowledging their success and efficiency, organizations also began to adopt these leadership strategies (Lawrence, 2013).

In 1860, Prussian General Helmuth Graf von Moltke faced a range of warfare situations. However, due to new technological developments, the already existing strategies were no longer efficient (Holborn, 1986). The Command-and-Control (C2) approach to leadership proved historically effective and was a "set of organizational and technical attributes and processes ... [that] employs human, physical, and information resources to solve problems and accomplish missions" to achieve the goals of an organization or enterprise (Vassiliou et al., 2014, p. 1). The C2 leadership style was effective in an environment where both change and competition were limited and a large margin of error existed (high profit margins) (Antonakis, 2012).

A similar situation has surfaced today. Carl von Clausewitz, Prussian general and military historian, was the first to acknowledge the necessity of increased flexibility, which enabled the army to meet warfare challenges. In his book, *On War*, he explained that complexity and unpredictability resulted from increased processes of interaction and interdependencies (Handel & Tzu, 1991). Clausewitz argued that the circumstances in warfare changed continuously, independently from the intentions of the commanders. Such circumstances involved the behavior of each subordinate, the enemy, physical endurance, and even the weather (Clausewitz, 1976).

Moltke proposed the following guidelines: commanders on the battlefield must understand the situation of their unit and their neighbor, create a mental picture of the situation, permanently assess their situation, and communicate with their neighbor and commander (Lyod, 1972). Nevertheless, the commander remained responsible for preventing things from following their own course in the absence of explicit orders (Moltke, 2000).

Command-and-Communicate Approach

A C2 approach is no longer feasible in the age of digitalization and telecommunications. In today's business environment, because of fast occurring changes and ICT, profit margins have been reduced (Müller et al., 2007). In addition, more events are taking place simultaneously and on a continuing basis than at any time in history. Due to the speed at which circumstances are changing, decision-making needs to be delegated down the organization to the level that has all the information at the time when a decision must be made (Turner & Müller, 2005).

VUCA, by its very nature, demands a democratic and flexible point of view, and thus, accountability must be delegated. These characteristics are not naturally present in the C2 approach (Northouse, 2021). In the First Industrial Revolution, C2 helped organize processes and foster a sense of accountability, order, and discipline (Dulewic & Higgs, 2005). C2 lacked flexibility, making the organization irresponsive to continuous internal and external environment changes.

Moltke's conception of command transformed the C2 approach of leaders into the Command-and-Communicate (C2+)approach, or as the United Nations calls it today in the military context, the Mission Command, which means:

> Exercising authority and leadership by the commander through mission orders that ensure the manifestation of the disciplined initiative within the commander's intention to give leaders the agility and adaptability needed to conduct unified land operations. (US Army, 2012, p. 1)

Moltke emphasized the importance of simplicity, clarity, and confident orders without too many details, for he believed that detailed orders hindered flexibility during operations (Holborn, 1986). Furthermore, due to Moltke's acceptance of uncertainty, he intended to maintain the ability to react in a rapidly changing environment by avoiding too many details and thus, confusion and demoralization during an action (Whitton, 1921).

According to this new approach, leaders in the VUCA world are responsible for establishing a clear vision or mission, which they must effectively communicate to their subordinates, enabling them to make decisions fast if the situation warrants, and in a manner that results in the subordinates' self-improvement. With the help of the newly acquired knowledge, the subordinate would be able to use it as a tool in similar future situations as well. This is new for both the leader and the follower or team member. Helping the team member to learn how to manage a situation in the future is an investment into the growth of the person and into the shared future.

Sadhguru, a yogi, mystic, and visionary and a contemporary Indian philosopher, established in 1992 the Isha Foundation in Coimbatore, Tamil Nadu in India. Sadhguru was a speaker at the World Economic Forum, where he was granted the Padma Vibhushan Award, (the highest annual civilian award accorded for exceptional and distinguished services by the Government of India for addressing social, environmental, and existential issues). The Isha Foundation has achieved a Special Consultative Status with Economic and Social Council of the United Nations. Sadhguru is also recognized by a range of international corporate CXOs as the thought leader of the emergent concept known as "Human is not a Resource." Sadhguru is in open exchange with universities around the globe, including US Ivy League institutions, and is the New York Times Bestselling author of *Inner Engineering: A Yogi's Guide to Joy*.

Sadhguru (Isha Foundation, 2015) proposed that leaders needed to develop the three I's: insight, inspiration, integrity. He led C-suite leaders to comprehend that they were not in the computer or automotive businesses, but that everybody is in the human *well-fare* business. Nonetheless, the business leaders may use different products and services to reach this lofty goal. Yet, each creative output of these firms supports well-being; albeit the original purpose may have been forgotten over time.

Sadhguru communicates the concept of *Insight* to his audience that every human is looking for well-being and that only the scale of delivery decides the potential reach of well-being: oneself, one's family, one's company, or one's nation. A leader is anybody whose scale of delivery is larger than one individual.

Inspiration pursues the cause of the lack of well-being with relentless commitment, whether events are going our way or not. *Integrity* is the state of the leaders' minds and actions and how they carry themselves. A leader's integrity is the coherence between what leaders say, what they do, what they think, and how they feel about life around them.

Sadhguru argued that every leader needs a spiritual trait. Spirituality was defined as expanding one's own horizons and perceptions. This approach to leadership and being a teacher within Sadhguru's Isha Foundation sparked a number of elements of the Internal–External Leadership Model. Everyone, in particular leaders, need to work on their internal perspectives of themselves, the situation, their vision to start leading, and respect for the people they lead.

In conclusion, a review of the range of leadership models and styles led the author to identify two styles that would activate and sustain the C2+ approach—the Authentic Leadership model and the Servant Leadership model. In the next section we will review these models and build toward an innovative synthesis of these models—the Internal–External Leadership Model.

The Authentic and Servant Leadership Models

Authentic Leadership theory and Servant Leadership theory offer two complementary frameworks or, in combination, one complex framework for developing effective and ethical leaders in the new VUCA ecosystem. Each theory is well established and supported within the literature, indicating a strong foundation for the researcher's Action Research. A range of complementary frameworks and models have been proposed by others, for example the functional-visionary leadership model for self-managing virtual teams (Eseryel et al., 2020);

Authentic Leadership theory suggested that an effective leader was honest, real, and authentic with their stakeholders (Avolio & Gardner, 2005). Implementing an authentic leadership style involved self-awareness of one's priorities and values and transparency in action, thus encouraging open sharing of information and positive relationships. Authentic leadership became a popular approach in the business world and gained empirical support in the academic world (Clapp-Smith et al., 2009; Kiersch & Byrne, 2015). Ilies et al. (2005) described a four-dimensional model of authentic leadership that may be useful in enhancing leadership development founded on this theory:

- Dimension 1: self-awareness, the awareness and trust of one's own personal values, motives, feelings, and cognition;

- Dimension 2: unbiased processing, including all relevant knowledge and experience in decision-making without denying, distorting, or exaggerating the evidence;
- Dimension 3: authentic behavior, acting in accord with one's true self rather than acting to please others or for the purpose of obtaining rewards or avoiding punishment;
- Dimension 4: authentic relational orientation, one's active process of self-disclosure, and the development of trust-based relationships.

Prabhat Ranjan (P. R.) Sarkar was an Eastern thought leader, activist, Indian philosopher, and guru. Often referred to as Bábá ("Father") by his disciples, Sarkar defined spirituality as the individual realizing the "true self." His social activism was an attempt to transform the Indian Caste System and envision a unique approach to leadership. He attempted to craft a global spiritual socialist revolution, based upon new ways of thought, voice, yoga, art, and culture (Inayatullah, 1990, par. 15):

> Thus, Sarkar would place the *sadvipra*, the compassionate servant leader ... at the center of society (not necessarily at the center of government). In his life, Sarkar's efforts were to create this type of leadership instead of building large bureaucratic organizations. He sought to create a new type of leadership that was humble and could serve, that was courageous and could protect, that was insightful and could learn and teach, and that was innovative and could use wealth–in a word, the *sadvipra*.

Sarkar's goal was to create individual opportunities to embrace a newfound spiritual presence, a prerequisite for transformation. This approach to leadership sparked a number of elements of the Internal–External Leadership Model.

Trust and being true to one's self are the hallmark of authentic leadership. The World Economic Forum (WEC) originated a foundational framework for trust as a catalyst in our post-pandemic world. Trust is the "salve" applied by emergent, resilient leaders to spearhead the human experience of recovery. The WEC framework encompassed four human dimensions of trust: Physical, Emotional, Financial, and Digital (Renjan, 2020, par. 10):

> The pandemic [offered] opportunities to act to build trust or lose it. ...Throughout the COVID-19 pandemic, organizations around the globe have demonstrated remarkable agility, changing business models literally overnight: setting up remote-work arrangements; offshoring entire business processes to less-affected geographies; initiating multi-company cooperation to redeploy furloughed employees across sectors. In each situation, the urgency for results prevailed over traditional bureaucratic responses.

Again, a useful framework that furnished additional rationales for the inception of the Internal–External Leadership Model.

On the other hand, Servant Leadership Theory is undergirded by the principle that the leader serves his or her followers or team (Greenleaf, 2002). From this perspective, effective leaders are humble and courageous at the same time, emphasizing follower empowerment and development. Servant leadership is also characterized by strong ethical and moral behavior, whereby leaders place the "greater good" above their self-interest (Greenleaf, 1991; van Dierendonck & Nuijten, 2011). Van Dierendonck and Nuijten (2011) identified eight characteristics of servant leadership:

1. accountability—addressing clear goals and visions and then perceiving others accountable for achieving set standards;
2. authenticity—presenting one's "true" self;
3. courage—daring to take risks and challenge conventional practices;
4. empowerment—believing in and enabling others' development;
5. humility—awareness of limitations and acceptance of any mistakes;
6. interpersonal acceptance, empathy, and understanding; and,
7. standing back—giving others credit, opportunity, and support;
8. stewardship—focusing on the common good above self-interest.

Combining the underlying competencies in the two models resulted in competencies that could present a unique framework for leadership development (van Dierendonck & Nuijten, 2011).

The Synthesized *Internal–External Leadership Model* Encompassing Authentic and Servant Leadership Styles

The increase in storage and speed of transmission has heightened interdependency and hyper-complexity. Because of this paradigm shift, we viewed the synthesis of the Authentic and Servant Leadership styles as a foundational approach to address the digital VUCA world. We propose that the C2 approach is no longer relevant within this new context. Thus, a transition to the C2+ approach is both prudent and wise to give authority to the person who has the information; hence the person understanding the need to act. We propose that the synthesized Internal–External Leadership Model (Fig. 27.2) involves a leader who exhibits:

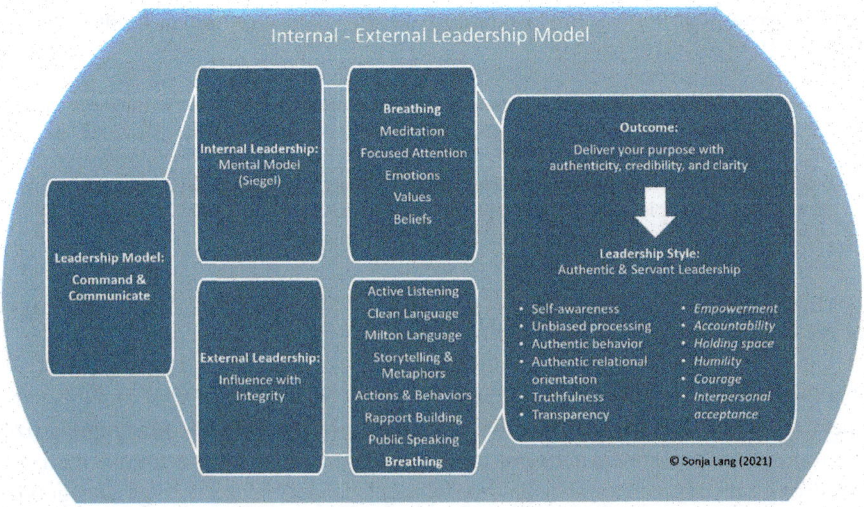

Fig. 27.2 Internal–External Leadership Model. © Copyright Mindful Clarity, 2021

- internally conscious, applying the mental model and methods, such as breathing and self-focused attention (meditation);
- externally able to influence with integrity by implementing active listening, Clean Language, Milton Language, and storytelling and metaphors .

By applying these methods to team members and subordinates, leaders could develop the capability to build rapport when delivering their purpose to the audience with authenticity, credibility, and clarity. White (2014) proposed a range of critical success factors for project leadership that echoes some of the elements of the Internal–External model:

- clear objectives,
- guidelines for facilitating virtual meetings,
- trust generated by team members,
- [clear] language training, and
- local achievement of global goals.

The Internal–External Leadership model is often interpreted as leading others through precise communication. Most communication is self-communication by looking to understand a situation and achieve clarity. However, this process is too often neglected. Applying the Internal Leadership mental model (Siegel, 2007) helps to distinguish between a filtered and perceived situation through unbiased facts. Knowing and being able to reduce one's filters and biases leads to clarity. Tools and methods to reach this goal in Internal Leadership are breathing, focused attention, and emotional control. Once this clarity is reached, visions can be shared with others with a positive intention for all through External Leadership. Effective tools exist for leaders to ensure that the vision can be transported and received by their audience (e.g., Milton Language, Storytelling, and Metaphors). Breath is the primary connection to reach internal clarity as well as external credibility. Applying all these insights and tools could enhance a leader's Authentic and Servant Leadership qualities.

The synthesized Internal–External Leadership Model enhances and sustains the C2+ approach. Authentic Leadership appears to contain essential elements to comprehend VUCA conditions without bias for what they are. Self-awareness establishes congruency between the outside world, self, and a leader's actions. The Servant Leadership style recognizes the interdependency between events, actors, and objects. For long-term success, we need a diverse and empowering range of inputs to the models to benefit individuals, businesses, industries, institutions, and societies. As Geerlof (2017) outlined in his grounded–detachment paradox explanation of the daily challenges in leadership practice:

> The grounded–detachment paradox refers to leadership that is on the one hand grounded in reality—and thus has the capacity to connect, engage, trust, and deal with uncertainty, headwind, and unpredictability—and is on the other hand detached, meaning not devoted to worldly possessions, status, relationships, security, and/or a pre-described outcome.

We are again presented with a bifurcated model that contrasts two ends of the spectrum: "grounded reality" with "detachment from reality" because of the VUCA world we operate within. The next section will describe how the synthesized Internal–External Leadership Model weaves the two leadership models into a unifying whole for coping and dealing with the VUCA world.

Internal Vs. External Leadership Principles

Leaders with internal clarity and positive intent combined with ability to connect externally and communicate with others can achieve their vision. In fact, they inspire and take along others–the positive effect of this can hence be multiplied and spread to a company, country, and the world. The Internal Leadership model is the foundation for so much, as it facilitates the leader to overcome unconscious/emotional distortion of self and the environment. Thus, external leadership creates teams and inspires followers with the vision.

In the digital age, which started in 2002, the C2 approach no longer effectively achieved its goal, e.g., to command a specific process for an expected return. Instead, we might wish to consider World Economic Forum's proclaimed need for competencies to not only manage the information flood and changes; but even benefit from the digital age's promises (Centre for the New Economy and Society, 2018). Intellectually, we know that as we desire a different outcome, we need a different input. The different input starts at the leader and his Internal Leadership.

Consilience has been used to describe the process of discovering common truths derived from divergent knowledge domains (Wilson, 1998). Siegal (1999) talks about using consilience *In the Developing Mind* to synthesize a wide range of dissimilar disciplines of science to construct a framework entitled "*Interpersonal Neurobiology*."This researcher used the outcomes of her Action Research united with consilience to architect the Internal–External Leadership Model. The tool could be used to build solutions for individuals and corporate executives in their quest to overcome the chaos of the VUCA environment. Thus, based upon Action Research in the workplace, the researcher identified numerous examples of how the C2+ approach could overcome the shortcomings of the C2 approach. The preliminary result was the emergence of a new model, synthesized from the Authentic and Servant Leadership models.

In fact, the author's Action Research in the workplace uncovered a pattern that was evident in a wide range of industries: the disconnect between proclaimed goals and pathways toward the goal as well as the praxis of management actions. The discrepancy appears between management communication of the vision and mission and the consequent actions of managers and staff. For example, Harris Polling conducted a recent *Interact* survey with over 2000 U.S. adults (Solomon, 2016). An impressive majority, almost 70%, were managers who expressed significant challenges associated with communicating to employees. Humankind could accumulate considerable benefits if appropriate, proven, and successful methods and tools were more widely adopted. In this section we will review the detailed elements of the Internal–External Leadership Model.

Internal Leadership Framework

We propose that not being aware of the multifaceted, deeply rooted perspectives held by all humans might be a root-cause for critical misunderstandings and misinterpretations during the communications process. Communication bears significant prominence in the corporate world and addressing the overall mission of a company appropriately is the responsibility of the leaders. Today, as creativity, authority, and action of the employee needs to be activated by the leader, the *what* do we want to achieve (goal) becomes essential and the *why* increases in importance to motivate the employee to find the solution (Sinek, 2009).

Mental Models

Siegel (2012, p. 38–8) defined the mind (the phenomenon of consciousness) as "an embodied and relational process that regulates the flow of energy and information." Siegel's Mindsight Theory concentrated on comprehending the fundamental elements comprising the human mind through mental models. The theory proposed that the mind "[emerged] from the mutual interconnectedness of the physical, mental, and relational (both human and environmental) domains of human reality" (Ogwu et al., 2020). The theory posited that the organization of these three domains arises from the communication patterns that occur through human relationships.

Cognitive science and psychology literature claim that mental models are the internal representations of reality in the individual's mind that makes it possible for them to interact with the environment (Craik, 1943; Johnson-Laird, 1983). Mental models are a cognitive structure, "the basis of reasoning, decision making, and, with the limitations also observed in the attitudes literature, behavior." (Jones et al., 2011, p. 1). The formation of the mental model originates through the workings of two processes within the mind: sensation and perception (DeLucia & Levulis, 2015). The unconscious mind is responsible for receiving, organizing, processing, and interpreting sensory information, which is the process of perception: the mechanism by which "with the help of the senses, environmental information is transformed into an experience of objects, events, sounds, tastes, and so on" (Roth, 1986, p. 81). The following steps are distinguished in the process (Roth, 1986):

1. the senses provide information, and,
2. the cognitive processes interpret information based on personal expectations, cultural values, and previous experiences .

The processed information then constructs the individual's perception (Eysenck & Keane, 2005). Thus, sensation is the input about the physical world obtained by the sensory receptors, and perception is the process by which the brain selects, organizes, and interprets these sensations. Therefore, the perception of the same senses may vary from one person to another because each person's unconscious mind interprets stimuli differently based on that individual's learning, memory, emotions, and expectations (Owsley & Sloane, 1987).

Emotions and Behavior within the Internal Leadership Approach

As emotions construct the foundation of thought, communication, and behavior (Bradley & Lang, 2000; Russell, 2003), leaders who want to lead need to regulate—not to suppress, yet to actively work on and with—their emotional process to control their own thoughts, communication, and behavior. Based on experience we propose that only two core emotions exist: love and fear. All other emotions are only derivatives of these two. Our experience shows that particularly the fear of failure can distort a leader's perception of situations, other emotions, and hence their responses. In a subsequent publication, we will describe more fully the relationship of love and fear to the Internal–External Leadership model. Suffice it to say that fear is associated with escape and avoidance behaviors and is almost always linked to future events, such as the continuation of a constantly deteriorating situation or a situation that is unacceptable. Fear can also be an immediate reaction to something happening right now (Lang et al., 2000).

In view of these emotions and behaviors, addressing clear vision has become a principle to maintain success in the corporate environment. Change often triggers fear and terminates logical thinking. Leaders must have ways to make themselves and others feel safe and secure to elicit the best and appropriate responses to the situation and align with the vision. Additionally, leaders must create the emotion of rapport and credibility to transfer their vision and mission.

The first stage of establishing credibility is during the declaration of the mission. This involves two significant steps: (1) bringing the mission to clarity within the framework of internal leadership, and (2) communicating it to the audience in an appropriate manner once the state of clarity is achieved. We have already concluded that emotions construct the basis of communication (Ekman, 1992). In the following, we propose that breathing practices could effectively enhance both internal and external leadership, and as a result, credibility, and authenticity—essential for an authentic and servant leader—can be successfully gained.

Let's look at a simple case study to demonstrate emotions and behavior:

> Chris manages a global team of a multinational corporation. He successfully developed go-to-market strategies but had difficulties in communicating with his peers and colleagues. Seeking advice, he was diagnosed with Social Anxiety Disorder (SAD). At the coaching's beginning, Chris unconsciously applied all his skills to the 7% of words, completely disregarding non-verbal communication. Focusing on inner leadership was his breakthrough. Chris acquired the skill of leading himself, to lead and influence his team authentically, credibly, and with clarity, and defeated the SAD. He now calls himself "a smart nerd."

Example Tools/Techniques for Mastering Mind and Emotions

Breathing

Eastern sciences have studied the role of breathing and breathing techniques in various contexts over many centuries. Furthermore, during previous decades, Western research of different fields has also paid increased attention to the benefits of breathing, and the application of breathing techniques has been adopted (Howe & Dwyer, 2007). Scientific evidence shows that despite the brain's central role and its specific parts, such as the amygdala in producing human emotions, emotions trigger responses throughout the entire body (Cacioppo & Decety, 2009).

Experts in physiology and health fields have observed that applying diaphragmatic breathing (also known as belly breathing or abdominal breathing) results in significantly decreased anxiety. Abdominal breathing involves a rising abdomen when inhaling and retracting when exhaling (Greenberg, 2003). Only a few researchers have investigated the benefits of using abdominal breathing in reducing general speech anxiety or even communication apprehension. Evidence from yoga practice also indicates that breathing practices reduce the sympathetic and increase the parasympathetic nervous system activity (Vempati & Telles, 2002; Raghuraj & Telles, 2003), leading to a balanced body and mental functions. According to Wilkinson et al. (2001), stress reduction methods often exclude simple breathing techniques that help individuals deal with stress and anxiety, and their role is underestimated. However, science has proven the physiological effects of inappropriate breathing and how carbon dioxide increases in the bloodstream inducing high stress and anxiety.

Focused Attention

Concerning Internal Leadership, the application of breathing practices such as abdominal breathing could enhance clear thinking and self-focused attention (Baer, 2009), which have a further beneficial effect on formulating a mission. Anxiety is reduced significantly so that a state of clarity is achieved. Thus, this pattern of breathing and other meditation practices can positively affect an individual's focus and approaches to problem-solving.

External Leadership Framework

Active Listening

Active Listening is a crucial element to servant leadership, first for the leader to understand a situation fully and secondly for the leader to establish a feedback loop with the follower (Brownlee, 2020). External leadership may be deemed successful if a speaker creates an intended effect on the listener, namely by making the listener recognize the speaker's intention to create that effect specifically (Searle, 2008). However, the listener plays at least as an important role as the speaker with attentive and focused listening to everything being said. The speaker and listener's roles shift naturally during communication. Therefore, the person in the momentary experience must listen to the other, then think, and only then speak instead of focusing on their role only as a speaker.

As Rogers (1980, p. 117) suggested:

Attentive listening means giving one's total and undivided attention to the other person and tells the other that we are interested and concerned. It shows Listening is challenging work that we will not undertake unless we have deep respect and care for the other... we listen not only with our ears but with our eyes, mind, heart, and imagination as well. We listen to what is going on within ourselves and what is taking place in the person we are hearing. We listen to the other's words, but we also listen to the messages buried in the words. We listen to the voice, the appearance, and the body language of the other... We simply try to absorb everything the speaker says verbally and nonverbally without adding, subtracting, or amending.

Active listening, thus, requires certain skills, which are the extension of the generic communication skills regarding both verbal and nonverbal communication (Silverman et al., 1998).

Clean Language

Another effective communication approach is the so-called Clean Language, based on the previously described Active Listening (Grove & Panzer, 1989). Clean Language is especially useful to those engaged in close working relationships. Clean Language is based on compassion and understanding, as opposed to "traditional" manipulative, persuasive communication techniques, the essence of which is persuasion with individual interests in mind. Clean Language allows the participants in the communication to convey their own interpretation of certain topics without others influencing their questioning through their own filter. Therefore, Clean Language as such allows for clearer, more neutral, and more objective (without emotional impact or prejudice) communication that results in understanding and cooperation. Active Listening and Clean Language could support the establishment of understanding, harmonizing relationships, and building rapport between the servant leader and their followers.

Public Speaking and Voice

The voice of a speaker often plays an even more critical role than the message itself (Mehrabian, 1971). People overwhelmingly deduce their feelings, attitudes, and beliefs about what is being said not by the actual words spoken, but by the speaker's body language and tone of voice. Mehrabian quantified this tendency: words are 7%, while 93% are not, 55% are body language, and 38% are tone of voice in personal communication. The nonverbal elements are particularly essential for communicating feelings and attitudes, especially when they are incongruent: if words and body language disagree, one's unconscious tends to believe the body language.

Voice is a part of the physical body and characterizes the individual even though the voice's basic role is to communicate, it expresses emotions, intentions, and also stress. Warren and Riedel (2004) suggested that distorted emotions have a distorting effect on the voice as well at the time of speaking. Therefore, when emotions or stress are uncontrolled during a conversation, the voice provides cues about the speaker's state (Scherer et al., 2001). According to earlier studies, facial and vocal expressions are the basic indicators of the emotions of an individual (Williams & Stevens, 1972; Cummings & Clements, 1995; Scherer, 1986; Scherer et al., 2001), thus managing voice is essential for speakers.

Milton Model

With Clean Language the leader's intent is to eliminate each disturbing element from the conversation to assist the speakers to be more specific or precise about their thoughts. The Milton Model is considered by some to be a useful tool for personal change and human communication (Bandler & Grinder, 1977). The Milton Model language patterns encourage the speaker to move away from the detail and the content and move to higher levels of thinking and deeper states of mind. The Milton Language creates a broader understanding of what has been said. The listener could receive the most appropriate meaning for them, which fits their perceptions. Milton Language patterns are a favorable tool for advertising and increasingly for politicians as well.

Storytelling and Metaphors

With storytelling and metaphors, the speaker reaches the listener on a deeper level. Storytelling is a favored tool and a crucial component to effective public speaking. It creates relevance for the audience, providing additional detail and mental visuals that bring to life otherwise remote or complex topics and most importantly connects on an emotional level. Stories give speakers the opportunity to convey narrations that relate to the audiences' experiences, thought processes, or values. Moreover, including stories in both interpersonal communication and public speaking helps the audience focus attention and increases recall.

According to psychologist Gary Klein (1999), stories are effective teaching tools because they illustrate causal relationships that people might not have recognized before, and they highlight resourceful ways in which people have solved problems. Additionally, stories motivate the audiences to act, i.e., to close the "action gap". The best stories captivate and immerse their audience, whose emotions can be inextricably tied to those of the story's characters. Most scientists agree that stories have such a powerful and universal appeal that the neurological roots of both telling tales and enjoying them are probably tied to crucial parts of our social cognition. We suggest that metaphors could enhance public speaking and storytelling significantly, which makes this technique popular in corporate leadership.

Metaphors can make communication more economical and efficient, filling lexical gaps and motivating semantic change (Gibbs & Colston, 2012). Metaphor is also a tool for explanation and persuasion (Lakoff, 2008), and the ability to generate and think with metaphors has been associated with everything from creativity to scientific innovation (Dunbar & Klahr, 2012). At the heart of these claims is the idea that metaphors both reflect underlying conceptual structures and processes and shape how people think. Studying metaphor can, therefore, lead to a better understanding of the relationship between language and thought (Lakoff & Johnson, 1980).

Conclusion

In this chapter, we suggested that leaders in the post COVID-19 VUCA world require a different mindset than those of the Third Industrial Revolution, which is achievable by applying the proposed framework of techniques in the Internal Leadership model. With the help of abdominal breathing, effective internal leadership supports the leader in bringing the mind to clarity. Proper breathing could combat anxiety and stress in situations and activate the conscious mind when "life-saving" decisions must be made. The tools of the External Leadership model, on the other hand, could support leaders in building rapport and gaining authenticity and credibility, making them able to inspire and empower the community.

We introduced that adopting a new mindset and new approaches in the leadership styles due to digitalization is critical for success. With machines winning the competition and work of processing more information and faster than humans, the pause in the struggle with work gives humans the opportunity to focus on what they are the best at: being human. Thus, the unique value proposition of being human is human qualities and human-to-human rapport, connections, and exchanges.

In the post COVID-19 digitalized VUCA world, the revival of human qualities facilitates connecting to others with clarity and integrity. Leaders can establish clarity for the purpose of creating and providing their vision and inspiration through effective communication and supporting, enabling, and empowering followers on their paths. The new leader can choose to be the authentic and servant leader who can even demonstrate acceptance of uncertainty and eliminate the fear from the volatile, uncertain, complex, and ambiguous information and data that otherwise could trigger fear and anxiety in the individuals. The new leader sets people free from fear and limitations to delegate power to achieve their best and the shared vision. Consequently, the new leader inspires people to do inspiring things. Inspiration is the spark for innovation. Innovation prepares us to embrace the unknown as an opportunity and even go beyond what digitalization is today.

Takeaways of "Internal–External Leadership Model in the Post-Covid-19, digital VUCA World"

1. People assume that digitalization has AI (artificial Intelligence) at its center. Yet, AI can free humans to focus on their unique selling proposition: **Being Human**. Only humans can create and have a human–human interaction, a natural connection. An exchange that also allows a connection between humans and human–natural ecosystems.
2. Key skills in a digital post COVID-19 world are creativity, originality, initiative, innovation, critical thinking, and complex problem-solving—skills that helped us to come through the COVID-19 era. Methods are available from a Swiss army knife of tools that can elicit the skills within oneself as well as in others.
3. Understanding the importance of one's own internal filters and "algorithms" brings unconscious biases to the conscious mind for active decision-making. Change begins within oneself and authentic breakthroughs come from within.

4. The leadership principles are logical, (including emotional patterns), yet simple. To be able to use them for oneself means to know one's ego and to know oneself.
5. Eckman has identified seven basic emotions. We propose there are two primary emotions, love and fear, the other emotions are a derivative of these two.
6. Traditional leadership models focused on managing others. By attempting to create external controls, those models became too rigid, both for changing environments and for situationally and emotionally-driven people.
7. Traditional leadership models focused on managing others. In contrast, the Internal–External Leadership Model is about clarity, integrity, and inspiration. The elements of leadership are first created internally and only then transferred externally.
8. Internal–External Leadership Model understands that without internal clarity, external control is pointless; internal clarity without ability to bring it across is ineffective. Both components are needed in a leader in the Post-COVID-19 and digital VUCA World.
9. Breathing is the key for internal clarity and external credibility.

Reflection Questions for "Internal–External Leadership Model in the Post COVID-19, Digital VUCA World"

1. A core question raised by the pandemic is: "Should we protect humans or the economy?" Various countries approached the challenge differently, such as Brazil, New Zealand, Germany, United States. Explain the underlying principles of each approach.
2. We should ask: "What is at the center of the Holonic Mode? Should the Holonic Model be rearranged? Should in 2021 society be at the center? Should it be ecology—considering 'Fridays for future'?"
3. Why is the internal state of someone so important? How can I control or influence my internal state?
4. What is the difference between a leader's style and a leader's behavior?
5. Does a leader need to be present? What comprised leadership prior to industrialization: The king in the Middle Ages, who no one saw and still was everywhere? Consider negative examples of leadership, e.g., the use of the Stasi in German Democratic Republic (GDR). Consider positive examples, e.g., in Bhutan, a king who measures gross domestic happiness.

References

Alvesson, M., & Sveningsson, S. (2003). Good visions, bad micro-management and ugly ambiguity: Contradictions of (non-) leadership in a knowledge-intensive organization. *Organization Studies, 24*(6), 961–988. https://doi.org/10.1177/0170840603024006007

Avanessian, A., & Malik, S. (Eds.). (2016). *Der Zeitkomplex: Postcontemporary*. Merve Verlag.

Avolio, B. J., & Gardner, W. L. (2005). Authentic leadership development: Getting to the root of positive forms of leadership. *Leadership Quarterly, 16*, 315–338. https://doi.org/10.1016/j.leaqua.2005.03.001

Baer, R. A. (2009). Self-focused attention and mechanisms of change in mindfulness-based treatment. *Cognitive Behaviour Therapy, 38*(S1), 15–20. https://doi.org/10.1080/16506070902980703

Baldoni, J. (2020, May 12). The next big thing: Virtual leadership. *Forbes*. https://www.forbes.com/sites/johnbaldoni/2020/05/12/the-next-big-thing-virtual-leadership/?sh=3dd2665b3e5e

Bandler, R., & Grinder, J. (1977). *Patterns of the hypnotic techniques of Milton H* (Vol. I). Meta Publications.

Bargh, J. A., & Morsella, E. (2008). The unconscious mind. *Perspectives on Psychological Science., 3*(1), 73–79. https://doi.org/10.1111/j.1745-6916.2008.00064.x

Bawany, S. (2014). Building high performance organizations with results-based leadership (RBL) framework. *Leadership Excellence Essentials, 31*(11), 46–47.

Bennis, W., & Nanus, B. (1985). *Leaders: The strategies for taking charge*. Harper & Row.

Berde, C. (2013). *Management Skill*. Debrecen, Hungary: University of Debrecen, Service Sciences Methodology Centre. Do. # TÁMOP-4.1.2.A/1–11/1–2011-0009. https://regi.tankonyvtar.hu/hu/tartalom/tamop412A/2011_0009_Berde_Csaba-Management_Skills/2011_0009_Berde_Csaba-Management_Skills.pdf.

Blanchard, K. H., Zigarmi, D., & Nelson, R. B. (1993). Situational leadership® after 25 years: A retrospective. *Journal of Leadership Studies, 1*(1), 21–36. https://doi.org/10.1177/107179199300100104

Bradley, M. M., & Lang, O. J. (2000). Measuring emotion: Behavior, feeling, and physiology. In R. D. Lane & L. Nadel (Eds.), *Cognitive neuroscience of emotion* (pp. 242–276). Oxford University Press.

Brownlee, D. (2020, May 7). Leadership traits for the post Covid-19 workplace. *Forbes*. https://www.forbes.com/sites/danabrownlee/2020/05/07/7-leadership-traits-for-the-post-covid-19-workplace/?sh=42fb38f82d4d

Brynjolfsson, E., & McAfee, A. (2011). *Race against the machine: How the digital revolution is accelerating innovation, driving productivity, and irreversibly transforming employment and the economy*. Digital Frontier Press.

Cacioppo, J. T., & Decety, J. (2009). What are the brain mechanisms on which psychological processes are based? *Perspectives on Psychological Science, 4*, 10–18. https://doi.org/10.1111/j.1745-6924.2009.01094.x

Centre for the New Economy and Society. (2018). *The future of jobs report 2018*. World Economic Forum. http://www3.weforum.org/docs/WEF_Future_of_Jobs_2018.pdf

Chen, J. C., & Silverthorne, C. (2005). Leadership effectiveness, leadership style and employee readiness. *Leadership & Organization Development Journal, 26*(4), 280–288. https://doi.org/10.1108/01437730510600652

Clapp-Smith, R., Vogelsang, G. R., & Avey, J. B. (2009). Authentic leadership and positive psychological capital: The mediating role of trust at the group level of analysis. *Journal of Leadership & Organizational Studies, 15*, 227–240. https://doi.org/10.1177/1548051808326596

Clausewitz, C. (1976). In M. Howard & P. Paret (Eds.), *On war*. Knopf.

Craik, K. J. W. (1943). *The nature of explanation*. Cambridge University Press.

Cummings, K. E., & Clements, M. A. (1995). Analysis of the glottal excitation of emotionally styled and stressed speech. *Journal of Acoustical Society of America, 98*, 88–98. https://doi.org/10.1121/1.413664

Daffara, P. (2004). Macrohistory and city futures. *Journal of Futures Studies, 9*(1), 13–30. http://jfsdigital.org/wp-content/uploads/2013/10/03.pdf

Dunbar, K. N., & Klahr, D. (2012). Scientific thinking and reasoning. In K. J. Holyoak & R. G. Morrison (Eds.), *The Oxford handbook of thinking and reasoning*. Oxford University Press.

Elkington, R., Van der Steege, M., Glick-Smith, J., Breen, M., & J. (Eds.). (2017). *Visionary leadership in a turbulent world: Thriving in the new VUCA context*. Emerald Publishing Limited.

Ekman, P. (1992). Are there basic emotions? *Psychological Review, 99*(3), 550–553. https://doi.org/10.1037/0033-295X.99.3.550

Eseryel, U. Y., Crowston, K., & Heckman, R. (2020). Functional and visionary leadership in self-managing virtual teams. *Group & Organization Management, 46*(2), 1–37. https://doi.org/10.1177/1059601120955034
Eysenck, M. W., & Keane, M. T. (2005). *Cognitive psychology: A student's handbook* (6th ed.). Psychology Press.
Galtung, J., Inayatullah, S., & (Eds.). (1997). *Macrohistory and macrohistorians - perspectives on individual, social and civilisational change*. Praeger.
Geerlof, J. (2017). Learning to embrace the paradox of leadership. *Integral Leadership Review, Aug 31*. http://integralleadershipreview.com/15719-learning-to-embrace-the-paradox-of-leadership/
Gerkhardt, M., Frey, D., & Fischer, P. (2008). The human factor in change processes: Success factors from a socio-psychological point of view. In J. Klewes & R. Langen (Eds.), *Change 2.0: Beyond organisational transformation* (pp. 11–25). Springer.
Gibbs, R. W., & Colston, H. L. (2012). *Interpreting figurative meaning*. Cambridge University Press.
Greenberg, J. S. (2003). *Comprehensive stress management*. McGraw-Hill.
Greenleaf, R. K. (1991). *The servant as leader*. The Robert Greenleaf Center.
Greenleaf, R. K. (2002). *Servant leadership: A journey into the nature of legitimate power and greatness*. Paulist Press.
Grove, D. J., & Panzer, B. I. (1989). *Resolving traumatic memories. Metaphors and symbols in psychotherapy*. Irvington.
Handel, M. I., & Tzu, S. (1991). *Clausewitz: The art of war and on war compared*. Strategic Studies Institute, US Army War College. https://apps.dtic.mil/sti/citations/ADA239084
Hilbert, M. (2012). How much information is there in the "information society"? *Significance, 9*(4), 8–12. https://doi.org/10.1111/j.1740-9713.2012.00584.x
Holborn, H. (1986). The Prusso-German school: Moltke and the rise of the general staff. In P. Paret (Ed.), *Makers of modern strategy, from Machiavelli to the nuclear age* (pp. 281–295). Princeton University Press.
Howe, M. M. & Dwyer, K. K. (2007). The influence of diaphragmatic breathing to reduce situational anxiety for basic course students. *Basic Communication Course Annual 19*, Article 9. https://ecommons.udayton.edu/bcca/vol19/iss1/9.
Ilies, R., Morgeson, F. P., & Nahrgang, J. D. (2005). Authentic leadership and eudemonic wellbeing: Understanding leader–follower outcomes. *The Leadership Quarterly, 16*, 373–394. https://doi.org/10.1016/j.leaqua.2005.03.002
Inayatullah, S. (1990). *Sarkar's theory of social change*. Metafuture. https://www.metafuture.org/sarkars-theory-of-social-change/
Isha Foundation. (2015). *Insight: The DNA of success*. Isha Foundation. https://www.ishaeducation.org/insight/insight-ebook/
Jandrić, P., Knox, J., Besley, T., Ryberg, T., Suoranta, J., & Hayes, S. (2018). Postdigital science and education. *Educational Philosophy and Theory, 50*(10), 893–899. https://doi.org/10.1080/00131857.2018.1454000
Johnson-Laird, P. N. (1983). *Mental models*. Cambridge University Press.
Jones, N. A., Ross, H., Lynam, T., Perez, P., & Leitch, A. (2011). Mental models: An interdisciplinary synthesis of theory and methods. *Ecology and Society, 16*(1), 46. https://www.ecologyandsociety.org/vol16/iss1/art46/
Kiersch, C. E., & Byrne, Z. S. (2015). Is being authentic being fair? Multilevel examination of authentic leadership, justice, and employee outcomes. *Journal of Leadership & Organizational Studies, 22*, 1–12. https://doi.org/10.1177/1548051815570035
Klewes, J., & Langen, R. (2008). A matter of trust—A journey through the five continents of change management. In J. Klewes & R. Langen (Eds.), *Change 2.0: Beyond organisational transformation* (pp. 11–25). Springer.
Lamm, E., & Gordon, J. R. (2010). Empowerment, predisposition to resist change, and support for organizational change. *Journal of Leadership & Organizational Studies, 17*(4), 426–437. https://doi.org/10.1177/1548051809355595
Lakoff, G. (2008). The neural theory of metaphor. In R. Gibbs (Ed.), *The metaphor handbook* (pp. 17–38). Cambridge University Press.

Lakoff, G., & Johnson, M. (1980). The metaphorical structure of the human conceptual system. *Cognitive Science, 4*, 195–208. https://doi.org/10.1016/S0364-0213(80)80017-6
Lang, P. J., Davis, M., & Öhman, A. (2000). Fear and anxiety: Animal models and human cognitive psychophysiology. *Journal of Affective Disorders, 61*(3), 137–159. https://doi.org/10.1016/S0165-0327(00)00343-8
Lawrence, K. (2013). *Developing leaders in a VUCA environment* (pp. 1–15). University of North Carolina Executive Development. https://www.emergingrnleader.com/wp-content/uploads/2013/02/developing-leaders-in-a-vuca-environment.pdf
Lenz, U. (2019). Coaching im Kontext der VUCA-Welt: Der Umbruch steht bevor. In J. Heller (Ed.), *Resilienz für die VUCA-welt* (pp. 49–68). Springer.
Lowe, I. (2016). *The lucky country? Reinventing Australia*. University of Queensland Press.
McChrystal, G. S., Collins, T., Silverman, D., & Fussell, C. (2015). *Team of teams: New rules of engagement for a complex world*. Portfolio/Penguin.
Mehrabian, A. (1971). *Silent messages*. Wadsworth.
Mengel, T. (2020, Sept.). Creative connections-fiction, futures studies, and leadership (for the future). *Creativity Matters, 01*, 72–79.
Müller, R., Geraldi, J. G., & Turner, J. R. (2007). Linking complexity and leadership competences of project managers. In *In proceedings of IRNOP VIII (international research network for organizing by projects) conference*. Universal Publishers. https://citeseerx.ist.psu.edu/viewdoc/download?doi=10.1.1.462.1858&rep=rep1&type=pdf
Negroponte, N. (1998). Beyond digital. In *Wired*. http://www.wired.com/wired/archive/6.12/negroponte.html
Northouse, P. G. (2021). *Leadership: Theory and practice*. SAGE Publications.
Ogwu, S., Sice, P., Keogh, S., & Goodlet, C. (2020). An exploratory study of the application of mindsight in email communication. *Heliyon, 6*(7), e04305. https://doi.org/10.1016/j.heliyon.2020.e04305
Peters, M. A. (2017). Technological unemployment: Educating for the fourth industrial revolution. *Educational Philosophy and Theory, 49*(1), 1–6. https://doi.org/10.1080/00131857.2016.1177412
Peters, M. A., & Jandrić, P. (2018). *The digital university: A dialogue and manifesto*. Peter Lang. Publishing. https://doi.org/10.3726/b11314
Petry, T. (2018). Digital leadership. In K. North, R. Maier, & O. Haas (Eds.), *Knowledge Management in Digital Change* (pp. 209–218). Springer. https://doi.org/10.1007/978-3-319-73546-7_12
Piel, M. A., & Johnson, K. K. (2015). Quantum leadership: Collapsing the wave function. In A. C. Andenoro, M. Sowcik, M. McNutt, & S. E. Murph (Eds.), *Leadership 2050: Critical challenges, key contexts, and emerging trends* (pp. 207–224). Emerald Group.
Raghuraj, P., & Telles, S. (2003). Effect of yoga-based and forced Uninostril breathing on the autonomic nervous system. *Perceptual and Motor Skills, 96*(1), 79–80. https://doi.org/10.2466/pms.2003.96.1.79
Renjan, P. (2020). *COVID-19: How leaders can create a new and better normal*. World Economic Forum. https://www.weforum.org/agenda/2020/05/leaders-should-use-their-vision-and-trust-to-create-a-new-and-better-normal
Rogers, C. R. (1980). *A way of being*. Houghton Mifflin Harcourt.
Roth, I. (1986). *Perception and representation: A cognitive approach*. Open University Press.
Russell, J. A. (2003). Core affect and the psychological construction of emotion. *Psychological Review, 110*(1), 145–172. https://doi.org/10.1037/0033-295X.110.1.145
Scharmer, C. O. (2016). *Theory U: Leading from the future as it emerges*. Berret-Koehler Publishers.
Scherer, K. R. (1986). Voice, stress and emotion. In H. Appley & R. Trumbull (Eds.), *Dynamics of stress: Physiological and psychological social perspective* (pp. 157–179). Plenum Press. https://doi.org/10.1007/978-1-4684-5122-1_9
Scherer, K. R., Banse, R., & Wallbott, H. G. (2001). Emotion inferences from vocal expression correlate across languages and cultures. *Journal of Cross Cultural Psychology, 32*, 76–92. https://doi.org/10.1177/0022022101032001009

Schwab, K. (2015). *The fourth industrial revolution: What it means and how to respond*. Foreign Affairs. https://www.foreignaffairs.com/articles/2015-12-12/fourth-industrial-revolution
Schwab, K. (2017). *The fourth industrial revolution*. Crown Business.
Searle, J. R. (2008). *Mind, language and society. Philosophy in the real world*. Basic Books.
Sinek, S. (2009). *Start with why: How great leaders inspire everyone to take action*. Penguin Group.
Siegel, D. (2007). *Mindsight: The new science of personal transformation*. Bantam.
Siegel, D. J. (2012). *Pocket guide to interpersonal neurobiology: An integrative handbook of the mind*. W. W. Norton & Company.
Silverman, J., Kurtz, S., & Draper, J. (1998). *Skills for communicating with patients*. Radcliffe Medical Press.
Solomon, L. (2016, March 9). Two-thirds of managers are uncomfortable communicating with employees. *Harvard Business Review*. https://hbr.org/2016/03/two-thirds-of-managers-are-uncomfortable-communicating-with-employees
Strack, R., Kugel, J., Dyrchs, S., & Tauber, M. (2020). *Leadership in the new now*. Boston Consulting Group (BCG). https://www.bcg.com/en-us/publications/2020/leadership-post-covid-19
Suderman, J. L., & Foster, P. A. (2015). Envisioning leadership in 2050: Four future scenarios. In A. C. Andenoro, M. Sowcik, M. McNutt, & S. E. Murph (Eds.), *Leadership 2050: Critical challenges, key contexts, and emerging trends* (pp. 23–38). Emerald Group.
Turner, J. R., & Müller, R. (2005). The project manager's leadership style as a success factor on projects: A literature review. *Project Management Journal, 36*(2), 49–61. https://doi.org/10.1177/875697280503600206
US Army. (2012). *Army doctrine publication (ADP) 6–22: Army leadership*. U.S. Government Printing Office [GPO]. https://capl.army.mil/repository/doctrine/adp-6-22.pdf
van Dierendonck, D., & Nuijten, I. (2011). The servant leadership survey: Development and validation of a multidimensional measure. *Journal of Business and Psychology, 26*, 249–267. https://doi.org/10.1007/s10869-010-9194-1
Vassiliou, M. S., Alberts, D. S., & Agre, J. R. (2014). *C2 re-envisioned: The future of the enterprise*. CRC Press.
Vempati, R. P., & Telles, S. (2002). Yoga-based guided relaxation reduces sympathetic activity judged from baseline levels. *Psychological Reports, 90*(2), 487–494. https://doi.org/10.2466/pr0.2002.90.2.487
Warren, J., & Riedel, R. (2004). *Emotional power: Tapping the inexhaustible energy of your spirit*. Axiom Publishers.
White, M. (2014). The management of virtual teams and virtual meetings. *Business Information Review, 31*(2), 111–117. https://doi.org/10.1177/0266382114540979
Whitton, F. E. (1921). *Moltke*. University of Michigan Library.
Wilkinson, L., Buboltz, W. C., Jr., & Seemann, E. (2001). Using breathing techniques to ease test anxiety. *Guidance & Counseling, 16*(3), 76–80.
Williams, C. E., & Stevens, K. N. (1972). Emotions and speech: Some acoustical correlates. *Journal of the Acoustical Society of America, 52*, 1238–1250. https://doi.org/10.1121/1.1913238
Wilson, E. O. (1998). Consilience among the great branches of learning. *Daedalus, 127*(1), 131–149. https://www.jstor.org/stable/20027479
Wittmann, J. (2017). Auftragstaktik for business organizations in volatile and uncertain environments: A competence-based view. *IAFOR Journal of Business & Management, 2*(2), 29–49. https://doi.org/10.22492/ijbm.2.2.02

Sonja Lang, inspires business leaders and executives across industries, continents, and cultures. Her coaching and training are based on Western and Eastern sciences combined with proven business practices. Sonja motivates leaders to transform internally and externally, as a certified coach and certified NLP master and trainer. She developed and promoted her *"Internal–External Leadership" Model* for the digital VUCA world, combining internal clarity with high-end communication: for unbiased processing, authentic behavior, and influencing with integrity. After achieving a bachelor in business administration in Frankfurt master's degree in business economics, Sonja enjoyed a successful 20-year career in investment banking in London. Sonja's monk-like Eastern sciences training at the Isha Institute of Inner Sciences in meditation, breathing, and courses on yoga psychology help her clients to adopt and successfully apply unique tools and techniques, and develop new competencies. Her speaking techniques and exemplary presentation skills position her as an exceptional keynote speaker and conceptual modeler.

Michael J. D. Sutton, PhD, CMC, FBEI, MIT, is an innovative researcher, knowledge scientist, and learning engineer. Over the past 50 years, he has distinguished himself as an interdisciplinary generalist working across several business and educational fields: Game-Based Learning, Online and Distance Education, Executive Coaching and Mentoring, Entrepreneurship/Edupreneurship, and Leadership and Executive Development. He has extensive experience in educating learners and leading strategic business and educational initiatives. He was an entrepreneur for over 40 years and a Practice Director for over 15 years in the emerging field of Knowledge Management. When he joined the academy, he motivated his learners in Business Schools to adopt an "entrepreneurial spirit" that is necessary to succeed in our complex world of volatility, uncertainty, complexity, and ambiguity (VUCA). He has coached and mentored founders of start-ups, SMEs, as well as executives and managers. As a life-long learner, Michael works to instill his vision of *Edupreneurship* in those he coaches and mentors.

The Prevalence of Upanishads in Sustainable Leadership: An Inevitable Influence of Spiritual Perception Towards the Context of the Dynamic Organizational Working

28

Nidhi Kaushal

Introduction

VUCA is the appellation given to the rapidly changing turbulent conditions of the business organization and transforms its strategic environment by providing new prospects for implementing innovative strategies from indigenous approaches. It is the synonym for chaos, terrific, insecurity, controversies, or unintended consequences and risks, but the concept of turbulence has been widely used in this phenomenon. Its conditions work as a challengeable approach and opportunity, which boosts the process of strategy development and motivational leadership in the organization. The components of the acronym VUCA are Volatility, Uncertainty, Complexity, and Ambiguity. Complexity refers to the various interconnected situations, which require restructuring in the organization, and volatility refers to the unexpected or unstable challenges, which require the consecration of resources to its control, while ambiguity refers to unclear and irregular connections, which require knowledge and expertise of the employees, and uncertainty refers to the event-based cause and effects, which require conjunction with structural changes. Its main reasons in human's life, society, and organizations are emotional imbalance in the behaviour, materialistic perspective, unethical conduct and indifferent approach, ill-usage of natural resources, extensive and infinite expectations, greediness, and immorality. The crisis period examines the integrity of the employees and changes their perspectives towards life by strengthening the belief that every problem has come with its solution ever.

VUCA conditions benefit the mind-set, which identifies various options as an opportunity (Ferrari et al., 2015). The changing work practices, multicultural workforce, endless and exciting opportunities, crisis, and corresponding adversities are some of the reasons for it (Steege, 2017), and its concept includes contemplation,

N. Kaushal (✉)
Leadership Practitioner/Researcher, Yamunanagar, India

S. K. Dhiman, J. F. Marques (eds.), *Leadership After COVID-19*, Future of Business and Finance, https://doi.org/10.1007/978-3-030-84867-5_28

strategic measures, and policy interventions (Tulder et al., 2019). Discernment has a significant aspect and a comprehensive approach (Kok et al., 2018), while the context of apathy, escalating change, and uncertainty makes leadership sharp and twisting (Bennis & Nanus, 1985). Leaders should create an environment of trust and transparency, of motivating challenges and stretch, of care and support to increase the people's performance during adverse conditions (Bogsnes, 2008), and those who are familiar with various organizational cultures express a global outlook to cope with it (Nandram & Bindlish, 2017). Modernism stresses coherence and order, while postmodernism emphasizes competing perspectives, which develops a diverse functional structure of the organization (Maanen, 2017). The culture of an enterprise has based on values and ethos, and for the survival of organizations during the crisis, required leaders to be more competitive and flexible (Vieira & Dixit, 2019). Excellent leaders collectively keep in mind their expectations and the wishes of the team to establish a unity of purpose among team members to achieve the goal (Kouzes & Posner, 2013). A multifaceted organizational environment with its hard intricacies gives wisdom to leaders to develop the capacity to lead from an ambiguous, emerging future as an outcome of leadership learning (Carvan, 2015). Value, understanding, contentment, and agility are the consistent characteristics to harmonize the modern components of VUCA in respect of volatile, uncertain, complex, and ambiguous situations. This chapter has examined its several forms and phases and classified into five sections such as (1) Influences and Motives Related to Today's Context of Complexities in Life and Work; (2) The Ancient Aspect of VUCA Reflecting the Valuable Approach of Truth and Discernment through the Wisdom of *Upanishads*; (3) The Implication of Spiritual Perception in the Crisis for a Psychological Change of New Insight; (4) The Importance of Agile Approach for Swift Leadership during Adversity; (5) VUCA as an Opportunity for Implementing Innovative Strategies of Well-being and Advancement.

Influences and Motives Related to Today's Context of Complexities in Life and Work

Human activities and behaviour are responsible for their favourable or unfavourable situations. Life's ups and downs are often concerned and acquired by himself rather than any other phenomenon, and his luck contributes very little to it because the mechanism of fate has based on the deeds only. It seems to be a crucial and sensitive phase of time, which tests the virtue of patience the most because various desires, needs, and perspectives also emphasize his mind-set that insists on engaging in moral and immoral acts. Consequently, it becomes very necessary to perform carefully, decisively, and judiciously by considering the inevitable prospective outcomes. Lazarus (1994) identifies that a person's personality struggles to manage transactions with the physical and social environment and changed accordingly. Greed and the extent of the materialistic perspective have a major contribution to the development of problematic conditions. Materialism means the value placed on the acquisition of material objects, which conflicts with collective-oriented values (Burroughs &

Rindfleisch, 2002). It is a state of mind that dehumanizes people and an innate drive to excel and oppose others (Scott, 2015), and forces one to compromise the personal freedom and value system and increases anxiety (Lambin, 2012). Materialism causes conflicting behaviour and choices, and a materialistic person places a high value on money and possessions rather than on family and relatedness needs (Promislo et al., 2010), while greed is a robust determinant and motivator of unethical actions (Piff et al., 2012). Another reason for the VUCA is to ignore the vulnerable and emerging threats and have an attitude of curt and indifference towards them because not paying attention to the smaller issues later take on a terrible form of crisis. Indifference is about the presence of an absence and usually object-oriented, and it is also a lack of empathy or a disregard for others' suffering and a lack of bias or impartiality (Leander et al., 2014). The manifestation of an attitude of 'indifference' produces measurable effects on the group members towards the goal and affects their aspiration levels for the group performance (Rosenthal & Cofer, 1948).

The extent of human desire and greed has been analyzed by several scholars for centuries, which has presented a parallel approach of an inexplicable objective with time, and they have emphasized overcoming the aspiration of the excessive collection of materialistic items. Because increasing competition and commercialism have an immense contribution to a complex organizational environment, so the greed of excess is also responsible for generating its conditions. Gluttony of greed has a significant approach in diverting the human's character from being moral to immoral while satisfying with existing resources proves to be a rational strategy and intellectualism to avoid the crisis. Learning is like making sense as a personal ability, which is also a process that leads to knowledge (Dixon, 1999). Folklore is the form of oral tradition and reflects the values of a social community, and develops along with the advancement of technology and human knowledge, which has excelled through ages (Hidayat et al., 2019). This term has evolved with remarkable semantic consistency throughout the decades (Fischman, 2012). Stories conveyed through cases have a lively and quick impact (Maanen, 2017), and below is a story depicting the factors involved in the causes of a problematic situation.

A monkey used to come to a man's house every day and make a fervour. Sometimes he even tore clothes, took away utensils and food items. All his family members were not sad, but they had fed up with that monkey's disturbance. One day the master of the house said, 'I will hold this monkey and send it out'. He asked for a small mouth pot (Handi) and put roasted gram into it, and buried it in the ground a hand above. Only its mouth was open, and everybody went away from that place. As usual, the monkey came into the house and kept jumping around for a while. When he saw the gram in the pot, he came and sat near to it. To get the gram, he put his hand into it and filled the gram in his fist. But the pot's mouth was small, and the fist tied to it could not come out. The monkey started pushing and jumping to get out of that dilemma. He shouted and leaped but did not leave the gram. Grabbing this opportunity, the master of the house tied the monkey and sent him out. Due to the greed of the gram, the monkey had to face that terrible situation and got caught. This tale shows that excessive desire or want can invites trouble and develops a situation of crisis (Poddhar, 1950).

Despite the necessary resources, higher expectations, and desires, and even excessive greed are also responsible for the circumstances of the crisis. It has been stated in this folktale that the desire to get more than enough can also disseminate one's happiness. Although all the items were present in that house for the monkey, but the greed of the monkey has created a problem for him, and he was deprived of his pleasure endlessly. Excessive indulgence of worldly pleasures also bestows the cause of the crisis and a reason for unethical conduct so, a person should understand the basis of VUCA and make a balance between his needs and wants. It gives the leader a rational and intellectual perspective of wisdom to avoid creating adverse situations in organizational functioning.

Expectations are interrelated with the external environment, which defines the natural selection of the organisms and their adaptation patterns (Lazarus, 1994), and reflect the rational attitude or psychological perspective, and moral or immoral behaviour as well as the strategy of the individuals during the realization process. Eternal expectations and the passion of fulfilling them, to an extent, create a situation of crisis in the organization. Therefore, it is vital to adjust favourably, amidst scarce resources and social inequality, to cope with the hard circumstances. Materialism reflects the individual's compatibility with experience and observations, while humanism treats knowledge or wisdom as a broad concept for internal development (Rummel, 2002), so spirituality makes the way to conquer, satisfy, or control the higher demands or expectations through understanding the aspect of supreme power and maintaining a balance between life and work.

Literature Review

Integrity is an act to express feelings in words, sincerely (Beebe, 2002). Spiritual awareness promotes soul-consciousness, which assures the feeling of achieving the real purpose of life (Culliford, 2011), and spiritual orientation is the intertwining of the inner personality to connect with the Supreme power (Danesh, 2000). The process of wakefulness occurs through adherence to spiritual practices, which involves diminishing the ego of one's self-system and rising of the inner self (Taylor, 2017). Spirituality is an interrelated aspect of various dimensions of religion, such as experiential, theistic, mythological, ritual, communal, or moral (Gollnick, 2005). Spirituality provides the emotional force that underlines the commitment to religious convictions (Ostow, 2007). It refers to life's most animating or vital issues and concerns (Thoresen & Harris, 2002), and it has a positive contribution to leading a healthy and happy life, which is important for day-to-day well-being (Idler, 2008). Recognition of spiritual issues is a significant aspect of multicultural education in enhancing religious competency (Hage, 2006), and Spirituality in the context of business retains new paradigms in anthropology, including the eternal rational conceptions (Kok et al., 2018). Business agility is about making purposeful efforts in alignment with corporate objectives (Evans, 2002), and it is the capability to manage organizational change (Worley et al., 2014). Emotional agility is about giving, calming, and living with more enthusiasm (David, 2016). It is the psychological power to change one's objective as well as the representation of a problem dynamically (Veale et al., 2013). Agile leaders are proactive and intended in the way of their work (Joiner & Josephs, 2007). Business flexibility makes the firm capable of responding to external pressure or threat with existing resolutions (Brown et al., 2009).

Morality and ethics as standards provide a behavioural approach to act and do correctly (Cremer & Vandekerckhove, 2017), and moral considerations, the concept of duty, and the natural tendency of persons or things are central in the meaning of dharma (Paranjpe, 2013). Ethics define the principles of noble life (Mandal, 2010). Unethical behaviour is responsible for diminishing well-being and rising stress levels among individuals (Promislo et al., 2014) and involves intentional aggressive behaviour for harming others. The absence of restrictions or lack of ethical norms leads to unethical behaviour, and it decreases the affective commitment of employees to the standards of the organization (Kaptein, 2011). In the volatility of a situation, people instinctively look to leaders, searching their words, actions, and gestures for guidance, when he appears assured and level-headed (Koehn, 2017). VUCA phenomenon is helpful to explore the creative processes and links with other concerns (Ferrari et al., 2015). No organization is an island because all organizations operate within their related frameworks (Bouée, 2014). The leadership task in the ambiguous world is to manage its inner psychological shifts, which is a developmental process (Fuchs, 2018). Responsible means being accountable for actions and answerable for decisions (Pless & Maak, 2011).

Learning from its historical structure is particularly effective for changes in the organization (Carley, 2000). Ancient wisdom has a rich source of learning indigenous policies of management (Thomas & Pillai, 2015). The literature of leadership examines the leadership roles at the individual (micro) level, performance at the organizational (meso) level, and attributes required for competencies and outcomes at the societal (meta) level (Kangas et al., 2019). Leaders should stringently implement values statements in the organization to develop an ethical culture (Jain, 2018). Develop managerial Effectiveness, inspire others, manage internal stakeholders, and politics are the challenges for leaders. As human cognition and emotion are integrated systems, so they should engage people emotionally by being visionary, passionate, and authentic (Gentry et al., 2016). VUCA provides opportunities to leaders by creating a flexible environment, adopting new technology, and conducting iterative dialogues information into differentiating capabilities in the organization (Raghuramapatruni & Kosuri, 2017), while rigidly adhering to current strategy means risk in missing opportunities (Waller et al., 2019). The role of a manager involves determining incremental tactics and implementation of the adaptive and flexible strategies confers his rationality during the complexity of organizational functioning (Parnell et al., 2012). The critical situation of VUCA empowers leaders to analyze and act quickly (Johansen, 2007).

Organizational cultures have become chaotic nowadays (Kumbhat & Sushil, 2018). Leaders must have an understanding of organizational business and master the nuances of global markets to foster innovation, communicate a compelling vision, and developed valuable teams (Phillips et al., 2012). Uncertain and turbulent conditions demand a breakage from the old customs and opt for the new changes, which appears to be an intellectual management act (Bogsnes, 2008). Being globally oriented means having an open heart to various cultures and traditions (Steege, 2017). Leadership involves the readiness to make decisions, the courage to take risks, the willingness to collaborate, and the ability to speak one's mind (Abidi & Joshi, 2015). Leaders working with considerable experience and responsible executive personalities get an opportunity to explore their valuable potential talent (Betof, 2009). Creating roles and units yields the benefits of specialization but creates problems of coordination and control. Every lateral coordination strategy has strengths and weaknesses, so a task force should analyze the problem carefully (Bolman & Deal, 2003). Impulsive people exhibit their inherent struggle in every aspect of life and relationships (Wishnie, 2012), and the best leaders, with their impressive style and enthusiasm, bring the vision alive for the upliftment of the team (Kouzes & Posner, 2013). The strategy has an inherent logic of suitability, feasibility, and acceptability (Yarger, 2006). Rigorous strategic planning deploys the available resources in the advancement mechanism of the organization and helps to mitigate employees in clarifying their goals (Prewitt & Weil, 2014).

Entrepreneurialism comes at the beginning of any organization, which has an ideal organizational structure in the form of a hierarchical pyramid or bureaucratic model (Crosby & Bryson, 2005). Working people have contributed enough time in performing their job effectively, so their job satisfaction factor has a vital aspect in determining their attitude towards the organization (Oraman et al., 2011). Leaders must understand the susceptibility of the underlying event and display a quick response during the crisis (Garcia, 2006), and Authentic leaders transmit their core values among employees, insist on fairness and integrity, and maintain harmony in the organization (Hegarty & Moccia, 2018). Crisis creates inconsistent implications in an organization's functioning (James et al., 2011). It is an occurrence that has not any anticipation or preparation (Munroe, 2015), and its management is a leadership imperative which opens opportunities for alternative possibilities (Taneja et al., 2014). Apathy is the basis for an indifferent attitude towards the objectives (Hendley, 2007). Materialism refers to a shift from intangible values to tangible goods (Scott, 2015). Intercultural sensitivity or mindfulness means being aware, open, and sympathetic to other people's experiences and cultural differences, which inclines people to be cooperative and tolerant (Shliakhovchuk, 2019). The consumer-oriented decision-making process enables managers to accommodate new changes and prevent their engagement in unethical practices (Singh, 2008). Discretion is a skill for making a quick and wise decision (Joubert, 2018), and servant leaders are always analyzed their decisions and actions carefully, and their holistic impact on the life of others (Gosling et al., 2012).

The Ancient Aspect of VUCA Reflecting the Valuable Approach of Truth and Discernment Through the Wisdom of *Upanishads*

Spirituality empowers a person to stand firm on the path of righteousness and maintains integrity despite all the troubles and obstacles because it provides an inner strength to deal with the complexities of life. The criteria under which VUCA is implied and categorized in today's world is not part of the modern pursuits, but these events or factors have also been present since ancient times. Various examples of ancient people grappling with complications and hindrances have been described in the *Upanishads* and *Puranas*. They have not only made a favourable ambiance from an obstinate environment with the strength of virtue, positive thinking, and the passion of struggle but also paved the way for ethics and justice to future generations. Gollnick (2005) defines that spirituality is an integral aspect of morality, and it has an active role in religion and a motivational influence (Culliford, 2011). It is an expression of refined energy that incorporates humanity and compassion while affirming the integrity of the personal experience (Mitchell & Roberts, 2009). Human spirituality has its source in psychological science, which is sought through experience (Worthington, 2012). *Upanishads* includes enigmatic sayings and sacred speeches of the Vedic tradition (Nelson, 2009), while spirituality provides the emotional force that underlines the commitment to religious convictions (Ostow, 2007). The psychology of spirituality perceives human nature as an integrated and unified reality with the powers of knowing, adoring, and feeling (Danesh, 2000), whereas spiritual belief is attached to an idea, while faith has linked with wisdom (Culliford, 2011). Learning from stories for developing the indigenous aspects works best in the organizational context and culture and as a paradigm for its practice (Betof, 2009). Reflecting the importance of spirituality, analyzing the aspects of VUCA, and contemplating its ancientness informs a relentless effort in this regard, so an ancient mythological story from *Puranas* as well as *Upanishads* has given here, which introduces the ancient phenomenon of it.

Once Ayodhya King Maharaja Harishchandra donated his kingdom to a Brahman, who was the sage Vishwamitra in reality. Taking the kingdom, he sought the king to give a thousand gold coins additional for the precedence of this donation. But all the glory of the donated kingdom, the treasure, and the palace had held to the sage. So he gave a month for providing that extra Dakshina (offering in the form of money) to him. The king who was till now wore ordinary clothes with his queen and the prince and left the palace like a poor. He did not even have a single penny or food because the food and water of his donated kingdom had forbidden for him, so he decided to go to the city Kashi of the benevolent God Vishwanath. After reaching there, in helplessness, he sold his wife queen Shaivya to pay the price of that donation, who was once serviced by the thousand maids. A Brahmin bought her and allowed her son Rohitashva to take along, but even by selling to the queen, the king could give only half of Dakshina to Vishwamitra. So, he sold himself to the executioner for paying the remaining half amount. The queen became the Brahmin's maid and had to do all the work of filling water, washing utensils, mopping, cleaning, and lifting cow dung, etc. On the other hand, the king was appointed as the cremation guard by the executioner.

The emperor, whose service was crowded by servants and soldiers, now roamed in the night alone in the cremation ground with sticks in his hands. But the sequence of trouble did not come to an end. The snake had bitten their son. Raising her dead son, the queen came to the cremation ground alone in the night while screaming. Hearing her cry, the king reached her to collect the tax of cremation. There were a thunderstorm and heavy clouds in the sky that night, and he recognized his son in the light incidentally. But he had made his heart thunderbolt and told her that without paying the charge, she could not cremate the body of the son. But she did not even have a shroud to cover the dead body of the son. Then, she decided to give half of her *Saree* (an Indian dress) in the form of tax, and the king agreed upon it. The period of examination had over. All of a sudden, the cremation ground lit up with divine light, and God Narayan appeared and grabbed the king's hand. He saw that his master executioner was none other than God itself, and his son also got up as soon as he called him. He was satisfied with his integrity and truthfulness and blessed him to live in heaven with his wife. At that time, Maharishi Vishwamitra also arrived there and had returned the entire kingdom and all prosperity to the king (Khemka, 2015).

This ancient story of the Vedic period realizes the prehistoric context of contemporary VUCA. Definitely, this term has related with the present organization's cultural dilemmas, and various policies have been devised to deal with it, but in every period, the most suitable approach of confronting it is through prudence and truth. Despite enduring all the hardships, the king remained adamant on the path of *Dharma* and did not get distraught at all. And his policy of following the path of truth proved victorious for him, and he got back his lost kingdom, family, and prosperity as the conducive gain of his all pains. There is a continuous change in an individual's conditions, which varies from time, and this phase examines his values of abstinence, discernment, and honesty to make a shift in the organizational environment as well as for personal improvement. This historical fiction offers modern leaders an inspirational model to pay attention to human values and work with emotional intelligence to stay driven during challenges.

The Implication of Spiritual Perception in the Crisis for a Psychological Change of New Insight

Spirituality brings an internal change of self-development. In the *Upanishads* discourse, the valuable wisdom of truth and discretion have asserted as effective attributes to get over from chaos and complexity because their collective power works psychologically to develop enthusiasm among individuals to take risks, make courageous judgments, and work diligently with persistence. An unpleasant event is not always destructive, but it also has another hidden aspect of positive alternatively, and an optimistic attitude gives the confidence to deal with complications and solve them gracefully for providing reliable results. Danesh (2000) finds that every living entity has an expression of either spiritual or materialistic reality, and ethics are the expressions exhibiting the standards of moral conduct governing the members of business and society (Mandal, 2010). Morally and spiritually oriented people always think about maintaining harmony and elatedness in the world, and Integrity is an ethic linked with spirituality with a sense of equality and justice while treating all (Beebe, 2002). Spirituality develops consciousness through self-development and empowers individuals to review and learn honesty from their own experiences (Mahida, 2015), and provides psychological and physical benefits (Idler, 2008).

Humanistic spirituality fosters a sense of closeness to the supreme power and connection to humankind (Worthington et al., 2011), and it serves as a foundation for personal growth and integration as well as life challenges (Kava, 2015).

Crises are often devastating events, but they can also be an opportunity to redesign and restructure a conventional system (Carmeli & Schaubroeck, 2008). It recognizes the most pressing issues of the changing environment, and a true leader knows to get benefited from those events that occurred during the shift and have confidence that the organization would emerge as a powerful entity better than before (Prewitt & Weil, 2014), and also measures the sense of perspective of the leader for organizational survival (Baldoni, 2011). They arouse due to paradoxical attitudes, and its management is an isolated endeavour (Pearson et al., 2007), so unprincipled mannerism of the organization has a strong contribution to reach the phase of crisis because unethical behaviour means deviance from morality (Promislo et al., 2014), and unethical business culture perpetually jeopardizes the organization because employees who engage in unethical behaviour impede the organization's ability to achieve goals (Askew et al., 2015). A volatile situation is unstable or unpredictable, and change may come quickly in it, while uncertainty is not volatility, and there may be no change inherent in it at all (Bennett & Lemoine, 2014). As organizations become flatter, so leaders should increasingly sensitive to diversity, generational, and geographical issues (Phillips et al., 2012). They must have an optimistic perspective for the complicated circumstances (Kadalie, 2006), and an effective crisis response enables an organization to make optimum changes and has a direct impact on quantitative measures of success (Garcia, 2006).

The wisdom of ancient Indian literature of the *Upanishads* serves to protect human beings from unethical conduct, guide them during complexity, and provide strength to trigger their tasks in the right direction. Various Scholars or humanists have analyzed these spiritual contexts with intensification and have considered them important towards behavioural and intellectual connections of human life, and also as a dynamic and inspiring source of wisdom to deal with the conditions of crisis. Here is a story that shows the power, help, and grace of God during VUCA and intensifies the spiritual connection of human beings towards the supreme power.

Once a merchant named Ramlal lived together with merchandized groups of related people for business purposes on an island in the southern part of primeval India. They were all wealthy businessmen and engaged in the trading of betel nut. Because of the holidays, all his family members have gone to visit Calcutta city. Once, he was sitting at his place with other business persons at night, then it was raining heavily, and an indication of the storm was as well. All of their labourers had used to work till 11 or 12 o'clock in the night. At that place, all the houses were made of tin metal. Suddenly a labour worker came and said that the warehouse had flooded. In the shop where all those traders were sitting, the water had started filling up, and its velocity got increasing. The storm was so fierce that the tin roof of the surrounding houses had flown, and the large trees of coconut and betel nut also fell. The scene of the disaster was before us. Now everyone started praying to God with a sincere heart as the last moment of life was present. Ramlal locked the entire bookkeeping in the vault. While meditating on the supreme almighty, he got an indication that he should go to his fellow Utpal Babu's house. His house was a double-story strong building made of brick-lime. So he asked all the people to go to his house, and they all walked together. He welcomed them and gave shelter in his house for a living before we said, and provided new clothes and food also. Several thoughts were roaming in his mind, and he started remembering his presiding deity. He was wondering what was there yesterday, what has happened today, and what will happen next morning. What to eat and how to live without money?

But what the little known creatures like him had known about the importance of omniscient God. Had he known, he would have thought about that God by not thinking so much for himself and for his sustenance, who has determined to eradicate all the sufferings always. The rain stopped as the dawn broke, and the storm had also stopped, and the light began to light up. He went to the roof and had seen a big catastrophic scene. After the water has run out, a person was sent to find the condition of our place. Their houses were safe, but due to floodwaters, all the goods had been soaked. Now he was worried about managing the food and drink, but the true God had arranged everything. They found an earthen pot, which contains half quintal rice, and remained floating on the water because the door of the room was closed and could not flow out. Everyone cooked food by using the rice, and the government's ponds of the city had situated on a high altitude, so they got their water to drink. Slowly the situation had started to improve. There was such a big catastrophe, but it seemed as if no heat has come. No loss of any kind had happened, either money or life. Those goods or items which were drenched by the floodwaters, their value got increased and sold at high prices. All this was the law of God and his graciousness. There is no cross of the mercy of the merciful God, the protector of the world. During the crisis, righteous conduct is necessary, and it emphasizes performing the tasks sincerely that embraces life with the perspective of ethics (Chaudari, 2016).

This narrative shows man's faith in God and his grace during the crisis that spiritual orientation works as an astounding power and helps him to overcome the VUCA period. It has a valuable lesson for today's impulsive leaders, who are ignorant of the omnipresence and infinite influence of the supreme power and give more importance to temporal enterprises and physical entities and consider spirituality to be a contradictory aspect. It strengthens the human's faith in the grace of God and his everlasting presence in good or bad circumstances, so everyone should believe in His sovereignty and patiently deal with adversity. It also extends the effectiveness of spiritual perceptions of the people and reflects their significant impact on their life's transformation, and also helpful in changing the psychological perspective of the employees positively during the stressful conditions by providing an optimal approach.

The Importance of Agile Approach for Swift Leadership during Adversity

An organization makes decisions in the present context of change, which reflects its future policies. Agility is the ability to identify new opportunities and their implementation in the pace of globalization, cultural and technical changes, and commoditization (Setili, 2014). Its aptitude is helpful to make critical changes in the right direction (Graham, 2014), so business agility is a desirable attribute for the enterprise for achieving its goal and mission (Evans, 2002), and included the concept of development and implementation of intelligent practices (Amos, 2014). The approach of the agile effort makes the firms more versatile and active to survive in the continuously changing environment (Worley et al., 2014), so it is the leading competency required by the leaders for sustained success in today's turbulent world of VUCA (Joiner & Josephs, 2007). The vision provides a context for day-to-day decisions about current work (Puri, 2009), and a clear picture of the set desire engages a person in taking action with agility (Goodrich, 2011), which enables leaders to think differently about the future as opposed to the past (Kelly & Hayes, 2012). Emotional agile people have dynamic characteristics (David, 2016). Reactive and proactive perspectives demand the need for flexibility in business to cope with changing environments (Sushil, 2014), so agile approaches are suitable in a changeable environment to provide a flexible system for further evolution (Boehm & Turner, 2004).

Responsiveness plays a key role in defining both the need for and the combination of old functions to meet the new reconstitution mission (Brown, 1987). A strategic response is required to cope with the immediate situation, which defines the ability of the leader to move from static plans towards pragmatic actions (Johannessen, 2017). Responsible leadership or quick responsive actions include reframing the rules of business practices and critical approaches (Pless et al., 2012), while quick response and mitigation strategies help an organization to achieve optimization in the business processes (King & Stevahn, 2003). Strategic intent provides a practical way to engage with chaotic situations, which facilitates agile response to anticipated events (Johansen, 2007), and flexibility addresses the strategy of conducting a quick response to change (Awwad, 2007). The Heroism of the hero's deeds in the heroic age is not a product of the imagination or brain of a later time. It originates there and then with the performance of the heroic actions (Sidhanta, 1929). Leaders should be aware of organizational dynamics while ignoring notable interactions of critical issues is vulnerable, so, from the perspective of performance, a leader should measure and diagnose the organization's overall functioning in the complex environment (Bushe & Marshak, 2016). Quick and early decisions are always better because decision delayed is often an opportunity lost in the VUCA world (Bouée, 2014). Agility is an underlying quality that reflects a person's activeness and sharp personality. It is essential to have the harmony of agility, cleverness, and prudence, to make rational decisions to get out of trouble during stressful conditions because entanglement is the attraction of many properties within a human's surroundings, which observes his internal values to aware of hidden qualities. A story signifying the human values and agile approach in the behaviour has given below:

Once a poor Brahmin lived in Asansol, India, and worked as a cook on occasion of weddings. One time, he went to a village to work as a cook for the marriage of a girl, and he was accompanied by an educated young man to attend the same festival. The young man had a box that contained thousands of precious clothes, jewellery, and cash for the marriage of the girl, but the cook had no idea that the person was going to the same destination with that exclusive luggage. On the way, he slept on the train, unfortunately, and he was to change another train at the junction ahead, but he slept till the last station. All passengers had landed at the station. Even the young man, who had the burden of carrying that box safely, left it and went away.

Suddenly he opened his eyes and saw that the train was empty, and all passengers had landed. He was the only one left on that train, and there was a heavy box in front of him. He was shocked and wondered, what to do with this ark, and in a state of helplessness, he lifted the box by the porter and decided to go Asansol without the ticket because he had no money to return. Then, he thought that it is not appropriate to travel without a ticket and to buy the ticket he opened the lock of the box, but he was speechless as soon as he opened the lock.

The box was filled with bundles of notes, a watch and shawl for the groom, and jewellery for the girl, and sesame, cash for wedding expenses. He started thinking seriously that this stuff should be of someone whose girl is going to be married. If he did not get this stuff, then the innocent girl will remain single. Perhaps, this box has belonged to the village person, where he was going for cooking, so he walked towards that village. Here, due to the loss of the ark, the whole work had stopped. Everyone in the family was sad and disappointed. On such an occasion, when he arrived with the box, everyone becomes relaxed, and the work of marriage moved ahead. This was a vicious situation for everybody there. Everything was going well and according to the program (Sharma, 2015). It is the honesty of a cook, and ideal for those people who, despite being rich, have bad intentions to seize the small possessions of others. If he wanted, he could easily grab that box, but his honesty, agility, and understanding had kept him firm and steady on his duty.

This story addresses the agility and intelligence of a person. Often, he is not able to make quick decisions and perform wrong deeds, and has to suffer, and his gain becomes paramount over the interest of others. Shrewdness and altruism have worked as a competent attributive strategy to deal with VUCA, because it was also possible that he would return to his place with the luggage, but takes a rational decision during the pressure and went to the village and handed over all the goods to the bride's family. His agile approach has not only saved the marriage but also exhibited his responsible behaviour of a humane character. So the strength of inner values and humanity has enabled a person to cope with complexity, and his agility has a meaningful approach to it.

VUCA as an Opportunity for Implementing Innovative Strategies of Well-being and Advancement

VUCA environment encourages strategies with the intensity of innovation. An organization could transform the crisis into an opportunity through focussing on business and customer requirements, developing innovative skills and strategies, compassionate about the team and his overall performance, and providing prospects for flexible approaches or resilience. Its conditions demand the skill of bounce back from adversity and to move ahead for making progress (Abidi & Joshi, 2015), and collaboration in the organization through trust, which has eroded by the propensity of competition (Kok et al., 2018). The restructuring is a powerful approach to cope with exceptional dilemmas in the organization (Bolman & Deal, 2003), which helps leaders to articulate the goal, and teams internalize them, and this internal motivation enables exploration (Puri, 2009). Characteristics of the internal dynamics of a team for the emergence and development of collective global leadership in diverse and complex contexts strengthens the team psychologically (Mohan & Lee, 2019). Mental agility is the power of people to become comfortable with complexity, examine problems, and connect with versatile factors (Gravett & Caldwell, 2016). It can be measured by keeping group learning logs that capture commitments, cognitive shifts, unanswered questions, and the group's ability to sustain thinking around the mind's states (Costa et al., 2014). An agile leader observes complexities to explore unknown possibilities (Veale et al., 2013). The challenges act as a call for change, and futuristic and optimistic perspectives turn them into opportunities because the crisis creates an opportunity for creativity and provides a powerful motivation to change (Munroe, 2015). In the inspiration mode of leadership, managers must inspire staff and employees to stretch and take risks, build trust, and create a climate conducive to ongoing change (Belasen, 2000).

Agility refers to a mind-set, business culture, or strategy (Waldock, 2015), and emotional agility means being responsive with feelings to respond optimally (David, 2016). Discipline makes the grounds for any flourishing endeavour, and agility is the counterpart of the disciplinary measures. The extent of task behaviour means spelling out the duties and responsibilities of a group by leaders (Gosling et al., 2012). Modern strategic dilemmas require a different orientation and a set of skills to formulate elegant and final solutions (Das & Ara, 2014), and assignmentology is a way of mapping standard leadership competencies to specific opportunities for development, such as serving on a task force, chairing a major initiative, or assuming a role with a greatly expanded scope (Phillips et al., 2012). A strategy has characterized by its complex approach of anticipating the future to maintain a holistic environment (Yarger, 2006), and a comprehensive strategic change makes the organizational functioning adaptive during environmental volatility (Carley, 2000). The change strategy manages a portfolio of change to transform performance in the business in its context (Gibbons, 2015), while a rational strategy shares a single vision at every stage of the organizational paradigm and enables versatility to adapt to changes in the working environment (Chakraborty, 2019). Leadership is about those people who operate effectively across organizational and jurisdictional limits and understand the importance of shared power (Crosby & Bryson, 2005). Creativity is related to innovation, which enables leaders to encourage people in conceptualizing organizational strategies (Luecke, 2003). Leadership is about those people who operate effectively across Emotions are the complex patterns and organismic reactions of humans (Lazarus, 1994), and impulsive means highly variable functional behaviour to immediate circumstances due to a skill deficit of emotional control (Farmer & Golden, 2009), and an impulsive individual generally attributes the outside environment responsible for his reflected behaviour (Wishnie, 2012). Thus the emotional intelligence of employees is significant to develop creativity and strategies for innovative outcomes (Gozukara, 2016).

Unfavourable conditions provide an opportunity to explore new avenues and to achieve distinctive success. A person often does not understand or recognize his potential and prevails monotonous life without any goal, whereas the changing circumstances give the possibility to implement innovative practices and provide new dimensions to his life, work, and relationships. These changes drive him to set new goals of finding alternative sources of subsistence and make him aware of his unique strength and expertise. In odd situations, a human either disintegrates or flourishes, therefore enduring the impulse of emotions with courage and discernment and make a judicious decision exhibits a wonderful power of human wisdom and awareness. A story reflecting the cleverness and awareness of a wise person for transforming the difficulty into a fruitful situation has given below:

Tenali Rama was an ancient scholar and had a prominent position in the king's court of Vijayanagar (a town in Southern India). One day he and his wife were resting at home, and they heard some leaves rustle in their garden. When he saw through the window, he found some thieves were hidden in the bushes. It was a big problem because both of them were alone in the house, and they did not even have any weapons, so he decided to teach them a lesson and make a plan to overcome this crisis and to confuse them. They know it was the group of thieves, and consequently, he raised his voice and told his wife that he was going to hide all the jewellery in the well. Both came out from the house to drop a big box into the well of his farms and then returned home and slept. The thieves in the garden heard their conversation and were overjoyed, and followed them, and after reaching the fields, they started drawing the water out of the well. They were indulged in their work the whole night. By daybreak, they were very tired and sat down to rest by the wall of the well. The next evening, Tenali Rama came to them and offered to pay money for watering his field all night. He told them that the box they worked so hard to get out, only stones were filled in it, and he had made this strategy to irrigate his farms and to teach them a lesson. After listening to all the matter, they remained stunned and were very ashamed after realizing their foolishness and promised him that they would not rob anyone. In this way, he had changed his crisis into a desirable situation through his intelligence and awareness (Board, 2013).

This fable has presented a framework for transforming a crisis into an opportunity and reflects the versatility of an intelligent and aware leader because, during the presence of alarming burglars, that wise man not only saved his money through his awareness but also got his farms irrigated by confusing them and turn the dangerous situation into an opportunity of watering the fields. A crisis not only creates situations of trouble but also provides opportunities for new possibilities of change. Challenges pave the way to explore new strategies alternatively and diversify the standard procedure of functioning, and also provide flexibility in the operations of organizational environment for new practices. Accordingly, it is the ability or potential of the leader that he takes the complication as trouble, or through talent and insight, turns the problem into a successful opportunity.

VUCA is an integral and underlying concept, which includes examining the reasons for its origin, the expression of its antiquity, the spiritual insights and psychological perspective, and practical understanding, and also the expertise to transform it into a successful opportunity. Its conditions arise in a natural or unnatural manner, particularly for the analysis and enhancement of human qualities, which signifies its universality throughout the ages. Life changes constantly, and its forms often deviate from normal, to complex, and complex, to normal, and the ability to keep pace with these instant turns or shifts recognizes a person's cognitive strength. Hence, with the dynamic power of spirituality and empirical knowledge, agility and intellectuality, truth, honesty and discernment, and emulation of the righteous conduct, an adverse situation or difficulty could be overcome or conquered.

Conclusion

Complex states affect various dimensions of an individual's life in all respects and enhance his personality through the mode of engagement of complexities, and spiritual perception paves the way for restraining a psychological balance with the external environment and inner turmoil during various ups and downs. Reconcile with limited resources and recognizing the difference between needs and wants has represented a functional mechanism and a significant strategy to make compatibility with adversities. The policy of dealing with difficulties through a sensible and agile approach has an influential aspect for leaders, which has presented through the concept of learning from folklore or narratives, as well as an ideology of transforming the unfavourable conditions into favourable. This work has analyzed VUCA's diverse forms, purposes, reasons, and notions from several domains, including its prospective compatibility in the organizational environment after Covid-19, which has served as an innovative mechanism in the field of sustainable leadership to counter the inevitable complications.

Key Takeaways from the Chapter

- Change in the highly materialistic perspective to control higher expectations, and satisfied with the available resources, a person can limit the situation of VUCA, to a great extent.
- The centuries-old references to ancient texts introduce VUCA conditions of human history and distinct strategies to deal with them, which also has a motivational approach for leaders.
- Spiritual perception and belief of being with God in every situation act as a unique force to cope with life's struggles and adversities.
- During complex situations, reasonable and rational decision-making and its quick execution build a leader's credibility in the organizational functioning and introduce his leadership skills.
- Eliminating problems through a prudent strategy and turning them into opportunities to explore new practices presents the sensible approach of a wise leader.

Reflection Questions

1. How higher expectations, materialism, and an indifferent attitude to prevailing issues are reasons or causes of the VUCA?
2. How ancient principles and narratives based on truth and discernment are effective to guide modern leaders during complexities in the organizational environment?
3. What is the implication of spiritual perceptions during the crisis, and the role of spirituality to change the psychological perspective of providing new insight?
4. How agility is a distinct quality, and why values are accountable for the ethical conduct of humans?
5. How can unfavourable circumstances be transformed into a positive and favourable environment?

References

Abidi, S., & Joshi, M. (2015). *The VUCA company*. Jaico Publishing House.

Amos, J. (2014). *Transformation to agility: Manufacturing in the market place of unanticipated change*. Taylor & Francis.

Askew, O. A., Beisler, J. M., & Kee, J. (2015). Current trends of unethical behavior within organizations. *International Journal of Management & Information Systems, 19*(3), 107–114.

Awwad, A. S. (2007). The role of flexibility in linking operations strategy to marketing strategy. In *POMS 18th Annual Conference, 4–7 May, 2007, Dallas, Texas, United States* (pp. 1–32).

Baldoni, J. (2011). How a good leader reacts to a crisis. *Harvard Business Review*, 1–2.

Beebe, J. (2002). The place of integrity in spirituality. In P. Young-Eisendrath & M. E. Miller (Eds.), *The psychology of mature spirituality integrity, wisdom, transcendence* (pp. 9–16). Taylor & Francis.

Belasen, A. T. (2000). *Leading the learning organization: Communication and competencies for managing change*. SUNY Press.

Bennett, N., & Lemoine, G. J. (2014). Organizational performance. What a difference a word makes: Understanding threats to performance in a VUCA world. *Business Horizons, 57*, 311–317.

Bennis, W. G., & Nanus, B. (1985). *Leaders: The strategies for taking charge*. Harper Collins.

Betof, E. (2009). *Leaders as teachers: Unlock the teaching potential of your company's best and brightest*. ASTD Press.

Board, M. P. (2013). *Treasure in the well. 151 stories of Tenali Raman*. Manoj Publications.

Boehm, B., & Turner, R. (2004). *Balancing agility and discipline: A guide for the perplexed.* Addison-Wesley.

Bogsnes, B. (2008). *Implementing beyond budgeting unlocking the performance potential*. Wiley.

Bolman, L. G., & Deal, T. E. (2003). *Reframing organizations: Artistry, choice, and leadership* (3rd ed.). Wiley.

Bouée, C. E. (2014). *Light footprint management: Leadership in times of change*. A&C Black.

Brown, K. N. (1987). *Strategics: The logistics—Strategy link*. DIANE Publishing.

Brown, W. A., Laird, R. G., Gee, C., & Mitra, T. (2009). *Soa governance: Achieving and sustaining business and it agility*. Pearson Education.

Burroughs, J. E., & Rindfleisch, A. (2002). Materialism and well-being: A conflicting values perspective. *Journal of Consumer Research, 29*(3), 348–370. https://doi.org/10.1086/344429

Bushe, G. R., & Marshak, R. J. (2016). The dialogic mind set: Leading emergent change in a complex world. *Organization Development Journal, 34*(1), 37–65.

Carley, K. M. (2000). Organizational adaptation in volatile environments. In C. L. Hulin & D. R. Ilgen (Eds.), *Computational modeling in organizational behavior: The third scientific discipline*. American Psychological Association.

Carmeli, A., & Schaubroeck, J. (2008). Organisational crisis preparedness: The importance of learning from failures. *Long Range Planning, 41*, 177–196.

Carvan, M. T. (2015). Leadership education for the volatile, uncertain, complex, and ambiguous now: A challenge to the field. *Journal of Leadership Education, Special Issue*, 3–10. https://doi.org/10.12806/V14/I4/C2

Chakraborty, D. (2019). Versatile performance in Vuca world: A case study. *Ushus-Journal of Business Management, 18*(4), 1–8.

Chaudari, R. (2016). *Rakhe Ram to Maare Kaun, Adarsh Maanav-Hriday, Prerna Dayak Satya Ghatnaye*. GitaPress.

Costa, A. L., Garmston, A. J., Zimmerman, D. P., & Fullan, M. (2014). *Cognitive capital: Investing in teacher quality*. Teachers College Press.

Cremer, D. D., & Vandekerckhove. (2017). Managing unethical behavior in organizations: The need for a behavioral business ethics approach. *Journal of Management & Organization, 23*(3), 437–455. https://doi.org/10.1017/jmo.2016.4

Crosby, B. C., & Bryson, J. M. (2005). *Leadership for the common good: Tackling public problems in a shared-power world* (2nd ed.). John Wiley & Sons.

Culliford, L. (2011). *The psychology of spirituality: An introduction*. Jessica Kingsley Publishers.

Danesh, H. B. (2000). *Psychology of spirituality: From divided self to integrated self*. Sterling Publishers Private Limited.

Das, K. K., & Ara, A. (2014). Leadership in VUCA world: A case of Lenovo. *International Journal of Current Research, 6*(04), 6410–6419.

David, S. (2016). *Emotional agility: Get unstuck, embrace change and thrive in work and life*. Penguin Books Limited.

Dixon, N. M. (1999). *The organizational learning cycle: How we can learn collectively* (2nd ed.). Gower Publishing, Ltd..

Evans, N. D. (2002). *Business solutions*. Financial Times/Prentice Hall.

Farmer, R. F., & Golden, J. A. (2009). The forms and functions of impulsive actions: Implications for behavioral assessment and therapy. *International Journal of Behavioral Consultation and Therapy, 5*(1), 12–30.

Ferrari, E., Sparrer, I., & Kibed, M. V. V. (2015). Simply more complex: A SySt® approach to VUCA. In T. Burgartz, A. Khare, A. Krämer, & O. Mack (Eds.), *Managing in a VUCA world* (pp. 21–40). Springer.

Fischman, F. (2012). Folklore and folklore studies in Latin America. In R. F. Bendix & G. Hasan-Rokem (Eds.), *A companion to folklore* (pp. 265–285). Blackwell Publishing Ltd..

Fuchs, M. (2018). *Leadership in a VUCA world: The Jedi path to agile mastery*. Haufe Lexware.

Garcia, H. F. (2006). Effective leadership response to crisis. *Strategy & Leadership's Editor's Letter, 34*(1), 4–10.

Gentry, W. A., Eckert, R. H., Stawiski, S. A., & Zhao, S. (2016). *The challenges leaders face around the world more similar than different* (pp. 1–20). Center for Creative Leadership, White Paper.

Gibbons, P. (2015). *The science of successful organizational change: How leaders set strategy, change behavior, and create an agile culture*. FT Press.

Gollnick, J. (2005). *Religion and spirituality in the life cycle*. Peter Lang.

Goodrich, L. (2011). *Seeing red cars: Driving yourself, your team, and your organization to a positive future*. Berrett-Koehler Publishers.

Gosling, J., Sutherland, I., & Jones, S. (2012). *Key concepts in leadership*. SAGE Publications.

Gozukara, E. (2016). Beyond the expected activities: The role of impulsivity between emotional intelligence and employee creativity. *International Business Research, 9*(3), 143–153.

Graham, J. F. (2014). *Agility training. Training for speed, agility, and quickness*. Human Kinetics.

Gravett, L. S., & Caldwell, S. A. (2016). *Learning agility: The impact on recruitment and retention*. Palgrave Macmillan.

Hage, S. M. (2006). A closer look at the role of spirituality in psychology training programs. *Professional Psychology: Research and Practice, 37*(3), 303–310.
Hegarty, N., & Moccia, S. (2018). Components of ethical leadership and their importance in sustaining organizations over the long term. *The Journal of Values-Based Leadership, 11*(1), 1–11.
Hendley, S. S. (2007). *Apathy: A cause not worth fighting for*. Crombie Jardine Publishing Limited.
Hidayat, H. N., Wasana, W., Pramono, P., Immerry, T., & Dahlan, F. (2019). Folklore in meme: Minangkabau folklore survival form in the digital world. In *INCOLWIS 2019, August 29–30, Padang, Indonesia* (pp. 1–7).
Idler, E. (2008). The psychological and physical benefits of spiritual/religious practices. *Spirituality in Higher Education Newsletter, 4*(2), 1–5.
Jain, K. (2018). When competition between co-workers leads to unethical behavior. *Harvard Business Review*, 1–2.
James, E., Prewitt, & Weil, R. (2011). Crisis Leadership -An Organizational Opportunity. *Australian Journal of Business and Management Research, 1*.
Johannessen, S. O. (2017). *Strategies, leadership and complexity in crisis and emergency operations*. Routledge.
Johansen, B. (2007). *Get there early: Sensing the future to compete in the present*. Berrett-Koehler Publishers.
Joiner, W. B., & Josephs, S. A. (2007). *Leadership agility: Five levels of mastery for anticipating and initiating change*. Wiley.
Joubert, S. (2018). A well-played life: Discernment as the constitutive building block of selfless leadership. In J. Kok & S. C. Heuvel (Eds.), *Leading in a VUCA world: Integrating leadership, discernment and spirituality* (pp. 139–150). Springer.
Kadalie, D. (2006). *Leader's resource kit: Tools and techniques to develop your leadership*. Evangel Publishing House.
Kangas, A., Kujala, J., Heikkinen, A., Lönnqvist, A., Laihonen, H., & Bethwaite, J. (2019). Introduction: Leadership for dealing with complex changes. In A. Kangas, J. Kujala, A. Lönnqvist, A. Heikkinen, & H. Laihonen (Eds.), *Leading change in a complex world: Transdisciplinary perspectives* (pp. 7–24). Tampere University Press.
Kaptein, M. (2011). Understanding unethical behavior by unraveling ethical culture. *Human Relations, 64*(6), 843–869. https://doi.org/10.1177/0018726710390536
Kava, L. F. (2015). Spirituality and the sense of self: An inductive analysis. *The Qualitative Report, 20*(5), 697–711.
Kelly, K., & Hayes, G. (2012). *Leading in turbulent times: The low down on the top job*. Pearson Education Limited.
Khemka, R. (2015). *Satya Paalan Ki Dhridta, Prernaprad Kathayen*. GitaPress.
King, J. A., & Stevahn, L. (2003). *Interactive evaluation practice: Mastering the interpersonal dynamics of program evaluation*. SAGE Publications.
Koehn, N. (2017). *Forged in crisis: The power of courageous leadership in turbulent times*. John Murray Press.
Kok, J., Steven, C., & Heuvel, V. D. (2018). Preface. In J. Kok, V. D. Heuvel, & C. Steven (Eds.), *Leading in a VUCA world: Integrating leadership, discernment and spirituality* (pp. v–xii). Springer Open.
Kouzes, J. M., & Posner, B. Z. (2013). *The five practices of exemplary leadership—Asia*. Wiley.
Kumbhat, A., & Sushil. (2018). Development stages and scaling issues of startups. In S. Dhir & Sushil (Eds.), *Flexible strategies in VUCA markets* (pp. 3–16).
Lambin, E. (2012). *An ecology of happiness*. University of Chicago Press.
Lazarus, R. S. (1994). *Emotion and adaptation*. Oxford University Press.
Leander, N. P., Shah, J. Y., & Sanders, S. (2014). Indifferent reactions: Regulatory responses to the apathy of others. *Journal of Personality and Social Psychology, 107*(2), 229–247.
Luecke, R. (2003). *Harvard business essentials managing creativity and innovation*. Harvard Business School Press.
Maanen, J. V. (2017). Foreword. In E. Gummesson (Ed.), *Case theory in business and management: Reinventing case study research* (pp. xv–xvii). SAGE Publications Ltd.

Mahida, A. (2015). The role of spiritual psychology for holistic living. *The International Journal of Indian Psychology, 2*(3), 141–148.

Mandal, S. K. (2010). Ethics in business & corp governance. McGraw-Hill Education (India) Pvt Limited.

Mitchell, S., & Roberts, G. (2009). Psychosis. In C. Cook, A. Powell, & A. Sims (Eds.), *Spirituality and psychiatry* (pp. 39–60). Royal College of Psychiatrists.

Mohan, G., & Lee, Y. (2019). Temporal dynamics of collective global leadership and team psychological safety in multinational teams: An empirical investigation. In B. S. Reiche, B. Szkudlarek, J. S. Osland, & M. E. Mendenhall (Eds.), *Advances in global leadership* (Vol. 12, pp. 29–47). Emerald Publishing Limited.

Munroe, M. (2015). *Overcoming crisis expanded edition: The secrets to thriving in challenging times*. Destiny Image, Incorporated.

Nandram, S. S., & Bindlish, P. K. (2017). Introduction to VUCA. In S. S. Nandram & P. K. Bindlish (Eds.), *Managing VUCA through integrative self-management: How to cope with volatility, uncertainty, complexity and ambiguity in organizational behavior* (pp. 3–14). Springer.

Nelson, J. M. (2009). Introduction to psychology, religion, and spirituality. In J. M. Nelson (Ed.), *Psychology, religion, and spirituality* (pp. 1–41). Springer.

Oraman, Y., Unakıtana, G., & Selen, U. (2011). Measuring employee expectations in a strategic human resource management research: Job satisfaction. *Procedia Social and Behavioral Sciences, 24*, 413–420.

Ostow, M. (2007). *Spirit, mind, & brain: A psychoanalytic examination of spirituality and religion*. Columbia University Press.

Paranjpe, A. C. (2013). The concept of dharma: Classical meaning, common misconceptions and implications for psychology. *Psychology and Developing Societies, 25*(1), 1–20.

Parnell, J. A., Dent, E. B., O'Regan, N., & Hughes, T. (2012). Managing performance in a volatile environment: Contrasting perspectives on luck and causality. *British Journal of Management, 23*, 104–118. https://doi.org/10.1111/j.1467-8551.2012.00815.x

Pearson, C. M., Roux-Dufort, C., & Clair, J. A. (2007). Introduction. In C. Roux-Dufort, J. A. Clair, & C. M. Pearson (Eds.), *International handbook of organizational crisis management* (pp. vii–xi). SAGE Publications.

Phillips, J., Phillips, P. P., & Ray, R. (2012). *Measuring leadership development: Quantify your Program's impact and ROI on organizational performance*. McGraw-Hill Education.

Piff, P. K., Stancato, D. M., Côté, S., Mendoza-Denton, R., & Keltner, D. (2012). Higher social class predicts increased unethical behavior. *Proceedings of the National Academy of Sciences of the United States, 109*(11), 4086–4091. https://doi.org/10.1073/pnas.1118373109

Pless, N., & Maak, T. (2011). Responsible leadership: Pathways to the future. *Journal of Business Ethics, 98*, 3–13. https://doi.org/10.1007/S10551-011-1114-4

Pless, N. M., Maak, T., & Jongh, D. D. (2012). Foreword to special issue on responsible leadership. In N. M. Pless & T. Maak (Eds.), *Responsible leadership* (p. 1). Springer.

Poddhar, H. (1950). *Lalchi Bandar. Upyogi Kahaniya*. Gita Press.

Prewitt, J. E., & Weil, R. (2014). Organizational opportunities endemic in crisis leadership. *Journal of Management Policy and Practice, 15*(2), 72–87.

Promislo, M. D., Deckop, J. R., & Giacalone, R. A. (2010). Valuing money more than people: The effects of materialism on work–family conflict. *Journal of Occupational and Organizational Psychology, 83*, 935–953. https://doi.org/10.1348/096317909X480167

Promislo, M. D., Giacalone, R. A., & Jurkiewicz, C. L. (2014). Ethical impact theory (EIT) unethical work behavior and well-being. In M. D. Promislo & R. A. Giacalone (Eds.), *Handbook of unethical work behavior* (pp. 3–22). Taylor & Francis.

Puri, C. P. (2009). *Agile management feature driven development*. Global India Publications Pvt Ltd..

Raghuramapatruni, R., & Kosuri, S. R. (2017). The straits of success in a VUCA world. *IOSR Journal of Business and Management*, 16–22.

Rosenthal, D., & Cofer, C. N. (1948). The effect on group performance of an indifferent and neglectful attitude shown by one group member. *Journal of Experimental Psychology, 38*(5), 568–577. https://doi.org/10.1037/h0057961

Rummel, R. (2002). A humanism between materialism and idealism. Hawaii: https://www.hawaii.edu/powerkills/DPF.CHAP32.HTM

Scott, G. (2015). *The materialistic world: Escape materialism. Refocus on what is truly important. Discover real joy*. Create Space Independent Publishing Platform.

Setili, A. (2014). *The agility advantage: How to identify and act on opportunities in a fast-changing world*. Jossey-Bass.

Sharma, S. (2015). *Imandaar Rasoiya. Upkar ka Badla*. Gita Press.

Shliakhovchuk, E. (2019). After cultural literacy: New models of intercultural competency for life and work in a VUCA world. *Educational Review*, 1–32. https://doi.org/10.1080/00131911.2019.1566211

Sidhanta, N. (1929). *The heroic age of India: A comparative study*. K. Paul, Trench, Trubner & Company, Limited.

Singh, S. (2008). Introduction. In S. Singh (Ed.), *Business practices in emerging and re-emerging markets* (pp. 1–13). Palgrave Macmillan.

Steege, M. V. D. (2017). Introduction. In R. Elkington, J. M. Breen, M. V. D. Steege, & J. Glick-Smith (Eds.), *Visionary leadership in a turbulent world: Thriving in the new VUCA context* (pp. 1–9). Emerald Publishing Limited.

Sushil. (2014). Diverse shades of flexibility and agility in business. In G. Chroust & Sushil (Eds.), *Systemic flexibility and business agility* (pp. 3–20). Springer.

Taneja, S., Pryor, M. G., Sewell, S., & Recuero, A. M. (2014). Strategic crisis management: A basis for renewal and crisis prevention. *Journal of Management Policy and Practice, 15*(1), 78–85.

Taylor, S. (2017). *The leap: The psychology of spiritual awakening*. New World Library.

Thomas, J., & Pillai, R. R. (2015). Globalizing Indian thought: Is there an 'Indian way of management'? *IIM Kozhikode Society & Management Review, 4*(1), vii–ix.

Thoresen, C. E. & Harris (2002). Spirituality and health: What's the evidence and what's needed? *Annals of Behavioral Medicine, 24*(1), 3–13.

Tulder, R., Jankowska, B., & Verbeke, A. (2019). Introduction: Progress in international business research in an increasingly VUCA world. In R. V. Tulder, A. Verbeke, P. J. Buckley, & B. Jankowska (Eds.), *International business in a VUCA world: The changing role of states and firms* (Vol. 14, pp. 1–22). Emerald Publishing Limited.

Veale, T., Feyaerts, K., & Forceville, C. (2013). Creativity and the agile mind. In T. Veale, C. Forceville, & K. Feyaerts (Eds.), *Creativity and the agile mind a multi-disciplinary study of a multi-faceted phenomenon* (Vol. 21, pp. 15–35). Walter de Gruyter.

Vieira, W., & Dixit, M. (2019). *The 5Gs of family business*. SAGE Publications India Pvt Ltd..

Waldock, B. (2015). *Being agile in business: Discover faster, smarter, leaner ways to work*. Pearson Education Limited.

Waller, R. E., Lemoine, P. A., Mense, E. G., Garretson, C. J., & Richardson, M. D. (2019). Global higher education in a VUCA world: Concerns and projections. *Journal of Education and Development, 3*(2), 73–83.

Wishnie, H. (2012). *The impulsive personality: Understanding people with destructive character disorders*. Springer.

Worley, C. G., Williams, T. D., & Lawler, E. E., III. (2014). *The agility factor: Building adaptable organizations for superior performance*. Jossey-Bass.

Worthington, E. L., Hook, J. N., Davis, D. E., & McDaniel, M. E. (2011). Religion and spirituality. *Journal of Clinical Psychology, 67*(2), 204–214. https://doi.org/10.1002/jclp.20760

Worthington, E. L. (2012). *The Oxford handbook of psychology and spirituality*. OUP.

Yarger, H. R. (2006). *Strategic theory for the 21st century: The little book on big strategy*. DIANE Publishing.

Nidhi Kaushal is a Ph.D. holder in Management Studies from the Indian Institute of Technology, Roorkee. She holds a Master's degree in Business Administration and a Bachelor's degree in Computer Science from Kurukshetra University, India, as well. She has been interested and indulged in research works related to Entrepreneurship, Leadership, Wisdom Literature, Management, and Indigenous Studies. During her Ph.D., she has identified the indigenous studies of literature and folklore related to Leadership and Management and presented her work in various international conferences and research publications across the globe. Working as a researcher, she is exploring Leadership with the study of Creative writings and ancient Indian scriptures, and this is her contribution to academic research.

Leadership Through Spiritual Economics: The Sustainable Model in the Post-Covid World

29

Bidyut K. Sarkar

The Covid affected world in general and the ocean of humanity in particular are getting churned like never before. The great churning, like that in the *Purāna*(s), is generating both ambrosia and poison. Amidst this turbulence, to guide the mankind in the right direction, utilizing the nectar to its fullest potential and minimizing the effect of the venom, we require an authority that has sufficient insight and foresight. What kind of leadership can bring about such a sustainable guidance is therefore the most important question.

'Looking from Within'

The same event looking from different level appears different—all may be valid to a certain extent, but the validity increases with the height of the level. For objective process, determination of height and validity are relatively easy; for subjective process they are difficult, but can be clearly determined through the dictum '*phalena pariciyate*' (effect indicates the cause).For instance, the apparently objective concept of electron, changes considerably as we move from secondary school level to the doctoral level through senior secondary, graduation and post-graduation—gradually the objectivity of classical physics merges into subjectivity of quantum-relativistic modern physics and then becomes omnijective in the contemporary field theories. To answer the question, how the post-Covid world scenario will be, in the short and the long term, so many researches are being conducted in several disciplines, reports are being prepared and published in public domain, most of them are based on mathematical modelling and statistical forecasting but effect on the individual and the society remains largely a subjective question, a matter of feeling and therefore cannot be calculated and expressed in numbers. 'Not everything that can

B. K. Sarkar (✉)
Founder-Managing Trustee, Prof. S. K. Chakraborty Memorial Trust, Kolkata, India

S. K. Dhiman, J. F. Marques (eds.), *Leadership After COVID-19*, Future of Business and Finance, https://doi.org/10.1007/978-3-030-84867-5_29

be counted counts and not everything that counts can be counted' (statement attributed to Einstein).Therefore, for the subjective assessment, which does count a lot, we need to respectfully prostate to such minds, who have reached a high level of spiritual attainment and can connect with the universal consciousness. For some purposeful prognostication, observing what is happening all around as the effect and applying some kind of subjective regression analysis to arrive at the cause, they support the application of Law of Karma. In this case, since the present collective scenario is on the whole bad, our collective karma in the past must be malafide also. This realization suggests, that if we are to move to a future which is on the whole good, we must make some fundamental changes in our life and management philosophy and initiate course corrections at the strategy and policy level, at present. Thus we should question some of the basic assumptions—should greed be the driver of national economy (let us remind ourselves, many investigative reports suggest that the genesis, spread and outcome of Covid-19 are results of commercial and imperialist greed and thus justifies the age-old maxim-greed leads to sin, sin to death); does obsession with GDP, etc. really help; should economic development be the supreme goal of life; is the present scenario not a wake-up call from the Providence to design a more holistic model of development which is sustainable and in which economic development is an important aspect but not the only aspect, etc.

Impact of the Pandemic

> The Covid-19 pandemic is far more than a health crisis: it is affecting societies and economies at their core. While the impact of the pandemic will vary from country to country, it will most likely increase poverty and inequalities at a global scale, making achievements of SDGs (Sustainability Development Goals) even urgent…Without urgent socioeconomic responses, global suffering will escalate, jeopardizing lives and livelihoods for years to come. Immediate development responses in the crisis must be undertaken with an eye to the future. Development trajectory in the long term will be affected by the choices countries make now and the support they receive. (UN's 'Framework for the Immediate Socio-economic Response, 2020)

'The impact of the pandemic has been felt across countries, societies and the economy' (The United Nations Development Programme (UNDP), June 2020, p. 2). It has affected almost all entities—urban or rural, rich or poor, high or low, human or non-human across the world; the degree and nature of the effect varies-for some it is positive, for some it is negative, for some it is mixed. The impact is both short-term as well as long term, both local as well as global. Moreover, the whole situation is dynamic and evolving fast. Amidst this vortex, so many variables are at work, some perceptible, some imperceptible, some operating at the surface both in time and space, some at much deeper level. Thus we are in a very interesting time when the 'great suffering' (*mahati vinastih*) of *Kena Upanishad* (verse-II.5) and 'welfare' (*bhuti*) of Srimad Bhagavad Gita (verse-18.78) (Radhakrishnan, 2006, p. 383) both appear as possibilities, may be one in the womb of the other. The situation echoes the sentiments of—'it was the best of times, it was the worst of times'(Dickens, 1859, p. 3). (The Sanskrit word '*vinastih*' is interpreted in various ways by different commentators, in the present context we have found the expression 'great suffering' used by Swami Lokeshwarananda (2003, p. 20) as an apt one.)

The all-encompassing impact may be classified into individual, organizational, societal, environmental, national and international level. The **individual level** impacts may be **further classified** into physical, mental and ethico-moral categories e.g. anxiety and fear of death affecting at the mental level, work from home (WFH) affecting at the physical level, loss of income and uncertainties affecting at the ethico-moral level—since these levels of human personality are not mutually exclusive, rather highly interrelated, the effects also have interrelated and multifarious dimensions.

Similarly at the **organizational level** we may have various categorization—sector specific (services, manufacturing, realty, etc.), function specific (HR, Marketing, Finance, IT, Production, etc.), organizational environment specific (macro/micro, internal/external) etc. e.g. Covid-19 induced lockdown affecting both supply and demand scenario of marketing, WFH is creating new challenges for HR, consequential revenue loss affecting the Finance and share-holder sentiments, fear of right-sizing (or downsizing?), layoff, etc. affecting employee-morale and so on.

The **Societal level** impacts are not always pronounced and vary widely from community to community but in general the prolonged and uncertain nature of the pandemic has increased both mistrust and compassion, familial discord and camaraderie, civil support and fearful indifference among the people.

The **environmental level** impacts may again be classified into effects on the natural environment (very pronounced during the lockdown e.g. huge reduction in all kinds of pollution due to decreased human activity and consequential impact on flora and fauna is well documented), technological environment (prominent changes and innovations can be observed in the health, pharmacy and IT related technology), etc.

The **national level** impacts may be classified into macro-economic (strain on national economic budget, fiscal scenario, etc.), political (communication and campaign are highly affected due to lockdown and physical distancing impediments), sociocultural (these effects are the slowest but deepest and therefore are not always easily perceptible but nevertheless always present in such wide-ranging churning).

At the **international level** we may observe some pronounced trends induced by Covid-19 at the levels of bilateral and multilateral relationships, international power dynamics, international organisations and multilateral groupings. Experts and observers are talking of **new world order** getting shaped.

The above is not a comprehensive list of impacts but a representative and indicative presentation of the same (till November 2020) for general guidance of the reader's thoughts.

Thus a quick scan of several dimensions of existence, suggests one thing-the post-Covid world will not be same as the pre-Covid one; there will be some fundamental changes. The nature, direction and intensity of the change are matters of deep contemplation.

Post-Covid World: A Likely Scenario

The post-Covid world is slowly emerging out of the present chaos. Almost all scholars and thinkers (whose viewpoints the author has gone through) agree that it will not be same as the pre-Covid one. The holocaust of such a magnitude in time and space will bring some fundamental changes at all levels, it remains to be seen whether these changes are on the whole for the better or for the worse. Two major forces will be operating—(1) reversal trend which will try to take the world back to the pre-Covid situation, (2) obversal trend which will try to establish the changes brought in during the Covid pandemic. Thus a new normal will be set as a resultant of these two forces which, in its widest magnitude and deepest connotations must be contrasted with our ancient eternal wisdom, manifested through 'perennial philosophy', to comprehend the effect of this. Some of the discernible trends observed during the Covid-induced crisis and the likely characteristics of the post-Covid world in the new normal may be presented below:

(a) **Individual level**—Covid has taught resilience and restraint. This learning of self-control will remain, at least for some time, till the fear subsides. Mental stress remains the most widespread characteristic after Covid—one fallout has been that Indian meditation and mental wellness (computer) applications are getting global takers (Venugopalan, 2020). On-line education, adopted as a compulsion during the pandemic will possibly lead to a hybrid model in the new normal with all its pros and cons. Mass religious, social, political gatherings may get reduced and replaced with on-line variants. Thus virtual space will become more and more important. New emphasis on cleanliness, health, and a new realization that all honest activities are important for the society esp. the menial works, like sanitation, etc. will be noticed. Reports suggest that cigarette and alcohol consumption got reduced in India after Covid—the trend may get reversed when economy revives. There is a great possibility of rise in mental illnesses. 'As Covid rises, so does depression' ("Covid…Depression", 2020). Heightened awareness of hygiene, clean living, protection, immunity, wellness, safety will be observed. Some more discernible trends are—fear factor, covid (hole) cocooning, obsession with cleanliness, contactless culture, protection, openness to change and experimentation. People will have to spend more time with smart-phone or laptop.

(b) **Organisational Level**—More focus will be on better health care system. Telemedicine, virtual medicine, virtual meetings and programmes, WFH will gain importance. Covid has highlighted the issue of capitalism becoming more humane and consider welfare of all stakeholders. The theory of CSR (Corporate Social Responsibility), stakeholder capitalism, etc. are appreciable, but one must realize, the successful implementation of these concepts requires a leadership which is humane, the man must stand behind the manager to make the management really purpose oriented. Focus will be on human factor and mental resilience. Increase in in-home consumption will remain at least for some more time. Speed, agility, innovation (both brand and product) will keep on influencing organizational strategies. Organisations will face volatile environment characterized by disruptions in economic activity, stressed asset valuation, volatile commodity prices, rising protectionism, political instability, reinvention of society and economy, greatest shocks to international trade since the Great Depression and a trend away from (economic) globalization. On the other hand, some organisations will discover, opportunities in adversities e.g. philip to e-commerce, digital business, digitization, on-line transactions, risk and crisis management. Proponents of the fourth industrial revolution (Industry 4.0) through automation, AI, ML, Robotics got a boost in the pandemic because the companies were in urgent need of remote solutions. It implies compression in supply chains preventing their disruptions; robots are helping where human social distancing is technically not possible. Automation is increasing productivity without job loss. Faster adoption of high end technologies will be the norm. Unprecedented alternative thinking, positive outcomes of humankind's innovations can be seen. Telemedicine, Tele-consultations are becoming common. Digitisation of almost any process has remained the new thrust-area. Technology for social good, culture-specific technological solutions are also observed.

(c) **Societal Level**—Increase in economic inequality and poverty, as indicated in the recent UNDP reports, if not addressed properly, will lead to social and political unrest. While WFH, social distancing, etc. are raising mental health problems (man being a social being), e.g. social distancing leading to social isolation, increasing domestic aberrations, substance abuse, OCD (Obsessive Compulsive Disorder), hypochondriasis have been reported. 'Years of work on gender-diversity undone'-solutions will be probably culture-specific. Both men and women have suffered, may be the natures of sufferings differ—there cannot be a one-size-fit-all kind of solution for all countries. Socially distant life-style will probably bring some relatively permanent behavioural changes. Some industry leaders have expressed lessons learnt by them in Human Values viz. empathy, patience, prayer, honesty, transparency, etc. which if sustained will have positive effect on the society. WFH will remain till there is a cure or effective vaccination. Thus there will be a mix of physical and remote working. Future of work will remain team oriented and fluid with a change in mindset—command and control to mentor and inspire. Undeterred entrepreneurial spirit and resolve of India's msme(s) are encouraging signs in this post-covid phase. Digitisation super cycle has started in this pandemic.

(d) **Environmental Level**—Decrease in various types of pollution during lockdown and its health benefits have increasingly pointed out the harmful effects of some conventional socioeconomic activities, hence signs of rethink on these issues are seen in the policy makers and intelligentsia.

(e) **National Level**—The covid-induced economic distress has prompted urgent reforms in labour and agricultural sectors, reducing the exploitative tendencies remains a challenge. Innovative cost-cutting ways to reduce travel, meeting, office space and other activities now consider routine will transform the corporate world and even social and environmental benefits. In the remote working environment, freelancing gets importance like never before. Formalization of economy will get increasing importance- unorganized sector, particularly women, are adversely affected, the sector will see more organization, formalization and social security efforts (Gender Responsive Recovery, 2020). Residential space demand will increase, office-space demand will decrease. As far as Covid is concerned, no cure protocol and ever-dynamic treatment protocol, changing from patient to patient, will possibly remain as a great challenge for the medical community.

(f) **International Level**—New world order is getting shaped with new power dynamics, multilateral groupings, new global supply chain, etc. India will hopefully play very crucial role in all these. Importance of India has increased in the post-covid world—previously for many world powers India was important but not urgent, in the post-covid world it will be both. Thus we may increasingly see new dialogues, pacts, arrangements and understanding. India, assertive than before, should show ways to international community in handling hegemony and nefarious designs. This new power dynamics may lead to less globalisation led by authoritarian, closed regime, a response to which may see a multipolar world where multilateral power centres will influence global politics. Restricted economic growth and reduced human movement/migration may be another characteristic. Global economic disruptions and shocks are almost inevitable.

Effective Leadership in the New Normal

The issue of leadership is to be seen in the light of the above imminent attributes of the likely new normal. If we contemplate deeply on these characteristics, we can infer certain key notes of the post-covid world viz. uncertainty, sudden disruptive changes in the macro as well as the micro business environment, socioeconomic hardships leading to political unrest, greater emphasis on technology-driven solutions, digitization, etc.

Keeping these keynotes in mind, we need to challenge ourselves to answer the question which we raised at the very outset. Indian spirituality presents a brief but very powerful response—an effective leader is one who directs himself as well as a group of individuals from a state of chaos to a state of order. According to Second Law of Thermodynamics in physics, in material world, there is a natural tendency to move towards chaos i.e. left to itself any entity generally moves towards disorder. This is also our everyday experience in both outer and inner world, e.g. (1) any material, if not maintained, starts decaying after some time, (2) students, if not disciplined, generally go astray,(3) mind, if not concentrated, cannot achieve perfection in any work (maintenance, discipline, control, concentration, etc., are various means to help this process of moving from chaos to order).

Now, one may ask-what does he achieve?—again, according to Indian Vedantic texts, the effective leader achieves four life-goals (the *purushārtha*(s)) viz. *dharma* (righteousness), *artha* (material prosperity), *kāma* (legitimate worldly desires), *moksha* (contextually speaking spiritual development). Now to ensure all these, the first step for the leader is to start with himself-Leader, lead thyself is an important maxim, i.e. at the outset he has to take his personality from a state of chaos or restlessness to a state of order or peace. He has to lead by example as emphasized in the Gita (verse–3.21) (Swarupananda, 2007). He has to cope with uncertainties and disruptive changes in almost all functional areas of management.

Crisis brings opportunities, provided one can identify them and translate them into practical and sustainable propositions. This requires deep concentration, comprehensive, rational and intuitive understanding of the situation i.e. profound insight and foresight, dynamism and above all a holistic personality.

Beyond that one has to be prompt and agile in implementing the proposition. This requires selfless courage and a sense of purpose. It remains to be seen what is that leadership model that promises to develop leaders with such attributes.

Rājarshi Leadership: The Indian Response

A deep introspection on the entire history of leadership in India starting from the days of the Vedic culture, Rāmāyana, Mahābhārata to the present times shows that there has been one ideal leadership theory working all throughout the ages in India and that is ***Rājarshi* Leadership**. This has been the Indian *paramparā* (tradition) [We get mention of this *Rājarshi paramparā* in many ancient texts e.g. *shloka(s)* 4.1 and 2 of Srimad Bhagavad Gita; Chapter 7 of Book I of Kautilya's Arthashastra, particularly verses 1.7.1–8; Mahabharata-Virat Parva, 65.14; In the famous history based epic-poem *Raghubamsam* of Kalidāsa, of the 23 kings all were trying to follow this ideal excepting one and the fallout in either case has been depicted in graphic detail to establish the importance of *Rājarshi* leadership.]

The *Rājarshi* concept is a combination of two dimensions—the *Rishi* and the *Rājā*. (One conventional understanding of the term *Rājarshi* is—a Rājā who has attained the highest spiritual wisdom and elevated himself to *Rishi*-hood, names of some such prominent *Rājarshi*(s) can be found in our Vedas and Upanishads).

Prof. S K Chakraborty, the doyen of Human Values Movement in Indian Management Education, has a pioneering contribution in encapsulating whole of the perennial *Rājarshi* Leadership theory into a comprehensive model and popularizing the same among corporate executives and university students in India and abroad through his executive and student development programmes. Referring to the viewpoints of many contemporary thinkers, like Einstein, Russell, Toynbee, Beer, Korten, Tagore, Abdul Kalam, Gandhi, Vivekananda, Aurobindo, Sorokin, R C Majumdar, R K Mukhrerjee, K M Panikkar, Netaji, J N Tata and many others as also that of our enlightened ancient texts, he established his thesis on a firm footing. The present author feels blessed to have worked with him for many years and delivered more than hundred such programmes in the last 9 years of his glorious life (Sarkar, 2019c). Following his leadership model, let us present very briefly the salient features of the profound leadership theory which has stood the test of time for thousands of years. (We are not presenting his model, the interested reader may refer to his books e.g. *Human Values and Ethics: In Search of Organizational Integrity*).

Rishi Dimensions

1. **Silence**: It has two aspects—external and internal i.e. absence of noise in the external environment as well as absence of conflicting thoughts. Achieving this internal silence is essential to prevent psychological burnout and rekindle adaptability.
2. **Solitude**: 'Withdrawal into solitude…(makes) control of the mind quite easy' (Gandhi, 1968, p. 473).
3. ***Antarmukhitā* (Interiorization)**: This regression or *antarmukhitā* is necessary to regain the 'subjective heaven' within.
4. **Seeing before Doing**: Rishi is the one who 'sees' the Truth 'looking within'. Then the manifestation of this truth for the good of the society is 'doing'.
5. **Insight to Foresight**: The above 'seeing' breaks the 'barrier of time' and he could perceive the past, present and future into a seamless continuity-thus develops foresight. This ability to foresee the unseen helps him to take right decisions regarding collaboration and likely involvement of the various stakeholders.
6. **Cosmic Intelligence above Human Intelligence**: Human mind is limited by *samskāra*(s) (*kārmic* impressions).The Rishi transcends this limitation by experiencing the Unity when the divine intelligence flows into and through him.
7. **Wisdom before Knowledge**: Wisdom connotes emotional and experiential unity, *sukshma dristi* (subtle comprehension), human values and *parā vidyā* whereas knowledge implies intellectual and empirical diversity, *sthula dristi* (gross understanding), operating skills and *aparā vidyā*. As Sri Aurobindo points out—'There are two allied powers in man: knowledge and wisdom. Wisdom looks behind the veil and sees…Reason divides…wisdom unifies…' (Aurobindo, 1999b, p. 718).
8. **Ego expansion**: The deficit driven lower-self expands and gives way to the ever-content Higher Self—an all-embracing selfless love is the fallout. Compassion and caring attitude spontaneously arise out of such love.
9. **Intuition**: 'Intellectuals frown upon Intuition, but wise men cultivate it by disciplined spiritual practice…' (Nixon(Krishna Prem), 1976, p. 302).
10. **Power flowing from the Divine**: The Rishi lives in communion with the Supreme and says 'if I have told you one word of truth, it was His and His alone…' (Vivekananda, 1990, p. 193)—thus 'instrument in the hands of the Lord' attitude is typical of him. This power is the actual source of transparency, honesty and resilience in any crisis.
11. **Unity**: The Rishi feels 'One in All' (Bhagavad Gita (BG), ch.10) and 'All in One' (BG, ch.11)—thus experiences spiritual unity amidst material diversity.

***Rājā* dimension**: Etymologically '*rājā*' is one who had pleased and became dear to all the subjects **following the just laws (*rājadharma*)** (*Māhābhārata, verse-12.59.125*).

Following are the characteristics of *Rājā* dimension:

1. ***Bahirmukhitā* (Exteriorization)**: The *rājā* is more concerned about the mundane aspects of the world. He is active, agile, prompt, courageous, ready to lay down his life for a just cause and fiercely honest.
2. **Humility**: The principles of righteousness (*dharma*) laid down by the Rishi demands that the raja should control all his internal vices including vanity which essentially implies that he be humble.
3. **Protecting the Righteous**: That is the significance of him being a *Kshatriya*.
4. **Punishing the Unrighteous**: This is a corollary of the previous attribute.
5. **Sense of Renunciation**: According to Rabindranath Tagore—'Renunciation means renouncing the part for the whole, renouncing the transient for the eternal, renouncing the ego for love, renouncing comfort for bliss' (Chakraborty & Bhattacharya, 1996, p. 266).
6. ***Sanyam* and Detachment**: 'Day and night, he must be engaged in conquering his senses; a king who has conquered his senses, is enabled to keep his subjects under control' (Manusmriti, 7.44). This detachment makes him flexible and pragmatic.
7. **Discipline**: The role of strict discipline in character building is emphasized in almost all our texts.
8. **Social Welfare**: Such selfless and service-oriented leaders dedicate their lives for the welfare of their followers, subject or people.
9. **Stress on Knowledge**: The leader is supposed to keep track of different areas of secular knowledge since he is to converse with all kinds of people. The need of continuous learning and constant updating of one's knowledge and skill is well documented in our sacred literature (e.g. *Taittiriya Upanishad*, verse-I.11.1).
10. **Obedience**: Such leaders exact obedience from their followers, not always through authority or command but mostly through the force of impersonal love.

    If we look at these two dimensions from the perspectives of the 'supreme knowledge' of Indian Psychology viz. the *Tri Guna Tattwa* ('Theory of Triple Psychological Forces' as named by Sri Aurobindo), we find the Rishi characteristics are essentially *Sāttwika* and *Rājā* attributes are mainly *Rājasika* and in the overall scheme of *Rājarshi* Leadership, we find the *Sāttwika* guiding the *Rājasika*, then only the dynamism of *rajo guna* becomes enlightened and beneficial to the society. ['The three *gunas—sattva, rajas, and tamas*—are the primal constituents of *Prakriti*, primordial nature, natura naturans, from which the whole universe, physical and mental, has evolved...*Sattva* is the principle of poise conducive to purity, knowledge, joy. *Rajas* is the principle of motivity leading to activity, desire, restlessness, or disquietude. *Tamas* is the principle of inertia resulting in inaction, dullness, delusion' (Satprakashananda, 1974), p. 261].

> Now if we compare the Rishi and the Raja dimensions of this *Rājarshi* model with the characteristics of the effective leader discussed earlier, we find they actually match. If that is what the crux of the matter is, then the solution lies in getting connected to our roots and derive strength therefrom. Even in this darkness, we have lights of wisdom in the form of stalwarts like Swami Vivekananda, Rabindranath Tagore, Sri Aurobindo and few others who were all deeply rooted and exemplified considerable *Rājarshi* characteristics. Therefore, it remains for us to ignite our minds in this light and be a part of the solution rather that of the problem. 'Whether the future of the race lies in a rational and an intelligently mechanized or in a spiritual, intuitive and religious civilization and culture—that then is the important issue (Aurobindo, 1968, p. 16). …the spiritual life of India is the first necessity of the world's future…for the spiritual emancipation of the human race…' (Aurobindo, as cited in Nahar, 2000, p. 25). Thus, this emancipation from the present chaos can be effected through *Rājarshi* leadership.

In the form of this leadership concept we have only highlighted certain general principles which have stood the test of time. It can be established through concrete illustrations that this model of leadership is applicable independent of space and time as well as across sectors, gender etc. (Sarkar, 2019a, b, c p. 42). Moreover, this indigenous leadership model of India, is based on the strong foundation of Vedāntic human values which are in consonance with the philosophical interpretations of New Physics and is therefore also highly scientific (Sarkar, 2020, p. 32). It may also be pointed out that since *Rājarshi* Leadership is primarily based on Vedanta, 'the most intellectual school' (Capra, 1988, p. 79) which is universally applicable, characteristics of such leadership may be discerned in the lives of the great leaders of the West and other parts of the world as well, e.g. in case of Abraham Lincoln (Brooks, 1894, pp. 50–70), Nelson Mandela (2010, pp. 122, 345) etc. we clearly observe such traits. The present scope will not allow us to elaborate on this.

Spirinomics: The Instrument of *Rājarshi*

Now we need to highlight how a *rājarshi* leader can be effective in the present scenario. As per the understanding of the *Rishi* (seer) any leader has to operate through the *purushārtha*(s) (life-goals) of the collective entity e.g. organisation, society, nation etc., which he is entrusted to guide in the right direction. Of the four life-goals, for the operational effectiveness of the leader, *Artha* (or Economics) happens to be the most important—this can be deduced from the arguments put forward by the famous ancient author on *Arthashastra* viz. Kautilya (or Chanakya) (Rangarajan, 1990, p. 14).

In Arthashāstra of Kautilya (there were many books on Arthashāstra but currently only one of them composed by Kautilya is extant) the expression '*artha*' has a very wide connotation:

> *Artha* is an all-embracing word with a variety of meanings. In (1.7.6-7), it is used in the sense of material well-being; in (15.1.1), livelihood; in (1.4.3), economically productive activity, particularly in agriculture, cattle-rearing and trade; and, in general, wealth as in the 'Wealth of Nations'. *Arthashāstra* is thus 'the science of politics' as it is used in (1.1.1) or (1.4.3).It is the art of government in its widest sense. The subjects covered include: administration, law, order and justice, taxation, revenue and expenditure, foreign policy; defence and war. Its three objectives follow one from the other: promotion of the welfare of the subjects leads to acquisition of wealth, in turn, makes it possible to enlarge the territory by conquest. (Ibid., p. 15)

In *Vārtā* 'subjects relating to agriculture, cattle-rearing and trade' (Mukherjee, 1989, p. 247) were covered.

The contemporary authors have defined Economics in different ways—some emphasize on the production and distribution of material wealth, some on the individual behaviour of the consumers, still others on the utilization of scarce resources and so on—accordingly we have various branches of Economics e.g. Macro-Economics, Micro-Economics, Welfare Economics, Behavioural Economics etc.—all of them agree with varying degree of emphasis that Economics is a science that deals with material wealth.

Thus we see that both in contemporary thought as well as in ancient Indian understanding Economics implies a vast field of activity (in theory and practice) covering almost all aspects of an individual, society and State involving the material dimensions.

Since the *Rājarshi* leadership draws its inspiration from spirituality, it is but natural that the Economics that is in consonance with this kind of leadership is spiritual economics or spirinomics (Chakraborty & Chakraborty, 2014, p. 188). In this context, therefore, it is imperative that we define this very important term.

At the mundane level, the connotation of the term 'spiritual' or 'spirituality' is dependent on space, time and person but at the transcendental level, the implications of these terms converge though their symbolic expressions vary, as our *Shāstra* (scriptures) says—'*Ekam Sad, Viprā Bahudhā Vadanti*'—The Truth is One, the sages express it in different ways (Rig Veda, 1.164.46). Hence we go to a realized soul like Sri Aurobindo to comprehend what do we mean by being spiritual.

> It is spirituality when you begin to become aware of another consciousness other than the ego and begin to live in it or under its influence more and more. It is that consciousness wide, infinite, self-existent, pure of ego etc. which is called spirit (Self, Brahman, Divine ...). (Aurobindo, 1999a, p. 362)

Let us go through one more relevant definition.

> Consciousness is a reality inherent in existence. It is there even when it is not active on the surface but silent and immobile...invisible...It is not...a phenomenon dependent on the reactions of personality to the forces of Nature...consciousness is usually identified with mind, but mental consciousness is only the human range...there are ranges of consciousness above and below the human range, with which normal human has no contact...supramental and sub-mental ranges. (Aurobindo, 1973, pp. 233–235)

Thus Spiritual Economics is a paradigm in which the pursuit of material wealth is carried out, not as an end in itself but as a means to achieve the higher goals of life viz. to be aware of the Highest Consciousness and realize the union with That following any of the numerous paths laid down in our scriptures. Once the mind gradually moves from the mundane material plane to the spiritual realm, philosophical questions pose themselves—generation of material wealth for what? Is it for personal enjoyment or sense pleasure? The answer comes from deep within—not for the personal enjoyment or aggrandizement, but for the general welfare of the society—that has always been the viewpoint of Indian thinkers. The spiritual outlook helps a man to be aware of wider perspectives in life beyond his parochial sense pleasures, it helps one to realize—'No one is satisfied with (material)wealth' (Katha Upanisad, 1.1.27) but material wealth is initially necessary for a householder person to sustain his body and others in his society so that they may go through right kind of daily practices (*sādhanā*) through righteousness (*Dharma*) to ultimately reach the highest realization (*Moksha*).Hence Spirinomics or Spiritual Economics may be defined as a system of generation of material wealth through judicious utilization of constrained resources through benevolent human responses with the objective of welfare of the society in general and realization of divine consciousness in particular.

It is to be carefully noted that by 'spiritual economics' we do not necessarily mean 'religious economics'. If we consider the widespread connotation of religion and then apply that to the expression 'religious economics' we arrive at certain methods and practices which are largely dependent on *Smriti* (i.e. tradition valid for only an epoch or an age) (Ranganathananda, 1995, p. 28) aspect of the religion (which has been the basis of many texts written on this subject and practised in some theological States). In our case we are developing the concept based on *Shruti* (i.e. tradition eternal) aspect of the religion which reveals some fundamental truths independent of space and time (and hence there is great unity of thought regarding these principles amongst all major world religions). Incidentally, it may be mentioned in the passing that if we consider the scriptural definition and socio-cultural application of the expression '*dharma*', [Considering the definition of the word '*dharma*' in Mahabharata (*Karnaparva, verse-69.59*) and that in Atharva Veda (XII.1.1) one may arrive at the very wide and all-encompassing connotation of the term], then spirituality and all other related concepts presented here may be accommodated within its ambit (Sarkar, 2019b, Cover Story).

Rājarshi and Philosopher-King

In the passing, it may be worthwhile, to present a brief comparative account of the *Rājarshi* Leadership theory and a similar concept from the West i.e. philosopher-king of Plato. In another article of the present author, an extensive comparative discussion on a classified basis is carried out and following inferences are deduced:

> Swami Vivekananda says—'The study of the Greeks was the outer infinite, while that of the Aryans (of India) was the inner infinite…In Pythagoras, Plato and the Egyptian

neo-Platonists, we can find traces of Indian thought' (Tathagatananda, 2005, p. 146). Keeping in mind the above perceptual differences and keeping aside the interesting idea of the influence of classical Indian mind on classical Greece, a careful study of the nature and characteristics of *rājarshi* and philosopher-king brings out some similarities and many differences:

- The 'philosopher' of Plato seems to be an intellectual person, whereas '*Rishi*' is a deeply spiritually awakened man. Rishi-hood is an outcome of rigorous *brahmacharya*, sustained *tapasyā* (austerity) & profound realization, whereas philosopher is an outcome of deep intellectual discourse and understanding of human nature in a sociopolitical setup. Thus it may be safely concluded that Rishi is not same as philosopher.
- The 'king' in the ancient Greek world-view is not exactly same as the '*rājā*' in ancient Indian thinking-whereas the king had legislative, executive and judicial authority, the raja mainly had the executive authority (his legislative and judicial power were subject to the Rule of Law laid down by the *Rishi*) though both were supposed to dedicate their lives for the welfare of the people.
- While stress on comprehensive knowledge and life-long education is common in both philosopher-king and *Rājarshi* leader, as per Indian spiritual scriptures, no amount of study of secular subjects can make a person a *Rishi* [Many instances and wisdom statements may be cited to support this e.g. the famous dialogue between Narada and *Rishi* Sanatkumara in *Chandogya Upanishad(Chapter 7)*]—the idea of *parā vidyā (Mundaka Upanishad, I.i.4.)* appears to be absent in Plato's concept.
- If we examine the Training and Development curricula, we find some similarities in the subjects taught, but the priority and stress seem to vary—in case of *Rājarshi*, the emphasis is clearly on the inner ethico-moral development.
- The *Rājarshi* model seems to accommodate both the concepts of Plato and Aristotle.
- The *Rājarshi* model has stood the test of time in India, she has continuously produced such kind of leaders from ancient time till date and the Indian mind only respects such kind of leaders since they strive for 'ultimate perfection' while Sri Aurobindo asserts—'An Indian mind faithful to its ideals would contend...that...the secret of our ultimate perfection is to be discovered deeper within us...' (Aurobindo, 1968, p. 17) though the intensity and applicability have got diminished over time. Swami Vivekananda opines—thus '...I challenge anybody to show one single period of her national life when India was lacking in spiritual giants capable of moving the world...' (Vivekananda, 1969a, p. 315).

Thus it may be opined that philosopher-king is more of an intellectual-rational model, whereas *Rājarshi* is more of a spiritually rooted concept going beyond conventional rationality which Sri Aurobindo supports thus—'...everything finite is striving to express an infinite...the reason deals successfully with the settled and finite...(therefore)the intellectual reason... cannot deal with life as its sovereign...the real sovereign is another than the reasoning intelligence...'. (Aurobindo, 1985, p. 112)

Rājarshi Leadership Through Spirinomics: A Sustainable Model

For thousands of years, India had consciously followed the *Rājarshi* leadership with respect and remained in the forefront in all human achievements. This may be established through several direct and indirect evidences e.g. in the OECD report titled World Economy, we find our *Bhāratvarsha* stood first for almost seventeen centuries (from 0 AD to 1700 AD roughly) in per capita GDP as well as contribution to world GDP (Organisation for Economic Cooperation and Development (OECD),

2007). Then we got confused, lost confidence in ourselves, looked without and faltered, but still the saving concept emanating from our *Rishi*(s) is very much alive in our subconscious, hence still we invariably respect the leaders having *Rājarshi* traits. Moreover, 'each race...has a peculiar bent...raison-d'etre...mission to fulfill... (our) mission...is to pour (all the spiritual energy) forth on the world whenever circumstances are propitious' (Vivekananda, 1969b, pp. 108–9) and 'we shall...follow our destiny' (Tagore, 2008, p. 457) notwithstanding the arguments of economic globalization.

An analysis of the economic history of India in the light of her leadership paradigms show that the *Rājarshi* leadership operating through spiritual economics has been a sustainable model. In her long unbroken history of about 10,000 years there are ample examples and research data to show that whenever, this model was upheld, there was long period of prosperity as is illustrated by the above OECD data and whenever, it was ignored or opposed, there was adversity—but the civilizational and cultural undercurrents remained so strong that, every time it was undermined, it got rejuvenated after sometime and was established, so that the national vitality was revived. Thus, 'The history of India shows that when the country was spiritually great it was also materially prosperous and culturally creative' (Nikhilananda, 1968, p. 14). Hence, on the whole we can say this combination of *Rājarshi* Leadership and spiritual economics has resulted in a sustainable civilization, the continuity of which is appreciated by the great contemporary historians also e.g. Will Durant (2011, p. 488). [Many experts have roughly calculated the period of written history of India as approx. 10,000 years. Swami Vivekananda also thinks so—'...our national life of these ten thousand years...' (1969c, vol. 5, pp. 459–60)].

The sustainability issue may be examined in the light of contemporary thoughts. The notion of 'sustainable development' was introduced into the political agenda by the World Commission on Environment and Development through its report called the Brundtland Report. As per the implication of the Report:

> Sustainable development is a development that meets the needs of the present without compromising the ability of future generations to meet their own needs. (1987, p. 43)

> More precisely, sustainability is defined as a requirement of our generation to manage the resource base such that the average quality of life that we ensure ourselves can potentially be shared by all future generations. The notion 'quality of life', includes everything that influences the situation in which people live. Hence, it includes much more than material consumption. It is intended to capture the importance of health, culture, and nature. (Asheim Geir, 1994)

The word 'development' generally implies economic development though some scholars have expanded the meaning of the term to include some more aspects of human living as we notice in the previous definition. General understanding as well as Indian spiritual comprehension regarding individual development points out that there are other important dimensions associated with the word. The most comprehensive connotation of individual development according to ancient Indian wisdom as pointed out earlier, includes four aspects viz. *Dharma* (righteous behaviour), *Artha* (material well-being), *Kāma* (legitimate worldly desires) and *Moksha* (spiritual development), which together is denoted by the expression '*Purushārthas*' or *Chaturvarga* (the four aims of human life)—economic development ensures *Artha* and *Kāma*. Thus comprehensive development of a typical human being (householder) involves positive change in all these dimensions simultaneously. Again the connotation of the term 'development' varies based on the Philosophy of Man e.g. if we consider a specific Vedāntic philosophy of man (Taittiriya Upanisad, Pancakosa etc.), we may say development of an individual involves upliftment in his physical, mental, intellectual, ethico-moral and spiritual dimensions. On the other hand, at the collective level, it may mean societal, regional, national or international enhancement. Now since individual is the cause and society or any other collective entity is the effect, in this article, by 'development' we will primarily mean positive changes at the individual level leading to overall welfare at the collective level.

Whither Contemporary Economics?

Given the profound and ubiquitous impact of Covid-19, in the post-covid world we require such a comprehensive development which may be sustained also. To achieve such an objective, we need to reexamine some of the basic ideas of conventional contemporary economics in the light of their outcome on common man as well as with respect to spiritual economics. Such an exercise yields serious doubt about the effectiveness of these ideas. Let us go through some extra-orbital viewpoints with an open mind:

- Modern economics turned the Hobbesian ideology of rational materialism into an applied science of human behaviour and social organization that embraces hedonism as the goal and measure of human progress, and absolves the individual of responsibility for moral choice.—D C Korten (1998, p. 27)
- Clearly, there was a need to transcend economics, without abandoning it...people realized that economic criteria alone could not provide a programme for human dignity and well-being.—The World Commission on Culture and Development (1995)
- Present-day society sees success and happiness in terms of ever-increasing economic affluence. The objective is not only economically unattainable but also spiritually unsatisfying.—Toynbee and Daisaku (1987, p. 103)

Now let us examine these in the light of some wisdom statements:

- In the West they are trying to solve the problem on how much a man can possess, and we here are trying to solve the problem on how little a man can live...But if history has any truth in it...it must be those who train themselves to live on the least...will in the end gain the battle, and those who run after enjoyment and luxury...will have to die...—Swami Vivekananda (1969b, vol. 3, p. 181)
- The aim of...economics would be not to create a huge engine of production, whether of the competitive or the cooperative kind but, to give men...the joy of work according to their own nature and free leisure to grow inwardly...—Sri Aurobindo (1985, p. 241)
- Unfortunately at the present day in almost all parts of the world the strain of money-making has been so great that many people are breaking down under it...Hinduism has

> no sympathy with the view that "to mix religion and business is to spoil two good things."...—Sarvapalli Radhakrishnan (1957, p. 110)

Hence spiritual economics is based on a low need, low greed model which essentially gives rise to sustainability at all levels .It does not try to generate demand or supply by hook or by crook, it is not obsessed with GDP or GNP, it tends to ensure holistic well-being and happiness of all through more equitable distribution of material wealth and generation of some which is really needed. It is not focused to scale of economies through undue emphasis on optimization (excluding other human dimensions) and application of high end technologies, rather it gives more emphasis on small scale industries (MSMEs) and Appropriate Technology (Schumacher, 1997, p. 45).

Toynbee, the great historian, conforms:

> I agree that we ought to aim not at gross national product but at gross national welfare. My tests of welfare would be...the average per capita spiritual welfare...the average standard of self-mastery, which is the key to spiritual welfare... (1987, p. 106)

The Synthesis

Since spirinomics is essentially rooted in spirituality, it leads to a sustainable paradigm. A non-spiritual system leads to greed and consumerism which ultimately leads to abuse of the resources disturbing the natural equilibrium of demand and supply. Moreover it results in concentration of material wealth and consequential unrest and violence in the society—an analysis of the contemporary economic and social history of the world yields ample illustrations to establish this argument e.g. it may be established that two world wars in close succession is a result of following such non-spiritual economic models. Indian Vedāntic spirituality essentially brings in self-control and control of the vices, which ultimately brings in the giving impulse as opposed to the grabbing tendency, as well as frugality and ascetic spirit. Thus it curbs consumerism, concentration of wealth and more equitable distribution of the produce—all leading to a more sustainable development.

All these again bring us back to the question of leadership. An effective leader can only bring such changes which will be sustainable. Sri Aurobindo hints at what kind of person can play such a role—'The individuals who will most help the future of humanity in the new age will be those who will recognize a spiritual evolution as the destiny and therefore the great need of the human being...They will especially not make the mistake of thinking that this (spiritual) change can be effected by machinery and outward institutions; they will know and never forget that it has to be lived out by each man inwardly or it can never be made a reality for the kind. They will adopt in its heart of meaning the inward view of the East which bids man seek the secret of his destiny and salvation within; but also they will accept, though with a different turn given to it, the importance which the West rightly attaches to life and to the making the best we know and can attain the general rule of all life' (Aurobindo, 2012, Back Cover).

Thus the ideal leader has to synthesize the best of the East and the West. Assimilation, not imitation, shall be his watchword. 'Living within' (Dalal, 2011) and 'growing within' (Dalal, 1995a), he shall analyze the problems of mankind 'looking from within' (Dalal, 1995b); thus he will realize that—no problem can be effectively solved staying at the level in which it has originated, one needs to move up to a higher level to have a comprehensive view of the situation and then only one can devise a lasting solution. Hence, considering the impacts of the pandemic, not in a piecemeal manner, but as an interconnected web of reality with dynamic positive and negative forces affecting the web, he will proceed to have control over the chaotic web with a dispassionate and detached sagacity. This will require him to develop the *Rishi* dimensions of 'Becoming' and then employ that character-energy in 'Doing' or executing the *Rājā* dimensions.

Chapter Takeaways/Lessons

1. The impact of Covid-19 induced pandemic is all-encompassing, having fundamental implications, leading to uncertainty and disruptive changes of both positive and negative character.
2. The effective leader in this calamitous disorder must learn to live within. It helps develop the insight and hence foresight, which ultimately enables him to guide his team in the right direction.
3. Leadership implies a transformation from a state of chaos to a state of order. Spiritual orientation helps achieve this change within and its manifestation without.
4. The eternal Indian concept of *Rājarshi*, a combination of *rājā*, the king and *Rishi*, the seer, promises to develop such a transformative leadership. *Rājarshi* is not exactly same as philosopher king.
5. Spirinomics is the most important instrument used by the *Rājarshi* to bring about this sustainable change and establish order both at the spiritual and at the material level.

Reflection Questions

1. What are the possible positive and negative effects of Covid-19 at the individual, organizational, societal, national and international level?
2. How the above effects may shape the world in the short and the long term?
3. What are the personality dimensions, the aspiring leader must develop, to face the challenge?
4. What kind of economics and public administration we require in the new normal?
5. If we have something called eternal truth, should we not have a time-tested, age-old and sustainable leadership model that can withstand the fury of this calamity? Hence, what kind of leadership is required in the present turmoil?

References

As Covid Rises, So Does Depression. (2020, September14). *The Economic Times* (p. 6).
Asheim Geir, B. (1994). *Policy research working paper 1302*. The World Bank Policy Research Department, Public Economics Division.
Aurobindo, S. (1968). *The foundations of Indian culture*. Sri Aurobindo Ashram.
Aurobindo, S. (1973). *Sri Aurobindo birth centenary library* (Vol. 22). Sri Aurobindo Society.
Aurobindo, S. (1985). *The human cycle*. Sri Aurobindo Ashrama.
Aurobindo, S. (1999a). *Essays-human and divine*. Sri Aurobindo Ashram Publication.
Aurobindo, S. (1999b). Synthesis of yoga. In *The complete works of Sri Aurobindo* (Vol. 23 and 24). Sri Aurobindo Ashrama Trust.
Aurobindo, S. (2012). *The human cycle/the ideal of human unity/war and self-determination*. Sri Aurobindo Ashram.
Brooks, N. (1894). *Abraham Lincoln: And the downfall of American slavery*. G.P. Putman's Sons.
Capra, F. (1988). *The Tao of physics*. Bantam Books.
Chakraborty, S. K., & Bhattacharya, P. (1996). *Human values: The Tagorean panorama*. New Age International.
Chakraborty, S. K., & Chakraborty, D. (2014). *Rajarshi leadership—The saving role of authentic spirituality*. Sri Aurobindo Society.
Dalal, A. S. (Ed.). (1995a). *Growing within: The psychology of inner development*. Sri Aurobindo Ashram.
Dalal, A. S. (Ed.). (1995b). *Looking from within: A seeker's guide to attitudes for mastery and inner growth*. Sri Aurobindo Ashram.
Dalal, A. S. (Ed.). (2011). *Living within: Selections from the works of Sri Aurobindo and the mother*. Sri Aurobindo Ashram.
Dickens, C. (1859). *A tale of two cities*. Chapman & Hall.
Durant, W. (2011). *The story of civilisation/our oriental heritage*. Simon & Schuster.
Gandhi, M. (1968). *Selected works of Mahatma Gandhi* (Vol. 5). Navjivan.
Korten, D. (1998). *The post-corporate world: Life after capitalism*. Berrett-Koehler.
Lokeswarananda, S. (2003). *Kena Upanishad*. The Ramakrishna Mission Institute of Culture.
Mandela, N. (2010). *Conversation with myself*. Macmillan.
Mukherjee, R. K. (1989). *Ancient Indian education: Brāhmanical & Buddhist*. Motilal Banarsidass.
Nahar, S. (2000). *India's rebirth*. Mira-Aditi.
Need A Gender-Responsive Recovery Strategy. (2020, September 7). *The Economic Times* (p. 5).
Nikhilananda, S. (1968). *Hinduism: Its meaning for the liberation of the spirit*. Sri Ramakrishna Math.
Nixon, R (Sri Krishna Prem). (1976). *Initiation into yoga*. Rider.
Organisation for Economic Cooperation and Development (OECD). (2007). *World economy, appendix*.
Radhakrishnan, S. (1957). *Hindu view of life*. George Allen and Unwin.
Radhakrishnan, S. (2006). *The Bhagavadgita*. HarperCollins Publishers.
Ranganathananda, S. (1995). *Eternal values for changing society* (Vol. III). Bharatiya Vidya Bhavan.
Rangarajan, L. N. (1990). *The Arthashastra*. Penguin Publication.
Sarkar, B. K. (2019a). Socially responsible leadership—Indian historical perspectives. *Globsyn Management Journal, XIII*(1 & 2), 34–47.
Sarkar, B. K. (2019b, December 16–31). Spiritual economics-the principle of sustainable development. *Business Economics*. Cover Story.
Sarkar, B. K. (2019c). *Beyond autumn clouds-A tribute to prof. S K Chakraborty*. Prof. S K Chakraborty Memorial Trust.
Sarkar, B. K. (2020). *Perennial values: Stress-free ethical leadership during crisis*. Eliva Press SRL.
Satprakashananda, S. (1974). *The goal and the way: The Vedāntic approach to life's problems*. Sri Ramakrishna Math.
Schumacher, E. F. (1997). *Small is beautiful*. Radhakrishna.

Swarupananda, S. (2007). *Srimad Bhagavad-Gita*. Advaita Ashrama.
Tagore, R. (2008). *The English writings of Tagore* (Vol. 2). Sahitya Akademi.
Tathagatananda, S. (2005). *Light from the orient*. Advaita Ashram.
The United Nations Development Programme (UNDP). (2020, June). *Brief#2: Putting the UN framework for socio-economic response to Covid19 into action: Insights*. https://www.undp.org
The World Commission on Culture and Development. (1995). *Annual report*.
Toynbee, A., & Daisaku, I. (1987). *Choose life: A dialogue*. Oxford University Press.
UN's 'Framework for the Immediate Socio-economic Response to the Covid19 Crisis'. (2020). UNDP.org. https://www.undp.org/
Venugopalan, A. (2020, October 17). Indian meditation and mental wellness apps are finding global takers. *The Economic Times* (p. 8).
Vivekananda, S. (1969a). *Complete works of Swami Vivekananda (CWSV)* (Vol. 4). Advaita Ashram.
Vivekananda, S. (1969b). *CWSV* (Vol. 3).
Vivekananda, S. (1969c). *CWSV* (Vol. 5, 8th ed.).
Vivekananda, S. (1990). *The sages of India. Lectures from Colombo to Almora*. Advaita Ashram.
World Commission on Environment and Development (WCED). (1987). *Brundtland report*.

Bidyut K. Sarkar has 23 years of formal teaching and administrative experience in reputed management institutions of India. He has been the vice principal and member-secretary of Tagore Centre for Human Values. As a corporate educator, he has conducted 75 workshops across India and abroad with top and middle level executives of public and private sector companies on Values, Ethics, Leadership and Stress Management. As a visiting professor, he has also delivered 48 courses and workshops at various academic institutions across India. His publications include 48 papers/articles, 3 monographs, 4 book chapters and one book. His academic and professional qualifications include MBA, MCA, MS (Psychotherapy), PGDCA, PGDI (Indology), BS (Physics), PG Diploma in International Understanding & Human Unity, Major World Religions, Functional Sanskrit, UGC-NET, AIMA-TEM, AIMA-AMT, etc. He takes interest in social work and conducts spiritual discourses on Bhagavad Gita, Sri Sri Chandi and Upanishads.

Forging a Roadmap for Post-Pandemic Global Leadership: A Preliminary Empirical Study of Citizen Perspectives

30

Natasha Brown and H. Eric Schockman

Show me the suffering of the most miserable;
So I will know my people's plight.

César E. Chávez

The novel coronavirus, COVID-19, burst onto the global stage in 2019, with cases first recorded in China and quickly spreading across people, communities, and nations. By March of 2020, the virus spread so invasively that it was acknowledged as a global pandemic. In its wake, the coronavirus left weakened health care systems and overly taxed people and economies strained by necessary lockdown measures (Pueyo, 2020). Though the virus' impact has been severe, there is a perception of weak government response to addressing the crisis (Fetzer et al., 2020). In addition, a socioeconomic dimension further exacerbates and complicates the ramifications of the pandemic; different countries and communities are not affected equally by the virus (Blanco & Rosales, 2020). Racism and discrimination amplify the hardships, difficulties, and suffering inflicted by the pandemic.

Inequality persists in the ramp-up to vaccination deployment, with wealthier nations uniquely well-positioned to provide for their citizens (Goodman, 2020). Despite the collective efforts of non-profits and global organizations to secure doses for poorer nations, concerns remain that those with the least will be vaccinated last (Benach, 2021). From a philosophical and moral design, this directly contradicts

N. Brown (✉)
Pepperdine University, Malibu, CA, USA
e-mail: natasha.brown@pepperdine.edu

H. E. Schockman
Woodbury University, Burbank, CA, USA
e-mail: eric.schockman@woodbury.edu

S. K. Dhiman, J. F. Marques (eds.), *Leadership After COVID-19*, Future of Business and Finance, https://doi.org/10.1007/978-3-030-84867-5_30

John Rawls *Theory of Justice*. Rawls (1971) posits in his "principle of equality" that the least advantaged in society should receive the greatest benefits. By some measure, it also appears that early distribution has led to a birthing of vaccine nationalism, with the world's wealthiest nations pre-ordering and stockpiling far more doses of the vaccine than its population could consume (Twohey et al., 2020). This race to vaccinate in the developed world may leave further carnage for those poorer nations left behind, demonstrating once again the parameters of decolonializing our global leadership.

The COVID-19 pandemic has revealed both bright spots and failures of international global leadership. The crisis has also heightened attention to and awareness of the need for such leadership. It is critical to understand the leadership traits that will be needed in the post-pandemic world from a global governance perspective. The purpose of this preliminary research essay is to investigate global leadership traits required for the post-pandemic world and to understand which leadership traits are needed more than, less than, or the same as pre-pandemic times. The coronavirus pandemic has introduced new and different challenges and presents a timely, relevant, and critical opportunity to investigate global leadership traits necessary for the future. We seek to understand, from a global citizen perspective, the type of global leadership needed in the post-pandemic era.

To fully explore the research question, first, a theoretical foundation is presented, anchoring the research in theories of constructivism, trait theory, and decolonization. Second, examples of failures of global leadership are cataloged. They include xenophobia, unilateralism, and inconsistent messaging based on disregard for science, which presents difficulties for followership and the global masses. Next, and in contrast to the previous section, a host of triumphs of pandemic-era global leadership is illuminated. These include developments in the rapid adoption of digital technologies, the victory of science, and the recognition of influential young women leaders on the international scene. Building on the exploration of triumphs and failures of global leadership during the pandemic, the focus then pivots to implications for the post-pandemic era. A series of hypotheses are presented, including that post-pandemic global leadership will need to be more agile, connected, and empathetic than in pre-pandemic times. Lastly, findings will be shared from a preliminary qualitative research study, specifically examining, through a rigorous questionnaire, views on necessary traits of global leadership in the post-pandemic era and whether they are needed the same as, more than, or less than in pre-pandemic times.

International Relations and Leadership Theory Anchors

Constructivism

Within the body of international relations theory, the school of constructivism provides a helpful lens for the analysis of pandemic-era global leadership. As a theoretical foundation, constructivism offers an approach to international relations theory in which meaning is created through observation and interpretation (Park,

2018). Constructivists posit that the context in which events occur is critical for understanding them. Social *facts*, therefore, are created through shared agreements among state and non-state actors. Global developments and historical moments can best be understood by paying attention to the social relations of the actors participating and engaging in the events.

In the case of COVID-19, constructivism can be applied to the analysis of global leadership during the coronavirus pandemic. Numerous actors, including nation-states, NGOs, corporations, and citizen groups, have been actively engaged in the creation of shared agreements and social facts. Scholars and researchers can observe the manifestation, or lack thereof, of global leadership during the pandemic, frame it within the context of current events and seek to understand and explain it through interpretation.

Constructivism constitutes the critical theoretical foundation for this study (along with two sub-theories) of current events and their implications for post-pandemic global leadership. It is argued that constructivism affords a helpful compromise (Adler, 1997). Located somewhere in between rationalist theory and interpretivism, constructivism carves out a space for new research and exploration to understand global events. A constructivist study by design, this post-pandemic global leadership research presented will focus on understanding citizen perspectives within the context of the pandemic-era. Specifically, constructivism is a critical choice for this study on post-pandemic leadership for three key reasons. First, constructivists argue that social relationships shared knowledge and norms shape the behavior of international actors (Wendt, 1999). During the pandemic in which the fates and futures of states and communities are intertwined due to the contagious nature of the coronavirus, it is more important than ever to investigate through a lens of shared meaning and connection. Second, for constructivists, absolute foundations of knowledge or fact are eschewed in place of new, created understanding (Kratochwil, 2008). In this context, information and communication take centerstage over "hard science" to explain social phenomena. In countless ways, the pandemic has turned what we know quite literally on its head globally. The coronavirus is new and quickly mutating. Addressing COVID-19 successfully will take the nimble and agile perspective that constructivism affords. Lastly, constructivists note that social action ultimately builds social order and can establish international structure (Ruggie, 1999). Amidst the backdrop of the social, political, and economic woes that have ravaged the nations of the world, a paradigm that provides insight into much-needed international structure is in order. Hence, we have elected to ground our research in constructivist theory. We supplement this framework with trait theory and decoloniality.

Trait Theory

In addition, to constructivism, trait theory grounds the research presented on post-pandemic leadership. Trait theorists explain that particular characteristics, or traits, of individuals affect and influence their leadership skills and abilities. Within this paradigm, leadership is a quantifiable and enduring set of traits specific to each person (Jago, 1982). Trait theorists note the relevance of individual characteristics, with some even arguing that there is evidence that effective leaders are distinct and different from others, based on a set of leadership traits (Kirkpatrick & Locke, 1991). In addition, perceived leadership traits can shape the way followers evaluate a leader's effectiveness (Dinh & Lord, 2012).

Criticisms of trait theory point out that it can be patriarchal and that it overlooks essential elements of social understandings of leadership (Northouse, 2019). Stogdill (1948, 1974) suggested that leadership could not be understood in terms of individual traits, but rather that a leader's actions and behaviors were a result of the overall environment and context of their situation. Some leadership theorists began to move away from examining leader traits as the focus for examination and moved more toward a behaviorist cannon. Stogdill and Shartle (1948) proposed that leadership exists not in the individual traits of a leader but instead in the interactions between people. For such behaviorists, the unit of study is leader action and activity more than leader traits.

Nevertheless, trait theory continues to provide a necessary grounding for understanding leadership in general and enables a specific focus on the leader. There are many benefits to using a trait approach, which make it a popular selection among leadership theories (Germain, 2012). Trait theory benefits from extensive research, validation, and credibility. It enables helpful benchmarking and zeroes in on the leader in the context of leadership. Trait theory also straightforward and affords a human perspective and fits into popular notions of leaders as unique and special individuals. Trait theory was the leading paradigm for understanding leadership until the 1940s and 1950s, then experienced a downturn in usage with refuting from the behaviorists and other theorists stressing the importance of context. However, trait theory enjoyed a new renaissance once again at the most recent turn of the century (Zaccaro, 2007). Based on its clarity and specificity, trait theory provides a useful lens for understanding leadership today.

In the context of the COVID-19, exploring the specific traits of leaders in terms of successes and failures helps garner an understanding of their applicability and functionality in the post-pandemic era. In addition, focusing on specific leadership traits enables a pulsing of global citizen perspectives to understand a collective sense of what the future might entail. Therefore, after analysis of the failures and triumphs of global leadership during the pandemic, the specific traits needed from global leaders in the post-pandemic will be explored to create a roadmap for the future. In order to supplement the trait analysis with the inclusion of behaviors and activities of leaders, the research study was designed using the holistic framework of the Multifactor Leadership Questionnaire (Bass & Avolio, 1995). Hence the unit of analysis for the study will be leadership *factors*, which enable a more broad interpretation of leadership traits with the incorporation of behaviors and activities.

Decoloniality

The ramifications of colonialism still echo in the modern world. The current reverberations of the decline and end of colonialism, whether in countries emerging 20 years ago or 200 years ago, profoundly impact the economic demographics of those societies and influence their ability to navigate through the COVID-19 pandemic and rebound. Overall, it should be noted that the pandemic affects nations unequally, with a disproportionate amount of consequence for poorer nations without the ability to isolate due to squalid living conditions, limited contract tracing, and sparse treatment options. In addition, the pandemic has demonstratively disproportionately impacted BIPOC (black, indigenous, and people of color) in the "advanced" world as well.

The core principle of decoloniality is that knowledge and being can be untangled from notions of Western cultural supremacy and Eurocentrism (Kataneksza et al., 2018). The untangling is necessary because definitions and "knowledge" of non-Western areas are inextricably linked to their imperialist histories of Western intervention and control, such as reflected in the term and concept of Orientalism (Said, 1978). No longer defined as in relation to "self" or "other," a sub-alternative perspective emerges in decoloniality that is independent. Decoloniality creates space for dialogue, disagreement, dismantling, and reconstruction of ideas, concepts, and knowledge. The idea of Western global dominance and hegemony is upended with a definitional liberation for regions such as Latin America, no longer dependent on Eurocentric ideals and definition as other (Quijano, 2000, 2002). Further, decoloniality offers a "delinking," or a separation of knowledge, thinking, and ways of being from previous colonial forms (Mignolo, 2007).

In shaping the research study presented below, decoloniality served as a foundational theory. The citizen perspective was sought and explored, not as "other," but as the core unit of analysis, and regarded as the critical source of knowledge. As researchers, we were also cautious to identify our own intellectual locale and to be wary of our own Eurocentrism or reliance on Western thinking as the locale for explorations of solutions to the global COVID-19 pandemic and the understanding of new leadership needed for the post-pandemic world. We intentionally sought to apply principles of decoloniality to our study both internally and externally. Internally, in developing countries, we observe that elites, many of whom are educated abroad, continue to manifest the Eurocentric top-down or trickle-down-economic suppression of wealth. Therefore, we need a process to begin decolonizing internal leadership domains so democratic theory can flourish. Decoloniality offers a critical assessment of those excluded from the dominant discourse. It forces us to rethink the belonging and citizenship of those marginalized by the binary divisions of self/other in mainstream International Relations theory. And with a focus externally, we note that while the de jure reality of the decolonial post-World War II era pushed the world order to grant independence to many former colonies, the de facto reality was the trap of globalization and dependency theory kept the developing world in a perpetual state of underdevelopment (Frank, 1980). We see this again with the COVID-19 vaccine deployment; the supply chain of life-saving doses prioritizes the rich over the poorer countries. Essentially there is a critical epistemology of geo-political realities of the "coloniality of power" at play, again. We need to reconceptualize the material and ideational residues of colonialism and the neo-colonialism of globalization.

Failures of Pandemic-Era Global Leadership

As the world's peoples navigate health, financial, and social woes inflicted by the coronavirus, they look to global leaders for direction, assurances, and guidance about the future. Unfortunately, the COVID-19 crisis has illuminated the consequential failures of modern global leadership. Firstly, pandemic global leadership has been marked by a resurgence of xenophobia, as exemplified by border and immigration restrictions, racialized rhetoric, and race-baiting, as well as finger-pointing and blame. Secondly, leaders have engaged in sharing mixed messages and inconsistent information on the virus. It has been, therefore, difficult for followers to develop clarity from leaders on expectations, forecasts, and actions needed. The failures of global leadership during that pandemic are consequential, have exacerbated the difficulties and negative experiences of individuals around the world. Finally, leadership around the globe during COVID-19 has mainly been siloed and lacking in collaboration and coordination.

The COVID-19 pandemic has unleashed a wave of xenophobic actions and a rise in nationalism around the world (United Nations Department of Communications, 2020). Borders have been closed in fear, migrants have been vilified, and immigration has been curtailed in some nations, blaming particular groups and nations for the spread of the virus (Yeung, 2020). Racializing rhetoric is active around the globe relating to the pandemic. For example, Chinese-Americans have faced discrimination on subways in New York and white foreigners have faced backlash in Thailand from the health ministry (Serhan & McLaughlin, 2020). In such cases, the virus is used to propagate bias and discrimination based on race, class, and origin. In addition, A racist interpretation of the pandemic has been on display from leaders like U.S. President Donald Trump, taking knowledge of the first recorded case in Wuhan and attributing it to people of Chinese descent (Blanco & Rosales, 2020). Misinformation and finger-pointing have also come from some Chinese leaders, returning blame with assertions that the virus was engineered in a U.S. lab (Sardarizadeh & Robinson, 2020).

A second failure of global leadership during the coronavirus pandemic, mixed messages from leaders, has resulted in a followership problem. The information shared by some global leaders, like Donald Trump, Boris Johnson, and Xi Jinping, during the coronavirus era has been plagued with confusing and conflicting guidelines, inconsistent messaging, and dizzying policy about-faces (Keaten & Cheng, 2020). There is also a lack of cohesion among and between leaders on coronavirus information. Some leaders are following scientific guidelines, while others are not. This inconsistency has created numerous problems from a followership point of view. There is a followership dichotomy amidst the mixed-messaging of failed pandemic global leadership; if the public doesn't understand public health messaging, then citizens cannot follow the health guidance set forth by leaders. Such confusion allows for the politicization of such a simple task as mask-wearing. According to followership theory, leaders must have a group of followers to lead (Uhl-Bien et al., 2014). It is when individuals accept the influence of others to move toward a shared goal that followership occurs. In the coronavirus pandemic, the troublesome inconsistent information dispensed from leaders has resulted in the absence of a coordinated response from a followership base. Such conflicting messaging also erodes trust, an essential factor by which followers evaluate their leaders (Chaleff, 2009).

In addition to xenophobia and confusing leader messaging, uncooperative unilateralism and siloed leadership has emerged as a failure in the post-pandemic era. In times of peace and crisis, global knowledge and advocacy networks enable the sharing of knowledge, information, and expertise across the globe (Stone, 2002). However, during the pandemic, we have seen a move away from such cooperative arrangements to more siloed activities. For example, we have seen in the Trump era an abandoning of global consortiums such as the U.S.'s call for defunding of, and later departure from, the World Health Organization, a critical international network dedicated to improving public health around the globe (Javed & Chattu, 2020; McNeil Jr. & Jacobs 2020; World Health Organization, 2020). Former military leaders in the United States have also expressed concern around the current retreat from allies, noting that the coronavirus is a force that needs to be addressed as a global collective (Lamb & Mattis, 2020). Siloed and unilateral actions have also impacted coordination and integration between public health agencies and health care institutions (Brownson et al., 2020).

The Unites States coronavirus response was marked by presidential leadership failures of Donald Trump and his administration, including looking to the states for direction versus providing federal support, fueling national division over unity, and attacking international organizations versus driving global cooperation (Fukuyama, 2020). While the current COVID-19 crisis has been marked with siloed actions of leaders like President Trump, examples of more collaborative leadership can be found in previous pandemic experiences. In her June, 2020 talk, "How the Pandemic Will Shape International Politics," at Yale University's Jackson Institute, Ambassador Samantha Powers compared leadership of the Trump administration during the coronavirus to the corollary leadership of Barack Obama during the Ebola outbreak in 2014, highlighting what she regarded as enduring lessons (Powers, 2020). The contrasts she drew between the two pandemic leadership examples were stark. During the Ebola mission, Obama's leadership included coordinating with medical experts, collaborating across international leadership, and inspiring contributions from other leaders. "Obama's logic was, at the heart of it, both humanitarian and this sense of connectedness and enlightened self-interest rooted a recognition that international institutions need leadership," Powers said (Powers, 2020). She noted that Obamas' deployment of troops of public health care workers and in the Ebola crisis troops were in part to inspire collective reciprocal actions of other nations. Trump's leadership, however, has been marked by unilateral action, disregard for medical guidance, and hostility toward other countries like China. "When you don't believe fundamentally in this connectedness, in global cooperation or that international institutions are useful venues, (or) in science, that is not an auspicious set of dispositions to confront the largest pandemic in more than a century," she said. Powers emphasized the criticality of global cooperation, noting the interconnectedness of nations around the globe. The siloed nature actions, such as those of the current Trump administration, represent a notable failure of COVID-19 global pandemic leadership. Lessons from the Ebola crisis point to a collective response as an essential ingredient in pandemic leadership (Sirleaf, 2020).

Triumphs of Global Leadership During COVID-19

Despite the marked failures of global leadership amid the worldwide pandemic, several meaningful bright spots have emerged as well. These triumphs are important for examination as they help illuminate implications for global leadership in the post-pandemic era. The COVID-19 leadership successes include an accelerated technological transformation around the world, marked by rapid digitization, adoption of remote work policies, and broader deployment of artificial intelligence (AI) technology. In addition, the pandemic has provided global exposure for the platform of a cadre of progressive women political leaders being recognized for their effective governance.

Borne out of necessity based on restrictions of travel and instituted health and safety quarantines, the world has seen rapid digitization and adoption of electronic tools for learning, work, and health during the pandemic. Microsoft President Brad Smith noted that during coronavirus times, the world has experienced "two years of digitization in two months" (Smith, 2020). In addition, landmark progress in e-learning protocols in the learning environment has been achieved, with significant strides in the innovation of both content and delivery (Smith, 2020). The necessity spurned by the pandemic has sparked innovation and technological adoption that has enabled employees to work differently and students to learn differently. In addition, provisions for telemedicine and virtual healthcare have enabled doctors and nurses to continue to deliver care for patients remotely (Nicola et al., 2020). The impact of these developments has been far-reaching and will likely bring benefits long beyond the end of the pandemic.

Rapid digital adoption has also meant that workplaces have successfully transformed to accommodate remote workforces practically overnight, and hospitals have accommodated patients virtually (Tynan, 2020). Critical ingredients for the remarkable enablement of telemedicine and teleworking have included advancements in technology, nimble actions of technologists, and a willingness of corporations and leaders to adopt new practices and policies promptly. The pandemic has also persuaded sometimes reluctant business decision-makers to develop options for employees to work from home. As the impact of COVID-19 progressed rapidly across the globe, companies, particularly technology firms, responded quickly by developing and adopting new remote work options and opportunities (Lerman & Greene, 2020).

In the COVID-era, many institutions have also adopted new policies that prioritize employee health and well-being. Corporations have begun to offer special affordances and reimbursement allocations for employees working from home, including provisions for the purchase of home equipment such as ergonomic desks and chairs, access to virtual fitness and mindfulness applications, and enhanced virtual mental health care. For example, funds have been allocated for workers in many companies to purchase equipment to make working from home more comfortable. Policies have been created in companies to help employees balance family and personal needs with the demands of work (Vasel, 2020; Bubb, 2020). In addition, some firms have announced plans to maintain work-from-home policies permanently beyond the reach of the coronavirus, opening up greater mobility and flexibility for the workforce (Conger, 2020).

The pandemic has also provided an opportunity for more widespread dissemination of artificial intelligence and other tools of technological advancement and internet of things technology. For example, drones, internet of things (IoT) technology, and 5G have been deployed throughout the pandemic-era with great benefit for communities and individuals (Chamola et al., 2020). And for many companies, the COVID-19 era has sparked incentives for, interest in, and the opportunity to test automation technology (Tan, 2020). In addition, it has been proposed that an opportunity exists for the corporate sphere to play an essential role in the mitigation of the global pandemic, including through leveraging drone and robotics IoT technologies for the delivery and deployment of vaccinations (Ebrahim et al., 2020). Concerns have been lodged about the potential for bias with the use of deep learning algorithms in artificial intelligence. (Marshall, 2019) Nevertheless, such technologies are proving valuable in times of crisis, and the pandemic has afforded an opportunity for usage, testing, and validation.

In addition to the triumphs of accelerated digital adoption, including the provisioning for and enablement of work-from-home scenarios and the rapid deployment of AI technologies for community good, the backdrop of the pandemic has provided an opportunity for global exposure to the platform of a cadre of progressive women political leaders. In some ways, the pandemic has reshaped notions of female leadership, highlighting a set of collective leadership traits involving courage, speed, and transparency (Carbonaro, 2020). New Zealand's Jacinda Ardern demonstrated proactive and innovative leadership, which garnered much public support when she announced a transparent COVID-19 alert system similar to an emergency system for tracking fires. This bold move came early in the pandemic, was executed swiftly, and proved significant in enabling the containment of the virus in New Zealand (Kerrissey & Edmondson, 2020). New Zealand continues to be a model nation in terms of containing the spread of the virus through enacting effective policies and procedures.

The effectiveness of Angel Merkel's leadership in Germany and Sanna Marin's leadership in Finland have been noted, especially when comparing COVID-19 related death rates of Germany and Finland to Britain, France, Italy, and Spain (Taub, 2020). Inviting diversity and dissent to the mix, communicating transparently, and taking proactive action have been part of the recipe for the success of strong women leaders. Merkel's coronavirus approach, for example, included considering broad information from a variety of sources versus relying on the modeling of her own advisers. And Sanna Marin, Finland's youngest Prime Minister, has drawn high approval ratings for clear communications and implementing swift and direct measures, including invoking an economic stimulus and closing public institutions like schools and museums, to address the virus (Mendoza, 2020). Finland continues to enjoy infection rates among the lowest in the world. However, thanks to early lockdown measures enacted by Prime Minister Marin, the nation has been able to navigate the fall and winter global spike while still maintaining a relatively open economy (Pancevski, 2020). In addition, Taiwan's President Tsai Ing-Wen has also been recognized for weathering the pandemic with resilience and determination and a remarkably low accompanying COVID-19 case level (Taub, 2020; Tsai, 2020). It has been remarkable to see the relative success of the national experience in New Zealand, Germany, Finland, and Taiwan in the midst of the pandemic and to correlate it to the styles of these countries' women leaders.

While the women leaders in these countries were no doubt active in successful leadership pre-pandemic, the coronavirus era brought spotlight, focus, and attention to their leadership styles, which are bold, fast-acting, compassionate, and team-focused (Chamorro-Premuzic & Wittenberg-Cox, 2020). The triumph here is two-fold. First, it is a triumph of pandemic-era leadership that Ardern, Merkel, Marin, Tsai have been able to manage and mitigate the spread of the virus in their nations to the extent they have. Secondly, it is a triumph that such leadership has been recognized and applauded worldwide. Further research, study, and exploration into the unique traits of women leaders and the resulting impact during the COVID-19 pandemic will benefit the fields of leadership studies and international affairs.

Framing the Roadmap for Post-Pandemic Leadership

Our cursory evaluation of pandemic-era global leadership demonstrates that there have been both failures and triumphs. But what are the implications for leadership in the post-pandemic era? Which leadership traits will be needed in the future more than, the same as, or less than pre-pandemic times? Most importantly, how can we "learn from" lessons of the coronavirus, versus "spurning" them, a task International Relations theorists have acknowledged is challenging to accomplish (Weiss & Wilkinson, 2018). Based on the analysis of COVID-era global leadership successes and misses, we hypothesized that three key leadership traits will be needed in the post-pandemic era: agility, connectedness, and empathy.

First, post-pandemic leadership will need to *be agile* in order to respond to changing demands on the health system, economy, and individual communities. In the business arena, agility is a trait of successful and effective leaders. At the most advanced levels, agile leaders are self-aware, take a holistic view of organizational needs, can move fluidly between leadership styles, and develop strong connections with others (Joiner & Josephs, 2007). In the context of achieving the United Nations Sustainable Development Goals (UN SDGs), adaptive leadership is flagged as most effective in meeting global objectives (Morgan, 2018). Adaptive leadership is an agile form of leadership. Like the issues in the spotlight by the UN SDGs, the coronavirus pandemic has affected communities worldwide and created a host of critical issues with a highly consequential need for resolution. Hence, agile leadership will be helpful in nimbly responding to quickly evolving needs and challenges.

In addition to agility, to be successful, post-pandemic leadership must be simultaneously global, local, and, most importantly, *connected*. In many ways, COVID-19 has changed the level of subsidiarity for public health. Subsidiarity is the lowest level at which an issue should be addressed (Kahler, 2009). Post-pandemic, broad public health issues need to be considered at a much higher, more global level. Our fates are now linked to the fates of others (Powers, 2020), and it is essential for post-pandemic leadership that we address our shared fate collectively. International relations scholars Stone and Ladi (2015) coined the phrase "transnational administration" to refer to "the regulation, management and implementation of global policies of a public nature by both private and public actors operating beyond the boundaries and jurisdictions of the state, but often in areas beneath the global level" (2015, p. 840). Using networks to pool knowledge globally on how to address problems of the pandemic and then produce advocacy is a primary example of connected leadership, a style that will likely serve us well in the post-pandemic era.

In addition to agility and connectedness, *empathy* is likely a third leadership characteristic that will be critical in the post-pandemic world. A critical component of emotional intelligence, empathy, helps leaders understand how others feel (Goleman, 1995). Empathy is considered an inclusive leadership competency because it takes into account the feelings and needs of others when planning for decisions and actions (Morgan, 2017). In broader terms, numerous thought leaders have expressed the importance of empathy in leadership. Bob Johansen (2017), for example, argues that creating and sustaining positive energy, including creating interpersonal wellbeing with others, is a critical component of leadership needed for the future (Johansen, 2017). Similarly, Colbert and Kurucz (2018) argue that humanistic leadership, by design complete with empathy, is needed for leadership globally in this century. It is hypothesized that empathy, agility, and connectedness, are required traits for post-pandemic global leaders to be effective and successful.

The COVID-19 pandemic has revealed both bright spots in and failures of international global leadership and has heightened attention to and awareness of the need for such leadership. The pandemic has brought a host of new challenges and has illuminated the need for global leadership in their resolution. It is critical to understand the leadership traits that will be needed in the post-pandemic world for global governance. The brief survey of international relations and leadership theory provide a helpful framework for post-pandemic global leadership in terms of a conjecture. A useful hypothesis has been presented in terms of a call for leadership that is agile, empathetic, and connected in the "new normal" era. However, empirical data is needed to validate further, define, and propose what will be required for global leadership in the times ahead, beyond the realm of the COVID-19 pandemic. In addition, the perspective of global citizens, whose shared lived experience documents the impact of the pandemic, is a necessary addition to a well-formed roadmap for post-pandemic global leadership.

The theoretical lens of constructivism affords an approach to examining citizen perspectives and the social context of the pandemic and explaining them through contextual interpretation. Within the framework of trait theory, we can identify the specific characteristics of leaders that are most desirable and necessary for guiding, orchestrating, and directing the activities and developments of the global new normal. Decoloniality challenges us to delink notions of progress and leadership for the new world order from Eurocentric and Western ideals of knowledge and power. Combining these three theoretical frameworks then, we endeavored to explore through our research the leadership traits needed in the post-pandemic world. We have endeavored to do so by examining and interpreting context and social interactions and considering the voices of many, and all, without limitation of the constructs of coloniality.

Harvesting Pandemic-Era Wisdom for the Future: A Preliminary Research Study

The COVID-19 pandemic has introduced new and different challenges and presents a timely, relevant, and critical opportunity to investigate global leadership traits necessary for the future. After following developments from a global leadership perspective throughout the spring and summer of 2020, in the autumn of 2020, the authors undertook a quantitative research study to collect the perspective of global citizens on post-pandemic global leadership. Specifically, the purpose of the study was to investigate global leadership traits needed in the post-pandemic world and to understand which leadership traits are needed more than, less than, or the same as pre-pandemic times. A quantitative methodology was used to explore common citizen perspectives. The study posed the following research question: To what extent, if any, are there differences in global leadership traits needed in the post-pandemic world compared to the pre-pandemic world?

Data from the survey was collected through the Amazon Mechanical Turk website, a crowdsourcing marketplace. Individuals were invited to self-select to take the survey with an informed consent letter attached to the invitation. Adults aged 18 and older were invited to participate. Well over 1200 responses were collected. The survey for the study was created from a list of leadership factors in the adapted version of the Multifactor Leadership Questionnaire (Xirasagar et al., 2005b), a compressed version of the longer Multifactor Leadership Questionnaire (Bass & Avolio, 1995), making it useful for research scenarios. The adapted questionnaire features 43 leadership factors and was initially designed to explore physician leadership styles and leadership effectiveness (Xirasagar et al. 2005a).

In our study, a scale was added to capture the relevancy of each of the 43 leadership factors from a pre- and post-pandemic global leadership perspective. In the survey, participants were asked to answer if each of the leadership factors is, in their opinion, needed "more than," "less than," or "the same as" in the post-pandemic world as compared to the pre-pandemic world. We hypothesized that post-pandemic leadership is a new and evolving phenomenon. The leadership factors from the adapted Multifactor Leadership Questionnaire was used as the basis for the formation of this survey, and the framework was used and adapted to capture an understanding of citizen perspectives of leadership needed post-pandemic.

The Citizen Perspective: Analysis and Findings

The research study conducted revealed a number of important conclusions about what is needed for post-pandemic global leadership. In general, respondents felt that positive leadership traits were more needed post-pandemic, and the negative leadership traits were less needed post-pandemic. Specifically, the leadership factors that fall into the dimensions *of transformational* leadership scored most highly for most needed post-pandemic. The *transactional* leadership dimensions such as laissez-faire and "passive management by exception" were ranked as being less important post-pandemic. Ultimately, the empirical data shows that there is a call for active and engaged leadership to lead the global community in the aftermath of COVID-19. There was a strong response indicating a preference for more transformational leadership in the post-pandemic world compared to more transactional leadership. Such decisiveness suggests a thirst for positive, transformational global leadership.

It should be noted that a sharp difference in view of what global leadership should look like post-pandemic compared to pre-pandemic emerged. Roughly 80% of answers reflected a point of view that either *more* or *less* of leadership factors is needed post-pandemic. Twenty percent or fewer respondents selected *of the same importance* when comparing leadership factors in the post-pandemic era to pre-pandemic times. In other words, there is not a steady-state by any measure in terms of citizen perspectives on post-pandemic global leadership. It seems that the pandemic has created a line of "before and after" historically in terms of calls for leadership or expressed in shorthand as LBC (leadership before coronavirus) or LAC (leadership after coronavirus), and they are notably different (Fig. 30.1).

The vision for post-pandemic leadership is one of hope and inspiration, optimism, and broad vision setting. The analysis from our study found the highest scoring answers for "more needed" post-pandemic included: Behavior inspiring respect and regard (73%), Communicating optimism about the future (68%), and Effectively communicating a collective sense of mission (66%). Curiously, "Respect and regard" tops the list at a strong rating. We hypothesize this result can be interpreted as a commentary on the lack of respect and regard in current global leadership.

When reviewing the top responses in terms of what is needed most for post-pandemic global leadership, distinct themes emerge. The data shows that leadership that encompasses ethics, morals, and values are in demand. There is a call for action from a global citizen perspective for leadership that inspires, unites, and rallies together populations. In particular, there is a call for collective over individual focus in leadership. Communication also tops the list as a desired action and behavior of global leaders. Post-pandemic, there is a need for more intentional information sharing. Overall, the empirical data reveal that transformational leadership will be most valuable following the aftermath of COVID-19 (Fig. 30.2).

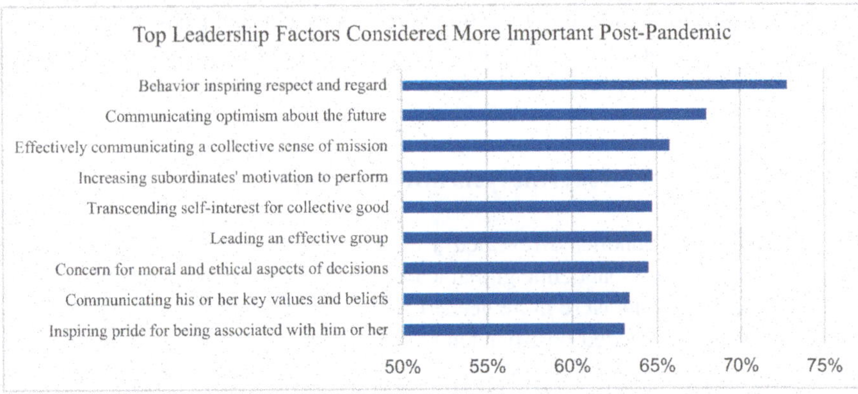

Fig. 30.1 Survey data to depict percentage of "more important post-pandemic" responses by leadership factor for the top cluster factors

% Less Important	Factor
46.19%	**Avoids decision making**
46.15%	**Unavailable when needed**
43.24%	**No action on the problem unless the situation worsens**

Fig. 30.2 Survey data to display the top three leadership factors respondents felt would be "less important" post-pandemic, and the percentage who answered accordingly

Although the responses weren't as drastic as for the "more needed" leadership types of leadership, a few factors stood out in the research as being less important post-pandemic. These factors include avoiding decision making, being unavailable when needed, and not taking action until the situation worsens. Global citizen survey respondents clearly identified the more transactional styles of leadership as ones that should be eschewed post-pandemic.

The Multifactor Leadership Questionnaire-Adapted Version, endeavors to measure both transformational and transactional leadership as well as laissez-faire features of leadership and perceptions of leader effectiveness (Xirasagar et al., 2005b). A number of dimensions fall under each of these categories of leadership. Transformational leadership is comprised of the leadership dimensions of idealized influence, both attributed and behavior-based, inspirational motivations, intellectual stimulation, and individualized consideration. Transactional leadership includes the contingent reward and active management by exception dimensions. Laissez-faire and passive management by exception comprise the laissez-faire leadership dimension. Lastly, the subjective measures of leader effectiveness dimension include rated effectiveness, subordinate satisfaction, and subordinate extra effort. The 43 leadership factors identified in the Multifactor Leadership Questionnaire-Adapter Version

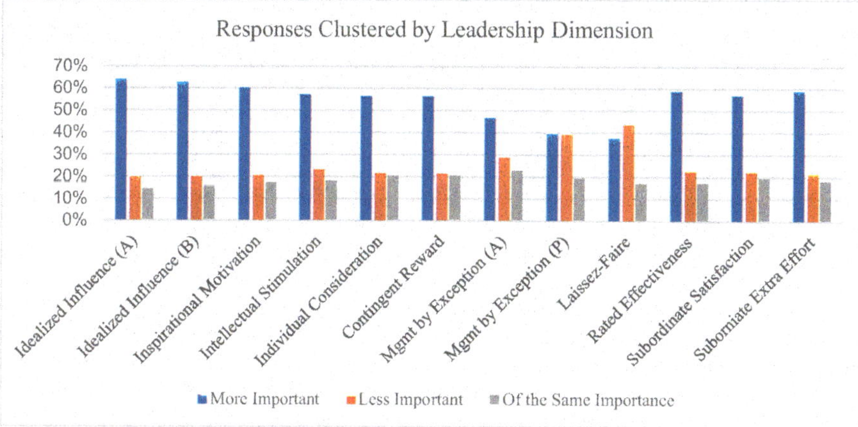

Fig. 30.3 Survey data to display survey responses for leadership factors grouped by dimension in terms of what will be "more important", "less importance" or "of the same importance" post-pandemic when compared to pre-pandemic

nest under the leadership dimensions, which, in turn, fall under the transformational, transactional, laissez-faire, and leader effectiveness categories (Fig. 30.3).

When analyzing the data from our survey of global citizen perspectives on post-pandemic leadership clustered by leadership dimensions and leadership type, a number of trends emerge. First, it is apparent that the less active and involved passive management by exception and laissez-faire leadership dimensions are less important for the post-pandemic world. However, the dimensions of idealized influence, inspirational motivation, intellectual stimulation, and individual consideration that comprise transformational leadership are more needed from our sample population. In addition, the citizen response reflects an emphasis on the dimension of leader effectiveness in the post-pandemic world, with nearly 60% of respondents ranking it as more important than in pre-pandemic times. Overall, our sample of the voice of global citizens seems to rally around the importance of transformation, effective, connected global leadership in the aftermath of COVID-19 (Fig. 30.4).

The research study on citizen perspectives of post-pandemic leadership helps to build and solidify the roadmap for post-pandemic leadership. Adding to the notion that the next era of leadership should be agile, empathetic, and connected, the research shows that post-pandemic leadership must focus on collective over individual interest, communicate optimism and purpose, and adhere to principles of universal morals and ethics. Ultimately, citizens are craving leadership that is respectful in style and transformational in nature. With this addition of our sample of citizen perspectives, the roadmap for post-pandemic global leadership begins to take clearer shape. Through the theoretical lens of trait theory, we can understand and evaluate the individual characteristics needed from our leaders internationally. Constructivist theory provides a foundation for examining, investigating, and understanding the social facts and interactions that have emerged. Further, decoloniality offers an opportunity to recognize the steep historical patterns and distribution of

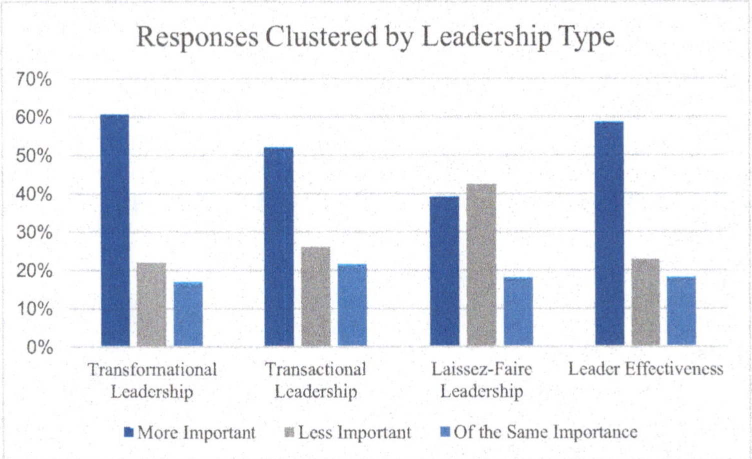

Fig. 30.4 Survey data to display survey responses for leadership factors grouped by leadership type in terms of what will be "more important", "less importance" or "of the same importance" post- pandemic when compared to pre-pandemic

power that have shaped the impact of the pandemic and pushes us to move beyond notions of Western ideals and hegemony as we explore solutions and options for a cure.

Conclusion

The global coronavirus pandemic in 2020 created tremendous strain on international systems, markets, and global leadership. Several leadership failures, such as xenophobia, siloed actions, and dissemination of mixed messages, have been documented during COVID-19 times. Nevertheless, a collection of triumphs of global leadership also emerged. These include accelerated digital adoption enabling telework, telemedicine, and telelearning, recognition of a group of strong global women leaders. Most importantly, lessons can be drawn from these failures and bright spots in terms of what is needed to cultivate future global leaders. A pattern emerges, which suggests that post-pandemic global leadership will need to be agile, connected, and empathetic. Empirical data further fleshes out this roadmap for post-pandemic global leadership with explicit calls for transformational leadership that communicates hope and optimism, stays grounded in ethical and moral principles, and favors collective over individual interest.

We see ample possibility in the realm of further research on post-pandemic global leadership and believe that, ultimately, such research could support relevant policy development aimed at easing some of the economic, social, political, and health consequences of the pandemic. At this juncture, we offer a few nascent ideas on policy recommendations for further exploration. First, we propose expanding some of the thinking on vaccination advocacy teams to be expanded from the national to the global scale (Polaha et al., 2020). Such teams could coordinate and tackle workstreams on ethical and equitable deployment, access, and information campaign to address vaccine hesitancy and the "anti-vaxxer movement". The initial work of UNICEF and the COVAX facility is remarkable but could benefit from the broader involvement of NGOs, nation-states, and the private sector (UNICEF, 2020). Second, at the international scale, we suggest a new framework for the 2030 UN Sustainable Development Goals, which are comprised of a set of interconnected umbrella initiatives ambitiously designed to better the planet ("United Nations," n.d.). Calls have been made for transformations in order to enable the attainment of these sustainable goals (Marien, 2020). We suggest specifically amending the current 17 sustainable development goals to include intentional initiatives in digital innovation, particularly in the realms of global telemedicine and remote learning, to help strengthen the post-pandemic world. Third, we proposed accelerated adoption and funding of AI technologies for smart cities globally. By design, the innovation -laden ecosystems of smart cities have always aimed to improve lives through focus areas such as mobility, public safety, and sustainability (De Guimarães et al., 2020). Adopting such technologies in the face of the pandemic affords an opportunity to save lives as well. For example, the drones that have successfully been used to provide monitoring surveillance and distribute information (Chamola et al., 2020) could also be used for the deployment of vaccines. Lastly, a rare opportunity exists at this moment in time to study and capture lessons learned from the successful cadre of women leaders globally who have helped their nations navigate the impact of the pandemic. We recommend harnessing the insight and advocacy of such women leaders through a global training institute for leadership after COVID (LAC) featuring proven women leaders as instructors and mentors. Our hope would be to garner learnings and plant seeds of knowledge for the next generation of leaders.

We conclude by reflecting on the 1960s farmworker plight, struggles for justice, the inspirational leader César E. Chávez, and his "Prayer of the Farm Workers' Struggle" (Chávez Foundation, n.d.). As a leader, Chávez prayed for the ability to see and understand the suffering of others, to forge a path of courage to help all, including enemies, so "that we can change the world." Although they were spoken so many years ago, and in a very different context and time, these words hold great value for inspiring the transformational leadership that is needed to navigate the world's "new normal". The rallying cry of the citizen voice is clear. The roadmap for post-pandemic leadership is infused with optimism, collectivism, hope, and ethics.

Five Chapter Takeaways

1. The COVID-19 pandemic tested the fabric of global leadership. Triumphs were unveiled including an accelerated digital transformation and recognition of an influential cadre of young women leaders. However, failures of global leadership were also exposed, including xenophobia, siloed actions, and mixed messages.
2. The COVID-19 pandemic also marks a clear line of "before and after" in history for global leadership. There is a marked difference in what is needed in the post-pandemic era compared to the pre-pandemic period.

3. The global citizen sample perspective on the post-pandemic era is that active and transformational leadership is needed most. There is a call for leadership that focuses on collective over individual interest, communicates optimism and a sense of purpose, and is mindful of the ethical and moral impact of decisions.
4. Transactional and passive leadership, however, will be less critical globally. Unavailable leadership that avoids decision making and doesn't proactively address problems will be far less needed in the post-pandemic world according to the global citizen perspective.
5. The strong response to this preliminary research survey in which over 1200 responses were collected is a snapshot of time that reflects that global citizens have an interest in post-pandemic global leadership.

Five Reflection Questions

1. Beyond the success of navigating the COVID-19 virus for their nations, what are the potentials of harnessing the style of female leadership which invites diversity and dissent, communicates transparently, and takes proactive action? What are the benefits and risks of examining gender-based leadership traits?
2. The survey research presented, which detailed a call for post-pandemic leadership that is transformational, collective, optimistic, and ethical, was conducted in September 2020. What might you anticipate would be different about these results had the survey been conducted in February of 2020? How about in February of 2021?
3. What strategies, tactics, and approaches should be used in order to execute on the roadmap for post-pandemic global leadership?
4. The empirical research data showed an interest in less transformational leadership that avoids decision making, is unavailable and doesn't act on problems until situations worsen. Do you read this as a commentary on the failures of the pandemic-era specifically? Why or why not?
5. The "Prayer of the Farm Worker's Struggle" in the 1960s' encapsulated leader César E. Chávez's humble hopes for humanity and devotion to service, action, and God. What might be the words of a "Prayer for the Citizens of the Globe Enduring the COVID-19 Pandemic"?

References

Adler, E. (1997). Seizing the middle ground: Constructive in world politics. *European Journal of International Relations, 3*(3), 319–363.

Bass, B. M., & Avolio, B. J. (1995). *Multifactor leadership questionnaire (MLQ)*. APA PsycTests.

Benach, J. (2021). We must take advantage of this pandemic to make a radical social change: The coronavirus as a global health, inequality, and eco-social problem. *International Journal of Health Services: Planning, Administration, Evaluation, 51*(1), 50–54.

Blanco, M. L., & Rosales, A. (2020, May 6). Global governance and COVID-19: The implications of fragmentation and inequality. *E-International Relations*. https://www.e-ir.info/2020/05/06/global-governance-and-covid-19-the-implications-of-fragmentation-and-inequality/

Brownson, R. C., Burke, T. A., Colditz, G. A., & Samet, J. M. (2020). Reimagining public health in the aftermath of a pandemic. *American Journal of Public Health, 110*(11), 1605–1610. https://doi.org/10.2105/AJPH.2020.305861

Bubb, D. (2020, May 7). *Inclusion matters more than ever. Your brain at work live podcast series.* The NeuroLeadership Institute.

Carbonaro, G. (2020, June 6). Why have female leaders been so successful in handling COVID-19? *CGTN.* https://newseu.cgtn.com/news/2020-06-06/Why-have-female-leaders-been-so-successful-in-handling-COVID-19--R6upTUoNTa/index.html

Chaleff, I. (2009). *The courageous follower: Standing up to & for our leaders* (3rd ed., Ser. A BK business book). Berrett-Koehler.

Chamola, V., Hassija, V., Gupta, V., & Guizani, M. (2020). A comprehensive review of the COVID-19 pandemic and the role of IoT, drones, A.I., blockchain and 5G in managing its impact. *IEEE Access*. https://doi.org/10.1109/ACCESS.2020.2992341

Chamorro-Premuzic, T., & Wittenberg-Cox, A. (2020, June 26). Will the pandemic reshape notions of female leadership? *Harvard Business Review.* https://hbr.org/2020/06/will-the-pandemic-reshape-notions-of-female-leadership

Chavez Foundation. (n.d.). César Chávez, *Prayer of the farm worker's struggle/Oración del Campesino en la Lucha.* Shared with permission from the Cesar Chavez Foundation.

Colbert, J., & Kurucz, E. (2018). Humanistic leadership for sustainable transformation. In S. Trevenna, S. Rappaport, S. Lowe Steffen, & J. Rezmovits (Eds.), *Evolving leadership for collective wellbeing: Lessons for implementing the United Nations sustainable development goals* (pp. 330–345). Emerald Publishing Limited.

Conger, K. (2020, May 21). Facebook starts planning for permanent remote workers. *The New York Times.* https://www.nytimes.com/2020/05/21/technology/facebook-remote-work-coronavirus.html

De Guimarães, J. C. F., Severo, E. A., Felix Júnior, L. A., Da Costa, W. P. L. B., & Salmoria, F. T. (2020). Governance and quality of life in smart cities: Towards sustainable development goals. *Journal of Cleaner Production, 253.* https://doi-org.lib.pepperdine.edu/10.1016/j.jclepro.2019.119926

Dinh, J. E., & Lord, R. G. (2012). Implications of dispositional and process views of traits for individual difference research in leadership. *The Leadership Quarterly, 23*(4), 651–669. https://doi.org/10.1016/j.leaqua.2012.03.003

Ebrahim, S. H., et al. (2020). All hands on deck: A synchronized whole-of-world approach for Covid-19 mitigation. *International Journal of Infectious Diseases, 98,* 208–215. https://doi.org/10.1016/j.ijid.2020.06.049

Fetzer, T., Witte, M., Hensel, L., Jachimowicz, J. M., Haushofer, J., Ivchenko, A., & National Bureau of Economic Research. (2020). *Global behaviors and perceptions at the onset of the covid-19 pandemic* (Working paper series, no. 27082). National Bureau of Economic Research. http://www.nber.org/papers/w27082

Frank, A. G. (1980). *Crisis in the world economy*. Holmes & Meier.

Fukuyama, F. (2020). The pandemic and political order. *Foreign Affairs, 99*(4).

Germain, M.-L. (2012). Traits and skills theories as the nexus between leadership and expertise reality or fallacy? *Performance Improvement, 51*(5), 32–39.

Goleman, D. (1995). *Emotional intelligence*. Bantam Books.

Goodman, P. (2020, December 25). One vaccine side effect: Global economic inequality. *New York Times*. https://www.nytimes.com/2020/12/25/business/coronavirus-vaccines-global-economy.html?searchResultPosition=2

Jago, A. G. (1982). Leadership: Perspectives in theory and research. *Management Science, 28*(3), 315–336. https://doi.org/10.1287/mnsc.28.3.315

Javed, S., & Chattu, V. K. (2020). Strengthening the COVID-19 pandemic response, global leadership, and international cooperation through global health diplomacy. *Health Promotion Perspectives, 10*(4), 300–305.

Johansen, R. (2017). *The new leadership literacies: Thriving in a future of extreme disruption and distributed everything* (First, Ser. A BK business book). Berrett-Koehler Publishers, BK Business book.

Joiner, B., & Josephs, S. (2007). Leadership agility: Five levels of mastery for anticipating and initiating change. *Reflections, 8*(1), 44–51.

Kahler, M. (2009). Global governance redefined. In A. C. Sobel (Ed.), *Challenges of globalization: Immigration, social welfare, global governance* (pp. 174–198). Routledge.

Kataneksza, J., et al. (2018). Decoloniality: (Re)making worlds. In T. G. Weiss & R. W. Wilkinson (Eds.), *International organization and global governance* (2nd ed., pp. 205–1217). Routledge, an imprint of the Taylor & Francis Group.

Keaten, J., & Cheng, M. (2020, July 13). WHO chief slams' mixed messages' from leaders on coronavirus. *Time Magazine*. https://time.com/5866524/world-health-organization-mixed-messages-coronavirus/

Kerrissey, M., & Edmondson, A. (2020, April 13). What good leadership looks like during this pandemic. *Harvard Business Review Online*. https://hbr.org/2020/04/what-good-leadership-looks-like-during-this-pandemic

Kirkpatrick, S., & Locke, E. A. (1991). Leadership: Do traits matter? *The Executive, 5*(2), 48–60.

Kratochwil, K. (2008). Constructivism: What it is (not) and how it matters. In D. Della Porta & M. Keating (Eds.), *Approaches and methodologies in the social sciences: A pluralist perspective* (pp. 80–99). Cambridge University Press.

Lamb, G., & Mattis, J. (2020, May 1). *The United States and its allies under stress*. Talk Presented in Yale University's Jackson Institute's Virtual Discussion Forum Series on COVID-19. Virtually through Zoom.

Lerman, R., & Greene, J. (2020, May 18). Big Tech was first to send workers home. Now it's in no rush to bring them back. *The Washington Post*. https://www.cnn.com/2020/06/04/success/google-wellness/index.html

Marien, M. (2020). COVID-19, human security, and global leadership. *Cadmus, 4*(3), 49–52.

Marshall, P. (2019). Algorithms and artificial intelligence. In *Global issues 2020 edition*. Sage/C.Q. Press.

McNeil, Jr., D., & Jacobs, A. (2020, May 29). Blaming China for the pandemic, trump says U.S. will leave the W.H.O. *The New York Times*. https://www.nytimes.com/2020/05/29/health/virus-who.html?searchResultPosition=4

Mendoza, K. A. (2020, June 23). *Meet Sanna Marin-Finland's female millennial prime minister, from an LGBT family, leading the war on coronavirus*. Style. https://www.scmp.com/magazines/style/news-trends/article/3090246/meet-sanna-marin-finlands-female-millennial-prime

Mignolo, W. D. (2007). Delinking the rhetoric of modernity, the logic of coloniality and the grammar of de-coloniality. *Cultural Studies Andover, 21*(2–3), 49–514.

Morgan, E. (2017). Breaking the zero-sum game. In A. Boitano de Moras, D. R. Lagomarsino, & H. E. Schockman (Eds.), *Breaking the zero-sum game: Transforming societies through inclusive leadership* (pp. 5–27) (First, Ser. Building leadership bridges). Emerald Publishing.

Morgan, E. (2018). Achieving a sustainable future through adaptive and strategic leadership. In S. Trevenna, S. Rappaport, S. Lowe Steffen, & J. Rezmovits (Eds.), *Evolving leadership for collective wellbeing: Lessons for implementing the United Nations sustainable development goals* (pp. 67–82). Emerald Publishing Limited.

Nicola, M., et al. (2020). The socio-economic implications of the coronavirus pandemic (covid-19): A review. *International Journal of Surgery, 78*, 185–193.

Northouse, P. (2019). *Leadership: Theory and practice* (8th ed.). SAGE Publications.

Pancevski, B. (2020, November 18). Finland and Norway avoid Covid-19 lockdowns but keep the virus at bay. *The Wall Street Journal*. https://www.wsj.com/articles/finland-and-norway-avoid-covid-19-lockdowns-but-keep-the-virus-at-bay-11605704407

Park, S. (2018). Constructivism. In T. G. Weiss & R. W. Wilkinson (Eds.), *International organization and global governance* (2nd ed., pp. 146–156). Routledge, an imprint of the Taylor & Francis Group.

Polaha, J., Johnson, L., Quinn, M., & Sunderji, N. (2020). Lessons from the team care playbook: Recommendations for COVID-19 vaccination dissemination and uptake. *Families, Systems, & Health.*

Powers, S. (2020, June 10). *How the pandemic will shape international politics.* Talk presented in Yale University's Jackson Institute's Virtual Discussion Forum Series on COVID-19. Virtually through Zoom.

Pueyo, T. (2020, March 19). *Coronavirus: The hammer and the dance: What the next 18 months can look like if leaders buy us time.* Medium. https://medium.com/@tomaspueyo/coronavirus-the-hammer-and-the-dance-be9337092b56

Quijano, A. (2000). Coloniality of power, eurocentrism, and Latin America. *Nepantla: Views from South, 1*(3), 533.

Quijano, A. (2002). The return of the future and questions about knowledge. *Current Sociology, 50*(1), 75–87. https://doi.org/10.1177/0011392102050001006

Rawls, J. (1971). *A theory of justice* (Original). Belknap Press of Harvard University Press.

Ruggie, J. G. (1999). What makes the world hang together? Neo-utilitarianism and the social constructivist challenge. In P. J. Katzenstein, R. O. Keohane, & S. D. Krasner (Eds.), *Exploration and contestation in the study of world politics* (pp. 215–245). MIT Press.

Said, E. W. (1978). Orientalism (First). Pantheon Books.

Sardarizadeh, S., & Robinson, O. (2020). Coronavirus: US and China trade conspiracy theories. *BBC News.* https://www.bbc.com/news/world-52224331

Serhan, Y., & McLaughlin, T. (2020, March 13). The other problematic outbreak: As the coronavirus spreads across the globe, so too does racism. *The Atlantic.* https://www.theatlantic.com/international/archive/2020/03/coronavirus-covid19-xenophobia-racism/607816/

Sirleaf, E. (2020, March 30). Coronavirus: What the world can learn from Ebola fight. *BBC.* https://www.bbc.com/news/world-africa-52061547

Smith, B. (2020, May 8). *Cyber threats and opportunities in the digital age.* Talk presented in Yale University's Jackson Institute's Virtual Discussion Forum Series on COVID-19. Virtually through Zoom.

Smith, K. (2020b, March 29). *Build a better normal: Insights from thousands of companies.* Your brain at work live podcast series. The NeuroLeadership Institute.

Stogdill, R. M. (1948). Personal factors associated with leadership: A survey of the literature. *The Journal of Psychology, 25*(1), 35–71.

Stogdill, R. M. (1974). *Handbook of leadership: A survey of theory and research.* Free Press.

Stogdill, R. M., & Shartle, C. L. (1948). Methods for determining patterns of leadership behavior in relation to organization structure and objectives. *Journal of Applied Psychology, 32*(3), 286–291.

Stone, D. (2002). Introduction: Global knowledge and advocacy networks. *Global Networks, 2*(1), 1–12. https://doi.org/10.1111/1471-0374.00023

Stone, D., & Ladi, S. (2015). Global public policy and transnational administration. *Public Administration, 93*(4), 839–855. https://doi.org/10.1111/padm.12207

Tan, A. (2020, June 12). *Coronavirus outbreak will speed up enterprise automation.* ComputerWeekly.com. https://www.computerweekly.com/news/252484564/Coronavirus-outbreak-will-speed-up-enterprise-automation

Taub, A. (2020, May 15). Why are women-led nations doing better with Covid-19? A new leadership style offers promise for a new era of global threats. *The New York Times.* https://www.nytimes.com/2020/05/15/world/coronavirus-women-leaders.html?smid=li-share

Tsai, I. (2020, April, 16). President of Taiwan: How my country prevented a major outbreak of COVID-19. *Time Magazine.* https://time.com/collection/finding-hope-coronavirus-pandemic/5820596/taiwan-coronavirus-lessons/

Twohey, M., et al. (2020, December 15). With first dibs on vaccines, rich countries have 'cleared the shelves'. *New York Times.* https://www.nytimes.com/2020/12/25/business/coronavirus-vaccines-global-economy.html?searchResultPosition=2

Tynan, D. (2020, March 19). IT heroes of the COVID-19 pandemic. *CIO.* https://www.cio.com/article/3563917/it-heroes-of-the-covid-19pandemic.html?upd=1595696038374

Uhl-Bien, M., Riggio, R. E., Lowe, K. B., & Carsten, M. K. (2014). Followership theory: A review and research agenda. *The Leadership Quarterly, 25*(1), 83–104. https://doi.org/10.1016/j.leaqua.2013.11.007

UNICEF. (2020). *COVAX: Ensuring global equitable access to COVID-19 vaccines*. https://www.unicef.org/supply/covax-ensuring-global-equitable-access-covid-19-vaccines

United Nations. (n.d.). *Sustainable development goals*. https://www.un.org/sustainabledevelopment/sustainable-development-goals/

United Nations Department of Communications. (2020). *COVID-19: UN counters pandemic-related hate and xenophobia*. Welcome to the United Nations. United Nations. https://www.un.org/en/coronavirus/covid-19-un-counters-pandemic-related-hate-and-xenophobia

Vasel, K. (2020, June 4). Google will give every employee $1,000 to WFH. Its head of wellness explains why. *CNN Business*. https://www.cnn.com/2020/06/04/success/google-wellness/index.html

Weiss, T., & Wilkinson, R. (2018). For international organization to global governance. In T. G. Weiss & R. W. Wilkinson (Eds.), *International organization and global governance* (2nd ed., pp. 3–16). Routledge, an imprint of the Taylor & Francis Group.

Wendt, A. (1999). *Social theory of international politics* (Ser. Cambridge studies in international relations, 67). Cambridge University Press.

World Health Organization. (2020). *About WHO*. World health Organization. https://www.who.int/about

Xirasagar, S., Samuels, M. E., & Stoskopf, C. H. (2005a). Physician leadership styles and effectiveness: An empirical study. *Medical Care Research and Review: MCRR, 62*(6), 720–740.

Xirasagar, S., Samuels, M. E., & Stoskopf, C. H. (2005b). Multifactor Leadership Questionnaire–Adapted Version [Data set]. In PsycTESTS Dataset. American Psychological Association (APA). https://doi.org/10.1037/t43935-000

Yeung, J. (2020, January 31). As the coronavirus spreads, fear is fueling racism and xenophobia. *CNN*. https://www.cnn.com/2020/01/31/asia/wuhan-coronavirus-racism-fear-intl-hnk/index.html

Zaccaro, S. J. (2007). Trait-based perspectives of leadership. *American Psychologist, 62*(1), 6–16. https://doi-org.lib.pepperdine.edu/10.1037/0003-066X.62.1.6

Natasha Brown holds a PhD in Global Leadership and Change from Pepperdine University's Graduate School of Psychology and Education, an MA in International Relations from Yale University, and a BA in Political Science from Occidental College. Natasha also studied at the University of Helsinki in Finland with a Fulbright fellowship. Professionally, she works in organizational development and business strategy and brings a deep passion for and expertise in large-scale enterprise transformation. Natasha has a background in international business, management consulting, and nonprofit. Her research interests include Post-Pandemic Global Leadership, Mentorship and Transformational Learning, Self-Awareness in Executive Development, Post-M&A Organizational Culture, and Crisis Leadership. Natasha lives in Oregon.

H. Eric Schockman is a professor of Political Science and International Relations and Director of the Center for Leadership, Equity and Diversity at Woodbury University. He also teaches in the PhD program in Global Leadership and Change at Pepperdine University. A public policy expert, Dr. Schockman previously served as associate dean and associate adjunct professor at the Sol Price School of Public Policy at the University of Southern California. He is president and founder of the Global Hunger Foundation, dedicated to helping women in the developing world break the chains of poverty by funding projects designed to provide sustainable development and organic farming. He has also written several books and edited many articles on leadership and politics in California, the nation, and international affairs, and presented on panels on these same topics. Dr. Schockman holds a PhD in political science and international relations from the University of California.

Leading in New VUCA Environment: Role of Positive Leadership Through Spiritual and Ethical Values

31

Varinder Kumar and Sanjay Modi

Introduction

The COVID-19 spread over more than 200 countries is expected to trim economy of different regions by 4–10% of GDP (World Bank, 2021), raise level of unemployment and poverty, and derail the career and happiness of people all over the world. It has compelled the leaders to think and lead differently in the present volatile, uncertain, complex, and ambiguous (VUCA) environment with new challenges like loss of comfort zones, disorganization, unpredictable speed and magnitude of change, sudden and severe fluctuations due to lockdowns, etc. They need to leverage creativity and compassion for taking decisions that will impact on large number of people. Positive leadership deeply rooted in spirituality, ethical and moral values like interconnectedness, universal responsibility, courage, meaning in life, patience and tolerance, learning and sharing, selfless service and self-awareness that have contributed to happiness and well-being of people, can promise shared and sustainable future. The present chapter attempts to explore the role of positive leadership in the present VUCA environment.

COVID Pandemic with Negative Effects and New Challenges

The COVID-19 spread over globe has caused havoc to lives and livelihood of people with severe negative economic and social impacts. More than 100 million cases (as on Jan 31, 2021) with death tolls near 2.4 million have been reported. More than

V. Kumar (✉)
NJSA Govt College, Kapurthala, India

S. Modi
Faculty of Business and Arts, Lovely Professional University, Phagwara, India
e-mail: sanjay.modi@lpu.co.in

S. K. Dhiman, J. F. Marques (eds.), *Leadership After COVID-19*, Future of Business and Finance, https://doi.org/10.1007/978-3-030-84867-5_31

96 million people have been reduced to extreme poverty and jobs equal to 495 million hours have been lost in just second quarter of 2020 alone with travel and tourism, and service industries most affected. This has contributed to stress and distress, social stigma and depression among people, and is likely to result in social unrest, political fragmentation and increased inequalities that will aggrieve the situation due to malfunctioning of social system.

Consequently COVID-19 is being viewed as era of new VUCA environment with new challenges like loss of comfort zones, disorganization of business, unpredictable speed and magnitude of change, sudden and severe fluctuations due to lockdowns, high volatility, sudden and severe multi-layered fluctuations in economy, unpredictable speed and magnitude of change, increased mobility of people to their home towns, lack of clarity, inability to make predictions, etc. Political, social and business leaders have been compelled to think and lead differently for minimizing the immediate and collateral damages.

Need for Compassion and Creativity

As the level of happiness has declined with COVID-19 due to increasing unemployment, widening income inequalities, derailing of business, deaths of near and dear ones—we human beings need to uplift each other economically, mentally and morally by viewing it as our universal responsibility as human being or global citizen of the world. Consequently we should act out of compassion to eradicate sufferings of others. This compassion according to Buddhism is an aspiration, a state of mind, wanting others to be free from suffering (Dalai Lama & Vreeland, 2001). Without compassion, solution of one problem may result in planting of seed of another problem. Therefore effective leaders before helping others, develop their "own compassion, altruistic love, and courage enough to be able to serve the others without betraying [their]original intention" (Ricard, 2013, p. 679). Their compassion embraces wisdom also because "if compassion without wisdom is blind, compassion without action is hypocritical" (Ricard, 2013, p. 7), and genuine compassion must have both wisdom and loving kindness. Compassion involves noticing or attending others' sufferings, feeling empathic concern and responding with aim at easing those sufferings (Batson, 1994; Frost et al., 2000; Lilius et al., 2011) and caring others with transformed attitude with altruistic love. To spiritualists, love is a journey from passion to compassion, and emotions to devotion with attitude of wishing and acting for the well-being and flourishing of others.

In this era of new VUCA with unprecedented, ferocious and fast change (Kotter, 2012) and changing paradigms (Barker, 1993) with lockdowns compelling to do business in different way with different thinking—leaders are expected to nurture an environment of collaborative creativity and innovation to survive and thrive. In the period of lockdowns, business has to be done through zoom and other technologies, as people have to work from home. Consequently it requires creativity and innovation to do business in different ways with "appropriate-useful and actionable idea" (Amabile, 1998) and "problem solving strategy" (Zhou & George, 2001). Like compassion, creativity requires spirit of loving and caring with mixture of intellect and intuition infused together. Leaders care and love their constituents to lead them in right and creative direction. Their kindness, love and caring attitude help to create soothing environment of mutual respect and trust, and engage people in effective way to promote creative solution to the problem. They have to be empathic (Yukl et al., 2013, p. 99) and caring (Spears, 2010) to induce creativity among people besides winning their willing cooperation.

Positive Leadership

It is imperative for business and political leaders to develop set of skills necessary to live and work mindfully and resiliently with this ever escalating volatility, uncertainty, complexity, and ambiguity as ordinary skills are insufficient to meet these challenges of New VUCA. Positive leadership-an umbrella term used for transformational, spiritual, ethical, authentic, servant and eupsychia leadership-deeply rooted in spiritual values can promise results for shared and sustainable future. Transformational leadership with idealized influence, inspiration, motivation, intellectual stimulation, and individualized consideration (Avolio, 1999; Bass, 1990; Bass & Avolio, 1993) has potential for enhancing the well-being of employees (Sivanathan et al., 2004). During the time of crisis, transformational leaders display idealized influence to win the willing cooperation of their followers and can consequently focus on the long-term health and well-being of the employees rather than adhering to short-term benefit approach like cutting costs through retrenchment, cutting costs on research and development, etc. Such leaders inspire their followers to aspire for higher challenges with realistic feelings of self-efficacy, stimulate them intellectually to innovate and give them individualized consideration by actively listening and valuing their options that give employees sense of well-being with shared and sustainable future. Transformational leadership occurs when one or more persons engage with others in such a way that leaders and followers raise one another to higher levels of motivation and morality with fused purposes (Burns, 1978). This type of leadership being elevating, mobilizing, inspiring, exalting, uplifting, exhorting, evangelizing—engages the hearts and minds of others, enlarges the shared vision, clarifies purposes, makes behavior congruent with principles and values and helps each other to achieve greater motivation, satisfaction and greater sense of achievement (Burns, 1978; Crainer, 1997, p. 50). As this leadership involves an ethical influence process (Kanungo & Mendonca, 1996), it contributes to employees' well-being.

Similarly, authentic leadership, another variant of transformational leadership talks about fostering positive self-development, bringing people together around a shared purpose and empowering them to set up and lead authentically in order to create value for all stakeholders (Luthans & Avolio, 2003). To Avolio et al. (2004), authentic leaders are deeply aware of their thinking pattern and behavior and are perceived by others as being aware of their own and others' values/moral perspective, knowledge, and strengths. They are aware of the context in which they operate and are confident, hopeful, optimistic, resilient, and high on moral character. Ethical leadership incorporates, demonstrates and promotes moral principles—like integrity, fairness, honesty, trust, etc. among followers through communication, reinforcement, and decision-making (Brown & Trevino, 2006). Such leaders engage in acts beneficial to others, refrain from causing harm to others (Kanungo, 2001). Ethical leadership behavior involves being very supportive and helpful when someone has a problem, being fair in distribution of rewards and benefits, being open and honest while communicating, making sacrifices to benefit others, setting clear ethical standards for the work and adhering them strictly by holding people accountable (Yukl et al., 2013). This behavior further contributes to happiness and well-being.

Another type of positive leadership-servant leadership (Greenleaf, 2003; Spears, 2010) is expression of inner spirituality in the service of others. This leadership attuned to basic spiritual values like service motive and taking care of others with sublimation of ego for higher purpose enables to enter into authentic relations (Covey, 2003). Responsible leadership (Freeman & Auster, 2011; Maak & Pless, 2009) cares for the needs of others and acts as global and responsible citizen (Maak, 2007). Authentic leaders are altruistic, honest, trustworthy, and principled decision-makers who care about the well-being of their followers and the needs of the broader society.

Positive leadership is deeply rooted in spiritual and ethical values as they emphasize moral values like liberty, equality, justice, and is guided by universal ethical principles-responsibility, fairness, etc.—along with empathy (Johnson, 2013, p. 190). Laura Reave (2005) reviewed 150 studies and finds consistency between spiritual values and practices in context of effective leadership. On the other end-without exercising values, leaders are more likely to exercise negative leadership styles like abusive supervision (Tepper, 2000; Bies, 2001; Keashly & Harvey, 2005), petty tyranny (Ashforth, 1997), workplace bullying (Hoel & Cooper, 2001), destructive leadership (Krasikova et al.,, 2013; Einarsen et al., 2007). Based upon authors' observation in context of educational institutions, different styles of functioning in VUCA environment as noticed due to Positive and Negative Leadership are illustrated in following table:

Positive leadership	Negative leadership
Engagement	Entanglement in activity without productivity
Fruitful and mutually beneficial direction	No sense of direction
Foster "bounded" optimism through creative thinking	Fear mongering and anxiety
Compassionate and caring	Callous and rubbing salt in the wounds
Shared and sustainable future	Focus on formalities or skin saving
Altruistic or shared	Selfish and corrupt
Developing the people	Depleting the time, talent and toil of its people
Looking at the opportunities in challenges	Looking challenges in opportunities

Values Contributing to Positive Leadership

Positive leadership is deeply rooted in spirituality and ethical values which this section attempts to explore. Practicing these values can contribute to happiness and well-being of people that can promise shared and sustainable future and can help to lead in COVID as new VUCA environment:

Interconnectedness

The word "interconnectedness" captures the essence of spirituality (Mitroff & Denton, 1999). This interconnectedness plays vital role in people's lives in the form of compassion, humanity, acceptance, holism, nonviolence, etc. with other human, animate and inanimate beings. According to Vedantist's perspective, different manifestations in existence are not isolated and discrete entities, as universal consciousness is flowing through all of us. Similarly Buddhist perspective of interconnectedness is reflected in desire to eradicate the sufferings of different beings. Physicists use phrase "the butterfly effect" that means if a butterfly flies in here and gets hurt, the effect of that accident would be felt in galaxies thousands of light years away (L'Engle, 1996, p. 256). Therefore Quantum scientist David Bohm (2003) views that we feel separate without separation as we are interconnected.

This feeling of interconnectedness enables the leader to experience the sacredness of human life, vibrating energies of different people functioning in harmonious manner, to act without ego and exercising of power mechanism, and to "relate to one another in less coercive and more creatively supporting ways" (Greenleaf, 2003, p. 23). Without feeling of interconnectedness, leaders may pretend feign kindness and empathy, but will exercise subtle forms of manipulation in an attempt to control others' behavior. As the leaders feel interconnectedness, they are more likely to understand the problems of people and will act out of compassion to contribute to their happiness and well-being in the period of COVID and VUCA.

Universal Responsibility

Positive leaders feel responsibility and inner calling for their contribution to the happiness of their organization, their people, society, family, nation, globe, and environmental protection. Their assumption of universal responsibility of conserving the environment in light of depleting resources and working on principles of sustainability, contributes to the peace of the planet and happiness of people by cultivating positive human qualities such as tolerance, generosity and love (Dalai Lama, 2012) and by transforming the lives of their people with positive influence. "The Tibetan term close to universal responsibility is *chi sem*, which literally means universal (chi) consciousness (sem), which implies that the sense of universal responsibility stems from developing universal consciousness with care for not only human but every sentient being as we exist in invisible network of relations" (Dalai

Lama & Muyzenberg, 2008, p. 101). Dalai Lama (1999, as quoted in Mathieu Ricard, 2013) advocates to pursue universal responsibility with elimination of petty self-interests and by viewing altruistic action as an opportunity to serve for other's happiness and to eradicate their sufferings:

> To acquire a sense of universal responsibility-to perceive the universal dimension of each of our actions and each person's duty towards happiness and non-suffering-is to acquire a state of mind that, when we see an opportunity to help others, drives us to seize it rather than worrying solely about our own petty self-interest. (p. 683)

As universal responsibility and community engagement require empathetic insights into the living conditions of people—it involves realizing that all things are interdependent, and altruism and compassion are intimately linked to this understanding of interdependence and bringing down the illusory wall between "myself" and "others," between "I" and "we" (Ricard, 2013, p. 682). This feeling of universal responsibility shall enable them to act for the betterment of the society at large especially in condition of crisis by making generous contribution through philanthropy, and protecting the jobs through creation of fruitful employment.

Courage

The situation of COVID-19 demands acting out of courage by leaders to contribute to the well-being of their followers especially those who are suffering more due to loss of job, disease or death of their near and dear one. Courage is verily the hinge of all virtues as it compels the person to take action for higher cause by harnessing inner strength and resources. A person though may be morally sensitive yet proves ethically failed and weak if s/he is wilted under pressure to act. Courage has been described as "willingness to face tough choices as well as overcoming the fear associated with them" (Clancy, 2003, p. 132), "ability to endure what is necessary to achieve a good end, even in the face of great obstacles" (Cavanagh & Monberg, 1999, p. 2), "(a) a willful, intentional act, (b) executed after mindful deliberation, (c) involving objective substantial risk to the actor, (d) primarily motivated to bring about a noble, good or worthy end (e) despite perhaps the presence of the emotion of fear" (Rate et al., 2007), wise and mindful action in the face of danger and risk, etc. Risk, fear, [higher] purpose and [mindful] action are key commonalities of courage (Hannah et al., 2010; Goud, 2005). Therefore courage being act of bravery requires action, in the condition of danger or risk for a higher purpose in mindful and conscious way.

Moral courage along with mental strength is needed to introspect, delve deep and prepare oneself for cultivating self-awareness and experiencing interdependence with other beings, otherwise its talks shall be shallow and superficial. This is high time to act out of courage to introspect what we as human beings have done as injustice to environment because of our greed than needs. In conditions of uncertainty and volatility, team leaders need to act with feelings of duty as well as moral identity which require demonstrating courage under conditions of risk (Amos &

Klimoski, 2014, p. 119). Leaders need to take risk while standing for the values they cherish. Bolman and Deal (2006) put the leader in wizard and warrior's role: the wizard role enables them to bring imagination, creativity, meaning and magic whereas the warrior role mobilizes strength, courage and willingness to fight as hard and long as necessary to fulfill their mission. Being in the role of warrior, they have to balance their conflicting impulses-with selfish and otherish motive, competition and collaboration, creation and destruction, and loyalty to oneself and to a greater cause. Their act of balancing requires them to act out of courage especially in situation of crisis like we face in case of COVID-19 situation.

Positive leadership like ethical and transformational leaders being principled worriers put combat in perspective as they are committed to overarching purpose rather than to power, self-aggrandizement or running roughshod over opponents, and sacrifice for worthy cause (Bolman & Deal, 2006, pp. 53–54). As they choose growth over safety and defensiveness in the light of danger, fear and risk (Goud, 2005) without being immobilized into fear of uncertainty and unknown, they act out of courage to help others and act for the humanity especially underprivileged and have-not section of the society. They regard their acts as their fulfillment and flourishing that contribute to not only their happiness but happiness of others.

Meaning in Life

The situation of COVID-19 calls for seeking and providing meaning in life not only for leaders but also for their followers. Meaning in life entails number of experiences and their interpretations with transformed attitude that fosters a sense of meaningfulness in life. Though the situation may be challenging, yet there are positive effects that leaders should search as hidden design of existence with profound life-altering experiences of life having "significance beyond the trivial or momentary [experiences of daily life] to have purpose , or to have coherence that transcend chaos" (King et al., 2006, p. 180). Steger (2012) calls it web of connections, understandings and interpretations that help us comprehend our experience and formulate plans directing our energies to the achievement of our desired future, as our lives matter, make sense and are more than days and years. Though the situation of COVID-19 is physically, mentally and economically challenging, yet it offers opportunities to introspect oneself about what we human beings have done to Mother Earth, to feel pollution free environment, to focus on responsible consumptions of essential commodities and services with avoidance of waste, to avoid unnecessary travel, etc. With searching and following meaning, they can lower depressive symptoms, hostility and other negative outcomes (Steger, 2012), alienation, frustration, increased stress, depression (Debats, 1996), post-traumatic stress disorder (Mascaro & Rosen, 2005), and cope with cancer and cardiovascular diseases (Steger, 2012) which have high causality rate in situation of COVID-19, etc.

Positive leadership not only overcomes meaninglessness but also creates supportive work environment. Their meaning in life is associated with satisfying transcendence needs-the highest type of needs in the hierarchy of needs model of

Maslow (1968). Transformational leaders and other variants of positive leadership—being fully evolved persons with deep-rooted ethical and spiritual values (Fry, 2003) actively search the meaning of their lives, facilitate in realizing meaning by others, and create work environment supportive of one's spiritual development along with organizational mission. Through their idealized influence and intellectual stimulation-they overcome meaninglessness manifested in the form of organizational dysfunction, ineffectiveness and stress impacting organizational performance (Mitroff & Denton, 1999). They also help others to find meaning and happiness at workplace with greater commitment and motivation by making the work more meaningful.

Meaning in life has great motivational power as it inspires and energizes people, gives them hope and optimism especially in adversity, and helps to maintain physical and psychological health. Victor Frankl's work *Man's search for meaning* (1959) being elaboration of Nietzsche's quote "He who has a *why* to live can bear with almost any *how*" with authenticity of his experiences as well as stories of his patients related with Nazi concentration camp demonstrates that though human beings cannot avoid suffering yet they can choose to cope with it in better and effective way by finding meaning in it and move forward with enlightened purpose with spiritual freedom. Meaning in life enables to develop resilience and cultivate a spiritual connectedness with something larger than the momentary experiences (Steger, 2012).

Patience and Tolerance

The situation of VUCA requires leaders to act out of patience and tolerance which positive leadership cultivates with profound peaceful state of mind. They respond in cool and calm manner with "calm, collected and concentrated mind" (Dalai Lama & Muyzenberg, 2008) undisturbed by reactive thoughts and negative emotions. In corporate world, leaders thrived because of resilience and their ability to view setbacks as learning experiences and challenges as opportunities to excel (Sonnenfeld & Ward, 2017). This helps them to check their negative emotions like anger, anxiety, fear and hostility overpowering them and getting transmitted to their followers as it increases susceptibility to diseases and worsens health outcomes (Anderson, 2003; Goleman, 2003). Their patience and tolerance prevent collateral damages occurring due to reactions and counter-reactions.

Learning and Sharing

Organizational learning and sharing has become the need than choice (Argyris & Schon, 1996; Senge, 1990) with organizations becoming more flexible without regard for occupying office space and functioning through zoom and other technologies, and employees working at home in the environment of COVID. In such situation, positive leadership like transformational leadership facilitates organizational learning and sharing by providing intellectual stimulation and inspiration (Bass, 1990; Bass & Avolio, 1993) and by acting as "catalyst, a mentor, a facilitator and trainer in organizational learning (García-Morales et al., 2012). They provoke curiosity for learning and generation of new ideas with trust among persons with positive resonance, and facilitate harmonious communication through effective coordination.

Selfless Service and Self-Sacrifice

The situation of COVID and crisis demands the leaders to put others' interest first as great leaders approach their work as contribution and service to the humanity. Service and self-sacrifice are hall marks of servant leadership, one of the types of positive leadership. Vedānta talks of *Nishkam karma*—doing actions without being attached to results or sense of doership, and treating work or actions as offering to the Divine. This selfless service can be offered in numerous ways like financial assistance, physical help, emotional and spiritual support, etc. The other related concept of selfless service is self-sacrificing behavior. The aim of selfless service is to contribute to the welfare and well-being of others through thoughts, words and actions without expectations of reward. Mahatma Gandhi—rare example of transformational, ethical and servant leadership remarked profoundly, "The best way to find yourself is to lose yourself in the service of others."

Self-Awareness

The first quality of positive leadership is self-awareness gained through self-knowledge. Advocates of emotional intelligence (Goleman, 2003) regarding self-awareness hold that knowledge about one's emotions is the first and foremost requirement of leadership. Without self-knowledge, service of others cannot be authentic or ethical as we cannot transcend our narrow self-interest. Vedanta teaches that seeking self-knowledge is a matter of "understanding" our true nature. Usually we identify ourselves with body-mind mechanism and consequently become egoist which superimposes the useless limitations due to selfishness. As a result, we fail to understand our real nature and identify the unreal as the real. Vedānta explains that one is not just the limited body-mind complex but pure awareness. This feeling gives one inexhaustible courage, freedom to act and abundant happiness not only for oneself, but for other beings that surround us. Self-awareness prevents the person to act and misuse power for selfish needs and to become open about their limits. This contributes to learning and sharing, and helps to harness the trust and cooperation of their members.

Earning Credibility Through Practising Ethical and Spiritual Values

With practicing these ethical and spiritual values, the leaders will not only get themselves as transformed leaders but also contribute to the happiness and well-being of their own as well as their followers (Kumar & Dhiman, 2021) which in turn help them to earn credibility which is "the foundation of leadership" (Kouzes & Posner,

2011, p. xi). Credibility enables the leaders to earn the trust and confidence of their followers which accelerate the speed along with lowering costs of functioning (Covey, 2003) besides earning employees' willing cooperation, and building learning organization with team of dedicated and devoted individuals. This credibility is manifested in trustworthiness, expertise and dynamism (Berlo et al., 1969). The intensive and ongoing research since 1980s, with interviews and focus group opinions of more than 100,000 people over more than three decades searching the qualities people most look for their willing cooperation-credibility is the answer (Kouzes & Posner, 2011, p. xv). Kouzes and Posner (2011) point out the characteristics of admired leaders in the form of 225 values as provided by more than 1500 nationwide managers, which are subsequently analyzed into 225 factors and then reduced to 15 categories with following the most frequent categories (pp. 4–5):

- Integrity (honesty, trustworthiness, character, convictions)
- Competence (capable, productive, efficient, professional)
- Leadership (inspiring, decisive, providing direction)

Concluding Thought

As COVID pandemic has adversely affected the lives and livelihood of people with timing of global economy, increased unemployment and poverty, derail the career and happiness of people all over the world. This has compelled the leaders to think and lead differently in VUCA environment with new challenges. Consequently they need to leverage compassion and creativity to protect and promote the well-being of different stakeholders. They need interconnectedness to feel the sufferings of different people, universal responsibility to eradicate their sufferings, courage to act to serve humanity at large and to take appropriate action, search meaning in life to infuse enthusiasm and hope, patience to act with equanimity, learn and share new ways, pursue selfless service without entitlements, and become self-aware to bring authenticity to their working. Positive leadership deeply rooted in spirituality and ethical values can contribute to the happiness and well-being of different people, and promise shared and sustainable future. Practicing these values helps them to earn the credibility and consequently willing cooperation of their followers that further help them to function in smooth way.

Reflection Questions

1. How can we describe COVID-19 challenges as VUCA challenges?
2. What are the negative effects and challenges of COVID-19?
3. Why there is need for creativity and compassion in COVID-19 situation?
4. What is the contrast between Positive and Negative Leadership?
5. What are the different ethical and spiritual values that positive leadership pursues to eradicate the sufferings of people?
6. Do practicing spiritual and ethical values help to eradicate sufferings of people?

References

Amabile, T. (1998). How to kill creativity. *Harvard Business Review, 76*(5), 76–87.
Amos, B., & Klimoski, R. J. (2014). Courage: Making teamwork work well. *Group & Organization Management, 39*(1), 110–128.
Anderson. (2003). *Emotional longevity*. Viking.
Argyris, C., & Schon, D. (1996). *Organizational learning II*. Addison Wesley.
Ashforth, B. E. (1997). Pretty tyranny in organizations: A preliminary examination of antecedents and consequences. *Canadian Journal of Administrative Science, 14*, 126–140.
Avolio, B. J. (1999). *Full leadership development building the vital forces in organization*. Sage.
Avolio, B., Luthans, F., & Walumbwa, F. O. (2004). *Authentic leadership: Theory building for veritable sustained performance. Working paper*. Gallup Leadership Institute, University of Nebraska.
Barker, J. A. (1993). *Paradigms: The business of discovering the future*. Harper Business.
Bass, B. M. (1990). From transactional to transformational leadership: Learning to share the vision. *Organizational Dynamics, 18*(3), 19–31.
Bass, B. M., & Avolio, B. J. (1993). Transformational leadership: A response to critiques. In M. M. Chamers & R. Ayman (Eds.), *Leadership theory and research: Perspectives and direction* (pp. 49–88). Academic Press.
Batson, C. D. (1994). Why act for the public good? Four answers. *Personality and Social Psychology Bulletin. Special Issue: The Self and the Collective, 20*(5), 603–610.
Berlo, D. K., Lemert, J. B., & Mertz, R. J. (1969). Dimensions for evaluating the acceptability of message source. *Public Opinion Quarterly, 33*(4), 563–576.
Bies, R. (2001). Interactional (in)justice: The sacred and profane. In J. Greenberg & R. Cropanzano (Eds.), *Advances in organizational behavior* (pp. 89–118). Stanford University Press.
Bohm, D. (2003). In L. Nichol (Ed.), *The essential David Bohm*. Routledge.
Bolman, L. G., & Deal, T. E. (2006). *The wizard and the warrior: Leading with passion and power*. Wiley.
Brown, M. E., & Trevino, L. K. (2006). Ethical Leadership: A review and future directions. *The Leadership Quarterly, 17*, 595–616.
Burns, J. (1978). *Leadership*. Harper & Row.
Cavanagh, G. F., & Monberg, D. J. (1999). The virtue of courage within the organization. In M. L. Pava & P. Primeaux (Eds.), *Research in ethical issues in organization* (pp. 1–25). JAI Press.
Clancy, T. R. (2003). Courage and today's nurse leader. *Nursing Administration Quarterly, 27*, 128–132.
Covey, S. R. (2003). In R. K. Greenleaf (1977). *Servant leadership*. Paulist Press.
Crainer, S. (1997). *The ultimate business library; 50 books that shaped management thinking*. American Management Association.
Dalai Lama. (2012). *Beyond religion: Ethics for the whole world*. Mariner Books.
Dalai Lama, & Muyzenberg, V. D. (2008). *The leader's way: Business, Buddhism and happiness in an interconnected world*. Nicholas Brealey Publishing.
Dalai Lama, & Vreeland, N. (2001). *An open heart: Practicing compassion in everyday life*. Little Brown.
Debats, D. L. (1996). Meaning in life: Clinical relevance and predictive power. *British Journal of Clinical Psychology, 35*, 503–516.
Einarsen, S., Aasland, M. S., & Skogstad, A. (2007). Destructive leadership behavior: A definition and conceptual model. *The Leadership Quarterly, 18*, 207–216.
Frankl, V. E. (1959). *Man's search for meaning: An introduction to logotherapy*. Random House.
Freeman, R. E., & Auster, E. R. (2011). Values, authenticity and responsible leadership. *Journal of Business Ethics, 98*, 15–23.
Frost, P. J., Dutton, J. E., Worline, M. C., et al. (2000). Narratives of compassion in organizations. In S. Fineman (Ed.), *Emotion in organizations* (pp. 25–45). Sage.

Fry, L. W. (2003). Toward a theory of spiritual leadership. *The Leadership Quarterly, 14*, 693–727.

García-Morales, V. J., Jiménez-Barrionuevo, M. M., & Gutiérrez-Gutiérrez, L. (2012). Transformational leadership influence on organizational performance through organizational learning and innovation. *Journal of Business Research, 65*, 1040–1050.

Goleman, D. (2003). *Healing emotions: Conversations with the Dalai Lama on mindfulness, emotions and health*. Shambhala.

Goud, N. H. (2005). Courage: Its nature and development. *Journal of Humanistic Counseling Education and Development., 44*, 102–116.

Greenleaf, R. K. (2003). *Servant leadership*. Paulist Press.

Hannah, S. T., Sweeney, P. J., & Lester, P. B. (2010). The courageous mind-set: A dynamic personality system approach to courage. In C. L. S. Pury & S. J. Lopez (Eds.), *The psychology of courage: Modern research on an ancient virtue* (pp. 125–148). American Psychological Association.

Hoel, H., & Cooper, C. L. (2001). Origins of bullying: Theoretical frameworks for explaining workplace bullying. In N. Tehrani (Ed.), *Building a culture of respect: Managing bullying at work* (pp. 3–19). Taylor & Francis.

Johnson, C. E. (2013). *Meeting the ethical challenges of leadership: Casting light or shadow* (4th ed.). Sage.

Kanungo, R. N. (2001). Ethical values of transactional and transformational leaders. *Canadian Journal of Administrative Sciences, 18*, 257–265.

Kanungo, R. N., & Mendonca, M. C. (1996). *Ethical dimensions of leadership*. Sage.

Keashly, L., & Harvey, S. (2005). Emotional abuse in the workplace. In S. Fox & P. E. Spector (Eds.), *Counterproductive work behavior: Investigations of actors and targets* (pp. 201–236). American Psychological Association.

King, L. A., Hicks, J., Krull, J., & Del Gaiso, A. K. (2006). Positive affect and the experience of meaning in life. *Journal of Personality and Social Psychology, 90*(1), 179–196.

Kotter, P. J. (2012). Leading Change. Boston: Harvard Business Review Press.

Kouzes, J. M., & Posner, B. (2011). *Credibility: How leaders gain and lose it, why people demand it*. Jossey Bass.

Krasikova, D. V., Green, S. G., & LeBreton, J. M. (2013). Destructive leadership: A theoretical review, integration, and future research agenda. *Journal of Management, 39*(5), 1308–1338.

Kumar, V., & Dhiman, S. (2021). Happiness and workplace well-being: Transformational leadership and the role of ethical and spiritual values. In S. Dhiman (Ed.), *The Palgrave handbook of workplace well-being*. Palgrave Macmillan.

L'Engle. (1996). As quoted in Csikszentmihalyi, Mihaly (1996). *Creativity: Flow and the psychology of discovery and invention* (p. 256). Harper Perennial.

Lilius, J. M., Worline, M. C., Dutton, J. E., Kanov, J. M., & Maitlis, S. (2011). Understanding compassion capacity. *Human Relations, 64*(7), 873–899.

Luthans, F., & Avolio, B. (2003). Authentic leadership: A positive developmental approach. In K. Cameron, J. Dutton, & R. Quinn (Eds.), *Positive organizational scholarship* (pp. 241–261). Barrett-Koehler.

Maak, T. (2007). Responsible leadership, stakeholder engagement, and the emergence of social capital. *Journal of Business Ethics, 74*, 329–343.

Maak, T., & Pless, N. M. (2009). Business leaders as citizens of the world: Advancing humanism on a global scale. *Journal of Business Ethics, 88*, 537–550.

Mascaro, N., & Rosen, D. H. (2005). Existential meaning's role in the enhancement of hope and prevention of depressive symptoms. *Journal of Personality, 73*, 985–1014.

Maslow, A. H. (1968). *Toward a psychology of being* (2nd ed.). Van Nostrand.

Mitroff, I. I., & Denton, E. A. (1999). *A spiritual audit of corporate America*. Jossey-Bass.

Rate, C. R., Clarke, J. A., Lindsay, D. R., & Sternberg, R. J. (2007). Implicit theories of courage. *Journal of Positive Psychology, 2*, 80–98.

Reave, L. (2005). Spiritual values and practices related to leadership effectiveness. *The Leadership Quarterly, 16*, 655–687.

Ricard, M. (2013). *Altruism: The power of compassion to change yourself and the world.* Atlantic Books.

Senge, P. (1990). *The fifth discipline, the art and practice of the learning organization.* Doubleday.

Sivanathan, N., Arnold, K., Turner, N., & Barling, J. (2004). Leading well: Transformational leadership and Well-being. In P. A. Lindey & S. Joseph (Eds.), *Positive psychology in practice* (pp. 241–255). Wiley.

Sonnenfeld, J., & Ward, A. (2017). Firing back: How great leaders rebound after career disasters: Managing big professional setback. In D. Goleman, Sonnenefeld, & S. Achor (Eds.), *Resilience (HBR emotional intelligence series)* (pp. 69–108). Harvard Business Review.

Spears, L. C. (2010). Character and servant leadership: Ten characteristics of effective, caring leaders. *The Journal of Virtues & Leadership, 1*(1), 25–30.

Steger, M. F. (2012). Experiencing meaning in life: Optimal functioning at the nexus of well-being, psychopathology and spirituality. In P. T. P. Wong (Ed.), *The human quest for meaning* (2nd ed., pp. 165–184). Routledge.

Tepper, B. J. (2000). Consequences of abusive supervision. *Academy of Management Journal, 43*(2), 178–190.

World Bank. (2021). *Global economic prospect.* Press Release.

Yukl, G., Mahsud, R., Hassan, S., & Prussia, G. E. (2013). An improved measure of ethical leadership. *Journal of Leadership & Organizational Studies, 20*(1), 38–48.

Zhou, J., & George, J. M. (2001). When job dissatisfaction leads to creativity: Encouraging the expression of voice. *Academy of Management Journal, 44*, 682–696.

Varinder Kumar is working as associate professor in commerce in Post Graduate Department of Commerce at the Government College in Kapurthala (North India). He has authored more than 30 books on Business Communication, Soft Skills, Human Values and Professional Ethics which are prescribed in syllabuses of different Indian Universities. His areas of interest include spirituality at workplace, transformational leadership, and creativity.

Sanjay Modi is a professor and executive dean of social sciences in Lovely Professional University at Phagwara (India). He has been associate editor of *Indian Management Studies Journal*, Punjabi University, Patiala, and has been author of three research books and 14 research papers published in different Indian Journals. His areas of interest are Human Resource Management, Employee Engagement, Trade Unionism, Life Skills, and Spirituality, and Work Behavior.

Sustainability and Organizational Longevity: Insights for Post-COVID-19 Organizations

32

William T. Craddock

Introduction

The title of this chapter suggests a clean, linear path that starts with leadership and organizational excellence that result in an organization's sustainability, which then leads to its organizational longevity. And then COVID-19 and its impacts are explored. This approach is not possible. The COVID-19 Pandemic has invaded all parts of our lives, regardless of who we are, what we do, and where we live. It is impossible to separate the Pandemic from the discussion that precedes the insights for organizations in the Post-COVID-19 era. This is addressed by discussing the Pandemic as appropriate in the sections preceding the summary discussion of the impact of the COVID-10 Pandemic on leadership.

The sources include academic articles, texts, popular business press articles, newspapers, and consulting firm reports. This cross-section of sources provides different perspectives and allows the most recent information to be considered in developing the insights.

Leadership

Leadership is a large general topic for business press books. An online bookseller search for "leadership" books peaked in early 2018 at a little over 196,000 thousand books. The actual number is probably lower due to some multiple entries for the same book in different formats and media. That number dropped to about 70,000 by mid-2018 and continues to fluctuate between 40,000 and 70,000 most likely due to

Author Note: I have no known conflict of interest to disclose.

W. T. Craddock (✉)
Craddock & Associates, Inc., Conway, AR, USA
e-mail: wtcraddock@conwaycorp.net

S. K. Dhiman, J. F. Marques (eds.), *Leadership After COVID-19*, Future of Business and Finance, https://doi.org/10.1007/978-3-030-84867-5_32

product pruning. This multitude of sources results in multiple definitions and frameworks for leadership, particularly when the on-line bookseller's books are combined with academic articles about leadership. This also creates a mismatch of definitions since some are grounded in research while others are based on opinions or a single author's personal experiences.

This chapter uses the definition of leadership proposed by Lussier and Achua (2013): "Leadership is the influencing process of leaders and followers to achieve organizational objectives through change" (p. 6). This definition has three notable characteristics aside from the influencing process: leadership requires both leaders and followers; their purpose is to achieve objectives; and leadership requires change. In much of the discussion that follows, adapt and adaptation are used to imply change.

Montuori (2000) noted: "Effective leadership requires an ability not only to recognize and navigate around the visible obstacles and threats, but also anticipate those that are not readily visible" (p. 68). Individuals who "lead into longevity" have the skill and abilities to differentiate environmental information as relevant or irrelevant, important or insignificant, and meaningful or meaningless. This can significantly increase response times during crises.

Some authors used a framework to describe the attributes or characteristics generally expected in leaders as opposed to defining leadership, per se. One example is *The Leadership Challenge* by Kouzes and Posner (2017). Their research began in the early-1980s and resulted in the first edition of *The Leadership Challenge* book in 1987. That book and each successive edition summarized insights from two different sets of interviews. At the time of their latest edition (2017) Kouzes and Posner's interviews collectively have resulted in millions of responses (p. xii).

The first set of interviews involved leaders and asked "What did you do when you were at your best as a leader?" (p. xii). This led to The Five Practices of Exemplary Leadership framework. These five practices are Model the Way; Inspire a Shared Vision; Challenge the Process; Enable Others to Act; and Encourage the Heart (pp. 12–13). This framework is particularly relevant as the world enters Year 2 of the Pandemic.

The second set of interviews involved the leaders' constituents, or followers. These interviews asked the respondents what they looked for in a leader. Analysis of the responses to these open-ended questions ultimately resulted in 20 traits or characteristics of admired leaders. For each new edition of their book, they summarized the characteristics from most cited to least cited. Four characteristics consistently appeared at the top of the list for each edition: honest, competent, inspiring, and forward-looking. If one assumes people enter the workforce around age 18–22, and exit the workforce around age 65, then the collective pool of survey respondents spans five generations: the silent generation, baby boomers, generation x, generation y (millennials), and generation z. This is good news for leaders of multigenerational workforces: the top four characteristics represent the most admired by people active in the workforce have remained consistent since the early-1980s.

Resilient and resiliency are two words that have become popular during the Pandemic in discussions of individuals, leaders, and organizations. For example, Renjen (2020) described five essential qualities of resilient leaders: their mindset regarding the situation, their focus, management skills, planning skills, and leadership attitude. Renjen also observed "... great leadership requires even greater followership—and followership is nurtured by trust" (p. 13). A synonym for trustworthiness is honesty. It is noteworthy that honesty was at the top of the four enduring characteristics of admired leaders identified by Kouzes and Posner in their multi-decade research. More specifically, honesty was at the top of each survey summary prepared for each edition of *The Leadership Challenge* by Kouzes and Posner from the first edition published in 1987 to the sixth edition published in 2017.

Montuori (2000) observed that leaders with a focus on organizational longevity must be transformational. Specifically, they must have the skills and abilities to "deal with complexity, uncertainty, ambiguity, and changes in the organization" (p. 63).

Rakowsky et al. (2020) described how COVID-19 caused abrupt changes in the leadership expectations for Chief Medical Residents at a major metropolitan hospital. The two primary leadership roles Chief Medical Residents served were to guide the residents in meeting the residency program goals and to operate as the interface between the residents and program directors. The traditional paths they had followed to accomplish this were no longer available. This led to five essential questions that apply to every leader regardless of sector.

These five essential questions addressed affirming and maintaining core values; managing communications; maintaining community with their workforce (the residents in their example) including mentoring; understanding how their roles had changed; and creating a sense of normalcy. In the midst of adapting their leadership roles to meet the demands created by the Pandemic, they remained optimistic based on some favorable unintended consequences. These included "innovation in our teaching strategies, development of novel methods to build community, elevation of the role of the chief resident, and the acquisition of leadership skills that could not have been gained elsewhere" (pp. 2–3).

Bennis and Thomas (2002) described a leadership development model that leverages moments like the chief medical residents described. Bennis and Thomas called these "crucible" moments as key to a leadership model "that explains how individuals make meaning out of often difficult events ... and how that process of 'meaning making' both galvanizes individuals and give them their distinctive voices" (p. 4). It is quite likely that the Pandemic created multiple crucibles across all sectors. Those leaders that rose to the challenge, like the chief medical residents, will likely be at the forefront of the recovery.

Organizational Excellence

Quinn and Cameron (1983) developed a composite framework for organizational excellence based on the analysis and integration of nine different excellence frameworks. They mapped their results into four existing models: rational goal, open systems, human relations, and internal processes. Elements of each of these models were used to describe an organization as it moved through its developmental stages.

Quinn and Rohrbaugh (1983) extended this work through a two-stage process using vetted experts to identify key elements. Their process resulted in three dyads used to assess an organization's effectiveness: (1) organizational focus: internal vs. external; (2) level of organizational control vs. its flexibility; and (3) its preference for ends vs. means; e.g., production and efficiency vs. growth (p. 369).

Craddock (2013) described the evolution of two Business Excellence Models (BEMs) that gained prominence in the late 1980s. The Malcolm Baldrige National Quality Award (MBNQA) and the European Foundation for Quality Management (EFQM) were established in 1987 and 1988, respectively. Both of these served as the basis for quality awards at the national level. The MBNQA is managed by the U.S. Department of Commerce, and is now known as the Baldrige Performance Excellence Program (BPEP). The EFQM is a not-for-profit organization headquartered in Belgium. Both frameworks are updated on a regular basis. The most recent versions are 2019 for the EFQM and 2020 for the Baldrige Criteria.

Use of the term Business Excellence Model continued even though articles discussed their broader applications to organizations in general. For example, Mohammad et al. (2011) noted: "Business Excellence Models (BEMs) are used by organisations to assess and improve their work practices and performance" (p. 1213). Non-business entities in the education, government, education, healthcare, and not-for-profit sectors also use BEMs for assessment and improvement.

Mann et al. (2011) determined that of the 86 countries using a BEM as the basis of their national quality award in that timeframe, 57 used one of two organizational excellence frameworks: The Malcolm Baldrige National Quality Award (MBNQA) and the European Foundation for Quality Management (EFQM). The MBNQA is managed by the U.S. Department of Commerce, and is now known as the Baldrige Performance Excellence Program (BPEP) (2021). The EFQM is a not-for-profit organization headquartered in Belgium (2019). Both frameworks are updated on a regular basis. The current version of the EFQM was published in 2019.

Although the Baldrige and EFQM frameworks are constructed differently, they address essentially the same organizational excellence issues. Ringrose (2014) updated a composite organizational excellence model that focused on the common features (principles and best management practices) of four major national business excellence models: Baldrige, EFQM, the Canadian Framework for Excellence, and the Australian Business Excellence Framework. Subsequently, Ringrose (2019) led a project use this model for a global assessment of organizational excellence. That first global assessment utilized responses from 1029 individuals representing multiple geographic regions, sectors, and organization sizes. "The respondents were asked to self-assess the degree to which their organization had a culture committed to excellence and had deployed best management practices found in excellence models. The aggregate results were shared by role, organization size, industry sector and region (country)." (D. Ringrose, personal communication, February 22, 2021). A major conclusion of the first global assessment was a validation of "the positive relationship between implementing an excellence model and developing a culture committed to excellence and improving organizational performance across a balanced system of measurement" (p. 5).

Bailey (2021) described how using a BEM process helped one small business remain viable during the Pandemic. This organization had used the Baldrige Framework for many years, including the process of having Baldrige Examiners review its applications that described its current processes and results. The Baldrige process includes a written feedback report for applicants. Each feedback report includes both strengths and opportunities for improvement. One organization credited a recent feedback report with helping prepare it for the (unknown at the time) COVID-19 Pandemic. Specifically, that feedback report "contained valuable insights that became improvements, which—fortuitously—helped us navigate this past year a little easier." One example cited was the improvement of communication with remote employees.

The Baldrige framework is updated every 2 years. The current version, Baldrige Excellence Framework for 2021–2022, was published in December 2020. The update addressed the Pandemic in a general sense rather than by name. Specifically, one process area to address (heading for a set of questions) changed from "Business Continuity" to "Business Continuity and Resilience" (p. 23). The definition for resilience includes the following: "To achieve resilience, leaders must cultivate the agility to respond quickly to both opportunities and threats, adapt strategy to changing circumstances, and have robust governance with a culture of trust" (p. 51).

Organizational Sustainability

Craddock established the linkages among Business Excellence Models (BEMs), Total Quality Management (TQM), Corporate Social Responsibility (CSR) and Sustainability. The definition used for sustainability was "a balanced approach to ensure an organization's financial, social (human), and environmental resources are sustained for both the present and the future" (p. 19). Craddock also quoted the original definition from the World Commission on Environment and Development: "Sustainable development is development the needs of the present without compromising the ability of future generations to meet their own needs" (p. 3). Sunkari (2015) summarized the evolution of the three components of sustainability and the metaphor of a three-legged stool where each leg represents one of the three components of sustainability. Sunkari also adopted the more colloquial phrase "profits, planet, and people" to represent the three legs (p. 7).

One impact of the COVID-19 Pandemic was a challenge to this definition. Hakovirta and Denuwara (2020) proposed to add human health explicitly as a fourth dimension. This more granular aspect of the societal dimension provided more clarity to the inequalities at the individual level that were exposed by the pandemic but not as readily visible in the more aggregate dimension of societal impact. Because of the recency of this proposal, the references for the remaining discussion still refer to the three dimensions of sustainability.

Kerrigan and Kulasooriya (2020) described a successful sustainability plan at Unilever where the corporation shifted from viewing sustainability efforts as risks to seeing them as opportunities. Unilever's efforts focused on all three sustainability components through a 10-year plan (2009–2019) "to double the company's revenue while simultaneously reducing its environmental footprint and increasing its social impact" during a turbulent time period (p. 128). The financial result was impressive; the total shareholder return over the 10-year period was 290%. Quantification for the other two sustainability dimensions was not provided. One explanation may be the difficulty of determining the outcome measures for the effects on environmental and societal sustainability efforts.

Based on the experiences at Unilever and other companies, Kerrigan and Kulasooriya identified three basic actions to reframe sustainability from a risk to an opportunity to guide sustainability journeys. These three basic actions are to look ahead for new growth opportunities sustainability; to look inside their organization to identify ways to accelerate the transformation toward greater sustainability; and to seek opportunities to leverage their business ecosystem and create competitive advantages.

The cover of the September 2019 issue of *Fortune* featured the pictures of three members of the Business Roundtable (BRT) at that time: the CEOs of IBM, J.P. Morgan Chase, and Johnson & Johnson. The magazine cover's headline was "Profits *and* Purpose: Can Big Business Have It Both Ways". The magazine article was titled "A New Purpose for the Corporation" (Murray, 2019) and included the Business Roundtable's "Statement on the Purpose of an Organization" published a month earlier in August 2019 (p. 94). This statement included a brief discussion of the BRT's five commitments in this order: delivery of customer value; investment in employees; fair and ethical treatment of suppliers; support for the communities where they work; and generation of long-term value for shareholders. While the list may have implied a hierarchy, the unstated expectation was that the needs of all stakeholders mattered and would be addressed.

Almost 5 months later the front page of the January 31, 2020 issue of *The Wall Street Journal* included as one of its front-page articles "CEO Out at IBM, Ending a Tough Tenure" with a brief subtitle explanation that the CEO had struggled to lift growth (Fitch, 2020). The article described how IBM "was slow to adapt as corporations shifted from storing data on big servers they owned to renting that computing capacity from service providers" (p. A10). On the surface, this seems as if one the BRT five commitments is more important than the others. However, an alternate conclusion could be that IBM was slow to address an imbalance among its five commitments.

Early in the Pandemic Cohen (2020) identified opportunities and challenges it could present for sustainability, particularly from a consumption perspective. An opportunity is the potential for permanent lifestyle changes dependent on large consumption of energy and materials. Cohen also identified a sustainability challenge related to the expectations for social distancing: the reinforcement of "commitments to individualized rather than public and shared modes consumption" (p. 2).

The fragility of the national and global supply chains emerged early in the Pandemic. Shortages of food and supplies were particularly visible to the general public. Sarkis (2020) summarized several virtual forums convened to discuss opportunities and challenges for the sustainability of supply chains. Although this is a specific topical area, it impacts the general population. Further, Sarkis' conclusions are also broadly applicable: "... there will be post-COVID-19 transformation of supply chain practices; but will these transformations stick? Technological and social innovations are important to supply chain sustainability transition" (p. 7). Again, these conclusions apply beyond the supply chain.

Sustainability and Corporate Social Responsibility (CSR) are related. Craddock (2013) described their relationship citing several definitions for CSR (p. 5). The common factors in these definitions were the elements of sustainability (balancing stakeholder needs and expectations among its financial, societal, and environmental contributions) and the expectation to do so in an ethical manner.

Ahn and Park (2018) examined the relationship of CSR and the longevity of eight long-lived Korean companies. One output of their analysis was a suggestion that "CSR principles play a critical role in maintaining the survival of companies by creating and leveraging social capital and moral legitimacy" (p. 131). This connection of CSR to organizational longevity is a good place to begin the discussion of organizational longevity.

Organizational Longevity

Sinek (2019) expanded the idea of an infinite game to describe the modern business environment. Sinek described a finite game using a sports analogy as a way to distinguish finite and infinite games from a business perspective. This concept should be applicable for the not-for-profit sector as well.

In a finite game the rules and competitors are known; there are people who enforce those rules; the end point of the game is well-defined; and there is a predetermined way to determine the winner of the game. In contrast, infinite games generally have limited rules with limited enforcement of those rules; all competitors are not known; there is no end point; and there are no winners—just remaining participants (pp. 3–4).

Sinek made the point that current businesses are in an infinite game even though many behave as if they were playing in a finite game. Competitors appear unexpectedly, and the rules change. Disruptive innovation is a good example of this. Sinek's advice to businesses for success in the infinite game was "stop thinking about who wins or who's the best and start thinking about how to build organizations that are strong enough and healthy enough to stay in the game for many generations to come" (p. 7). This is organizational longevity.

Ahmad et al. (2019) divided the literature on organizational longevity into two categories: corporate longevity (CL) and corporate sustained longevity (CSL). Their distinction between the two terms was that CL refers to surviving beyond the average life of comparable organizations; and CSL refers to an organization sustaining its longevity well beyond the average life (p. 2). Their research approach was a literature review and input from experts using a Delphi approach to identify elements contributing to CSL. They then examined a set of family-owned manufacturing companies to determine which of the initial list of CSL attributes were most important. Their result was identification of five key strategies for CSL. These were a shared vision, customer orientation, financial strength, organizational learning and adaptation, and efficient utilization of organizational resources and capabilities (p. 14).

The study by Ahn and Park (2018) introduced in the previous section used a similar panel of experts' methodology. This resulted in four conclusions: CSR principles represent a critical role in organizational longevity; CSR is both a management style and a strategic tool; the CSR expectations may vary among stakeholders; and the common management style and strategic tool; CSR expectations may vary among stakeholders; and the common management principles reflect the seven CSR principles identified in the study (p. 131). These seven CSR principles were summarized in Table 4: promise fulfillment, self-sacrifice, humanitarianism, openness, long-term employment, pro-social goals, and corporate giving. While these conclusions focused on CSR principles and actions, the authors acknowledged that economic performance was also a prerequisite for a company's long-term survival (p. 117).

Galadanchi and Bakar (2018) used two definitions for longevity: business longevity is "the sustained existence of companies even after the dead of the founder" and business firm longevity is "the continuity of the firm beyond the career span of its founders" (p. 53). It is clear that their focus is on family-owned or operated businesses. They proposed a business longevity model with five factors: capability for innovation; organizational systems; resources (financial & human); organizational culture; and strategy. Strategy is important to maintain competitive advantages and core competencies. They also noted that organizational excellence "is vital for business longevity" (p. 55).

Moya et al. (2020) also focused on the longevity of large European family businesses. Longevity was defined as "the successful generational transfer of strategic family influence in business" (p. xx). The statistics for generational transfers of family businesses between 1994 and 2009 cited by Moya were not encouraging: about 30% survived into the second generation, and under 15% made it into the third generation. This was based on their literature review. However, Moya et al. point out that the context for these low survival rates was mostly not provided.

Montuori's (2000) description of effective leadership skills was included in the Leadership section earlier. Montuori also discussed the longevity of organizations as their durability. Perhaps more to the point, "the inability to adapt to change, uncertainty, and turbulence leads to organizational mortality" (p. 70).

Napolitano et al. (2015) noted that statistics for long-lived companies are contradictory. Some suggest that longevity favors SME-sized family-owned companies. Others point to large and publicly owned companies that may exist longer because of better access to resources. Regardless, Napolitano et al. cited multiple factors identified in earlier research that might result in organizational longevity: "branch of industry, size of company, stage of maturity, privileges, transformation capability, cultural context, historical time, and pure good luck" (p. 955).

Sharma and Dixit (2017) described four keys to organizational longevity. First, long-lived firms are conservative when it comes to change. That doesn't mean they cannot adapt. Instead, they are selective about large-scale change to ensure they remain consistent with their core values and principles. Second, their attention is focused on exploiting segments and markets where they already excel. Third, their strategy is to diversify selectively when needed to reduce the risk focusing the organization too narrowly. Finally, long-lived organizations recognize when cooperation with other firms is needed, even with competitors.

In spite of the odds, there are some extraordinarily long-lived companies surviving the odds against longevity. Both Napolitano et al. (2015) and Sharma and Dixit (2017) described global examples of long-lived organizations. As examples they mentioned loose association or fraternal relationships among Japanese organizations over 100-years old ("Shinise"), French organizations over 200-years old ("Les henokiens"), and British organizations over 300-years old ("Tercentenarians Club"). Napolitano et al. also noted that the oldest continuously operating company ended its reign in 2006 after 1428 years of existence. This was the Japanese temple builder Kongo Gumi.

Davis (2014) took a more pragmatic view: "... survival is the ultimate performance indicator" (p. 2). Also, according to Davis, different industries and sectors have different rates for new product/service expectations, different barriers to entry, and different level of importance for customer trust. Context is obviously important. Davis proposed that 15 years of successful operations for a tech company is equivalent to 30 successful years as a consumer-product company. The antidote proposed by Davis was to measure organizational longevity in innovation cycles instead of years.

Davis described the characteristics of organizations that "successfully adapt over multiple product and innovation cycles." These included a relentless customer focus, key supplier engagement in solving problems, and purposely discerning external trends that may impact them (pp. 4–5).

Krell (2000) described two approaches to the analysis of organizational longevity: the internal processes of the organization; and how the organization interacts with its broader environment. Krell noted that an organization's management failure in either of these approaches is problematic. These implications are still relevant for the COVID-19 Pandemic 20 years after Krell's article. Leaders must address both the internal and external environments simultaneously.

Role of Innovation in Organizational Longevity

The International Organization for Standardization (2019) defined innovation as a "new or changed entity, realizing or redistributing value" in the international standard ISO 56000 (p. 1). Simply put, innovation is something new that results in value. Innovation is not the same as invention since inventions do not automatically create value. The invention must be used for this to occur. Academic papers and business press books have suggested multiple adjectives to describe different types of innovation. ISO 56000 offered only four: radical, breakthrough, incremental, and disruptive. It also described a continuum that encompasses all types of innovation, with radical or breakthrough innovation at one end of the continuum and incremental innovation at the other end. Disruptive innovation occurs somewhere along the continuum. It may be easier to envision the continuum with incremental innovation on the left end and breakthrough or radical innovation on the right end. In this verbal picture, incremental innovation is either adjacent to or the same as continuous improvement from a quality perspective.

Kim and Huh (2015) described the need to balance exploitive innovation and explorative innovation. In this context, exploitive innovation means exploiting the products and services in the organization's portfolio through incremental innovation to create additional value. In the verbal picture, this is on the left end of the continuum, and involves a lower level of risk. Explorative innovation essentially means exploring new opportunities. This typically involves a higher level of risk to successfully create a radical or breakthrough innovation.

According to Kim and Huh, exploitive innovation focused on "incremental innovation that reinforces existing knowledge" while exploration innovation focused on "radical innovation requiring new knowledge" (p. 392). As an aside, Kim and Huh adopted the ISO 56000 description of innovation as a continuum.

Kim and Huh also explored the impact of exploratory innovation and exploitive innovation on a firm's longevity by examining the 118 firms in the Korean IT industry over a 30-year period from 1981 to 2011. An extreme focus on one or the other can result in a decrease in organizational longevity. The balance between the two types of innovation is a function of both the organization's strategies and its environment. When either or both of these changes, so must the balance. Three of their conclusions were "clear empirical evidence that the exploration-exploitation balance plays an important role in organizational longevity" (p. 406); "excessive exploratory innovation can be more dangerous than excessive exploitative innovation" (p. 409); and "the fit between the exploration-exploitation balance and a firm's strategies is more important than the balance itself" (p. 411). Aleksic (2013) also emphasized the impacts of the two types of innovation: exploitation focused on an organization's sustainability and exploration on its future viability (p. 69).

Taneja et al. (2016) identified innovation is a key driver of an organization's sustainable competitive advantage. Small and medium sized enterprises (SMEs) have strengths and challenges regarding innovation. SME strengths that favor innovation could include innovation cultures, a low resistance to change, low risk aversion, high tolerance for ambiguity, and agility. SME often have less formal strategic planning processes, a key adjunct to successful innovation. This could be an organizational challenge. In particular, decisions regarding the balance between exploitive innovation and explorative innovation efforts are strategic. This balance between relatively low risk, low return innovation efforts and high risk, high return is both critical and situational. Since these decisions are strategic, a more formal strategic planning process should facilitate those timely decisions. "Organizations that can achieve appropriate balance between explorative innovation and exploitative innovation will have the best capability for long-term survival and viability" (Taneja et al., p. 47). In other words, decisions regarding the balance of exploitive and explorative innovation directly impact organizational longevity.

Stadler (2007) identified four principles of enduring success: exploitation before exploration, a diversified business portfolio, leverage mistakes for future organizational learning, and approach change conservatively. Stadler's observations were made well before the Pandemic, so not all of the four principles will necessarily apply in times of crisis. In particular, the conservative approach to change may be insufficient in the rapidly changing supply chain and customer interactions during a global Pandemic. The product/service portfolio diversification may require more urgency during a time of crisis. In addition, the exploitation before exploration may require a rebalance of the innovation portfolio.

Gittleson (2012) noted "Although there are exceptions to every rule, the most important factor for survival is an emphasis on innovation and reinvention." and "Innovation in general is not always easy, however, especially for publicly listed companies that must balance the concerns of capital markets and shareholders, who demand quarterly profits and who are not necessarily interest in decades-long research projects." The earlier description of Unilever's experience by Kerrigan and Kulasooriya provided an example of a public company successfully balancing competing demands for corporate resources. A restatement of Gittleson's observation could be "not easy but possible" when a company is considering investing in innovation capabilities.

Serendipity also plays in an important role in innovation. Alcock (2010) provided two definitions of serendipity that represent two ends of a spectrum in a sense. "At one end of the spectrum, as a kind of lowest common denominator, the word has come to mean chance, coincidence, sheer dumb luck" (p. 12). Alcock's other definition is a bit more specific: "... 'serendipity strong' revolves around the finding of what you didn't know you were looking for; and it involves both accidents and sagacity" (p. 13).

Kamprath and Henike (2019) described the role of serendipity in innovation. In particular they identified and defined seven patterns of serendipitous discoveries: sanctum, detour, momentum, combinatorial, data, communal, and aftermath. The names of these patterns seem daunting, but they involve combining "accidentally" with additional descriptors such as being in the right place, observing at the right time, combining the right materials, combining the right people. Two patterns are of particular interest. The first is combinatorial serendipity or "discovering something by accidentally combining the right materials." The second is communal serendipity or "accidentally discovering something by combining the right people" (Table 17.1, p. 348). These two patterns are used in the following discussion.

The cover of the February/March 2021 issue of *Fortune* stated: "What Comes Next • For Business • For the Economy • For the Battle Against COVID-19." The initial article in this issue was "The Conversation; Albert Bourla" (Leaf, 2021, pp. 9–12). Bourla was the CEO of Pfizer at the time, and the interview involved Pfizer's approach to producing its COVID-19 vaccine, the first COVID-19 vaccine that received emergency use authorization in the U.S. from the Food & Drug Administration.

Bourla described how their ongoing work on the mRNA technology for a flu vaccine, its partnership with BioNtech, and its end-to-end process from early research and development through manufacturing and finally distribution contributed to its success. Using Kamprath and Heinke's innovation serendipity terminology, this is a merger of combinatorial serendipity and communal serendipity. Innovation has and will play an important role in moving through the Pandemic to the new (somewhat) steady state.

Additional COVID-19 Pandemic Impact on Leadership

The COVID-19 Pandemic has created high uncertainty, high risk, and often enormous consequences for the decisions an organization's leaders must now make on a routine basis. There is optimism that recovery is just around the corner. What else is around that corner and what are their consequences are unclear.

McCardle (2020) wrote an opinion article for *The Washington Post* titled "What changes after covid-19? I'm betting on everything." In this article McCardle states that "large chunks of the old normal are due for a post-covid-10 rethink." Organizational leaders pressed with those high uncertainty, high risk, big consequence decisions may be operating with ad hoc processes, waiting for a return to the regular routine. If McCardle is correct, the overhaul of many operating processes may be on hold while leaders deal with the current crisis. So, when the "new normal" finally arrives, those organizations that have been very focused on the tactics may be at a decided disadvantage strategically.

Finn (2020) stated "Uncertainty can be measured in magnitude and duration. By both measures, the extreme uncertainty accompanying the public-health and economic damage created by the COVID-19 pandemic is unprecedented in modern history" (p. 2). There is likely agreement on the magnitude of the current uncertainty. The debate about the duration continues and has two parts. The first is about when the COVID-19 Pandemic will end, or at least abate. The second part is more personal, and involves when will the impacts of the COVID-19 Pandemic on my sector and my organization end, or at least diminish.

Dua et al. (2020) forecasted the recovery from the Pandemic to the 2019-level contributions to the GDP for various sectors using two scenarios: a virus-contained scenario and a muted-recovery scenario. Except for the healthcare and social assistance sector, the projections for the muted-recovery scenario extended into 2022. For the arts, entertainment, and recreation sector and the accommodation and food services sector the recovery projections are early 2024 to early 2025. These two sectors represent 68% and 53% of the small-business share of the respective sector GDP. This study was published in July 2020, based on a survey of 2174 global executives during the period of Jun 1–5, 2020. The assumptions about the COVID-19 recovery scenarios may be impacted by the experiences of the second half of 2020. This additional uncertainty compounds the leadership demands for all sectors, but particularly those with the most pessimistic projections.

Tompkins (2020), a supply chain executive, made a keynote presentation during the 2020 IISE Virtual Annual Conference and Expo. The title of the presentation was *2020: One Heck of a Decade*. At the beginning of the presentation Tompkins noted that the draft presentation had to be returned to the graphics specialist two or three times before the title was listed correctly. The subtle point was that the projected changes expected to occur in the supply chain industry during the next 10 years were all occurring in 2020. This acceleration of 10 years of projected new processes, requirements, etc. into 2020 was a compression that added to the uncertainty facing leaders in that sector.

Llopis (2020, April 6) noted "Crisis has a way of revealing, course-correcting and recalibrating what leadership really means." Bourla, the Pfizer CEO discussed in the last section about innovation, also described the thought process behind the decision to invest $2 billion of Pfizer's money into a project that had never been attempted before. Bourla said "It was a massive bet, but a very necessary one. ... So the question in my mind was, 'If not us, then who?'" (Leaf, 2021, p. 9). Bourla's decision was more than a financial one. It also involved the two non-financial legs of the sustainability stool, infused with an innovative, but untried, approach.

The compression of events described by Tompkins and the pressures on Pfizer's leadership suggest one mostly unnoticed aspect of the pandemic is the multiple, at times unrelenting, pressures facing leadership. These pressures suggest the need for another type of innovation to add to the list of seven patterns of serendipitous discoveries (for innovation) described by Kamprath and Henike (2019). This eighth pattern is concatenated serendipity since leaders now have to address multiple issues in parallel, under immense pressure, and a singular focus on only the most relevant pieces of information. (F. Voehl & R. Fernandez, personal communications, February 17 & 25, 2021).

Renjen (2020) discussed the three critical timeframes for leaders: "Respond, Recover, and Thrive" (p. 10). Moving from the Respond to Recover timeframe requires a shift in the leaders' mindset: From unpredictability, inward focus, crisis management, contingency planning and reacting in the Respond timeframe to the new "interim" normal, market focus, program management, scenario planning, and reinventing in the Recover timeframe (p. 11). Reinvention usually implies some form of innovation.

The subsequent decision to move from the Recover to the Thrive timeframe depends on successfully completing four actions: describing the vision of organizational success, focusing on stakeholder outcomes, using agile sprint principles to enable quickly addressing uncertainties as they arise, and picking the right time to pivot.

ISO 56000 defined disruptive innovation as "initially addressing less demanding needs, displacing established offerings." (p. 2). Business model shifts to digital platforms, particularly in retail including both home delivery and curb-side pickup has been evolving for some retailers in the past few years, and has created a competitive advantage against competitors who have not or cannot make the shift. However, this same digital platform approach for the restaurant industry is a business model disruptive innovation, even though it has been emerging steadily over the past few years in the fast-food industry. However, making business model shifts such as these may be difficult for many organizations in certain industries with low margins. For example, Dua et al. reported that "Many small businesses across sectors came into the COVID-19 crisis with low financial resilience" (p. 3).

Taylor (2020, June 15) described leadership challenge (during) and after COVID-19 as having to deal with the tensions surrounding key decisions. Taylor described four. First, there will be tensions between raised expectations and diminished resources. "However compelling is the case for change, the priority will be survival." Second, there will be tensions between the centralized hierarchical model and the decentralized work-from-home model. The third tension involves the decisions (and investments) for innovation or a preservation of funds that creates a form of dependency. Taylor asked "Will debt be the enemy of innovation?". Decisions to spend money to save money; e.g., technology investments or implementing new business models may be difficult.

The last tension leaders (will) face is planning for the new normal with incomplete information. Business conditions will not return to the Pre-COVID-19 model. The operating performance during the Pandemic is not a steady reference for future planning and projections. Taylor mentioned the fragility of the economy, the weariness of both stakeholders (customers, workforce, suppliers, et al.). Taylor also noted: "The best material to bridge the gap between high hopes and expectations, on the one hand, and tough choices on the other, is truth. As far as possible share and trust your colleagues with the challenges the organisation faces". This last statement reaches back to the opening discussion about leadership and honesty as the most admired characteristic of leaders.

Taylor ended with a personal story that illustrates leadership post-COVID-19. "I'll give the final word to a friend, an advisor to many leaders; I explained my argument: that I was trying to get across some of the tensions organisations may face in hard times. 'No,' he replied. 'It's simpler than that; quite simply, owning those tensions is what defines leadership'".

Additional authors published articles about the COVID-19 impacts on leaders and the leadership function. Dirani et al. (2020) viewed the leadership impacts from a Human Resource Development (HRD) perspective and identified five roles for leaders during the Pandemic and beyond. The first role was sensemaking for their stakeholders, particularly their workforce. Bennis and Thomas called this meaning making in their leadership development model. The primary difference is that Bennis and Thomas were focused on the leader, and Dirani et al. were focused on everyone else. The second role was technology enabler, including the vision for how technology will enable the organization to accomplish its purpose.

The third role was emotional stability and employee well-being. This will require leaders to understand their followers' personal needs and challenges. While some of the roles appeared to be focused on the senior leaders, this role would have to be cascaded to leadership at all levels. The fourth role was innovative communication to overcome typical communication problems during crises, both message content and delivery of those messages. This was one of the five essential questions described by Rakowsky et al. The fifth and last role identified by Dirani et al. was to maintain the financial health of the organization. This is particularly relevant for smaller businesses that may have limited financial reserves and all organizations in the sectors most acutely impacted adversely by the Pandemic. This is particularly critical for the small business in those impacted sectors as described by Dua et al.

The fourth leadership role described by Dirani et al. (effective communications) was also addressed by Bodenheimer and Leidenberger (2020) in their response to the editorial by Cohen. Bodenheimer and Leidenberger focused most of their attention on strategies for the crisis and post-crisis communication. They listed six characteristics of (effective) crisis communication: truthful (similar to Kouzes and Posner's top leader characteristic); understandable; timely; consistent; providing explanations (similar to Dirani et al.'s sensemaking); and customizing the delivery mechanisms for each target group of stakeholders (p. 63).

McGuinness (2020) made four observations about effective CEOs a few months into the Pandemic. According to McGuinness, effective CEOs showed positive accountability for managing the crisis, including checking in with their teams and expressing gratitude; foresight about the ability to sift out data unnecessary for their decision making; putting people first in words and actions; and exhibiting decisive adaptability through making decisions and moving on to the next issue. McGuinness' third observation, the ability to sift out unnecessary data, was very similar to the second definition of serendipity provided by Alcock. Specifically, Alcock noted that serendipity involves both accidentally observing and the sagacity to recognize it. Sagacity is the mental discernment about what is important and what is not.

Lastly, Shepard et al. (2020) identified challenges that will emerge in the Post COVID-19 world. They noted: "COVID-19 accelerates the trends transforming the world" (p. 35). This was the same message Tomkins delivered in the IISE Keynote Presentation, except Tomkins' topic was limited to the supply chain. Shepard et al. devised the ADAPT acronym to describe these expected accelerated trends: Asymmetry, Disruption, Age, Polarization, and Trust. Asymmetry described the disproportionate distribution of wealth, both within and among countries. Disruption addressed both technological and climate change issues. Age referred to demographic pressures at both ends of the workforce. Polarization identified the increasing difficulty in achieving consensus, again both within and among countries. Trust noted the declining confidence and event mistrust in societal institutions. These issues will require significant and consolidated efforts along with the recent leadership lessons to adequately address.

Concluding Thoughts

This chapter reviewed organizational sustainability in terms of the three traditional areas of profits, people, and planet. These three components may be unbalanced in the short term because of current conditions, but all must be balanced in the long term to achieve organizational longevity. Organizations and leaders struggle with balancing decisions regarding financial, societal, and environmental contributions. This chapter also explored the relationships among an organization's leadership, its pursuit of excellence, the balance of traditional sustainability components, the part innovation plays in organizational longevity. Finally, it reexamined these relationships through the lens of the COVID-19 Pandemic that has affected both organizations and individuals in unequal ways. Insights from both failed and surviving organizations were discussed that may provide lessons for future organizational resiliency. Leaders must learn to manage the inherent uncertainty caused by disruptive events like the pandemic, tensions of incomplete information, short timeframes for quick decisions, and the need to quickly pivot to innovative business models while maintaining their creditability with stakeholders, starting with transparency, honesty, and trustworthiness.

Chapter Takeaways

1. The three components of organizational sustainability (profits, people, and planet) may be unbalanced in the short term because of current conditions, but all must be balanced in the long-term to achieve organizational longevity.
2. There is some disagreement about which organizational structure (public or private) increases the likelihood of organizational longevity. Each structure has benefits and liabilities. Leadership (and leadership succession) may affect the ultimate determination.
3. Innovation plays a key role in both organizational longevity and the recovery from the COVID-19 Pandemic. Leaders must balance the exploitive and explorative innovation projects to ensure their innovation portfolio has an appropriate amount of risk.
4. The role of serendipity in innovation success is emerging. The patterns of innovation serendipity may help leaders orchestrate the right combination of people, timing, and other inputs to increase the likelihood of innovation success.
5. Leaders must manage the tensions of incomplete information, short timeframes for quick decisions, and the need to quickly pivot to new business models while maintaining their creditability with stakeholders, starting with their honesty and trustworthiness.

Reflection Questions

1. The literature suggests that, on average, family-owned SMEs survive longer than larger public organizations although there are some exceptions. How can an organizational leader of a public company embrace and leverage the apparent longevity advantages of a successful family-owned SME?
2. How does organizational culture impact the decisions that define the right balance between exploitive and explorative innovation for the organization? How do the organizational leaders affect this?
3. How does a leader demonstrate honesty and engender trust among the workforce and other stakeholders when there are ongoing but incomplete analyses and pending decisions that could potentially impact stakeholders adversely?
4. Which organizations do you believe have survived (or even thrived) during the Pandemic thus far? What lessons from those organizations could help other organizations that are struggling to stay in business?
5. How can small organizations without internal resources (human or financial) engage in innovation to increase their strategic advantages or address strategic challenges?

References

Ahmad, S., Omar, R., & Quoquab, F. (2019). Corporate sustainable longevity: Scale development and validation. *SAGE Open, 9*(1), 1–19. https://doi.org/10.1177/2158244018822379

Ahn, S. Y., & Park, D. J. (2018). Corporate social responsibility and corporate longevity: The mediating role of social capital and moral legitimacy in Korea. *Journal of Business Ethics, 150*(1), 117–134. https://doi.org/10.1007/s10551-016-3161-3

Alcock, A. (2010). The stratigraphy of serendipity. In M. de Rond & I. Morley (Eds.), *Serendipity: Fortune and the prepared mind* (pp. 11–25). Cambridge University Press.

Aleksic, A. (2013). How organizations achieve longevity: The role of change management in building their sustainability. *International Journal of the Academy of Organizational Behavior Management, 4*, 65–78.

Bailey, D. (2021, January 12). *MESA: A most excellent quest continues*. https://www.nist.gov/blogs/blogrige/mesa-most-excellent-quest-continues

Baldrige Performance Excellence Program. (2021). *2021–2022 Baldrige excellence framework: Proven leadership and management practices for high performance*. U.S. Department of Commerce, National Institute of Standards and Technology. https://www.nist.gov/baldrige

Bennis, W. G., & Thomas, R. J. (2002). *Geeks & geezers; How era, values, and defining moments shape leaders*. Harvard Business School Press.

Bodenheimer, M., & Leidenberger, J. (2020). COVID-19 as a window of opportunity for sustainability transitions? Narratives and communication strategies beyond the pandemic. *Sustainability: Science, Practice and Policy, 16*(1), 61–66. https://doi.org/10.1080/15487733.2020.1766318

Cohen, M. J. (2020). Does the COVID-19 outbreak mark the onset of a sustainable consumption transition? *Sustainability: Science, Practice and Policy, 16*(1), 1–3. https://doi.org/10.1080/15487733.2020.1740472

Craddock, W. T. (2013). How business excellence models contribute to project sustainability and project success. In G. Silvius & J. Tharp (Eds.), *Sustainability integration for effective project management* (pp. 1–19). IGI Global). https://doi.org/10.4018/978-1-4666-4177-8.ch001

Davis, I. (2014). Reflections on corporate longevity. *McKinsey Quarterly*. https://www.mckinsey.com/business-functions/strategy-and-corporate-finance/our-insights/reflections-on-corporate-longevity

Dirani, K. M., Mehrangiz, A., Alizadeh, A., Barhate, B., Garza, R. C., Gunasekara, N.,Ibrahim, G., & Majzun, Z. (2020). Leadership competencies and the essential role of human resource development in times of crisis: A response to Covid-19 pandemic. *Human Resource Development International, 23*(4), 380–394. https://doi.org/10.1080/13678868.2020.1780078.

Dua, A., Mahajan, D., Oyer, L., & Ramaswamy, S. (2020). *US small-business recovery after the COVID-19 crisis*. https://www.mckinsey.com/industries/public-and-social-sector/our-insights/us-small-business-recovery-after-the-covid-19-crisis#

European Foundation for Quality Management. (2019). *The EFQM model*.

Finn, P., Mysore, M., & Usher, O. (2020). *When nothing is normal: Managing in extreme uncertainty*. https://www.mckinsey.com/~/media/McKinsey/Business%20Functions/Risk/Our%20Insights/When%20nothing%20is%20normal%20Managing%20in%20extreme%20uncertainty/When-nothing-is-normal-Managing-in-extreme-uncertainty-vF.pdf?shouldIndex=false

Fitch, A. (2020, January 31). CEO out at IBM, ending a tough tenure. *The Wall Street Journal, A1*.

Galadanchi, H., & Bakar, L. J. (2018). A study of factors that support longevity of business enterprises. *IOSR Journal of Business and Management, 20*(1), 53–59.

Gittleson, K. (2012, January 19). *Can a company live forever?* https://www.bbc.com/news/business-16611040

Hakovirta, M., & Denuwara, N. (2020). How COVID-19 redefines the concept of sustainability. *Sustainability, 12*(9), 3727. https://doi.org/10.3390/su12093727

International Organization for Standardization. (2019). *International Standard ISO 56000: Innovation management—Fundamentals and vocabulary*. IOS.

Kamprath, M., & Henike, T. (2019). Serendipity and innovation; Beyond planning and experimental-driven exploration. In J. Chen, A. Brem, E. Viardot, & P. K. Wong (Eds.), *The Routledge companion to innovation management* (pp. 343–360). Routledge.

Kerrigan, S., & Kulasooriya, D. (2020). The sustainability transformation; Look ahead, look inside, and look around. *Deloitte Review, 27*, 126–139. https://www2.deloitte.com/content/dam/insights/us/articles/6771_deloitte-review-27/DI_Deloitte-Review-27.pdf

Kim, G., & Huh, M. G. (2015). Exploration and organizational longevity: The moderating role of strategy and environment. *Asia Pacific Journal of Management, 32*(2), 389–414. https://doi.org/10.1007/s10490-014-9399-3

Kouzes, J. M., & Posner, B. Z. (2017). *The leadership challenge; How to make extraordinary things happen in organizations* (6th ed.). Wiley.

Krell, T. C. (2000). Organizational longevity and technological change. *Journal of Organizational Change Management, 13*(1), 8–14. https://doi.org/10.1108/09534810010310203

Leaf, C. (2021, February/March). The conversation; Albert Bourla. *Fortune, 183*(1), 8–12.

Llopis, G. (2020, April 6). *Leadership will change forever after the Coronavirus Pandemic*. https://www.forbes.com/sites/glennllopis/2020/04/06/leadership-will-change-forever-after-the-coronavirus-pandemic/?sh=50f5fe1a61eb

Lussier, R. N., & Achua, C. F. (2013). *Leadership; Theory, application, & skill development* (5th ed.). South-Western.

Mann, R., Adebanjo, D., & Tickle, M. (2011). Deployment of business excellence in Asia: An exploratory study. *International Journal of Quality & Reliability Management, 28*(6), 604–627.

McCardle, M. (2020, November 29). *Opinion: What changes after covid-19? I'm betting on everything*. https://www.washingtonpost.com/opinions/2020/11/29/what-changes-after-covid-19-im-betting-everything/?utm_campaign=wp_todays_headlines&utm_medium=email&utm_source=newsletter&wpisrc=nl_headlines

McGuinness, J. (2020, May 12). 4 COVID-19 leadership lessons. *Chief Executive*. https://chiefexecutive.net/4-covid-19-leadership-lessons/

Mohammad, M., Mann, R., Grigg, N., & Wagner, J. P. (2011). Business excellence model: An overarching framework for managing and aligning multiple organisational improvement initiatives. *Total Quality Management, 22*(11), 1213–1236.

Montuori, L. A. (2000). Organizational longevity; Integrating systems thinking, learning and conceptual complexity. *Journal of Organizational Change Management, 13*(1), 61–73.

Moya, M. F., Perez, P. F., & Lubinski, C. (2020). Standing the test of time: External factors influencing family firm longevity in Germany and Spain during the twentieth century. *Journal of Evolutionary Studies in Business, 5*(1), 221–264. https://doi.org/10.1344/JESB2020.1.j073

Murray, A. (2019, September). A new purpose for corporations. *Fortune, 180*(3), 88–94.

Napolitano, M. R., Marino, V., & Ojala, J. (2015). In search of an integrated framework of business longevity. *Business History, 57*(7), 955–969. https://doi.org/10.1080/00076791.2014.993613

Quinn, R. E., & Cameron, K. (1983). Organizational life cycles and shifting criteria of effectiveness: Some preliminary evidence. *Management Science, 29*(1), 33–51.

Quinn, R. E., & Rohrbaugh, J. (1983). A spatial model of effectiveness criteria: Towards a competing values approach to organizational analysis. *Management Science, 29*(3), 363–377.

Rakowsky, S., Flashner, B. M., Doolin, J., Reese, Z., Shpilsky, J., Yang, S., Smith, C. C., & Graham, K. (2020). Five questions for residency leadership in the time of COVID-19: Reflections of chief medical residents from an internal medicine program. *Academic Medicine: Journal of the Association of American Medical Colleges, 95*(8), 1152–1154. https://doi.org/10.1097/ACM.0000000000003419

Renjen, P. (2020). The essence of resilient leadership; Business recovery from COVID-19. *Deloitte Review, 27*, 9–23. https://www2.deloitte.com/content/dam/insights/us/articles/6771_deloitte-review-27/DI_Deloitte-Review-27.pdf

Ringrose, D. (2014). *Organizational excellence framework*. https://organizationalexcellencespecialists.ca/

Ringrose, D. (2019). *First global assessment on the current state of organizational excellence*. https://organizationalexcellencespecialists.ca/wp-content/uploads/2019/04/First-Global-Assessment-on-Current-State-of-OE-final.pdf

Sarkis, J. (2020). Supply chain sustainability: Learning from the COVID-19 pandemic. *International Journal of Operations & Production Management, 41*(1), 63–73. https://doi.org/10.1108/IJOPM-08-2020-0568

Sharma, K., & Dixit, M. R. (2017). Live long and prosper: The search for business longevity. *Strategic Direction, 33*(11), 1–3. https://doi.org/10.1108/SD-06-2017-0088

Shepard, B., Zarubina, D., & Jenkins, A. (2020). Adapting to a new world; Facing the challenges of the post-COVID-19 landscape. *Strategy + Business, 100*, 32–41. https://www.strategy-business.com/article/Adapting-to-a-new-world?gko=5b5d0

Sinek, S. (2019). *The infinite game*. Portfolio/Penguin.

Stadler, C. (2007). Four principles of enduring success. *Harvard Business Review, 85*(7–8), 62–72.

Sunkari, P. A. (2015). *Using the triple bottom line to select sustainable suppliers for a major oil and gas company*. Master's thesis, University of Arkansas Fayetteville. http://scholarworks.uark.edu/etd/1114

Taneja, S., Pryor, M. G., & Hayek, M. (2016). Leaping innovation barriers to small business longevity. *Journal of Business Strategy, 37*(3), 44–51. https://doi.org/10.1108/JBS-12-2014-0145

Taylor, M. (2020, June 15). *Leadership after Covid-19*. https://medium.com/bridges-to-the-future/leadership-after-covid-19-12746d8fa2f5

Tompkins, J. (2020, November 3). *2020: One heck of a decade* [keynote address]. IISE Annual Conference & Expo 2020, Virtual.

William T. Craddock is a global trainer, author, and consultant. He previously led staff and operations groups for a Fortune 300 company, and now works with organizations to improve their organizational effectiveness and sustainability. Assignments have included strategic planning, organizational excellence, and various workshops. His certifications include Lean Six Sigma Black Belt (LSSBB) and Project Management Professional (PMP). Bill has made presentations at various Global Congresses, and authored a PMI Thought Leadership White Paper on Change Management. He has served as a Master Examiner for the Baldrige Performance Excellence Program as a team leader and site visit team leader. He has been a member of two U.S. Delegations for ISO international Committees—TC/176 (Quality Assurance & Quality Management) and TC/279 (Innovation Management), and has served in leadership roles for the respective U.S. ISO committees. Bill has undergraduate/graduate Engineering degrees, a Doctorate in Higher Education, and is a Registered Professional Engineer (PE).

Correction to: Towards Developing a Framework of Emergency Leadership

Mohammed Aboramadan and Yasir Mansoor Kundi

Correction to:
Chapter 26 in: S. K. Dhiman, J. F. Marques (eds.), *Leadership After COVID-19*, Future of Business and Finance, https://doi.org/10.1007/978-3-030-84867-5_26

A belated correction was received from the author Yasir Mansoor Kundi to change his affiliation from:

Y. M. Kundi
IAE Aix-Marseille Graduate School of Management, Aix-Marseille University, Aix-en-Provence, France
e-mail: yasir-mansoor.kundi@iae-aix.com

To:

Y. M. Kundi
Institute of Business Administration (IBA), Karachi, Karachi, Pakistan
e-mail: ymkundi@iba.edu.pk

The book and chapter have been updated with this change.

The updated version of this chapter can be found at
https://doi.org/10.1007/978-3-030-84867-5_26

S. K. Dhiman, J. F. Marques (eds.), *Leadership After COVID-19*, Future of Business and Finance, https://doi.org/10.1007/978-3-030-84867-5_33

Index

S. K. Dhiman, J. F. Marques (eds.), *Leadership After COVID-19*, Future of Business and Finance, https://doi.org/10.1007/978-3-030-84867-5

F

Printed by Printforce, United Kingdom